TAKING SIDES

Clashing Views in

Science, Technology, and Society

NINTH EDITION, EXPANDED

TAKING SIDES

Clashing Views in

Science, Technology, and Society

NINTH EDITION, EXPANDED

Selected, Edited, and with Introductions by

Thomas A. Easton
Thomas College

TAKING SIDES: CLASHING VIEWS IN SCIENCE, TECHNOLOGY, AND SOCIETY, NINTH EDITION, EXPANDED

Published by McGraw-Hill, a business unit of The McGraw-Hill Companies, Inc., 1221 Avenue of the Americas, New York, NY 10020. Copyright © 2010 by The McGraw-Hill Companies, Inc. All rights reserved. Previous edition(s) 2009, 2008, 2006. No part of this publication may be reproduced or distributed in any form or by any means, or stored in a database or retrieval system, without the prior written consent of The McGraw-Hill Companies, Inc., including, but not limited to, in any network or other electronic storage or transmission, or broadcast for distance learning.

Some ancillaries, including electronic and print components, may not be available to customers outside the United States.

Taking Sides® is a registered trademark of The McGraw-Hill Companies, Inc.
Taking Sides is published by the **Contemporary Learning Series** group within the McGraw-Hill Higher Education division.

1 2 3 4 5 6 7 8 9 0 DOC/DOC 1 0 9 8 7 6 5 4 3 2 1 0

MHID: 0-07-738197-1
ISBN: 978-0-07-738197-4
ISSN: 1098-5417

Managing Editor: *Larry Loeppke*
Senior Managing Editor: *Faye Schilling*
Senior Developmental Editor: *Jill Meloy*
Editorial Coordinator: *Mary Foust*
Production Service Assistant: *Rita Hingtgen*
Permissions Coordinator: *DeAnna Dausener*
Senior Marketing Manager: *Julie Keck*
Marketing Communications Specialist: *Mary Klein*
Marketing Coordinator: *Alice Link*
Project Manager: *Erin Melloy*
Design Coordinator: *Brenda A. Rolwes*
Cover Graphics: *Rick D. Noel*

Compositor: MPS Limited, A Macmillan Company
Cover Image: Roger Angel/Tom Connors/Johanan L. Codona, The University of Arizona (Arizona Board of Regents, all rights reserved)

Library of Congress Cataloging-in-Publication Data

Main entry under title:
  Taking sides: clashing views on science, technology, and society/selected, edited, and with introductions by Thomas A. Easton.—9th ed., expanded.

  1. Science—Social Aspects. 2. Technology—Social Aspects. I. Easton, Thomas A., *comp.*

306.45

Editors/Academic Advisory Board

Members of the Academic Advisory Board are instrumental in the final selection of articles for each edition of TAKING SIDES. Their review of articles for content, level, and appropriateness provides critical direction to the editors and staff. We think that you will find their careful consideration well reflected in this volume.

TAKING SIDES: Clashing Views in SCIENCE, TECHNOLOGY, AND SOCIETY

Ninth Edition, Expanded

EDITOR

Thomas A. Easton
Thomas College

ACADEMIC ADVISORY BOARD MEMBERS

Himanshu Baral
California State University–East Bay

Don Booker
Pace University

Claudius A. Carnegie
Florida International University

Robert Cole
Saint Louis University

Paul DiBara
Curry College

Michael Efthimiades
Vaughn College of Aeronautics and Technology

Malynnda A. Johnson
Carroll University

JoAnne Juett
University of Wisconsin–Eau Claire

John A. Kromkowski
Catholic University of America

Joseph B. Mosca
Monmouth University

R. Waldo Roth
Taylor University

Nicholas Rowland
Pennsylvania State University

Viveca Sulich
Raritan Valley Community College

Mike Theiss
University of Wisconsin–Marathon County

Linda Wright-Smith
Cameron University

Preface

Those who must deal with scientific and technological issues—scientists, politicians, sociologists, business managers, and anyone who is concerned about energy policy, genetically modified foods, government intrusiveness, expensive space programs, or the morality of medical research, among many other issues—must be able to consider, evaluate, and choose among alternatives. Making choices is an essential aspect of the scientific method. It is also an inescapable feature of every public debate over a scientific or technological issue, for there can be no debate if there are no alternatives.

The ability to evaluate and to select among alternatives—as well as to know when the data do not permit selection—is called critical thinking. It is essential not only in science and technology but in every other aspect of life as well. *Taking Sides: Clashing Views in Science, Technology, and Society* is designed to stimulate and cultivate this ability by holding up for consideration 21 issues that have provoked substantial debate. Each of these issues has at least two sides, usually more. However, each issue is expressed in terms of a single question in order to draw the lines of debate more clearly. The ideas and answers that emerge from the clash of opposing points of view should be more complex than those offered by the students before the reading assignment.

The issues in this book were chosen because they are currently of particular concern to both science and society. They touch on the nature of science and research, the relationship between science and society, the uses of technology, and the potential threats that technological advances can pose to human survival. And they come from a variety of fields, including computer and space science, biology, environmentalism, law enforcement, and public health.

Organization of the book   For each issue, I have provided an *issue introduction,* which provides some historical background and discusses why the issue is important. I then present two selections, one pro and one con, in which the authors make their cases. Each issue concludes with a *postscript* that brings the issue up to date and adds other voices and viewpoints. I have also provided relevant Internet site addresses (URLs) on the *Internet References* page that accompanies each part opener. At the back of the book is a listing of all the *contributors to this volume,* which gives information on the scientists, technicians, professors, and social critics whose views are debated here.

Which answer to the issue question—yes or no—is the correct answer? Perhaps neither. Perhaps both. Students should read, think about, and discuss the readings and then come to their own conclusions without letting my or their instructor's opinions (which sometimes show!) dictate theirs. The additional readings mentioned in both the introductions and the postscripts should prove helpful. It is worth stressing that the issues covered in this book are all *live* issues; that is, the debates they represent are active and ongoing.

Changes to this edition   This expanded ninth edition represents a considerable revision of its predecessor. There are three completely new issues: "Should 'Intelligent Design' Be Taught in Public Schools?" (Issue 2); "Are 'Space Sunshades' a Possible Answer to Global Warming?" (Issue 4); and "Can Machines Be Conscious?" (Issue 15). Three issues have been renamed and given two new essays: "Is NASA Doing Enough to Protect the Earth from Asteroid and Comet Impacts?" (Issue 12); "Is 'Manned Space Travel' a Delusion?" (Issue 14); and "Is 'Animal Rights' Just Another Excuse for Terrorism?" (Issue 18). One issue has been renamed and given one new essay: "Is Information Technology a Threat to Privacy?" (Issue 16).

In addition, for six of the issues retained from the previous edition, one or both readings have been replaced to bring the debate up to date. Three issues have had both essays replaced: "Does Politics Come Before Science in Current Government Decision Making?" (Issue 1); "Should the Internet Be Neutral?" (Issue 3); and "Is It Time to Revive Nuclear Power?" (Issue 5). Three issues have had one essay replaced: "Will Hydrogen Replace Fossil Fuels for Cars?" (Issue 6); "Do Falling Birth Rates Pose a Threat to Human Welfare?" (Issue 7); and "Are Genetically Modified Foods Safe to Eat?" (Issue 11). In all, there are 22 new selections. The book's introduction and the issue introductions and postscripts in the retained issues have been revised and updated where necessary.

A word to the instructor   An *Instructor's Resource Guide with Test Questions* (multiple-choice and essay) is available through the publisher for the instructor using *Taking Sides* in the classroom. It includes suggestions for stimulating in-class discussion for each issue. A general guidebook, *Using Taking Sides in the Classroom,* which discusses methods and techniques for integrating the pro-con approach into any classroom setting, is also available. An online version of *Using Taking Sides in the Classroom* and a correspondence service for *Taking Sides* adopters can be found at http://www.mhcls.com/usingts/.

Taking Sides: Clashing Views in Science, Technology, and Society is only one title in the Taking Sides series. If you are interested in seeing the table of contents for any of the other titles, please visit the Taking Sides Web site at http://www.mhcls.com/takingsides/.

Thomas A. Easton
Thomas College

Contents In Brief

Contents

Professor of law Lawrence Lessig argues that in order to protect the growth
and economic vitality of the Internet, Congress should enact "network
neutrality" legislation to prevent broadband providers from interfering with
free competition among application and content providers. Kyle McSlarrow,
president and chief executive officer of the National Cable &
Telecommunications Association, argues that "net neutrality" mandates
would interfere with the ability of broadband providers to improve Internet
access and thus would ultimately undermine consumer choice and welfare.

UNIT 2   ENERGY AND THE ENVIRONMENT   59

Professor of astronomy Roger Angel argues that if dangerous changes in
global climate become inevitable, despite greenhouse gas controls, it
may be possible to solve the problem by reducing the amount of solar
energy that hits the Earth, using reflective spacecraft. James R. Fleming,
professor of science, technology, and society, argues that climate
engineers such as Roger Angel fail to consider both the risks of unintended
consequences to human life and political relationships and the ethics of
the human relationship to nature.

Iain Murray argues that the world's experience with nuclear power has
shown it to be both safe and reliable. Costs can be contained, and if one is
concerned about global warming, the case for nuclear power is unassailable.
Professor Kristin Shrader-Frechette argues that nuclear power is one of the
most impractical and risky of energy sources. Renewable energy sources
such as wind and solar are a sounder choice.

Professor David L. Bodde argues that there is no question whether
hydrogen can satisfy the nation's energy needs. The real issue is how to

handle the transition from the current energy system to the hydrogen system. Robert Zubrin argues that so far hydrogen-fueled vehicles are little better than display models and there are too many obstacles to replacing gasoline with hydrogen. What is needed is legislation to mandate that all new cars sold in the United States be "flex-fueled"—able to burn any mixture of gasoline and alcohol.

Anne Platt McGinn, a senior researcher at the Worldwatch Institute, argues that although DDT is still used to fight malaria, there are other, more effective and less environmentally harmful methods. She maintains that DDT should be banned or reserved for emergency use. Donald R. Roberts argues that the scientific evidence regarding the environmental hazards of DDT has been seriously misrepresented by anti-pesticide activists. The hazards of malaria are much greater and, properly used, DDT can prevent them and save lives.

John Balbus, Richard Denison, Karen Florini, and Scott Walsh of Environmental Defense in Washington, D.C., argue that much more needs to be done to assess risks to health and the environment before nanotechnology-based products are put on the market. Mike Treder, executive director of the Center for Responsible Nanotechnology, argues that the task at hand is to realize the benefits of nanotechnology while averting the dangers but that attempts to control all risks may lead to abusive restrictions and wind up exacerbating the hazards.

Henry I. Miller and Gregory Conko of the Hoover Institution argue that genetically modified (GM) crops are safer for the consumer and better for the environment than non-GM crops. Jeffrey M. Smith, director of the Institute for Responsible Technology and the Campaign for Healthier Eating in America, argues that GM foods are dangerous to health and should be removed from the marketplace.

Physics professor J. Anthony Tyson argues that NASA can fulfill its congressionally mandated mission of surveying near-Earth objects (NEOs) that may pose future hazards to Earth by funding the proposed Large Synoptic Survey Telescope (LSST) project. Russell L. Schweickart, chairman of the B612 Foundation, argues that NASA should do much more than just survey and catalog NEOs. Not only should it mount a more aggressive survey effort, but it should also accept the job of protecting the Earth from NEO impacts as a public safety responsibility.

Radio astronomer and SETI researcher Seth Shostak argues that if the assumptions behind the SETI search are well grounded, signals of extraterrestrial origin will be detected soon, perhaps within the next generation. Peter Schenkel argues the SETI's lack of success to date, coupled with the apparent uniqueness of Earth, suggest that intelligent life is probably rare in our galaxy and that the enthusiastic optimism of SETI proponents should be reined in.

Astronomer Neil deGrasse Tyson argues that large, expensive projects such as space exploration are driven only by war, greed, and the celebration of power. The dream of colonizing space became a delusion as soon as we beat the Russians to the moon, and it remains so. President George W. Bush argues for his vision of renewed and expanded manned space travel because it improves our lives and lifts the national spirit.

UNIT 5   THE COMPUTER REVOLUTION   279

Christof Koch and Giulio Tononi argue that because consciousness is a natural phenomenon, it will eventually be artificially created. To test for such consciousness, however, will require something other than the classic Turing test. John Horgan argues that no one has the foggiest idea of what consciousness really is, and it seems highly unlikely that we will ever be able to create an artificial consciousness. "Engineers and scientists should be helping us face the world's problems and find solutions to them, rather than indulging in escapist, pseudoscientific fantasies like the singularity."

Amitai Etzioni argues that privacy is under attack by new technologies. There is a need for oversight and accountability, but the mechanisms of accountability must not lie solely in the hands of government. Stuart Taylor, Jr., contends that those who object to surveillance—particularly the government surveillance—have their priorities wrong. Curbing "government powers in the name of civil liberties [extracts] too high a price in terms of endangered lives."

Brendan Rapple argues that as Google scans, indexes, and makes available for online searching the books of the world's major libraries, it will increase access, facilitate scholarship, and in general benefit human civilization. Keith Kupferschmid argues that there is no justification in law for Google's massive copying of books. If the Google Print Library Project is allowed to continue, the interests of publishers, authors, and creators of all kinds will be seriously damaged.

UNIT 6   ETHICS   333

Journalist John J. Miller argues that animal rights extremists have adopted terrorist tactics in their effort to stop the use of animals in scientific research. Because of the benefits of such research, if the terrorists win, everyone loses. Professor Steven Best argues that new laws against animal rights "terrorism" represent the efforts of animal exploitation industries that seek immunity from criticism. The new Animal Enterprise Protection Act is excessively broad and vague, imposes disproportionate penalties, endangers free speech, and detracts from prosecution of real terrorism. The animal liberation movement, on the other hand, is both a necessary effort to emancipate animals from human exploitation, and part of a larger resistance movement opposed to exploitation and hierarchies of any and all kinds.

Introduction

Analyzing Issues in Science and Technology

Civilization in the twenty-first century cannot escape science and technology. Their fruits—the clothes we wear, the foods we eat, the tools we use—surround us. They also fill us with both hope and dread for the future, for although new discoveries promise us cures for diseases and other problems, new insights into the wonders of nature, new gadgets, new industries, and new jobs (among other things), the past has taught us that technological developments can have unforeseen and terrible consequences.

Those consequences do *not* belong to science, for science is nothing more (or less) than a systematic approach to gaining knowledge about the world. Technology is the application of knowledge (including scientific knowledge) to accomplish things we otherwise could not. It is not just devices such as hammers and computers and jet aircraft, but also management systems and institutions and even political philosophies. And it is of course such *uses* of knowledge that affect our lives for good and ill.

We cannot say, "for good *or* ill." Technology is neither an unalloyed blessing nor an unmitigated curse. Every new technology offers both new benefits and new problems, and the two sorts of consequences cannot be separated from each other. Automobiles provide rapid, convenient personal transportation, but precisely because of that benefit, they also create suburbs, urban sprawl, crowded highways, and air pollution, and even contribute to global climate change.

Optimists vs. Pessimists

The inescapable pairing of good and bad consequences helps to account for why so many issues of science and technology stir debate in our society. Optimists focus on the benefits of technology and are confident that we will be able to cope with any problems that arise. Pessimists fear the problems and are sure their costs will outweigh any possible benefits.

Sometimes the costs of new technologies are immediate and tangible. When new devices—steamship boilers or space shuttles—fail or new drugs prove to have unforeseen side effects, people die. Sometimes the costs are less obvious.

The proponents of technology answer that if a machine fails, it needs to be fixed, not banned. If a drug has side effects, it may need to be refined or its permitted recipients may have to be better defined (the banned tranquilizer thalidomide is famous for causing birth defects when taken early in pregnancy; it is apparently quite safe for men and nonpregnant women).

Certainty vs. Uncertainty

Another root for the debates over science and technology is uncertainty. Science is by its very nature uncertain. Its truths are provisional, open to revision.

Unfortunately, most people are told by politicians, religious leaders, and newspaper columnists that truth is certain. They therefore believe that if someone admits uncertainty, their position is weak and they need not be heeded. This is, of course, an open invitation for demagogues to prey upon fears of disaster or side-effects or upon the wish to be told that the omens of greenhouse warming and ozone holes (etc.) are mere figments of the scientific imagination. Businesses may try to emphasize uncertainty to forestall government regulations; see David Michaels, *Doubt Is Their Product: How Industry's Assault on Science Threatens Your Health* (Oxford University Press, 2008).

Is Science Just Another Religion?

Science and technology have come to play a huge role in human culture, largely because they have led to vast improvements in nutrition, health care, comfort, communication, transportation, and humanity's ability to affect the world. However, science has also enhanced understanding of human behavior and of how the universe works, and in this it frequently contradicts what people have long thought they knew. Furthermore, it actively rejects any role of God in scientific explanation.

Many people therefore reject what science tells us. They see science as just another way of explaining how the world and humanity came to be; in this view, science is no truer than religious accounts. Indeed, some say science is just another religion, with less claim on followers' allegiance than other religions that have been divinely sanctioned and hallowed by longer traditions. Certainly, they see little significant difference between the scientist's faith in reason, evidence, and skepticism as the best way to achieve truth about the world and the religious believer's faith in revelation and scripture. This becomes very explicit in connection with the debates between creationists and evolutionists. Even religious people who do not favor creationism may reject science because they see it as denying both the existence of God and the importance of "human values" (meaning behaviors that are affirmed by traditional religion). This leads to a basic antipathy between science and religion, especially conservative religion, and especially in areas—such as human origins—where science and scripture seem to be talking about the same things but are contradicting each other. This point can be illustrated by mentioning the Italian physicist Galileo Galilei (1564–1642), who in 1616 was attacked by the Roman Catholic Church for teaching Copernican astronomy and thus contradicting the teachings of the Church. Another example arose when evolutionary theorist Charles Darwin first published *On the Origin of Species by Means of Natural Selection* in 1859. Mano Singham notes in "The Science and Religion Wars," *Phi Delta Kappan* (February 2000) that "In the triangle formed by science, mainstream religion, and fringe beliefs, it is the conflict between science and fringe beliefs that is usually the source of the most heated, acrimonious, and public debate." Michael Ruse takes a more measured tone when he asks "Is Evolution a Secular Religion?" *Science* (March 7, 2003); his answer is that "Today's professional evolutionism is no more a secular religion than is industrial chemistry" but there is also a "popular evolutionism" that treads on religious ground and must be carefully distinguished. In recent years, efforts to counter "evolutionism" by mandating the teaching of creationism or "intelligent design" (ID) in public schools have made frequent appearances in the news, but so have the defeats of those efforts. One of the most recent defeats was in Dover, Pennsylvania, where the judge declared that "ID is not science." See Jeffrey Mervis, "Judge Jones Defines Science—And Why Intelligent Design Isn't," *Science* (January 6, 2006), and Sid Perkins, "Evolution in Action," *Science News* (February 25, 2006).

Even if religion does not enter the debate, some people reject new developments in science and technology (and in other areas) because they seem "unnatural." For most people, "natural" seems to mean any device or procedure to which they have become accustomed. Very few realize how "unnatural" are such ordinary things as circumcision and horseshoes and baseball.

Yet new ideas are inevitable. The search for and the application of knowledge is perhaps the human species' single most defining characteristic. Other creatures also use tools, communicate, love, play, and reason. Only humans have embraced change. We are forever creating variations on our religions, languages, politics, and tools. Innovation is as natural to us as building dams is to a beaver.

Voodoo Science

Public confusion over science and technology is increased by several factors. One is the failure of public education. In 2002, the Committee on Technological Literacy of the National Academy of Engineering and the National Research Council published a report (*Technically Speaking: Why All Americans Need to Know More About Technology*) that said that although the United States is defined by and dependent on science and technology, "its citizens are not equipped to make well-considered decisions or to think critically about technology. As a society, we are not even fully aware of or conversant with the technologies we use every day."

A second factor is the willingness of some to mislead. Alarmists stress awful possible consequences of new technology without paying attention to actual evidence, they demand certainty when it is impossible, and they reject the new because it is untraditional or even "unthinkable." And then there are the marketers, hypesters, fraudsters, activists, and even legitimate scientists and critics who oversell their claims. Robert L. Park, author of *Voodoo Science: The Road from Foolishness to Fraud* (Oxford University Press, 2002), lists seven warning signs "that a scientific claim lies well outside the bounds of rational scientific discourse" and should be viewed warily:

- The discoverer pitches his claim directly to the media, without permitting peer review.
- The discoverer says that a powerful establishment is trying to suppress his or her work.

- The scientific effect involved is always at the very limit of detection.
- Evidence for a discovery is only anecdotal.
- The discoverer says a belief is credible because it has endured for centuries.
- The discoverer has worked in isolation.
- The discoverer must propose new laws of nature to explain an observation.

The Soul of Science

The standard picture of science—a world of observations and hypotheses, experiments and theories, a world of sterile white coats and laboratories and cold, unfeeling logic—is a myth of our times. It has more to do with the way science is presented by both scientists and the media than with the way scientists actually do their work. In practice, scientists are often less orderly, less logical, and more prone to very human conflicts of personality than most people suspect.

The myth remains because it helps to organize science. It provides labels and a framework for what a scientist does; it may thus be especially valuable to student scientists who are still learning the ropes. In addition, it embodies certain important ideals of scientific thought. It is these ideals that make the scientific approach the most powerful and reliable guide to truth about the world that human beings have yet devised.

The Ideals of Science: Skepticism, Communication, and Reproducibility

The soul of science is a very simple idea: *Check it out.* Scholars used to think that all they had to do to do their duty by the truth was to say "According to . . ." some ancient authority such as Aristotle or the Bible. If someone with a suitably illustrious reputation had once said something was so, it was so. Arguing with authority or holy writ could get you charged with heresy and imprisoned or burned at the stake.

This attitude is the opposite of everything that modern science stands for. As Carl Sagan says in *The Demon-Haunted World: Science as a Candle in the Dark* (Random House, 1995, p. 28), "One of the great commandments of science is, 'Mistrust arguments from authority.'" Scientific knowledge is based not on authority but on reality itself. Scientists take nothing on faith. They are *skeptical.* When they want to know something, they do not look it up in the library or take others' word for it. They go into the laboratory, the forest, the desert—wherever they can find the phenomena they wish to know about— and they ask those phenomena directly. They look for answers in the book of nature. And if they think they know the answer already, it is not of books that they ask, "Are we right?" but of nature. This is the point of "scientific experiments"—they are how scientists ask nature whether their ideas check out.

This "check it out" ideal is, however, an ideal. No one can possibly check everything out for himself or herself. Even scientists, in practice, look things up in books. They too rely on authorities. But the authorities they rely on are other scientists who have studied nature and reported what they learned. In principle, everything those authorities report can be checked. Observations in the lab or in the field can be repeated. New theoretical or computer models can be designed. What is in the books can be confirmed.

In fact, a good part of the official "scientific method" is designed to make it possible for any scientist's findings or conclusions to be confirmed. Scientists do not say, "Vitamin D is essential for strong bones. Believe me. I know." They say, "I know that vitamin D is essential for proper bone formation because I raised rats without vitamin D in their diet, and their bones turned out soft and crooked. When I gave them vitamin D, their bones hardened and straightened. Here is the kind of rat I used, the kind of food I fed them, the amount of vitamin D I gave them. Go thou and do likewise, and you will see what I saw."

Communication is therefore an essential part of modern science. That is, in order to function as a scientist, you must not keep secrets. You must tell others not just what you have learned by studying nature, but how you learned it. You must spell out your methods in enough detail to let others repeat your work.

Scientific knowledge is thus *reproducible* knowledge. Strictly speaking, if a person says "I can see it, but you can't," that person is not a scientist. Scientific knowledge exists for everyone. Anyone who takes the time to learn the proper techniques can confirm it. They don't have to believe in it first.

⋘◈⋙

As an exercise, devise a way to convince a red-green colorblind person, who sees no difference between red and green, that such a difference really exists. That is, show that a knowledge of colors is reproducible, and therefore scientific, knowledge, rather than something more like belief in ghosts or telepathy.

Here's a hint: Photographic light meters respond to light hitting a sensor. Photographic filters permit light of only a single color to pass through.

⋘◈⋙

The Standard Model of the Scientific Method

As it is usually presented, the scientific method has five major components. They include *observation, generalization* (identifying a pattern), stating a *hypothesis* (a tentative extension of the pattern or explanation for why the pattern exists), and *experimentation* (testing that explanation). The results of the tests are then *communicated* to other members of the scientific community, usually by publishing the findings. How each of these components contributes to the scientific method is discussed briefly below.

Observation

The basic units of science—and the only real facts the scientist knows—are the individual *observations*. Using them, we look for patterns, suggest explanations, and devise tests for our ideas. Our observations can be casual, as when we notice a black van parked in front of the fire hydrant on our block. They may also be more deliberate, as what a police detective notices when he or she sets out to find clues to who has been burglarizing apartments in our neighborhood.

Generalization

After we have made many observations, we try to discern a pattern among them. A statement of such a pattern is a *generalization*. We might form a generalization if we realized that every time there was a burglary on the block, that black van was parked by the hydrant.

Cautious experimenters do not jump to conclusions. When they think they see a pattern, they often make a few more observations just to be sure the pattern holds up. This practice of strengthening or confirming findings by *replicating* them is a very important part of the scientific process. In our example, the police would wait for the van to show up again and for another burglary to happen. Only then might they descend on the alleged villains. Is there loot in the van? Burglary tools?

The Hypothesis

A tentative explanation suggesting why a particular pattern exists is called a *hypothesis*. In our example, the hypothesis that comes to mind is obvious: The burglars drive to work in that black van.

The mark of a good hypothesis is that it is *testable*. The best hypotheses are *predictive*. Can you devise a predictive test for the "burglars use the black van" hypothesis?

Unfortunately, tests can fail even when the hypothesis is perfectly correct. How might that happen with our example?

Many philosophers of science insist on *falsification* as a crucial aspect of the scientific method. That is, when a test of a hypothesis shows the hypothesis to be false, the hypothesis must be rejected and replaced with another.

The Experiment

The *experiment* is the most formal part of the scientific process. The concept, however, is very simple: An experiment is nothing more than a test of a hypothesis. It is what a scientist—or a detective—does to check an idea out.

If the experiment does not falsify the hypothesis, that does not mean the hypothesis is true. It simply means that the scientist has not yet come up with the test that falsifies it. The more times and the more different ways that falsification fails, the more probable it is that the hypothesis is true. Unfortunately, because it is impossible to do all the possible tests of a hypothesis, the scientist can never *prove* it is true.

Consider the hypothesis that all cats are black. If you see a black cat, you don't really know anything at all about all cats. If you see a white cat, though, you certainly know that not all cats are black. You would have to look at every cat on Earth to prove the hypothesis. It takes just one to disprove it.

This is why philosophers of science say that *science is the art of disproving,* not proving. If a hypothesis withstands many attempts to disprove it, then it may be a good explanation of what is going on. If it fails just one test, it is clearly wrong and must be replaced with a new hypothesis.

However, researchers who study what scientists actually do point out that the truth is a little different. Almost all scientists, when they come up with what strikes them as a good explanation of a phenomenon or pattern, do *not* try to disprove their hypothesis. Instead, they design experiments to *confirm* it. If an experiment fails to confirm the hypothesis, the researcher tries another experiment, not another hypothesis.

Police detectives may do the same thing. Think of the one who found no evidence of wrongdoing in the black van but arrested the suspects anyway. Armed with a search warrant, he later searched their apartments. He was saying, in effect, "I *know* they're guilty. I just have to find the evidence to prove it."

The logical weakness in this approach is obvious, but that does not keep researchers (or detectives) from falling in love with their ideas and holding onto them as long as possible. Sometimes they hold on so long, even without confirmation of their hypothesis, that they wind up looking ridiculous. Sometimes the confirmations add up over the years and whatever attempts are made to disprove the hypothesis fail to do so. The hypothesis may then be elevated to the rank of a *theory, principle,* or *law.* Theories are explanations of how things work (the theory of evolution *by means of* natural selection). Principles and laws tend to be statements of things that happen, such as the law of gravity (masses attract each other, or what goes up comes down) or the gas law (if you increase the pressure on an enclosed gas, the volume will decrease and the temperature will increase).

Communication

Each scientist is obligated to share her or his hypotheses, methods, and findings with the rest of the scientific community. This sharing serves two purposes. First, it supports the basic ideal of skepticism by making it possible for others to say, "Oh, yeah? Let me check that." It tells those others where to see what the scientist saw, what techniques to use, and what tools to use.

Second, it gets the word out so that others can use what has been discovered. This is essential because science is a cooperative endeavor. People who work thousands of miles apart build with and upon each other's discoveries, and some of the most exciting discoveries have involved bringing together information from very different fields, as when geochemistry, paleontology, and astronomy came together to reveal that what killed off the dinosaurs 65 million years ago was apparently the impact of a massive comet or asteroid with the Earth.

Scientific cooperation stretches across time as well. Every generation of scientists both uses and adds to what previous generations have discovered. As Isaac Newton said, "If I have seen further than [other men], it is by standing upon the shoulders of Giants" (Letter to Robert Hooke, February 5, 1675/6).

The communication of science begins with a process called "peer review," which typically has three stages. The first occurs when a scientist seeks funding—from government agencies, foundations, or other sources—to carry out a research program. He or she must prepare a report describing the intended work, laying out background, hypotheses, planned experiments, expected results, and even the broader impacts on other fields. Committees of other scientists then go over the report to see whether the scientist knows his or her area, has the necessary abilities, and is realistic in his or her plans.

Once the scientist has the needed funding, has done the work, and has written a report of the results, that report will go to a scientific journal. Before publishing the report, the journal's editors will show it to other workers in the same or related fields and ask whether the work was done adequately, the conclusions are justified, and the report should be published.

The third stage of peer review happens after publication, when the broader scientific community gets to see and judge the work.

This three-stage quality-control filter can, of course, be short-circuited. Any scientist with independent wealth can avoid the first stage quite easily, but such scientists are much, much rarer today than they were a century or so ago. Those who remain are the object of envy. Surely it is fair to say that they are not frowned upon as are those who avoid the later two stages of the "peer review" mechanism by using vanity presses and press conferences.

On the other hand, it is certainly possible for the standard peer review mechanisms to fail. By their nature, these mechanisms are more likely to approve ideas that do not contradict what the reviewers think they already know. Yet unconventional ideas are not necessarily wrong, as Alfred Wegener proved when he tried to gain acceptance for the idea of continental drift in the early twentieth century. At the time, geologists believed the crust of the Earth—which was solid rock, after all—did not behave like liquid. Yet Wegener was proposing that the continents floated about like icebergs in the sea, bumping into each other, tearing apart (to produce matching profiles like those of South America and Africa), and bumping again. It was not until the 1960s that most geologists accepted his ideas as genuine insights instead of hare-brained delusions.

The Need for Controls

Many years ago, I read a description of a wish machine. It consisted of an ordinary stereo amplifier with two unusual attachments. The wires that would normally be connected to a microphone were connected instead to a pair of copper plates. The wires that would normally be connected to a speaker were connected instead to a whip antenna of the sort we usually see on cars.

To use this device, one put a picture of some desired item between the copper plates. It could be a photo of a person with whom one wanted a date, a lottery ticket, a college, anything. One test case used a photo of a pest-infested cornfield. One then wished fervently for the date, a winning ticket, a college acceptance, or whatever else one craved. In the test case, that meant wishing that all the cornfield pests should drop dead.

Supposedly the wish would be picked up by the copper plates, amplified by the stereo amplifier, and then sent via the whip antenna wherever wish-orders have to go. Whoever or whatever fills those orders would get the message, and then. . . . Well, in the test case, the result was that when the testers checked the cornfield, there was no longer any sign of pests.

What's more, the process worked equally well whether the amplifier was plugged in or not.

I'm willing to bet that you are now feeling very much like a scientist—skeptical. The true, dedicated scientist, however, does not stop with saying, "Oh, yeah? Tell me another one!" Instead, he or she says something like, "Mmm. I wonder. Let's check this out." (Must we, really? After all, we can be quite sure that the wish machine does not work because if it did, it would be on the market. Casinos would then be unable to make a profit for their backers. Deadly diseases would not be deadly. And so on.)

Where must the scientist begin? The standard model of the scientific method says the first step is observation. Here, our observations (as well as our necessary generalization) are simply the description of the wish machine and the claims for its effectiveness. Perhaps we even have an example of the physical device itself.

What is our hypothesis? We have two choices, one consistent with the claims for the device, one denying those claims: The wish machine always works, or the wish machine never works. Both are equally testable, but perhaps one is more easily falsifiable. (Which one?)

How do we test the hypothesis? Set up the wish machine, and perform the experiment of making a wish. If the wish comes true, the device works. If it does not, it doesn't.

Can it really be that simple? In essence, yes. But in fact, no.

Even if you don't believe that wishing can make something happen, sometimes wishes do come true by sheer coincidence. Therefore, if the wish machine is as nonsensical as most people think it is, sometimes it will *seem* to work. We therefore need a way to shield against the misleading effects of coincidence. We need a way to *control* the possibilities of error.

Coincidence is not, of course, the only source of error we need to watch out for. For instance, there is a very human tendency to interpret events in such a way as to agree with our preexisting beliefs, our prejudices. If we believe in wishes, we therefore need a way to guard against our willingness to interpret near misses as not quite misses at all. There is also a human tendency not to look for mistakes when the results agree with our prejudices. That cornfield, for instance, might not have been as badly infested as the testers said it was, or a farmer might have sprayed it with pesticide whether the testers had wished or not, or the field they checked might have been the wrong one.

We would also like to check whether the wish machine does indeed work equally well plugged in or not, and then we must guard against the tendency to wish harder when we know it's plugged in. We would like to know whether the photo between the copper plates makes any difference, and then we must guard against the tendency to wish harder when we know the wish matches the photo.

Coincidence is easy to protect against. All that is necessary is to repeat the experiment enough times to be sure we are not seeing flukes. This is one major purpose of replication.

Our willingness to shade the results in our favor can be defeated by having someone else judge the results of our wishing experiments. Our eagerness to overlook "favorable" errors can be defeated by taking great care to avoid any errors at all; peer reviewers also help by pointing out such problems.

The other sources of error are harder to avoid, but scientists have developed a number of helpful *control* techniques. One is "blinding." In essence, it means setting things up so the scientist does not know what he or she is doing.

In the pharmaceutical industry, this technique is used whenever a new drug must be tested. A group of patients are selected. Half of them—chosen randomly to avoid any unconscious bias that might put sicker, taller, shorter, male, female, homosexual, black, or white patients in one group instead of the other—are given the drug. The others are given a dummy pill, or a sugar pill, also known as a placebo. In all other respects, the two groups are treated exactly the same. Drug (and other) researchers take great pains to be sure groups of experimental subjects are alike in every way but the one way being tested. Here that means the only difference between the groups should be which one gets the drug and which one gets the placebo.

Unfortunately, placebos can have real medical effects, apparently because we *believe* our doctors when they tell us that a pill will cure what ails us. We have faith in them, and our minds do their best to bring our bodies into line. This mind-over-body "placebo effect" seems to be akin to faith healing.

Single Blind. The researchers therefore do not tell the patients what pill they are getting. The patients are "blinded" to what is going on. Both placebo and drug then gain equal advantage from the placebo effect. If the drug seems to work better or worse than the placebo, then the researchers can be sure of a real difference between the two.

Double Blind. Or can they? Unfortunately, if the researchers know what pill they are handing out, they can give subtle, unconscious cues. Or they may interpret any changes in symptoms in favor of the drug. It is therefore best to keep the researchers in the dark too; since both researchers and patients are now blind to the truth, the experiment is said to be "double blind." Drug trials often use pills that differ only in color or in the number on the bottle, and the code is not broken until all the results are in. This way nobody knows who gets what until the knowledge can no longer make a difference.

Obviously, the double-blind approach can work only when there are human beings on both sides of the experiment, as experimenter and as experimental subject. When the object of the experiment is an inanimate object such as a wish machine, only the single-blind approach is possible.

With suitable precautions against coincidence, self-delusion, wishful thinking, bias, and other sources of error, the wish machine could be convincingly tested. Yet it cannot be perfectly tested, for perhaps it works only sometimes, when the aurora glows green over Copenhagen, in months without an "r," or when certain people use it. It is impossible to rule out all the possibilities, although we can rule out enough to be pretty confident as we call the gadget nonsense.

Very similar precautions are essential in every scientific field, for the same sources of error lie in wait wherever experiments are done, and they serve very much the same function. However, we must stress that no controls and no peer review system, no matter how elaborate, can completely protect a scientist—or science—from error.

Here, as well as in the logical impossibility of proof (experiments only fail to disprove) and science's dependence on the progressive growth of knowledge (its requirement that each scientist make his or her discoveries while standing on the shoulders of the giants who went before, if you will) lies the uncertainty that is the hallmark of science. Yet it is also a hallmark of science that its methods guarantee that uncertainty will be reduced (not eliminated). Frauds and errors will be detected and corrected. Limited understandings of truth will be extended.

Those who bear this in mind will be better equipped to deal with issues of certainty and risk.

Something else to bear in mind is that argument is an inevitable part of science. The combination of communication and skepticism very frequently leads scientists into debates with each other. The scientist's willingness to be skeptical about and hence to challenge received wisdom leads to debates with everyone else. A book like this one is an unrealistic portrayal of science only because it covers such a small fraction of all the arguments available.

Is Science Worth It?

What scientists do as they apply their methods is called *research*. Scientists who perform *basic or fundamental research* seek no specific result. Basic research is motivated essentially by curiosity. It is the study of some intriguing aspect of nature for its own sake. Basic researchers have revealed vast amounts of detail about the chemistry and function of genes, explored the behavior of electrons in semiconductors, revealed the structure of the atom, discovered radioactivity, and opened our minds to the immensity in both time and space of the universe in which we live.

Applied or strategic research is more mission-oriented. Applied scientists turn basic discoveries into devices and processes, such as transistors, computers, antibiotics, vaccines, nuclear weapons and power plants, and communications and weather satellites. There are thousands of such examples, all of which are answers to specific problems or needs, and many of which were quite surprising to the basic researchers who first gained the raw knowledge that led to these developments.

It is easy to see what drives the effort to put science to work. Society has a host of problems that cry out for immediate solutions. Yet there is also a need for research that is not tied to explicit need because such research undeniably supplies a great many of the ideas, facts, and techniques that problem-solving researchers then use in solving society's problems. Basic researchers, of course, use the same ideas, facts, and techniques as they continue their probings into the way nature works.

In 1945—after the scientific and technological successes of World War II—Vannevar Bush argued in *Science, the Endless Frontier* (Washington, DC: National Science Foundation, 1990) that science would continue to benefit society best if it were supported with generous funding but not controlled by society. On the record, he was quite right, for the next half-century saw an unprecedented degree of progress in medicine, transportation, computers, communications, weapons, and a great deal more.

There have been and will continue to be problems that emerge from science and its applications in technology. Some people respond like Bill Joy, who argues in "Why the Future Doesn't Need Us," *Wired* (April 2000), that some technologies—notably robotics, genetic engineering, and nanotechnology—are so hazardous that we should refrain from developing them. On the whole, however, argue those like George Conrades ("Basic Research: Long-Term Problems Facing a Long-Term Investment," *Vital Speeches of the Day,* May 15, 1999), the value of the opportunities greatly outweighs the hazards of the problems. Others are less sanguine. David H. Guston and Kenneth Keniston ("Updating the Social Contract for Science," *Technology Review,* November/December 1994) argue that despite the obvious successes of science and technology, public attitudes toward scientific research also depend on the vast expense of the scientific enterprise and the perceived risks. As a result, the public should not be "excluded from decision making about science." That is, decisions should not be left to the experts alone.

Conflict also arises over the function of science in our society. Traditionally, scientists have seen themselves as engaged in the disinterested pursuit of knowledge, solving the puzzles set before them by nature with little concern for whether the solutions to these puzzles might prove helpful to human enterprises such as war, health care, and commerce, among many more. Yet again and again the solutions found by scientists have proved useful. They have founded industries. And scientists love to quote Michael Faraday, who, when asked by politicians what good the new electricity might be, replied: "Someday, sir, you will tax it."

Not surprisingly, society has come to expect science to be useful. When asked to fund research, it feels it has the right to target research on issues of social concern, to demand results of immediate value, to forbid research it deems dangerous or disruptive, and to control access to research results that might be misused by terrorists or others (the issue of "unclassified but sensitive" research was included in the 8th edition of this book; see also Donald Kennedy, "Science and Security, Again," *Science,* August 22, 2008).

Private interests such as corporations often feel that they have similar rights in regard to research they have funded. For instance, tobacco companies have displayed a strong tendency to fund research that shows tobacco to be safe and to cancel funding for studies that come up with other results, which might interfere with profits.

One argument for public funding is that it avoids such conflict-of-interest issues. Yet politicians have their own interests, and their control of the purse strings—just like a corporation's—can give their demands a certain undeniable persuasiveness.

Public Policy

The question of targeting research is only one way in which science and technology intersect the broader realm of public policy. Here the question becomes how society should allocate its resources in general: toward education or prisons? health care or welfare? research or trade? encouraging new technologies or cleaning up after old ones?

The problem is that money is finite. Faced with competing worthy goals, we must make choices. We must also run the risk that our choices will turn out, in hindsight, to have been wrong.

The Purpose of This Book

Is there any prospect that the debates over the proper function of science, the acceptability of new technologies, or the truth of forecasts of disaster will soon fall quiet? Surely not, for some of the old issues will forever refuse to die (think of evolution vs. creationism), and there will always be new issues to debate afresh. Some of the new issues will strut upon the stage of history only briefly, but they will in their existence reflect something significant about the way human beings view science and technology. Some will remain controversial as long as has evolution or the population explosion (which has been debated ever since Thomas Malthus' 1798 "Essay on the Principle of Population"). Some will flourish and fade and return to prominence; early editions of this book included the debate over whether the last stocks of smallpox virus should be destroyed; they were not, and the war on terrorism has brought awareness of the virus and the need for smallpox vaccine back onto the public stage. The loss of the space shuttle *Columbia* reawakened the debate over whether space should be explored by people or machines. Some issues will remain live but change their form, as has the debate over government interception of electronic communications. And there will always be more issues than can be squeezed into a book like this one—think, for instance, of the debate over whether elections should use electronic voting machines (discussed by Steve Ditlea, "Hack the Vote," *Popular Mechanics*, November 2004).

Since almost all of these science and technology issues can or will affect the conditions of our daily lives, we should know something about them. We can begin by examining the nature of science and a few of the current controversies over issues in science and technology. After all, if one does not know what science, the scientific mode of thought, and their strengths and limitations are, one cannot think critically and constructively about any issue with a scientific or technological component. Nor can one hope to make informed choices among competing scientific, technological, or political and social priorities.

Internet References . . .

Union of Concerned Scientists

The Union of Concerned Scientists is an independent nonprofit alliance of more than 100,000 concerned citizen and scientist advocates dedicated to building a cleaner, healthier environment and a safer world.

http://www.ucsusa.org/

Science and Technology Policy

The Federal Office of Science and Technology Policy advises the president on how science and technology affects domestic and international affairs.

http://www.ostp.gov/

SavetheInternet.Com

The SavetheInternet.com Coalition believes that the Internet is a crucial engine for economic growth and free speech and lobbies to preserve network neutrality.

http://www.savetheinternet.com

Discovery Institute

The Discovery Institute's Center for Science and Culture questions the validity of evolutionary theory and promotes the teaching of intelligent design.

http://discovery.org/csc/aboutCSC.php/

National Center for Science Education

The National Center for Science Education provides information and advice to keep evolution in the science classroom and "scientific creationism" out.

http://www.natcenscied.org/

The Place of Science and Technology in Society

*T*he partnership between human society and science and technology is an uneasy one. Science and technology offer undoubted benefits, in both the short and long term, but they also challenge received wisdom and political ideology. The issues in this section deal with whether public policy should follow science or ideology, whether religion should supplant science in public schools, and whether commerce or freedom is a better foundation for regulation.

- Does Politics Come Before Science in Current Government Decision Making?
- Should "Intelligent Design" Be Taught in Public Schools?
- Should the Internet Be Neutral?

ISSUE 1

Does Politics Come Before Science in Current Government Decision Making?

YES: **Francesca T. Grifo**, from Hearing on "EPA's New Ozone Standards," Testimony before the House Committee on Oversight and Government Reform (May 20, 2008)

NO: **Susan E. Dudley**, from Hearing on "EPA's New Ozone Standards," Testimony before the House Committee on Oversight and Government Reform (May 20, 2008)

ISSUE SUMMARY

YES: Francesca T. Grifo, director of the Union of Concerned Scientists' Scientific Integrity Program, argues that the Bush administration established a pattern of interfering in federal scientific reports and science-based decision making, notably with the Environmental Protection Agency's (EPA) setting of an air quality standard for ground-level ozone.

NO: Susan E. Dudley, administrator of the Office of Management and Budget's (OMB) Office of Information and Regulatory Affairs, argues that regulations and guidance documents such as scientific reports must be consistent with the president's priorities, among other things.

The history of science is also the history of struggle against those who insist—from religious, political, or other motives—that truth is what they say it is. Scientists insist on evidence and reason rather than creed or ideology, and the monuments on the field of battle between the two opposing forces include the tombstones of Galileo and Lysenko, among others.

Galileo Galilei used an early telescope to discover that Venus showed phases like Earth's moon and to find moons around Jupiter. The Roman Catholic Church, upset that Galileo's discoveries contradicted traditional teachings of the Church, demanded in 1633 that he recant. (See The Galileo Project at http://galileo.rice.edu/index.html.) Trofim Lysenko concluded that plants could be, in effect, trained to grow in inhospitable conditions. This view found favor with Soviet dictator Josef Stalin (whose ideology insisted on the "trainability" of human nature), who put Lysenko in charge of Soviet genetic and agricultural research and thereby set Soviet progress in these fields back by decades. (See http://www.wsws.org/articles/1999/feb1999/sov-gen.shtml.)

In the United States, science has enjoyed a very special relationship with government. Largely because science has generated answers to many pressing problems in areas ranging from war to medicine, the government has chosen to fund science with a liberal hand and, as well, to sponsor organizations such as the National Academies of Science, Engineering, and Medicine (http://www.nas.edu/) to provide objective advice to Congress and government agencies. Historically, the role of government has been to pose questions to be answered, or to offer money for research into specific problem areas. Government has *not* specified the answers sought or required that scientists belong to a particular political party or religion.

There have been exceptions. Robert Buderi, in "Technological McCarthyism," *Technology Review* (July/August 2003), reminds us that in 1954, J. Robert Oppenheimer, who played a crucial role in the development of the atomic bomb, was investigated for his opposition to the hydrogen bomb and for his "alleged left-wing associations." Oppenheimer lost his security clearance and was thereby barred from further work in his field. "Scientific McCarthyism" has become the term of choice for using a scientist's political or religious beliefs to judge their scientific work. It arises in connection with research into sexual behavior, AIDS, environmental science, and many other areas, notably where the conservative and religious right already "know" the answers the scientists seek in their research. (For example, do abstinence-only sex education programs keep young people from contracting HIV, or should they be taught about condoms?)

Another method of avoiding the scientific evidence and the need to make decisions that conflict with political or corporate agendas is to create the appearance of doubt. According to David Michaels, "Doubt Is Their Product," *Scientific American* (June 2005), "this administration has tried to facilitate and institutionalize the corporate strategy of manufacturing uncertainty," in part by putting industry representatives or industry-funded scientists on advisory panels. "Instead of allowing uncertainty to be an excuse for inaction," he says, "regulators . . . should use the best science available."

In February 2004, and again in March, the Union of Concerned Scientists (UCS) released a report that assembled numerous charges that the Bush administration had repeatedly and on an unprecedented scale used political "litmus tests" to choose members of scientific advisory panels, suppressed and distorted scientific findings, and otherwise tried to stack the scientific deck in favor of its policies, with important consequences for human health, public safety, and community well-being. In April 2008, the Union of Concerned Scientists released a new report on political interference, specifically at the Environmental Protection Agency (EPA). In the following selections, Francesca T. Grifo, director of the Union of Concerned Scientists' Scientific Integrity Program, summarizes that report in congressional testimony, arguing that the Bush administration has established a pattern of interfering in federal scientific reports and science-based decision making, notably with the EPA's setting of an air quality standard for ground-level ozone. Susan E. Dudley, administrator of the Office of Management and Budget's (OMB) Office of Information and Regulatory Affairs, argues that regulations and guidance documents such as scientific reports must be consistent with the president's priorities, among other things.

YES

Francesca T. Grifo

EPA's New Ozone Standards

I. Introduction

The United States has enjoyed prosperity and health in large part because of its strong and sustained commitment to independent science. As the nation faces new challenges at home and growing competitiveness abroad, the need for a robust federal scientific enterprise remains critical. Unfortunately an epidemic of political interference in federal science threatens this legacy, promising serious and wide-ranging consequences.

The U.S. Environmental Protection Agency (EPA) has been especially harmed by political interference in its work to protect human health and the environment. The flagrant political interference in EPA's decision regarding the national ambient air quality standard (NAAQS) for ground-level ozone is emblematic of this epidemic.

Despite the unanimous recommendation from the EPA's scientific advisors that the ozone NAAQS should be set no higher than 70 parts per billion (ppb), in March 2008 EPA Administrator Stephen Johnson issued the final ozone standard at 75 ppb—a level not based on the best science and not sufficiently protective of public health. This decision followed multiple edits to EPA documents by the White House that played up uncertainties in scientific knowledge of the health effects of ozone exposure and laid the groundwork for Johnson's decision. The White House also directly overruled the EPA's attempt to set a secondary standard to protect crops and plant life from ozone exposure.

These and other EPA decisions based on tainted science have consequences for the health and safety of Americans that can be measured in numbers of hospital visits and premature deaths. The White House has also rewritten EPA scientific documents concerning climate change, pressured EPA scientists to support predetermined conclusions regarding mercury pollution and has pushed for rules that politicize the scientific findings contained in the IRIS toxics database.

To assess the breadth and depth of political interference at the EPA, and to give voice to the thousands of civil servant scientists working at the agency, the Union of Concerned Scientists (UCS) distributed a 44-question survey to nearly 5,500 scientists at the EPA in the summer of 2007 and received responses from 1,586 scientists. The results of that survey, as well as additional investigations, are contained in our recently released report *Interference at the EPA: Politics and Science at the U.S. Environmental Protection Agency*. We summarize

From U.S. House of Representatives, May 20, 2008, excerpts.

here the problems with scientific integrity across the federal government, the major findings of this latest report, and outline the solutions needed to restore scientific integrity to federal decision making.

Political interference has penetrated deeply into the culture and practices of federal agencies. This interference in science threatens our nation's ability to respond to complex challenges to public health, the environment, and national security. It risks demoralizing the federal scientific workforce and raises the possibility of lasting harm to the federal scientific enterprise. It betrays public trust in our government and undermines the democratic principles upon which this nation was founded. The thousands of scientists in the employ of the federal government represent a tremendous resource and their knowledge and advice should not be manipulated or ignored. Without strong action to restore integrity to federal science our nation will be ill-prepared to deal with the challenges we face.

II. Scientific Integrity

Successful application of science has played a large part in the policies that have made the United States of America the world's most powerful nation and its citizens increasingly prosperous and healthy.

Although scientific input to the government is rarely the only factor in public policy decisions, scientific input should always be weighted from an objective and impartial perspective. Presidents and administrations of both parties have long adhered to this principle in forming and implementing policies. However, the current Bush administration has consistently undermined this legacy by manipulating, censoring, and suppressing the work of federal government scientists—with serious consequences for our health, safety, and environment.

Misrepresenting and suppressing scientific knowledge for political purposes can have serious consequences. For example, if the Nixon administration suppressed air quality studies and vetoed the Clean Air Act of 1970, Americans would have suffered more than 200,000 premature deaths and millions of cases of respiratory and cardiovascular disease over the next 20 years.

This misuse of science has led Russell Train, the EPA administrator under Presidents Nixon and Ford, to observe: "How radically we have moved away from regulation based on independent findings and professional analysis of scientific, health and economic data by the responsible agency to regulation controlled by the White House and driven primarily by political considerations."

Political interference in the work of federal scientists has become widespread in the past several years. To catalog these abuses, UCS launched the A-to-Z Guide to Political Interference in Science . . . a webpage that now documents 85 case studies of such interference, involving 24 government agencies. In our February 2008 report, *Federal Science and the Public Good*, we outlined the patterns of interference with government science. The report also highlights the deeper systemic changes that have been made to the structure and policies of the executive branch that threaten to enshrine politicized science even after George W. Bush leaves office. These findings are summarized below.

Patterns of Abuse

Specific examples of the misuse of science have occurred across a broad range of issues such as childhood lead poisoning, toxic mercury emissions, climate change, reproductive health, and nuclear weapons. Experts at the FDA charged with ensuring the safety of our food and drug supply report being pressured to alter their scientific conclusions. Political appointees in the Department of the Interior have been exposed for overruling the scientific consensus and refusing to protect endangered species. Scientists nominated to serve on scientific advisory boards report being asked about their political leanings. And scientists studying what may very well be the most profound global change of this century—global warming—are effectively barred from communicating their findings to the news media and the public.

Interference can take many different forms, including:

- Falsifying data and fabricating results. Federal officials with little or no scientific background have misrepresented scientific data and presented scientific results not based on actual research.
- Selectively editing reports and creating false uncertainty. Political appointees have selectively deleted evidence from scientific documents and exaggerated uncertainty in scientific findings.
- Tampering with scientific procedures. Federal agencies have replaced standard scientific procedures with flawed methodologies, biased toward finding predetermined results.
- Intimidating and coercing scientists. High-level administration officials have directly pressured researchers at federal agencies to alter scientific findings, threatening reprisal if they refuse.
- Censoring and suppressing scientists. Federal officials have prevented scientists from communicating with their colleagues, the media, and the public.
- Hiding, suppressing, and delaying release of scientific findings. Federal officials have buried scientific findings and prevented their public release.
- Disregarding legally mandated science. Federal agencies have repeatedly ignored scientific research that by law must form the basis for certain policy decisions.
- Allowing conflicts of interest. Officials with clear conflicts of interest have held key positions throughout the federal government, from which they have made decisions harming the integrity of federal science.
- Corrupting scientific advisory panels. Political interests have manipulated the process for selecting members of independent scientific advisory panels.

Changing the Rules

Beyond the system-wide epidemic of interference, the Bush administration has instituted deeper changes in the structure and policies of the executive branch. Without a strong commitment to scientific integrity from the next president and Congress, these changes may ensure that politicization of science will continue after President Bush leaves office.

- Centralizing decision making and the unitary executive. The Bush administration has invoked the theory of the "unitary executive" to justify tight White House control over federal agencies. For example, President Bush has greatly expanded the use of signing statements. He has used them to assert his right to ignore or disobey any laws or requests he considers unconstitutional, including congressional requests for scientific information and whistle-blower rights for federal employees. Executive order 13422 dramatically expands the role of the Office of Management and Budget (OMB) in reviewing all agency regulations, including the scientific basis for regulations.
- Homogenizing agency decision making. The White House has sought to replace the policies of individual agencies regarding peer review of scientific findings, risk assessment, and cost–benefit analysis with inappropriate government-wide standards, ignoring the reality that each federal agency requires different tools to best fulfill its mission.
- Reducing transparency. The Bush administration has limited government transparency and accountability by preventing public disclosure of information on the internal workings of the federal government. New policies regarding Freedom of Information Act requests and classification of government documents have created a "presumption of secrecy." In this approach, agencies automatically keep information from public view unless someone specifically requests it, or the law requires them to disclose it.
- Adding unnecessary bureaucracy. New demands, including interagency review and excessive legal challenges from industry, have prevented federal agencies from acting promptly to protect public health and safety.
- Retaliating against whistle-blowers. The Bush administration's penchant for secrecy and centralizing executive power has increased the vulnerability of federal employees who blow the whistle on government waste, fraud, or abuse.
- Foxes guarding the henhouse. The revolving door for officials who shuttle between high-level government positions and regulated industries has harmed the integrity of federal science. The legacy of political appointees with conflicts of interest lives on in the agencies after their departure—through both the flawed policies they helped enact and the erosion of public trust in agency integrity.
- Removing science from decision making. Administration officials have often simply shut out scientists and scientific information from the policy discussion.
- Weakening enforcement and monitoring. Many federal agencies have seen their ability to enforce the nation's laws decline under the Bush administration. In many cases, agencies are simply not collecting the data they need to ensure robust enforcement.

Scientist Surveys

To move beyond anecdotes and to gather information about the extent and nature of the interference, UCS has conducted a series of surveys of federal scientists. Previous surveys have given voice to scientists at the Fish and Wildlife Service, the National Ocean and Atmospheric Administration Fisheries, the Food and Drug Administration, and climate scientists working in seven federal agencies. The survey of EPA scientists is the fifth in the series.

Collectively 3,400 federal government scientists responded to these five surveys. Several common themes ran through their responses:

- 1,301 scientists across nine federal agencies reported that they fear retaliation for openly expressing their concerns about the mission driven work of their agencies.
- 688 scientists from four agencies reported that they were not able to publish work in peer reviewed journals if it did not adhere to agency policies.
- 150 federal climate scientists from seven agencies personally experienced at least one incident of political interference in the past five years.
- And from our most recent report, 889 EPA scientists personally experienced at least one incident of inappropriate interference in their work over the past five years. . . .

III. Interference at the EPA

The U.S. Environmental Protection Agency (EPA) has the simple yet profound charge "to protect human health and the environment." EPA scientists apply their expertise to protect the public from air and water pollution, clean up hazardous waste, and study emerging threats such as global warming. Because each year brings new and potentially toxic chemicals into our homes and workplaces, because air pollution still threatens our public health, and because environmental challenges are becoming more complex and global, a strong and capable EPA is more important than ever.

Yet challenges from industry lobbyists and some political leaders to the agency's decisions have too often led to the suppression and distortion of the scientific findings underlying those decisions—to the detriment of both science and the health of our nation. While every regulatory agency must balance scientific findings with other considerations, policy makers need access to the highest-quality scientific information to make fully informed decisions.

Concern over this problem led the Union of Concerned Scientists (UCS) to investigate political interference in science at the EPA. In the summer of 2007, UCS, working with the Center for Survey Statistics and Methodology at Iowa State University, distributed a 44-question survey to nearly 5,500 EPA scientists, asking for information about political interference in their scientific work, the use of science in EPA decision making, barriers to communication, employee morale, and the agency's effectiveness. . . .

The results of these investigations show an agency under siege from political pressures. On numerous issues—ranging from mercury pollution to groundwater contamination to climate change—political appointees of the George W. Bush administration have edited scientific documents, manipulated scientific assessments, and generally sought to undermine the science behind dozens of EPA regulations.

These findings highlight the need for strong reforms to protect EPA scientists, make agency decision making more transparent, and reduce politicization of the regulatory process.

Political Interference in Scientific Work

Large numbers of EPA scientists reported widespread and inappropriate interference by EPA political appointees, the White House, and other federal agencies in their scientific work:

- 889 scientists (60 percent of respondents) personally experienced at least one incident of political interference during the past five years.
- Among EPA veterans (scientists with more than 10 years experience at the agency), 409 (43 percent) said interference occurred more often in the past five years than in the previous five-year period.

EPA scientists also reported personally experiencing specific forms of political interference, from the explicit to the subtle:

- 94 scientists (7 percent) had frequently or occasionally been "directed to inappropriately exclude or alter technical information from an EPA scientific document."
- 191 scientists (16 percent) had personally experienced frequent or occasional "situations in which scientists have actively objected to, resigned from, or removed themselves from a project because of pressure to change scientific findings."
- 232 scientists (18 percent) had personally experienced frequent or occasional "changes or edits during review that change the meaning of scientific findings."
- 285 scientists (22 percent) had personally experienced frequent or occasional "selective or incomplete use of data to justify a specific regulatory outcome."
- 153 scientists (13 percent) had personally experienced frequent or occasional "pressure to ignore impacts of a regulation on sensitive populations."
- 299 scientists (24 percent) had personally experienced frequent or occasional "disappearance or unusual delay in the release of websites, press releases, reports, or other science-based materials."
- 394 scientists (31 percent) had personally experienced frequent or occasional "statements by EPA officials that misrepresent scientists' findings."

Respondents indicated that political interference arose from both internal and external sources:

- 516 scientists (43 percent) knew of "many or some" cases where EPA political appointees had inappropriately involved themselves in scientific decisions.

- 560 scientists (49 percent) knew of "many or some" cases where political appointees at other federal agencies had inappropriately involved themselves in decisions.
- 507 scientists (42 percent) knew of "many or some" cases where "commercial interests have inappropriately induced the reversal or withdrawal of EPA scientific conclusions or decisions through political intervention."
- 329 scientists (28 percent) knew of such interference by "nongovernmental or advocacy groups."

In essay responses, nearly 100 scientists identified the White House Office of Management and Budget (OMB), which oversees the federal budget and coordinates all federal regulations, as the primary source of external interference. . . .

To place these results in context, we cite specific incidents of interference. For example, political appointees at the White House and in top positions at the EPA manipulated scientific findings and analyses regarding mercury pollution and climate change. These incidents involved pressure to change scientific methods and findings, direct editing of scientific documents by nonscientists, and delayed release of scientific reports.

A third case—involving interagency review of the EPA's assessment of toxic chemicals—illustrates the growing ability of the OMB and other federal agencies to review and second-guess the work of the EPA's scientific experts.

Barriers to the Free Communication of Science

The free communication of scientific results is a critical part of the scientific process. Despite statements by EPA leaders asserting that the agency supports scientific openness, many scientists report that it restricts free communication of the results of taxpayer-funded research:

- 783 scientists (51 percent) disagreed or strongly disagreed that EPA policies allow scientists to "speak freely to the news media about their findings." Another 556 scientists (36 percent) had no opinion or were unsure. Only 197 scientists (13 percent) agreed that the EPA allows scientists to communicate freely with the media.
- 291 scientists (24 percent) disagreed or strongly disagreed that they are "allowed to publish work in peer-reviewed scientific journals regardless of whether it adheres to agency policies or positions."

Beyond these restrictive policies, hundreds of scientists said they fear retaliation for speaking candidly about the EPA's work. More scientists feared retaliation for speaking candidly inside the agency than outside it:

- 492 scientists (31 percent) disagreed or strongly disagreed that they could openly express concerns about the EPA's work inside the agency without fear of retaliation.
- 382 scientists (24 percent) disagreed or strongly disagreed that they could openly express concerns about the EPA's work outside the agency without fear of retaliation.

Interviews with current and former EPA scientists revealed new examples of problems in communicating scientific research. In two cases, EPA scientists were barred from presenting research on climate change at scientific conferences. Other scientists reported difficulties speaking with the media and obtaining EPA clearance to publish their findings in scientific journals.

Political interference in scientific work combined with barriers to the free communication of scientific findings affect the amount and quality of information the U.S. public receives. . . .

IV. The Ozone NAAQS: A Case Study in Political Interference

The EPA's recent rulemaking setting the national ambient air quality standards (NAAQS) for ground-level ozone provides a perfect case study for understanding the extent of political interference in EPA's science and the consequences of this interference for the health of Americans.

Despite the unanimous recommendation from the EPA's scientific advisors that the ozone NAAQS should be set no higher than 70 parts per billion (ppb), in March 2008 EPA Administrator Stephen Johnson issued the final ozone standard at 75 ppb—a level not based on the best science and not sufficiently protective of public health. This decision followed multiple edits to EPA documents by the White House that played up uncertainties in scientific knowledge of the health effects of ozone exposure and laid the groundwork for Johnson's decision. The White House also directly overruled the EPA's attempt to set a secondary standard to protect crops and plant life from ozone exposure.

Ground-level ozone—a component of smog—is created by chemical reactions between oxides of nitrogen and volatile organic compounds in the presence of sunlight. Multiple studies indicate that exposure to ozone pollution can cause and exacerbate a variety of respiratory health problems, and can even lead to premature death. The EPA's recent decisions contradict both the letter and spirit of the Clean Air Act, which requires that the NAAQS be based on the "latest scientific knowledge" and be sufficiently protective of public health. Interference in the ozone standard is only the latest example of political meddling with air pollution standards, a disturbing trend that has serious consequences for the health and well-being of Americans.

This example illustrates many of the findings of our survey of EPA scientists, including the intrusive role of the White House Office of Management and Budget (OMB), direct interference in the work of EPA's staff scientists, and systemic disregard for the expertise of EPA's advisory committees. . . .

Background

The Clean Air Act requires the EPA to set NAAQS for six "criteria" air pollutants (ozone, fine and coarse particulate matter, lead, nitrogen dioxide, sulfur oxides, and carbon monoxide), and to review each standard every five years. Under the act, the EPA must base the NAAQS on the "latest scientific knowledge" and in 2001 the Supreme Court affirmed that the agency cannot consider costs or other factors in setting the NAAQS. While the EPA has rarely kept to the five-year schedule, the strong scientific mandate of the Clean Air Act has ensured that standards for these air pollutants eventually reflect advances in scientific understanding. These standards are responsible for widespread improvements in air quality and public health.

In 2006, the EPA's Clean Air Science Advisory Committee (CASAC) unanimously recommended tightening the ozone standard from 80 parts per billion (ppb) to a level as strict as 60 ppb, and in no case higher than 70 ppb. To support that standard, the committee cited recent controlled clinical studies documenting "statistically significant decrements in lung function" at concentrations of 80 ppb, and "adverse lung function effects" in some individuals at 60 ppb. CASAC also cited several new studies providing evidence of increased likelihood of premature death at ozone exposure levels below 80 ppb, a connection that was recently confirmed by a recent report of the National Research Council.

The Clean Air Act provides a strong mandate to the EPA to rely on the consensus opinions of its scientific staff and independent advisers. However, Administrator Johnson overruled these experts by setting the primary ozone standard at 75 ppb, and after direct intervention by President Bush, adopted a secondary standard for ozone that was also weaker than the scientific experts recommended. The decision by Johnson mirrors his earlier decision to overrule his scientific advisers regarding the NAAQS for fine particulate matter pollution. Even more troubling is the EPA's attempt to cut science out of the standard setting process entirely.

Regulatory Impact Statement

Although the law does not allow the EPA to account for economic costs when setting the NAAQS, the EPA is required to perform a regulatory impact analysis (RIA) that weighs net costs and benefits for any proposed or final regulation. Agencies must adhere to strict guidelines set forth by the OMB when preparing RIAs. The Office of Information and Regulatory Affairs (OIRA, a part of OMB) requested that EPA make a number of changes to the RIA for the ozone NAAQS that undermined the scientific evidence of the benefits of a stronger regulation.

The connection between ozone exposure and premature mortality emphasized by CASAC leads to the single largest economic benefit to a stronger ozone standard in the RIA. Despite the scientific evidence for this connection, OIRA altered statements in the RIA to cast doubt on the findings and requested that EPA include cost–benefit analyses that assume no connection to premature mortality. OIRA's edits resulted in a downward shift in the range of possible net economic benefits ascribed to a stronger ozone standard.

Primary Standard

In addition to interfering in the scientific information contained in the RIA, OMB also introduced last-minute changes to the proposed ozone rule released in July 2007. These changes played up "uncertainties" in several aspects of the scientific findings and sought to provide justification for maintaining the 80 ppb standard. Other OMB edits also attempted to lay the groundwork for a weakened standard, including a suggestion for legally bypassing the Supreme Court's opinion in *Whitman v. American Trucking Assns., Inc.*

Industry groups and local governments actively lobbied both the White House and the EPA to leave the 80 ppb standard unchanged, an option left open by the EPA's proposed rule. On March 12, 2008, Administrator Johnson overruled CASAC to set the primary NAAQS for ozone at 75 ppb—a level unsupported by the best available science. In defending this level, Johnson followed OMB's lead and pointed to "uncertainties" in the scientific evidence for health effects from ozone. Yet Johnson made no allowance for "uncertainties" in the science that might support a stronger standard (such as a lack of controlled human exposure studies focusing on sensitive populations such as children or asthmatics), despite the fact that the Clean Air Act directs the administrator to choose a more protective standard when faced with scientific uncertainty.

Johnson also called for changing the Clean Air Act to allow the EPA to consider the costs of complying with the standards when setting the NAAQS—a move that drew immediate condemnation from Congress.

Secondary Standard

President Bush personally intervened to prevent the EPA from also adopting a stronger secondary standard for ozone. The Clean Air Act allows the EPA to set secondary standards to protect the "public welfare"—a broad term that includes lower visibility, ecological damage, and other concerns—beyond the primary standards designed to protect public health. The EPA often sets secondary NAAQS that are identical to the primary standards.

However, the agency, with CASAC's support, initially proposed a more stringent seasonal standard for ozone to protect crops and other plant life during times of intense exposure. A March 6, 2008, memorandum from OIRA head Susan Dudley to Administrator Johnson questioned the EPA's scientific basis for the secondary standard, and called on the agency to consider "economic values, personal comfort and well-being." EPA Deputy Administrator Marcus Peacock replied that the EPA was barred by law from considering economic costs, and that the EPA was unaware of "any information indicating beneficial effects of ozone on public welfare." Confidential talking points prepared for Administrator Johnson's March 11 meeting with President Bush also emphasized strong scientific support for the EPA's proposal.

Despite this pushback from the EPA, a last-minute intervention by President Bush overruled the agency's proposal and established a secondary standard identical to the primary one. *The Washington Post* reported that Solicitor General Paul Clement warned that Bush's decision contradicted the agency's past submissions to the Supreme Court defending against industry challenges, and touched off a "scramble" to create new legal justifications for the weakened secondary standard. Following the final decision, CASAC sent a letter to Johnson re-emphasizing that the ozone review panel does "not endorse the new primary ozone standard as being sufficiently protective of public health." . . .

V. Solutions and Reforms

The results of our survey and interviews with EPA scientists show widespread problems at the agency. Hundreds of scientists report direct and indirect interference with their scientific work by political appointees at the EPA and the White House. Despite claims to the contrary from EPA leaders, scientists also report institutional barriers to freely communicating their findings through both the media and scientific publications. EPA scientists are not confident that environmental decision makers respect their expertise. And the agency's effectiveness needs to improve on several fronts.

Wide-ranging political interference in EPA science requires a suite of reforms in five major arenas: protecting EPA scientists, improving the agency's transparency, reforming its regulatory framework, strengthening its system of scientific advice, and depoliticizing funding, monitoring, and enforcement. These efforts to revitalize the EPA and allowing it to fulfill its mission of protecting human health and the environment will require strong leadership from Congress, the next president, and the next EPA administrator, joined by EPA scientists and the broader scientific community. . . .

VI. Concluding Thoughts

The EPA's scientific enterprise is our nation's first line of defense against threats to public health and the environment. These threats are growing more complex and global, with the potential to harm the nation's health and prosperity. Despite notable successes, air and water pollution remain serious public health problems. Each year brings new and untested chemicals into our homes, schools, and workplaces. Climate change alone is projected to have profound impacts on public health, agriculture, the economy, and even national security.

These problems are not insurmountable. The environmental and public health successes of the past several decades show that the country can rise to the challenge of environmental threats—but only if the EPA has the proper tools. Given the complexity of today's environmental challenges, a credible scientific knowledge base is essential to an effective response. To foster and sustain a healthy scientific enterprise, Congress and the next president should take concrete steps to protect EPA's scientists, make the agency more transparent, reform the regulatory process, strengthen the scientific advisory system, and depoliticize funding, monitoring, and enforcement.

Science is not the only element of effective policy making. However, because science enjoys widespread respect, appointed officials will always be tempted to manipulate or suppress scientific findings to support predetermined policies. Such manipulation is not only dishonest; it undermines the EPA's credibility and affects the health and safety of Americans.

The Bush administration's direct abuse of science—combined with systemic changes to the regulatory system that threaten the integrity of EPA science—highlight the need for strong action by the next president and Congress to restore scientific integrity to the agency's decision making. Only then can the EPA fully mobilize to serve the public good and ensure the nation's health. . . .

Susan E. Dudley  **NO**

EPA's New Ozone Standards

. . . Thank you for inviting me to testify about the Environmental Protection Agency's recent final regulation strengthening the national ambient air quality standard (NAAQS) for ozone.

In the interest of public transparency, as part of the rulemaking, and before your Committee's inquiry was initiated, both OMB and EPA placed the key correspondence related to this rulemaking in the public record to ensure a clear presentation of the issues involved. Letters between EPA Administrator Stephen Johnson, Deputy Administrator Marcus Peacock, and me are available on OIRA's website. . . .

This testimony (1) lays out the procedures by which OIRA oversees inter-agency review of agency regulations generally, and then (2) provides informa-tion on the specific discussions related to the secondary ozone NAAQS.

Regulatory coordination and review operates under authority of Execu-tive Order 12866, issued by President Clinton in 1993. This Executive Order establishes principles and procedures for regulatory review, including require-ments for disclosure. It also sets forth regulatory principles and procedures that are relevant to today's hearing. The Executive Order establishes OIRA as the entity that reviews significant regulations, observing that "[c]oordinated review of agency rulemaking is necessary to ensure that regulations and guid-ance documents are consistent with applicable law, the President's priorities, and the principles set forth in this Executive Order and that decisions made by one agency do not conflict with the policies or actions taken or planned by another agency."

The confidential nature of interagency deliberations is necessary to allow the Executive Branch to engage in open and candid discussions as policy deci-sions are debated. Over several administrations, OIRA has sought to strike a balance between this legitimate need to protect the deliberative process and the Congress's and the public's need for information. As part of this effort to strike a balance, E.O. 12866 provides specific procedures on the disclosure of information associated with the review of rules. This Administration has expanded public disclosure by providing on OIRA's website lists of any meet-ings held with outside parties on rules under review. We also list on our web-site all regulations under review. Additionally, once a rule has been published, the public has access to the OIRA docket which contains, among other things, a copy of the draft rule as originally submitted to OIRA by the agency and a copy of the draft rule at the conclusion of interagency review.

From U.S. House of Representatives, May 20, 2008.

Executive Order 12866 embraces the regulatory philosophy that "Federal agencies should promulgate only such regulations as are required by law, are necessary to interpret the law, or are made necessary by compelling public need, such as material failures of private markets to protect or improve the health and safety of the public, the environment, or the well-being of the American people," and lays out regulatory principles to which agencies should adhere, to the extent permitted by law. Some of these principles cannot be applied to NAAQS regulations. However, others do apply, for example:

- In setting regulatory priorities, each agency shall consider, to the extent reasonable, the degree and nature of the risks posed by various substances or activities within its jurisdiction.
- Wherever feasible, agencies shall seek views of appropriate State, local, and tribal officials before imposing regulatory requirements that might significantly or uniquely affect those governmental entities . . .
- Each agency shall draft its regulations and guidance documents to be simple and easy to understand, with the goal of minimizing the potential for uncertainty and litigation arising from such uncertainty.

Pursuant to Executive Order 12866 and its regulatory principles and philosophies, OIRA oversees the regulatory process for the Executive Branch by coordinating interagency review of significant agency regulations. When agencies submit draft regulations for review under Executive Order 12866, OIRA shares these with other agencies so as to ". . . avoid regulations and guidance documents that are inconsistent, incompatible, or duplicative with its other regulations and guidance documents or those of other Federal agencies."

In most cases, OIRA is able to work with the regulatory agency to resolve any issues that arise during the interagency review process. For those rare circumstances when such resolution is not possible, the Executive Order provides a process for conflict resolution:

To the extent permitted by law, disagreements or conflicts between or among agency heads or between OMB and any agency that cannot be resolved by the Administrator of OIRA shall be resolved by the President, with the assistance of the Chief of Staff to the President ("Chief of Staff"), acting at the request of the President, with the relevant agency head (and, as appropriate, other interested government officials). Presidential consideration of such disagreements may be initiated only by the Director, by the head of the issuing agency, or by the head of an agency that has a significant interest in the regulatory action at issue. Such review will not be undertaken at the request of other persons, entities, or their agents.

Under the Executive Order, "[a]t the end of this review process, the President, or the Chief of Staff acting at the request of the President, shall notify the affected agency and the Administrator of OIRA of the President's decision with respect to the matter."

EPA's NAAQS ozone rule is a significant regulation under Executive Order 12866, and as such was submitted to OIRA for interagency review on February 22, 2008.

The Clean Air Act (the Act) provides the authority for setting NAAQS. Section 109 of the Act directs the Administrator to propose and promulgate "primary" and "secondary" NAAQS for pollutants listed under section 108 of the Act. Section 109(b)(1) defines a primary standard as one "the attainment and maintenance of which in the judgment of the Administrator, based on such criteria and allowing an adequate margin of safety, are requisite to protect the public health." A secondary standard, as defined in section 109(b)(2), must "specify a level of air quality the attainment and maintenance of which, in the judgment of the Administrator, based on such criteria, are requisite to protect the public welfare from any known or anticipated adverse effects associated with the presence of the pollutant in the ambient air." Section 302(h) of the Act defines "welfare" broadly, by setting forth a non-exhaustive list of criteria: ". . . welfare includes, but is not limited to, effects on soils, water, crops, vegetation, man-made materials, animals, wildlife, weather, visibility, and climate, damage to and deterioration of property, and hazards to transportation, as well as effects on economic values and on personal comfort and well-being, whether caused by transformation, conversion, or combination with other air pollutants."

The draft final rule as initially submitted to OIRA included a primary (health-based) standard of 75 parts per billion (ppb) measured over an 8-hour period, and a separate secondary (welfare-based) standard of 21 parts-per-million hours (ppm-hrs) cumulated over three consecutive months during the ozone season.

In the course of interagency review, concerns were raised with the secondary (welfare-based) standard, which is based on ozone effects other than direct human health effects. These concerns focused on the form of the standard, not the level. EPA's proposed rule had sought comment on two alternative forms, one form identical to the form of the primary standard, and another form based on cumulative ozone levels over a growing season.

Establishing a separate seasonal standard would have deviated from EPA's past practice, which has been to set a secondary ozone NAAQS equal to the primary NAAQS. The preamble to the 1997 final regulation, promulgated pursuant to President Clinton's July 16, 1997, directive to the EPA Administrator, explained the rationale for deciding not to establish a separate secondary standard, as follows:

The decision not to set a seasonal secondary standard at this time is based in large part on the Administrator's recognition that the exposure, risk, and monetized valuation analyses presented in the proposal contain substantial uncertainties, resulting in only rough estimates of the increased public welfare protection likely to be afforded by each of the proposed alternative standards. . . . In light of these uncertainties, the Administrator has decided it is not appropriate at this time to establish a new separate seasonal secondary standard given the potentially small incremental degree of public welfare protection that such a standard may afford.

Neither the draft initially submitted for review nor its accompanying analysis clearly supported a different conclusion than that reached in 1997 regarding the need for a separate secondary standard.

First, as EPA observed in the preamble to the proposed rule issued in 2007, a secondary standard set at a level identical to the proposed new primary standard would provide a significant degree of additional protection for vegetation as compared to the standard established in 1997.

Second, EPA's analysis indicated that a separate secondary standard set at 21 ppm-hrs cumulated over a season would be unlikely to be more protective than one set equal to the primary (public-health based) standard of 75 ppb averaged over 8 hours. In fact, the preamble to the final rule states: "[t]he Staff Paper analysis shows that at that W126 standard level [21 ppm-h], there would be essentially no counties with air quality that would be expected both to exceed such an alternative W126 standard and to meet the revised 8-hour primary standard—that is, based on this analysis of currently monitored counties, a W126 standard would be unlikely to provide additional protection in any areas beyond that likely to be provided by the revised primary standard." Since EPA's analysis showed the seasonal secondary standard is unlikely to be more protective than one set equal to the revised primary standard, concerns were raised that the draft rule did not contain a reasoned basis for concluding that a separate secondary standard was "requisite to protect the public welfare."

On March 6, 2008, I sent Administrator Johnson a memorandum outlining these concerns. Given the public interest in this regulatory proceeding, I wanted to ensure that these concerns were laid out clearly to avoid misunderstandings. On March 7, 2008, EPA Deputy Administrator Peacock responded to my memorandum in writing. I then advised EPA's Deputy Administrator that OIRA was still not in a position to conclude interagency review of the rule with the proposed secondary standard unaltered.

Pursuant to section 7(a) of the Executive Order as discussed above, EPA then sought further consideration of this disagreement regarding the form of the secondary standard. Following the established Presidential review process, the President concluded that, consistent with Administration policy, added protection should be afforded to public welfare by strengthening the secondary ozone standard and setting it to be identical to the new primary standard. This policy recognized the Administrator's judgment that the secondary standard needed to be adjusted to provide increased protection to public welfare and avoided setting a standard lower or higher than is necessary.

On March 12, 2008, I sent a memorandum to Administrator Johnson memorializing the process. EPA cited this memorandum in the preamble to the final rule but also noted that the final decision was the EPA Administrator's: "While the Administrator fully considered the President's views, the Administrator's decision, and the reasons for it, are based on and supported by the record in this rulemaking."

As the preamble to the final rule states:

Based on his consideration of the full range of views . . . , the Administrator judges that the appropriate balance to be drawn is to revise the secondary standard to be identical in every way to the revised primary standard. The Administrator believes that such a standard would be sufficient to protect public welfare from known or anticipated adverse effect, and does not believe that an alternative cumulative, seasonal standard is needed to provide this degree of protection. This judgment by the Administrator appropriately considers the requirement for a standard that is neither more nor less stringent than necessary for this purpose.

In summary, let me reiterate a few key points. First, in the course of interagency review of EPA's final ozone NAAQS decision under Executive Order 12866, both OMB and EPA have been forthright in making key correspondence regarding initial disagreements over the form of the secondary standard available to the public. Second, the focus of my correspondence with EPA was not the primary (health-based) standard, but the secondary (welfare-based) standard. No changes were made to the level or form of the health-based standard. Third, the discussion regarding the secondary standard related exclusively to the form of the standard, and did not affect the level of protection from ozone exposure provided to vegetation. Contrary to some media accounts, the 8-hour form ultimately selected by the EPA Administrator is not lower, nor is it generally expected to be less protective than the alternative seasonal form of the standard. As EPA observed, "based on [its] analysis of currently monitored counties, a W126 standard would be unlikely to provide additional protection in any areas beyond that likely to be provided by the revised primary standard." . . .

POSTSCRIPT

Does Politics Come Before Science in Current Government Decision Making?

One might think that questions of what to do when confronted with problems such as air pollution and climate change should depend more on scientific data than on politics. John F. Kavanaugh, "The Values Vote," *America* (November 29, 2004), argues that there is a place for morality or ethics, but neither the Republicans nor the Democrats have suitable versions of either. Tibor R. Machan, "Faith and Public Controversy," *The Humanist* (May/June 2005), disagrees, arguing that resting public policy on faith "places it on wobbly foundations." Robert Costanza, "When Scoundrels Rule," *Bioscience* (May 2005), notes in reviewing David W. Orr's *The Last Refuge: Patriotism, Politics, and the Environment in an Age of Terror* (Washington, DC: Island Press, 2004), that "scientists abhor (as well they should) faith-based or politically driven conclusions to important questions of science and policy" and asks "But what happens when these rules of conduct are disrespected, as they have been in the last four years? What happens when religious beliefs and political power are allowed to influence science and policy?" See also Chris Mooney, *The Republican War on Science* (Basic Books, 2005). However, Cameron Wilson and Peter Harsha, "Science Policy Isn't Always About Science," *Communications of the ACM* (September 2008), stress that "the nexus of science and technology and public policy is layered over a political system." Public policy is about balancing competing interests.

In April 2004, the U.S. Department of Health and Human Services (HHS) announced that henceforth, when the World Health Organization (WHO) invited scientists employed by the HHS (including scientists at the National Institutes of Health and the Centers for Disease Control), it could no longer send invitations directly to those scientists whom it deemed experts in particular fields (such as avian flu, carcinogenic chemicals, and SARS) and whose assistance it particularly desired. Instead, WHO must send invitations to the office of the HHS global health chief, who would then choose the appropriate experts. There was no suggestion that "appropriate" would mean anything other than scientific expertise, but Steiger did note in a letter to WHO that "regulations require HHS experts to serve as representatives of the U.S. government at all times and advocate U.S. government policies." See "Politics Manipulating Scientific Decisions, Recent Report Shows," *Nation's Health* (September 2004).

The problem of political interference is not new, as Madelon Lubin Finke stresses in *Truth, Lies, and Public Health: How we Are Affected when Science and*

Politics Collide (Praeger, 2007). But the Bush administration has drawn a great deal of attention to its attempts to dictate what scientists say in reports, to Congress, and to the public. In October 2007, Juliet Eilperin, "Sen. Boxer Seeks Answers on Redacted Testimony: White House Cut Climate Warnings," *The Washington Post* (October 25, 2007), reported that when Julie L. Gerberding, director of the Centers for Disease Control, testified before Congress on the dangers of climate change, the Bush administration removed almost half of that testimony to keep Congress from hearing that climate change could adversely affect human health, apparently because of fears that mentioning health effects would help the drive to regulate carbon dioxide emissions as an air pollutant (the full and censored versions of the testimony are available at http://www.climatesciencewatch.org/index.php/csw/details/censored_cdc_testimony/). In July 2008, reports surfaced that Vice President Dick Cheney's office had insisted on the changes; see Robert Davis, "Cuts in Climate Testimony Fire up Debate," *USA Today* (July 9, 2008). Perhaps because not all such efforts succeeded, when the EPA concluded (under pressure from the Supreme Court) that carbon dioxide was a pollutant, the White House simply refused to open the e-mails that reported that conclusion; see Felicity Barringer, "White House Refused to Open Pollutants E-Mail," *The New York Times* (June 25, 2008).

Soon thereafter, the Bush administration apparently decided to leave the matter for the next president to deal with; see David Malakoff, "Bush Takes a Final Swipe, and Salute, at CO_2 Emission Curbs," *Science* (July 18, 2008). When the U.S. Climate Change Science Program released its latest report, *Analyses of the Effects of Global Change on Human Health and Welfare and Human Systems* (CCSP, 2008) (http://www.climatescience.gov/Library/sap/sap4-6/final-report/), its authors reported that there were no attempts to meddle with the content; see Eli Kintisch, "EPA Calls for More Studies on Health Risks of Climate Change," *Science* (July 25, 2008).

ISSUE 2

Should "Intelligent Design" Be Taught in Public Schools?

YES: J. Scott Turner, from "Signs of Design," *The Christian Century* (June 12, 2007)

NO: National Academy of Sciences and Institute of Medicine of the National Academies, from *Science, Evolution, and Creationism* (National Academies Press, 2008)

ISSUE SUMMARY

YES: Professor J. Scott Turner argues that the real issue is whether the world is purposeful. Intelligent design can in fact be usefully taught, and doing so avoids intrusions on academic freedom.

NO: The National Academy of Sciences and Institute of Medicine of the National Academies argue that evolution is so firmly ensconced in the foundations of modern science that nonscientific alternatives to evolution such as creationism (including intelligent design) have no place in the public school science curriculum.

It has long been an article of faith for scientists that teleological questions ("why" questions that presume there is an intent behind the phenomena they study) should not be asked, largely because "intent" implies an intender, which is generally taken to mean a divinity of some sort. As a result, there is a continuing conflict between the forces of faith—which are predicated on the existence of an intender—and the forces of reason. Conservative Christians in many states—California, Texas, Louisiana, and Pennsylvania, among others—have mounted vigorous campaigns to require public school biology classes to give equal time to both biblical creationism and Darwinian evolution. For many years, this meant that evolution was barely mentioned in high school biology textbooks. In Christian schools it still isn't; see Liza Lentini, "One Universe, Under God," *Discover* (October 2007).

For a time, it looked like evolution had scored a decisive victory. In 1982 federal judge William K. Overton struck down an Arkansas law that would have required the teaching of straight biblical creationism, with its explicit talk of God the Creator, as an unconstitutional intrusion of religion into a government activity: education. But the creationists have not given up. They have returned to the fray with something called "scientific creationism" or "intelligent design" (ID), and they have shifted their campaigns from state legislatures and school boards to local school boards, where it is harder for lawyers and biologists to mount effective counterattacks. "Scientific creationism" tries to show that the evolutionary approach is incapable of providing satisfactory explanations. For one thing it says that natural selection relies on random chance to produce structures whose delicate intricacy could only be the product of deliberate design. Therefore, there must have been a designer. There is no mention of God—but, of course, that is the only possible meaning of "designer" (unless one believes in ancient extraterrestrial visitors). For an excellent presentation of the various threads in the debate over intelligent design, see Robert T. Pennock, *Intelligent Design Creationism and Its Critics: Philosophical, Theological, and Scientific Perspectives* (MIT Press, 2001), and Eugenie C. Scott and Glenn Branch, "Antievolutionism: Changes and Continuities," Bioscience (March 2003).

William Johnson, associate dean of academic affairs at Ambassador University in Big Sandy, Texas, offered another argument for replacing the theory of evolution in a 1994 speech, "Evolution: The Past, Present, and Future Implications," *Vital Speeches of the Day* (February 15, 1995). He argued that the triumph of Darwin's theory "meant the end of the traditional belief in the world as a purposeful created order . . . and the consequent elimination of God from nature has played a decisive role in the secularization of Western society. Darwinian theory broke man's link with God and set him adrift in a cosmos without purpose or end." Johnson suggested that evolution—and perhaps the entire scientific approach to nature—should be abandoned in favor of a return to religion because of the untold damage it has done to the human values that underpin society. See also Evan Ratliff, "The Crusade Against Evolution," *Wired* (October 2004), and Sid Perkins, "Evolution in Action," *Science News* (February 25, 2006).

In the following selections, Professor J. Scott Turner argues that the real issue is whether the world is purposeful. Intelligent design can in fact be usefully taught, and doing so avoids intrusions on academic freedom. The National Academy of Sciences and Institute of Medicine of the National Academies argue that evolution is so firmly ensconced in the foundations of modern science that nonscientific alternatives to evolution such as creationism (including intelligent design) have no place in the public school science curriculum.

YES

J. Scott Turner

Signs of Design

Because I am a biologist, evolution is at the core of virtually everything I think about. Like most of my colleagues, I've kept an eye on the emerging "intelligent design" movement. Unlike most of my colleagues, however, I don't see ID as a threat to biology, public education or the ideals of the republic. To the contrary, what worries me more is the way that many of my colleagues have responded to the challenge.

ID proponents claim that Darwinism is insufficient to explain the origin and evolution of life on Earth. All is better explained, they say, if there is some kind of designing intelligence guiding things. These assertions are based on two core ideas. The first is essentially a scientific theory of miracles that is the brain-child of philosopher and mathematician William Dembski, one of ID's leading intellectual lights. According to Dembski, one can use rules of probability and information theory to construct "explanatory filters" that can objectively distinguish between purely natural phenomena that come about on their own and phenomena that require some kind of intelligent guidance—a miracle, in a word. Applying an explanatory filter to, say, the origin of life reveals that the probability that life arose by chance is infinitesimal. This in itself is not a particularly novel or controversial idea—no biologist I know would disagree. But Dembski parts company with the rest of us when he insists that a designing intelligence is the only agency that could bring such an improbable event to pass. What heats people up, of course, is that Dembski's "designing intelligence" strikes many as code for "God."

The second core idea comes from microbiologist Michael Behe, who is another of ID's leading lights. He asserts that living systems exhibit a sort of "irreducible complexity" that cannot be derived from the piecemeal evolution that Darwinism demands. The poster child for this argument is the bacterial flagellum, a whiplike device that bacteria use to propel themselves around their environment. This remarkable contrivance, which resembles an electric motor, is built from protein parts and will work only when all the parts are assembled into the complex whole—and this is why Behe calls its complexity irreducible. Whether the flagellum actually is irreducibly complex is questionable: scientists have proposed reasonable models for how its design could have emerged via piecemeal evolution.

Nevertheless, Behe considers irreducible complexity to be proof positive of a designing intelligence at work: how could the flagellum have developed by natural selection if none of its elements by themselves would have made the organism's predecessor more fit to survive? Behe claims that many other attributes of living systems, including the complicated structure of genomes, mechanisms for gene replication, and complex metabolic pathways in cells, are likewise irreducibly complex. What stirs the pot is ID's claim that all this irreducible complexity constitutes a rhetorical dagger pointed at the heart of Darwinism.

If all this sounds familiar, it should: it is essentially natural theology and the argument from design dressed up in modern clothes—William Paley equipped with a computer and electron microscope. Looked at in this way, ID seems not so much like the radical alternative to Darwinism that it claims to be, and more like nostalgia for the Platonic tradition in natural history that prevailed prior to Darwin.

The nostalgia is puzzling: for centuries, the Platonic tradition tied natural history into knots, with some of the most intractable tangles woven around the nature of species and the meaning of the apparent design that abounds in the living world. In a single decisive stroke, Darwin cut a wide path through this Platonic morass with a simple and, most important, reasonable natural explanation for why species exist and why they exist in such marvelous diversity and complexity. To extend Richard Dawkins's famous quip that Darwin made it possible to be an intellectually fulfilled atheist, so too did Darwin make it difficult to be an intellectually credible Platonist.

Nevertheless, ID is as popular as it is controversial, and Platonic nostalgia is not enough to explain why. Something deeper is obviously at play.

⋅◈⋅

To most people who contemplate the natural world, it seems self-evident that the world is a designed place. Despite its many difficulties, the Platonic tradition endured because it offered a satisfying explanation for why: the world reflects God's purposeful design for creation. In dethroning the Platonic tradition, Darwin seemed to take that purpose away, and this has obviously been a difficult pill for many to swallow. It's not so clear, however, that Darwin did divorce design and purpose so decisively from the living world. Indeed, to claim that he did is to misread the history of Darwinism.

Consider, for example, the bedrock concept of Darwinian fitness. Natural selection operates because "fit" individuals are more fecund than "unfit" individuals. This should, over time, produce populations of fitter creatures, even though there is no purpose at work here, no striving for perfection. However, a problem lurks in this seemingly simple explanation. For a scientific idea to be credible, there must at least be the possibility that one can show it to be incorrect. Darwin ran into early difficulty on this score because the conventional depiction of fitness cannot be false—fecundity is fitness, and fitness is fecundity. To Darwin's early critics, a veritable fountain of doubt gushed from this tautology at the heart of his theory.

Edward Drinker Cope, a 19th-century American paleontologist, probably expressed the issue best. The problem is not so much the origin of species as it is the origin of fitness: how, precisely, do organisms become well-crafted—*fit*—things? To Cope, and to many of Darwin's contemporary critics, the way out of the tautology was the very purposefulness that Darwin so adamantly insisted we reject.

Interestingly, Darwin himself was a little muddy on the issue. Asa Gray, the Harvard botanist who was Darwin's most energetic advocate in the 19th-century U.S., actually saw in Darwinian adaptation the vindication of purposefulness in biology—to Darwin's chagrin. Darwin's most enthusiastic German convert, Ernst Haeckel, did Gray one better, crafting his own theory of evolution by melding Darwinian natural selection with the purposeful *Naturphilosophie* of romantics like Goethe—and leaving Darwin not just exasperated but aghast.

One could argue that Gray and Haeckel simply failed to understand Darwin's elegantly simple idea, but that argument doesn't hold water. Alfred Russell Wallace, who independently conceived the idea of natural selection and whose thinking surely would be most closely aligned to Darwin's own, thought that purpose in some form had to have guided the origin of life and the origin of consciousness in the higher animals, particularly humans. One finds similar doubts cropping up among thinkers throughout the late 19th and early 20th centuries—Freud, Louis Agassiz, Carl Jung and Henri Bergson, to name a few—and all were concerned about Darwin's insistence that a purposeless materialism is all there is.

To be fair, much of the ambiguity and unease swirling around during Darwinism's early years was fueled by a lack of knowledge about how another core Darwinian concept—heredity—works. For a time, it was thought that we could resolve Cope's question about how organisms came to be fit by clarifying the material nature of the gene, Mendel's "atom of heredity." That quest succeeded spectacularly, culminating in today's remarkable revolution in molecular biology, and engendering along the way our modern answer to Cope's question: the gene-centered conception of Darwinism—neo-Darwinism, as it is called—in which fitness arises by way of the selection of "good-function genes" at the expense of "poor-function genes."

For a time, neo-Darwinism triumphantly swept away quaint notions of purposeful evolution, to the point where Will Provine, the eminent Darwin historian, could confidently say that there are "no designing agents in evolution." That confident pronouncement may have been premature, however. As we discover more about how genes work, the stranger they become; they are far from the simple specifiers of good and poor function that they were classically thought to be. Paradoxically, this has breathed new life into Cope's question making it more acute, not less so. Indeed, my own scientific work has led me to a conclusion that is precisely the opposite of Provine's: designing agents are in fact everywhere, if only you know how to spot them. The ubiquity of these designing agents may make evolution a far more purposeful phenomenon than neo-Darwinists have been willing to allow.

This puts intelligent design into what I believe is its proper perspective: it is one of multiple emerging critiques of materialism in science and evolution. Unfortunately, many scientists fail to see this, preferring the gross caricature that ID is simply "stealth creationism." But this strategy fails to meet the challenge. Rather than simply lament that so many people take ID seriously. scientists would do better to ask *why* so many take it seriously. The answer would be hard for us to bear: ID is popular not because the stupid or ignorant like it, but because neo-Darwinism's principled banishment of purpose seems less defensible with each passing day.

·❀·

A more constructive response to the ID challenge would ask whether ID is a credible critique of Darwinian materialism. In my opinion, that judgment should turn on one simple criterion: Will ID pose testable answers to Cope's question? By this measure, a fair reading of ID's prospects shows that it is in the game, though it has stepped up to the plate with two self-inflicted strikes against it. The first strike is its philosophical commitment to the argument from design and to the Platonic intelligent designer it implies. The second strike is that the testable ideas it has produced, like Behe's irreducible complexity, have not so far measured up. Whether ID gets a third strike will depend on whether it can come up with a credible and scientific theory of purposeful evolution. Most scientists, including me, doubt that it will be able to, but of all people scientists should know that the world is full of surprising things. ID might surprise us still.

It seems less than sporting, then, to call the pitch while it's still in the air, which is precisely what many of my colleagues insists on doing, sometimes quite vehemently. This, to me, is the most problematic thing about the controversy: it's not ID that keeps me awake at nights, but the tactics and attitudes of certain colleagues who really should know better. In Pogo's immortal words, "We have met the enemy and he is us."

One doesn't have to look far to find examples of conduct unbecoming. There is the recent case of Richard Sternberg, an unpaid staffer at the National Museum of Natural History (part of the Smithsonian), who became the object of a malicious campaign to oust him from the museum. Sternberg's crime? As managing editor of a Smithsonian-affiliated journal, he decided to publish an article that was sympathetic to ID on the seemingly reasonable grounds that a scientific journal is the appropriate venue for an advocate of a controversial theory to state his case. The Justice Department rapped the museum's knuckles for its treatment of Sternberg.

It would be comforting if one could dismiss such incidents as the actions of a misguided few. But the intolerance that gave rise to the Sternberg debacle is all too common: you can see it in its unfiltered glory by taking a look at Web sites . . . and following a few of the threads on ID. The attitudes on display there, which at the extreme verge on antireligious hysteria, can hardly be squared with the relatively innocuous (even if wrong-headed) ideas that sit at ID's core. Why, then, are such attitudes commonplace? The only explanation I can come up with is that many biologists regard ID as a dire existential threat. And that is what really troubles me about the ID controversy: the animal that feels threatened is the one most likely to do something irrational and destructive.

Consider, for example, the most emotionally charged issue related to ID—whether it has any place in our classrooms. One can render plausible arguments that it does: even if ID is wrong, students are interested in the issue, and it offers a wealth of teachable moments to explore deeper issues of the philosophical roots of biology and the nature of science. What, then, is the harm in allowing teachers to deal with the subject as each sees fit? Advance this seemingly reasonable proposition, and you are likely to see scientists rolling their eyes; some may even become apoplectic.

When pressed to explain why normal standards of tolerance and academic freedom should not apply in the case of ID, scientists typically reply with all manner of evasions and prevarications that are quite out of character for otherwise balanced, intelligent and reasonable people. To give just one argument that has turned up frequently in my correspondence with colleagues: because ID has its roots in fundamentalist Christianity (a dubious proposition in itself), admitting it into our classrooms will foster an exclusionary and hurtful climate, as would admitting other exclusionary sins such as racism or sexism.

Even setting aside the numerous head-turning non sequiturs that weave through this argument, a stroll through most modern universities will quickly reveal how hollow the argument is. Each day as I make my way to my office, for example, I pass the usual gauntlet of Bushitler cartoons and "Duck, it's Dick" posters, and doors plastered with lame jokes and cartoons about Republicans, Christians and conservatives. "Abortion Stops a Beating Heart" posters, on the other hand, are as rare as four-leaf clovers. The display is a stark panorama of what the modern academy is evolving into: a tedious intellectual monoculture where conformity and not contention is the norm. Reflexive hostility to ID is largely cut from that cloth: some ID critics are worried not so much about a hurtful climate as they are about a climate in which people are free to disagree with them.

⋅⟨⊙⟩⋅

Such things are easily laughed off as the foibles of the modern academy. My blood chills, however, when these essentially harmless hypocrisies are joined with the all-American tradition of litigiousness, for it is in the hands of courts and lawyers that real damage to cherished academic ideals is likely to be done. This is not mere lawyer-bashing: as universities become more corporatized and politicized, academic freedom and open inquiry are coming under an ever more grave threat. A case in point is the recent federal court decision in *Mayer v. Monroe County Community School Corporation,* which essentially dismisses the notion of academic freedom in high schools. The court found that teachers have no academic autonomy but are only instruments for advancing the interests of school boards.

My university colleagues should not take much comfort in the fact that this decision involved a high school, because it would require only a short step to apply the same logic to them—a step that some administrators are eager to take. A high-level administrator at the prestigious university near my own has gone on record saying that First Amendment rights of free speech do not apply at an "educational corporation" like a private university. We should take heed: courts, ambitious attorneys and lawsuit-averse administrators are manifestly not academics' friends when it comes to unfettered free speech. Yet the courts are where many of my colleagues seem determined to go with the ID issue. I believe we will ultimately come to regret this.

Take, for example, the recent case in Dover, Pennsylvania, where a group of parents sued the local school board over its requirement that a statement be read to biology students encouraging them to keep an open mind about alternatives to Darwinism. The plaintiffs regarded this requirement as "stealth creationism"—an unanswerable criticism if you think about it—and, backed by the ACLU, they sought relief in the federal courts. There were few heroes to be found in the spectacle that followed. The only bright spot was when a larger group of grown-ups, the Dover electorate, put a stop to the circus by voting out the school board that had put the offending policy in place. Unfortunately, this happy outcome did not keep the judge from ruling for the plaintiffs, decreeing that teaching about ID is constitutionally proscribed.

Many of my scientific colleagues were involved in this case. One would hope that they would have taken a stance of principled neutrality, offering a robust defense of academic freedom tempered with the sober recognition that freedom means that sometimes people will think, speak and even teach things one disagrees with. Instead, my colleagues took sides; many were actively involved as advocates for the plaintiffs, and they were cheered on by many more from the sidelines. Although there was general jubilation at the ruling, I think the joy will be short-lived, for we have affirmed the principle that a federal judge, not scientists or teachers, can dictate what is and what is not science, and what may or may not be taught in a classroom. Forgive me if I do not feel more free.

**National Academy of Science
and Institute of Medicine
of the National Academies**

 **NO**

Science, Evolution,
and Creationism

Scientific and technological advances have had profound effects on human life. In the 19th century, most families could expect to lose one or more children to disease. Today, in the United States and other developed countries, the death of a child from disease is uncommon. Every day we rely on technologies made possible through the application of scientific knowledge and processes. The computers and cell phones which we use, the cars and airplanes in which we travel, the medicines that we take, and many of the foods that we eat were developed in part through insights obtained from scientific research. Science has boosted living standards, has enabled humans to travel into Earth's orbit and to the Moon, and has given us new ways of thinking about ourselves and the universe.

Evolutionary biology has been and continues to be a cornerstone of modern science. This booklet documents some of the major contributions that an understanding of evolution has made to human well-being, including its contributions to preventing and treating human disease, developing new agricultural products, and creating industrial innovations. More broadly, evolution is a core concept in biology that is based both in the study of past life forms and in the study of the relatedness and diversity of present-day organisms. The rapid advances now being made in the life sciences and in medicine rest on principles derived from an understanding of evolution. That understanding has arisen both through the study of an ever-expanding fossil record and, equally importantly, through the application of modern biological and molecular sciences and technologies to the study of evolution. Of course, as with any active area of science, many fascinating questions remain, and this booklet highlights some of the active research that is currently under way that addresses questions about evolution.

However, polls show that many people continue to have questions about our knowledge of biological evolution. They may have been told that scientific understanding of evolution is incomplete, incorrect, or in doubt. They may be skeptical that the natural process of biological evolution could have produced such an incredible array of living things, from microscopic bacteria to whales and redwood trees, from simple sponges on coral reefs to humans capable of contemplating life's history on this planet. They may wonder if it is possible to accept evolution and still adhere to religious beliefs.

This publication speaks to those questions. It is written to serve as a resource for people who find themselves embroiled in debates about evolution. It provides information about the role that evolution plays in modern biology and the reasons why only scientifically based explanations should be included in public school science courses. Interested readers may include school board members, science teachers and other education leaders, policy makers, legal scholars, and others in the community who are committed to providing students with quality science education. This booklet is also directed to the broader audience of high-quality school and college students as well as adults who wish to become more familiar with the many strands of evidence supporting evolution and to understand why evolution is both a fact and a process that accounts for the diversity of life on Earth.

This booklet also places the study of evolution in a broader context. It defines what "theory" means in the scientific community. It shows how evolutionary theory reflects the nature of science and how it differs from religion. It explains why the overwhelming majority of the scientific community accepts evolution as the basis for modern biology. It shows that some individual scientists and religious organizations have described how, for them, evolution and their faith are not in opposition to each other. And it explains why nonscientific alternatives to evolution such as creationism (including intelligent design creationism) should not be part of the science curriculum in the nation's public schools. . . .

Much has happened in evolutionary biology since the release of the first two editions of this booklet, and this new edition provides important updates about these developments. Fossil discoveries have continued to produce new and compelling evidence about evolutionary history. New information and understanding about the molecules that make up organisms has emerged, including the complete DNA sequences of humans. DNA sequencing has become a powerful tool for establishing genetic relationships among species. DNA evidence has both confirmed fossil evidence and allowed studies of evolution where the fossil record is still incomplete. An entirely new field, evolutionary developmental biology, enables scientists to study how the genetic changes that have occurred throughout history have shaped the forms and functions of organisms. The study of biological evolution constitutes one of the most active and far-reaching endeavors in all of modern science.

The public controversies that swirl around evolution also have changed. In the 1980s many people opposed to the teaching of evolution in public schools supported legislation that would have required biology teachers to discuss "scientific creationism"—the assertion that the fossil record and the planet's geological features are consistent with Earth and its living things being created just a few thousand years ago. Major court cases—including a Supreme Court case in 1987—ruled that "creation science" is the product of religious convictions, not scientific research, and that it cannot be taught in public schools because to do so would impose a particular religious perspective on all students.

Since then, the opponents of evolution have taken other approaches. Some have backed the view known as "intelligent design," a new form of creationism based on the contention that living things are too complex to have evolved through natural mechanisms. In 2005 a landmark court case in Dover, Pennsylvania, deemed the teaching of intelligent design unconstitutional, again because it is based on religious conviction and not science.

Others have argued that science teachers should teach the "controversies" surrounding evolution. But there is no controversy in the scientific community about whether evolution has occurred. On the contrary, the evidence supporting descent with modification, as Charles Darwin termed it, is both overwhelming and compelling. In the century and a half since Darwin, scientists have uncovered exquisite details about many of the mechanisms that underlie biological variation, inheritance, and natural selection, and they have shown how these mechanisms lead to biological change over time. Because of this immense body of evidence, scientists treat the occurrence of evolution as one of the most securely established of scientific facts. Biologists also are confident in their understanding of how evolution occurs. . . .

As . . . [this publication] makes clear, the evidence for evolution can be fully compatible with religious faith. Science and religion are different ways of understanding the world. Needlessly placing them in opposition reduces the potential of each to contribute to a better future.

Frequently Asked Questions

Aren't evolution and religion opposing ideas?

Newspaper and television stories sometimes make it seem as though evolution and religion are incompatible, but that is not true. Many scientists and theologians have written about how one can accept both faith and the validity of biological evolution. Many past and current scientists who have made major contributions to our understanding of the world have been devoutly religious. At the same time, many religious people accept the reality of evolution, and many religious denominations have issued emphatic statements reflecting this acceptance. . . .

To be sure, disagreements do exist. Some people reject any science that contains the word "evolution"; others reject all forms of religion. The range of beliefs about science and about religion is very broad. Regrettably, those who occupy the extremes of this range often have set the tone of public discussions. Evolution is science, however, and only science should be taught and learned in science classes. . . .

Isn't belief in evolution also a matter of faith?

Acceptance of evolution is not the same as a religious belief. Scientists' confidence about the occurrence of evolution is based on an overwhelming amount of supporting evidence gathered from many aspects of the natural world. To be accepted, scientific knowledge has to withstand the scrutiny of testing, retesting, and experimentation. Evolution is accepted within the scientific community because the concept has withstood extensive testing by many thousands of scientists for more than a century. As a 2006 "Statement on the Teaching of Evolution" from the Interacademy Panel on International Issues, a global network of national science academies, said, "Evidence-based facts about the origins and evolution of the Earth and of life on this planet have been established by numerous observations and independently derived experimental results from a multitude of scientific disciplines" (emphasis in original). . . .

Many religious beliefs do not rely on evidence gathered from the natural world. On the contrary, an important component of religious belief is faith, which implies acceptance of a truth regardless of the presence of empirical evidence for or against that truth. Scientists cannot accept scientific conclusions on faith alone because all such conclusions must be subject to testing against observations. Thus, scientists do not "believe" in evolution in the same way that someone believes in God.

How can random biological changes lead to more adapted organisms?

Contrary to a widespread public impression, biological evolution is not random, even though the biological changes that provide the raw material for evolution are not directed toward predetermined, specific goals. When DNA is being copied, mistakes in the copying process generate novel DNA sequences. These new sequences act as evolutionary "experiments." Most mutations do not change traits or fitness. But some mutations give organisms traits that enhance their ability to survive and reproduce, while other mutations reduce the reproductive fitness of an organism.

The process by which organisms with advantageous variations have greater reproductive success than other organisms within a population is known as "natural selection." Over multiple generations, some populations of organisms subjected to natural selection may change in ways that make them better able to survive and reproduce in a given environment. Others may be unable to adapt to a changing environment and will become extinct.

Aren't there many questions that still surround evolution? Don't many famous scientists reject evolution?

As with all active areas of science, there remain questions about evolution. There are always new questions to ask, new situations to consider, and new ways to study known phenomena. But evolution itself has been so thoroughly tested that biologists are no longer examining whether evolution has occurred and is continuing to occur. Similarly, biologists no longer debate many of the mechanisms responsible for evolution. As with any other field of science, scientists continue to study the mechanisms of how the process of evolution operates. As new technologies make possible previously unimaginable observations and allow for new kinds of experiments, scientists continue to propose and examine the strength of evidence regarding the mechanisms for evolutionary change. But the existence of such questions neither reduces nor undermines the fact that evolution has occurred and continues to occur.

Nor do such questions diminish the strength of evolutionary science. Indeed, the strength of a theory rests in part on providing scientists with the basis to explain observed phenomena and to predict what they are likely to find when exploring new phenomena and observations. In this regard, evolution has been and continues to be one of the most productive theories known to modern science.

Even scientific theories that are firmly established continue to be tested and modified by scientists as new information and new technologies become available. For example, the theory of gravity has been substantiated by many observations on Earth. But theoretical scientists, using their understanding of the physical universe, continue to test the limits of the theory of gravity in more extreme situations, such as close to a neutron star or black hole. Someday, new phenomena may be discovered that will require that the theory be expanded or revised, just as the development of the theory of general relativity in the first part of the 20th century expanded knowledge about gravity.

With evolutionary theory, many new insights will emerge as research proceeds. For example, the links between genetic changes and alterations in an organism's form and function are being intensively investigated now that the tools and technologies to do so are available.

Some who oppose the teaching of evolution sometimes use quotations from prominent scientists out of context to claim that scientists do not support evolution. However, examination of the quotations reveals that the scientists are actually disputing some aspect of how evolution occurs, not whether evolution occurred.

What evidence is there that the universe is billions of years old?

This is an important question because evolution of the wide variety of organisms currently existing on Earth required a very long period of time. Several independent dating techniques indicate that the Earth is billions of years old. Measurements of the radioactive elements in materials from the Earth, the Moon, and meteorites provide ages for the Earth and the solar system. These measurements are consistent with each other and with the physical processes of radioactivity. Additional evidence for the ages of the solar system and the galaxy includes the record of crater formation on the planets and their moons, the ages of the oldest stars in the Milky Way, and the rate of expansion of the universe. Measurements of the radiation left over from the Big Bang also support the universe's great age.

What's wrong with teaching critical thinking or "controversies" with regard to evolution?

Nothing is wrong with teaching critical thinking. Students need to learn how to reexamine their ideas in light of observations and accepted scientific concepts. Scientific knowledge itself is the result of the critical thinking applied by generations of scientists to questions about the natural world. Scientific knowledge must be subjected to continued reexamination and skepticism for human knowledge to continue to advance.

But critical thinking does not mean that all criticisms are equally valid.

Critical thinking has to be based on rules of reason and evidence. Discussion of critical thinking or controversies does not mean giving equal weight to ideas that lack essential supporting evidence. The ideas offered by intelligent design creationists are not the products of scientific reasoning. Discussing these ideas in science classes would not be appropriate given their lack of scientific support.

Recent calls to introduce "critical analysis" into science classes disguise a broader agenda. Other attempts to introduce creationist ideas into science employ such phrases as "teach the controversy" or "present arguments for and against evolution." Many such calls are directed specifically at attacking the teaching of evolution or other topics that some people consider as controversial. In this way, they are intended to introduce creationist ideas into science classes, even though scientists have thoroughly refuted these ideas. Indeed, the application of critical thinking to the science curriculum would argue against including these ideas in science classes because they do not meet scientific standards.

There is no scientific controversy about the basic facts of evolution. In this sense the intelligent design movement's call to "teach the controversy" is unwarranted. Of course, there remain many interesting questions about evolution, such as the evolutionary origin of sex or different mechanisms of speciation, and discussion of these questions is fully warranted in science classes. However, arguments that attempt to confuse students by suggesting that there are fundamental weaknesses in the science of evolution are unwarranted based on the overwhelming evidence that supports the theory. Creationist ideas lie outside of the realm of science, and introducing them in science courses has been ruled unconstitutional by the U.S. Supreme Court and other federal courts.

What are common ideas regarding creationism?

"Creationism" is a very broad term. In the most general sense, it refers to views that reject scientific explanations of certain features of the natural world (whether in biology, geology, or other sciences) and instead posit direct intervention (sometimes called "special creation") in these features by some transcendent being or power. Some creationists believe that the universe and Earth are only several thousand years old, a position referred to as "young Earth" creationism. Creationism also includes the view that the complex features of organisms cannot be explained by natural processes but require the intervention of a nonnatural "intelligent designer.". . .

Wouldn't it be "fair" to teach creationism along with evolution?

The goal of science education is to expose students to the best possible scholarship in each field of science. The science curriculum is thus the product of centuries of scientific investigation. Ideas need to become part of the base of accepted scientific knowledge before they are appropriately taught in schools. For example, the idea of continental drift to explain the movements and shapes of the continents was studied and debated for many years without becoming part of the basic science curriculum. As data accumulated, it became clearer that the surface of the Earth is composed of a series of massive plates, which are not bounded by the continents, that continually move in relation to each other. The theory of plate tectonics (which was proposed in the mid-1960s) grew from these data and offered a more complete explanation for the movement of continents. The new theory also predicted important phenomena, such as where earthquakes and volcanoes are likely to occur. When enough evidence had accumulated for the concept of plate tectonics to be accepted by the scientific community as fact, it became part of the earth sciences curriculum.

Scientists and science educators have concluded that evolution should be taught in science classes because it is the only tested, comprehensive scientific explanation for the nature of the biological world today that is supported by overwhelming evidence and widely accepted by the scientific community. The ideas supported by creationists, in contrast, are not supported by evidence and are not accepted by the scientific community.

Different religions hold very different views and teachings about the origins and diversity of life on Earth. Because creationism is based on specific sets of religious convictions, teaching it in science classes would mean imposing a particular religious view on students and thus is unconstitutional, according to several major rulings in federal district courts and the Supreme Court of the United States.

Does science disprove religion?

Science can neither prove nor disprove religion. Scientific advances have called some religious beliefs into question, such as the ideas that the Earth was created very recently, that the Sun goes around the Earth, and that mental illness is due to possession by spirits or demons. But many religious beliefs involve entities or ideas that currently are not within the domain of science. Thus, it would be false to assume that all religious beliefs can be challenged by scientific findings.

As science continues to advance, it will produce more complete and more accurate explanations for natural phenomena, including a deeper understanding of biological evolution. Both science and religion are weakened by claims that something not yet explained scientifically must be attributed to a supernatural deity. Theologians have pointed out that as scientific knowledge about phenomena that had been previously attributed to supernatural causes increases, a "god of the gaps" approach can undermine faith. Furthermore, it confuses the roles of science and religion by attributing explanations to one that belong in the domain of the other.

Many scientists have written eloquently about how their scientific studies have increased their awe and understanding of a creator. . . . The study of science need not lessen or compromise faith.

POSTSCRIPT

Should "Intelligent Design" Be Taught in Public Schools?

In 1999, the Kansas Board of Education deleted evolution—as well as much other science that would support the idea of an Earth and universe older than 6,000 years—from coverage in state competency tests. Since most teachers could be expected to focus their efforts on material their students would need to score well on the tests, and since the Board had vocal anti-evolution, pro-creation members, the Board's move was widely seen as supporting the pro-creation agenda. See Marjorie George, "And Then God Created Kansas . . . ," *University of Pennsylvania Law Review* (January 2001). Early in 2001, a new Kansas Board of Education took office and promptly put evolution back in the curriculum. See Eugene Russo, "Fighting Darwin's Battles," *The Scientist* (March 19, 2001). Yet the battle is hardly won. Not even Pope John Paul II's 1996 announcement that "new knowledge leads us to recognize that the theory of evolution is more than a hypothesis" had much impact. Indeed, in November 2004, the balance of power on the Kansas Board of Education had changed again and an effort to move "intelligent design" (ID) into the curriculum was growing. See Yudhijit Bhattacharjee, "Kansas Gears Up for Another Battle over Teaching Evolution," *Science* (April 29, 2005). A similar battle was raging in Dover, Pennsylvania; it was settled in the end by federal district court judge John Jones III, who emphatically declared that intelligent design is not science and thus has no place in a science curriculum. He wrote in his decision that urging that teaching the controversy, if not ID itself, "is at best disingenuous and, at worst, a canard. The goal of the ID movement is not to encourage critical thought, but to foment a revolution that would supplant evolutionary theory with ID." See Jeffrey Mervis, "Judge Jones Defines Science—And Why Intelligent Design Isn't," *Science* (January 6, 2006). Harold Morowitz, Robert Hazen, and James Trefil, "Intelligent Design Has No Place in the Science Curriculum," *Chronicle of Higher Education* (September 2, 2005), make similar points.

Yet proponents of ID—and/or opponents of Darwinism—never give up. ID was itself an attempt to bypass opposition to creationism. Now the watchword appears to have changed again. In June 2008, the Louisiana House of Representatives approved a bill to promote "critical thinking" on controversial topics such as evolution, the origins of life, global warming, and human cloning. The bill is widely seen as an attempt to slip ID into the curriculum as an alternative to evolution, which it plainly is not according to "Louisiana's Latest Assault on Darwin," an editorial in *The New York Times* (June 21, 2008). Pro-creationists such as the Discovery Institute are elated, according to senior fellow John G. West's "Louisiana Confounds the Science Thought Police," *National Review Online* (July 8, 2008).

Among recent books on this issue, Thomas Woodward's *Doubts About Darwin: A History of Intelligent Design* (Baker Books, 2003) argues the case in favor of intelligent design, as does H. Wayne House, ed., *Intelligent Design 101: Leading Experts Explain the Key Issues* (Kregel Publications, 2008). Michael Ruse's *Darwin and Design: Does Evolution Have a Purpose?* (Harvard University Press, 2003) also covers the history but concludes that those who study evolution have an almost religious response to the marvels they find. More critical efforts include Niall Shanks, *God, the Devil, and Darwin: A Critique of Intelligent Design Theory* (Oxford University Press, 2004), Barbara Forrest and Paul R. Gross, *Creationism's Trojan Horse: The Wedge of Intelligent Design* (Oxford University Press, 2004), and Matt Young and Taner Edis, eds., *Why Intelligent Design Fails: A Scientific Critique of the New Creationism* (Rutgers University Press, 1984). John Brockman, ed., *Intelligent Thought: Science versus the Intelligent Design Movement* (Vintage, 2006), gathers a number of often quite pungent essays by scientists on ID.

The 2008 movie *Expelled: No Intelligence Allowed* charges that Darwinians are guilty of suppressing valid alternatives to the theory of evolution, but Peter Manseau, "Is I.D. Ready for Its Close-Up?" *Science & Spirit* (May–June, 2008), says that "the greatest flaw in this deeply flawed film [is that] not only does *Expelled* treat evolution dishonestly, it does the same with design. Playing fast and loose with the question of whether ID is religion or science (swearing it is the latter but reaching for 'a loving God' when it wants to drive its message home), *Expelled* manages to miss the most intriguing facet of the discussion."

ISSUE 3

Should the Internet Be Neutral?

YES: Lawrence Lessig, from "The Future of the Internet," Testimony before the Senate Committee on Commerce, Science, and Transportation Hearing (April 22, 2008)

NO: Kyle McSlarrow, from "The Future of the Internet," Testimony before the Senate Committee on Commerce, Science, and Transportation Hearing (April 22, 2008)

ISSUE SUMMARY

YES: Professor of law Lawrence Lessig argues that in order to protect the growth and economic vitality of the Internet, Congress should enact "network neutrality" legislation to prevent broadband providers from interfering with free competition among application and content providers.

NO: Kyle McSlarrow, president and chief executive officer of the National Cable & Telecommunications Association, argues that "net neutrality" mandates would interfere with the ability of broadband providers to improve Internet access and thus would ultimately undermine consumer choice and welfare.

When the Internet was young—barely more than a decade ago—any content provider could send any kind of data they wished to any and all users. It was all bits—ones and zeroes—and from the standpoint of the computers or servers that accepted, transferred, and delivered the data, there was no difference between one stream of bits and another. The Communications Act of 1934, which regulated the phone companies that owned the wires over which almost all network traffic then ran, outlawed treating one kind of traffic or one source's traffic differently from any other. The result was that if one could figure out a way to turn a new kind of data into bits, or a new way to package the bits, or a new way to coordinate different bit streams, one could create a new business. It didn't matter whether one was a teenager in a bedroom in Indiana or a big business in New York. It also didn't matter whether the bits—or "content"—meant stock tips or porn. Everyone had a chance to innovate and make money.

The result was a virtual explosion of innovation. Today it is hard to imagine a world without e-mail, instant messaging, file sharing, Web pages, eBay,

PayPal, Google, blogging, MySpace, Monster, wireless connectivity, Web cameras, PDAs, Blackberries, Internet (VOIP) phones, and Web-enabled cell phones, among many other things. We have also gone from an Internet that ran on slow dial-up connections to one dominated by much faster broadband—DSL and cable—connections, which make it possible to deliver television and film over the Internet. Media and phone companies now deliver content, and at least some of them would like to facilitate the flow of their own content to their own customers and to interfere with the flow of content from other sources, unless those other sources pay a fee. Such a change has been likened to turning the open highway of the present Internet into a toll road. See Wendy M. Grossman, "Who Pays?" *Scientific American* (July 2006). At the same time, traffic on the Internet has increased tremendously, to the point where the flow of content is sometimes greatly slowed. Tom Giovanetti, "Network Neutrality? Welcome to the Stupid Internet," *Mercury News* (June 9, 2006), argues that a nonneutral Internet that gave priority to such things as VOIP (Internet phone) traffic from police and fire departments, 911 calls, and so on would be vastly preferable to a neutral Internet that did not. The debate has been vigorous, and legislation now before Congress would require "net neutrality." Opposition from broadband providers remains strong, however.

Should the Internet be neutral? In the following selections, Professor of law Lawrence Lessig argues that in order to protect the growth and economic vitality of the Internet, Congress should enact "network neutrality" legislation to prevent broadband providers from interfering with free competition among application and content providers. Kyle McSlarrow, president and chief executive officer of the National Cable & Telecommunications Association, argues that "net neutrality" mandates would interfere with the ability of broadband providers to improve Internet access and thus would ultimately undermine consumer choice and welfare.

YES

Lawrence Lessig

The Future of the Internet

Introduction

. . . For more than a decade, I have been studying the relationship between technology and Internet policy, and in particular, the relationship between the architecture of the Internet and innovation. I am honored to have the oportunity to address the question that is before this Committee—the future of the Internet.

This is the third time that I have addressed this Committee about essentially the same question. In October 2002, I testified about "network neutrality." That was, I believe, the first time that idea had been presented to this Committee. In February 2006, I testified at a hearing devoted to "network neutrality" exclusively. And in my view, the question before this Committee today, "The Future of the Internet," is directly tied to the future of network neutrality.

Yet while these questions are not new, in my view, Congress has yet to address them adequately. For the reasons I outline below, this failure to act continues to threaten the growth and economic vitality of the Internet. Thus, I would urge Congress to enact legislation that sets the basic framework for this critical economic infrastructure in a way that assures the greatest innovation and economic growth. That framework would embed a design principle that gave birth to the Internet—network neutrality.

Network Neutrality

The term "network neutrality" was introduced into the academic debate by Professor Tim Wu in early 2003. But the idea behind the term has been a central focus of network theorists since the early 1980s. "Network neutrality" builds upon a fundamental recognition about the relationship between a certain network design (what network architects Jerome Saltzer, David Clark, and David Reed called the "end-to-end" principle) and economic innovation. As former FCC Chief Economist, Professor Gerald R. Faulhauber, described the relationship at a Stanford conference in 2000,

> if I translate this into . . . economics, ["end-to-end"] in engineering is the equivalent of . . . perfect competitive market [in] economi[cs]. It's the thing that makes it all transparent, open, [where] anybody can do anything.

U.S. Senate, April 22, 2008.

"End-to-end" or, to update the language, "network neutrality," is the equivalent of perfect competition because it creates an environment, or platform, upon which competition among applications and content happens with minimum interference by the network or platform owner. Like a traditional marketplace, or a modern stock market, a neutral network assures that in the negotiation between buyer and seller, or innovator and consumer, the network itself plays little or no substantive role. All the power within this negotiation is shifted to the edge, to those economic actors directly responsible for innovation and growth in network applications and content—namely, consumers and innovators.

The original Internet achieved this architecture of competition unintentionally. The framers of the network's original design were not economists. They were not focused on building an engine of economic growth. Yet that was the consequence of a technical design intended to facilitate development flexibility. A network designed to enable anyone to develop new applications to run was also a network designed to maximize competition among applications and content.

The reason for this is simple but technical: under the Internet's original design, there was no easy way within the network to discriminate among applications or content. The network was built without the knowledge to discriminate built-in. Just as the Post Office can't cheaply pick and choose which letters to deliver based upon the sentiments expressed in the letters, so too the original Internet couldn't easily pick and choose which packets of data to send based on the content of those packets. It was blind to that content. That blindness encouraged a wide range of innovation.

This technical feature of the original network is now changing. Network owners increasingly have the ability to in effect open the Internet's letters—to peek inside the packets, and choose which go faster, or which get blocked. And while there are plenty of legitimate reasons why a network owner might need to "manage" network behavior, there are anticompetitive, or strategic reasons as well. Which reason motivates a network owner turns upon the business model that the network owner has adopted—either a business model of abundance and neutrality, serving whatever legal applications and content users and innovators want, or a business model of scarcity and control, leveraging financial return out of the scarcity their gate-keeping role allows them to create or maintain. If policymakers were confident network owners were following a model of abundance, there would be less reason to be concerned about how they manage the packets on their network. But because policymakers are uncertain about the ultimate motive for this "management," extensive inquiry into the technical questions of network management become important.

In my view, Congress could substantially simplify this area by setting a strong policy in favor of networks with a business model of abundance and neutrality. A clear set of network neutrality principles would do just that. If Congress made it perfectly clear that the FCC had the charge and authority to assure that the providers of this critical economic infrastructure were deploying this infrastructure with abundance in view, businesses would conform to that requirement. The economic question here is much more important than the financial returns to one particular industry. A powerful and vibrant broadband infrastructure is crucial to the economic growth of the Nation generally.

In addressing the question before this Committee, I would offer four points to consider.

1. The question of effective regulation for critical economic infrastructure did not begin with the Internet. Though the Internet is certainly "new" within the history of critical economic infrastructures, the regulatory questions it raises are as old as the Republic. Throughout our history, policymakers have weighed how best to encourage the spread of critical economic infrastructure, recognizing that sometimes subsidy is required, and at other times, simple regulation is sufficient. The Post Office, for example, was perhaps this Nation's first communication infrastructure, and as many have noted, the federal government played a critical role in assuring that that infrastructure supported the rapid growth of commercial newspaper and periodical publications, both for economic and political reasons. Likewise with the telegraph, railroads, electricity, the national highway system, and telephones: In each case, the policy question was how best to encourage broad scale, and relatively inexpensive infrastructure to support critical economic growth. How, in other words, to encourage an infrastructure of abundance rather than an infrastructure of scarcity.

Throughout this history, to achieve abundance it has sometimes been necessary to limit the freedom of infrastructure providers. Common carrier regulation did that substantially. But even without common carrier regulation, some limits have been essential to assuring that the interests of those who build this economic infrastructure are aligned with the interests of the Nation that depends upon it.

One critical limitation has been upon the ability of infrastructure owners to discriminate. Consider, for example, the infrastructure for electricity. As I have testified before, the electricity grid is a fundamentally neutral network. Innovators (like Sony, or Panasonic) are invited to develop applications (televisions, and radios) that use that network. They don't need permission from the network owners (PG&E, Commonwealth Edison) to deploy those innovations. When you plug your television set into an outlet, the network doesn't ask (as it well could, given modern technology) whether the television set is made by Sony or Panasonic. It doesn't ask whether the function of the appliance is to provide television or radio service. Instead, so long as application developers develop appliances that comply with the protocols of the network, the electricity grid will provide service to those appliances neutrally. That doesn't mean for free—for obviously, we all pay for the electricity we consume. It doesn't mean unmetered—obviously, we pay more if we use more. But it does mean that Sony doesn't need to pay a special tax to PG&E for the right to develop Sony television sets, or digital music players. Sony, in this model, is free to innovate without permission from the infrastructure owners—the electricity network.

We could of course imagine a different system. And indeed, we could well build that different system into our electricity grid right now. The electricity grid could be architected to ask the application who made it, or what its function is. The network could then decide whether or how to serve electricity depending upon the answer to that question. Providers of appliances could then be taxed depending upon the elasticity of demand for their products. Electricity providers could then enjoy greater revenue for their product from this tax.

I take it there are few who believe that this alternative electricity system would be better than the system we have today—even though economists could well describe the conditions under which this alternative may well be more "efficient."

My point, however, is not about whether those conditions obtain, either for the electricity grid, or the Internet. It is instead to emphasize the value of being conservative in policymaking in both contexts. Anyone arguing that the electricity network should be rebuilt to permit PG&E to discriminate among applications using its network should bear a significant burden before that change was allowed. And likewise for anyone arguing that the core competitive feature of the original Internet should be altered: he or she too should bear a significant burden before that change is allowed to alter the critical competitive environment that the Internet presents.

Giving up on network neutrality would be like permitting PG&E to tax appliance manufacturers for the privilege of using electricity on its network: No doubt, that would be a boon for PG&E, and its shareholders. It would not be a boon for the economy.

2. Policymakers should adopt policies that drive network providers towards business models of broadband abundance rather than business models that exploit scarcity. There are at least two clear business models for broadband deployment—one that drives to broadband abundance, the other that leverages broadband scarcity to maximize network provider returns. There is a critical economic justification for government to try to tilt broadband providers towards the model of abundance.

Again, the broadband Internet is infrastructure. Like electricity grids, and national highways, it supports a wide range of economic and social activity. As scholars have demonstrated, private actors providing public infrastructure but focused on private gain alone would rationally maximize their own return at the expense of this broader public gain. Interventions that create the incentive among infrastructure providers to support these broader interests produce real economic return to the economy, even if they mean less financial return to the infrastructure providers.

For example, consider by contrast policy decisions affecting the growth of cable. Though cable television obviously provides valuable free speech opportunities and economic return through the incentives it creates to produce new content, it is plausible that cable television is not a core infrastructure technology, since it does not generate a diverse range of technology and applications building upon the cable platform. For this reason, it may well have been sensible for Congress to grant to cable owners an almost unlimited range of freedom to structure production decisions as they want, and develop cable offerings and prices as the market will bear. The product of these policy decisions is obviously not uncontested—families continue to resist the bundling of cable providers, making it hard, for example, for parents to select a mix of content that minimizes advertising; consumers generally resist significant price increases; developers of independently produced content point to the radical drop in independently produced television content after the relaxation of government ownership regulations. All of these "problems" are the predictable result of allowing cable owners the degree of economic freedom the law now permits them. And while I share with many the wish that things were different, I can well understand that there are limited public policy reasons for regulatory intervention.

But when the platform is not just a video delivery system, but instead, a general purpose digital innovation platform, the justification for regulatory intervention changes dramatically. In the world of entertainment, cable TV is just one option. But in the world of digital communication infrastructures, the Internet is everything. And assuring that this infrastructure gets built with maximum capacity at the lowest cost, and with minimal burdens on application and content developers, is a critical public policy objective.

3. Investment decisions by venture capitalists are driven by expectations of future, not present, behavior. In both of the earlier hearings at which I was invited to testify about network neutrality issues, critics of regulation argued that there was no reason to intervene, because there was no actual evidence of discrimination. In the two years since my last testimony, however, network owners have provided this Congress with a significant number of examples of exactly the kind of harmful discrimination that network theorists have long predicted. In 2005, the FCC was forced to intervene to stop a DSL provider from blocking voice-over-IP technologies. In 2007, AT&T technologists acted to block the audio of Pearl Jam performer as he criticized the President in a webcast carried by AT&T. Verizon has been accused of blocking text messages that it found too controversial. And most recently, Comcast has been shown to be blocking particular Internet applications that might compete with its video service, using network management practices not approved by any independent standards body. If "network neutrality" was "a solution in search of a problem" in 2002, and 2006, the network owners have been very kind to network neutrality advocates by now providing plenty of examples of the problem to which network neutrality rules would be a solution.

But there is one very practical point that this debate about whether there is significant current discrimination misses. Venture capitalists don't choose whether to invest in new innovation based upon what is happening on the Internet today. They base their decisions upon what they expect behavior on the Internet will be tomorrow. They decide, for example, whether to fund a new Internet application today based upon whether they believe the entrepreneur will be able to deploy that application profitably in 2 or 5 years. That question in turn will depend upon whether network owners will be free to discriminate against that application in the future. Or more generally, whether network owners will be free to tax that application to extract some portion of that application's profit. If venture capitalists believe that network owners will have that freedom tomorrow, then for a certain range of innovations, they will choose not to invest in that innovation today.

It is for this reason that I and others have consistently argued that Congress could well be slowing the growth of the Internet economy by not setting today a clear principle about the rules that will govern Internet innovation tomorrow. This "wait and see" attitude ignores that sector of the economy that can't afford to wait and see: investors. The "wait and see" argument is thus oblivious to the real economic costs that uncertainty here creates.

If Congress were clear in its direction to the FCC about the policy the FCC is required to implement, then any uncertainty about network owner behavior could be eliminated. And any costs from that uncertainty could also be eliminated. So long as a simple and clear rule signaled to the markets that network owners would be in the business of producing abundant broadband by encouraging innovation rather than leveraging value from scarcity, markets would react to that signal in a way that encouraged greater investment in new innovation.

4. Congress should direct the FCC to implement, with the minimal regulatory intervention necessary, a policy that drives network providers to a business model of abundance. It has been my view for the past decade that Congress needs to signal a clear policy supporting neutral and abundant broadband growth. Without doubt, however, such a policy can go too far. The objective of regulators must be the minimum intervention necessary to steer broadband providers to a business model of abundance rather than scarcity, while recognizing the limited competence of regulators in any field of new technological innovation. That limited competence means regulators should focus on the behavior that they can monitor well, using the levers they have over that regulable behavior, so that they can have confidence about behavior at the layers of the network that they can't regulate as well.

Congress can achieve that end by setting out clear neutrality principles in legislation, while charging the FCC with the responsibility for carrying those principles into effect. Congress' principle, again, should be to encourage broadband abundance, by steering providers away from a business model that leverages scarcity. But in pursuing that clear legislative objective, the FCC should proceed in a careful and limited way, escalating regulatory intervention only when existing strategies have been proven to fail. Put differently, if a clear objective has been set by Congress, then an FCC strategy of "shock and awe" is both unnecessary and counter productive. Instead, the interventions by the FCC should be directed to the end of convincing broadband providers that the legislative policy choice of Congress will be achieved. A consistent regulatory practice to that end will convince investors of the only profitable broadband investment strategy. That will drive providers to the economically optimal broadband strategy.

As I testified in 2006, in my view that minimal strategy right now marries the basic principles of "Internet Freedom" first outlined by Chairman Michael Powell, and modified more recently by the FCC, to one additional requirement—a ban on discriminatory access tiering. While broadband providers should be free, in my view, to price consumer access to the Internet differently—setting a higher price, for example, for faster or greater access— they should not be free to apply discriminatory surcharges to those who make content or applications available on the Internet. As I testified, in my view, such "access tiering" risks creating a strong incentive among Internet providers to favor some companies over others; that incentive in turn tends to support business models that exploit scarcity rather than abundance. If Google, for example, knew it could buy a kind of access for its video content that iFilm couldn't, then it could exploit its advantage to create an even greater disadvantage for its competitors; network providers in turn could deliver on that disadvantage only if the non-privileged service was inferior to the privileged service.

Put differently, "fast lanes" on the Internet are only valuable if "slow lanes" are really slow. Depending upon the market, this fact can create a perverse incentive among network providers not to build the fastest network possible.

Conclusion

As I testified in 2002 and 2006, the Internet was the great economic surprise of the 20th century. No one who funded or initially developed the network imagined it would have the economic and social consequences that it has had.

But though the success of the network was a surprise, policymakers have yet to learn just why it was a success: Built into its basic design was a guarantee of maximum competition. A free market in applications was coded into its architecture. The growth of that network followed from this basic design. The world economy benefited dramatically from this growth.

The threat facing the Internet today is that network owners will convince regulators to go back on that original design. Through regulatory policies that permit broadband providers to act however their private interests dictate, these regulatory policies would threaten the economic potential of the network generally. New innovation always comes from outsiders. If insiders are given both technical and legal control over innovation on the Internet, innovation will be stifled.

Unlike many other industrialized nations, we in the United States have failed to preserve the extraordinary competition among ISPs that characterized early Internet growth. But despite that loss in access competition, network neutrality still provided significant opportunity for application and content competition. The changes now being spoken of by the effective duopoly of broadband providers will weaken that application and content competition.

It is my view that any policy that weakens competition is a policy that will weaken the prospects for Internet and economic growth. I therefore urge this Committee to secure and supplement the work begun originally by Chairman Powell, and continued now by Chairman Martin, by enacting legislation that sets a clear policy to protect the environment for Internet innovation and competition.

Kyle McSlarrow

 **NO**

The Future of the Internet

. . . The cable industry is the nation's largest provider of high-speed Internet access, making cable broadband service available to 92 percent of Americans, and has invested $130 billion to build a two-way interactive network with fiber-optic technology. Cable companies also provide state-of-the-art digital telephone service to more than 15 million American consumers. Cable operators are committed to delivering an open and satisfying Internet experience to their customers, and the dramatic growth in cable broadband subscribers is evidence of their success in doing so.

The cable industry has consistently demonstrated its commitment to policies that ensure all Americans have access to affordable broadband. We supported, for example, proposals advanced by Senator Dorgan and Senator Stevens to create a fund tailored to expanding broadband into unserved areas. We support Senator Inouye's Broadband Data Improvement Act, because we believe that improving federal data collection and dissemination regarding where broadband services have been deployed in the United States is necessary in order to achieve the goal of ubiquitous broadband availability for all Americans. And we continue to support:

- Tax credits or other tax incentives to providers that build out in rural areas that are unserved by an existing broadband provider.
- Reform of the RUS broadband loan program so that funding is targeted specifically to unserved areas.
- Expansion of the FCC's Lifeline and Link-Up Programs to help ensure that broadband access is extended to low-income households.
- Public–private partnerships to provide broadband in unserved areas.

We support these initiatives because we recognize that the government can play an important role in making certain that the economic and social benefits of broadband connectivity are extended to all areas of this country, and we look forward to working with you further to achieve these goals. But while broadband deployment to every community in America merits the full attention of policymakers, legislation calling for "network neutrality" or government intervention into the operation of networks would undermine the goals of broadband deployment and adoption. The development of the Internet, expansion of broadband networks, and creation of innovative Internet applications we have seen would not have occurred at such a rapid pace if providers were restricted in how they could engineer their networks to accommodate

U.S. Senate, April 22, 2008.

these dynamic developments. The government's consistent light regulatory touch since the introduction of broadband has worked. And only that continued regulatory freedom is likely to spur the investment and innovation that consumers have come to expect.

Today, I would like to focus on three points that illustrate why the Internet and broadband services should not be subject to greater and more intrusive government regulation. First, cable broadband providers have demonstrated and remain committed to providing Americans the very best broadband service available. Second, every cable modem subscriber today can access the content he or she seeks over the Internet. Broadband providers do not block access to content. Reasonable network optimization techniques not only enable the growth and development of the Internet, they protect consumers and their legitimate expectations.

Finally, the national policy of leaving the Internet unregulated has been a resounding success. Government intervention in broadband network management would only slow the pace of innovation and prevent the natural development of traffic solutions that is already occurring today.

I. Cable Brought Broadband to America

The industry's commitment to the deployment of broadband is reflected in the plain statistics. By any benchmark, the cable industry is leading efforts to spur broadband use and deployment.

Investment. The cable industry has done more to stimulate broadband growth and innovation than any other industry. Cable operators have invested $130 billion in private capital since the passage of the Telecommunications Act of 1996 to build broadband networks across the United States. Today 92% of American households, or about 117 million homes, have access to cable broadband service, including 96% of American homes to which cable television service is available. This investment and expansion took place without any government subsidies.

Competition. The cable industry's efforts to deploy broadband have stimulated tremendous investment in the provision of Internet access by competing providers, first by telephone companies and now wireless and satellite companies. This competition has spurred cable broadband providers and their competitors to develop better and better networks and applications to meet consumer demand and compete for their business. As former FTC Chairman Timothy Muris has explained, "competition [among providers] spurs producers to meet consumer expectations because the market generally imposes strict discipline on sellers who disappoint consumers and thus lose sales to producers who better meet consumer needs. These same competitive pressures also encourage producers to provide truthful information about their offerings."

Most notably, as the availability of broadband service has grown, the price-per-megabit has fallen significantly, and the speeds cable broadband offers have shot up dramatically. When cable first offered high-speed broadband service as an alternative to dial-up access in the mid-90s, the speeds were approximately 1–1.5 Mbps. Today, most cable operators offer broadband speeds topping 5 Mbps and some operators, such as Cablevision and Comcast, offer speeds up to 50 Mbps. Comcast and Cox Communications also offer a service that provides for "boosts" of higher speeds that double the throughput on an on-demand, capacity-available basis.

Now the cable industry is on the verge of making the next leap—from "broadband" to "wideband"—with a technology which can enable dramatically higher download and upload speeds well above 100 Megabits per second. Several weeks ago, for example, Comcast launched a "wideband" service in Minneapolis–St. Paul that offers speeds of 50 Megabits per second. Comcast expects to have wideband available to 20% of its systems by year-end 2008 and to all homes passed by mid-2010.

Increased Use and Demand. The high quality and easy availability of cable broadband has led to the widespread adoption of broadband use. Today, the cable industry has more than 35 million broadband customers. Overall, approximately 64 million broadband households nationwide have broadband service, and that number continues to grow.

New Content, Web Services, and Applications. The efforts of broadband network providers to build larger and faster networks have helped ensure the success of countless numbers of new Internet businesses and applications—online video services, social networking websites, data-sharing services, and online interactive game services, to name a few. Despite concerns about alleged limited access to broadband, use of Internet video on demand has grown at the most dramatic rate. In July 2006, 107 million Americans watched video online and about 60% of Internet users downloaded more than 7 billion videos off the Internet. In February 2008, nearly 135 million U.S. Internet users spent an average of 204 minutes viewing 10.1 billion online videos. YouTube represented 34% of those online videos, or nearly 3.5 billion in total. To put it into context, in 2006, YouTube consumed as much bandwidth as the entire Internet consumed in the year 2000.

Television networks are now offering cable modem and other broadband customers video online, such as NBC Universal and News Corp.'s new Hulu service. Book retailers are now offering online digital novels; and music sales websites, such as iTunes, continue to grow. Social networking websites, where users share home videos, pictures, and music content, are also on the rise—in 2007, an estimated 126.5 million people in North America participated in an online social networking website. Internet commerce also continues to grow. Last year, over $135 billion was spent purchasing goods and services over the Internet.

For years, net neutrality proponents have argued that without government intervention, broadband providers would stifle competing services and content providers; Internet development and usage would stagnate; and consumers would be unable to use their broadband connections to download video or access other emerging applications. In fact, cable's investment in broadband has driven innovation and investment in new content and applications

. the edge—the exact opposite of what was predicted by advocates of net regulation.

There is no better proof that there presently exists no "problem" needing a "solution" than YouTube. YouTube would have been a pipe dream in 2002. Six years later, however, YouTube—the proverbial "two guys in a garage" who allegedly could not survive, let alone thrive, unless the Internet were regulated—has become a multibillion dollar enterprise. And YouTube is now owned by Google, which itself has grown to become one of the largest companies in the world with a market capitalization of $169 billion.

Here's an incontrovertible truth: the staggering growth of these companies would not have occurred without cable's investment in and deployment of the reliable high-speed broadband service that provides the ecosystem in which Google, YouTube, Yahoo! and other Internet services can flourish.

II. Network Optimization Enhances and Enables the Internet Experience

In 2006, I testified before this Committee and stated that cable operators do not and would not block subscribers' access to any lawful content, applications or services. That statement remains true today. Cable modem subscribers have the ability to do anything they want to on the Internet. They can download or stream videos, upload and send pictures to friends, or call family across the world. They can also attach gaming devices, or any other computing device they want to use to the network. They can use file-sharing software from peer-to-peer networks. If they couldn't do what they wanted, they would soon not be cable modem subscribers. They would go to our competitors.

Cable subscribers can enjoy the most advanced and cutting-edge Internet sites and applications because of the extensive efforts cable operators constantly undertake to make all content and applications flow smoothly and work seamlessly together over the network. In 1999, there were only 2 million households with broadband service in the United States; today there are approximately 64 million. This is a great success story—but with this success comes the need to manage the network so that every household has good user experience.

Cable providers built a smart infrastructure that has the capability to evolve and meet the challenges of multimedia, file sharing, and other bandwidth-intensive applications. But cable broadband subscribers currently enjoy the full benefits of broadband only because cable operators manage their networks on a content-agnostic basis to provide seamless connectivity, deter spam and viruses, and make sure that a tiny minority of users don't slow down the Internet for everyone else. Various estimates are that as few as 5% of customers use from 50 to 90% of the total capacity of the network. In Japan, it is estimated that 1% of Internet users consume 47% of the total Internet traffic. Faced with these voracious bandwidth consumers, cable operators may engage in reasonable, content-agnostic network management practices—triggered by objective criteria based upon network traffic levels—to ensure that the relatively few customers who utilize bandwidth-heavy applications do not degrade or otherwise adversely affect broadband Internet access for the vast majority of customers.

There have been some recent concerns that network management practices affecting certain high-bandwidth-consuming peer-to-peer (P2P) applications are "discriminatory." P2P traffic can consume a disproportionately large amount of network resources—far, far more than any other Internet use. If even a small fraction of customers are using these bandwidth-intensive applications at the same time, it can interfere with the ability of the vast majority of all other customers in that area to surf the web, watch streaming video, make voice-over-IP calls, or engage in other routine uses of the Internet.

Providers can't build their way out of this problem—in spite of increasing capacity, many P2P protocols are written specifically to commandeer as much bandwidth as is available. Instead, providers optimize their networks in order to balance the needs of all of their customers.

Far from inhibiting access, smart network techniques protect the ability of our customers to make the greatest and most flexible use of the Internet. They are a reasonable response to an identified congestion problem that has the benefit of allowing all other applications—particularly latency-sensitive applications like VoIP and streaming video—to work better. As the Institute for Policy Innovation recently stated, "[i]n almost all cases, network management today is unnoticed by consumers. The opposite, a total lack of management, would not be true. If network operators were precluded from managing their networks, consumers would be negatively affected." Sound network management is essential to ensuring a stable broadband platform. Google, Yahoo!, Amazon, and service providers like Vonage could not carry on their businesses if bandwidth-consuming applications were allowed to block customers from accessing their Web sites or completing their transactions. Because of network management, such businesses can develop business models that hinge on the expectation that their service will not be crowded out by congestion caused by heavy bandwidth-using software. Far from being "neutral," a network that is not managed simply allows those who want to demand all the bandwidth for themselves to do so unchecked.

Reasonable network management practices are also vital to combating the well-documented, illegal distribution of copyrighted material on the Internet. We cannot ignore the problem of piracy. It is a problem that affects not just broadband service providers, legitimate broadband application providers and content providers, but also law-abiding consumers. Ultimately they are the ones that bear the burden of congestion caused by those who abuse their network access to engage in the widespread distribution of infringing works. Technology is agnostic, but, according to one source, 90 percent of P2P downloads are pirated material. Broadband providers, content owners and others all have a stake in exploring technology solutions that address piracy in ways that respect our customers' expectations and respect the copyright owner's rights, not simply to curtail congestion but for reasons of fairness to those who invest in content and make an important contribution to our economy. Government action that would inhibit development of innovative approaches to thwarting piracy and enhancing the online experience for the vast majority of Internet users would harm content creation and ultimately consumers.

is there evidence that these challenges are insurmountable and
more government regulation? Quite the contrary. The same techno-
al innovation that gives rise to some of these challenges has produced
ative ways to fight spam and viruses. The same private sector collaboration
nat allowed the countless number of networks that make up the Internet to
exchange traffic and engage in peering has and continues to focus on new
challenges.

Some P2P developers are creating new ways to make that technology
more bandwidth-efficient and network-friendly, so that it may continue to
emerge as a useful way to distribute legal content. Cable companies and other
broadband providers are working hard to find ways to address concerns about
network congestion and create consumer-friendly options that allow the
majority of users to access content at the speeds needed. The "P4P Working
Group"—a collaborative industry effort to develop network management solutions that benefit cable and other broadband operators, P2P software firms,
and consumers—is one such effort.

Broadband providers have also begun testing and dialogue with P2P
applications providers to make networks and P2P applications friendlier to one
another. For example, Verizon has been working with Pando Networks, a P2P
software developer, and the P4P Working Group to develop a more bandwidth
efficient file-sharing protocol. Just last week, Comcast and Pando announced
their intention to lead an industry-wide effort to create a "P2P Bill of Rights
and Responsibilities." And Comcast and BitTorrent recently reached an agreement in which Comcast pledged to adopt a capacity management technique
based on individual users' consumption during peak periods rather than based
on a particular protocol.

Broadband providers and Internet content and service providers have
mutual incentives to develop workable solutions that enhance customers'
Internet experiences. Cable operators' tremendous investments have laid the
foundation for robust broadband networks that have spurred the remarkable
explosion of new services and innovations on the Internet. In turn, the vast
array of applications and services now available on the Internet drive more
and more people to become broadband users.

III. The Government Should Continue to Refrain from Regulation

Congress should resist calls to interfere with broadband providers' freedom
to manage their respective networks in order to satisfy the evolving needs of
American consumers. Cable modem service has never been subject to regulation. Six years after the FCC classified cable's broadband offering as an unregulated information service and nearly three years after the FCC determined
that no regulation was needed to encourage broadband deployment and preserve and promote Internet usage and demand, there has been no evidence
of any practices that would change those conclusions or warrant government
intervention generally or specifically with respect to permissible network

management activities. The disaster scenarios voiced by network neutrality proponents for many years have never happened. In fact, the opposite has happened—the Internet is booming without regulation. There is quite simply no problem requiring a government solution.

Under the guise of preventing discrimination, "net neutrality" proponents would have the government determine which network management techniques are permissible. But putting every network management strategy up for debate before regulators would severely hamper the ability of network providers to ensure high-quality and reliable Internet access for their subscribers. Depriving network operators of certain bandwidth management tools only makes the network less efficient for everyone. Ultimately, interfering with an operator's ability to manage its network would harm consumers and prevent them from accessing the content they desire. Adept network optimization techniques are fundamental to creating and preserving the stable "ecosystem" for online service providers that ensures an optimal customer experience.

Government intervention in a fast-changing technological world could result in very real problems developing very quickly. Network management practices are constantly changing and evolving—as networks grow, consumer usage patterns change, and new technologies emerge. It would be impossible for any regulation to keep up with these changes. Nor does the government have the expertise or resources to second-guess the thousands of network management decisions broadband network engineers must make every day. It is far more likely that government interference in the development of the market could foreclose or prevent the emergence of cross-industry efforts that are more likely to get the solutions right.

Conclusion

Misplaced concerns over legitimate and reasonable network management practices do not justify the enactment of open-ended regulation of the Internet, particularly where the costs of such regulation are foreseeable and substantial. Given the growth of broadband competition and the breathtaking pace of technological change, government intervention is unwarranted. As the Federal Trade Commission has warned, regulation of Internet access at this stage of market development could have "potentially adverse and unintended effects," including reduced product and service innovation. And net neutrality requirements would frustrate the Federal policy of "preserv[ing] the vibrant and competitive free market that presently exists for the Internet . . . , unfettered by Federal or State regulation." Today's hands-off policy has given us the flexibility to innovate and respond to consumer demand. By contrast, proposals for "net neutrality" amount to regulation of the Internet that would undermine—not promote—consumer choice and welfare.

OSTSCRIPT

Should the Internet Be Neutral?

In June 2006, the U.S. House of Representatives passed the Communications Opportunity, Promotion, and Enhancement Act after deleting a provision that would have mandated network neutrality. As passed, the Act "would let the [Federal Communications Commission] investigate complaints about broadband providers blocking Internet content only after the fact." See Grant Gross, "House Rejects 'Net Neutrality,' Passes Telecom Reform Bill," *Network World* (June 12, 2006) (http://www.networkworld.com/). In the Senate, attempts to amend a similar bill to mandate network neutrality failed. See Tom Abate, "Net Neutrality Amendment Dies: Telecommunications Bill Goes to Senate Without Provision Sought by Web Firms," *San Francisco Chronicle* (June 29, 2006). Some have credited the telecommunications industry's heavy investment in lobbyists and campaign contributions with the result to that point. Lauren Weinstein, "Ma Bell's Revenge: The Battle for Network Neutrality," *Communications of the ACM* (January 2007), says that "much of the anti-neutrality argument is simple greed in action" and warns that "most Internet users simply don't realize how drastically and negatively they could be affected if anti-neutrality arguments hold sway. Getting true network neutrality back after it's been lost is likely to be effectively impossible. Except for the anti-neutrality camp itself, we'd all be worse off with a non-neutral Internet, and that's a risk we simply must not accept."

The overall significance of the issue is discussed by Daniel Krauss, "Net Neutrality and How It Just Might Change Everything," *American Libraries* (September 2006), and Michael Baumann, "Net Neutrality: The Internet's World War," *Information Today* (September 2006). Since then, the debate has gained new impetus with the proposal of new legislation and charges that Comcast and other broadband providers are surreptitiously causing large file downloads to fail (see "Comcast, Cox Slowing P2P Traffic 24 × 7," *Network World* (May 19, 2008), and "Elude Your ISP's BitTorrent Blockade," *PC World* (July 2008). In August 2008, the Federal Communications Commission declared network blocking illegal and told Comcast to stop interfering with its customers' use of the Internet (John Eggerton, "FCC: Comcast Violated Internet Open-Access Guidelines," *Broadcasting & Cable* (August 1, 2008) (http://www.broadcastingcable.com/article/CA6583586.html).

Net neutrality is not just a matter of promoting innovation, growth, and economic vitality. Joe Dysart, "The Quest for Net Neutrality," *American School Board Journal* (May 2008), says that broadband providers such as AT&T and Comcast are pushing for a two-tiered Internet, with first tier free but slow and a second tier that provides more speed at a premium price. Dysart notes that this would adversely impact institutions such as public schools, whose limited

budgets would confine them to the inferior tier. Religious groups have simila
concerns. Testifying at the same "The Future of the Internet" hearing that provided the selections for this issue, Michele Combs, vice president of Communications for the Christian Coalition of America, argued that net neutrality has
been abused by many ISPs: "Verizon Wireless censored text messages sent by
the pro-choice advocacy group, NARAL, to its own members who had voluntarily signed up to receive them. . . . AT&T [has] cut off political speech during
live concerts . . . [and] Comcast was blocking consumers' ability to download
the King James Bible." Combs says, "Increasingly, faith-based groups are turning to the Internet to promote their political rights, to engage in what Ronald
Reagan called 'the hard work of freedom.' We should not let the phone and
cable companies interfere with that work."

Net neutrality laws are not the only possible solution, of course. According
to David Hatch, "Gutierrez Affirms Opposition to 'Net Neutrality' Measures,"
CongressDaily AM (May 20, 2008), the Bush administration would prefer to
encourage expansion of Internet capacity.

Internet References . . .

University Corporation for Atmospheric Research

The University Corporation for Atmospheric Research and the National Center for Atmospheric Research are part of a collaborative community dedicated to understanding the atmosphere—the air around us—and the interconnected processes that make up the Earth system, from the ocean floor to the Sun's core. The *UCAR Quarterly* is a journal that presents reports on many issues, including geoengineering (e.g., http://www.ucar.edu/communications/quarterly/fall06/bigfix.jsp).

http://www.ucar.edu/

Department of Energy

The U.S. Department of Energy provides information on nuclear power, hydrogen, and other energy sources, as well as such energy-related issues as global warming.

http://www.energy.gov

Global Warming

The Environmental Protection Agency maintains this site to summarize the current state of knowledge about global warming.

http://www.epa.gov/climatechange/index.html

Intergovernmental Panel on Climate Change

The Intergovernmental Panel on Climate Change (IPCC) was formed by the World Meteorological Organization (WMO) and the United Nations Environment Programme (UNEP) to assess any scientific, technical, and socioeconomic information that is relevant to the understanding of the risk of human-induced climate change.

http://www.ipcc.ch

National Renewable Energy Laboratory

The National Renewable Energy Laboratory (NREL) is the leading center for renewable energy research in the United States.

http://www.nrel.gov

Heritage Foundation

The Heritage Foundation is a think tank whose mission is to formulate and promote conservative public policies based on the principles of free enterprise, limited government, individual freedom, traditional American values, and a strong national defense.

http://www.heritage.org

Energy and the Environment

As the damage that human beings do to their environment in the course of obtaining food, water, wood, ore, energy, and other resources has become clear, many people have grown concerned. Some of that concern is for the environment—the landscapes and living things with which humanity shares its world. Some of that concern is more for human welfare; it focuses on the ways in which environmental damage threatens human health, prosperity, or even survival.

Among the major environmental issues are those related to energy. By releasing vast amounts of carbon dioxide, fossil fuels threaten to change the world's climate. Potential solutions include warding off excess solar heating, greatly expanding the use of nuclear power, and changing our automobile fuel from gasoline to hydrogen.

- Are "Space Sunshades" a Possible Answer to Global Warming?

- Is It Time to Revive Nuclear Power?

- Will Hydrogen Replace Fossil Fuels for Cars?

ISSUE 4

Are "Space Sunshades" a Possible Answer to Global Warming?

YES: **Roger Angel,** from "Feasibility of Cooling the Earth with a Cloud of Small Spacecraft near the Inner Lagrange Point (L1)," *Proceedings of the National Academy of Sciences of the United States of America* (November 14, 2006)

NO: **James R. Fleming,** from "The Climate Engineers," *Wilson Quarterly* (Spring 2007)

ISSUE SUMMARY

YES: Professor of astronomy Roger Angel argues that if dangerous changes in global climate become inevitable, despite greenhouse gas controls, it may be possible to solve the problem by reducing the amount of solar energy that hits the Earth, using reflective spacecraft.

NO: James R. Fleming, professor of science, technology, and society, argues that climate engineers such as Roger Angel fail to consider both the risks of unintended consequences to human life and political relationships and the ethics of the human relationship to nature.

It has been known for a very long time that natural events such as volcanic eruptions can cool climate, sometimes dramatically, by injecting large quantities of dust and sulfates into the stratosphere, where they serve as a "sunshade" that reflects a portion of solar heat back into space before it can warm the Earth. In 1815, the Tambora volcano on Sumbawa island, Indonesia, put so much material (especially sulfates) into the atmosphere that 1816 was known in the United States, Canada, and Europe as the "year without a summer." There was crop-killing frost, snow, and ice all summer long, which gave the year its other name of "eighteen-hundred-and-froze-to-death." See Clive Oppenheimer, "Climatic, Environmental and Human Consequences of the Largest Known Historic Eruption: Tambora Volcano (Indonesia) 1815," *Progress in Physical Geography* (June 2003). In 1992, Mount Pinatubo, in the Philippines, had a similar, if smaller, effect and hid for a time the climate warming otherwise produced by increasing amounts of greenhouse gases. See Alan Robock, "The

Climatic Aftermath," *Science* (February 15, 2002). Changes in solar activity can also have effects. Periods of climate chilling and climate warming have been linked to decreases and increases in the amount of energy released by the sun and reaching the Earth. See Caspar M. Ammann et al., "Solar Influence on Climate During the Past Millennium: Results from Transient Simulations with the NCAR Climate System Model," *Proceedings of the National Academy of Sciences of the United States of America* (March 6, 2007).

Such effects have prompted many researchers to think that global warming is not just a matter of increased atmospheric content of greenhouse gases such as carbon dioxide (which slow the loss of heat to space and thus warm the planet) but also of the amount of sunlight that reaches Earth from the sun. So far, most attempts to find a solution to global warming have focused on reducing human emissions of greenhouse gases. But it does not seem unreasonable to consider the other side of the problem, the energy that reaches Earth from the sun. After all, if you are too warm in bed at night, you can remove the blanket *or* turn down the furnace.

Paul Crutzen suggested in "Albedo Enhancement by Stratospheric Sulfur Injections: A Contribution to Resolve a Policy Dilemma?" *Climate Change* (August 2006) that adding sulfur compounds to the stratosphere (as volcanoes have done) could reflect some solar energy and help relieve the problem. According to Bob Henson, "Big Fixes for Climate?" *UCAR Quarterly* (Fall 2006), the National Center for Atmospheric Research is currently testing the idea with computer simulations; one conclusion is that a single Pinatubo-sized stratospheric injection could buy 20 years of time before we would have to cut back carbon dioxide emissions in a big way. Such measures would not be cheap, and at present there is no way to tell whether they would have undesirable side-effects, although G. Bala, P. B. Duffy, and K. E. Taylor, "Impact of Geoengineering Schemes on the Global Hydrological Cycle," *Proceedings of the National Academy of Sciences of the United States of America* (June 3, 2008), suggest it is likely that precipitation would be significantly reduced. Suggestions that something similar might be done on a global scale go back more than 40 years; see Robert Kunzig, "A Sunshade for Planet Earth," *Scientific American* (November 2008).

In the following selections, professor of astronomy Roger Angel argues that if dangerous changes in global climate become inevitable, despite greenhouse gas controls, it may be possible to solve the problem by reducing the amount of solar energy that hits the Earth, using reflective spacecraft. James R. Fleming, professor of science, technology, and society, argues that climate engineers such as Roger Angel fail to consider both the risks of unintended consequences to human life and political relationships and the ethics of the human relationship to nature. They also, he says, display signs of over confidence in technology as a solution of first resort.

YES

Roger Angel

Feasibility of Cooling the Earth with a Cloud of Small Spacecraft near the Inner Lagrange Point (L1)

Projections by the Intergovernmental Panel on Climate Change are for global temperature to rise between 1.5 and 4.5°C by 2100, but recent studies suggest a larger range of uncertainty. Increases as high as 11°C might be possible given CO_2 stabilizing at twice preindustrial content. Holding to even this level of CO_2 will require major use of alternative energy sources and improvements in efficiency. Unfortunately, global warming reasonably could be expected to take the form of abrupt and unpredictable changes, rather than a gradual increase. If it were to become apparent over the next decade or two that disastrous climate change driven by warming was in fact likely or even in progress, then a method to reduce the sun's heat input would become an emergency priority. A 1.8% reduction is projected to fully reverse the warming effect of a doubling of CO_2, although not the chemical effects.

One way known to reduce heat input, observed after volcanic eruptions, is to increase aerosol scattering in the stratosphere. Deployment of 3 to 5 million tons/year of sulfur would be needed to mitigate a doubling of CO_2. This amount is not incompatible with a major reduction in the current atmospheric sulfur pollution of 55 million tons/year that goes mostly into the troposphere. The approach we examine here to reduce solar warming is to scatter away sunlight in space before it enters the Earth's atmosphere. The preferred location is near the Earth–sun inner Lagrange point (L1) in an orbit with the same 1-year period as the Earth, in-line with the sun at a distance [from Earth] ≥1.5 million km (Gm). From this distance, the penumbra shadow covers and thus cools the entire planet.

A major technical hurdle to be overcome is the instability of the orbit, which is at a saddle point. A cloud of scattering particles introduced there would dissipate in a few months. But a cloud of spacecraft holding their orbits by active station-keeping could have a lifetime of many decades. Stabilizing forces could be obtained by modulating solar radiation pressure, with no need for expendable propellants. The same controls could be used, if desired, to stop the cooling at any time by displacing the orbit slightly. In addition to longevity, space shading has the advantages that the composition of the atmosphere and ocean would not be altered further, beyond their loading with

From *Proceedings of the National Academy of Sciences,* by Roger Angel, vol. 103, no. 46, November 14, 2006, excerpts pp. 17184–17189. Copyright © 2006 by National Academy of Sciences, USA. Reprinted by permission.

greenhouse gases, and because only a single parameter is modified, the flux of solar radiation, the results should be predictable.

Because of its enormous area and the mass required, shading from space has in the past been regarded as requiring manufacture in space from lunar or asteroid material and, thus, as rather futuristic. Here we explore quantitatively an approach aimed at a relatively near-term solution in which the sunshade would be manufactured completely and launched from Earth, and it would take the form of many small autonomous spacecraft ("flyers").

Shading Efficiency and Radiation Pressure

Early recognized that the orbit of a lightweight sunshade would be disturbed by radiation pressure. With the balance point moved farther away from L1 toward the sun, the area would need to be increased for a given flux reduction. This effect can be characterized by the blocking efficiency ε, defined as the fraction of the light blocked by a spacecraft that otherwise would have illuminated the Earth. It depends on the Earth's motion within the Earth–moon system as well as the orbital distance. Although the barycenter of the combined system and the L1 point sweep around the sun with uniform angular speed, the Earth's wobble in reaction to the moon can carry it partly out of the penumbral shadow. . . . $\varepsilon = 68\%$ for L1 at distance 1.5 Gm, and it drops to 25% at 3 Gm. To reduce the solar flux by a fraction f, the total area A of sunlight that must be blocked by the spacecraft at a given distance is given by $A = f\pi R_E^2/\varepsilon$, where R_E is the Earth's radius. The sunshade area for our goal of $f = 0.018$ varies from 3.4 million km^2 at 1.5 Gm distance to 9.4 million km^2 at 3 Gm. The total mass of the sunshade is given by $M = A\rho_s$, where ρ_s is its average areal density. . . .

In general, the total mass is reduced for sunshades with low areal density, but very low densities can be orbited near the L1 point only if they have very low reflectivity to minimize radiation pressure. For sunshades with density ≤ 40 g/m^2, for any given reflectivity, the total mass is minimized at a distance of ≈ 2.5 Gm. Thus, for a high reflectivity ($R \sim 1$), the density required at this distance is 40 g/m^2 and the mass is ≈ 270 million tons. Such a sunshade might be manufactured in space from an iron asteroid, which would have to be formed into ≈ 10-µm-thick foil. An opaque sunshade could be built with lower mass if its reflectivity were reduced by applying coatings that absorb light energy on the sunward side and reemit it as heat mostly on the Earthward side. Reflectivity as low as $R = 0.3$ might be achievable, given a sun-side coating with 90% solar absorption and 10% emissivity. The corresponding minimum mass at 2.5 Gm would be 80 million tons. . . .

Further reduction of the overall mass will be crucially important for a sunshade that could be launched relatively soon from Earth. To achieve the required lower reflectivities, a transparent screen is needed that deflects the transmitted sunlight by a couple of degrees, enough to miss the Earth but not enough to transfer significant radiation pressure. Early envisaged a 10-µm-thick glass Fresnel screen with dielectric reflectivity $R = 8\%$ and areal density 25 g/m^2. Together with 5 g/m^2 of supporting structure, $\rho_s \approx 30$ g/m^2. The equilibrium distance is then 1.58 Gm, and for $f = 1.8\%$ the required area is 3.6 million km². But, still, the mass is high at 100 million tons. . . .

A more efficient optical design is needed to deflect the light with a screen of lower areal density. A sunshade with $R = 10\%$ and $\rho_s \approx 5.6$ g/m² could be orbited at 2.25 Gm distance, where it would need area 5 million km² and would weigh 27 million tons. A still lower mass of 11 million tons could be achieved with $R = 3.2\%$ and $\rho_s = 2.5$ g/m². . . .

From the Earth to L1

Is it at all realistic to transport a total payload mass of 20 million tons from Earth? If, for the sake of argument, we allow $1 trillion for the task, a transportation cost of $50/kg of payload would be needed. The present cost for multi-stage rocket transportation to high orbit is $\approx$$20,000/kg. For very high volume, it is reasonable to suppose that the cost might brought to a level approaching fuel cost, not unlike car and airline transportation. Thus, the cost to low-Earth orbit for a two-stage system using kerosene liquid oxygen fuel might approach $100/kg, with additional costs to get to L1. Here, we explore the potential for still lower costs by using electromagnetic launch followed by ion propulsion.

In electromagnetic launch, the payload is driven by a current-carrying armature in a magnetic field. From the analysis below, it seems that there is no fundamental reason why launch from Earth by linear acceleration to escape velocity of 11.2 km/sec should not be possible, even allowing for atmospheric slowing and heating. Once the launch vehicle is clear of Earth's gravity, additional propulsion will be necessary to reach L1. If auxiliary rockets were used, the potential for large savings from the initial electromagnetic launch could not be fully realized. But ion propulsion is an ideally suited, low-cost alternative that adds only a small additional mass to the vehicle and is now space-proven by the SMART1 spacecraft to the moon.

The potential for very low transportation cost can be seen by consideration of launch energy cost. Kinetic energy at escape velocity is 63 MJ/kg = 17kW $\cdot$ hr/kg (1kW $\cdot$ hr = 3.6×10^6 J). Taking into account the mass of the armature and the ion-propulsion fuel, and the loss in conversion from electrical to kinetic energy, the energy for launch (as shown below) will be $\approx$10 times this final payload energy. At the current cost to industry of 5.3¢/kW $\cdot$ hr, the launch energy cost would be $9/kg of payload. The additional major cost for energy storage is likely to be comparable, thus the $50/kg target for transportation is not unrealistic.

Atmospheric drag and heating.   On exiting the evacuated launch tube, the launch vehicle will be subject for about a second to strong drag and heating as it transits the atmosphere. . . . To minimize the energy loss, the launch would be vertical from a high site. A realistic goal would be an atmospheric entry point at 5.5 km elevation (18,000 feet) where [the atmospheric pressure is] half that at sea level. Setting as a goal $\Delta v/v = 1/8$, an initial velocity of 12.8 km/sec would be needed for escape velocity of 11.2 km/sec above the atmosphere, and the vehicle will need an areal density $\rho v = 4$ tons/m².

The drag results in loss of 25% of the initial kinetic energy. Most will go into moving and heating the displaced air, but some will heat the vehicle itself. To prevent damage, an ablative shield must be used, as for space vehicles designed for atmospheric reentry. Based on past experience, it would seem that such a shield could be designed to weigh only a small fraction of the total vehicle mass. Measurements of a test vehicle with a low-drag ($\delta = 0.06$) carbon nosecone entering the Earth's atmosphere at 6 km/sec showed an ablative loss of ≈ 0.1 kg, for a mass-loss to energy-loss ratio of 0.14 kg/GJ. A similar ratio of 0.25 kg/ GJ was measured for the Galileo probe, which entered Jupiter's atmosphere at 47 km/sec and was brought to rest by a carbon ablation shield designed for high drag. In our case, a 4 ton/m^2 vehicle losing 77 GJ/m^2 would suffer an ablation loss of 20 kg/m^2, if the loss rate were 0.25 kg/GJ. Even if the rate were twice as much, and the ablator including safety factor weighed 100 kg/m^2, it would still make up only 2.5% of the vehicle total of 4,000 kg/m^2. Based on the above considerations, it seems reasonable to suppose that atmospheric drag should not prevent Earth launch, but clearly modeling with codes such as those used for the Galileo heat shield needs to be undertaken. A full-scale test at 12.8 km/sec could be made with a rocket-propelled reentry vehicle.

Electromagnetic launch to 12.8 km/sec. Two types of electromagnetic launchers, rail and coil, have been studied over the years. In the rail type, the current in the armature is delivered by rails with sliding contact, and the driving magnetic field perpendicular to the armature current provided by a combination of the rail current and external coils. Laboratory experiments with rail systems have demonstrated acceleration of projectiles of a few grams to ≈ 8 km/sec and ≈ 1 kg to 2–3 km/sec. In the coil type, the armature is a cylinder with no contact, carrying a ring current maintained by magnetic induction. The magnetic field is provided by a long solenoid comprised of many short coils that are energized successively in synchronization with the armature accelerating along the axis. A 30-coil test system has been used in the laboratory to accelerate a 240-g armature to 1 km/sec with a comoving field of 30 T. The average accelerating pressure measured at 150 MPa reached nearly half the theoretical limit of $B^2/2\mu_0$. For comparison, the same pressure applied to a 1-m-diameter armature would yield a thrust of 10^8 N, four times that of the Saturn V first stage.

Designs to harness such prodigious magnetic force to deliver payloads into orbit have been worked out for both launcher types but have never been attempted. The reasons are high up-front costs, the restriction to payloads able to survive very high acceleration, and the difficulty of launch into low-Earth orbits. Such orbits can be reached only by launch at low elevation angle, which incurs substantial aerodynamic drag, and with the addition of a supplemental rocket. However, these difficulties do not apply in our case, where a high volume is to be carried to very high orbit, and there is the possibility of ruggedizing the simple payloads to withstand high g force. The coil type is the better choice to survive a very large number of launches, given active control to prevent mechanical contact during launch. (Rail launchers inevitably suffer wear from the electrical connection required between the armature and rails.) . . .

Ion propulsion. Going from a highly eccentric orbit with 2-month period and 1.5 Gm apogee to L1 requires changes in velocity totaling ≈1 km/sec. Given also some margin to correct for errors in launch velocity, a total of $\Delta v = 2$ km/sec is wanted. The propulsion force of ≈0.2 N available from ion propulsion will be sufficient, when applied over a few months. The mass of fuel needed is relatively low, because of its high ejection velocity, ≥20 km/sec. Thus, the Dawn spacecraft to the asteroids will carry 30% of its mass in xenon fuel to obtain a total Δv of 11 km/sec. For our task, a mass of ≈5% of the launch vehicle should be sufficient. Argon, which might be stored by adsorption in carbon, would be preferred to xenon to remove fuel as a significant factor in the transportation cost.

The Sunshade as a Cloud of Autonomous Spacecraft

Previous L1 concepts have envisaged very large space structures. The alternative described here has many free-flyers located randomly within a cloud elongated along the L1 axis. The cloud cross-section would be comparable to the size of the Earth and its length much greater, ≈100,000 km. This arrangement has many advantages. It would use small flyers in very large numbers, eliminating completely the need for on-orbit assembly or an unfolding mechanism. The requirements for station-keeping are reduced by removing the need for the flyers to be regularly arrayed or to transmit any signals.

The cross-sectional area of the cloud with random placement must be several times larger than the area of sunlight to be blocked, or the individual flyers will shadow one another and lose efficiency. On the other hand, if they are spread out too far off the axis, their penumbral shadows will move off the Earth. For randomly distributed flyers with the design parameters established above, namely a residual on-axis transmission of 10% and 1.85 Gm of distance, the optimum cloud cross-section size is a 6,200 × 7,200-km ellipse. For this choice, the average off-axis shadowing efficiency is 51% (compared with 54% on-axis), and the loss from shadows overlapping is 6.5%. These two losses combined result in a 13% reduction in blocking, compared with the maximum achievable for the same number of elements in a tightly controlled, close-packed array, which would have a 7.6 times smaller cross-sectional area. The additional flyers needed to make up for the losses of the random configuration result in an increase in the total mass from 20 to 23 million tons, given the same areal density. In reality, the mass penalty may be smaller or even negative because small flyers will require lighter structural supports and simpler controls for station keeping.

Position and momentum control. The key requirements for autonomous control are to hold within the cloud envelope, to move slowly, and to keep facing the sun. The position must be actively controlled to prevent axial instability, which if left uncorrected will result in exponential increase in velocity with an *e*-folding time of 22 days. There is an independent need to control velocity, to minimize the chance of collisions between the randomly moving flyers, which even at low speed could set them spinning out of control. Control to ≤1 cm/sec, for example, will keep the collision probability to 10% per century per flyer.

To provide position and velocity information, special spacecraft with radio beacons in a global positioning system (GPS)-like system will be scattered through the cloud. Each flyer will incorporate a radio receiver to sense its velocity and position. In addition, it will carry two small tracker cameras mounted back-to-back to track the sun, Earth, and moon, to determine orientation.

Control of lateral and rotational motion will be accomplished by varying the radiation pressure on each flyer, with mirrors covering 2% of the flyer area and tiltable about an axis pointing to the flyer center. In the normal equilibrium configuration, half the mirrors would be turned so as to let the sunlight pass by and half would be set close to normal incidence to reflect back the sunlight. By appropriate rotations of the different mirrors, the lateral and angular acceleration in all six degrees of freedom can be set independently. . . . Thus, flyers can easily be held within the elliptical envelope, requiring an outward acceleration of $\approx 8 \times 10^{-7}$ m/sec² 5,000 km off the axis. Shadowing could be stopped temporarily if desired by placing the flyers into halo orbits about the L1 axis.

Flyer size and design for launch at high acceleration. The preferred option is to eliminate completely construction, assembly, or unfurling in space by having rigid flyers completely fabricated on Earth and launched in stacks. A mechanism built into the launch vehicle would be used to deal the flyers off the stack, a steady process that could take around a year. This approach avoids any requirement for space rendezvous or infrastructure of any sort, except for the local beacon system.

Although aerodynamic considerations constrain the vehicle mass density to be ≥4,000 kg/m², they do not favor a specific diameter. However, several factors argue for keeping the flyers small. To survive the high acceleration of launch, the smaller the flyers are, the less overhead will be needed for structural elements, and the easier it will be to make the sail-tilting mechanisms and to achieve high stacking density. A lower limit will be set ultimately by how small the control sensors and computer can be made, but a mass of no more than 0.1 g total seems reasonable. Based on these arguments, a flyer size of <1 m is adopted, to fit in a launch vehicle diameter of 1 m with cross-sectional area of 0.78 m² and total mass of 3,100 kg. . . .

Once rugged flyer prototypes are developed, their operation with radiation pressure control would be tested in space. They would be taken to L1 initially by conventional rocket propulsion.

The mass of 3,100 kg for the launch vehicle will break down approximately as 1 ton for the flyers, 1 ton for the armature (scaled by area from the Lipinski design), and 1 ton for the structure and remaining items. To prevent the build up of very high loads, the flyers will be stowed in a number of short stacks, each supported by a shelf to transfer the local load to the outer cylindrical wall and thence down to the armature. Each 1,000-kg payload will contain 800,000 flyers. The payload height, set by the stacking separation of 5 µm, will be 4 m plus the thickness of the shelves. The remaining elements with 1,000-kg budget will include the structure and nonstructural items whose mass was already estimated, the ablation shield ($\approx$80 kg), and the ion-propulsion fuel ($\approx$150 kg) and motor, along with the mechanism to destack and release the flyers and vehicle spacecraft elements for communications and orientation.

Discussion

None of the technical issues explored above invalidate the space sunshade concept. To take it further, more analysis and experiments are needed, and the benefits and costs must be further explored, particularly in relation to Earth-based approaches. In making such a comparison, it will be important to understand flyer lifetime. Currently, spacecraft in high orbits such as communications satellites last for $\approx$20 years, failing in part from loss of solar power of 1% a year caused by cosmic rays. Lifetimes $\geq$50 years should be achievable for the much simpler flyers, provided that radiation damage is mitigated by derating the solar cells, and the control electronics is made highly redundant. The mirror mechanisms should not be a limitation, because lifetimes $>10^{10}$ operations are achieved by MEMS mirrors in TV displays.

At the end of their life, the flyers will have to be replaced if atmospheric carbon levels remain dangerously high. The dead ones that find their way back to Earth could present a threat to Earth-orbiting spacecraft, but hopefully no greater than the annual flux of a million, 1-g micrometeorites, or the 30 million debris objects in low-Earth orbit that weigh $\approx$1 g. This issue needs to be analyzed. Similarly, the 20 million spent armatures would be directed into solar orbit or to the moon, but a small fraction might take up eccentric orbits and eventually reach the Earth intact. It seems, however, that this threat could be held to a level no more than that presented by the $\approx$100 1-ton natural objects that hit the Earth annually.

The total cost of the first full sunshade implementation will include development and ground operations, as well as the flyer production and transportation. Of these, transportation is the best understood at present, although a significant cost not yet addressed will be for storing the electrical energy for release during the short launch interval. Here, because of the large scale of the project, the key parameter is the cost per launch amortized over the lifetime of the storage medium. Capacitors of the type used to store 0.3 GJ at the National Ignition Facility would be suitable, if upgraded for million shot lifetime. Flywheel storage such as used currently to deliver $\approx$5 GJ to the JET torus at rates up to 800 MW also could be adapted to supply high power over the 0.3-sec launch interval and should have potential for even longer lifetime. Batteries optimized for very fast discharge and long life are another possibility. A reasonable goal for cost of highly mass-produced storage with million cycle lifetime is 2¢/J. This corresponds to 7¢/kW · hr, comparable to the cost of the electrical energy itself.

To transport the total sunshade mass of 20 million tons, a total of 20 million launches will be needed, given flyer payloads of 1,000 kg. If it became necessary to complete the sunshade deployment in as little as 10 years, a number of launchers working in parallel would be needed. If each one were operated a million times on a 5-min cycle, in all, 20 would be required. To propel the 3.1-ton vehicles to escape velocity with 40% efficiency, each launcher will need 640 GJ of energy storage, which at 2¢/J will cost $13 billion. Allowing also $10 billion for the 2-km-high, largely underground launch structure, and another $6 billion for other costs such as for magnet wire and high-speed switches, then the total capital cost of each launcher would be ≈$30 billion. The first such launcher could serve not only to verify and start sunshade construction but also to test other systems requiring large mass in high orbit. (It could be used, for example, to transport a prototype space solar electric system weighing ≥100,000 tons to geosynchronous orbit, at a cost less than the National Research Council target for financial viability of $400/kg, or to deliver a similar mass of freight to the moon.) For all 20 million launchings the capital cost would be ≈$600 billion and the electrical energy cost $150 billion.

The environmental impact of launch must be considered in addition to its cost. In the worst case, if electrical energy were generated with coal, ≈30 kg would be required for each kg transported to L1. But each kilogram of the sunshade mitigates the warming effect of 30 tons of atmospheric carbon, a thousand times more. Note that if the launch were by rockets with kerosene/liquid oxygen fuel, the carbon consumed would be comparable. It takes ≈20 kg of kerosene to place 1 kg in low-Earth orbit with an efficient two-stage rocket, and likely twice this to escape the Earth. On the other hand, the fuel cost for rocket launch is much higher. Kerosene costs currently $0.73/kg, compared with ≈$0.02/kg for coal delivered to power stations. This difference underlies in part the economy of magnetic launch.

The production costs for the flyers as described here are unclear, as a completely unprecedented scale of mass-production is needed. An aggressive target would be the same $50 cost per kilogram as for launch, for $1 trillion total. To date, spacecraft have been mass-produced only in quantities ≤100. The Iridium satellites, for example, at $5 million each cost ≈$7,000/kg, an order of magnitude less than for one-off spacecraft but still over a hundred times too high. Strategies for completely automated production of 16 trillion flyers will have to draw on, but go far beyond, experience from the highest volume mass production in other fields. Some highly complex systems produced by the millions already come close to our cost target, for example, laptop computers at ≈$100/kg. At a volume a million time larger still, new economies of scale should further reduce cost, for example, mass-production of flyer mass-production lines themselves. Although further studies are needed, it seems that $50/kg for the flyers is not unreasonable. And if flyer construction and transportation costs each can be held in the region of $1 trillion total, then a project total including development and operations of <$5 trillion seems also possible. If the 50-year lifetime is achieved, the cost per year averages to $100 billion (0.2% of current world gross domestic product) and would decrease after that when only flyer and energy storage renewal is needed.

In conclusion, it must be stressed that the value of the space sunshade is its potential to avert dangerous abrupt climate change found to be imminent or in progress. It would make no sense to plan on building and replenishing ever larger space sunshades to counter continuing and increasing use of fossil fuel. The same massive level of technology innovation and financial investment needed for the sunshade could, if also applied to renewable energy, surely yield better and permanent solutions. A number of technologies hold great promise, given appropriate investment.

James R. Fleming  **NO**

The Climate Engineers

Beyond the security checkpoint at the National Aeronautics and Space Administration's Ames Research Center at the southern end of San Francisco Bay, a small group gathered in November for a conference on the innocuous topic of "managing solar radiation." The real subject was much bigger: how to save the planet from the effects of global warming. There was little talk among the two dozen scientists and other specialists about carbon taxes, alternative energy sources, or the other usual remedies. Many of the scientists were impatient with such schemes. Some were simply contemptuous of calls for international cooperation and the policies and lifestyle changes needed to curb greenhouse-gas emissions; others had concluded that the world's politicians and bureaucrats are not up to the job of agreeing on such reforms or that global warming will come more rapidly, and with more catastrophic consequences, than many models predict. Now, they believe, it is time to consider radical measures: a technological quick fix for global warming.

"Mitigation is not happening and is not going to happen," physicist Lowell Wood declared at the NASA conference. Wood, the star of the gathering, spent four decades at the University of California's Lawrence Livermore National Laboratory, where he served as one of the Pentagon's chief weapon designers and threat analysts. (He reportedly enjoys the "Dr. Evil" nickname bestowed by his critics.) The time has come, he said, for "an intelligent elimination of undesired heat from the biosphere by technical ways and means," which, he asserted, could be achieved for a tiny fraction of the cost of "the bureaucratic suppression of CO_2." His engineering approach, he boasted, would provide "instant climatic gratification."

Wood advanced several ideas to "fix" the earth's climate, including building up Arctic sea ice to make it function like a planetary air conditioner to "suck heat in from the mid-latitude heat bath." A "surprisingly practical" way of achieving this, he said, would be to use large artillery pieces to shoot as much as a million tons of highly reflective sulfate aerosols or specially engineered nanoparticles into the Arctic stratosphere to deflect the sun's rays. Delivering up to a million tons of material via artillery would require a constant bombardment—basically declaring war on the stratosphere. Alternatively, a fleet of B-747 "crop dusters" could deliver the particles by flying continuously around the Arctic Circle. Or a 25-kilometer-long sky hose could be tethered to a military superblimp high above the planet's surface to pump reflective particles into the atmosphere.

Far-fetched as Wood's ideas may sound, his weren't the only Rube Goldberg proposals aired at the meeting. Even as they joked about a NASA staffer's apology for her inability to control the temperature in the meeting room, others detailed their own schemes for manipulating earth's climate. Astronomer J. Roger Angel suggested placing a huge fleet of mirrors in orbit to divert incoming solar radiation, at a cost of "only" several trillion dollars. Atmospheric scientist John Latham and engineer Stephen Salter hawked their idea of making marine clouds thicker and more reflective by whipping ocean water into a froth with giant pumps and eggbeaters. Most frightening was the science-fiction writer and astrophysicist Gregory Benford's announcement that he wanted to "cut through red tape and demonstrate what could be done" by finding private sponsors for his plan to inject diatomaceous earth—the chalk-like substance used in filtration systems and cat litter—into the Arctic stratosphere. He, like his fellow geoengineers, was largely silent on the possible unintended consequences of his plan.

⋅⟨⊙⟩⋅

The inherent unknowability of what would happen if we tried to tinker with the immensely complex planetary climate system is one reason why climate engineering has until recently been spoken of only sotto voce in the scientific community. Many researchers recognize that even the most brilliant scientists have a history of blindness to the wider ramifications of their work. Imagine, for example, that Wood's scheme to thicken the Arctic icecap did somehow become possible. While most of the world may want to maintain or increase polar sea ice, Russia and some other nations have historically desired an ice-free Arctic ocean, which would liberate shipping and open potentially vast oil and mineral deposits for exploitation. And an engineered Arctic ice sheet would likely produce shorter growing seasons and harsher winters in Alaska, Siberia, Greenland, and elsewhere, and could generate super winter storms in the midlatitudes. Yet Wood calls his brainstorm a plan for "global climate stabilization," and hopes to create a sort of "planetary thermostat" to regulate the global climate.

Who would control such a "thermostat," making life-altering decisions for the planet's billions? What is to prevent other nations from undertaking unilateral climate modification? The United States has no monopoly on such dreams. In November 2005, for example, Yuri Izrael, head of the Moscow-based Institute of Global Climate and Ecology Studies, wrote to Russian president Vladimir Putin to make the case for immediately burning massive amounts of sulfur in the stratosphere to lower the earth's temperature "a degree or two"—a correction greater than the total warming since pre-industrial times.

There is, moreover, a troubling motif of militarization in the history of weather and climate control. Military leaders in the United States and other countries have pondered the possibilities of weaponized weather manipulation for decades. Lowell Wood himself embodies the overlap of civilian and military interests. Now affiliated with the Hoover Institution, a think tank at Stanford University, Wood was a protégé of the late Edward Teller, the weapons scientist who was credited with developing the hydrogen bomb and was the architect of the Reagan-era Star Wars missile defense system (which Wood worked on, too). Like Wood, Teller was known for his advocacy of controversial military and technological solutions to complex problems, including the chimerical "peaceful uses of nuclear weapons." Teller's plan to excavate an artificial harbor in Alaska using thermonuclear explosives actually came close to receiving government approval. Before his death in 2003, Teller was advocating a climate control scheme similar to what Wood proposed.

Despite the large, unanswered questions about the implications of playing God with the elements, climate engineering is now being widely discussed in the scientific community and is taken seriously within the U.S. government. The Bush administration has recommended the addition of this "important strategy" to an upcoming report of the Intergovernmental Panel on Climate Change, the UN-sponsored organization whose February study seemed to persuade even the Bush White House to take global warming more seriously. And climate engineering's advocates are not confined to the small group that met in California. Last year, for example, Paul J. Crutzen, an atmospheric chemist and Nobel laureate, proposed a scheme similar to Wood's, and there is a long paper trail of climate and weather modification studies by the Pentagon and other government agencies.

As the sole historian at the NASA conference, I may have been alone in my appreciation of the irony that we were meeting on the site of an old U.S. Navy airfield literally in the shadow of the huge hangar that once housed the ill-starred Navy dirigible U.S.S. *Macon*. The 785-foot-long *Macon*, a technological wonder of its time, capable of cruising at 87 miles per hour and launching five Navy biplanes, lies at the bottom of the Pacific Ocean, brought down in 1935 by strong winds. The Navy's entire rigid-airship program went down with it. Coming on the heels of the crash of its sister ship, the *Akron*, the *Macon's* destruction showed that the design of these technological marvels was fundamentally flawed. The hangar, built by the Navy in 1932, is now both a historic site and a Superfund site, since it has been discovered that its "galbestos" siding is leaching PCBs into the drains. As I reflected on the fate of the Navy dirigible program, the geoengineers around the table were confidently and enthusiastically promoting techniques of climate intervention that were more than several steps beyond what might be called state of the art, with implications not simply for a handful of airship crewmen but for every one of the 6.5 billion inhabitants of the planet.

Ultimate control of the weather and climate excites some of our wildest fantasies and our greatest fears. It is the stuff of age-old myths. Throughout history, we mortals have tried to protect ourselves against harsh weather. But weather *control* was reserved for the ancient sky gods. Now the power has seemingly devolved to modern Titans. We are undoubtedly facing an uncertain future. With rising temperatures, increasing emissions of greenhouse gases, and a growing world population, we may be on the verge of a worldwide climate crisis. What shall we do? Doing nothing or too little is clearly wrong, but so is doing too much.

Largely unaware of the long and checkered history of weather and climate control and the political and ethical challenges it poses, or somehow considering themselves exempt, the new Titans see themselves as heroic pioneers, the first generation capable of alleviating or averting natural disasters. They are largely oblivious to the history of the charlatans and sincere but deluded scientists and engineers who preceded them. If we fail to heed the lessons of that history, and fail to bring its perspectives to bear in thinking about public policy, we risk repeating the mistakes of the past, in a game with much higher stakes.

Three stories (there are many more) capture the recurring pathologies of weather and climate control schemes. The first involves 19th-century proposals by the U.S. government's first meteorologist and other "pluviculturalists" to make artificial rain and relieve drought conditions in the American West. The second begins in 1946 with promising discoveries in cloud seeding that rapidly devolved into exaggerated claims and attempts by cold warriors to weaponize the technique in the jungles of Vietnam. And then there is the tale of how computer modeling raised hopes for perfect forecasting and ultimate control of weather and climate—hopes that continue to inform and encourage present-day planetary engineers. . . .

⋅◈⋅

Weather warfare took a macro-pathological turn between 1967 and '72 in the jungles over North and South Vietnam, Laos, and Cambodia. Using technology developed at the naval weapons testing center at China Lake, California, to seed clouds by means of silver iodide flares, the military conducted secret operations intended, among other goals, to "reduce trafficability" along portions of the Ho Chi Minh Trail, which Hanoi used to move men and materiel to South Vietnam. Operating out of Udorn Air Base, Thailand, without the knowledge of the Thai government or almost anyone else, but with the full and enthusiastic support of presidents Lyndon B. Johnson and Richard M. Nixon, the Air Weather Service flew more than 2,600 cloud seeding sorties and expended 47,000 silver iodide flares over a period of approximately five years at an annual cost of some $3.6 million. The covert operation had several names, including "POPEYE" and "Intermediary-Compatriot."

In March 1971, nationally syndicated columnist Jack Anderson broke the story about Air Force rainmakers in Southeast Asia in *The Washington Post,* a story confirmed several months later with the leaking of the Pentagon Papers and splashed on the front page of *The New York Times* in 1972 by Seymour Hersh. By 1973, despite stonewalling by Nixon administration officials, the U.S. Senate had adopted a resolution calling for an international treaty "prohibiting the use of any environmental or geophysical modification activity as a weapon of war." The following year, Senator Claiborne Pell (D.-R.I.), referring to the field as a "Pandora's box," published the transcript of a formerly top-secret briefing by the Defense Department on the topic of weather warfare. Eventually, it was revealed that the CIA had tried rainmaking in South Vietnam as early as 1963 in an attempt to break up the protests of Buddhist monks, and that cloud seeding was probably used in Cuba to disrupt the sugarcane harvest. Similar technology had been employed, yet proved ineffective, in drought relief efforts in India and Pakistan, the Philippines, Panama, Portugal, and Okinawa. All of the programs were conducted under military sponsorship and had the direct involvement of the White House.

Operation POPEYE, made public as it was at the end of the Nixon era, was dubbed the "Watergate of weather warfare." Some defended the use of environmental weapons, arguing that they were more "humane" than nuclear weapons. Others suggested that inducing rainfall to reduce trafficability was preferable to dropping napalm. As one wag put it, "Make mud, not war." At a congressional briefing in 1974, military officials downplayed the impact of Operation POPEYE, since the most that could be claimed were 10 percent increases in local rainfall, and even that result was "unverifiable." Philip Handler, president of the National Academy of Sciences, represented the mainstream of scientific opinion when he observed, "It is grotesquely immoral that scientific understanding and technological capabilities developed for human welfare to protect the public health, enhance agricultural productivity, and minimize the natural violence of large storms should be so distorted as to become weapons of war."

At a time when the United States was already weakened by the Watergate crisis, the Soviet Union caused considerable embarrassment to the Ford administration by bringing the issue of weather modification as a weapon of war to the attention of the United Nations. The UN Convention on the Prohibition of Military or Any Other Hostile Use of Environmental Modification Techniques (ENMOD) was eventually ratified by nearly 70 nations, including the United States. Ironically, it entered into force in 1978, when the Lao People's Democratic Republic, where the American military had used weather modification technology in war only six years earlier, became the 20th signatory.

The language of the ENMOD Convention may become relevant to future weather and climate engineering, especially if such efforts are conducted unilaterally or if harm befalls a nation or region. The convention targets those techniques having "widespread, longlasting or severe effects as the means of destruction, damage, or injury to any other State Party." It uses the term "environmental modification" to mean "any technique for changing—through the deliberate manipulation of natural processes—the dynamics, composition, or structure of the Earth, including its biota, lithosphere, hydrosphere, and atmosphere, or of outer space."

✎☜☞

A vision of perfect forecasting ultimately leading to weather and climate control was present at the birth of modern computing, well before the GE cloud seeding experiments. In 1945 Vladimir Zworykin, an RCA engineer noted for his early work in television technology, promoted the idea that electronic computers could be used to process and analyze vast amounts of meteorological data, issue timely and highly accurate forecasts, study the sensitivity of weather systems to alterations of surface conditions and energy inputs, and eventually intervene in and control the weather and climate. He wrote:

> The eventual goal to be attained is the international organization
> of means to study weather phenomena as global phenomena and

to channel the world's weather, as far as possible, in such a way as to minimize the damage from catastrophic disturbances, and otherwise to benefit the world to the greatest extent by improved climatic conditions where possible.

Zworykin imagined that a perfectly accurate machine forecast combined with a paramilitary rapid deployment force able literally to pour oil on troubled ocean waters or even set fires or detonate bombs might someday provide the capacity to disrupt storms before they formed, deflect them from populated areas, and otherwise control the weather.

John von Neumann, the multi-talented mathematician extraordinaire at the Institute for Advanced Study in Princeton, New Jersey, endorsed Zworykin's view, writing to him, "I agree with you completely. . . . This would provide a basis for scientific approach[es] to influencing the weather." Using computer-generated predictions, von Neumann wrote, weather and climate systems "could be controlled, or at least directed, by the release of perfectly practical amounts of energy" or by "altering the absorption and reflection properties of the ground or the sea or the atmosphere." It was a project that neatly fit von Neumann's overall philosophy: "All stable processes we shall predict. All unstable processes we shall control." Zworykin's proposal was also endorsed by the noted oceanographer Athelstan Spilhaus, then a U.S. Army major, who ended his letter of November 6, 1945, with these words: "In weather control meteorology has a new goal worthy of its greatest efforts."

In a 1962 speech to meteorologists, "On the Possibilities of Weather Control," Harry Wexler, the MIT-trained head of meteorological research at the U.S. Weather Bureau, reported on his analysis of early computer climate models and additional possibilities opened up by the space age. Reminding his audience that humankind was modifying the weather and climate "whether we know it or not" by changing the composition of the earth's atmosphere, Wexler demonstrated how the United States or the Soviet Union, perhaps with hostile intent, could alter the earth's climate in a number of ways. Either nation could cool it by several degrees using a dust ring launched into orbit, for example, or warm it using ice crystals lofted into the polar atmosphere by the explosion of hydrogen bombs. And while most practicing atmospheric chemists today believe that the discovery of ozone-destroying reactions dates to the early 1970s, Wexler sketched out a scenario for destroying the ozone layer using chlorine or bromine in his 1962 speech.

"The subject of weather and climate control is now becoming respectable to talk about," Wexler claimed, apparently hoping to reduce the prospects of a geophysical arms race. He cited Soviet premier Nikita Khrushchev's mention of weather control in an address to the Supreme Soviet and a 1961 speech to the United Nations by John F. Kennedy in which the president proposed "cooperative efforts between all nations in weather prediction and eventually in weather control." Wexler was actually the source of Kennedy's suggestions, and had worked on them behind the scenes with the President's Science Advisory Committee and the State Department. But if weather control's "respectability" was not in question, its attainability—even using computers, satellites, and 100-megaton bombs—certainly was.

⚜

In 1965, the President's Science Advisory Committee warned in a report called *Restoring the Quality of Our Environment* that increases in atmospheric carbon dioxide due to the burning of fossil fuels would modify the earth's heat balance to such an extent that harmful changes in climate could occur. This report is now widely cited as the first official statement on "global warming." But the committee also recommended geoengineering options. "The possibilities of deliberately bringing about countervailing climatic changes . . . need to be thoroughly explored," it said. As an illustration, it pointed out that, in a warming world, the earth's solar reflectivity could be increased by dispersing buoyant reflective particles over large areas of the tropical sea at an annual cost, not considered excessive, of about $500 million. This technology might also inhibit hurricane formation. No one thought to consider the side effects of particles washing up on tropical beaches or choking marine life, or the negative consequences of redirecting hurricanes, much less other effects beyond our imagination. And no one thought to ask if the local inhabitants would be in favor of such schemes. The committee also speculated about modifying high-altitude cirrus clouds to counteract the effects of increasing atmospheric carbon dioxide. It failed to mention the most obvious option: reducing fossil fuel use.

After the embarrassment of the 1978 ENMOD Convention, federal funding for weather modification research and development dried up, although freelance rainmakers continued to ply their trade in the American West with state and local funding. Until recently, a 1991 National Academy of Sciences report, *Policy Implications of Greenhouse Warming,* was the only serious document in decades to advocate climate control. But the level of urgency and the number of proposals have increased dramatically since the turn of the new century.

In September 2001, the U.S. Climate Change Technology Program quietly held an invitational conference, "Response Options to Rapid or Severe Climate Change." Sponsored by a White House that was officially skeptical about global warming, the meeting gave new status to the control fantasies of the climate engineers. According to one participant, "If they had broadcast that meeting live to people in Europe, there would have been riots." . . .

[The] National Research Council issued a study, *Critical Issues in Weather Modification Research,* in 2003. It cited looming social and environmental challenges such as water shortages and drought, property damage and loss of life from severe storms, and the threat of "inadvertent" climate change as justifications for investing in major new national and international programs in weather modification research. Although the NRC study included an acknowledgment that there is "no convincing scientific proof of the efficacy of intentional weather modification efforts," its authors nonetheless argued that there should be "a renewed commitment" to research in the field of intentional and unintentional weather modification.

The absence of such proof after decades of efforts has not deterred governments here and abroad from a variety of ill-advised or simply fanciful undertakings. . . .

With great fanfare, atmospheric chemist Paul J. Crutzen, winner of a 1995 Nobel Prize for his work on the chemistry of ozone depletion, recently proposed to cool the earth by injecting reflective aerosols or other substances into the tropical stratosphere using balloons or artillery. He estimated that more than five million metric tons of sulfur per year would be needed to do the job, at an annual cost of more than $125 billion. The effect would emulate the 1991 eruption of Mount Pinatubo in the Philippines, which covered the earth with a cloud of sulfuric acid and other sulfates and caused a drop in the planet's average temperature of about 0.5°C for roughly two years. Unfortunately, Mount Pinatubo may also have contributed to the largest ozone hole ever measured. The volcanic eruption was also blamed for causing cool, wet summers, shortening the growing season, and exacerbating Mississippi River flooding and the ongoing drought in the Sahel region of Africa.

Overall, the cooling caused by Mount Pinatubo's eruption temporarily suppressed the greenhouse warming effect and was stronger than the influence of the El Niño event that occurred at the same time. Crutzen merely noted that if a Mount Pinatubo-scale eruption were emulated every year or two, undesired side effects and ozone losses should not be "as large," but some whitening of the sky and colorful sunsets and sunrises would occur. His "interesting alternative" method would be to release soot particles to create minor "nuclear winter" conditions.

Crutzen later said that he had only reluctantly proposed his planetary "shade," mostly to "startle" political leaders enough to spur them to more serious efforts to curb greenhouse-gas emissions. But he may well have produced the opposite effect. The appeal of a quick and seemingly painless technological "fix" for the global climate dilemma should not be underestimated. The more practical such dreams appear, the less likely the world's citizens and political leaders are to take on the difficult and painful task of changing the destiny that global climate models foretell.

These issues are not new. In 1956, F. W. Reichelderfer, then chief of the U.S. Weather Bureau, delivered an address to the National Academy of Sciences, "Importance of New Concepts in Meteorology." Reacting to the widespread theorizing and speculation on the possibilities of weather and climate control at the time, he pointed out that the crucial issue was "practicability" rather than "possibility." In 1956 it was possible to modify a cloud with dry ice or silver iodide, yet it was impossible to predict what the cloud might do after seeding and impracticable to claim any sense of control over the weather. This is still true today. Yet thanks to remarkable advances in science and technology, from satellite sensors to enormously sophisticated global climate models, the fantasies of the weather and climate engineers have only grown. Now it is possible to tinker with scenarios in computer climate models—manipulating the solar inputs, for example, to demonstrate that artificially increased solar reflectivity will generate a cooling trend in the model.

But this is a far cry from conducting a practical global field experiment or operational program with proper data collection and analysis; full accounting for possible liabilities, unintended consequences, and litigation; and the necessary international support and approval. Lowell Wood blithely declares that if his proposal to turn the polar icecap into a planetary air conditioner were implemented and didn't work, the process could be halted after a few years. He doesn't mention what harm such a failure could cause in the meantime.

There are signs among the geoengineers of an overconfidence in technology as a solution of first resort. Many appear to possess a too-literal belief in progress that produces an anything-is-possible mentality, abetted by a basic misunderstanding of the nature of today's climate models. The global climate system is a "massive, staggering beast," as oceanographer Wallace Broecker describes it, with no simple set of controlling parameters. We are more than a long way from understanding how it works, much less the precise prediction and practical "control" of global climate.

Assume, for just a moment, that climate control were technically possible. Who would be given the authority to manage it? Who would have the wisdom to dispense drought, severe winters, or the effects of storms to some so that the rest of the planet could prosper? At what cost, economically, aesthetically, and in our moral relationship to nature, would we manipulate the climate?

These questions are never seriously contemplated by the climate wizards who dream of mastery over nature. If, as history shows, fantasies of weather and climate control have chiefly served commercial and military interests, why should we expect the future to be different? . . .

_&_

When Roger Angel was asked at the NASA meeting last November how he intended to get the massive amount of material required for his space mirrors into orbit, he dryly suggested a modern cannon of the kind originally proposed for the Strategic Defense Initiative: a giant electric rail gun firing a ton or so of material into space roughly every five minutes. Asked where such a device might be located, he suggested a high mountaintop on the Equator.

I was immediately reminded of Jules Verne's 1889 novel _The Purchase of the North Pole_. For two cents per acre, a group of American investors gains rights to the vast and incredibly lucrative coal and mineral deposits under the North Pole. To mine the region, they propose to melt the polar ice. Initially the project captures the public imagination, as the backers promise that their scheme will improve the climate everywhere by reducing extremes of cold and heat, making the earth a terrestrial heaven. But when it is revealed that the investors are retired Civil War artillerymen who intend to change the inclination of the earth's axis by building and firing the world's largest cannon, public enthusiasm gives way to fears that tidal waves generated by the explosion will kill millions. In secrecy and haste, the protagonists proceed with their plan, building the cannon on Mount Kilimanjaro. The plot fails only when an error in calculation renders the massive shot ineffective. Verne concludes, "The world's inhabitants could thus sleep in peace." Perhaps he spoke too soon.

POSTSCRIPT

Are "Space Sunshades" a Possible Answer to Global Warming?

Roger Angel does not suggest that climate engineering solutions such as injecting sulfur compounds into the stratosphere or orbiting reflective space-craft should be tried *instead of* reducing greenhouse gas emissions. Rather, he suggests that such solutions should be evaluated for use *in extremis,* if green-house gas reductions are not sufficient or if global warming runs out of control. This position makes a good deal of sense. To some people, it gained sense when reports that methane was bubbling out of melting permafrost off the Arctic coasts of Siberia and Norway raised alarm; see Steve Connor, "Hundreds of Methane 'Plumes' Discovered," *The Independent* (September 25, 2008) (http://www.independent.co.uk/news/science/hundreds-of-methane-plumes-discovered-941456.html). Methane is a more powerful greenhouse gas than carbon dioxide, and rapid release of large amounts may increase greenhouse warming rapidly. Newspaper columnists were soon calling for more research into geoengineer-ing. In January 2009, a survey of climate scientists found broad support for exploring the geoengineering approach and even developing techniques; see "What Can We Do to Save Our Planet?" *The Independent* (January 2, 2009) (http://www.independent.co.uk/environment/climate-change/what-can-we-do-to-save-our-planet-1221097.html).

Some geoengineering proposals focus on applying such measures before or instead of reducing greenhouse gas emissions. Jeff Goodell, "Can Dr. Evil Save the World?" *Rolling Stone* (November 16, 2006), discusses Lowell Wood's proposal to inject sulfur compounds, notes the expense seems low, and reports that computer simulations say it could work.

However, Wood has already moved away from a strong "instead of" posi-tion. Fred C. Iklé and Lowell Wood, "Climatic Engineering," *The National Interest* (January/February 2008), argue that "Programs should be funded to conduct seri-ous research in climate geoengineering and to carefully evaluate the most prom-ising options, while international efforts to curtail greenhouse gas emissions continue." Chris Mooney, "Climate Repair Made Simple," *Wired* (July 2008), notes that geoengineering proposals such as Wood's might actually work for climate control, but increasing carbon dioxide levels have other consequences too, such as increasing acidity of the oceans. Alan Robock lists this among "20 Reasons Why Geoengineering May Be a Bad Idea," *Bulletin of the Atomic Scientists* (May/June 2008). Alternative methods such as ocean fertilization to stimulate algae to remove carbon dioxide from the atmosphere do not seem likely to be success-ful; see Noreen Parks, "Fertilizing the Seas for Climate Mitigation—Promising Strategy or Sheer Folly?" *Bioscience* (February 2008).

James R. Fleming, "The Pathological History of Weather and Climate Modification: Three Cycles of Promise and Hype," *Historical Studies in the Physical and Biological Sciences* (vol. 37, no. 1, 2006), finds the history of attempts to modify weather and climate so marred by excessive optimism that we should doubt the rationality of present climate engineering proposals. Thomas Sterner et al., "Quick Fixes for the Environment: Part of the Solution or Part of the Problem?" *Environment* (December 2006), say that "Quick fixes are sometimes appropriate because they work sufficiently well and/or buy time to design longer term solutions . . . [but] When quick fixes are deployed, it is useful to tie them to long-run abatement measures." Fundamental solutions (such as reducing emissions of greenhouse gases to solve the global warming problem) are to be preferred, but they may be opposed because of "lack of understanding of ecological mechanisms, failure to recognize the gravity of the problem, vested interests, and absence of institutions to address public goods and intergenerational choices effectively."

A basic problem with solutions such as sulfate injections or reflective spacecraft is that even if they work as intended, with few or no undesirable side effects, they must be maintained indefinitely, while the underlying problem continues. If the maintenance falters—as seems reasonable to expect, given the nature of human politics—the underlying problem will still be there. In fact, atmospheric levels of greenhouse gases will be higher than before because emissions will have continued to rise. The climate will then warm relatively suddenly, to an extent determined largely by how long we have been able to suppress the greenhouse effect.

Such solutions also fail to recognize that we face more than one problem. Fossil fuels are finite in supply. We will eventually run out of them. At that time, if we have failed to develop alternative energy sources, we will face a tremendous crisis. But if we reduce greenhouse gas emissions in part by developing alternative energy sources, that crisis may never arrive. One question with which human society is presently struggling is whether we can shift away from fossil fuels despite the vested interests mentioned by Sterner et al.

It is perhaps worth noting that similar climate modification schemes have also been proposed for other purposes. In the 1970s, when some people were worrying about a coming ice age, darkening polar ice with soot was suggested as a way of boosting heat absorption. More recently, adding chlorofluorocarbons to the atmosphere of Mars has been suggested as a way to warm the planet and prepare it for "terraforming." See Jeffrey Kluger, "Mars, in Earth's Image," *Discover* (September 1992).

ISSUE 5

Is It Time to Revive Nuclear Power?

YES: Iain Murray, from "Nuclear Power? Yes, Please," *National Review* (June 16, 2008)

NO: Kristin Shrader-Frechette, from "Five Myths About Nuclear Energy," *America* (June 23–30, 2008)

ISSUE SUMMARY

YES: Iain Murray argues that the world's experience with nuclear power has shown it to be both safe and reliable. Costs can be contained, and if one is concerned about global warming, the case for nuclear power is unassailable.

NO: Professor Kristin Shrader-Frechette argues that nuclear power is one of the most impractical and risky of energy sources. Renewable energy sources such as wind and solar are a sounder choice.

The technology of releasing for human use the energy that holds the atom together did not get off to an auspicious start. Its first significant application was military, and the deaths associated with the Hiroshima and Nagasaki explosions have ever since tainted the technology with negative associations. It did not help that for the ensuing half-century, millions of people grew up under the threat of nuclear Armageddon. But almost from the beginning, nuclear physicists and engineers wanted to put nuclear energy to more peaceful uses, largely in the form of power plants. Touted in the 1950s as an astoundingly cheap source of electricity, nuclear power soon proved to be more expensive than conventional sources, largely because safety concerns caused delays in the approval process and prompted elaborate built-in precautions. Safety measures have worked well when needed—Three Mile Island, often cited as a horrific example of what can go wrong, released very little radioactive material to the environment. The Chernobyl disaster occurred when safety measures were ignored. In both cases, human error was more to blame than the technology itself. The related issue of nuclear waste has also raised fears and proved to add expense to the technology.

It is clear that two factors—fear and expense—impede the wide adoption of nuclear power. If both could somehow be alleviated, it might become possible to gain the benefits of the technology. Among those benefits are that nuclear power does not burn oil, coal, or any other fuel, does not emit air pollution and thus contribute to smog and haze, does not depend on foreign sources of fuel and thus weaken national independence, and does not emit carbon dioxide. Avoiding the use of fossil fuels is an important benefit; see Robert L. Hirsch, Roger H. Bezdek, and Robert M. Wendling, "Peaking Oil Production: Sooner Rather Than Later?" *Issues in Science and Technology* (Spring 2005). But avoiding carbon dioxide emissions may be more important at a time when society is concerned about global warming, and this is the benefit that prompted James Lovelock, creator of the Gaia Hypothesis and hero to environmentalists everywhere, to say, "If we had nuclear power we wouldn't be in this mess now, and whose fault was it? It was [the anti-nuclear environmentalists']." See his autobiography, *Homage to Gaia: The Life of an Independent Scientist* (Oxford University Press, 2001). Others have also seen this point. The OECD's Nuclear Energy Agency ("Nuclear Power and Climate Change" [Paris, France, 1998] [http://www.nea.fr/html/ndd/climate/climate.pdf]) found that a greatly expanded deployment of nuclear power to combat global warming was both technically and economically feasible. Robert C. Morris published *The Environmental Case for Nuclear Power: Economic, Medical, and Political Considerations* (Paragon House) in 2000. "The time seems right to reconsider the future of nuclear power," say James A. Lake, Ralph G. Bennett, and John F. Kotek in "Next-Generation Nuclear Power," *Scientific American* (January 2002). Stewart Brand, long a leading environmentalist, predicts in "Environmental Heresies," *Technology Review* (May 2005), that nuclear power will soon be seen as the "green" energy technology. David Talbot, "Nuclear Powers Up," *Technology Review* (September 2005), notes that "While the waste problem remains unsolved, current trends favor a nuclear renaissance. Energy needs are growing. Conventional energy sources will eventually dry up. The atmosphere is getting dirtier." Peter Schwartz and Spencer Reiss, "Nuclear Now!" *Wired* (February 2005), argue that nuclear power is the one practical answer to global warming and forthcoming shortages of fossil fuels.

In the following selections, Iain Murray of the Competitive Enterprise Institute argues that the world's experience with nuclear power has shown it to be both safe and reliable. Costs can be contained, and if one is concerned about global warming, the case for nuclear power is unassailable. Professor Kristin Shrader-Frechette argues that nuclear power is one of the most impractical and risky of energy sources. Renewable energy sources such as wind and solar are a sounder choice.

YES

Iain Murray

Nuclear Power? Yes, Please

My grandfather was a coal miner. My father was an electrical engineer. Energy appears to be in my blood. In the late 1960s and early 1970s, when I was growing up in the north of England, we seemed to be heading for a new age of energy production. Just to the south of us was a community called Seaton Carew, in the county of Durham. It needed more electricity, and a new coal-fired power station was proposed. The people objected. As Ian Fells, emeritus professor of energy conversion at the nearby University of Newcastle-upon-Tyne puts it, they said, "Why can't we have one of those new, clean nuclear power stations?" My neighbors got their wish. In 1969, work began on the Hartlepool Nuclear Plant. Since 1983, it has provided 3 percent of the United Kingdom's energy.

Next year, decommissioning work will begin on the plant. The local people are opposed to a replacement nuclear facility. What happened? The answer is strangely universal. Around the Western world, environmentalists did what they do best: They exploited fear and massaged science to make nuclear power morally unacceptable, impeding progress and innovation. Yet today they find their case weakened—perhaps fatally—by another concern born from another campaign of fear: global warming. The hysteria environmentalists have built up around carbon emissions may lead to a new dawn for nuclear power. Given that, the case for new nuclear is almost unassailable.

Throughout the late 1960s and early 1970s, there was considerable technical discussion about the safety of nuclear power throughout the world, and local court cases against new construction had been common. The Calvert Cliffs Coordinating Committee, for example, delayed the building of a reactor in Maryland after a court victory over the Atomic Energy Commission in 1971. Construction on subsequent projects slowed as a result. Mass popular opposition to the "new, clean nuclear power stations" worldwide, however, seems to have begun in Germany. Shortly after work started in Hartlepool, a new plant was proposed for the tiny southwest German village of Wyhl. Opposition grew and, by the time work began in 1975, a mass movement was ready. Thirty thousand protesters gathered, seized control of the site, and occupied it. The plant was never built.

The German protesters did not rest on their laurels after this victory. In 1977, 20,000 people protested the use of salt mines at Gorleben for nuclear-waste storage. Growing bolder, they turned to open violence. At Brokdorf in

1981, 100,000 demonstrators surrounded the site of a proposed nuclear plant, confronting 10,000 police. According to the *New York Times* report, "groups of hundreds of demonstrators armed with gasoline bombs, sticks, stones and high-powered slingshots" attacked the police, injuring 21 of them.

It was about this time that I noticed a cultural invasion of England by Germany. Dozens of students at my high school started sporting large yellow buttons depicting a smiley-faced sun surrounded by the German words "ATOMKRAFT? NEIN DANKE!" ("Nuclear power? No thanks!") In 1979, the movement had reached such levels of power that it was able to establish its own sustainable political party. Die Grünen (the Greens) had among their early leaders a roll call of radical leftists. Among them was the tiny and articulate Petra Kelly, a former European Commission bureaucrat who had been educated in the United States and had worked on the Robert F. Kennedy and Hubert Humphrey campaigns in 1968. Others included former student radical Rudi Dutschke, who followed Gramsci in advocating a "long march through the institutions," the novelist Heinrich Böll, and the artist Joseph Beuys. Anti-nuclear activism was the core of their appeal and remains a central plank today. They have indeed marched through the institutions, even claiming the foreign ministry from 1998 to 2005 and entering into a state-level coalition with Germany's nominal conservatives, the Christian Democrats. The Green virus spread dramatically out from Germany, infecting the politics of most developed nations.

I have spent a little time outlining this early history because it is important to recognize that the anti-nuclear movement was already ascendant before the Three Mile Island incident in 1979. On May 2, 1977, no doubt inspired by the German protesters, 1,414 people were arrested protesting a nuclear plant in Seabrook, N.H. Three Mile Island merely galvanized an already-active movement. Nuclear-plant orders had in fact peaked in 1973, and fell off sharply after 1974 as energy-conservation concerns reigned supreme in the wake of the Arab oil embargo. . . . The anti-nuclear movement's achievement was not to stop nuclear power, but to take it off the table as an option after 1979.

Fear and Loathing

How did they succeed? By creating a global zeitgeist—an appropriately German word—holding as an article of faith that nuclear power is a severe danger in all sorts of ways. Their arguments revolved around three main propositions: that nuclear plants are dangerous because they can blow up or melt down; that nuclear waste is extremely and persistently dangerous; and that nuclear power and nuclear weapons are intrinsically linked. All these arguments are overstated.

As to the safety of nuclear power stations, there is now a significant history to demonstrate that these concerns are no longer justified, even if they may have had some precautionary legitimacy in the 1970s. It has long been recognized that the Chernobyl accident was caused by features unique to the Soviet-style RBMK (*reaktor bolshoy moshchnosti kanalniy*—high-power channel reactor). When reactors of that sort get too hot, the rate of the nuclear reaction increases—the reverse of what happens in most Western reactors. Moreover, RBMK reactors do not have containment shells that prevent radioactive material from getting out. The worst incident in the history of nuclear power, Chernobyl killed just 56 people and made 20 square miles of land uninhabitable. (The exclusion zone has now become a haven for wildlife, which is thriving.) There are suggestions that hundreds or thousands more may die because of long-term effects, but these estimates are based on the controversial Linear Non-Threshold (LNT) theory about the effects of radiation.

Official EPA doctrine, based on the LNT theory, holds that no level of radiation is safe, and that the maximum allowable exposure to radiation is an extremely stringent 15 millirems (mrem) per year. After Hiroshima and Nagasaki, researchers discovered that 600,000 mrem was a sufficient dose of radiation to kill anyone exposed to it, and 400,000 mrem killed half the people exposed. Symptoms of radiation sickness develop at 75,000–100,000 mrem. By extrapolating linearly, the model holds that there is no level of radiation at which someone is not adversely affected (hence "nonthreshold"). Therefore, if a million people are exposed to a very low dose of radiation—say 500 mrem— then 6,250 of them will die of cancer brought on by the exposure. At least according to the theory.

But this is mere assumption, with no epidemiological evidence to back it up. As Prof. Donald W. Miller Jr. of the University of Washington School of Medicine wrote in 2004, "Known and documented health-damaging effects of radiation—radiation sickness, leukemia, and death—are only seen with doses greater than 100 rem [which is to say, 100,000 mrem]. The risk of doses less than 100 rem is a black box into which regulators extend 'extrapolated data.' There are no valid epidemiologic or experimental data to support linearly extrapolated predictions of cancer resulting from low doses of radiation."

In fact, Americans are naturally exposed to around 200 mrem a year of background radiation. In some places around the world that background level is much higher. In Ramsar, Iran, thanks to the presence of natural radium in the vicinity, residents get 26,000 mrem a year, but there is no increased incidence of cancer or shortened lifespan. This is a real problem for the LNT theory. The predicted deaths and cancer cases haven't materialized.

In Britain, much hay was made by Greenpeace and other organizations of the emergence of greater incidences of leukemia in children living near the nuclear-reprocessing plant at Sellafield in the early 1990s. But such "cancer clusters" appear all over the place, and are just as likely to appear next to an organic farm—to borrow the formulation of British environment writer Rob Johnston—as next to a nuclear facility. There does not appear to be any greater incidence of leukemia in the children of those who work in the nuclear industry. In fact, there is so little evidence of significant safety risks related to nuclear power that the British government "continues to believe that new nuclear power stations would pose very small risks to safety, security, health and proliferation," according to a recent analysis it undertook. It also believes that "these risks are minimized and sensibly managed by industry."

Nuclear waste is a stickier problem, but one that can be safely managed. In most American reactors, fuel rods need to be replaced every 18 months or so. When they are taken out, they contain large amounts of radioactive fission products and produce enough heat that they need to be cooled in water. Radioactivity declines as the isotopes decay and the rods produce less heat. It is the very nature of radioactivity that, as materials decay, they become less dangerous and easier to handle. The question is what to do with the waste when space runs out.

In most of the rest of the world, fuel reprocessing extracts usable uranium and plutonium. The highly radioactive waste that remains is not a large amount. By 2040, Britain will have just 70,000 cubic feet of such waste. This volume could be contained in a cube measuring 42 feet on each side. Moreover, most of Britain's waste is left over from its nuclear-weapons program. The British government has determined that "geological disposal"—burial deep underground—provides the best available approach to dealing with existing and also with new nuclear waste, arguing that "the balance of ethical considerations does not rule out the option of new nuclear power."

In the U.S., unfortunately, reprocessing was stopped during the Carter administration, in the naïve belief that other countries would follow suit and thereby reduce the amount of plutonium available for weapons proliferation. For that reason, the U.S. has rather more nuclear waste than any other nation, about 144 million pounds of it. Since 1987, the U.S. has focused its own efforts at geological disposal at a remote Nevada site called Yucca Mountain, located within a former nuclear-test facility.

The story of Yucca Mountain is well-known—it has become a political football as pro- and anti-nuclear forces try to accelerate or delay (or even stop) the facility's commissioning. Legal challenges have focused on the question of how much radiation will escape to the public from the facility—over a timeline of a million years. The Department of Energy has calculated that exposure will be no more than 0.98 mrem per year, up to a million years into the future. Even those who hold to the stringent LNT view of radiation should be satisfied.

With that settled, the Department of Energy announced in 2006 that Yucca Mountain would open for business in 2017. But later that year, when Harry Reid was chosen as Senate majority leader, he announced, "Yucca Mountain is dead. It'll never happen." The project's budget has been slashed. As a result, the question of storing America's nuclear waste remains open, even as more and more of that waste piles up around the country.

On the issue of persistence, bear in mind that reprocessing the fuel means that, after ten years, the fission products are only one-thousandth as radioactive as they were initially. After 500 years, they will be less radioactive than the uranium ore they originally came from. The waste question is therefore simply one of storage. It is a political, not a scientific, dispute.

As for the problem of nuclear proliferation, the unpleasant fact is that every country that has been willing to invest the time and effort required to make a nuclear weapon has succeeded. The existence of nuclear power plants in Western countries has nothing to do with this. In fact, in order to keep plants economical, fuel rods are kept in the reactor long enough that the weapons-grade plutonium, Pu-239, absorbs another neutron and becomes the much less dangerous Pu-240. To be effective in a weapon, a given volume of plutonium must contain no more than 7 percent Pu-240. Spent fuel from civilian nuclear plants is typically composed of about 26 percent Pu-240. This makes it extremely difficult even for experts to use in the manufacture of nuclear weapons—and well nigh impossible for amateurs.

There is some concern that nuclear power plants present an attractive target for terrorists. After the attacks of Osama bin Laden's impromptu air force in 2001, the Department of Energy commissioned a study into the effects of a fully fueled jetliner's hitting a reactor containment vessel at maximum speed. In none of the simulations was containment breached. Given the massive investment that would be needed to compromise a nuclear power station, it is highly unlikely that terrorists would seek to attack such a hard target—especially when their revealed preference has been for soft targets offering the maximum possible loss of civilian life.

The world's experience with nuclear power, therefore, has confounded the arguments of the environmentalists. It has proven safe and reliable—and if you still need convincing of this, remember that the second-worst nuclear incident, Three Mile Island, saw a destroyed reactor confined with no casualties.

Environmental Economics

With safety concerns off the table, the real question remaining as to whether we should move forward with nuclear power is one of economics. Up until now, the high costs of construction and decommissioning have made nuclear more expensive than coal and natural gas. That, however, is likely to change, and it is the environmentalists who will have brought about the change.

The Congressional Budget Office recently released a report finding that nuclear power costs around $72 per megawatt-hour of energy, compared with $55 for coal and $57 for natural gas. But those estimates reflect very high construction costs. When it comes to operating costs, nuclear power is much less expensive. Therefore, the economics of nuclear power depend to a large extent on reducing those construction costs—both the direct costs of building (which is highly dependent on construction time) and the costs of regulation. It should be feasible to reduce significantly the costs of regulation by various means. Under its Nuclear Power 2010 program, for example, the U.S. Department of Energy has offered interested parties the opportunity to operate under a surprisingly non-bureaucratic model for licensing based on the French system. (Less responsibly, for the first six plants, the program also offers to subsidize 25 percent to 50 percent of any construction-cost overruns due to delays.) Nuclear plants have never been built anywhere in an environment of low regulatory costs, so it is hard to estimate to what degree deregulation could reduce expenses without jeopardizing safety.

Those high construction costs have led many to argue that nuclear power is intrinsically uneconomic without subsidy. This is contradicted by the British government's recent analysis, which found that nuclear power is viable without subsidies. The British government received confirmation from potential nuclear operators that subsidy was neither needed nor desired. In the U.S., there have been 30 announcements of plans for new nuclear plants, totaling 40,000 megawatts of capacity, which would power 32 million households.

In all the hysteria about global warming, environmentalists have, for the most part, agreed on one thing above all—that the use of fossil fuels must be made more expensive. Every proposal currently under consideration for the reduction of greenhouse-gas emissions seeks to raise prices as a brake on emissions, through either a cap-and-trade system or a carbon tax. Once this expense is included in the calculations, nuclear power becomes extremely competitive, and remains considerably cheaper than wind power. The Congressional Budget Office found that nuclear power is the most attractive source of electricity once the price of carbon emissions reaches $45 a ton. If natural-gas prices increase as rapidly as they have done recently, then that figure will come down even further. The British-government review found that nuclear provides "economic benefit regardless of the carbon price." Moreover, it provides carbon reductions much more cheaply than wind power does. Using nuclear power, it costs 60 cents to eliminate a ton of CO_2 emissions, as opposed to a staggering $100 per ton for onshore wind power. It is true that a carbon tax amounts to a subsidy for nuclear power. But if carbon emissions are to be taxed, then that is the only subsidy that nuclear power will ever need.

Keep in mind that many of the current arguments used against nuclear power by environmentalists are economic in tone—that uranium is running out (not true even in the medium term); that decommissioning is expensive and/or will be a burden on the taxpayer (it is expensive, but the cost could be met by requiring the operator to pay into a fund during the reactor's life); or that building reactors takes too long (true, but most of that is the fault of red tape). The Canadian company ACEL has managed to shorten the time for building a reactor—from groundbreaking to coming online—to four years. Such a schedule should significantly reduce construction costs which, as we have seen, are the main impediment to nuclear cost-effectiveness.

Nuclear Is Greener

Beyond economics, if you take seriously the issue of greenhouse gases—whether as a climate alarmist or as someone with an open mind who believes in a degree of prudence—then the case for nuclear power is unassailable. James Lovelock, famous as the father of the "Gaia Hypothesis," has said nuclear power represents humanity's only hope to escape runaway global warming. Yet most environmental groups refuse to recognize the impracticality of opposing both greenhouse-gas emissions and our most effective way of reducing them. For those groups, the problem isn't "dirty" energy, but energy itself. They presumably agree with one of their sages, Amory Lovins, who told *Playboy* in 1977, "It'd be a little short of disastrous for us to discover a source of clean, cheap, abundant energy because of what we might do with it."

For the rest of us, what we might do with it is the whole point—we might increase human prosperity and welfare. If we're determined to price coal out of the energy market, then nuclear is it. If we're determined to cure our "addiction to oil," then we will need nuclear facilities to power our plug-in hybrid electric cars or to make the hydrogen for our fuel cells. This is not a green pipe dream. In fact, given the way automotive technology is developing, it is plausible that a majority of vehicles sold in the U.S. by 2020 will use electric power trains, increasing our need for electricity. We might not even need to close our coal mines, since we can get more energy from the uranium found in coal than from burning the coal itself.

Those denizens of Seaton Carew had it right. Nuclear power is clean. In a sense it is still new. Thirty years after their radical predecessors took nuclear energy away from the people of the world, environmentalists might have inadvertently given it back. *Atomkraft? Ja, bitte!*

Kristin Shrader-Frechette  **NO**

Five Myths About Nuclear Energy

Atomic energy is among the most impractical and risky of available fuel sources. Private financiers are reluctant to invest in it, and both experts and the public have questions about the likelihood of safely storing lethal radioactive wastes for the required million years. Reactors also provide irresistible targets for terrorists seeking to inflict deep and lasting damage on the United States. The government's own data show that U.S. nuclear reactors have more than a one-in-five lifetime probability of core melt, and a nuclear accident could kill 140,000 people, contaminate an area the size of Pennsylvania, and destroy our homes and health.

In addition to being risky, nuclear power is unable to meet our current or future energy needs. Because of safety requirements and the length of time it takes to construct a nuclear-power facility, the government says that by the year 2050 atomic energy could supply, at best, 20 percent of U.S. electricity needs; yet by 2020, wind and solar panels could supply at least 32 percent of U.S. electricity, at about half the cost of nuclear power. Nevertheless, in the last two years, the current U.S. administration has given the bulk of taxpayer energy subsidies—a total of $20 billion—to atomic power. Why? Some officials say nuclear energy is clean, inexpensive, needed to address global climate change, unlikely to increase the risk of nuclear proliferation and safe.

On all five counts they are wrong. Renewable energy sources are cleaner, cheaper, better able to address climate change and proliferation risks, and safer. The government's own data show that wind energy now costs less than half of nuclear power; that wind can supply far more energy, more quickly, than nuclear power; and that by 2015, solar panels will be economically competitive with all other conventional energy technologies. The administration's case for nuclear power rests on at least five myths. Debunking these myths is necessary if the United States is to abandon its current dangerous energy course.

Myth 1. Nuclear Energy Is Clean

The myth of clean atomic power arises partly because some sources, like a pro-nuclear energy analysis published in 2003 by several professors at the Massachusetts Institute of Technology, call atomic power a "carbon-free source" of energy. On its Web site, the U.S. Department of Energy, which is also a proponent of nuclear energy, calls atomic power "emissions free." At best, these claims are half-truths because they "trim the data" on emissions.

While nuclear reactors themselves do not release greenhouse gases, reactors are only part of the nine-stage nuclear fuel cycle. This cycle includes mining uranium ore, milling it to extract uranium, converting the uranium to gas, enriching it, fabricating fuel pellets, generating power, reprocessing spent fuel, storing spent fuel at the reactor and transporting the waste to a permanent storage facility. Because most of these nine stages are heavily dependent on fossil fuels, nuclear power thus generates at least 33 grams of carbon-equivalent emissions for each kilowatt-hour of electricity that is produced. (To provide uniform calculations of greenhouse emissions, the various effects of the different greenhouse gases typically are converted to carbon-equivalent emissions.) Per kilowatt-hour, atomic energy produces only one-seventh the greenhouse emissions of coal, but twice as much as wind and slightly more than solar panels.

Nuclear power is even less clean when compared with energy-efficiency measures, such as using compact-fluorescent bulbs and increasing home insulation. Whether in medicine or energy policy, preventing a problem is usually cheaper than curing or solving it, and energy efficiency is the most cost-effective way to solve the problem of reducing greenhouse gases. Department of Energy data show that one dollar invested in energy-efficiency programs displaces about six times more carbon emissions than the same amount invested in nuclear power. Government figures also show that energy-efficiency programs save $40 for every dollar invested in them. This is why the government says it could immediately and cost-effectively cut U.S. electricity consumption by 20 percent to 45 percent, using only existing strategies, like time-of-use electricity pricing. (Higher prices for electricity used during daily peak-consumption times—roughly between 8 a.m. and 8 p.m.—encourage consumers to shift their time of energy use. New power plants are typically needed to handle only peak electricity demand.)

Myth 2. Nuclear Energy Is Inexpensive

Achieving greater energy efficiency, however, also requires ending the lopsided system of taxpayer nuclear subsidies that encourage the myth of inexpensive electricity from atomic power. Since 1949, the U.S. government has provided about $165 billion in subsidies to nuclear energy, about $5 billion to solar and wind together, and even less to energy-efficiency programs. All government efficiency programs—to encourage use of fuel-efficient cars, for example, or to provide financial assistance so that low-income citizens can insulate their homes—currently receive only a small percentage of federal energy monies.

After energy-efficiency programs, wind is the most cost-effective way both to generate electricity and to reduce greenhouse emissions. It costs about half as much as atomic power. The only nearly finished nuclear plant in the West, now being built in Finland by the French company Areva, will generate electricity costing 11 cents per kilowatt-hour. Yet the U.S. government's Lawrence Berkeley National Laboratory calculated actual costs of new wind

WHAT DOES THE CHURCH SAY?

Though neither the Vatican nor the U.S. bishops have made a statement on nuclear power, the church has outlined the ethical case for renewable energy. In *Centesimus Annus* Pope John Paul II wrote that just as Pope Leo XIII in 1891 had to confront "primitive capitalism" in order to defend workers' rights, he himself had to confront the "new capitalism" in order to defend collective goods like the environment. Pope Benedict XVI warned that pollutants "make the lives of the poor especially unbearable." In their 2001 statement *Global Climate Change,* the U.S. Catholic bishops repeated his point: climate change will "disproportionately affect the poor, the vulnerable, and generations yet unborn."

The bishops also warn that "misguided responses to climate change will likely place even greater burdens on already desperately poor peoples." Instead they urge "energy conservation and the development of alternate renewable and clean-energy resources." They argue that renewable energy promotes care for creation and the common good, lessens pollution that disproportionately harms the poor and vulnerable, avoids threats to future generations and reduces nuclear-proliferation risks.

plants, over the last seven years, at 3.4 cents per kilowatt-hour. Although some groups say nuclear energy is inexpensive, their misleading claims rely on trimming the data on cost. The 2003 M.I.T. study, for instance, included neither the costs of reprocessing nuclear material, nor the full interest costs on nuclear-facility construction capital, nor the total costs of waste storage. Once these omissions—from the entire nine-stage nuclear fuel cycle—are included, nuclear costs are about 11 cents per kilowatt-hour.

The cost-effectiveness of wind power explains why in 2006 utility companies worldwide added 10 times more wind-generated, than nuclear, electricity capacity. It also explains why small-scale sources of renewable energy, like wind and solar, received $56 billion in global private investments in 2006, while nuclear energy received nothing. It explains why wind supplies 20 percent of Denmark's electricity. It explains why, each year for the last several years, Germany, Spain and India have each, alone, added more wind capacity than all countries in the world, taken together, have added in nuclear capacity.

In the United States, wind supplies up to 8 percent of electricity in some Midwestern states. The case of Louis Brooks is instructive. Utilities pay him $500 a month for allowing 78 wind turbines on his Texas ranch, and he can still use virtually all the land for farming and grazing. Wind's cost-effectiveness also explains why in 2007 wind received $9 billion in U.S. private investments, while nuclear energy received zero. U.S. wind energy has been growing by nearly 3,000 megawatts each year, annually producing new electricity equivalent to what three new nuclear reactors could generate. Meanwhile, no new U.S. atomic-power reactors have been ordered since 1974.

Should the United States continue to heavily subsidize nuclear technology? Or, as the distinguished physicist Amory Lovins put it, is the nuclear industry dying of an "incurable attack of market forces"? Standard and Poor's, the credit- and investment-rating company, downgrades the rating of any utility that wants a nuclear plant. It claims that even subsidies are unlikely to make nuclear investment wise. *Forbes* magazine recently called nuclear investment "the largest managerial disaster in business history," something pursued only by the "blind" or the "biased."

Myth 3. Nuclear Energy Is Necessary to Address Climate Change

Government, industry and university studies, like those recently from Princeton, agree that wind turbines and solar panels already exist at an industrial scale and could supply one-third of U.S. electricity needs by 2020, and the vast majority of U.S. electricity by 2050—not just the 20 percent of electricity possible from nuclear energy by 2050. The D.O.E. says wind from only three states (Kansas, North Dakota and Texas) could supply all U.S. electricity needs, and 20 states could supply nearly triple those needs. By 2015, according to the D.O.E., solar panels will be competitive with all conventional energy technologies and will cost 5 to 10 cents per kilowatt hour. Shell Oil and other fossil-fuel companies agree. They are investing heavily in wind and solar.

From an economic perspective, atomic power is inefficient at addressing climate change because dollars used for more expensive, higher-emissions nuclear energy cannot be used for cheaper, lower-emissions renewable energy. Atomic power is also not sustainable. Because of dwindling uranium supplies, by the year 2050 reactors would be forced to use low-grade uranium ore whose greenhouse emissions would roughly equal those of natural gas. Besides, because the United States imports nearly all its uranium, pursuing nuclear power continues the dangerous pattern of dependency on foreign sources to meet domestic energy needs.

Myth 4. Nuclear Energy Will Not Increase Weapons Proliferation

Pursuing nuclear power also perpetuates the myth that increasing atomic energy, and thus increasing uranium enrichment and spent-fuel reprocessing, will increase neither terrorism nor proliferation of nuclear weapons. This myth has been rejected by both the International Atomic Energy Agency and the U.S. Office of Technology Assessment. More nuclear plants means more weapons materials, which means more targets, which means a higher risk of terrorism and proliferation. The government admits that Al Qaeda already has targeted U.S. reactors, none of which can withstand attack by a large airplane. Such an attack, warns the U.S. National Academy of Sciences, could cause fatalities as far away as 500 miles and destruction 10 times worse than that caused by the nuclear accident at Chernobyl in 1986.

Nuclear energy actually increases the risks of weapons proliferation because the same technology used for civilian atomic power can be used for weapons, as the cases of India, Iran, Iraq, North Korea and Pakistan illustrate. As the Swedish Nobel Prize winner Hannes Alven put it, "The military atom and the civilian atom are Siamese twins." Yet if the world stopped building nuclear-power plants, bomb ingredients would be harder to acquire, more conspicuous and more costly politically, if nations were caught trying to obtain them. Their motives for seeking nuclear materials would be unmasked as military, not civilian.

Myth 5. Nuclear Energy Is Safe

Proponents of nuclear energy, like Patrick Moore, cofounder of Greenpeace, and the former Argonne National Laboratory adviser Steve Berry, say that new reactors will be safer than current ones—"meltdown proof." Such safety claims also are myths. Even the 2003 M.I.T. energy study predicted that tripling civilian nuclear reactors would lead to about four core-melt accidents. The government's Sandia National Laboratory calculates that a nuclear accident could cause casualties similar to those at Hiroshima or Nagasaki: 140,000 deaths. If nuclear plants are as safe as their proponents claim, why do utilities need the U.S. Price-Anderson Act, which guarantees utilities protection against 98 percent of nuclear-accident liability and transfers these risks to the public? All U.S. utilities refused to generate atomic power until the government established this liability limit. Why do utilities, but not taxpayers, need this nuclear-liability protection?

Another problem is that high-level radioactive waste must be secured "in perpetuity," as the U.S. National Academy of Sciences puts it. Yet the D.O.E. has already admitted that if nuclear waste is stored at Nevada's Yucca Mountain, as has been proposed, future generations could not meet existing radiation standards. As a result, the current U.S. administration's proposal is to allow future releases of radioactive wastes, stored at Yucca Mountain, provided they annually cause no more than one person—out of every 70 persons exposed to them—to contract fatal cancer. These cancer risks are high partly because Yucca Mountain is so geologically unstable. Nuclear waste facilities could be breached by volcanic or seismic activity. Within 50 miles of Yucca Mountain, more than 600 seismic events, of magnitude greater than two on the Richter scale, have occurred since 1976. In 1992, only 12 miles from the site, an earthquake (5.6 on the Richter scale) damaged D.O.E. buildings. Within 31 miles of the site, eight volcanic eruptions have occurred in the last million years. These facts suggest that Alvin Weinberg was right. Four decades ago, the then-director of the government's Oak Ridge National Laboratory warned that nuclear waste required society to make a Faustian bargain with the devil. In exchange for current military and energy benefits from atomic power, this generation must sell the safety of future generations.

Yet the D.O.E. predicts harm even in this generation. The department says that if 70,000 tons of the existing U.S. waste were shipped to Yucca Mountain, the transfer would require 24 years of dozens of daily rail or truck shipments. Assuming low accident rates and discounting the possibility of terrorist attacks on these lethal shipments, the D.O.E. says this radioactive-waste transport likely would lead to 50 to 310 shipment accidents. According to the D.O.E., each of these accidents could contaminate 42 square miles, and each could require a 462-day cleanup that would cost $620 million, not counting medical expenses. Can hundreds of thousands of mostly unguarded shipments of lethal materials be kept safe? The states do not think so, and they have banned Yucca Mountain transport within their borders. A better alternative is onsite storage at reactors, where the material can be secured from terrorist attack in "hardened" bunkers.

Where Do We Go From Here?

If atomic energy is really so risky and expensive, why did the United States begin it and heavily subsidize it? As U.S. Atomic Energy Agency documents reveal, the United States began to develop nuclear power for the same reason many other nations have done so. It wanted weapons-grade nuclear materials for its military program. But the United States now has more than enough weapons materials. What explains the continuing subsidies? Certainly not the market. *The Economist* (7/7/05) recently noted that for decades, bankers in New York and London have refused loans to nuclear industries. Warning that nuclear costs, dangers and waste storage make atomic power "extremely risky," *The Economist* claimed that the industry is now asking taxpayers to do what the market will not do: invest in nuclear energy. How did *The Economist* explain the uneconomical $20 billion U.S. nuclear subsidies for 2005–7? It pointed to campaign contributions from the nuclear industry.

Despite the problems with atomic power, society needs around-the-clock electricity. Can we rely on intermittent wind until solar power is cost-effective in 2015? Even the Department of Energy says yes. Wind now can supply up to 20 percent of electricity, using the current electricity grid as backup, just as nuclear plants do when they are shut down for refueling, maintenance and leaks. Wind can supply up to 100 percent of electricity needs by using "distributed" turbines spread over a wide geographic region—because the wind always blows somewhere, specially offshore.

Many renewable energy sources are safe and inexpensive, and they inflict almost no damage on people or the environment. Why is the current U.S. administration instead giving virtually all of its support to a riskier, more costly nuclear alternative?

POSTSCRIPT

Is It Time to Revive Nuclear Power?

Robert Evans, "Nuclear Power: Back in the Game," *Power Engineering* (October 2005), reports that a number of power companies are considering new nuclear power plants. See also Eliot Marshall, "Is the Friendly Atom Poised for a Comeback?" and Daniel Clery, "Nuclear Industry Dares to Dream of a New Dawn," *Science* (August 19, 2005). Nuclear momentum is growing, says Charles Petit, "Nuclear Power: Risking a Comeback," *National Geographic* (April 2006), thanks in part to new technologies. Karen Charman, "Brave Nuclear World?" (Part I) *World Watch* (May/June 2006), objects that producing nuclear fuel requires huge amounts of electricity derived from fossil fuels, so going nuclear can hardly prevent all releases of carbon dioxide (although using electricity derived from nuclear power would reduce the problem). She also notes that "Although no comprehensive and integrated study comparing the collateral and external costs of energy sources globally has been done, all currently available energy sources have them. . . . Burning coal—the single largest source of air pollution in the U.S.—causes global warming, acid rain, soot, smog, and other toxic air emissions, and generates waste ash, sludge, and toxic chemicals. Landscapes and ecosystems are completely destroyed by mountaintop removal mining, while underground mining imposes high fatality, injury, and sickness rates. Even wind energy kills birds, can be noisy, and, some people complain, blights landscapes."

Michael J. Wallace tells us that there are 103 nuclear reactors operating in the United States today. Stephen Ansolabehere et al., "The Future of Nuclear Power," an interdisciplinary MIT study (MIT, 2003), note that in 2000 there were 352 nuclear reactors operating in the developed world as a whole, and a mere 15 in developing nations, and that even a very large increase in the number of nuclear power plants—from 1,000 to 1,500—will not stop all releases of carbon dioxide. In fact, if carbon emissions double by 2050 as expected, from 6,500 to 13,000 million metric tons per year, the 1,800 million metric tons not emitted because of nuclear power will seem relatively insignificant. Nevertheless, say John M. Deutch and Ernest J. Moniz, "The Nuclear Option," *Scientific American* (September 2006), such a cut in carbon emissions would be "significant." Christine Laurent, in "Beating Global Warming with Nuclear Power?" *UNESCO Courier* (February 2001), notes that "For several years, the nuclear energy industry has attempted to cloak itself in different ecological robes. Its credo: nuclear energy is a formidable asset in battle against global warming because it emits very small amounts of greenhouse gases. This stance, first presented in the late 1980s when the extent of the phenomenon was still the subject of controversy, is now at the heart of policy debates over how to avoid droughts, downpours and floods." Laurent adds that it makes more sense to focus on reducing carbon emissions by reducing energy consumption.

The debate over the future of nuclear power is likely to remain vigorous for some time to come. But as Richard A. Meserve says in a *Science* editorial ("Global Warming and Nuclear Power," *Science* [January 23, 2004]), "For those who are serious about confronting global warming, nuclear power should be seen as part of the solution. Although it is unlikely that many environmental groups will become enthusiastic proponents of nuclear power, the harsh reality is that any serious program to address global warming cannot afford to jettison any technology prematurely. . . . The stakes are large, and the scientific and educational community should seek to ensure that the public understands the critical link between nuclear power and climate change." Paul Lorenzini, "A Second Look at Nuclear Power," *Issues in Science and Technology* (Spring 2005), argues that the goal must be energy "sufficiency for the foreseeable future with minimal environmental impact." Nuclear power can be part of the answer, but making it happen requires that we shed ideological biases. "It means ceasing to deceive ourselves about what might be possible."

Alvin M. Weinberg, former director of the Oak Ridge National Laboratory, notes in "New Life for Nuclear Power," *Issues in Science and Technology* (Summer 2003), that to make a serious dent in carbon emissions would require perhaps four times as many reactors as suggested in the MIT study. The accompanying safety and security problems would be challenging. If the challenges can be met, says John J. Taylor, retired vice president for nuclear power at the Electric Power Research Institute, in "The Nuclear Power Bargain," *Issues in Science and Technology* (Spring 2004), there are a great many potential benefits. Are new reactor technologies needed? Richard K. Lester, "New Nukes," *Issues in Science and Technology* (Summer 2006), says that better centralized waste storage is what is needed, at least in the short term.

Environmental groups such as Friends of the Earth are adamantly opposed, but there are signs that some environmentalists do not agree; see William M. Welch, "Some Rethinking Nuke Opposition," *USA Today* (March 23, 2007). Judith Lewis, "The Nuclear Option," *Mother Jones* (May/June 2008), concludes that "When rising seas flood our coasts, the idea of producing electricity from the most terrifying force ever harnessed may not seem so frightening—or expensive—at all."

ISSUE 6

Will Hydrogen Replace Fossil Fuels for Cars?

YES: David L. Bodde, from "Fueling the Future: The Road to the Hydrogen Economy," Statement Presented to the Committee on Science, Subcommittee on Research and Subcommittee on Energy, U.S. House of Representatives (July 20, 2005)

NO: Robert Zubrin, from "The Hydrogen Hoax," *The New Atlantis* (Winter 2007)

ISSUE SUMMARY

YES: Professor David L. Bodde argues that there is no question whether hydrogen can satisfy the nation's energy needs. The real issue is how to handle the transition from the current energy system to the hydrogen system.

NO: Robert Zubrin argues that so far hydrogen-fueled vehicles are little better than display models and there are too many obstacles to replacing gasoline with hydrogen. What is needed is legislation to mandate that all new cars sold in the United States be "flex-fueled"—able to burn any mixture of gasoline and alcohol.

$\mathbf{T}$he 1973 "oil crisis" heightened awareness that the world—even if it was not yet running out of oil—was extraordinarily dependent on that fossil fuel (and therefore on supplier nations) for transportation, home heating, and electricity generation. Recent rapid price increases have repeated the lesson. Since the supply of oil and other fossil fuels is clearly finite, some people have worried that there would come a time when demand could not be satisfied, and our dependence would leave us helpless. At the same time, we have become acutely aware of the many unfortunate side effects of fossil fuels, including air pollution, strip mines, oil spills, global warming, and more.

The 1970s saw the modern environmental movement gain momentum. The first Earth Day was in 1970. Numerous steps were taken by the government to deal with air pollution, water pollution, and other environmental problems. In response to the oil crisis, a great deal of public money went into developing alternative energy supplies. The emphasis was on "renewable" energy, meaning conservation, wind, solar, and fuels such as hydrogen gas (which when burned with pure oxygen produces only water vapor as exhaust). However, when the crisis passed and oil supplies were once more ample (albeit it did cost more to fill a gasoline tank), most public funding for alternative-energy research and demonstration projects vanished. What work continued was at the hands of a few enthusiasts and those corporations that saw future opportunities. In 2001, the Worldwatch Institute published Seth Dunn's *Hydrogen Futures: Toward a Sustainable Energy System*. In 2002, MIT Press published Peter Hoffman's *Tomorrow's Energy: Hydrogen, Fuel Cells, and the Prospects for a Cleaner Planet*.

What drives the continuing interest in hydrogen and other alternative or renewable energy systems is the continuing problems associated with fossil fuels—concern about dependence on petroleum producing countries and potential political instability, rising oil and gasoline prices, and the growing realization that the availability of petroleum will peak in the near future. Will that interest come to anything? There are, after all, a number of other ways to meet the need. Coal can be converted into oil and gasoline (though the air pollution and global warming problems remain). Cars can be made more efficient (and mileage efficiency is much greater than it was in the seventies despite the popularity of SUVs). Cars can be designed to use natural gas or battery power; "hybrid" cars use combinations of gasoline and electricity, and some are already on the market. See Mark K. Solheim, "How Green Is My Hybrid?" *Kiplinger's Personal Finance* (May 2006), and Seth Fletcher, "Tomorrow's Hybrid," *Popular Science* (April 2008).

Perhaps people are just waiting for hydrogen. The hydrogen enthusiasts remain. In the selections that follow, Clemson University professor David L. Bodde argues that there is no question whether hydrogen can satisfy the nation's energy needs. The real issue is how to handle the transition from the current energy system to the hydrogen system. He recommends research, education, and support for entrepreneurs. Engineer Robert Zubrin argues that so far hydrogen-fueled vehicles are little better than display models and there are too many obstacles to replacing gasoline with hydrogen. What is really needed is legislation to mandate that all new cars sold in the United States be "flex-fueled"—able to burn any mixture of gasoline and alcohol.

YES

David L. Bodde

Fueling the Future: The Road to the Hydrogen Economy

T hank you, ladies and gentlemen, for this opportunity to discuss the *Road to the Hydrogen Economy,* a road I believe we must travel if we are to ensure a world well supplied with clean, affordable energy derived from secure sources. I will speak to this from the perspective of motor vehicle transportation and address the questions posed by the Committee within the framework of three basic ideas.

First, research policy should view the hydrogen transition as a marketplace competition. For the next several decades, three rival infrastructures will compete for a share of the world auto market: (a) the current internal combustion engine and associated fuels infrastructure; (b) the hybrid electric vehicles, now emerging on the market; and (c) the hydrogen fueled vehicles, now in early demonstration. We can judge policy alternatives and applied research investments by their ability to accelerate the shift in market share among these competing infrastructures.

Second, and in parallel with the marketplace transition, fundamental research should focus on sustaining the hydrogen economy into the far future. Key issues include: (a) storing hydrogen on-board vehicles at near-atmospheric pressure; (b) sequestering the carbon-dioxide effluent from manufacturing hydrogen from coal; (c) sharply reducing the cost of hydrogen produced from non-coal resources, especially nuclear, photobiological, photoelectrochemical, and thin-film solar processes; (d) improving the performance and cost of fuel cells; and (e) storing electricity on-board vehicles in batteries that provide both high energy performance and high power performance at reasonable cost.

And third, the results of this research must be brought swiftly and effectively to the marketplace. This requires economic policies that encourage technology-based innovation, both by independent entrepreneurs and those operating from the platform of established companies. Clemson University, through its International Center for Automotive Research and its Arthur M. Spiro Center for Entrepreneurial Leadership, intends to become a major contributor to this goal.

In what follows, I will set out my reasoning and the evidence that supports these three basic ideas.

U.S. House of Representatives, July 20, 2005.

The Hydrogen Transition: A Marketplace Competition

Much thinking about the hydrogen economy concerns "what" issues, visionary descriptions of a national fuels infrastructure that would deliver a substantial fraction of goods and services with hydrogen as the energy carrier. And yet, past visions of energy futures, however desirable they might have seemed at the time, have not delivered sustained action, either from a public or private perspective. The national experience with nuclear power, synthetic fuels, and renewable energy demonstrates this well.

The difficulty arises from insufficient attention to the transition between the present and the desired future—the balance between forces that lock the energy economy in stasis and the entrepreneurial forces that could accelerate it toward a more beneficial condition.

In effect, the present competes against the future, and the pace and direction of any transition will be governed by the outcome. Viewing the transition to a hydrogen economy through the lens of a competitive transition can bring a set of "how" questions to the national policy debate—questions of how policy can rebalance the competitive forces so that change prevails in the marketplace.

A Model of the Competitive Transition

The competitive battle will be fought over a half century among three competing infrastructures:[1]

- The internal combustion engine (ICE), either in a spark-ignition or compression-ignition form, and its attendant motor fuels supply chain;
- The hybrid electric vehicle (HEV), now entering the market, which achieves superior efficiency by supplementing an internal combustion engine with an electric drive system and which uses the current supply chain for motor fuels; and,
- The hydrogen fuel cell vehicle (HFCV), which requires radically distinct technologies for the vehicle, for fuel-production, and for fuel distribution.

Figure 1 shows one scenario, based on the most optimistic assumptions, of how market share could shift among the contending infrastructures (NRC 2004). Several aspects of this scenario bear special mention. First, note the extended time required for meaningful change: these are long-lived assets built around large, sunk investments. They cannot be quickly changed under the best of circumstances. Second, the road to the hydrogen economy runs smoothest through the hybrid electric vehicle. The HEV offers immediate gains in fuel economy and advances technologies that will eventually prove useful for hydrogen fuel cell vehicles, especially battery and electric system management technologies. Although this scenario shows significant market penetration for the HEV, its success cannot be assured. The HEV might remain a niche product, despite its current popularity if consumers conclude that the value of the fuel savings does not

Figure 1

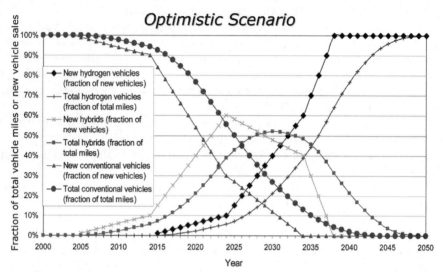

Competition for Market Share

Optimistic Scenario

• *Complete replacement of ICE and HEV vehicles with fuel cell vehicles in 2050*

Source: NRC 2004

compensate for the additional cost of the HEV. Or, its gains in efficiency might be directed toward vehicle size and acceleration rather than fuel economy. Either circumstance would make an early hydrogen transition even more desirable.

Any transition to a HFCV fleet, however, will require overcoming a key marketplace barrier that is unique to hydrogen—widely available supplies of fuel. And to this we now turn.

The Chicken and the Egg[2]

Most analyses suggest that large-scale production plants in a mature hydrogen economy can manufacture fuel at a cost that competes well with gasoline at current prices (NRC 2004). However, investors will not build these plants and their supporting distribution infrastructure in the absence of large-scale demand. And, the demand for hydrogen will not be forthcoming unless potential purchasers of hydrogen vehicles can be assured widely available sources of fuel. Variants of this "chicken and egg" problem have limited the market penetration of other fuels, such as methanol and ethanol blends (M85 and E85) and compressed natural gas. This issue—the simultaneous development of the supply side and demand sides of the market—raises one of the highest barriers to a hydrogen transition.

Distributed Hydrogen Production for the Transition

To resolve this problem, a committee of the National Academy of Sciences (NRC 2004) recommended an emphasis on distributed production of hydrogen.

Figure 2

A Supply Chain Infrastructure

Delivered H₂ Costs of Alternative Technologies

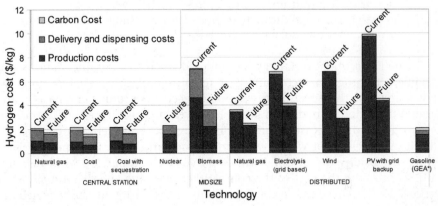

* GEA = Gasoline Efficiency Adjusted – scaled to hybrid vehicle efficiency

Source: NRC 2004

In this model, the hydrogen fuel would be manufactured at dispensing stations conveniently located for consumers. Once the demand for hydrogen fuel grew sufficiently, then larger manufacturing plants and logistic systems could be built to achieve scale economies. However, distributed production of hydrogen offers two salient challenges.

The first challenge is cost. Figure 2 shows the delivered cost of molecular hydrogen for a variety of production technologies. The "distributed" technologies, to the right in Figure 2, offer hydrogen at a cost between 2 and 5 times the cost of the large-scale, "central station" technologies, on the left in Figure 2. Technological advances can mitigate, but not remove entirely, this cost disadvantage.

The second challenge concerns the environment. Carbon capture and sequestration do not appear practical in distributed production. During the opening stage of a hydrogen transition, we might simply have to accept some carbon releases in order to achieve the later benefits.

Research to Accelerate a Transition by Distributed Hydrogen Production

A study panel convened by the National Academy of Sciences (NAS) recently recommended several research thrusts that could accelerate distributed production for a transition to hydrogen (NRC 2004). These include:

- Development of hydrogen fueling "appliance" that can be manufactured economically and used in service stations reliably and safely by relatively unskilled persons—station attendants and consumers.

- Development of an integrated, standard fueling facility that includes the above appliance as well as generation and storage equipment capable of meeting the sharply varying demands of a 24-hour business cycle.
- Advanced technologies for hydrogen production from electrolysis, essentially a fuel cell operated in reverse, to include enabling operation from intermittent energy sources, such as wind.
- Research on breakthrough technologies for small-scale reformers to produce hydrogen from fossil feedstocks.

The Department of Energy has adopted the NAS recommendations and modified its programs accordingly. It remains too early to judge progress, but in any case these technologies should receive continued emphasis as the desired transition to hydrogen nears. However, progress in research is notoriously difficult to forecast accurately. This suggests consideration be given to interim strategies that would work on the demand side of the marketplace, either to subsidize the cost of distributed hydrogen production while demand builds or to raise the cost of the competition, gasoline and diesel fuels. Such actions would relieve the research program of the entire burden for enabling the transition.

Fundamental Research to Sustain a Hydrogen Economy

At the same time that the marketplace transition advances, several high-payoff (but also high-risk) research campaigns should be waged. These include:

- Storing hydrogen on-board vehicles at near-atmospheric pressure;
- Sequestering the carbon-dioxide effluent from manufacturing hydrogen from coal;
- Sharply reducing the cost of hydrogen produced from non-coal resources, especially nuclear, photobiological, photoelectrochemical, and thin-film solar processes;
- Improving the performance and cost of fuel cells; and,
- Storing electricity on-board vehicles in batteries that provide both high energy performance and high power performance at reasonable cost.

On-Vehicle Hydrogen Storage

The most important long-term research challenge is to provide a more effective means of storing hydrogen on vehicles than the compressed gas or cryogenic liquid now in use. In my judgment, failure to achieve this comes closer to a complete "show-stopper" than any other possibility. I believe this true for two reasons: hydrogen leakage as the vehicle fleet ages, and cost.

With regard to leakage, high pressure systems currently store molecular hydrogen on demonstration vehicles safely and effectively. But these are new and specially-built, and trained professionals operate and maintain. What can we expect of production run vehicles that receive the casual maintenance afforded most cars? A glance at the oil-stained pavement of any parking lot offers evidence of the leakage of heavy fluids stored in the current ICE fleet at atmospheric pressure. As high pressure systems containing the lightest element in the universe age, we might find even greater difficulties with containment. With regard to cost, the energy losses from liquefaction and even compression severely penalize the use of hydrogen fuel, especially when manufactured at distributed stations.

The NAS Committee, cited earlier (NRC 2004), strongly supported an increased emphasis on game-changing approaches to on-vehicle hydrogen storage. One alternative could come from novel approaches to generating the hydrogen on board the vehicle.[3] Chemical hydrides, for example, might offer some promise here, such as the sodium borohydride system demonstrated by Daimler-Chrysler.

Carbon Sequestration

Domestic coal resources within the United States hold the potential to relieve the security burdens arising from oil dependence—but only if the environmental consequences of their use can be overcome. Further, as shown in Figure 2, coal offers the lowest cost pathway to a hydrogen-based energy economy, once the transient conditions have passed. Thus, the conditions under which this resource can be used should be established as soon as possible. The prevailing assumption holds that the carbon effluent from hydrogen manufacturing can be stored as a gas (carbon dioxide, or CO_2) in deep underground formations. Yet how long it must be contained and what leakage rates can be tolerated remain unresolved issues (Socolow 2005). Within the Department of Energy, the carbon sequestration program is managed separately from hydrogen and vehicles programs. The NAS committee recommended closer coordination between the two as well as an ongoing emphasis on carbon capture and sequestration (NRC 2004).

Producing Hydrogen Without Coal

Manufacturing hydrogen from non-fossil resources stands as an important hedge against future constraints on production from coal, or even from natural gas. And under any circumstance, the hydrogen economy will be more robust if served by production from a variety of domestic sources.

The non-fossil resource most immediately available is nuclear. Hydrogen could be produced with no CO_2 emissions by using nuclear heat and electricity in the high-temperature electrolysis of steam. Here the technology issues include the durability of the electrode and electrolyte materials, the effects of high pressure, and the scale-up of the electrolysis cell. Alternatively, a variety of thermochemical reactions could produce hydrogen with great efficiency. Here the needed research concerns higher operating temperatures (700°C to 1000°C) for the nuclear heat as well as research into the chemical cycles themselves. In both cases, the safety issues that might arise from coupling the nuclear island with a hydrogen production plant bear examination (NRC 2004).

In addition, hydrogen production from renewable sources should be emphasized, especially that avoiding the inefficiencies of the conventional chain of conversions: (1) from primary energy into electricity; (2) from electricity to hydrogen; (3) from hydrogen to electricity on-board the vehicle; (4) from electricity to mobility, which is what the customer wanted in the first place. Novel approaches to using renewable energy, such as photobiological or photoelectrochemical, should be supported strongly (NRC 2004).

Improved Fuel Cells

The cost and performance of fuel cells must improve significantly for hydrogen to achieve its full potential. To be sure, molecular hydrogen can be burned in specially designed internal combustion engines. But doing so foregoes the efficiency gains obtainable from the fuel cell, and becomes a costly and (from an energy perspective) inefficient process. The NAS Committee thought the fuel cell essential for a hydrogen economy to be worth the effort required to put it in place. They recommended an emphasis on long-term, breakthrough research that would dramatically improve cost, durability, cycling capacity, and useful life.

Improved Batteries

The battery is as important to a hydrogen vehicle as to a hybrid because it serves as the central energy management device. For example, the energy regained from regenerative braking must be stored in a battery for later reuse. Though energy storage governs the overall operating characteristics of the battery, a high rate of energy release (power) can enable the electric motor to assist the HEV in acceleration and relieve the requirements for fuel cells to immediately match their power output with the needs of the vehicle. Thus, advanced battery research becomes a key enabler for the hydrogen economy and might also expand the scope of the HEV.

Entrepreneurship for the Hydrogen Economy

For the results of DoE research to gain traction in a competitive economy, entrepreneurs and corporate innovators must succeed in bringing hydrogen-related innovations to the marketplace. In many cases, independent entrepreneurs provide the path-breaking innovations that lead to radical improvements in performance, while established companies provide continuous, accumulating improvement. The federal government, in partnership with states and universities, can become an important enabler of both pathways to a hydrogen economy.

Federal Policies Promoting Entrepreneurship

From the federal perspective, several policies could be considered to build an entrepreneurial climate on the "supply" side of the market. These include:

- Special tax consideration for investors in new ventures offering products relevant to fuel savings. The intent would be to increase the amount of venture capital available to startup companies.

- Commercialization programs might enable more entrepreneurs to bring their nascent technologies up to investment grade. For example, an enhanced and focused *Small Business Innovation Research* (SBIR) program might increase the number of participating entrepreneurs participating in fuel-relevant markets. A portion of the *Advanced Technology Program* (ATP) could be focused in like manner.
- Outreach from the National Laboratories to entrepreneurs might be improved. Some laboratories, the National Renewable Energy Laboratory (NREL) for example, offer small, but effective programs. But more systematic outreach, not to business in general, but to entrepreneurial business, would also increase the supply of market-ready innovations.

On the demand side, any policy that increases consumer incentives to purchase fuel efficient vehicles will provide an incentive for ongoing innovation—provided that the policy is perceived as permanent. Entrepreneurs and innovators respond primarily to opportunity; but that opportunity must be durable for the 10 year cycle required to establish a new, high-growth company.

States and Universities as Agents of Innovation/Entrepreneurship

Innovation/entrepreneurship is a contact sport, and that contact occurs most frequently and most intensely within the context of specific laboratories and specific relationships. I will use Clemson's International Center for Automotive Research (ICAR) to illustrate this principle. Most fundamentally, the ICAR is a partnership among the State of South Carolina, major auto makers,[4] and their Tier I, Tier II, and Tier III suppliers. The inclusion of these suppliers will be essential for the success of ICAR or any similar research venture. This is because innovation in the auto industry has evolved toward a global, networked process, much as it has in other industries like microelectronics. The "supply chain" is more accurately described as a network, and network innovation will replace the linear model.

For these reasons, the ICAR, when fully established, will serve as a channel for research and innovation to flow into the entire cluster of auto-related companies in the Southeast United States. We anticipate drawing together and integrating the best technology from a variety of sources:

- Research performed at Clemson University and at the ICAR itself;
- Research performed at the Savannah River National Laboratory and the University of South Carolina; and,
- Relevant science and technology anywhere in the world.

Beyond research, the ICAR will include two other components of a complete innovation package: education, and entrepreneur support. With regard to education, the Master of Science and PhD degrees offered through the ICAR will emphasize the integration of new technology into vehicle design, viewing the auto and its manufacturing plant as an integrated system. In addition, courses on entrepreneurship and innovation, offered through Clemson's

Arthur M. Spiro Center for Entrepreneurial Leadership, will equip students with the skills to become effective agents of change within the specific context of the global motor vehicle industry.

With regard to entrepreneur support, the ICAR will host a state-sponsored innovation center to nurture startup companies that originate in the Southeast auto cluster and to draw others from around the world into that cluster. In addition, the ICAR innovation center will welcome teams from established companies seeking the commercial development of their technologies. The State of South Carolina has provided significant support through four recent legislative initiatives. The Research University Infrastructure and the Research Centers of Economic Excellence Acts build the capabilities of the state's universities; and the Venture Capital Act and Innovation Centers Act provide support for entrepreneurs.

None of these elements can suffice by itself; but taken together they combine to offer a package of technology, education, and innovation that can serve the hydrogen transition extraordinarily well.

A Concluding Observation

Revolutionary technological change of the kind contemplated here is rarely predictable and never containable. Every new technology from the computer to the airplane to the automobile carries with it a chain of social and economic consequences that reach far beyond the technology itself. Some of these consequences turn out to be benign; some pose challenges that must be overcome by future generations; but none have proven foreseeable.

For example, a hydrogen transition might bring prolonged prosperity or economic decline to the electric utility industry depending upon which path innovation takes. A pathway that leads through plug-hybrids to home appliances that manufacture hydrogen by electrolysis would reinforce the current utility business model. A pathway in which hydrogen fuel cell vehicles serve as generators for home electric energy would undermine that model. The same holds true for the coal industry. A future in which carbon sequestration succeeds will affect coal far differently from one in which it cannot be accomplished.

The only certainty is that the energy economy will be vastly different from that which we know today. It will have to be.

Notes

1. Another concept, the battery electric vehicle (BEV), offers an all-electric drivetrain with all on-board energy stored in batteries, which would be recharged from stationary sources when the vehicle is not in operation. I have not included this among the competitors because battery technology has not advanced rapidly enough for it to compete in highway markets. In contrast, BEV have proven quite successful in the personal transportation niche.

2. Alternatively framed: "Which comes first, the vehicle or the fuel?"

3. I do not include on-board reforming of fossil feedstocks, like gasoline, among these. These systems offer little gain beyond that achievable with the HEV, and most industrial proponents appear to have abandoned the idea.

4. BMW was the founding OEM and most significant supporter of the ICAR.

References

Socolow, Robert H. "Can We Bury Global Warming?" *Scientific American,* July 2005, pp. 49–55.

Sperling, Daniel and James D. Cannon, *The Hydrogen Transition,* Elsevier Academic Press, 2004.

U.S. National Research Council, *The Hydrogen Economy: Opportunities, Costs, Barriers, and R&D Needs,* The National Academies Press, 2004.

Robert Zubrin

 **NO**

The Hydrogen Hoax

Nearly everyone in American politics believes we face an energy crisis, and nearly everyone believes we need a technological solution that will make America "energy independent." Americans are, as President Bush put it in his 2006 State of the Union address, "addicted to oil," and in this case our addiction is enriching and empowering those who seek to destroy us. We are funding, if indirectly, the madrassahs that teach vile hatred of Western civilization and the backward cultures that create death-seeking soldiers for Islam. We are, if unwittingly, arming those who wish to kill us. To cure this self-destructive addiction, the Bush administration has placed a major bet on the so-called "hydrogen economy," both in policy and in rhetoric. Former Energy Secretary Spencer Abraham laid out this vision, in rhapsodic language, in 2002:

> Hydrogen can fuel much more than cars and light trucks, our area of interest. It can also fuel ships, airplanes, and trains. It can be used to generate electricity, for heating, and as a fuel for industrial processes. We envision a future economy in which hydrogen is America's clean energy choice—flexible, affordable, safe, domestically produced, used in all sectors of the economy, and in all regions of the country. . . .
>
> Imagine a world running on hydrogen later in this century: Environmental pollution will no longer be a concern. Every nation will have all the energy it needs available within its borders. Personal transportation will be cheaper to operate and easier to maintain. Economic, financial, and intellectual resources devoted today to acquiring adequate energy resources and to handling environmental issues will be turned to other productive tasks for the benefit of the people. Life will get better.

In 2003, President Bush reaffirmed this vision, offering a presidential primer on the scientific, economic, and foreign-policy dimensions of hydrogen power:

> The sources of hydrogen are abundant. The more you have of something relative to demand for that, the cheaper it's going to be, the less expensive it'll be for the consumer. . . . Hydrogen power is also clean to use. Cars that will run on hydrogen fuel produce only water, not exhaust fumes. . . . One of the greatest results of using hydrogen power, of course, will be energy independence for this nation. . . . If we develop hydrogen power to its full potential, we can reduce our demand for oil by over 11 million barrels per day by the year 2040.

It certainly sounds great. Hydrogen, after all, is "the most common element in the universe," as Secretary Abraham pointed out. Since it is so plentiful, surely President Bush must be right when he promises it will be cheap. And when you use it, the waste product will be nothing but water—"environmental pollution will no longer be a concern." Hydrogen will be abundant, cheap, and clean. Why settle for anything less?

Unfortunately, it's all pure bunk. To get serious about energy policy, America needs to abandon, once and for all, the false promise of the hydrogen age.

The New Energy Charlatans

The idea of hydrogen as the fuel of the future dates back to Jules Verne, and by the 1930s was a staple of science fiction. With the advent of nuclear energy after World War II, technologists expected that atomic power would provide electricity "too cheap to meter"—electricity that could be used to produce pure hydrogen at low cost, which could then be used as a fuel. By the 1970s, however, it was apparent that nuclear energy, while potentially competitive with conventional power, did not usher in a new golden age of cheap electricity. Still, researchers devoted to the idea of the "hydrogen economy" soldiered on, and with increased public concern about carbon dioxide emissions in the 1990s and about America's dependence on foreign oil after 9/11, the pro-hydrogen crowd seized a new opportunity to make their pitch. Incredibly, the Bush administration swallowed it, hook, line, and sinker. As a result, over the past six years, billions of dollars have been dished out to national labs, auto companies, fuel-cell firms, and other beneficiaries of government largesse on hydrogen show projects that have no practical application.

The problem with this expenditure is not simply the waste; the government throws away vaster sums on any number of other useless programs all the time. Rather, the real issue is that the myth of the hydrogen economy has masked the administration's total failure to address the nation's vulnerability to energy blackmail. In consequence, despite the obvious relationship between oil dependence and the war with Islamist terrorism, no competent policy for achieving energy security has been put forth. If we are to achieve any progress on this most critical issue, the myth of the hydrogen economy needs to be debunked. It is bad science, bad economics, and bad public policy.

The Real Science of Hydrogen

Hydrogen is only a source of energy if it can be taken in its pure form and reacted with another chemical, such as oxygen. But all the hydrogen on Earth, except that in hydrocarbons, has already been oxidized, so none of it is available as fuel. . . .

The only way to get free hydrogen on Earth is to make it. The trouble is that making hydrogen requires more energy than the hydrogen so produced can provide. Hydrogen, therefore, is not a *source* of energy. It simply is a *carrier* of energy. And it is, as we shall see, an extremely poor one.

The spokesmen for the hydrogen hoax claim that hydrogen will be manufactured from water via electrolysis. It is certainly possible to make hydrogen this way, but it is very expensive—so much so that only four percent of all hydrogen currently produced in the United States is produced in this manner. The rest is made by breaking down hydrocarbons through processes like pyrolysis of natural gas or steam reforming of coal.

Neither type of hydrogen is even remotely economical as fuel. The wholesale cost of commercial grade liquid hydrogen (made the cheap way, from hydrocarbons) shipped to large customers in the United States is about $6 per kilogram. High purity hydrogen made from electrolysis for scientific applications costs considerably more. Dispensed in compressed gas cylinders to retail customers, the current price of commercial grade hydrogen is about $100 per kilogram. For comparison, a kilogram of hydrogen contains about the same amount of energy as a gallon of gasoline. This means that even if hydrogen cars were available and hydrogen stations existed to fuel them, no one with the power to choose otherwise would ever buy such vehicles. This fact alone makes the hydrogen economy a non-starter in a free society. . . .

The situation is much worse than this, however, because before the hydrogen can be transported anywhere, it needs to be either compressed or liquefied. To liquefy it, it must be refrigerated down to a temperature of 20 K (20 degrees above absolute zero, or −253 degrees Celsius). At these temperatures, the fundamental laws of thermodynamics make refrigerators extremely inefficient. As a result, about 40 percent of the energy in the hydrogen must be spent to liquefy it. This reduces the actual net energy content of our product fuel to 792 kilocalories. In addition, because it is a cryogenic liquid, still more energy could be expected to be lost as the hydrogen boils away during transport and storage.

As an alternative, one could use high pressure pumps to compress the hydrogen as gas instead of liquefying it for transport. This would only require wasting about 20 percent of the energy in the hydrogen. The problem is that safety-approved, steel compressed-gas tanks capable of storing hydrogen at 5,000 psi weigh approximately 65 times as much as the hydrogen they can contain. So to transport 200 kilograms of compressed hydrogen, roughly equal in energy content to just 200 gallons of gasoline, would require a truck capable of hauling a 13-ton load. Think about that: an entire large truckload delivery would be needed simply to transport enough hydrogen to allow *ten* people to fill up their cars with the energy equivalent of 20 gallons of gasoline each.

Instead of steel tanks, one could propose using (very expensive) lightweight carbon fiber overwrapped tanks, which only weigh about ten times as much as the hydrogen they contain. This would improve the transport weight ratio by a factor of six. Thus, instead of a 13-ton truck, a mere two-ton truckload would be required to supply enough hydrogen to allow a service station to provide fuel for ten customers. This is still hopeless economically, and could probably not be allowed in any case, since carbon fiber tanks have low crash resistance, making such compressed hydrogen transport trucks deadly bombs on the highway.

In principle, a system of pipelines could, at enormous cost, be built for transporting gaseous hydrogen. Yet because hydrogen is so diffuse, with less than one-third the energy content per unit volume as natural gas, these pipes would have to be very big, and large amounts of energy would be required to move the gas along the line. Another problem with this scheme is that the small hydrogen molecules are brilliant escape artists. Hydrogen can not only penetrate readily through the most minutely flawed seal, it can actually diffuse right through solid steel itself. The vast surface area offered by a system of hydrogen pipelines would thus afford ample opportunity for much of the hydrogen to leak away during transport.

As hydrogen diffuses into metals, it also embrittles them, causing deterioration of pipelines, valves, fittings, and storage tanks used throughout the entire distribution system. These would all have to be constantly monitored and regularly inspected, tested, and replaced. Otherwise the distribution system would become a continuous source of catastrophes.

Given these technical difficulties, the implementation of an economically viable method of retail hydrogen distribution from large-scale central production factories is essentially impossible. Because of this, an alternative concept has been proposed wherein methane or methanol fuel would be transported by pipeline or truck, and then steam-reformed into hydrogen at the filling station itself. This would eliminate most of the cost of hydrogen transport, but would increase the cost of the hydrogen itself, since small-scale reformers are less efficient, both economically and energetically, than large-scale industrial units. Also, it is questionable how many service stations would want to buy, operate, and maintain their own steam reforming facility. The station would also need to operate its own 5,000 psi explosion-proof high pressure hydrogen pump, or a cryogenic refrigeration plant, both of which are very unappealing prospects. Such a scheme of distributed production stations would also eliminate any hope of implementing the hydrogen economy's advertised plan to sequester underground the carbon dioxide produced as a byproduct of its hydrogen manufacturing operations. At bottom, the whole idea is ridiculous, since either the methane or methanol used as feedstock at the station to make the hydrogen would be a better automobile fuel, containing more energy, in less volume, at less cost, than the hydrogen it yields. . . .

The Trouble with Hydrogen Cars

The Queen in Lewis Carroll's *Through the Looking Glass* says that she could believe "six impossible things before breakfast." Such an attitude is necessary to discuss the hydrogen economy, since no part of it is possible. Putting aside the intractable issues of fundamental physics, hydrogen production costs, and distribution show stoppers, let us proceed to discuss the problems associated with the hydrogen cars themselves. In order for hydrogen to be used as fuel in a car, it has to be stored in the car. As at the station, this could be done either in the form of cryogenic liquid hydrogen or as highly compressed gas.

In either case, we come up against serious problems caused by the low density of hydrogen. For example, if liquid hydrogen is the form employed, then storing 20 kilograms onboard (equivalent in energy content to 20 gallons of gasoline) would require an insulated cryogenic fuel tank with a volume of some 280 liters (70 gallons). This cryogenic hydrogen would always be boiling away, which would create concerns for those who have to leave their cars parked for any length of time, and which would also turn the atmospheres in underground or otherwise enclosed parking garages into explosive fuel-air mixtures. Public parking garages containing such cars could be expected to explode regularly, since hydrogen is flammable over concentrations in air ranging from 4 to 75 percent, and the minimum energy required for its ignition is about one-twentieth that required for gasoline or natural gas.

Compressed hydrogen is just as unworkable as liquid hydrogen. If 5,000 psi compressed hydrogen were employed, the tank would need to be 650 liters (162 gallons), or eight times the size of a gasoline tank containing equal energy. Because it would have to hold high pressure, this huge tank could not be shaped in an irregular form to fit into the vehicle's empty space in some convenient way. Instead it would have to be a simple shape like a sphere or a domed cylinder, which would make its spatial demands much more difficult to accommodate, and significantly reduce the usable vehicle space within a car of a given size. If made of (usually) crash-safe steel, such a hydrogen tank would weigh 1,300 kilograms (2,860 pounds)—about as much as an entire small car! Lugging this extra weight around would drastically increase the fuel consumption of the vehicle, perhaps doubling it. If, instead of steel, a lightweight carbon fiber overwrapped tank were employed to avoid this penalty, the car would become a deadly explosive firebomb in the event of a crash.

While hydrogen gas can be used as a fuel in internal combustion engines, there is no advantage in doing so. In fact, hydrogen reduces the efficiency of such engines by 20 percent compared to what they can achieve using gasoline. For this reason, nearly all discussion of hydrogen vehicles has centered on power systems driven by fuel cells.

Fuel cells are electrochemical systems that generate electricity directly through the combination of hydrogen and oxygen in solution. Essentially electrolyzers operating in reverse, they are attractive because they have no moving parts (other than small water pumps), and under conditions where the quality of their hydrogen and oxygen feed can be perfectly controlled, they are quite efficient and reliable. These features have provided sufficient advantages to make fuel cells the technology of choice for certain specialty applications, such as the power system for NASA's Apollo capsules and the space shuttle.

Yet despite their successful use for four decades in the space program, and many billions of dollars of research and development funds expended over the years for their improvement and refinement, fuel cells have thus far found little use in broader commercial applications. The reasons for this are threefold. First, in ordinary terrestrial applications, a practical power system must last years, not just the few weeks required to support a manned space flight. Second, on Earth, the oxygen supply for the fuel cell must come from the atmosphere, which contains not only nitrogen (which decreases the fuel cell efficiency compared to a pure oxygen source), but carbon dioxide, carbon monoxide, and many other pollutants. Even in trace form, such pollutants can contaminate the catalysts used in the fuel cells and cause permanent degradation, ultimately rendering the system inoperable. Finally, and decisively, fuel cells are very expensive. For NASA, which spends hundreds of millions of dollars on every shuttle launch, it makes little difference if its 10 kilowatt fuel cell system costs $100,000, a million dollars, or ten million dollars. For a member of the public, however, such costs matter a great deal.

There are many kinds of fuel cells, including alkaline, phosphoric acid, and molten carbonate systems, but for purposes of motor vehicle use the only kind that is suitable and being pursued for development is the proton exchange membrane fuel cell (PEMFC). These, for example, are the kind used by all vehicle fuel cell engines manufactured by the Ballard Power company, of Vancouver, British Columbia, which for the past decade has produced nearly 80 percent of all fuel cell engines worldwide.

PEMFCs use a platinum catalyst, which is very expensive, and despite billions of dollars of R&D efforts to reduce the amount required, it has proven impossible to cut the cost of such systems below about $7,000/kW. This is very unfortunate, because an electric car with a 100-horsepower motor needs about 75 kilowatts of electricity to make it go. At this price, the cost *for just the fuel cell stack* powering the car would be about half a million dollars. Actual costs for *complete* Ballard fuel cell engine systems have been well over a million dollars each. Then there's still the rest of the car to pay for, although with the propulsion system costing this much, the additional cost would seem like a rounding error.

That, however, is not even the worst of it. Operating under road conditions in the real atmosphere, which contains such powerful catalyst poisons (chemicals that will reduce the effectiveness of the fuel cell) as sulfur dioxide, nitrogen dioxide, hydrogen sulfide, carbon monoxide, and ammonia that can permanently incapacitate a PEMFC, the operating lifetimes of fuel cell stacks have been shown to be less than 20 percent those of conventional diesel engines. As the trenchant industry analyst F. David Doty pointedly put it:

> We're still waiting to see a fuel-cell vehicle driven from Miami to Maine via the Smoky Mountains in the winter—even one time, with a few stops and restarts in Maine. Then, we need to see one hold up to a forty-minute daily commute for more than two years (preferably at least fifteen years) with minimal maintenance, and come through a highway accident with less than $200,000 in damages. . . . When lifetime and maintenance are considered, one can argue that vehicle-qualified PEMFCs are currently 400 times more expensive than diesel engines.

It is true that the costs of PEMFC might conceivably be reduced over time due to technology improvements (although no real cost reduction has been achieved over the past decade despite several billion dollars in research investment). Moreover, if somehow the vehicles ever went into mass production, increased demand would likely drive the price of the platinum they contain, and thus the overall system cost, through the roof.

Taken together, the outrageously high costs of fuel-cell cars and hydrogen fuel, combined with the non-existence of a hydrogen distribution and sales infrastructure, and the danger to life and limb involved in driving around a vehicle containing a crash-detonatable hydrogen gas bomb, make the possibility of mass consumer purchases of hydrogen fuel-cell vehicles a non-starter. But let's say some benevolent government bureaucrat with a great deal of your money decided to spend $700 billion to buy, at $1 million each, 700,000 PEMFC powered vehicles (this would represent about four-tenths of one percent of the total U.S. automobile fleet), and then another $300 billion to establish a hydrogen distribution infrastructure. Wouldn't we at least get some environmental benefit for our trillion bucks?

No, we would get no benefit at all. As discussed above, hydrogen is actually produced commercially using fossil fuel energy, much of which is lost in the process, meaning that more fossil fuels need to be burned, and thus more carbon dioxide produced, to provide a vehicle with a given amount of energy using hydrogen than if the vehicle were allowed to burn fossil fuels directly. Even if we ignore costs completely and generate hydrogen for vehicle fuel using water electrolysis, that would also *increase* pollution, since most electricity is actually generated by burning coal and natural gas. Even if the electricity in question came from nuclear, hydro, wind, or solar power, wasting it on hydrogen generation would still increase overall carbon dioxide emissions relative to the alternative of simply putting the power into the grid.

Furthermore, despite all their cost and hype, the fuel cell vehicles themselves offer no increase in efficiency relative to more conventional systems. (In this context, "efficiency" means the percentage of energy in the fuel that is spent on actual work rather than wasted.) While the theoretical efficiency of a hydrogen/oxygen fuel cell approaches 85 percent, the actual efficiency of real PEMFC stacks using hydrogen and air near maximum output (where they must operate, because fuel cell capacity is so expensive) is about 38 percent. If we then factor in an estimated efficiency for the power electronics of 92 percent and a real-world motor efficiency of 85 percent, we obtain an estimate of about 30 percent efficiency for a fuel-cell vehicle. Ordinary internal combustion engine cars can already match this, with systems offering up to 38 percent efficiencies well in sight. Conventional diesel engines operate *today* at about 42 percent efficiency. With variable valve timing, they should be able to attain 58 percent efficiency. That's nearly *twice* the efficiency offered by a fuel cell vehicle, at 1/400th the cost.

Despite these inconvenient facts, the U.S. Department of Energy has continued to hand out billions of dollars of the taxpayers' money to major auto companies and their fuel-cell development partners to produce hydrogen-powered auto-show display vehicles. The agency issues repeated predictions claiming that tens of thousands of these cars will soon be appearing on America's highways, when in fact the Department's past projections of the growth of hydrogen vehicles have all been at least two orders of magnitude higher than reality. As a result, stocks in all the major fuel-cell companies, pumped high by such hype at the expense of naïve investors, are currently selling at less than one-tenth their peak values. Eventually, real markets catch up with reality; hype and hoaxes can only take us so far.

A Real Energy Solution

The problem, however, is not simply economic but political, and the reality check on politicians is not always so swift or so reliable. The longer we buy into the hydrogen hoax, the longer we will avoid developing an energy policy that truly serves America's interests—economic, environmental, and geopolitical. Fortunately, on this front, there is good news, if only we have the will to be serious. Ethanol and methanol are practical liquid fuels that can be handled by the existing fuel distribution infrastructure and produced at prices roughly competitive with gasoline. During 2006, for example, methanol was selling at unsubsidized prices as low as $0.80 per gallon, equivalent on an energy basis to gasoline at $1.50 per gallon. As a path toward energy security, methanol is also extremely attractive, since it can be made from any kind of biomass, coal, natural gas, or municipal waste—resources plentiful in the United States and many other non-OPEC nations. Unfortunately, however, the vast majority of cars on the road cannot use it.

What is needed is government action to break the vertical monopoly on the automobile fuel supply currently held by the petroleum cartel. This could most efficiently be done simply by mandating that all new cars—whether of foreign or domestic manufacture—sold in the United States be "flex-fueled." Such cars, which can run on any mixture of alcohol or gasoline, are currently being produced in the United States for little more (typically an extra $100 to $200) than the same vehicles in non-flex-fueled form. But they only command about 3 percent of the market, because there are so few high-alcohol gas pumps to serve them. Conversely, the reason why there are few high-alcohol pumps is because there are not enough flex-fuel cars on the road to warrant them. If you own a fuel station with three pumps, you are not going to waste one distributing a type of fuel that only 3 percent of cars can use.

Yet within three years of a flex-fuel mandate, there would be at least 50 million cars on the road in the United States capable of using high-alcohol fuel, and at least an equal number overseas. This would be a sufficient market to create a widespread network of high-alcohol fuel pumps. Moreover, this dramatically increased demand for alcohol fuels would greatly exceed the supply capacity of American corn-ethanol producers, which means that we could drop our current tariffs against Latin American sugar-ethanol. A similar circumstance would pertain in Europe and Japan, enabling the elimination of their protectionist measures against Third World agricultural imports. This would solve the problem of trade barriers against farm products that scuttled the recent Doha round of international trade talks, thus benefiting rich and poor nations alike.

By simply exposing the oil cartel to competition from such alternative fuel sources, we could impose a powerful constraint on its ability to run up prices. Combined with an unrelenting tariff policy favoring alcohol over imported oil, we could destroy OPEC completely, and effectively redirect over $600 billion per year that is now going to the treasury of terrorism to the global agricultural and mining sectors. Instead of sending our money to the Islamists to spread fanatical ideology, we could give our business to the world's farmers, coal miners, and other people who actually work for a living. Instead of selling off blocks of stock in Western media companies to Saudi princes, we could be selling tractors to Honduras. Instead of funding terrorism, we could be using our energy dollars to finance world development. That's what a serious energy policy would look like.

POSTSCRIPT

Will Hydrogen Replace Fossil Fuels for Cars?

Hydrogen as a fuel offers definite benefits. As Joan M. Ogden notes in "Hydrogen: The Fuel of the Future?" *Physics Today* (April 2002), the technology is available and compared to the alternatives, it "offers the greatest potential environmental and energy-supply benefits." To put hydrogen to use, however, will require massive investments in facilities for generating, storing, and transporting the gas, as well as manufacturing hydrogen-burning engines and fuel cells. Currently, large amounts of hydrogen can easily be generated by "reforming" natural gas or other hydrocarbons. Hydrolysis—splitting hydrogen from water molecules with electricity—is also possible, and in the future this may use electricity from renewable sources such as wind or from nuclear power. The basic technologies are available right now. See Thammy Evans, Peter Light, and Ty Cashman, "Hydrogen—A Little PR," *Whole Earth* (Winter 2001). Daniel Sperling notes in "Updating Automotive Research," *Issues in Science and Technology* (Spring 2002), that "Fuel cells and hydrogen show huge promise. They may indeed prove to be the Holy Grail, eventually taking vehicles out of the environmental equation," but making that happen will require research, government assistance in building a hydrogen distribution system, and incentives for both industry and car buyers. First steps along these lines are already visible in a few places; see Bill Keenan, "Hydrogen: Waiting for the Revolution," *Across the Board* (May/June 2004), and Annie Birdsong, "California Drives the Future of the Automobile," *World Watch* (March/April 2005). M. Z. Jacobson, W. G. Colella, and D. M. Golden, "Cleaning the Air and Improving Health with Hydrogen Fuel-Cell Vehicles," *Science* (June 24, 2005), conclude that if all onroad vehicles are replaced with fuel-cell vehicles using hydrogen generated by wind power, air pollution and human health impacts will both be reduced and overall costs will be less than for gasoline. Joan Ogden, "High Hopes for Hydrogen," *Scientific American* (September 2006), agrees that the potential is great but stresses that the transition to a hydrogen future will take decades. Tim Moran, "Fuel for the Future," *Automotive News* (November 20, 2006), describes General Motors' plans to bring hydrogen-fueled cars to market. Michael K. Heiman and Barry D. Solomon, "The Hydrogen Economy and Its Alternatives," *Environment* (October 2007), argue that hydrogen may serve as a bridge to the future in some ways, but it is not likely to play much role in the transportation sector.

Jeremy Rifkin, "Hydrogen: Empowering the People," *Nation* (December 23, 2002), says local production of hydrogen could mean a much more decentralized energy system. He may be right, as John A. Turner makes clear in "Sustainable

Hydrogen Production," *Science* (August 13, 2004), but Henry Payne and Diane Katz, "Gas and Gasbags . . . or, the Open Road and Its Enemies," *National Review* (March 25, 2002), contend that a major obstacle to hydrogen is market mechanisms that will keep fossil fuels in use for years to come, local hydrogen production is unlikely, and adequate supplies will require that society invest heavily in nuclear power. Robert Zubrin extends his argument in favor of flex cars and alcohol fuels in *Energy Victory: Winning the War on Terror by Breaking Free of Oil* (Prometheus, 2007). Jim Motavalli, "Hijacking Hydrogen," *E—The Environmental Magazine* (January/February 2003), worries that the fossil fuel and nuclear industries will dominate the hydrogen future. The former wish to use "reforming" to generate hydrogen from coal, and the latter see hydrolysis as creating demand for nuclear power. In Iceland, Freyr Sverrisson, "Missing in Action: Iceland's Hydrogen Economy," *World Watch* (November/December 2006), notes that the demand of industry for electricity has shifted plans to develop hydrogen to the development of hydroelectric dams instead.

In January 2003, President George W. Bush proposed $1.2 billion in funding for making hydrogen-powered cars an on-the-road reality. Gregg Easterbrook, "Why Bush's H-Car Is Just Hot Air," *New Republic* (February 24, 2003), thinks it would make much more sense to address fuel-economy standards; Bush should "leave futurism to the futurists." Peter Schwartz and Doug Randall, "How Hydrogen Can Save America," *Wired* (April 2003), commend Bush's proposal but say the proposed funding is not enough. We need, they say, "an Apollo-scale commitment to hydrogen power. The fate of the republic depends on it."

The difficulty of the task is underlined by Robert F. Service in "The Hydrogen Backlash," *Science* (August 13, 2004) (the lead article in a special section titled "Toward a Hydrogen Economy"). Michael Behar, "Warning: The Hydrogen Economy May Be More Distant Than It Appears," *Popular Science* (January 2005), argues that the public has been misled about the prospects of the "hydrogen economy." Before it can arrive, we must overcome major technological, financial, and political obstacles. However, in the summer of 2008, Honda introduced the FCX Clarity, a car that runs on hydrogen (with fuel cells and a battery) and is twice as efficient as a gas–electric hybrid.

Internet References . . .

Facing the Future: People and the Planet

Facing the Future strives to educate people about critical global issues, including population growth, poverty, overconsumption, and environmental destruction.

http://www.facingthefuture.org/

Cell Phone Facts

The Food and Drug Administration (FDA) summarizes current knowledge of health risks from cell phone use at its Cell Phone Facts page.

http://www.fda.gov/cellphones/

World Health Organization

The World Health Organization of the United Nations provides links to recent reports and meetings about the safety of GM foods on its Biotechnology page.

http://www.who.int/foodsafety/biotech/en/

Malaria Foundation International

The Malaria Foundation International seeks "to facilitate the development and implementation of solutions to the health, economic and social problems caused by malaria."

http://www.malaria.org/

The Foresight Nanotech Institute

The Foresight Nanotech Institute works closely with governments, environmental groups, the policy community, professional associations, and civic sector organizations to improve education on and public policy on nanotechnology.

http://www.foresight.org/

National Institute of Environmental Health Sciences

The National Institute of Environmental Health Sciences studies the health risks of numerous environmental factors, many of which are associated with the use of technology.

http://www.niehs.nih.gov

Human Health and Welfare

***M**any people are concerned about new technological and scientific discoveries because they fear their potential impacts on human health and welfare. In the past, fears have been expressed concerning nuclear bombs and power plants, irradiated food, the internal combustion engine, medications such as thalidomide and diethylstilberstrol, vaccines, pesticides and other chemicals, and more. Not too long ago, people worried that the population explosion would harm both the environment and human well-being. Today the trend appears to be toward a population "implosion," and human well-being remains of concern. On the technology front, people worry about the possible health risks of cell phones, nanotechnology, and genetically modified foods, among other things. It is worth stressing that risks may be real (as they are with insecticides such as DDT), but there may be a trade-off for genuine health benefits.*

- Do Falling Birth Rates Pose a Threat to Human Welfare?
- Is There Sufficient Scientific Evidence to Conclude That Cell Phones Cause Cancer?
- Should DDT Be Banned Worldwide?
- Should Potential Risks Slow the Development of Nanotechnology?
- Are Genetically Modified Foods Safe to Eat?

ISSUE 7

Do Falling Birth Rates Pose a Threat to Human Welfare?

YES: Michael Meyer, from "Birth Dearth," *Newsweek* (Atlantic Edition) (September 27, 2004)

NO: Dave Foreman, from "The Human Population Explosion and the Future of Life," *Uncle Dave Foreman's Around the Campfire* (March 11, 2008)

ISSUE SUMMARY

YES: Michael Meyer argues that when world population begins to decline after about 2050, economies will no longer continue to grow, government benefits will decline, young people will have to support an elderly population, and despite some environmental benefits, quality of life will suffer.

NO: Environmental activist Dave Foreman argues that although levels of consumption and technology play large parts in threatening both the natural world and human welfare, a far more significant factor is population numbers and population growth. It is crucial that the world stabilize population as soon as possible.

In 1798 the British economist Thomas Malthus published his *Essay on the Principle of Population.* In it, he pointed with alarm at the way the human population grew geometrically (a hockey-stick curve of increase) and at how agricultural productivity grew only arithmetically (a straight-line increase). It was obvious, he said, that the population must inevitably outstrip its food supply and experience famine. Contrary to the conventional wisdom of the time, population growth was not necessarily a good thing. Indeed, it led inexorably to catastrophe. For many years, Malthus was something of a laughingstock. The doom he forecast kept receding into the future as new lands were opened to agriculture, new agricultural technologies appeared, new ways of preserving food limited the waste of spoilage, and the birth rate dropped in the industrialized nations (the "demographic transition"). The food supply kept ahead of population growth and seemed likely—to most observers—to continue to do so. Malthus's ideas were dismissed as irrelevant fantasies.

Yet overall population kept growing. In Malthus's time, there were about 1 billion human beings on Earth. By 1950—when Warren S. Thompson worried that civilization would be endangered by the rapid growth of Asian and Latin American populations during the next five decades (see "Population," *Scientific American* [February 1950])—there were a little over 2.5 billion. In 1999 the tally passed 6 billion. By 2025 it will be over 8 billion. Statistics like these, which are presented in *World Resources 2005—The Wealth of the Poor: Managing Ecosystems to Fight Poverty* (World Resources Institute, 2005) (http://www.wri.org/biodiv/pubs_description.cfm?pid=4073), published in collaboration with the United Nations Development Programme, the United Nations Environment Programme, and the World Bank, are positively frightening. The Worldwatch Institute's yearly *State of the World* reports (W. W. Norton) are no less so. By 2050 the UN expects the world population to be about 9 billion (see *World Population Prospects: The 2006 Revision Population Database;* http://esa .un.org/unpp/; United Nations, 2007). While global agricultural production has also increased, it has not kept up with rising demand, and—because of the loss of topsoil to erosion, the exhaustion of aquifers for irrigation water, and the high price of energy for making fertilizer (among other things)—the prospect of improvement seems exceedingly slim to many observers.

Two centuries never saw Malthus' forecasts of doom come to pass. Population continued to grow, and environmentalists pointed with alarm at a great many problems that resulted from human use of the world's resources (air and water pollution, erosion, loss of soil fertility and groundwater, loss of species, and a great deal more). "Cornucopian" economists such as the late Julian Simon insisted that the more people there are on Earth, the more people there are to solve problems and that humans can find ways around all possible resource shortages. See Simon's essay, "Life on Earth Is Getting Better, Not Worse," *The Futurist* (August 1983).

Was Malthus wrong? Both environmental scientists and many economists now say that if population continues to grow, problems are inevitable. But earlier predictions of a world population of 10 or 12 billion by 2050 are no longer looking very likely. The UN's population statistics show a slowing of growth, to be followed by an actual decline in population.

Some people worry that such a decline will not be good for human welfare. Michael Meyer argues that a shrinking population will mean that the economic growth that has meant constantly increasing standards of living must come to an end, government programs (from war to benefits for the poor and elderly) will no longer be affordable, a shrinking number of young people will have to support a growing elderly population, and despite some environmental benefits, quality of life will suffer. Environmental activist Dave Foreman argues that although levels of consumption and technology play large parts in threatening both the natural world and human welfare, a far more significant factor is population numbers and population growth. It is crucial that the world stabilize population as soon as possible.

YES

Michael Meyer

Birth Dearth

Everyone knows there are too many people in the world. Whether we live in Lahore or Los Angeles, Shanghai or Sao Paulo, our lives are daily proof. We endure traffic gridlock, urban sprawl and environmental depredation. The evening news brings variations on Ramallah or Darfur—images of Third World famine, poverty, pestilence, war, global competition for jobs and increasingly scarce natural resources.

Just last week the United Nations warned that many of the world's cities are becoming hopelessly overcrowded. Lagos alone will grow from 6.5 million people in 1995 to 16 million by 2015, a miasma of slums and decay where a fifth of all children will die before they are 5. At a conference in London, the U.N. Population Fund weighed in with a similarly bleak report: unless something dramatically changes, the world's 50 poorest countries will triple in size by 2050, to 1.7 billion people.

Yet this is not the full story. To the contrary, in fact. Across the globe, people are having fewer and fewer children. Fertility rates have dropped by half since 1972, from six children per woman to 2.9. And demographers say they're still falling, faster than ever. The world's population will continue to grow—from today's 6.4 billion to around 9 billion in 2050. But after that, it will go sharply into decline. Indeed, a phenomenon that we're destined to learn much more about—depopulation—has already begun in a number of countries. Welcome to the New Demography. It will change everything about our world, from the absolute size and power of nations to global economic growth to the quality of our lives.

This revolutionary transformation will be led not so much by developed nations as by the developing ones. Most of us are familiar with demographic trends in Europe, where birthrates have been declining for years. To reproduce itself, a society's women must each bear 2.1 children. Europe's fertility rates fall far short of that, according to the 2002 U.N. population report. France and Ireland, at 1.8, top Europe's childbearing charts. Italy and Spain, at 1.2, bring up the rear. In between are countries such as Germany, whose fertility rate of 1.4 is exactly Europe's average. What does that mean? If the U.N. figures are right, Germany could shed nearly a fifth of its 82.5 million people over the next 40 years—roughly the equivalent of all of east Germany, a loss of population not seen in Europe since the Thirty Years' War.

And so it is across the Continent. Bulgaria will shrink by 38 percent, Romania by 27 percent, Estonia by 25 percent. "Parts of Eastern Europe, already sparsely populated, will just empty out," predicts Reiner Klingholz, director of the Berlin Institute for Population and Development. Russia is already losing close to 750,000 people yearly. (President Vladimir Putin calls it a "national crisis.") So is Western Europe, and that figure could grow to as much as 3 million a year by midcentury, if not more.

The surprise is how closely the less-developed world is following the same trajectory. In Asia it's well known that Japan will soon tip into population loss, if it hasn't already. With a fertility rate of 1.3 children per woman, the country stands to shed a quarter of its 127 million people over the next four decades, according to U.N. projections. But while the graying of Japan (average age: 42.3 years) has long been a staple of news headlines, what to make of China, whose fertility rate has declined from 5.8 in 1970 to 1.8 today, according to the U.N.? Chinese census data put the figure even lower, at 1.3. Coupled with increasing life spans, that means China's population will age as quickly in one generation as Europe's has over the past 100 years, reports the Center for Strategic and International Studies in Washington. With an expected median age of 44 in 2015, China will be older on average than the United States. By 2019 or soon after, its population will peak at 1.5 billion, then enter a steep decline. By midcentury, China could well lose 20 to 30 percent of its population every generation.

The picture is similar elsewhere in Asia, where birthrates are declining even in the absence of such stringent birth-control programs as China's. Indeed, it's happening despite often generous official incentives to procreate. The industrialized nations of Singapore, Hong Kong, Taiwan and South Korea all report subreplacement fertility, says Nicholas Eberstadt, a demographer at the American Enterprise Institute in Washington. To this list can be added Thailand, Burma, Australia and Sri Lanka, along with Cuba and many Caribbean nations, as well as Uruguay and Brazil. Mexico is aging so rapidly that within several decades it will not only stop growing but will have an older population than that of the United States. So much for the cliche of those Mexican youths swarming across the Rio Grande? "If these figures are accurate," says Eberstadt, "just about half of the world's population lives in subreplacement countries."

There are notable exceptions. In Europe, Albania and the outlier province of Kosovo are reproducing energetically. So are pockets of Asia: Mongolia, Pakistan and the Philippines. The United Nations projects that the Middle East will double in population over the next 20 years, growing from 326 million today to 649 million by 2050. Saudi Arabia has one of the highest fertility rates in the world, 5.7, after Palestinian territories at 5.9 and Yemen at 7.2. Yet there are surprises here, too. Tunisia has tipped below replacement. Lebanon and Iran are at the threshold. And though overall the region's population continues to grow, the increase is due mainly to lower infant mortality; fertility rates themselves are falling faster than in developed countries, indicating that over the coming decades the Middle East will age far more rapidly than other regions of the world. Birthrates in Africa remain high, and despite the AIDS epidemic its population is projected to keep growing. So is that of the United States.

We'll return to American exceptionalism, and what that might portend. But first, let's explore the causes of the birth dearth, as outlined in a pair of new books on the subject. "Never in the last 650 years, since the time of the Black Plague, have birth and fertility rates fallen so far, so fast, so low, for so long, in so many places," writes the sociologist Ben Wattenberg in "Fewer: How the New Demography of Depopulation Will Shape Our Future." Why? Wattenberg suggests that a variety of once independent trends have conjoined to produce a demographic tsunami. As the United Nations reported last week, people everywhere are leaving the countryside and moving to cities, which will be home to more than half the world's people by 2007. Once there, having a child becomes a cost rather than an asset. From 1970 to 2000, Nigeria's urban population climbed from 14 to 44 percent. South Korea went from 28 to 84 percent. So-called megacities, from Lagos to Mexico City, have exploded seemingly overnight. Birthrates have fallen in inverse correlation.

Other factors are at work. Increasing female literacy and enrollment in schools have tended to decrease fertility, as have divorce, abortion and the worldwide trend toward later marriage. Contraceptive use has risen dramatically over the past decade; according to U.N. data, 62 percent of married or "in union" women of reproductive age are now using some form of nonnatural birth control. In countries such as India, now the capital of global HIV, disease has become a factor. In Russia, the culprits include alcoholism, poor public health and industrial pollution that has whacked male sperm counts. Wealth discourages childbearing, as seen long ago in Europe and now in Asia. As Wattenberg puts it, "Capitalism is the best contraception."

The potential consequences of the population implosion are enormous. Consider the global economy, as Phillip Longman describes it in another recent book, "The Empty Cradle: How Falling Birthrates Threaten World Prosperity and What to Do About It." A population expert at the New America Foundation in Washington, he sees danger for global prosperity. Whether it's real estate or consumer spending, economic growth and population have always been closely linked. "There are people who cling to the hope that you can have a vibrant economy without a growing population, but mainstream economists are pessimistic," says Longman. You have only to look at Japan or Europe for a whiff of what the future might bring, he adds. In Italy, demographers forecast a 40 percent decline in the working-age population over the next four decades—accompanied by a commensurate drop in growth across the Continent, according to the European Commission. What happens when Europe's cohort of baby boomers begins to retire around 2020? Recent strikes and demonstrations in Germany, Italy, France and Austria over the most modest pension reforms are only the beginning of what promises to become a major sociological battle between Europe's older and younger generations.

That will be only a skirmish compared with the conflict brewing in China. There market reforms have removed the cradle-to-grave benefits of the planned economy, while the Communist Party hasn't constructed an adequate social safety net to take their place. Less than one quarter of the population is covered by retirement pensions, according to CSIS. That puts the burden of elder care almost entirely on what is now a generation of only children. The one-child policy has led to the so-called 4-2-1 problem, in which each child will be potentially responsible for caring for two parents and four grandparents.

Incomes in China aren't rising fast enough to offset this burden. In some rural villages, so many young people have fled to the cities that there may be nobody left to look after the elders. And the aging population could soon start to dull China's competitive edge, which depends on a seemingly endless supply of cheap labor. After 2015, this labor pool will begin to dry up, says economist Hu Angang. China will have little choice but to adopt a very Western-sounding solution, he says: it will have to raise the education level of its work force and make it more productive. Whether it can is an open question. Either way, this much is certain: among Asia's emerging economic powers, China will be the first to grow old before it gets rich.

Equally deep dislocations are becoming apparent in Japan. Akihiko Matsutani, an economist and author of a recent best seller, "The Economy of a Shrinking Population," predicts that by 2009 Japan's economy will enter an era of "negative growth." By 2030, national income will have shrunk by 15 percent. Speculating about the future is always dicey, but economists pose troubling questions. Take the legendarily high savings that have long buoyed the Japanese economy and financed borrowing worldwide, especially by the United States. As an aging Japan draws down those assets in retirement, will U.S. and global interest rates rise? At home, will Japanese businesses find themselves competing for increasingly scarce investment capital? And just what will they be investing in, as the country's consumers grow older, and demand for the latest in hot new products cools off? What of the effect on national infrastructure? With less tax revenue in state coffers, Matsutani predicts, governments will increasingly be forced to skimp on or delay repairs to the nation's roads, bridges, rail lines and the like. "Life will become less convenient," he says. Spanking-clean Tokyo might come to look more like New York City in the 1970s, when many urban dwellers decamped for the suburbs (taking their taxes with them) and city fathers could no longer afford the municipal upkeep. Can Japanese cope? "They will have to," says Matsutani. "There's no alternative."

Demographic change magnifies all of a country's problems, social as well as economic. An overburdened welfare state? Aging makes it collapse. Tensions over immigration? Differing birthrates intensify anxieties, just as the need for imported labor rises—perhaps the critical issue for the Europe of tomorrow. A poor education system, with too many kids left behind? Better fix it, because a shrinking work force requires higher productivity and greater flexibility, reflected in a new need for continuing job training, career switches and the health care needed to keep workers working into old age.

In an ideal world, perhaps, the growing gulf between the world's wealthy but shrinking countries and its poor, growing ones would create an opportunity. Labor would flow from the overpopulated, resource-poor south to the depopulating north, where jobs would continue to be plentiful. Capital and remittance income from the rich nations would flow along the reverse path, benefiting all. Will it happen? Perhaps, but that presupposes considerable labor mobility.

Considering the resistance Europeans display toward large-scale immigration from North Africa, or Japan's almost zero-immigration policy, it's hard to be optimistic. Yes, attitudes are changing. Only a decade ago, for instance, Europeans also spoke of zero immigration. Today they recognize the need and, in bits and pieces, are beginning to plan for it. But will it happen on the scale required?

A more probable scenario may be an intensification of existing tensions between peoples determined to preserve their beleaguered national identities on the one hand, and immigrant groups on the other seeking to escape overcrowding and lack of opportunity at home. For countries such as the Philippines—still growing, and whose educated work force looks likely to break out of low-status jobs as nannies and gardeners and move up the global professional ladder—this may be less of a problem. It will be vastly more serious for the tens of millions of Arab youths who make up a majority of the population in the Middle East and North Africa, at least half of whom are unemployed.

America is the wild card in this global equation. While Europe and much of Asia shrinks, the United States' indigenous population looks likely to stay relatively constant, with fertility rates hovering almost precisely at replacement levels. Add in heavy immigration, and you quickly see that America is the only modern nation that will continue to grow. Over the next 45 years the United States will gain 100 million people, Wattenberg estimates, while Europe loses roughly as many.

This does not mean that Americans will escape the coming demographic whammy. They, too, face the problems of an aging work force and its burdens. (The cost of Medicare and Social Security will rise from 4.3 percent of GDP in 2000 to 11.5 percent in 2030 and 21 percent in 2050, according to the Congressional Budget Office.) They, too, face the prospect of increasing ethnic tensions, as a flat white population and a dwindling black one become gradually smaller minorities in a growing multicultural sea. And in our interdependent era, the troubles of America's major trading partners—Europe and Japan—will quickly become its own. To cite one example, what becomes of the vaunted "China market," invested in so heavily by U.S. companies, if by 2050 China loses an estimated 35 percent of its workers and the aged consume an ever-greater share of income?

America's demographic "unipolarity" has profound security implications as well. Washington worries about terrorism and failing states. Yet the chaos of today's fragmented world is likely to prove small in comparison to what could come. For U.S. leaders, Longman in "The Empty Cradle" sketches an unsettling prospect. Though the United States may have few military competitors, the technologies by which it projects geopolitical power—from laser-guided missiles and stealth bombers to a huge military infrastructure—may gradually become too expensive for a country facing massively rising social entitlements in an era of slowing global economic growth. If the war on terrorism turns out to be the "generational struggle" that national-security adviser Condoleezza Rice says it is, Longman concludes, then the United States might have difficulty paying for it.

None of this is writ, of course. Enlightened governments could help hold the line. France and the Netherlands have instituted family-friendly policies that help women combine work and motherhood, ranging from tax credits for kids to subsidized day care. Scandinavian countries have kept birthrates up with generous provisions for parental leave, health care and part-time employment. Still, similar programs offered by the shrinking city-state of Singapore—including a state-run dating service—have done little to reverse the birth dearth. Remember, too, that such prognoses have been wrong in the past. At the cusp of the postwar baby boom, demographers predicted a sharp fall in fertility and a global birth dearth. Yet even if this generation of seers turns out to be right, as seems likely, not all is bad. Environmentally, a smaller world is almost certainly a better world, whether in terms of cleaner air or, say, the return of wolves and rare flora to abandoned stretches of the East German countryside. And while people are living longer, they are also living healthier—at least in the developed world. That means they can (and probably should) work more years before retirement.

Yes, a younger generation will have to shoulder the burden of paying for their elders. But there will be compensations. As populations shrink, says economist Matsutani, national incomes may drop—but not necessarily per capita incomes. And in this realm of uncertainty, one mundane thing is probably sure: real-estate prices will fall. That will hurt seniors whose nest eggs are tied up in their homes, but it will be a boon to youngsters of the future. Who knows? Maybe the added space and cheap living will inspire them to, well, do whatever it takes to make more babies. Thus the cycle of life will restore its balance. . . .

Dave Foreman  **NO**

The Human Population Explosion and the Future of Life

Shortly after the end of World War Two, visionary conservationists and scientists such as Fairfield Osborn began to warn that continued human population growth would cause all kinds of problems including heightened plundering of wild Nature. It was not until the late 1960s, however, that population growth moved to the front burner of the conservation stove as shown by the Sierra Club's publication of a book called *The Population Bomb* by a young biologist named Paul Ehrlich. During the next decade those who were worried studied, wrote, and warned about human population growth and its consequences.

Ehrlich and physicist John Holdren (currently in the highly prestigious position of president of the American Association for the Advancement of Science) suggested a formula for understanding the consequences of human growth: I=PAT. This formula, once recognizable but now widely forgotten, means that human impact is a production of population, affluence (consumption), and some measure of technology. At the time, P (population size) was seen as the underlying and key factor for determining the magnitude of human impact. During the last two decades, however, it has become fashionable to discount P and stress A (affluence or consumption).

The level of consumption is a key multiplier of population's impact and individuals worldwide have vastly different levels of consumption of goods and services. Nevertheless, some "environmentalists" and social engineers (right and left) now argue that population size or even continued growth is relatively unimportant; they say it is the level of consumption of certain groups that is key for calculating how much damage an individual or population causes. Such activists argue that reducing consumption is much more important than stabilizing population. Others of us still see population as the big rock. Consumption vs. population may be an intractable debate since it is grounded in worldview as much as in evidence. In general, those who are biologically (or scientifically) oriented are more likely to see population as paramount in I=PAT, while those socially and economically directed tend to stress consumption. I would argue that biologists deal with a more fundamental and real world than do culturalists.

Let me offer just two examples to show how total population is the key. China's remarkable and frightening economic explosion in the last few years has now thrust it into the lead of nations cranking out greenhouse gases. However, were it not for the draconian population policies of China since the 1960s, the population of China would be closer to two billion instead of a billion and a half. How much more greenhouse pollution would China be pumping out had it not taken extreme measures to reduce the birth rate?

Had the United States instituted reasonable immigration policies in the 1960s before immigration became such a volatile issue, our population would likely have stabilized around 250 million. Because we didn't deal wisely with immigration, our population is now over 300 million and rapidly headed toward 400 million. How much less sprawl, greenhouse gas production, resource consumption, etc., would the U.S. boast today, had we stabilized our population then?

We can sort out the kinds of impacts population growth or PAT cause into five stacks:

Land degradation

Resource depletion

Famine

Social, political disruption

Ecological/Evolutionary wounds

Overall, discussion about the problems of population growth has looked at the first four sets. As a conservationist and Nature lover, however, I believe the impact of the population explosion on the rest of Nature is paramount. I also agree with Virginia Tech Professor Eileen Crist that population stabilization and resource depletion activists have made a strategic error by focusing on the first four. As she points out, we cannot predict when we will run out of a resource such as oil or when famine will strike. Indeed, attempting to do so has harmed our credibility. On the other hand, we can accurately and strikingly show how the spread and population growth of humans is harming Nature.

In *Rewilding North America* [Island Press, 2004], I sorted out how humans harm Nature into Seven Ecological Wounds: direct killing, habitat loss and modification, habitat fragmentation, exotic species invasion, loss and disruption of ecological and evolutionary processes, biocide pollution, and the greenhouse gas effect. These different wounds are cumulative and synergistic.

Taken simplistically, the I=PAT equation lumps together the impacts of all kinds of people. This is how we get comparisons such as the one claiming that one typical American causes thirty-five times the impact of one typical Bangladeshi. To more accurately understand ecological wounds, though, we need to shake out how global and local populations have differing effects. For example, an average American is responsible for much more greenhouse gas production, but a poor Bangladeshi farmer may be much more dangerous to the survival of tigers. Someone with a million-dollar starter castle certainly consumes more than someone living in an old shack on a national forest inholding. But the relatively poorer rural dweller might contribute more to the extinction of the Mexican wolf in the wild. So, we need to look at both IG=PAT and IL=PAT.

Seventy years ago, Aldo Leopold saw the protection of rare species as the most important task of conservation. Since the mid-1970s, we've known that mass extinction caused by humans is the leading problem, conservation or otherwise, facing us. In addition to wiping out many of our fellow Earthlings, mass extinction destroys raw material for evolution and disrupts evolutionary processes. Therefore the shocking, explosive growth of human population has not just short-term but also very long-term catastrophic consequences. Indeed, should the vast, sprawling human population break off major limbs of the tree of life instead of just plucking twigs and leaves, our impact will last forever in terms of Earthly life.

If we are to bring back population stabilization as a bedrock goal of conservation, I think it is essential to show how high human populations and continued growth cause and exacerbate the Seven Ecological Wounds. What I sketch here is just a beginning, only a few examples of what conservationists need to document on how the human population explosion drives the biodiversity crisis. For each of the wounds, I'll give an example of how both global and local populations drive them. (It can be more complicated when global and local people work together to cause wounds, but I will save that issue for a later time.)

Direct Killing

I remember how as a kid I read the *Weekly Reader* telling us how better exploitation of the oceans would feed growing populations. Well, we did that. The consequences are collapsing fisheries around the world, die-off of coral reefs, and the functional extinction of once abundant and/or highly interactive species such as cod, sharks, and tuna. As hungry rural populations swell and spread, they vacuum the rainforest and other semi-wild ecosystems of larger animals for food. Experienced tropical researchers have told how even a small village with primitive technology can clean out the larger animals in a nearby protected area. As their population grows, hunters go ever farther afield with snares, nets, and old guns.

Habitat Destruction and Modification

Other factors, such as lust for larger homes and moving to the Sunbelt, grow the cancerous sprawl of suburban and exurban bedroom communities in the United States. But the absolute growth of numbers of Americans also contributes to the destruction of wildlife habitat by new home developments. In the United States, immigration plays the big role in increasing our population. Even if people come here poor, their goal is to increase their standard of living—which they do, thereby consuming more than had they stayed home. Regardless of overconsumption, if the U.S. had fifty or sixty million fewer residents, there would be fewer home developments in the California coastal chaparral, the Sonoran Desert around Phoenix, woods and forests surrounding Atlanta, and so on.

In India, rapid growth of very poor peasants and tribal peoples is putting irresistible pressure on tiger reserves. Plans are afoot to allow people to move into once-well-protected areas that provide the last secure habitat for tigers and other species. Indian conservationists predict that tigers will vanish where this is allowed to happen.

Fragmentation

No matter if it is starter-castle suburbs and wide freeways in the United States or new slash-and-burn crop patches and logging roads in poorer countries, humans create barriers and fracture zones in wildlife habitats that isolate animal and plant populations into smaller and smaller areas and that will prevent migration north (south below the equator) or to higher elevations with radical climate change. Increased numbers of people are a key cause of our spread into once unpopulated or lightly populated regions where wild critters could range as widely as they needed before the human invasion.

Ecological/Evolutionary Processes

High population densities and the further spread of humans lead to disruption of vital ecological and evolutionary processes, such as wildfire, river flooding and drying, predation, and pollination. Growing numbers of people crowd fertile river bottoms creating pressure for upstream flood-control dams, which, of course, stop normal hydrological processes. In the United States and Canada, the spread of homes to forested areas leads to suppression of naturally occurring wildfires, which harms forest health and creates conditions for larger, unnatural, uncontrollable conflagrations in the future. Humans, whether Denver suburbanites or Indian peasants, are intolerant of big cats, wolves, and other carnivores, leading to their extermination and the loss of essential top-down regulation of prey species.

Exotic Species

The spread of people spreads invasive species. Increased global trade between growing (in numbers and affluence) populations spreads invasive species. The impacts people have on the ground when they move into a new area create the conditions most beneficial for invasive, exotic, weedy species that outcompete native species. Among the most destructive organisms spread by growing populations are plant diseases, which play absolute havoc with native plants and forests.

Biocide Pollution

People use biocides and cause pollution. On a global scale, wealthy populations cause much more pollution than do poor populations. But locally, all people produce pollution of varying kinds and growing population density leads inevitably to more local pollution, which acts as biocides to many species.

Greenhouse Gases

It can be hard to tell what the limiting resource will be when a population of any species grows to approach a point of overshooting the carrying capacity of its habitat. Unlike other species and other communities of humans before the industrial revolution, we are now a global species. The entire Earth is our habitat. For the global human community, the resource in most short supply has turned out to be the ability of the atmosphere and the seas to handle industrial farts of carbon dioxide and methane, among other gases. By industry, I do not just include factories, smelters, motor vehicles, and such, but also the industrial exploitation of forests and other lands. Wealthy people throughout the world share the greatest guilt for producing greenhouse gases, but poorer people with their fires in forests, grasslands, and woodlands also contribute.

Here affluence (A) and technology (T) play large roles in how much impact individuals may have. However, the influence of sheer numbers of people cannot be brushed aside on the greenhouse gas question. What drives the clearing and burning of the Amazon? Too many people and too high a rate of growth in Brazil, plus the burgeoning numbers of hungry people in the world who need food the "virgin lands" of Brazil supposedly can produce—resulting in a speedy increase in Brazil's greenhouse gas production and loss of forests that could continue to sequester carbon from the atmosphere and sea. China passed the United States as the number one greenhouse gas emitting country in the world because of its massive population charging after greater affluence and technology. But if China had only half a billion people instead of close to a billion and a half, it would not have passed the U.S. If China's population growth had not been harshly curtailed, China would be producing much more greenhouse pollution and may have by this time already pushed past a deeply consequential tipping point. The one-child policy in China may be giving us a few more years to deal with the staggering greenhouse problem.

As I ponder what factors cause each of these wounds on global and local scales, I do not deny that affluence and technology play big parts. My point, however, is that we cannot allow that obvious reality to overshadow the probably even-greater role of high population numbers and population growth rates in driving ecological wounds, from direct killing of threatened species to production of carbon dioxide.

Should conservationists find the wisdom and courage to come back to calling for population stabilization, we must stress how the population explosion causes the ecological wounds that result in mass extinction and destruction of the biosphere. There is our expert province. Because species extinction and destruction of wilderness has consistently been overshadowed by the other consequences of the population explosion, pointing this out as a new concern in a thoughtful, convincing way could help return the world community to a more rational approach about population growth. . . .

POSTSCRIPT

Do Falling Birth Rates Pose a Threat to Human Welfare?

Resources and population come together in the concept of "carrying capacity," defined very simply as the size of the population that the environment can support, or "carry," indefinitely, through both good years and bad. It is not the size of the population that can prosper in good times alone, for such a large population must suffer catastrophically when droughts, floods, or blights arrive or the climate warms or cools. It is a long-term concept, where "long term" means not decades or generations, nor even centuries, but millennia or more. See Mark Nathan Cohen, "Carrying Capacity," *Free Inquiry* (August/September 2004), and T. C. R. White, "The Role of Food, Weather, and Climate in Limiting the Abundance of Animals," *Biological Reviews* (August 2008).

What is Earth's carrying capacity for human beings? It is surely impossible to set a precise figure on the number of human beings the world can support for the long run. As Joel E. Cohen discusses in *How Many People Can the Earth Support?* (W. W. Norton, 1996), estimates of Earth's carrying capacity range from under a billion to over a trillion. The precise number depends on our choices of diet, standard of living, level of technology, willingness to share with others at home and abroad (including wildlife and natural environments) and desire for an intact physical, chemical, and biological environment, as well as on whether or not our morality permits restraint in reproduction and our political or religious ideology permits educating and empowering women. The key, Cohen stresses, is human choice, and the choices are ones we must make within the next 50 years. Phoebe Hall, "Carrying Capacity," *E Magazine* (March/April 2003), notes that even countries with large land areas and small populations, such as Australia and Canada, can be overpopulated in terms of resource availability. The critical resource appears to be food supply; see Russell Hopfenberg, "Human Carrying Capacity Is Determined by Food Availability," *Population & Environment* (November 2003).

Andrew R. B. Ferguson, in "Perceiving the Population Bomb," *World Watch* (July/August 2001), sets the maximum sustainable human population at about 2 billion. Sandra Postel, in the Worldwatch Institute's *State of the World 1994* (W. W. Norton, 1994), says, "As a result of our population size, consumption patterns, and technology choices, we have surpassed the planet's carrying capacity. This is plainly evident by the extent to which we are damaging and depleting natural capital" (including land and water).

If population growth is now declining and world population will actually begin to decline during this century, there is clear hope. But the question of carrying capacity remains. Most estimates of carrying capacity put it at well below the current world population size, and it will take a long time for global population to fall far enough to reach such levels. We seem to be moving in the right direction, but it remains an open question whether our numbers will decline far enough soon enough (i.e., before environmental problems become critical). On the other hand, Jeroen Van den Bergh and Piet Rietveld, "Reconsidering the Limits to World Population: Meta-Analysis and Meta-Prediction," *Bioscience* (March 2004), set their best estimate of human global carrying capacity at 7.7 billion, which is distinctly reassuring. However, there is still concern that global population will not stop at that point; see David R. Francis, "'Birth Dearth' Worries Pale in Comparison to Overpopulation," *Christian Science Monitor* (July 14, 2008).

How high a level will population actually reach? Fertility levels are definitely declining in many developed nations; see Alan Booth and Ann C. Crouter (eds.), *The New Population Problem: Why Families in Developed Countries Are Shrinking and What It Means* (Lawrence Erlbaum Associates, 2005). The visibility of this fertility decline is among the reasons mentioned by Martha Campbell, "Why the Silence on Population?" *Population and Environment* (May 2007). Is there an actual "birth dearth"? Not according to Doug Moss, "What Birth Dearth?" *E Magazine* (November–December 2006), who reminds us that there is still a large surplus of births—and therefore a growing population—in the less developed world. If we think globally, there is no shortage of people. However, many countries are so concerned about changing age distributions that they are trying to encourage larger—not smaller—families. See Robert Engelman, "Unnatural Increase? A Short History of Population Trends and Influences," *World Watch* (September/October 2008—a special issue on population issues), and his book *More: Population, Nature, and What Women Want* (Island Press, 2008).

ISSUE 8

Is There Sufficient Scientific Evidence to Conclude That Cell Phones Cause Cancer?

YES: George Carlo and Martin Schram, from "Follow the Science: Piecing Together the Cancer Puzzle," *An Insider's Alarming Discoveries About Cancer and Genetic Damage* (Carroll & Graf, 2001)

NO: United Kingdom's National Radiation Protection Board, from *Mobile Phones and Health 2004: Report by the Board of NRPB* (Doc NRPB 15(5), 2004)

ISSUE SUMMARY

YES: Public health scientist George Carlo and journalist Martin Schram argue that there is a definite risk that the electromagnetic radiation generated by cell phone antennae can cause cancer and other health problems.

NO: The National Radiation Protection Board (now the Radiation Protection Division, http://www.hpa.org.uk/radiation/, of the United Kingdom's Health Protection Agency) argues that there is no clear indication of adverse health effects, including cancer, from the use of mobile phones, but precautions are nevertheless in order.

It seems inevitable that new technologies will alarm people. For example, in the late 1800s, when electricity was new, people feared the new wires that were strung overhead. See Joseph P. Sullivan, "Fearing Electricity: Overhead Wire Panic in New York City," *IEEE Technology and Society Magazine* (Fall 1995). More recently, electromagnetic fields (EMFs) have drawn attention. Now cell phones and other forms of wireless communications technology, including wireless networks (wi-fi), are the focus of controversy.

EMFs are emitted by any device that uses electricity. They weaken rapidly as one gets farther from the source, but they can be remarkably strong close to the source. Users of electric blankets (before the blankets were redesigned to minimize EMFs) and personal computers are thus subject to high exposures. Since EMF strength also depends on how much electricity is flowing through the source, people who live near power lines, especially high-tension, long-distance transmission lines, are also open to high EMF exposure.

Are EMFs dangerous? There have been numerous reports suggesting a link between EMF exposure and cancer, but inconsistency has been the curse of research in this area. In 1992 the Committee on Interagency Radiation Research and Policy Coordination, an arm of the White House's Office of Science and Technology Policy, released *Health Effects of Low Frequency Electric and Magnetic Fields,* a report that concluded, "There is no convincing [published] evidence . . . to support the contention that exposures to extremely low frequency electric and magnetic fields generated by sources such as household appliances, video terminals, and local powerlines are demonstrable health hazards." Jon Palfreman, in "Apocalypse Not," *Technology Review* (April 1996), summarized the controversy and the evidence against any connection between cancer and EMFs. And in "Residential Exposure to Magnetic Fields and Acute Lymphoblastic Leukemia in Children," *The New England Journal of Medicine* (July 3, 1997), Martha S. Linet et al. report that they failed to find any support for such a connection.

Since cell phones are electrical devices, they emit EMFs. But they—or their antennae—also emit electromagnetic radiation in the form of radio signals. And after a few cell phone users developed brain cancer and sued the phone makers, people began to worry. See Gordon Bass, "Is Your Cell Phone Killing You?" *PC Computing* (December 1999). Professor John Moulder and his colleagues published a review of the evidence in "Cell Phones and Cancer: What Is the Evidence for a Connection?" *Radiation Research* (May 1999). In it, they concluded, "Overall, the existing evidence for a causal relationship between RF radiation from cell phones and cancer is found to be weak to nonexistent." Tamar Nordenberg, "Cell Phones and Brain Cancer: No Clear Connection," *FDA Consumer* (November–December 2000), reported no real signs that cell phones caused cancer but noted that the evidence was sufficient to justify continuing research.

In the following selections, George Carlo and Martin Schram argue that there is a definite risk that the electromagnetic radiation generated by cell phone antennae can cause cancer and other health problems. Furthermore, wireless Internet devices also emit such radiation and may pose similar risks. The National Radiation Protection Board (now the Radiation Protection Division of the United Kingdom's Health Protection Agency) argues that the widespread adoption of mobile phones has not been accompanied by any clear increase in adverse health effects, including cancer, but the technology is still young, there has not been enough time for epidemiological studies of users, especially in subgroups of users, and there have been some suggestive laboratory studies. There are no clear indications of risk, but precautions are nevertheless in order.

YES    George Carlo and Martin Schram

Follow the Science: Piecing Together the Cancer Puzzle

Scientific findings are like pieces of a puzzle. Individually, they may not seem to show anything clearly. But by trying to fit the pieces together, it is possible to see if they form a big, coherent picture.

In the puzzle of cell phone radiation research, the pieces of scientific evidence we have now do fit together. Although many pieces are still missing, those that are in place indicate a big picture of cancer and health risk. The picture is alarming, because even if the risk eventually proves to be small, it will still be real—and that means millions of people around the world will develop cancer or other health problems due to using mobile phones.

Even more alarming, however, is that many in the industry, who are paid by the industry—and some who are paid by the public to oversee and regulate the industry—have persisted in talking publicly as if they cannot see the picture that is taking shape even as they speak.

In the study of public health, there is a well-known template that researchers use to put together individual scientific findings—like the pieces of a puzzle—to see if they show evidence of a public-health hazard. This template, known as the Koch-Henle Postulates, is a means of determining whether the findings indicate a true cause-and-effect process, from biological plausibility to exposure and dose-response. The postulates are:

1. If there is a biological explanation for the association derived from separate experiments that is consistent with what is known about the development of the disease, then the association is more likely to be causal. Scientists term this *biological plausibility*.
2. If several studies of people are showing the same finding while employing different methods and different investigators, the association that is being seen is more likely to be cause and effect, or causal. Scientists term this *consistency*.
3. If it is clear that the exposure precedes the development of the disease, then the association is more likely to be causal. Scientists term this *temporality*.

4. If the increase in risk is significant—more than a doubling in the risk or an increase that is statistically significant—the association is more likely to be causal. Scientists term this *significance.*
5. If the more severe the level of exposure, the higher the risk for the disease or the biological effect that is being studied, the association is more likely to be causal. Scientists term this *dose–response upward.*
6. If the absence of exposure corresponds to the absence of the disease, the more likely the association is to be causal. Scientists term this *dose–response downward.*
7. If there are similar findings in human, animal, and *in vitro* studies—in other words, if the same conclusions can be drawn from all—the more likely the association that is seen is causal. Scientists term this *concordance.*

Researchers use the Koch-Henle Postulates as a checklist. The greater the number of postulates that are met, the greater the likelihood that a hazard exists. For some of the more commonly recognized carcinogens, it has taken decades for the hazards to be judged as valid. For example, in the case of cigarette smoking, it took two decades of study and more than 100 years of consumer use to gather enough information that could be judged against the Koch-Henle standards to demonstrate the need for the U.S. Surgeon General's warning label on cigarette packs.

In the case of cellular telephones, consumers are fortunate that the health-hazard picture can be seen much sooner than that. Each of the red-flag findings about cell phone radiation provides a vital piece of information that fits into the overall cancer puzzle. A number of the other earlier studies, which on their own were inconclusive or seemed uninterpretable, now appear to fit into the puzzle as well. They clarify a troubling picture of cancer and health risk that is just now becoming clear.

Here is how the scientific pieces fit into the larger cancer puzzle:

Human blood studies   These studies—by Drs. Ray Tice and Graham Hook, and most recently [corroborated by] Dr. Joseph Roti Roti—show genetic damage in the form of micronuclei in blood cells exposed to cell phone radiation. They provide evidence of the Koch-Henle postulate of *biological plausibility* for the development of the tumors following exposure to radio waves. Without some type of genetic damage, it is unlikely that radio waves would be able to cause cancer. Every direct mechanism that has been identified in the development of cancer involves genetic damage; the linkage is so strong that if an absence of genetic damage had been proven in these studies, scientists would have considered that to be reason enough to conclude that cancer is not caused by cell phones. (Indeed, that is what scientists were justified in saying prior to 1999.) Scientific literature has repeatedly confirmed that brain cancer is clearly linked to chromosome damage; brain tumors have consistently been shown to have a variety of chromosomal abnormalities. The studies by Tice, Hook, and Roti Roti consistently showed chromosomal damage in blood exposed to wireless phone radio waves.

Breakdown in the blood brain barrier The findings of genetic damage by Tice, Hook, and Roti Roti now give new meaning and importance to Dr. Leif Salford's 1994 studies that showed a breakdown in the blood brain barrier of rats when they were exposed to radio waves. The blood brain barrier findings now fit into the overall cancer picture by providing a two-step explanation for how cancer could be caused by cell phone radiation. (The blood brain barrier filters the blood by not allowing dangerous chemicals to reach sensitive brain tissue.)

Step One: A breakdown in the blood brain barrier filter would provide an avenue for chemical carcinogens in the bloodstream (from tobacco, pesticides, or air pollution, for example) to leak into the brain and reach sensitive brain tissue that would otherwise be protected. Those chemicals, upon reaching sensitive brain tissue, could break the DNA in the brain or cause other harm to reach those cells.

Step Two: While a number of studies showed that cell phone radiation by itself does not appear to break DNA, the micronuclei findings of Tice, Hook, and Roti Roti suggest that DNA repair mechanisms in brain cells could be impaired by mobile phone radiation. (One reason micronuclei occur is that there has been a breakdown in the cell's ability to repair itself.) If the brain cells become unable to repair themselves, the process of chemically induced carcinogenesis—the creation of tumors—could begin.

This is further evidence of the Koch-Henle postulate of *biological plausibility* for cell phone radiation involvement in the development of brain cancer.

Studies of tumors in people who use cell phones There have been four studies of tumors in people who use cellular phones—Dr. Ken Rothman's study of deaths among cell phone users, Joshua Muscat's two studies of brain cancer and acoustic neuroma, and Dr. Lennart Hardell's study of brain tumors. All four epidemiological studies, done by different investigators who used different methods, show some evidence of an increased risk of tumors associated with the use of cellular phones. This is evidence of the Koch-Henle postulate of *consistency*.

All four epidemiological studies provide some assurance in the methods used by the investigators that the people studied had used cellular telephones before they were clinically diagnosed as having tumors. This is evidence of the Koch-Henle postulate of *temporality*.

All four epidemiological studies showed increases in risk of developing brain tumors. Muscat's study of cell phone users showed a doubling of the risk of developing neuro-epithelial tumors. (The result was statistically significant.) Hardell's study showed that among cell phone users, tumors were twice as likely to occur in areas of the brain at the side where the user normally held the phone. (This result was also statistically significant.) Rothman's study showed that users of handheld cell phones have more than twice the risk of dying from brain cancer than do car phone users—whose antennas are mounted on the body of the car, far removed from the users' heads. (That finding was not statistically significant.) Muscat's study of acoustic neuroma indicates that cell phone users have a 50-percent increase in risk of developing tumors of the auditory nerve. (This finding was statistically significant only when correlated with the years of cell phone usage by the patient.) These findings are evidence of the Koch-Henle postulate of *significance*.

Studies of cell phone radiation dosage and response   In Dr. Michael Repacholi's study of mice, the risk of lymphoma increased significantly with the number of months that mice were exposed to the radio waves.

In the work by Tice, Hook, and Roti Roti, the risks of genetic damage as measured by the formation of micronuclei increased as the amount of radiation increased.

In the three epidemiological studies—two by Muscat and one by Hardell—that were able to estimate radiation exposure to specific parts of the brain, the risk of tumors was greater in the areas of the brain near where the cell phone was held.

These findings are all evidence of the Koch-Henle postulate known as *dose–response upward*. (In cell phones, minutes of phone usage are not a reliable indication of dosage, because the distance of the telephone from a base station during the call and any physical barriers to the signal are the most important factors in the amount of radiation the phone antenna emits during the call.)

The Hardell epidemiological study showed that patients with tumors in areas of the brain that could not be reached by radiation from a cell phone antenna were likely not to have been cell phone users. Similarly, in Muscat's study, when all brain-tumor patients were included in his analysis—those with tumors that were outside the range of radiation from the cellular phone antenna and those whose tumors were within that range—there was no increase in the risk of brain cancer. This is evidence of the Koch-Henle postulate that is called *dose–response downward*—which simply means that if there is no chance that cell phone radiation dosage could have been received, chances are the tumor was caused by something else.

Agreement of findings from in vitro and in vivo studies   The test-tube studies by Tice and Hook; the mouse study by Repacholi; and the four epidemiological studies by Rothman, Muscat, and Hardell are all in agreement in that they suggest an increase in the risk of cancer among people who use mobile phones. This is evidence of the Koch-Henle postulate of *concordance*.

. . . And the Largest Piece of the Puzzle

As the officials of the government, officials of the industry, and just plain unofficial people try to fit together jigsaw pieces to see whether mobile phones indeed pose a cancer risk, the cancer experts themselves have provided what is by far the biggest and most revealing piece of the puzzle. Writing in the U.S. government's own *Journal of the National Cancer Institute*, and other prestigious professional publications, these experts have made it clear that, if there are findings that micronuclei develop in blood cells exposed to mobile phone radiation, that is in itself evidence of a cancer risk. The risk is so persuasive, the experts have written, that preventative treatment should be given in order to best protect those people whose levels of micronuclei have increased.

The Big Picture

The pieces of the cell phone puzzle do indeed fit together to form the beginnings of a picture that researchers, regulators, and mobile phone users can all see for themselves. Many pieces are still missing. But enough pieces are already in place to see that there are legitimate reasons to be concerned about the health of people who use wireless phones.

Most alarming to public health scientists should be the fact that all seven of the Koch-Henle postulates have been met within the first decade of widespread mobile phone usage.

The big picture is becoming disturbingly clear: There is a definite risk that the radiation plume that emanates from a cell phone antenna can cause cancer and other health problems. It is a risk that affects hundreds of millions of people around the world. It is a risk that must be seen and understood by all who use cell phones so they can take all the appropriate and available steps to protect themselves—and especially to protect young children whose skulls are still growing and who are the most vulnerable to the risks of radiation.

Safety First: Health Recommendations

As the big picture becomes clear and we see that radiation from mobile phones poses a real cancer and health risk, it also becomes clear that there are basic recommendations that now demand the urgent attention of all who use, make, research, or regulate cell phones.

Mobile telephones are a fact of life and a fixture in the lifestyles of more than half a billion people around the world. That only makes it all the more vital that we understand and follow the recommendations by which all who use mobile phones can minimize their health risk, and especially can protect our children. Here are some basic suggestions for mobile phone users, manufacturers, and science and medical researchers.

Recommendations for Consumers

To avoid radiation exposure and minimize health risks when using wireless phones:

1. The best advice is to keep the antenna away from your body by using a phone with a headset or earpiece. Another option is a phone with speakerphone capability.
2. If you must use your phone without a headset, be sure the antenna is fully extended during the phone's use. Radiation plumes are emitted mainly from the mid-length portion of the antenna; when the antenna is recessed inside the phone, the entire phone functions as the antenna—and the radiation is emitted from the entire phone into a much wider area of your head, jaw, and hand.

3. Children under the age of ten should not use wireless devices of any type; for children over the age of ten, pagers are preferable to wireless phones because pagers are not put up to the head and they can be used away from the body.
4. When the signal strength is low, do not use your phone. The reason: The lower the signal strength, the harder the instrument has to work to carry the call—and the greater the radiation that is emitted from the antenna.
5. Emerging studies, and common sense, make clear that handheld phones should not be used while driving a vehicle.

A Few Words of Caution for Consumers

The public is bombarded with waves of claims that are made at times by individuals who are well-meaning but not well-informed—and at other times by special interests who really want to sell a product. For example, there is no scientific basis for recommendations that have been made by some groups to limit phone use as a means of minimizing the risk of health effects. It is not possible to determine scientifically the difference in radiation exposure from one ten-minute call and ten one-minute calls. The total number of minutes is the same, but the pattern and amount of radiation could be very different. Also, the amount of radiation emitted by a mobile phone depends on the distance of the phone from a base station; the further the distance, the harder the phone has to work and the greater the radiation. Finally, the greatest amount of radiation emitted by a phone is during dialing and ringing. People who keep their phones on their belts or in their pockets should move the phones away from their bodies when the phones are ringing. (The amounts of radiation in a single call can vary by factors of ten to 100 depending on all of these variables.)

Consumers also need to be cautious about unverified claims that seem to have scientific backing. For example: The media recently carried an account published in Britain's *Which?* magazine that said a group called the Consumers' Association (with which the magazine is affiliated) had shown in tests that some cell phone headsets actually cause more radiation to go to the brain than the phones themselves. But the claim is unsubstantiated by any scientific evidence, and has been refuted by a number of studies by recognized researchers using established scientific methods. The only conclusion that can be drawn from existing scientific evidence is that headsets are the best option for mobile phone users to minimize exposure to wireless phone radiation.

Also, a number of devices on the market claim to eliminate the effects of antenna radiation and are being marketed as alternatives to using headsets or speakerphones. These products need to be tested to see if they will really protect consumers—a caution expressed by Great Britain's Stewart Commission. They recommended that their government set in place "a national system which enables independent testing of shielding devices and hands-free kits . . . which enable clear information to be given about the effectiveness of such devices. A kite mark or equivalent should be introduced to demonstrate conformity with the testing standard." In the United States, the FDA has been silent on the matter.

Recommendations for the Mobile Phone Industry

To enhance consumer protection:

1. Phones should be redesigned to minimize radiation exposure to consumers—antennas that extend out at an angle, away from the head, or that carry the radiation outward should be developed.
2. Headsets and other accessories that minimize radiation exposure should be redesigned so they are more durable and can be conveniently used.
3. Consumers should be given complete information about health risks and solutions through brochures, product inserts, and Internet postings so they can make their own decisions about how much of the risk inherent to mobile telephone use they wish to assume.
4. Emerging and advancing phone technologies need to be premarket tested for biological effects so dangerous products do not make it to the market.
5. Post-market surveillance is necessary for all phone users—surveys of analog and digital phone users to see if they experience any adverse health effects, and databases should be maintained where people can report any health effects they have experienced due to their phones.

Recommendations for Scientific, Medical, and Public Health Officials

To help consumers:

1. Science, medicine, and government must move immediately and aggressively with the goal of minimizing the impact of radio waves on adults, children, and pregnant women.
2. One federal agency must be designated as the lead agency for protecting people who use wireless communications devices, rather than having the responsibility remain undefined and shared among multiple agencies including the FDA, FCC, EPA, and others.
3. A genuine safety standard needs to be established to serve as the basis for future regulatory decisions. Since the specific absorption rate alone does not measure biological effects on humans, it does not serve the safety needs of consumers. . . .

Recommendations for Industry and Government Concerning the Wireless Internet

We need to recognize and learn from the mistakes we made when cellular phones were first introduced. The phones were sold to the public before there had been any premarket testing to determine whether they were safe or posed a potential health risk. Because the cell phones were not tested initially, by the time they were on the market, efforts to research the problem became intertwined with the forces of politics and profit. Consumer protection was not the highest priority.

As we enter the age of the wireless Internet, no one can say for sure whether or not the radio waves of these new wireless products will prove harmless or harmful. But this much is known: The concern about mobile phones focuses on the near-field radiation that extends in a 2-to-3-inch plume from an antenna, and the radiation from the many wireless laptop and handheld computer products is just about the same. It would seem that these latter products should be safer because users don't hold their laptops and handheld computers against their heads. But no one has researched what the effect will be of a roomful of wireless products all being used simultaneously, with radio waves invisibly crisscrossing the space that is occupied by people. Will these passive occupants run a risk similar to nonsmokers in a room filled with smokers, who end up affected by passive smoke?

Thus, it is important that these new products must be formally testing under official regulatory control that includes specific premarket screening guidelines. There must also be post-market surveys of people who use the wireless Internet to see if health problems emerge that were not found in the premarket testing.

United Kingdom's National
Radiation Protection Board

 **NO**

Mobile Phones and Health 2004

Executive Summary

Background

1. There are currently about 50 million mobile phones in use in the UK compared with around 25 million in 2000 and 4.5 million in 1995. These are supported by about 40,000 base stations in the UK network. The majority of these base stations operate under the Global System for Mobile Communications (GSM).

2. In less than ten years since the first GSM network was commercially launched as the second generation of mobile phones, it has become the world's leading and fastest growing telecommunications system. It is in use by more than one-sixth of the world's population and it has been estimated that at the end of January 2004 there were 1 billion GSM subscribers across more than 200 countries. The growth of GSM continues unabated with more than 160 million new customers in the last 12 months.

3. The revolution in communications continues world-wide. The third generation of mobile phones, 3G, is now being marketed in the UK and in many other countries and it is to be expected that further developments will become available in due course. In addition, there are many other telecommunications and related systems in use, all of which result in exposure of the population to radiofrequency (RF) fields.

4. The UK government has given strong encouragement to the development of mobile phone technology. Operators have been given support for the installation of the cellular networks and government has seen this as an important area for UK-based firms to establish themselves as world leaders. There have also been extensive developments in security-related equipment that utilise radiocommunications systems.

Public Health Concerns

5. The extensive use of mobile phones suggests that users do not in general judge them to present a significant health hazard. Rather they have welcomed the technology and brought it into use in their everyday lives. Nevertheless, since their introduction, there have

From DOC NRPB 15(5) 1-116 (2004), 2004, pp. 1–89 (excerpts). Copyright © 2004 by HPA/CRCE. Reprinted by permission. References omitted.

been persisting concerns about the possible impact of mobile phone technologies on health.

6. This was appreciated by the UK government, which in 1999 took the early initiative of setting up the Independent Expert Group on Mobile Phones (IEGMP) to review the situation. Its report, *Mobile Phones and Health* (the Stewart Report), was published in May 2000. It stated:

   "The balance of evidence to date suggests that exposures to RF radiation below NRPB and ICNIRP (International Commission on Non-Ionizing Radiation Protection) guidelines do not cause adverse health effects to the general population."

   "There is now scientific evidence, however, which suggests that there may be biological effects occurring at exposures below these guidelines."

   "We conclude therefore that it is not possible at present to say that exposure to RF radiation, even at levels below national guidelines, is totally without potential adverse health effects, and that the gaps in knowledge are sufficient to justify a precautionary approach."

   "We recommend that a precautionary approach to the use of mobile phone technologies be adopted until much more detailed and scientifically robust information on any health effects becomes available."

7. The Board notes that a central recommendation in the Stewart Report was that a precautionary approach to the use of mobile phone technologies be adopted until much more detailed and scientifically robust information on any health effects becomes available.

8. The Stewart Report was welcomed by government, the general public and by industry. Various subsequent reports from across the world have supported the main thrust of its general conclusions.

9. Since then, the widespread development in the use of mobile phones world-wide has not been accompanied by associated, clearly established increases in adverse health effects. Within the UK, there is a lack of hard information showing that the mobile phone systems in use are damaging to health. It is important to emphasise this crucial point.

10. Nevertheless, the following issues have to be taken into consideration.

11. First, the widespread use of mobile phone technologies is still fairly recent and technologies are continuing to develop at a pace which is outstripping analyses of any potential impact on health (see paragraphs 55–57, 84 and 85).

12. Second, there are data which suggest that RF fields can interfere with biological systems.

13. Third, because the use of mobile phone technologies is a fairly recent phenomenon, it has not yet been possible to carry out necessary long-term epidemiological studies and evaluate the findings. However, an increase in the risk of acoustic neuromas has recently been reported in people in Sweden with more than ten years' use of mobile phones. This study has been able to obtain long-term follow-up data and highlights the need for extended follow-up studies on phone users, as has been noted in a number of reviews. Epidemiological studies, because of a lack of sensitivity, may miss any effects in small subsets of the general populations studied. This is a reason why the Board welcomes the large international cohort study proposed for support by the Mobile

Telecommunications and Health Research (MTHR) programme (see paragraph 89). A recent German study has also suggested concerns.

14. Fourth, a recent paper has suggested possible effects on brain function resulting from the use of 3G phones, although the study has some limitations and needs replication. The Stewart Report had previously identified the need for research on brain function.

15. Fifth, populations are not homogeneous and people can vary in their susceptibility to environmental and other challenges. There are well-established examples in the literature of the genetic predisposition of some groups that could influence sensitivity to disease. This remains an outstanding issue in relation to RF exposure and one on which more information is needed. A number of people also report symptoms they ascribe to electromagnetic hypersensitivity arising from exposure to a range of electromagnetic fields (EMFs) encountered in everyday life. There is concern by an increasing number of individuals, although relatively small in relation to the total UK population, that they are adversely affected by exposure to RF fields from mobile phones (see also paragraphs 58–64).

16. Sixth, IEGMP considered that children might be more vulnerable to any effects arising from the use of mobile phones because of their developing nervous system, the greater absorption of energy in the tissues of the head and a longer lifetime of exposure. Data on the impact on children have not yet been forthcoming. The potential for undertaking studies to examine any possible effects on children, however, are limited for ethical reasons.

17. Seventh, there are ongoing concerns in the UK about the use of Terrestrial Trunked Radio (TETRA) by the police and the nature of the signals emitted as well as about exposures to RF from other telecommunications technologies.

18. Eighth, there remain particular concerns in the UK about the impact of base stations on health, including well-being. Despite current evidence which shows that exposures of individuals are likely to be only a small fraction of those from phones, they may impact adversely on well-being. The large numbers of additional base stations which will be necessary to effectively roll out the 3G and other new networks are likely to exacerbate the potential impact. People can also be concerned about effects on property values when base stations are built near their homes.

19. The Board believes that the main conclusions reached in the Stewart Report in 2000 still apply today and that a precautionary approach to the use of mobile phone technologies should continue to be adopted.

Progress Made in Addressing Public Health Concerns

20. The recommendation in the Stewart Report to adopt a precautionary approach was immediately accepted by government. It also endorsed many of the other recommendations in the Report.

21. The Stewart Report made a number of other recommendations that were designed to provide more information about the operation of mobile phones and base stations and to address public concerns

about this technology. This sought to allow individuals, local communities and local authorities to make informed choices about how the technology should be developed.

22. The responses to the recommendations in the Stewart Report are reviewed in the report by the Board and issues where further progress is needed have been identified. The key findings are summarised below.

Tightening of Exposure Guidelines

23. A recommendation in the Stewart Report was that, as a precautionary approach, the ICNIRP guidelines for public exposure be adopted for use in the UK for mobile phone frequencies. It was felt that this would bring the UK into line with other countries in the European Union. These guidelines have now been adopted by government for application across the UK and provide for a five-fold reduction in exposure guidelines for members of the public compared with the recommended values for people whose work brings them into contact with sources of RF fields.

24. The Board welcomes the introduction by government of tighter exposure guidelines for the general public.

Base Stations

25. A wide variety of types of base stations make up the UK network. Macrocells provide the main framework of the system. Where there are areas of high demand, as in busy streets and shopping areas, microcells are used to infill the network and help to prevent 'lost' calls. Picocells may be installed in buildings or other enclosed areas to improve signal strength and to infill the network in areas of high demand for calls. . . .

31. The Board recommends that monitoring of potential exposures from 3G base stations should be concomitant with the rollout of the network.

Mobile Phones and SAR Values

32. In September 2001 the European Committee for Electrical Standardisation (CENELEC) published a standard testing procedure for the measurement of specific energy absorption rate (SAR) from mobile phones. Information on all phones marketed in the UK, using this standard testing procedure, is now available.

33. However, it is still difficult for people to readily and easily acquire the necessary information so that comparisons of different phones can be made.

34. The Board welcomes the provision of information on the SAR from phones by all manufacturers using a standard testing procedure. This is an important contribution to providing information to the public about the potential for exposure and informs consumer choice. It recommends that comparative information on the SAR from phones is readily available to the consumer. The inclusion of comparative data on the SAR from phones in its promotional literature by at least one

retailer is a welcome development. The public also need to be able to understand the merits and limitations of published SAR values.

Planning Guidance on Base Station Locations

35. IEGMP was concerned that anxiety about the presence of local base stations and resulting exposure to RF fields could affect people's health, including well-being. IEGMP also heard at open meetings that information about base station developments was frequently not provided to the local community.

36. A number of recommendations were made in the Stewart Report to improve the transparency of the local planning process and to improve the planning procedure. A specific recommendation was that permitted development rights for the erection of masts under 15 m should be revoked and that the siting of all new base stations should be subject to the normal planning process.

37. Following publication of the Stewart Report reviews of the planning process were put in place throughout the UK. Revised guidance that was issued aimed to provide for more discussions between operators and local authorities on the development of all proposals for telecommunications equipment and to minimise visual intrusion. . . .

40. The Board notes that whilst there has been a plethora of documents about planning issues for base stations, public concerns have not abated.

41. The Board supports the government view that whilst planning is necessarily a local issue, the assessment of evidence related to possible health concerns associated with exposures to RF fields from base stations is best dealt with nationally.

42. Accepting that, the Board believes that it is timely for there to be set in place a much clearer and more readily understandable template of protocols and procedures to be followed by local authorities and phone operators across the UK. It is clear that at present the application of guidance is very variable and that the extent to which the underpinning facts are presented can also be variable. It recommends that there should be an independent review of the extent to which implementation of good practice guidelines by operators and local authorities is being carried out.

43. The Board considers that it is important that 'best practice' in relation to network development operates consistently across the country and that how planning applications are dealt with should be an open and transparent process.

44. The Board welcomes the ODPM *Code of Best Practice on Mobile Phone Network Development*, that incorporates the 'ten commitments on best siting practice'. . . .

Developing Technologies

55. A variety of additional technologies are now being progressively developed and implemented in the field of telecommunications. New technologies include third-generation (3G) mobile telephony, wireless local area networks (WLANs), Bluetooth and

ultra-wideband (UWB) technology, and radio-frequency identification (RFID) devices.

56. The Board considers that it is important to understand the signal
characteristics and field strengths arising from new telecommunications systems and related technologies, to assess the RF exposure
of people, and to understand the potential biological effects on the
human body.

57. The Board also believes it important to ensure that the exposure
of people from all new and existing systems complies with ICNIRP
guidelines.

Sensitive Groups

58. Populations as a whole are not genetically homogeneous and people can vary in their susceptibility to environmental hazards. There
could also be a dependency on age. The issue of individual sensitivity
remains an outstanding one in relation to RF exposure and one on
which more information is needed.

59. IEGMP considered that children might be more vulnerable to any
effects arising from the use of mobile phones. The potential for
undertaking studies to examine any possible effects on children
are, however, limited for ethical reasons. It was recommended in the
Stewart Report that the use of mobile phones by children should be
minimised and this was supported by the Departments of Health.
Text messaging has considerable advantages as the phone is in use
for only a short time, when the phone transmits the message, compared with voice communication.

60. The Board concludes that, in the absence of new scientific evidence,
the recommendation in the Stewart Report on limiting the use of
mobile phones by children remains appropriate as a precautionary
measure.

61. The Board also welcomes an initiative by the World Health Organization in its EMF programme to focus attention on research relevant to
the potential sensitivity of children.

62. Additionally, there is concern by an increasing number of individuals, although relatively small in relation to the total UK population,
that they are adversely affected by exposure either to EMFs in general
or specifically to RF fields from mobile phones. A European Commission group of experts termed the syndrome 'electromagnetic hypersensitivity'. Similar concerns have been raised in the past in relation
to exposure to agricultural chemicals and other materials. . . .

64. The Board considers that the issue of electromagnetic hypersensitivity needs to be carefully examined in the UK. It supports the strengthening of work designed to understand the reasons for the reported
electromagnetic hypersensitivity of some members of the public.

Occupational Exposure

65. Levels of exposure to RF fields can be higher through occupational
exposure than for members of the public and sometimes approach
guideline levels.

66. The Board welcomes the establishment of a register of occupationally exposed people at the Institute of Occupational Health, Birmingham. This should facilitate the determination of whether, occupationally, there are health effects from exposure to RF fields not observed in the general public. . . .

Mobile Phones and Driving

69. The Stewart Report demonstrated that there is good experimental evidence that the use of mobile phones whilst driving has a detrimental effect on drivers' responsiveness. This translates into a substantial increased risk of an accident. The evidence suggested that the negative effects of phone use while driving were similar whether the phone was hand-held or hands-free.

70. The Board welcomes the intention of government to increase the penalty for the offence of using a hand-held mobile phone while driving by making it endorsable with three penalty points and an increased fine of £60.

71. The Board notes that the UK legislation on the use of phones in motor vehicles, making it illegal to use any hand-held phone, is tailored to the practicality of enforcement. The evidence remains, however, that the use of mobile phones in moving vehicles, both hand-held and hands-free, can significantly increase the risk of an accident. . . .

Health-Related Research

84. Outstanding health-related concerns can be addressed by epidemiological (human health) studies, experimental investigations with animals, and the use of cell-based techniques. Dosimetric studies are important for understanding the exposure of people from various sources and human volunteer studies can investigate short-term interactions of RF fields, for example, with brain function. In the area of telecommunications, however, technological change is rapid and it is a challenge to carry out comprehensive research and to determine the possibility of any health effects.

85. Research into any health effects of exposure to RF fields is still in a developmental phase. There are analogies with work on the consequences of exposure to EMFs from power lines. In the early 1980s, the epidemiological studies on exposure to extremely low frequency (ELF) EMFs lacked methods to directly assess exposure of individuals and instead surrogates for exposure were frequently used. Subsequently portable measurement equipment became available in the late 1980s/early 1990s and the quality of studies providing exposure-response information, for both occupational and domestic exposures, rapidly improved. Studies on RF exposure were in a similar position in the 1990s to those on ELF EMFs in the early 1980s. In recent years, however, considerable effort has gone into developing RF-related studies that combine high quality dosimetry with well-designed studies in experimental biology and epidemiology. Inevitably it will be some time before the present generation of studies comes to fruition. The MTHR programme

in the UK has been at the forefront of this advance in RF-related research.

86. The MTHR programme was launched in February 2001 with an initial budget of £7.36 million funded by government and industry on a 50 : 50 basis. To date around 30 projects have been funded through MTHR with additional support from the Home Office, the Department of Trade and Industry, and industry. It presently has a budget of £8.8 million, all of which has now been allocated to the ongoing research programme. The RF-related research in the UK is complementary to further research being carried out world-wide, much of it co-ordinated through the WHO EMF programme.

87. The Board considers that the MTHR programme, which was first announced in December 2000, has set the standard for independent, high quality, health-related research on RF exposure.

88. The Board further recommends that government and industry should provide support for a continuation of the programme.

89. The Board particularly supports the need for further research, in the following areas:

   a. an international cohort study of mobile phone users aimed at pooling and sharing experimental design, findings and expertise internationally,

   b. an expanded programme of research on TETRA signals and biological effects,

   c. effects of RF exposure on children,

   d. investigation of public concerns about mobile phone technology,

   e. electromagnetic hypersensitivity and its possible impact on health, including well-being, associated with mobile phone technology,

   f. studies of RF effects on direct and established measures of human brain function and investigations of possible mechanisms involved,

   g. complementary dosimetry studies focused on ascertaining the exposure of people to RF fields.

In developing the MTHR and other research programmes, care needs to be taken to prevent unnecessary duplication of studies whilst at the same time seeking to replicate significant findings.

POSTSCRIPT

Is There Sufficient Scientific Evidence to Conclude That Cell Phones Cause Cancer?

Is the cell phone cancer scare nothing more than media hype, as Sid Deutsch called the EMF cancer scare in "Electromagnetic Field Cancer Scares," *Skeptical Inquirer* (Winter 1994)? Or do cell phones pose a genuine hazard? L. Hardell et al. reported in "Cellular and Cordless Telephones and the Risk for Brain Tumours," *European Journal of Cancer Prevention* (August 2002), that long-term users of older, analog phones were more likely to suffer brain tumors. U.S. District Judge Catherine Blake, presiding over the most famous phone-cancer lawsuit, was not swayed. She declared that the claimant had provided "no sufficiently reliable and relevant scientific evidence" and said she intended to dismiss the case (Mark Parascandola, "Judge Rejects Cancer Data in Maryland Cell Phone Suit," *Science*, October 11, 2002). Robert Clark, "Clean Bill of Health for Cell Phones," *America's Network* (April 1, 2004), reports that "A survey by the Danish Institute of Cancer Epidemiology . . . says there is no short-term danger of developing brain tumors." A Swedish study found no breast cancer link to electromagnetic fields; see Janet Raloff, "Study Can't Tie EMFs to Cancer," *Science News* (February 26, 2005), and U. M. Forssen et al., "Occupational Magnetic Fields and Female Breast Cancer: A Case-Control Study Using Swedish Population Registers and New Exposure Data," *American Journal of Epidemiology* (vol. 161, no. 3, 2005). In early 2006, three European studies reported an increased risk of some kinds of brain tumors in people who had used cell phones for more than ten years; see, for example, Joachim Schuz et al., "Cellular Phones, Cordless Phones, and the Risks of Glioma and Meningioma," *American Journal of Epidemiology* (March 2006). In September, a Danish study reported that cell phone users suffer no more risk that nonusers; see Joachim Schuz, "Cellular Telephone Use and Cancer Risk: Update of a Nationwide Danish Cohort," *Journal of the National Cancer Institute* (December 6, 2006). An Israeli study reports that heavy cell phone users face a 50 percent greater risk of tumors in the parotid (cheek) salivary gland; see Siegal Sadetzki et al., "Cellular Phone Use and Risk of Benign and Malignant Parotid Gland Tumors—A Nationwide Case-Control Study," *American Journal of Epidemiology* (February 15, 2008). However a 2006 study did not find such a risk. If there are any effects, they do not seem to be large and, say Reetta Nylund and Darius Leszczynski, "Mobile Phone Radiation Causes Changes in Gene and Protein Expression in Human Endothelial Cell Lines and the Response Seems to Be Genome- and Proteome-Dependent," *Proteomics* (September 2006), they may depend upon differences in the genes possessed by those exposed. There are apparently reasons to doubt reports of DNA damage from cell phone radiation; see Gretchen Vogel, "Fraud Charges Cast Doubt on Claims of DNA Damage from Cell Phone Fields," *Science* (August 29, 2008).

Skeptics insist that the threat is real. However, if it is real, this is not yet clear beyond a doubt. Unfortunately, society cannot always wait for certainty. In connection with EMFs, Gordon L. Hester, in "Electric and Magnetic Fields: Managing an Uncertain Risk," *Environment* (January/February 1992), asserts that just the possibility of a health hazard is sufficient to justify more research into the problem. The guiding principle, says Hester, is "'prudent avoidance,' which was originally intended to mean that people should avoid fields 'when this can be done with modest amounts of money and trouble.'" The same guideline surely applies to cell phone radiation. Sari N. Harar, "Do Cell Phones Cause Cancer?" *Prevention* (August 2006), notes that the consensus answer is that the risks are low and adds that risk can easily be reduced even further by using hands-free headsets and keeping calls short. In July 2008, Ronald B. Herberman, director of the University of Pittsburgh Cancer Institute, warned staff and faculty to limit cell phone use because of the possible risks, basing his warning on early unpublished data. His memo is posted at http://www.upci .upmc.edu/news/upci_news/2008/072308_celladvisory.html.

Is it possible to prove that cell phones do *not* cause cancer? Unfortunately, no, because small, sporadic effects might not be detected even in massive studies. Thus, for some people, the jury will forever be out. Meanwhile, the jury is getting new charges to consider: George Carlo is now contending that wireless computer networks (wi-fi) also involve radiation that can cause tumors (see "Wi-Fi Fear," *The Ecologist,* April 2007). As with cell phones, there is a lack of evidence to support the charges.

What should society do in the face of weak, uncertain, and even contradictory data? Can we afford to conclude that there is no hazard? Or must we ban or redesign a useful technology with no justification other than our fear that there might be a real hazard? Many scientists and politicians argue that even if there is no genuine medical risk, there is a genuine impact in terms of public anxiety. See Gary Stix, "Closing the Book," *Scientific American* (March 1998). It is therefore appropriate, they say, to fund further research and to take whatever relatively inexpensive steps to minimize exposure are possible. Failure to do so increases public anxiety and distrust of government and science.

Some of those "relatively inexpensive steps" are pretty simple. As Carlo and Schram note, they include repositioning cell phone antennae and using headsets. As Tamar Nordenberg, "Cell Phones and Brain Cancer: No Clear Connection," *FDA Consumer* (November–December 2000), says, quoting Professor John Moulder, using a cell phone while driving is much more hazardous even than using a conventional high-radiation cell phone. By 2003, cell phones were being broadly indicted as hazards on the highway. The basic problem is that using a cell phone increases the mental workload on the driver, according to Roland Matthews, Stephen Legg, and Samuel Charlton, "The Effect of Cell Phone Type on Drivers' Subjective Workload During Concurrent Driving and Conversing," *Accident Analysis & Prevention* (July, 2003); they too recommend using a hands-free phone. As a result of such studies, several states have already banned handheld phones while driving, with initial good effect; see Anne T. McCartt, Elisa R. Braver, and Lori L. Geary, "Drivers' Use of Handheld Cell Phones Before and After New York State's Cell Phone Law," *Preventive Medicine* (May 2003). Unfortunately, the initial good results have not lasted. See "Motorists' Cell Phone Use Rising: NHTSA," *Safety & Health* (May 2005).

ISSUE 9

Should DDT Be Banned Worldwide?

YES: Anne Platt McGinn, from "Malaria, Mosquitoes, and DDT," *World Watch* (May/June 2002)

NO: Donald R. Roberts, from "The Role of Science in Environmental Policy-Making," Statement before U.S. Senate Committee on Environment & Public Works (September 28, 2005)

ISSUE SUMMARY

YES: Anne Platt McGinn, a senior researcher at the Worldwatch Institute, argues that although DDT is still used to fight malaria, there are other, more effective and less environmentally harmful methods. She maintains that DDT should be banned or reserved for emergency use.

NO: Donald R. Roberts argues that the scientific evidence regarding the environmental hazards of DDT has been seriously misrepresented by anti-pesticide activists. The hazards of malaria are much greater and, properly used, DDT can prevent them and save lives.

The story of DDT is a crucial element in the story of how science and technology interact with society. The chemical was first synthesized in 1874. Its insecticidal properties were first noticed by Paul Mueller, and it was very quickly realized that this implied the chemical could save human lives. It had long been known that in wars, more soldiers died because of disease than because of enemy fire. During World War I, some 5 million lives were lost to typhus, a disease carried by body lice. DDT was first deployed during World War II to halt a typhus epidemic in Naples, Italy. Dramatic success soon meant that DDT was used routinely as a dust for soldiers and civilians. During and after the war, it was also successfully deployed against the mosquitoes that carry malaria and other diseases. In the United States, cases of malaria fell from 120,000 in 1934 to 72 in 1960. Yellow fever cases dropped from 100,000 in 1878 to none. In 1948, Mueller received the Nobel Prize for Medicine and Physiology because DDT had saved so many civilian lives. Roger Bate, director of Africa Fighting Malaria, argues in "A Case of the DDTs," *National Review* (May 14, 2001), that DDT remains the cheapest and most effective way to combat malaria and that it should remain available for use.

DDT was by no means the first pesticide. But its predecessors were such things as arsenic, strychnine, cyanide, copper sulfate, and nicotine, all of which had such marked toxicity to humans that they gave rise to a host of murder mysteries such as the play "Arsenic and Old Lace." DDT was not only more effective as an insecticide; it was also less hazardous to users (not to mention potential murder victims). It is thus not surprising that DDT was seen as a beneficial substance, and was soon applied routinely to agricultural crops and used to control mosquito populations in American suburbs ("Rachel Carson's Silent Spring," a PBS American Experience video, includes footage of children at a picnic being engulfed in a cloud of DDT). However, insects quickly became resistant to the insecticide (in any population of insects, some will be more resistant than others; when the insecticide kills the more vulnerable members of the population, the resistant ones are left to breed and multiply; this is an example of natural selection). In *Silent Spring* (1961), Rachel Carson documented that DDT was concentrated in the food chain and affected the reproduction of predators such as hawks and eagles. In 1972, the U.S. Environmental Protection Agency banned almost all DDT uses (it could still be used to protect public health). Other developed countries soon banned it as well, but developing nations, especially in the tropics, saw it as an essential tool for fighting diseases such as malaria, which infects up to half a billion people per year and kills over a million, most of them under age five. See Michael Finkel, "Bedlam in the Blood," *National Geographic* (July 2007).

DDT is by no means the only pesticide or organic toxin with environmental effects. On May 24, 2001, the United States joined 90 other nations in signing the Stockholm Convention on Persistent Organic Pollutants (POPs). This treaty aims to eliminate from use the entire class of chemicals to which DDT belongs, beginning with the "dirty dozen" pesticides, DDT, aldrin, dieldrin, endrin, chlordane, heptachlor, mirex, toxaphene, and the industrial chemicals polychlorinated biphenyls (PCBs), hexachlorobenzene (HCB), dioxins, and furans. Since then, 59 countries, not including the United States and the European Union, have formally ratified the treaty, which took effect in May 2004. Fiona Proffitt, "U.N. Convention Targets Dirty Dozen Chemicals," *Science* (May 21, 2004), notes that "About 25 countries will be allowed to continue using DDT against malaria-spreading mosquitoes until a viable alternative is found."

In the following selections, Worldwatch researcher Anne Platt McGinn grants that malaria remains a serious problem in the developing nations of the tropics, especially in Africa. DDT is still used to fight malaria in these nations, but because of resistance, it is far less effective than it used to be and environmental effects are serious concerns. She argues that alternative measures such as mosquito nets impregnated with pyrethrin insecticides are more effective and less environmentally harmful. DDT should be banned or reserved for emergency use. In the second selection, Professor Donald R. Roberts argues that the scientific evidence regarding the environmental hazards of DDT has been seriously misrepresented by anti-pesticide activists. The hazards of malaria are much greater and, properly used, DDT can prevent them and save lives. Efforts to prevent the use of DDT have produced a "global humanitarian disaster."

YES

Anne Platt McGinn

Malaria, Mosquitoes, and DDT

This year, like every other year within the past couple of decades, uncountable trillions of mosquitoes will inject malaria parasites into human blood streams billions of times. Some 300 to 500 million full-blown cases of malaria will result, and between 1 and 3 million people will die, most of them pregnant women and children. That's the official figure, anyway, but it's likely to be a substantial underestimate, since most malaria deaths are not formally registered, and many are likely to have escaped the estimators. Very roughly, the malaria death toll rivals that of AIDS, which now kills about 3 million people annually.

But unlike AIDS, malaria is a low-priority killer. Despite the deaths, and the fact that roughly 2.5 billion people (40 percent of the world's population) are at risk of contracting the disease, malaria is a relatively low public health priority on the international scene. Malaria rarely makes the news. And international funding for malaria research currently comes to a mere $150 million annually. Just by way of comparison, that's only about 5 percent of the $2.8 billion that the U.S. government alone is considering for AIDS research in fiscal year 2003.

The low priority assigned to malaria would be at least easier to understand, though no less mistaken, if the threat were static. Unfortunately it is not. It is true that the geographic range of the disease has contracted substantially since the mid-20th century, but over the past couple of decades, malaria has been gathering strength. Virtually all areas where the disease is endemic have seen drug-resistant strains of the parasites emerge—a development that is almost certainly boosting death rates. In countries as various as Armenia, Afghanistan, and Sierra Leone, the lack or deterioration of basic infrastructure has created a wealth of new breeding sites for the mosquitoes that spread the disease. The rapidly expanding slums of many tropical cities also lack such infrastructure; poor sanitation and crowding have primed these places as well for outbreaks—even though malaria has up to now been regarded as predominantly a rural disease.

What has current policy to offer in the face of these threats? The medical arsenal is limited; there are only about a dozen antimalarial drugs commonly in use, and there is significant malaria resistance to most of them. In the absence of a reliable way to kill the parasites, policy has tended to focus on killing the mosquitoes that bear them. And that has led to an abundant use of synthetic pesticides, including one of the oldest and most dangerous: dichlorodiphenyl trichloroethane, or DDT.

DDT is no longer used or manufactured in most of the world, but because it does not break down readily, it is still one of the most commonly detected pesticides in the milk of nursing mothers. DDT is also one of the "dirty dozen" chemicals included in the 2001 Stockholm Convention on Persistent Organic Pollutants [POPs]. The signatories to the "POPs Treaty" essentially agreed to ban all uses of DDT except as a last resort against disease-bearing mosquitoes. Unfortunately, however, DDT is still a routine option in 19 countries, most of them in Africa. (Only 11 of these countries have thus far signed the treaty.) Among the signatory countries, 31—slightly fewer than one-third—have given notice that they are reserving the right to use DDT against malaria. On the face of it, such use may seem unavoidable, but there are good reasons for thinking that progress against the disease is compatible with *reductions* in DDT use.

❦

Malaria is caused by four protozoan parasite species in the genus *Plasmodium*. These parasites are spread exclusively by certain mosquitoes in the genus *Anopheles*. An infection begins when a parasite-laden female mosquito settles onto someone's skin and pierces a capillary to take her blood meal. The parasite, in a form called the *sporozoite*, moves with the mosquito's saliva into the human bloodstream. About 10 percent of the mosquito's lode of sporozoites is likely to be injected during a meal, leaving plenty for the next bite. Unless the victim has some immunity to malaria—normally as a result of previous exposure—most sporozoites are likely to evade the body's immune system and make their way to the liver, a process that takes less than an hour. There they invade the liver cells and multiply asexually for about two weeks. By this time, the original several dozen sporozoites have become millions of *merozoites*—the form the parasite takes when it emerges from the liver and moves back into the blood to invade the body's red blood cells. Within the red blood cells, the merozoites go through another cycle of asexual reproduction, after which the cells burst and release millions of additional merozoites, which invade yet more red blood cells. The high fever and chills associated with malaria are the result of this stage, which tends to occur in pulses. If enough red blood cells are destroyed in one of these pulses, the result is convulsions, difficulty in breathing, coma, and death.

As the parasite multiplies inside the red blood cells, it produces not just more merozoites, but also *gametocytes*, which are capable of sexual reproduction. This occurs when the parasite moves back into the mosquitoes; even as they inject sporozoites, biting mosquitoes may ingest gametocytes if they are feeding on a person who is already infected. The gametocytes reproduce in the insect's gut and the resulting eggs move into the gut cells. Eventually, more sporozoites emerge from the gut and penetrate the mosquito's salivary glands, where they await a chance to enter another human bloodstream, to begin the cycle again.

Of the roughly 380 mosquito species in the genus *Anopheles*, about 60 are able to transmit malaria to people. These malaria vectors are widespread throughout the tropics and warm temperate zones, and they are very efficient at spreading the disease. Malaria is highly contagious, as is apparent from a measurement that epidemiologists call the "basic reproduction number," or BRN. The BRN indicates, on average, how many new cases a single infected person is likely to cause. For example, among the nonvectored diseases (those in which the pathogen travels directly from person to person without an intermediary like a mosquito), measles is one of the most contagious. The BRN for measles is 12 to 14, meaning that someone with measles is likely to infect 12 to 14 other people. (Luckily, there's an inherent limit in this process: as a pathogen spreads through any particular area, it will encounter fewer and fewer susceptible people who aren't already sick, and the outbreak will eventually subside.) HIV/AIDS is on the other end of the scale: it's deadly, but it burns through a population slowly. Its BRN is just above 1, the minimum necessary for the pathogen's survival. With malaria, the BRN varies considerably, depending on such factors as which mosquito species are present in an area and what the temperatures are. (Warmer is worse, since the parasites mature more quickly.) But malaria can have a BRN in excess of 100: over an adult life that may last about a week, a single, malaria-laden mosquito could conceivably infect more than 100 people.

Seven Years, Seven Months

"Malaria" comes from the Italian "mal'aria." For centuries, European physicians had attributed the disease to "bad air." Apart from a tradition of associating bad air with swamps—a useful prejudice, given the amount of mosquito habitat in swamps—early medicine was largely ineffective against the disease. It wasn't until 1897 that the British physician Ronald Ross proved that mosquitoes carry malaria.

The practical implications of Ross's discovery did not go unnoticed. For example, the U.S. administration of Theodore Roosevelt recognized malaria and yellow fever (another mosquito-vectored disease) as perhaps the most serious obstacles to the construction of the Panama Canal. This was hardly a surprising conclusion, since the earlier and unsuccessful French attempt to build the canal—an effort that predated Ross's discovery—is thought to have lost between 10,000 and 20,000 workers to disease. So the American workers draped their water supplies and living quarters with mosquito netting, attempted to fill in or drain swamps, installed sewers, poured oil into standing water, and conducted mosquito-swatting campaigns. And it worked: the incidence of malaria declined. In 1906, 80 percent of the workers had the disease; by 1913, a year before the Canal was completed, only 7 percent did. Malaria could be suppressed, it seemed, with a great deal of mosquito netting, and by eliminating as much mosquito habitat as possible. But the labor involved in that effort could be enormous.

That is why DDT proved so appealing. In 1939, the Swiss chemist Paul Müller discovered that this chemical was a potent pesticide. DDT was first used during World War II, as a delousing agent. Later on, areas in southern Europe, North Africa, and Asia were fogged with DDT, to clear malaria-laden mosquitoes from the paths of invading Allied troops. DDT was cheap and it seemed to be harmless to anything other than insects. It was also long-lasting: most other insecticides lost their potency in a few days, but in the early years of its use, the effects of a single dose of DDT could last for up to six months. In 1948, Müller won a Nobel Prize for his work and DDT was hailed as a chemical miracle.

A decade later, DDT had inspired another kind of war—a general assault on malaria. The "Global Malaria Eradication Program," launched in 1955, became one of the first major undertakings of the newly created World Health Organization [WHO]. Some 65 nations enlisted in the cause. Funding for DDT factories was donated to poor countries and production of the insecticide climbed.

The malaria eradication strategy was not to kill every single mosquito, but to suppress their populations and shorten the lifespans of any survivors, so that the parasite would not have time to develop within them. If the mosquitoes could be kept down long enough, the parasites would eventually disappear from the human population. In any particular area, the process was expected to take three years—time enough for all infected people either to recover or die. After that, a resurgence of mosquitoes would be merely an annoyance, rather than a threat. And initially, the strategy seemed to be working. It proved especially effective on islands—relatively small areas insulated from reinfestation. Taiwan, Jamaica, and Sardinia were soon declared malaria-free and have remained so to this day. By 1961, arguably the year at which the program had peak momentum, malaria had been eliminated or dramatically reduced in 37 countries.

One year later, Rachel Carson published *Silent Spring,* her landmark study of the ecological damage caused by the widespread use of DDT and other pesticides. Like other organochlorine pesticides, DDT bioaccumulates. It's fat soluble, so when an animal ingests it—by browsing contaminated vegetation, for example—the chemical tends to concentrate in its fat, instead of being excreted. When another animal eats that animal, it is likely to absorb the prey's burden of DDT. This process leads to an increasing concentration of DDT in the higher links of the food chain. And since DDT has a high chronic toxicity—that is, long-term exposure is likely to cause various physiological abnormalities—this bioaccumulation has profound implications for both ecological and human health.

With the miseries of malaria in full view, the managers of the eradication campaign didn't worry much about the toxicity of DDT, but they were greatly concerned about another aspect of the pesticide's effects: resistance. Continual exposure to an insecticide tends to "breed" insect populations that are at least partially immune to the poison. Resistance to DDT had been reported as early as 1946. The campaign managers knew that in mosquitoes, regular exposure to DDT tended to produce widespread resistance in four to seven years. Since it took three years to clear malaria from a human population, that didn't leave a lot of leeway for the eradication effort. As it turned out, the logistics simply couldn't be made to work in large, heavily infested areas with high human populations, poor housing and roads, and generally minimal infrastructure. In 1969, the campaign was abandoned. Today, DDT resistance is widespread in *Anopheles,* as is resistance to many more recent pesticides.

Undoubtedly, the campaign saved millions of lives, and it did clear malaria from some areas. But its broadest legacy has been of much more dubious value. It engendered the idea of DDT as a first resort against mosquitoes and it established the unstable dynamic of DDT resistance in *Anopheles* populations. In mosquitoes, the genetic mechanism that confers resistance to DDT does not usually come at any great competitive "cost"—that is, when no DDT is being sprayed, the resistant mosquitoes may do just about as well as nonresistant mosquitoes. So once a population acquires resistance, the trait is not likely to disappear even if DDT isn't used for years. If DDT is reapplied to such a population, widespread resistance will reappear very rapidly. The rule of thumb among entomologists is that you may get seven years of resistance-free use the first time around, but you only get about seven months the second time. Even that limited respite, however, is enough to make the chemical an attractive option as an emergency measure—or to keep it in the arsenals of bureaucracies committed to its use.

Malaria Taxes

In December 2000, the POPs Treaty negotiators convened in Johannesburg, South Africa, even though, by an unfortunate coincidence, South Africa had suffered a potentially embarrassing setback earlier that year in its own POPs policies. In 1996, South Africa had switched its mosquito control programs from DDT to a less persistent group of pesticides known as pyrethroids. The move seemed solid and supportable at the time, since years of DDT use had greatly reduced *Anopheles* populations and largely eliminated one of the most troublesome local vectors, the appropriately named *A. funestus* ("funestus" means deadly). South Africa seemed to have beaten the DDT habit: the chemical had been used to achieve a worthwhile objective; it had then been discarded. And the plan worked—until a year before the POPs summit, when malaria infections rose to 61,000 cases, a level not seen in decades. *A. funestus* reappeared as well, in KwaZulu-Natal, and in a form resistant to pyrethroids. In early 2000, DDT was reintroduced, in an indoor spraying program. (This is now a standard way of using DDT for mosquito control; the pesticide is usually applied only to walls, where mosquitoes alight to rest.) By the middle of the year, the number of infections had dropped by half.

Initially, the spraying program was criticized, but what reasonable alternative was there? This is said to be the African predicament, and yet the South African situation is hardly representative of sub-Saharan Africa as a whole.

Malaria is considered endemic in 105 countries throughout the tropics and warm temperate zones, but by far the worst region for the disease is sub-Saharan Africa. The deadliest of the four parasite species, *Plasmodium falciparum,* is widespread throughout this region, as is one of the world's most effective malaria vectors, *Anopheles gambiae.* Nearly half the population of sub-Saharan Africa is at risk of infection, and in much of eastern and central Africa, and pockets of west Africa, it would be difficult to find anyone who has not been exposed to the parasites. Some 90 percent of the world's malaria infections and deaths occur in sub-Saharan Africa, and the disease now accounts for 30 percent of African childhood mortality. It is true that malaria is a grave problem in many parts of the world, but the African experience is misery on a very different order of magnitude. The average Tanzanian suffers more infective bites each *night* than the average Thai or Vietnamese does in a year.

As a broad social burden, malaria is thought to cost Africa between $3 billion and $12 billion annually. According to one economic analysis, if the disease had been eradicated in 1965, Africa's GDP would now be 35 percent higher than it currently is. Africa was also the gaping hole in the global eradication program: the WHO planners thought there was little they could do on the continent and limited efforts to Ethiopia, Zimbabwe, and South Africa, where eradication was thought to be feasible.

But even though the campaign largely passed Africa by, DDT has not. Many African countries have used DDT for mosquito control in indoor spraying programs, but the primary use of DDT on the continent has been as an agricultural insecticide. Consequently, in parts of west Africa especially, DDT resistance is now widespread in *A. gambiae*. But even if *A. gambiae* were not resistant, a full-bore campaign to suppress it would probably accomplish little, because this mosquito is so efficient at transmitting malaria. Unlike most *Anopheles* species, *A. gambiae* specializes in human blood, so even a small population would keep the disease in circulation. One way to get a sense for this problem is to consider the "transmission index"—the threshold number of mosquito bites necessary to perpetuate the disease. In Africa, the index overall is 1 bite per person per month. That's all that's necessary to keep malaria in circulation. In India, by comparison, the TI is 10 bites per person per month.

And yet Africa is not a lost cause—it's simply that the key to progress does not lie in the general suppression of mosquito populations. Instead of spraying, the most promising African programs rely primarily on "bednets"—mosquito netting that is treated with an insecticide, usually a pyrethroid, and that is suspended over a person's bed. Bednets can't eliminate malaria, but they can "deflect" much of the burden. Because *Anopheles* species generally feed in the evening and at night, a bednet can radically reduce the number of infective bites a person receives. Such a person would probably still be infected from time to time, but would usually be able to lead a normal life.

In effect, therefore, bednets can substantially reduce the disease. Trials in the use of bednets for children have shown a decline in malaria-induced mortality by 25 to 40 percent. Infection levels and the incidence of severe anemia also declined. In Kenya, a recent study has shown that pregnant women who use bednets tend to give birth to healthier babies. In parts of Chad, Mali, Burkina Faso, and Senegal, bednets are becoming standard household items. In the tiny west African nation of The Gambia, somewhere between 50 and 80 percent of the population has bednets.

Bednets are hardly a panacea. They have to be used properly and retreated with insecticide occasionally. And there is still the problem of insecticide resistance, although the nets themselves are hardly likely to be the main cause of it. (Pyrethroids are used extensively in agriculture as well.) Nevertheless, bednets can help transform malaria from a chronic disaster to a manageable public health problem—something a healthcare system can cope with.

So it's unfortunate that in much of central and southern Africa, the nets are a rarity. It's even more unfortunate that, in 28 African countries, they're taxed or subject to import tariffs. Most of the people in these countries would have trouble paying for a net even without the tax. This problem was addressed in the May 2000 "Abuja Declaration," a summit agreement on infectious diseases signed by 44 African countries. The Declaration included a pledge to do away with "malaria taxes." At last count, 13 countries have actually acted on the pledge, although in some cases only by reducing rather than eliminating the taxes. Since the Declaration was signed, an estimated 2 to 5 million Africans have died from malaria.

This failure to follow through with the Abuja Declaration casts the interest in DDT in a rather poor light. Of the 31 POPs treaty signatories that have reserved the right to use DDT, 21 are in Africa. Of those 21, 10 are apparently still taxing or imposing tariffs on bednets. (Among the African countries that have *not* signed the POPs treaty, some are almost certainly both using DDT and taxing bednets, but the exact number is difficult to ascertain because the status of DDT use is not always clear.) It is true that a case can be made for the use of DDT in situations like the one in South Africa in 1999—an infrequent flare-up in a context that lends itself to control. But the routine use of DDT against malaria is an exercise in toxic futility, especially when it's pursued at the expense of a superior and far more benign technology.

Learning to Live with the Mosquitoes

A group of French researchers recently announced some very encouraging results for a new anti-malarial drug known as G25. The drug was given to infected aotus monkeys, and it appears to have cleared the parasites from their systems. Although extensive testing will be necessary before it is known whether the drug can be safely given to people, these results have raised the hope of a cure for the disease.

Of course, it would be wonderful if G25, or some other new drug, lives up to that promise. But even in the absence of a cure, there are opportunities for progress that may one day make the current incidence of malaria look like some dark age horror. Many of these opportunities have been incorporated into an initiative that began in 1998, called the Roll Back Malaria (RBM) campaign, a collaborative effort between WHO, the World Bank, UNICEF, and the UNDP [United Nations Development Programme]. In contrast to the earlier WHO eradication program, RBM grew out of joint efforts between WHO and various African governments specifically to address African malaria. RBM focuses on household- and community-level intervention and it emphasizes apparently modest changes that could yield major progress. Below are four "operating principles" that are, in one way or another, implicit in RBM or likely to reinforce its progress.

1. Do away with all taxes and tariffs on bednets, on pesticides intended for treating bednets, and on antimalarial drugs. Failure to act on this front certainly undercuts claims for the necessity of DDT; it may also undercut claims for antimalaria foreign aid.

2. Emphasize appropriate technologies. Where, for example, the need for mud to replaster walls is creating lots of pothole sized cavities near houses—cavities that fill with water and then with mosquito larvae—it makes more sense to help people improve their housing maintenance than it does to set up a program for squirting pesticide into every pothole. To be "appropriate," a technology has to be both affordable and culturally acceptable. Improving home maintenance should pass this test; so should bednets. And of course there are many other possibilities. In Kenya, for example, a research institution called the International Center for Insect Physiology and Ecology has identified at least a dozen native east African plants that repel *Anopheles gambiae* in lab tests. Some of these plants could be important additions to household gardens.

3. Use existing networks whenever possible, instead of building new ones. In Tanzania, for example, an established healthcare program (UNICEF's Integrated Management of Childhood Illness Program) now dispenses antimalarial drugs—and instruction on how to use them. The UNICEF program was already operating, so it was simple and cheap to add the malaria component. Reported instances of severe malaria and anemia in infants have declined, apparently as a result. In Zambia, the government is planning to use health and prenatal clinics as the network for a coupon system that subsidizes bednets for the poor. Qualifying patients would pick up coupons at the clinics and redeem them at stores for the nets.

4. Assume that sound policy will involve action on many fronts. Malaria is not just a health problem—it's a social problem, an economic problem, an environmental problem, an agricultural problem, an urban planning problem. Health officials alone cannot possibly just make it go away. When the disease flares up, there is a strong and understandable temptation to strap on the spray equipment and douse the mosquitoes. But if this approach actually worked, we wouldn't be in this situation today. Arguably the biggest opportunity for progress against the disease lies, not in our capacity for chemical innovation, but in our capacity for *organizational innovation*—in our ability to build an awareness of the threat across a broad range of policy activities. For example, when government officials are considering loans to irrigation projects, they should be asking: has the potential for malaria been addressed? When foreign donors are designing antipoverty programs, they should be asking: do people need bednets? Routine inquiries of this sort could go a vast distance to reducing the disease.

Where is the DDT in all of this? There isn't any, and that's the point. We now have half a century of evidence that routine use of DDT simply will not prevail against the mosquitoes. Most countries have already absorbed this lesson, and banned the chemical or relegated it to emergency only status. Now the RBM campaign and associated efforts are showing that the frequency and intensity of those emergencies can be reduced through systematic attention to the chronic aspects of the disease. There is less and less justification for DDT, and the futility of using it as a matter of routine is becoming increasingly apparent: in order to control a disease, why should we poison our soils, our waters, and ourselves?

Donald R. Roberts

The Role of Science in Environmental Policy-Making

Thank you, Chairman Inhofe, and distinguished members of the Committee on Environment and Public Works, for the opportunity to present my views on the misuse of science in public policy. My testimony focuses on misrepresentations of science during decades of environmental campaigning against DDT.

Before discussing how and why DDT science has been misrepresented, you first must understand why this misrepresentation has not helped, but rather harmed, millions of people every year all over the world. Specifically you need to understand why the misrepresentation of DDT science has been and continues to be deadly. By way of explanation, I will tell you something of my experience.

I conducted malaria research in the Amazon Basin in the 1970s. My Brazilian colleague—who is now the Secretary of Health for Amazonas State—and I worked out of Manaus, the capitol of Amazonas State. From Manaus we traveled two days to a study site where we had sufficient numbers of cases for epidemiological studies. There were no cases in Manaus, or anywhere near Manaus. For years before my time there and for years thereafter, there were essentially no cases of malaria in Manaus. However, in the late 1980s, environmentalists and international guidelines forced Brazilians to reduce and then stop spraying small amounts of DDT inside houses for malaria control. As a result, in 2002 and 2003 there were over 100,000 malaria cases in Manaus alone.

Brazil does not stand as the single example of this phenomenon. A similar pattern of declining use of DDT and reemerging malaria occurs in other countries as well, Peru for example. Similar resurgences of malaria have occurred in rural communities, villages, towns, cities, and countries around the world. As illustrated by the return of malaria in Russia, South Korea, urban areas of the Amazon Basin, and increasing frequencies of outbreaks in the United States, our malaria problems are growing worse. Today there are 1 to 2 million malaria deaths each year and hundreds of millions of cases. The poorest of the world's people are at greatest risk. Of these, children and pregnant women are the ones most likely to die.

We have long known about DDT's effectiveness in curbing insect-borne disease. Othmar Zeidler, a German chemistry student, first synthesized DDT in 1874. Over sixty years later in Switzerland, Paul Müller discovered the

U.S. Senate Committee on Environment and Public Works, September 28, 2005.

insecticidal property of DDT. Allied forces used DDT during WWII, and the new insecticide gained fame in 1943 by successfully stopping an epidemic of typhus in Naples, an unprecedented achievement. By the end of the war, British, Italian, and American scientists had also demonstrated the effectiveness of DDT in controlling malaria-carrying mosquitoes. DDT's proven efficacy against insect-borne diseases, diseases that had long reigned unchecked throughout the world, won Müller the Nobel Prize for Medicine in 1948. After WWII, the United States conducted a National Malaria Eradication Program, commencing operations on July 1, 1947. The spraying of DDT on internal walls of rural homes in malaria endemic counties was a key component of the program. By the end of 1949, the program had sprayed over 4,650,000 houses. This spraying broke the cycle of malaria transmission, and in 1949 the United States was declared free of malaria as a significant public health problem. Other countries had already adopted DDT to eradicate or control malaria, because wherever malaria control programs sprayed DDT on house walls, the malaria rates dropped precipitously. The effectiveness of DDT stimulated some countries to create, for the first time, a national malaria control program. Countries with pre-existing programs expanded them to accommodate the spraying of houses in rural areas with DDT. Those program expansions highlight what DDT offered then, and still offers now, to the malaria endemic countries. As a 1945 U.S. Public Health Service manual explained about the control of malaria: "Drainage and larviciding are the methods of choice in towns of 2,500 or more people. But malaria is a rural disease. Heretofore there has been no economically feasible method of carrying malaria control to the individual tenant farmer or sharecropper. Now, for the first time, a method is available—the application of DDT residual spray to walls and ceilings of homes." Health workers in the United States were not the only ones to recognize the particular value of DDT. The head of malaria control in Brazil characterized the changes that DDT offered in the following statement: "Until 1945–1946, preventive methods employed against malaria in Brazil, as in the rest of the world, were generally directed against the aquatic phases of the vectors (draining, larvicides, destruction of bromeliads, etc. . . .). These methods, however, were only applied in the principal cities of each state and the only measure available for rural populations exposed to malaria was free distribution of specific drugs."

DDT was a new, effective, and exciting weapon in the battle against malaria. It was cheap, easy to apply, long-lasting once sprayed on house walls, and safe for humans. Wherever and whenever malaria control programs sprayed it on house walls, they achieved rapid and large reductions in malaria rates. Just as there was a rush to quickly make use of DDT to control disease, there was also a rush to judge how DDT actually functioned to control malaria. That rush to judgment turned out to be a disaster. At the heart of the debate—to the extent there was a debate—was a broadly accepted model that established a mathematical framework for using DDT to kill mosquitoes and eradicate malaria. Instead of studying real data to see how DDT actually worked in controlling malaria, some scientists settled upon what they thought was a logical conclusion: DDT worked solely by killing mosquitoes.

This conclusion was based on their belief in the model. Scientists who showed that DDT did not function by killing mosquitoes were ignored. Broad acceptance of the mathematical model led to strong convictions about DDT's toxic actions. Since they were convinced that DDT worked only by killing mosquitoes, malaria control specialists became very alarmed when a mosquito was reported to be resistant to DDT's toxic actions. As a result of concern about DDT resistance, officials decided to make rapid use of DDT before problems of resistance could eliminate their option to use DDT to eradicate malaria. This decision led to creation of the global malaria eradication program. The active years of the global malaria eradication program were from 1959 to 1969. Before, during, and after the many years of this program, malaria workers and researchers carried out their responsibilities to conduct studies and report their research. Through those studies, they commonly found that DDT was functioning in ways other than by killing mosquitoes. In essence, they found that DDT was functioning through mechanisms of repellency and irritancy. Eventually, as people forgot early observations of DDT's repellent actions, some erroneously interpreted new findings of repellent actions as the mosquitoes' adaptation to avoid DDT toxicity, even coining a term, "behavioral resistance," to explain what they saw. This new term accommodated their view that toxicity was DDT's primary mode of action and categorized behavioral responses of mosquitoes as mere adaptations to toxic affects. However this interpretation depended upon a highly selective use of scientific data. The truth is that toxicity is not DDT's primary mode of action when sprayed on house walls. Throughout the history of DDT use in malaria control programs there has always been clear and persuasive data that DDT functioned primarily as a spatial repellent. Today we know that there is no insecticide recommended for malaria control that rivals, much less equals, DDT's spatial repellent actions, or that is as long-acting, as cheap, as easy to apply, as safe for human exposure, or as efficacious in the control of malaria as DDT. . . . The 30 years of data from control programs of the Americas plotted . . . illustrate just how effective DDT is in malaria control. The period 1960s through 1979 displays a pattern of malaria controlled through house spraying. In 1979 the World Health Organization (WHO) changed its strategy for malaria control, switching emphasis from spraying houses to case detection and treatment. In other words, the WHO changed emphasis from malaria prevention to malaria treatment. Countries complied with WHO guidelines and started to dismantle their spray programs over the next several years. . . .

I find it amazing that many who oppose the use of DDT describe its earlier use as a failure. Our own citizens who suffered under the burden of malaria, especially in the rural south, would hardly describe it thus.

Malaria was a serious problem in the United States and for some localities, such as Dunklin County, Missouri, it was a very serious problem indeed. For four counties in Missouri, the average malaria mortality from 1910 to 1914 was 168.8 per 100,000 population. For Dunklin County, it was 296.7 per 100,000, a rate almost equal to malaria deaths in Venezuela and actually greater than the mortality rate for Freetown, Sierra Leone. Other localities in other states were equally as malarious. Growing wealth and improved living conditions were gradually reducing malaria rates, but cases resurged during WWII. The advent of DDT, however, quickly eradicated malaria from the United States.

DDT routed malaria from many other countries as well. The Europeans who were freed of malaria would hardly describe its use as a failure. After DDT was introduced to malaria control in Sri Lanka (then Ceylon), the number of malaria cases fell from 2.8 million in 1946 to just 110 in 1961. Similar spectacular decreases in malaria cases and deaths were seen in all the regions that began to use DDT. The newly formed Republic of China (Taiwan) adopted DDT use in malaria control shortly after World War II. In 1945 there were over 1 million cases of malaria on the island. By 1969 there were only 9 cases and shortly thereafter the disease was eradicated from the island and remains so to this day. Some countries were less fortunate. South Korea used DDT to eradicate malaria, but without house spray programs, malaria has returned across the demilitarized zone with North Korea. As DDT was eliminated and control programs reduced, malaria has returned to other countries such as Russia and Argentina. Small outbreaks of malaria are even beginning to appear more frequently in the United States.

These observations have been offered in testimony to document first that there were fundamental misunderstandings about how DDT functioned to exert control over malaria. Second, that regardless of systematic misunderstandings on the part of those who had influence over malaria control strategies and policies, there was an enduring understanding that DDT was the most cost-effective compound yet discovered for protecting poor rural populations from insect-borne diseases like malaria, dengue, yellow fever, and leishmaniasis. I want to emphasize that misunderstanding the mode of DDT action did not lead to the wholesale abandonment of DDT. It took an entirely new dimension in the misuse of science to bring us to the current humanitarian disaster represented by DDT elimination.

The misuse of science to which I refer has found fullest expression in the collection of movements within the environmental movement that seek to stop production and use of specific man-made chemicals. Operatives within these movements employ particular strategies to achieve their objectives. By characterizing and understanding the strategies these operatives use, we can identify their impact in the scientific literature or in the popular press.

The first strategy is to develop and then distribute as widely as possible a broad list of claims of chemical harm. This is a sound strategy because individual scientists can seldom rebut the scientific foundations of multiple and diverse claims. Scientists generally develop expertise in a single, narrow field and are disinclined to engage issues beyond their area of expertise. Even if an authoritative rebuttal of one claim occurs, the other claims still progress. A broad list of claims also allows operatives to tailor platforms for constituencies, advancing one set of claims with one constituency and a different combination for another. Clever though this technique is, a list of multiple claims of harm is hardly sufficient to achieve the objective of a ban. The second strategy then is to mount an argument that the chemical is not needed and propose that alternative chemicals or methods can be used instead. The third strategy is to predict that grave harm will occur if the chemical continues to be used.

The success of Rachel Carson's *Silent Spring* serves as a model for this tricky triad. In *Silent Spring*, Rachel Carson used all three strategies on her primary target, DDT. She described a very large list of potential adverse effects of insecticides, DDT in particular. She argued that insecticides were not really needed and that the use of insecticides produces insects that are insecticide resistant, which only exacerbates the insect control problems. She predicted scary scenarios of severe harm with continued use of DDT and other insecticides. Many have written rebuttals to Rachel Carson and others who have, without scientific justification, broadcast long lists of potential harms of insecticides. . . .

[T]ime and science have discredited most of Carson's claims. Rachel Carson's descriptions of inappropriate uses of insecticides that harmed wildlife are more plausible. However, harm from an inappropriate use does not meet the requirements of anti-pesticide activists. They can hardly lobby for eliminating a chemical because someone used it wrongly. No, success requires that even the proper use of an insecticide will cause a large and systematic adverse effect. However, the proper uses of DDT yield no large and systematic adverse effects. Absent such adverse actions, the activists must then rely on claims about insidious effects, particularly insidious effects that scientists will find difficult to prove one way or the other and that activists can use to predict a future catastrophe.

Rachel Carson relied heavily on possible insidious chemical actions to alarm and frighten the public. Many of those who joined her campaign to ban DDT and other insecticides made extensive use of claims of insidious effects. These claims were amplified by the popular press and became part of the public perception about modern uses of chemicals. For example, four well-publicized claims about DDT were:

1. DDT will cause the obliteration of higher trophic levels. If not obliterated, populations will undergo reproductive failure. Authors of this claim speculated that, even if the use of DDT were stopped, systematic and ongoing obliterations would still occur.
2. DDT causes the death of algae. This report led to speculations that use of DDT could result in global depletion of oxygen.
3. DDT pushed the Bermuda petrel to the verge of extinction and that full extinction might happen by 1978.
4. DDT was a cause of premature births in California sea lions.

Science magazine, the most prestigious science journal in the United States, published these and other phantasmagorical allegations and/or predictions of DDT harm. Nonetheless, history has shown that each and every one of these claims and predictions were false.

1. The obliteration of higher trophic levels did not occur; no species became extinct; and levels of DDT in all living organisms declined precipitously after DDT was de-listed for use in agriculture. How could the prediction have been so wrong? Perhaps it was so wrong because the paper touting this view used a predictive model based

on an assumption of no DDT degradation. This was a startling assertion even at the time as *Science* and other journals had previously published papers that showed DDT was ubiquitously degraded in the environment and in living creatures. It was even more startling that *Science* published a paper that flew so comprehensively in the face of previous data and analysis.

2. DDT's action against algae reportedly occurred at concentrations of 500 parts per billion. But DDT cannot reach concentrations in water higher than about 1.2 parts per billion, the saturation point of DDT in water.

3. Data on the Bermuda petrel did not show a cause-and-effect relationship between low numbers of birds and DDT concentrations. DDT had no effect on population numbers, for populations increased before DDT was de-listed for use in agriculture and after DDT was delisted as well.

4. Data gathered in subsequent years showed that "despite relatively high concentrations [of DDT], no evidence that population growth or the health of individual California sea lions have been compromised. The population has increased throughout the century, including the period when DDT was being manufactured, used, and its wastes discharged off southern California."

If time and science have refuted all these catastrophic predictions, why do many scientists and the public not know these predictions were false? In part, we do not know the predictions were false because the refutations of such claims rarely appear in the literature.

When scientists hear the kinds of claims described above, they initiate research to confirm or refute the claims. After Charles Wurster published his claim that DDT kills algae and impacts photosynthesis, I initiated research on planktonic algae to quantify DDT's effects. From 1968–1969, I spent a year of honest and demanding research effort to discover that not enough DDT would even go into solution for a measurable adverse effect on planktonic algae. In essence, I conducted a confirmatory study that failed to confirm an expected result. I had negative data, and journals rarely accept negative data for publication. My year was practically wasted. Without a doubt, hundreds of other scientists around the world have conducted similar studies and obtained negative results, and they too were unable to publish their experimental findings. Much in the environmental science literature during the last 20–30 years indicates that an enormous research effort went into proving specific insidious effects of DDT and other insecticides. Sadly, the true magnitude of such efforts will never be known because while the positive results of research find their way into the scientific literature, the negative results rarely do. Research on insidious actions that produce negative results all too often ends up only in laboratory and field notebooks and is forgotten. For this reason, I place considerable weight on a published confirmatory study that fails to confirm an expected result.

The use of the tricky triad continues. A ... recent paper ... published in *The Lancet* illustrates the triad's modern application. Two scientists at the National

Institute of Environmental Health Sciences, Walter Rogan and Aimin Chen, wrote this paper, entitled "Health risks and benefits of bis(4-chlorophenyl)-1,1,1-trichloroethane (DDT)." It is interesting to see how this single paper spins all three strategies that gained prominence in Rachel Carson's *Silent Spring*.

The journal *Emerging Infectious Diseases* had already published a slim version of this paper, which international colleagues and I promptly rebutted. The authors then filled in some parts, added to the claims of harm, and republished the paper in the British journal, *The Lancet*. To get the paper accepted by editors, the authors described studies that support (positive results) as well as studies that do not support (negative results) each claim. Complying with strategy number 1 of the triad, Rogan and Chen produce a long list of possible harms, including the charge that DDT causes cancer in nonhuman primates. The literature reference for Rogan and Chen's claim that DDT causes cancer in nonhuman primates was a paper by Takayama et al. Takayama and coauthors actually concluded from their research on the carcinogenic effect of DDT in nonhuman primates that "the two cases involving malignant tumors of different types are inconclusive with respect to a carcinogenic effect of DDT in nonhuman primates." Clearly, the people who made the link of DDT with cancer were not the scientists who actually conducted the research.

The authors enacted strategy number two of the triad by conducting a superficial review of the role of DDT in malaria control with the goal of discrediting DDT's value in modern malaria control programs. The authors admitted that DDT had been very effective in the past, but then argued that malaria control programs no longer needed it and should use alternative methods of control. Their use of the second strategy reveals, in my opinion, the greatest danger of granting authority to anti-pesticide activists and their writings. As *The Lancet* paper reveals, the NIEHS scientists assert great authority over the topic of DDT, yet they assume no responsibility for the harm that might result from their erroneous conclusions. After many malaria control specialists have expressed the necessity for DDT in malaria control, it is possible for Rogan and Chen to conclude that DDT is not necessary in malaria control only if they have no sense of responsibility for levels of disease and death that will occur if DDT is not used.

Rogan and Chen also employ the third strategy of environmentalism. Their list of potential harms caused by DDT includes toxic effects, neurobehavior effects, cancers, decrements in various facets of reproductive health, decrements in infant and child development, and immunology and DNA damage. After providing balanced coverage of diverse claims of harm, the authors had no option but to conclude they could not prove that DDT caused harm. However, they then promptly negated this honest conclusion by asserting that if DDT is used for malaria control, then great harm might occur. So, in an amazing turn, they conclude they cannot prove DDT causes harm, but still predict severe harm if it is used.

Rogan and Chen end their paper with a call for more research. One could conclude that the intent of the whole paper is merely to lobby for research to better define DDT harm, and what's the harm in that? Surely increasing knowledge is a fine goal. However, if you look at the specific issue of the relative need for research, you will see that the harm of this technique is great. Millions of children and pregnant women die from malaria every year, and the disease sickens hundreds of millions more. This is an indisputable fact: impoverished people engage in real life and death struggles every day with malaria. This also is a fact: not one death or illness can be attributed to an environmental exposure to DDT. Yet, a National Library of Medicine literature search on DDT reveals over 1,300 published papers from the year 2000 to the present, almost all in the environmental literature and many on potential adverse effects of DDT. A search on malaria and DDT reveals only 159 papers. DDT is a spatial repellent and hardly an insecticide at all, but a search on DDT and repellents will reveal only 7 papers. Is this not an egregiously disproportionate research emphasis on non-sources of harm compared to the enormous harm of malaria? Does not this inequity contribute to the continued suffering of those who struggle with malaria? Is it possibly even more than an inequity? Is it not an active wrong?

Public health officials and scientists should not be silent about enormous investments into the research of theoretical risks while millions die of preventable diseases. We should seriously consider our motivations in apportioning research money as we do. Consider this: the U.S. used DDT to eradicate malaria. After malaria disappeared as an endemic disease in the United States, we became richer. We built better and more enclosed houses. We screened our windows and doors. We air conditioned our homes. We also developed an immense arsenal of mosquito control tools and chemicals. Today, when we have a risk of mosquito borne disease, we can bring this arsenal to bear and quickly eliminate risks. And, as illustrated by aerial spray missions in the aftermath of hurricane Katrina, we can afford to do so. Yet, our modern and very expensive chemicals are not what protect us from introductions of the old diseases. Our arsenal responds to the threat; it does not prevent the appearance of old diseases in our midst. What protects us is our enclosed, screened, air-conditioned housing, the physical representation of our wealth. Our wealth is the factor that stops dengue at the border with Mexico, not our arsenal of new chemicals. Stopping mosquitoes from entering and biting us inside our homes is critical in the prevention of malaria and many other insect-borne diseases. This is what DDT does for poor people in poor countries. It stops large proportions of mosquitoes from entering houses. It is, in fact, a form of chemical screening, and until these people can afford physical screening or it is provided for them, this is the only kind of screening they have.

DDT is a protective tool that has been taken away from countries around the world, mostly due to governments acceding to the whims of the anti-pesticide wing of environmentalism, but it is not only the anti-pesticide wing that lobbies against DDT. The activists have a sympathetic lobbying ally in the pesticide industry. As evidence of insecticide industry working to stop countries from using DDT, I am attaching an email message dated 23rd September and authored by a Bayer official. . . . The Bayer official states

"[I speak] Not only as the responsible manager for the vector control business in Bayer, being the market leader in vector control and pointing out by that we know what we are talking about and have decades of experiences in the evolution of this very particular market. [but] Also as one of the private sector representatives in the RBM Partnership Board and being confronted with that discussion about DDT in the various WHO, RBM et al circles. So you can take it as a view from the field, from the operational commercial level—but our companies [sic] point of view. I know that all of my colleagues from other primary manufacturers and internationally operating companies are sharing my view."

The official goes on to say that

"DDT use is for us a commercial threat (which is clear, but it is not that dramatical because of limited use), it is mainly a public image threat."

However the most damning part of this message was the statement that

"we fully support EU to ban imports of agricultural products coming from countries using DDT"

[There is] . . . clear evidence of international and developed country pressures to stop poor countries from using DDT to control malaria. This message also shows the complicity of the insecticide industry in those internationally orchestrated efforts.

Pressures to eliminate spray programs, and DDT in particular, are wrong. I say this not based on some projection of what might theoretically happen in the future according to some model, or some projection of theoretical harms, I say this based firmly on what has already occurred. The track record of the anti-pesticide lobby is well documented, the pressures on developing countries to abandon their spray programs are well documented, and the struggles of developing countries to maintain their programs or restart their uses of DDT for malaria control are well documented. The tragic results of pressures against the use of DDT, in terms of increasing disease and death, are quantified and well documented. How long will scientists, public health officials, the voting public, and the politicians who lead us continue policies, regulations and funding that have led us to the current state of a global humanitarian disaster? How long will support continue for policies and programs that favor phantoms over facts?

POSTSCRIPT

Should DDT Be Banned Worldwide?

Professor Roberts is not alone in his disapproval of the efforts to halt the use of DDT. Angela Logomasini comes close to accusing environmentalists of condemning DDT more on the basis of politics or ideology than of science in "Chemical Warfare: Ideological Environmentalism's Quixotic Campaign Against Synthetic Chemicals," in Ronald Bailey, ed., *Global Warming and Other Eco-Myths: How the Environmental Movement Uses False Science to Scare Us to Death* (Prima Publishing, 2002). Her admission that public health demands have softened some environmentalists' resistance to the use of DDT points to a basic truth about environmental debates. Over and over again, they come down to what we should do first: Should we meet human needs whether or not species die and air and water are contaminated? Or should we protect species, air, water, and other aspects of the environment even if some human needs must go unmet? Even if those human needs are the lives of children? This opposition is very clear in the debate over DDT. The human needs are clear, for insect-borne diseases have killed and continue to kill a great many people. Yet the environmental needs are also clear; the title of Rachel Carson's *Silent Spring* says it all. The question is one of choosing priorities and balancing risks. See John Danley, "Balancing Risks: Mosquitoes, Malaria, Morality, and DDT" (*Business & Society Review [1974]*, Spring 2002). It is worth noting that John Beard, "DDT and Human Health," *Science of the Total Environment* (February 2006), finds the evidence for the ill effects of DDT more convincing and says that it is still too early to say it does not contribute to human disease.

Malaria can be treated with drugs, but the parasite has developed resistance to standard medications such as chloroquine. A new medication based on a Chinese plant extract (from Artemisia, or sweet wormwood or Qinghao) has shown promise but is in far too short supply; see Martin Enserink, "Source of New Hope Against Malaria in Short Supply," *Science* (January 7, 2005). Mosquitoes can be controlled in various ways: Swamps can be drained (which carries its own environmental price), other breeding opportunities (such as old tires containing pools of water) can be eliminated, and larvae can be destroyed by hand (see Jeffrey Marlow, "Malaria," *World Watch*, May/June 2008). Fish can be introduced to eat mosquito larvae. Bednets can keep the mosquitoes away from people. But these (and other) alternatives do not mean that there does not remain a place for chemical pesticides. In "Pesticides and Public Health: Integrated Methods of Mosquito Management," *Emerging Infectious Diseases* (January–February 2001), Robert I. Rose, an arthropod biotechnologist with the Animal and Plant Health Inspection Service of the U.S. Department of

Agriculture, says, "Pesticides have a role in public health as part of sustainable integrated mosquito management. Other components of such management include surveillance, source reduction or prevention, biological control, repellents, traps, and pesticide-resistance management." "The most effective programs today rely on a range of tools," says Anne Platt McGinn in "Combating Malaria," *State of the World 2003* (W. W. Norton, 2003).

Today some countries see DDT as essential. See Tina Rosenberg, "What the World Needs Now Is DDT," *The New York Times Magazine* (April 11, 2004). However, when the World Health Organization (WHO) endorsed the use of DDT to fight malaria, there was immediate outcry; see Allan Schapira, "DDT: A Polluted Debate in Malaria Control," *Lancet* (December 16, 2006).

It has proven difficult to find effective, affordable drugs against malaria; see Ann M. Thayer, "Fighting Malaria," *Chemical and Engineering News* (October 24, 2005), and Claire Panosian Dunavan, "Tackling Malaria," *Scientific American* (December 2005). A great deal of effort has gone into developing vaccines against malaria; the parasite has demonstrated a persistent talent for evading all attempts to arm the immune system against it, but the work goes on. See Michael Finkel, "Bedlam in the Blood," *National Geographic* (July 2007). A newer approach is to develop genetically engineered (transgenic) mosquitoes that either cannot support the malaria parasite or cannot infect humans with it; see George K. Christophides, "Transgenic Mosquitoes and Malarial Transmission," *Cellular Microbiology* (March 2005). On the other hand, Nicholas J. White, "Malaria—Time to Act," *The New England Journal of Medicine* (November 9, 2006), argues that rather than wait for a perfect solution, we should recognize that present tools—including DDT—are effective enough now that there is no excuse to avoid using them.

It is worth stressing that malaria is only one of several mosquito-borne diseases that pose threats to public health. Two others are yellow fever and dengue. A new arrival in the United States is West Nile virus, which mosquitoes can transfer from birds to humans. However, West Nile virus is far less fatal than malaria, yellow fever, or dengue fever. Pesticides are already being used in the United States to kill the mosquitoes that carry West Nile virus, and health effects are being seen; see Grace Ziem, "Pesticide Spraying and Health Effects," *Environmental Health Perspectives* (March 2005). Fortunately, a vaccine is in development. See Dwight G. Smith, "A New Disease in the New World," *The World & I* (February 2002), and Michelle Mueller, "The Buzz on West Nile Virus," *Current Health 2* (April/May 2002). But "West Nile Virus Still a Threat," says *Clinical Infectious Diseases* (April 15, 2006).

It is also worth stressing that global warming (see Issue 4) means climate changes that may increase the geographic range of disease-carrying mosquitoes. Many climate researchers are concerned that malaria, yellow fever, and other now mostly tropical and subtropical diseases may return to temperate-zone nations and even spread into areas where they have never been known. See Atul A. Khasnis and Mary D. Nettleman, "Global Warming and Infectious Disease," *Archives of Medical Research* (November 2005).

ISSUE 10

Should Potential Risks Slow the Development of Nanotechnology?

YES: John Balbus, Richard Denison, Karen Florini, and Scott Walsh, from "Getting Nanotechnology Right the First Time," *Issues in Science and Technology* (Summer 2005)

NO: Mike Treder, from "Molecular Nanotech: Benefits and Risks," *The Futurist* (January–February 2004)

ISSUE SUMMARY

YES: John Balbus, Richard Denison, Karen Florini, and Scott Walsh of Environmental Defense in Washington, D.C., argue that much more needs to be done to assess risks to health and the environment before nanotechnology-based products are put on the market.

NO: Mike Treder, executive director of the Center for Responsible Nanotechnology, argues that the task at hand is to realize the benefits of nanotechnology while averting the dangers but that attempts to control all risks may lead to abusive restrictions and wind up exacerbating the hazards.

The concept of nanotechnology dates back to 1959, when the late physicist Richard Feynman discussed in an American Physical Society talk ("There's Plenty of Room at the Bottom," *Engineering and Science* [February 1960]) the possibility of building machines the size of viruses. As described by K. Eric Drexler in his 1986 book *Engines of Creation,* such machines would be able to manipulate and position single atoms and molecules. For a time, enthusiasts talked of the devices as self-reproducing robots that needed only suitable programming to manufacture practically anything from dirt, air, and water, or to disassemble anything into its component atoms. Consumer goods—from steaks to cars—would be essentially free! Furthermore, nanomachines would repair wounds, destroy cancer, and scrub the cholesterol from our arteries. It sounded like magic, and it stirred debate over the possibility that out-of-control nanobeasties might turn everything into grey goo. Bill Joy, "Why the Future Doesn't Need Us," *Wired* (April 2000), argues that the hazards of nanotechnology, robotics, and genetic engineering are so serious that they threaten to make humans an endangered species; research into these areas should be halted immediately. However, Ken Donaldson and Vicki Stone, "Nanoscience Fact versus Fiction," *Communications of the ACM* (November 2004), say that the gray goo scenario "is a scientific fantasy, more in the tradition of *King Kong* than the realms of scientific plausibility."

Enthusiasts such as the Foresight Institute (founded by Eric Drexler) remain optimistic. The National Heart, Lung, and Blood Institute published a report in 2003 (Denis B. Buxton, et al., "Recommendations of the National Heart, Lung, and Blood Institute Nanotechnology Working Group," *Circulation*, vol. 108, pp. 2737–2742) that called the medical prospects encouraging and called for increased research effort and funding. On February 15, 2006, Mark E. Davis, professor of chemical engineering at California Institute of Technology, told the Senate Committee on Commerce, Science, and Transportation that "The benefits of treating human disease with nanoparticle therapeutics far exceed the potential safety risks." Chuck Lenatti, in "Nanotech's First Blockbusters?" *Technology Review* (March 2004), reports that the effort to learn how to make tiny things is having some practical payoffs already. No one is building tiny robots of any kind, but some companies are making tiny components (such as "nanowires") from which they hope to build marketable photovoltaic cells, improved batteries, electronic devices, and so on. See, for instance, "Nanotechnology, Fuel Cells, and the Future," *Global Environmental Change Report* (June 2005).

How long will it take to go from the first primitive nanomachines able to build very simple things to the tiny robots that can make or unmake virtually anything? Most people have thought that if the step is possible at all, it will take decades. But in summer 2003, the Center for Responsible Nanotechnology concluded that instead it could be a matter of weeks, because even simple nanomanufacturing, combined with computer-aided design and manufacturing techniques, would enable extraordinarily rapid progress. This prospect, despite admittedly enticing potential benefits, alarms some people. So far, however, nanotechnology is reaching the market in the much more limited form of "nanomaterials" containing nano-sized particles whose toxicity and other potential ill effects are largely unknown. John Balbus, Richard Denison, Karen Florini, and Scott Walsh of Environmental Defense in Washington, D.C., argue that much more needs to be done to assess risks to health and the environment before nanotechnology-based products are put on the market. "With the right mix of increased risk research, improved regulatory oversight, self-initiated corporate standards, and inclusive stakeholder engagement, we have the opportunity to get nanotechnology right the first time." Mike Treder, executive director of the Center for Responsible Nanotechnology, argues that the task at hand is to realize the benefits of nanotechnology while averting the dangers but that attempts to control all risks may lead to abusive restrictions and wind up exacerbating the hazards.

YES

John Balbus et al.

Getting Nanotechnology Right the First Time

Nanotechnology—the design and manipulation of materials at the molecular and atomic scale—has great potential to deliver environmental as well as other benefits. The novel properties that emerge as materials reach the nanoscale (changes in surface chemistry, reactivity, electrical conductivity, and other properties) open the door to innovations in cleaner energy production, energy efficiency, water treatment, environmental remediation, and "lightweighting" of materials, among other applications, that provide direct environmental improvements.

At the same time, these novel properties may pose new risks to workers, consumers, the public, and the environment. The few data now available give cause for concern: Some nanomaterials appear to have the potential to damage skin, brain, and lung tissue, to be mobile or persistent in the environment, or to kill microorganisms (potentially including ones that constitute the base of the food web). This trickle of data only highlights how little is known about the environmental and health effects of engineered nanomaterials. . . .

As illustrated by the problems caused by asbestos, chlorofluorocarbons, DDT, leaded gasoline, PCBs, and numerous other substances, the fact that a product is useful does not ensure that it is benign to health or the environment. And if the danger becomes known after the product is widely used, the consequences can go beyond human suffering and environmental harm to include lengthy regulatory battles, costly cleanup efforts, expensive litigation quagmires, and painful public-relations debacles. So far, rapid development and commercial introduction of nanomaterials in varied applications are outpacing efforts to understand their implications, let alone ensure their safety. Fortunately, nanotechnology development and commercialization are still at an early stage, so it is not too late to begin managing this process wisely.

Nanotechnology offers an important opportunity to apply the lessons from prior mistakes by identifying risks up front, taking the necessary steps to address them, and meaningfully engaging stakeholders to help shape this technology's trajectory. There is an opportunity to get nanotechnology right the first time.

Reason for Concern

Nanoparticles can be naturally occurring or generated as byproducts of chemical reactions such as combustion. But attention now is focusing on the large number of engineered nanomaterials—fullerenes (also known as buckyballs), carbon nanotubes, quantum dots, and nanoscale metal oxides, among others—that are beginning to reach the market in growing quantities and in a wide variety of applications.

Studies performed to date are inadequate to provide a full picture of the risks of these engineered nanomaterials and leave open even more questions about other variants and types of engineered nanomaterials. Even so, they offer reason for concern. Studies have demonstrated that some nanomaterials can be mobile or persist in the environment and can be toxic to animals as diverse as fish and rats. A recent Rice University study of buckyballs found that although individual buckyballs do not dissolve well in water, they have a tendency to form aggregates that are both very water-soluble and bacteriocidal, a property that raises strong concerns about ecosystem impacts, because bacteria constitute the bottom of the food chain in many ecosystems. In addition, nanoparticles are deposited throughout the respiratory tract when inhaled. Some of the particles settle in the nasal passages, where they have been shown to be taken up by the olfactory nerves and carried past the blood-brain barrier directly into brain cells. Nanoparticles in the 30- to 50-nanometer range have been shown to penetrate deeply into the lungs, where they readily cross through lung tissue and enter the systemic circulation. This potential for rapid and widespread distribution within the body offers promise of a new array of diagnostic and therapeutic applications for these substances, but it also heightens the importance of having a full understanding of their toxicity.

A variety of nanomaterials have the capacity to cause tissue and cellular damage by causing oxidative stress (the same type of damage that people take antioxidant pills to protect against). Buckyballs caused oxidative damage to brain and liver cells in a study in largemouth bass; other nanoparticles have also been shown to cause oxidative stress in skin cells and in the liver. Most research has used prototypical or "plain" nanoparticles, such as uncoated buckyballs and carbon nanotubes. The few studies that have looked at the effects of variations and coatings have shown that these changes modify the toxicity of the original particle, further complicating the picture and raising the question of how these coatings may degrade over time within the body or in the environment. Oxidative stress may also be part of the mechanism behind the damage to lung tissue that has been observed in several studies of carbon nanotubes. Carbon nanotubes instilled into the lungs of rats and mice have caused unusual localized immune lesions (granulomas) within 30 days, and a separate aspiration study noted this effect as well as dose-dependent lung fibrosis throughout the lung tissue. These and other studies suggest that some nanomaterials can evade the lung's normal clearance and defense mechanisms.

Although the doses and methods of administration used in these studies may not perfectly mirror likely exposure scenarios, these studies strongly suggest the potential for some nanomaterials to pose significant risks.

Urgent Need for Action

These initial studies highlight how little is known about the health and environmental effects of engineered nanomaterials. Thousands of tons of nanomaterials are already being produced each year, and hundreds of products incorporating nanomaterials are reportedly already on the market. The global market for nanotechnology products is expected to reach at least $1 trillion over the next decade. Given the length of time it will take to develop an adequate understanding of the potential risks posed by a wide variety of nanomaterials and to apply this knowledge to inform appropriate regulation, it is imperative to take action now.

Both the public and private sector's best interests are served by an investment to identify and manage potential risks from nanomaterials now, rather than waiting until problems arise and then struggling to remediate or otherwise cope with them. History demonstrates that embracing a technology without a careful assessment and control of its risks can be extremely costly from both human and financial perspectives. The failure to sufficiently consider the adverse effects of using lead in paint, plumbing, and gasoline has resulted in widespread health problems that continue to this day and burden us with extremely high cleanup costs. Asbestos is another example where enormous sums of money are being spent by private companies for remediation, litigation, and compensation, even beyond that spent by the public sector to alleviate harm to human health and the environment. Standard & Poor's has estimated that the total cost of liability for asbestos-related losses could reach $200 billion.

The risks at issue here are not only those related to health and the environment but also risks to the very success of this promising set of technologies. If the public is not convinced that nanomaterials are being developed in a way that identifies and minimizes negative consequences to human health and the environment, a backlash could develop that delays, reduces, or even prevents the realization of many of the potential benefits of nanotechnology. As demonstrated with genetically modified organisms just a few years ago, rapid commercialization combined with a failure to address risks early on can lead to product bans and closed markets, resulting in that case in hundreds of millions of dollars in annual export losses for U.S. farmers and companies.

Timely implementation of the following four actions will allow for the most efficient and safest use of nanotechnology.

Increase risk research. The U.S. government, as the largest single investor in nanotechnology R&D, needs to spend more to assess the health and environmental implications of nanotechnology and ensure that the critical research needed to identify potential risks is done, and done expeditiously. Of the roughly $1 billion that the federal government spends annually on nanotechnology, spending for environmental and health implications research accounted for only $8.5 million (less than 1 percent) in fiscal year (FY) 2004 and is proposed to increase to only $38.5 million (less than 4 percent) for FY 2006.

Environmental Defense has called on the U.S. government to increase federal funding for nanomaterial risk research under the National Nanotechnology

Initiative (NNI) to at least $100 million annually for the next several years. Although an annual expenditure of $100 million is a significant increase over current levels, it is still a small fraction of the overall federal budget for nano-technology development. Moreover, it is a modest investment compared to the potential benefits of risk avoidance and to the $1 trillion or more that nanotech-nology is projected to provide to the world economy by 2015. Given the com-plexity of the task, the scope of the necessary research, and available benchmarks for comparison, $100 million per year is a reasonable lower-bound estimate of what is needed.

Broad agreement exists among stakeholders that addressing the potential risks of nanotechnology will be an unusually complex task. Nanotechnology is a potentially limitless collection of technologies and associated materials. The sheer diversity of potential materials and applications, which is a source of nanotechnology's enormous promise, also poses major challenges with respect to characterizing potential risks. Nanotechnology entails many fundamentally different types of materials (and hundreds or thousands of potential variants of each); many novel properties that are potentially relevant to risk; many potential types of applications; and multiple sources and routes of exposure over the full life cycle of a given material or application.

Even before the research is done that will allow hazards and exposures to be evaluated in detail, a number of more fundamental needs must be addressed. At present, even a basic understanding of which specific properties determine nanomaterials' risk potential is lacking. Many of the methods, protocols, and tools needed to characterize nanomaterials or to detect and measure their pres-ence in a variety of settings, including the workplace environment, the human body, and environmental media, are still in a very early stage of development.

Nor is it clear the extent to which existing knowledge about conventional chemicals can be used to predict risks of nanomaterials. The defining character of nanotechnology—the emergence of novel properties when materials are reduced to or assembled at the nanoscale—carries with it the potential for novel risks and even novel mechanisms of toxicity that cannot be predicted from the properties and behavior of their bulk counterparts. Risk research is needed to understand nanomaterial characterization, biological and environ-mental fate and transport, and acute and chronic toxicity.

In each of these areas, existing testing and assessment methods and pro-tocols need to be reexamined to determine the extent to which they can be modified to account for nanomaterials' novel characteristics or need to be sup-plemented with new methods. Similar challenges will arise with respect to methods and technologies for sampling, analysis and monitoring, all of which will be needed to detect nanomaterials and their transformation products in living systems and in various environmental media.

The view that significantly more money needs to be spent on nano-technology risk research is further supported by experts' assessments, known testing costs associated with hazard characterization programs for conven-tional chemicals, and the research budgets for a roughly analogous risk-characterization effort, namely the Environmental Protection Agency's (EPA's) research on risks of airborne particulate matter (PM).

Experts' assessments. Experts from a variety of fields have declared that the NNI's current funding for nanotechnology risk research needs to be significantly increased. Invited government, industry, and academic experts at a September 2004 workshop sponsored by the NNI called for at least a 10-fold increase in federal spending on nanotechnology risk-related research, relative to the approximately $10 million spent in fiscal year 2004. The United Kingdom's Royal Society and Royal Academy of Engineering called for the UK government to devote £5 million to £6 million ($9 million to $11 million) per year for 10 years just to do its part to develop the methodologies and instrumentation needed to set the stage for actual testing of nanomaterials. The chemical industry's "nanotechnology development roadmap," requested by the NNI, indicates that the assessment of hazards to human health and the environment will require a level of cumulative R&D investment that is among the highest of any assigned to the industry's priority research requirements. President Bush's science advisor John H. Marburger III noted that the current toxicity studies now under way through the NNI are "a drop in the bucket compared to what needs to be done."

Hazard endpoint testing costs. Several estimates available from chemical hazard assessment programs can be used to provide at least a lower bound on the costs of testing a nanomaterial for hazardous properties. These costs are for the testing of a conventional chemical for an assortment of hazard endpoints of concern (toxicity plus environmental fate); notably, they do not include costs associated with assessing exposure, which is also needed to assess risk. Generating the Screening Information Data Set, a basic set of hazard information designed to screen chemicals only in order to set priorities for further scrutiny, is estimated to cost roughly $250,000 per chemical. Estimates for filling the more extensive data requirements applicable to high-volume chemicals under the European Union's proposed Registration, Evaluation, and Authorization of Chemicals program exceed $2 million per chemical. The test battery required to register a pesticide under U.S. law can reportedly cost as much as $10 million per pesticide.

EPA research budgets for risks of airborne PM. In response to recommendations from the National Research Council, the EPA spent $40 million to $60 million annually for the first 6 years of a multiyear research program on risks posed by airborne PM. The scope of needed research on nanomaterials is considerably broader and thus likely to cost much more than for airborne PM. This is because airborne PM is a relatively well-studied mixture of chemicals to which exposure arises from a discrete (though highly diffuse) set of sources and through a single route: inhalation. In contrast, nanomaterials

- are composed of many entirely novel, often poorly characterized classes of materials
- will be applied and used in ways that will create the potential for release and exposure through many more pathways, including breathing, ingesting drinking water, and skin absorption

- may be present in wastes, water discharges, and a wide array of products
- may result in the exposure of consumers, as well as the general public and workers, through incorporation into products
- pose potential environmental as well as human health risks that need to be considered

Hence, regardless of the ultimate magnitude of risk identified, the research needed to assess the risks is likely to be considerably more involved and costly for nanomaterials than for airborne PM.

The President's Subcommittee on Nanoscale Science, Engineering and Technology already plays a role in coordinating and exchanging information on federal R&D spending for nanotechnology. That coordinating role needs to be enhanced to include the ability to shape and direct the overall federal risk research agenda across agencies to ensure that all critical needs are being addressed, as well as the responsibility and authority to ensure that individual agencies have sufficient resources to conduct the needed research in their areas. In light of the rapidity with which nanomaterials are reaching the market, this added authority is essential to ensure that the fight questions are asked and answered on a timely basis.

This is not to say that the U.S. government should be the sole, or even the principal, funder of nanomaterial risk research. Other governments are also spending heavily to promote nanotechnology R&D, and they too should allocate some portion of their spending to address nanotechnology risks. And although government risk research has a critical role to play in developing the infrastructure needed to characterize and assess the risks of nanomaterials, private industry should fund the majority of the research and testing on the products they are planning to bring to market. Clearly, all parties will benefit if governments and industry coordinate their research to avoid redundancy and optimize efficiency.

Improve regulatory policy. Although the United States has many regulatory programs in place to address environmental and health risks, those programs are neither comprehensive in their design nor without flaws in their implementation. As a result, some substances can fall through regulatory cracks and go unregulated or underregulated, posing risks that are not discovered until adverse effects are widespread. There are signs that some nanomaterials may be poised to fall between those cracks. Consider a few examples:

- For many substances and products, there is little or no governmental review before they are marketed; regulation occurs only after a problem has arisen.
- Other programs are triggered only if a substance is considered "new." Yet at least some nanomaterial producers are apparently proceeding on the assumption that their products are not new despite their novel properties, and government agencies have not clarified the regulatory status of these materials. As a result, nanomaterials with novel properties are entering commerce without the scrutiny of potential health and environmental effects they warrant.

- Some programs for "new" substances have historically required very limited data to be submitted by producers, relying instead on extrapolation from information on existing chemicals, an approach that is highly questionable for nanomaterials, given how few hazard data now exist.
- Under many regulatory programs, coverage is triggered by mass-based thresholds or standards. Yet because of their high surface-area-to-mass ratios or other properties, nanomaterials often exhibit dramatically increased potency or other activity relative to their bulk counterparts, a distinction not reflected in existing mass-based measures.
- Some potential nanotechnology applications may fall through the cracks between the jurisdictions of multiple regulatory programs. For example, sunscreens using nanoparticles of titanium dioxide were reviewed by the Food and Drug Administration (FDA) for potential immediate health effects on consumers, but neither the FDA nor the EPA reviewed how titanium dioxide nanoparticles may affect aquatic ecosystems when these sunscreens wash off.

At this point, federal agencies need to vigorously use their existing statutory authorities to address potential nanomaterial risks as effectively as possible. Regrettably, there are few signs of action on this score. For example, the EPA has been conspicuously silent regarding the extent to which nanomaterials are "new" or "existing" chemical substances for purposes of the Toxic Substances Control Act, an important distinction because only new chemicals trigger premanufacture notification and review requirements. The EPA can and should clarify the principle that nanomaterials are new unless they demonstrably lack novel properties as compared to a conventional counterpart. Further, the EPA should clarify that nanomaterials do not automatically qualify for the exemptions from premanufacture notice provisions that are allowed for materials produced in low volumes or thought to result in low exposure, at least until appropriate nanomaterial-specific definitions of "low volume" and "low exposure" can be set. Likewise, before assuming that the existing exemption of polymers from the premanufacture notification program applies to nanomaterials, the EPA needs to determine whether nanomaterials meet the rationale for the exemption; namely, that the molecules are too large to be biologically available and that they degrade only into substances that have already been evaluated. The EPA should also state publicly that it is unlikely to approve the commercial manufacture of a nanomaterial in the absence of hazard and exposure data sufficient to characterize its potential risks.

As agencies apply their existing authorities (or fail to do so), the need for further steps may well become evident. A comprehensive and independent process that identifies deficiencies as well as steps to address them will be vital.

Develop corporate standards of care.   Even under the most optimistic scenario, it appears unlikely that federal agencies will put into place adequate provisions for nanomaterials quickly enough to address the materials now entering or poised to enter the market. Out of enlightened self-interest, industry must take the lead in evaluating and managing nanomaterial risks for the near term, working with other stakeholders to quickly establish and implement life cycle-based "standards of care" for nanomaterials.

These standards should include a framework and a process by which to identify and manage nanomaterials' risks across a product's full life cycle, taking into account worker safety, manufacturing releases and wastes, product use, and product disposal. Standards of care should also include and be responsive to feedback mechanisms, including environmental and health monitoring programs to check the accuracy of the assumptions about a material's risks and the effectiveness of risk management practices. Such standards should be developed and implemented in a transparent and accountable manner, including by publicly disclosing the assumptions, processes, and results of the risk identification and risk management systems.

Ideally, such standards of care would help provide a model for sensible regulatory policies as they emerge. This would assure the public that all companies, not just those who participate in voluntary programs, are taking the steps needed to safely manage nanomaterials. This would also set a level playing field for companies, so that responsible companies are not at a disadvantage relative to those that cut corners.

Engage a diverse range of stakeholders.   To date, neither government nor industry has sufficiently engaged the wide array of stakeholders—including labor groups, health organizations, consumer advocates, community groups, and environmental organizations—whose constituencies both stand to benefit from this technology and are most likely to bear any risks that arise. Government and industry need to engage these various stakeholders and consider their views in deciding how to develop and manage this promising technology in a way that maximizes its benefits and minimizes its risks.

All too often, "stakeholder involvement" translates in practice into either communicating the end result of a process to those who have been excluded (whether intentionally or by default) from participating in it, or seeking to "educate" the public in order to promote a technology and allay concerns that the technology's proponents believe to be unfounded. Engagement is not simply top-down communication. It means involving stakeholders from the outset in helping to identify expectations and concerns, and providing a role for them in helping to set priorities for research and action. And many of these stakeholders not only have a stake or interest in nanotechnology, they also have relevant perspective, experience, and expertise to offer.

Here again, there is an opportunity to get this right the first time. The potential payoff in terms of reduced risks and increased market and public acceptance will almost certainly greatly exceed the investment necessary to draw these important voices into the discussion.

The rapid commercialization of nanotechnology, coupled with the potential risks from at least certain nanomaterials as demonstrated in initial studies, lend urgency to the need for government and industry to direct more of their investments in nanotechnology development toward identifying the potential risks and addressing them. Government and industry have done a great job so far in accentuating nanotechnology's potential up sides and in accelerating its development, but they have yet to come to terms with their equally critical roles in identifying and avoiding the down sides. A far better balance between these two roles must be struck if nanotechnology is to deliver on its promise without delivering unintended adverse consequences. With the right mix of increased risk research, improved regulatory oversight, self-initiated corporate standards, and inclusive stakeholder engagement, we have the opportunity to get nanotechnology right the first time.

Mike Treder

 **NO**

Molecular Nanotech: Benefits and Risks

T he future shock of rapid change and technology run amok described by Alvin Toffler in his 1970 best seller has perhaps been less debilitating for most people than predicted, but even Toffler could not have envisioned the tidal wave of change that will hit us when *nanofactories* make the scene.

Imagine a world with billions of desktop-size, portable, nonpolluting, cheap machines that can manufacture almost anything—from clothing to furniture to electronics, and much more—in just a few hours. Today, such devices do not exist. But in the years ahead, this advanced form of nanotechnology could create the next Industrial Revolution—or the world's worst nightmare.

The technology described in this article is *molecular nanotechnology* (MNT). This is a big step beyond most of today's nanotech research, which deals with exploring and exploiting the properties of materials at the nanoscale. Industry has begun using the term *nanotechnology* to cover almost any technology significantly smaller than microtechnology, such as those involving nanoparticles or nanomaterials. This broad field will produce important and useful results, but their societal effects—both positive and negative—will be modest compared with later stages of the technology.

MNT, by contrast, is about constructing shapes, machines, and products at the atomic level—putting them together molecule by molecule. With parts only a few nanometers wide, it may become possible to build a supercomputer smaller than a grain of sand, a weapon smaller than a mosquito, or a self-contained nanofactory that sits on your kitchen counter.

"Picture an automated factory, full of conveyor belts, computers, and swinging robot arms," writes scientist and engineer K. Eric Drexler, who first brought nanotechnology to public attention with his 1986 book *Engines of Creation*. "Now imagine something like that factory, but a million times smaller and working a million times faster, with parts and workpieces of molecular size."

Unlike any machine ever built, the nanofactory will be assembled from the bottom up, constructed of specifically designed and placed molecules. Drexler says, "Nanotechnology isn't primarily about miniaturizing machines, but about extending precise control of molecular structures to larger and larger scales. Nanotechnology is about making precise things *big*."

Virtually every previous technological improvement has been accomplished by making things smaller and more precise. But as the scales at which we work get smaller and smaller, we approach limits imposed by physics. The smallest unit of matter we can build with is the atom, or combinations of atoms known as molecules. The earthshaking insight of molecular nanotechnology is that, when we reach this scale, we can reverse direction and begin building *up*, making products by placing individual atoms and molecules exactly where we want them.

Ever since Richard Feynman enunciated MNT's basic concepts in 1959, and especially since Drexler began detailing its amazing possibilities in the 1980s, proposals for building products in various ways have been put forth. Some of these have been fanciful and many have been impractical. At this point, it appears that the idea of a nanofactory is the safest and most useful method of building general-purpose products by molecular manufacturing.

Inside a Nanofactory

The inner architecture of a nanofactory will be a stunning achievement, outside the realm of anything previously accomplished. Nanofactories will make use of a vast number of moving parts, each designed and precisely constructed to do a specific job. Some of these parts will be visible to the human eye. Most will be microscopic or even nanoscale, smaller than a human cell. An important feature of a nanofactory is that all of its parts will be fixed in place. This is significant because it greatly simplifies development of the device. Engineers won't have to figure out how to tell each little nanobot in a swarm where to go and how to get there, and none of the parts can get lost or go wild.

Perhaps the easiest way to envision the inner workings of a nanofactory is to picture a large city, with all the streets laid out on a grid. Imagine that in this city everyone works together to build gigantic products—ocean liners, for instance. To build something that big, you have to start with small parts and put them together. In this imaginary city, all the workers stand along the streets and pass the parts along to each other. The smallest parts are assembled on the narrowest side streets, and then handed up to the end of the block. Other small parts from other side streets are joined together to make medium-sized parts, which are joined together to make large parts. At the end, the largest parts converge in one place, where they are joined together to make the finished product. A nanofactory performs in this way, with multiple assembly lines operating simultaneously and steadily feeding into each other.

The first and hardest step in building a nanofactory is building an *assembler,* a tiny device that can combine individual molecules into useful shapes. An early plan for molecular manufacturing imagined lots of free-floating assemblers working together to build a single massive product, molecule by molecule. A more efficient approach is to fasten down the assemblers in orderly arrays of chemical fabricators, instruct each fabricator to create a tiny piece of the product, and then fasten the pieces together, passing them along to the next level within the nanofactory.

A human-scale nanofactory will consist of trillions of fabricators, and it could only be built by another nanofactory. But at the beginning, an assembler could build a very small nanofactory, with just a few fabricators. A smaller nanofactory could build a bigger one, and so on. According to the best estimates we have today, a fabricator could make its own mass in just a few hours. So a small nanofactory could make another one twice as big in just a few days—maybe less than a day. Do that about 60 times, and you have a tabletop model.

By the time the first working assembler is ready, the blueprint for a basic nanofactory may already be prepared. But until we have an assembler, we can't make a nanofactory.

Building an assembler is one of the ambitious research projects of Zyvex, a Texas firm that bills itself as "the first molecular nanotechnology company." Zyvex has gathered many leading minds in physics, chemistry, mechanical engineering, and computer programming to focus on the long-range goal of molecular assembler manufacturing technology. Along the way, the company has developed some of the world's most precise tools for manipulating and testing materials and structures at the nanoscale. Numerous other projects at research universities and in corporations around the world are contributing valuable knowledge to the field.

How far are we from having a working assembler? A 1999 media report on nanotech said, "Estimates vary. From five to 10 years, according to Zyvex, or from eight to 15 years, according to the research community."

And how long will it take from building a single assembler to having a fully functional nanofactory? The report continues, "After that, it could be decades before we'll be able to manufacture finished consumer goods." This reflects the common wisdom, but it's wrong. Very wrong.

The Center for Responsible Nanotechnology (CRN), a non-profit think tank co-founded by this author, published a detailed study in summer 2003 of the work required to progress from a single assembler to a full-fledged nanofactory that can create a wide variety of low-cost products. The startling conclusion of this report is that the span of time could be measured in weeks—probably less than two months. And what will the first nanofactory build? Another one, and another one.

Each nanofactory will be able to duplicate itself in as little as a few hours, or perhaps a half a week at most. Even using the most conservative estimate, in a couple of months you could have a million nanofactories, and a few months after that, a billion. Less than a year after the first basic assembler is completed, every household in the world conceivably could have its own nanofactory.

Creativity Unleashed

Before a tidal wave strikes, another dramatic event—usually an earthquake or major landslide—must occur to trigger it. The first generation of products to come out of nanofactories—inexpensive but high quality clothing, furniture, electronics, household appliances, bicycles, tools, building supplies, and more—may be like that: a powerful landslide of change, but only a portent of the gigantic wave that is to follow.

Most of these early products will probably be similar to what are current at the time nanofactories begin production. Because they are built by MNT, with every atom precisely placed, they will be better in every way—stronger, lighter, cheaper—but they still will be built on existing models.

The world-changing shock wave will hit when we realize that we no longer need be restricted to existing models—not when a supercomputer smaller than a grain of sand can be integrated into any product, and not when people everywhere—young, old, male, female, technical, nontechnical, practical, artistic, and whimsical—will have the opportunity to be designers.

MNT product design will be eased by CAD (computer-aided design) programs so simple that a child can do it—and that's no exaggeration. New product prototypes can be created, tested, and refined in a matter of hours instead of months and without the expense of traditional production facilities. No special expertise is needed beyond the skill for using CAD programs—only imagination, curiosity, and the desire to create.

Within months, conceivably, even the most up-to-date appliances, machines, communication media, and other electronics will be outmoded. Imagine embedding "smart" gadgetry into everything you own or might want to have. Demand for these new products will be intense. The cost of manufacturing them may be almost negligible.

To maximize the latent innovation potential in nanofactory proliferation, and to help prevent illicit, unwise, or malicious product design and manufacture, CRN recommends that designers work (and play) with modular *nanoblocks* of various compositions and purposes to create a wide variety of products, from consumer goods and educational tools to building supplies and even new modes of transportation. When combined with automated verification of design safety and protection of intellectual property, this should open up huge new areas for originality and improvement while maintaining safety and commercial viability.

Working with nanoblocks, designers can create to their hearts' content. The combination of user-friendly CAD and rapid prototyping will result in a spectacular synergy, enabling unprecedented levels of innovation and development. Among the many remarkable benefits accruing to humanity from nanofactory proliferation will be this unleashing of millions of eager new minds, allowed for the first time to freely explore and express their brilliant creative energy.

It becomes impossible to predict what might be devised then. The smart components and easy design systems of the nanotech revolution will rewrite the rules.

Benefits and Dangers

This all adds up to change that is sudden and shocking and could be extremely disruptive.

On the plus side, MNT could solve many of the world's problems. Simple products like plumbing, water filters, and mosquito nets—made cheaply on the spot—would greatly reduce the spread of infectious diseases. The efficient, cheap construction of strong and lightweight structures, electrical equipment, and power storage devices will allow the use of solar thermal power as a primary and abundant energy source.

Many areas of the world could not support a twentieth-century manufacturing infrastructure, with its attendant costs, difficulties, and environmental impacts, but MNT should be self-contained and clean. A single packing crate or suitcase could contain all the equipment required for a village-scale industrial revolution.

Computers and display devices will become stunningly inexpensive and could be made widely available. Much social unrest can be traced directly to material poverty, ill health, and ignorance. Nanofactories could greatly reduce these problems.

On the other hand, all this sudden change—the equivalent of a century's development packed into a few years—has the potential to disrupt many aspects of society and politics.

When a consumer purchases a manufactured product today, he is paying for its design, raw materials, the labor and capital of manufacturing, transportation, storage, marketing, and sales. Additional money—usually a fairly low percentage—goes to the owners of each of these businesses, and eventually to the employed workers. If nanofactories can produce a wide variety of products when and where they are wanted, most of this additional effort will become superfluous. This raises many questions about the nature of a post-MNT economy: Who will own the technology for molecular manufacturing? Will it be heavily restricted, or widely available? Will products become cheaper? Will major corporations disappear? Will new monopolies arise? Will most people retire—or be unemployed? What will it do to the gap between rich and poor?

It seems clear that molecular manufacturing could severely disrupt the present economic structure, greatly reducing the value of many material and human resources, including much of our current infrastructure. Despite utopian postcapitalist hopes, it is unclear whether a workable replacement system could appear in time to prevent the human consequences of massive job displacement.

MNT manufacturing will allow the cheap creation of incredibly powerful devices and products. Stronger materials will allow the creation of much larger machines, capable of excavating or otherwise destroying large areas of the planet at a greatly accelerated pace. It is too early to tell whether there will be economic incentive to do this. However, given the large number of activities and purposes that would damage the environment if taken to extremes, and the ease of taking them to extremes with molecular manufacturing, it seems likely that this problem is worth worrying about.

Some forms of damage can result from an aggregate of individual actions, each almost harmless by itself. For example, the extreme compactness of nanomanufactured machinery may lead to the use of very small products, which can easily turn into nanolitter that will be hard to clean up and may cause health problems. Collection of solar energy on a sufficiently large scale—by corporations, municipalities, and individuals—could modify the planet's albedo and directly affect the environment. In addition, if we are not careful, the flexibility and compactness of molecular manufacturing may allow the creation of free-floating, foraging self-replicators—a "gray goo" that could do serious damage to the biosphere by replicating out of control.

Molecular manufacturing raises the possibility of horrifically effective weapons. As an example, the smallest insect is about 200 microns; this creates a plausible size estimate for a nanotech-built antipersonnel weapon capable of seeking and injecting toxin into unprotected humans. The human lethal dose of botulism toxin is about 100 nanograms, or about 1/100 the volume of the weapon. As many as 50 billion toxin-carrying devices—theoretically enough to kill every human on earth—could be packed into a single suitcase. Guns of all sizes would be far more powerful, and their bullets could be self-guided. Aerospace hardware would be far lighter and offer higher performance; built with minimal or no metal, such craft would be much harder to spot on radar.

The awesome power of MNT may cause two or more competing nations to enter into an unstable arms race. Increased uncertainty of the capabilities of an adversary, less time to respond to an attack, and better targeted destruction of the enemy's resources during an attack all make nanotech arms races less stable than a nuclear arms race. Also, unless nanotech is tightly controlled on an international level, the number of nanotech nations in the world could be much higher than the number of nuclear nations, increasing the chance of a regional conflict expanding globally.

Criminals and terrorists with stronger, more powerful, and more compact devices could do serious damage to society. Chemical and biological weapons could become much deadlier and easier to conceal. Many other types of terrifying devices are possible, including several varieties of remote assassination weapons that would be difficult to detect or avoid. If such devices were available from a black market or a home factory, it would be nearly impossible to detect them before they were used; a random search capable of spotting them would be a clear violation of current human rights standards in most civilized countries.

Surveillance devices could be made microscopically small, low-priced, and very numerous—leading to questions of pervasive invasions of privacy, from illicit selling of sexual or other images to ubiquitous covert government or industrial spying. Attempts to control all these risks may lead to abusive restrictions, or create a black market that would be very risky and almost impossible to stop, because small nanofactories will be very easy to smuggle and fully dangerous.

Searching for Solutions

If you knew that in one year's time you would be forced to walk a tightrope without a net hundreds of feet above a rocky canyon, how soon would you begin practicing? The analogy applies to nanofactory technology. Because we know it is possible—maybe even probable—that everything we've reviewed here could happen within a decade, how soon should we start to prepare?

A report issued by the University of Toronto Joint Centre for Bioethics in February 2003 calls for serious consideration of the ethical, environmental, economic, legal, and social implications of nanotechnology. Report co-author

Peter Singer says, "Open public discussion of the benefits and risks of this new technology is urgently needed."

There's no doubt that such discussion is warranted and urgent. But beyond talking about ethics, immediate research into the need, design, and building of an effective global administration structure is crucial. Unwise regulation is a serious hazard. Simple solutions won't work.

"A patchwork of extremist solutions to the wide-ranging risks of advanced nanotechnology is a grave danger," says Chris Phoenix, research director for the Center for Responsible Nanotechnology. "All areas of society stand to be affected by molecular manufacturing, and unless comprehensive international plans are developed, the multiplicity of cures could be worse than the disease. The threat of harm would almost certainly be increased, while many extraordinary benefits could go unrealized."

We have much to gain, and much to lose. The advantages promised by MNT are real, and they could be ours soon. Living conditions worldwide could be dramatically improved, and human suffering greatly diminished. But everything comes at a cost. The price for safe introduction of the miracles of nanofactory technology is thorough, conscientious preparation.

Several organizations are stepping up to this challenge. For example:

- The Foresight Institute has drafted a set of molecular nanotechnology guidelines for researchers and developers. These are mostly aimed at restricting the development of MNT to responsible parties and preventing the production of free-ranging self-replicating nanobots.
- The Millennium Project of the American Council for the United Nations University is exploring various scenarios for safe and socially conscious implementation of molecular manufacturing and other emerging technologies. These scenarios depict the world in 2050, based on various policy choices we might make between now and then.
- The Center for Responsible Nanotechnology is studying all the issues involved—political, economic, military, humanitarian, technological, and environmental—and developing well-grounded, complete, and workable proposals for effective administration and safe use of advanced nanotechnology. Current results of CRN's research lead to the conclusion that establishing a single international program to develop molecular manufacturing technology may be the safest course. The leading nations of the world would have to agree to join—or at least not to oppose—this effort, and a mechanism to detect and deter competing programs would have to be devised.

It will take all this and more. The brightest minds and clearest thinkers, the most energetic activists and committed organizers, the smartest scientists, most dedicated ethicists, and most creative social planners desperately will be needed.

Will it be easy to realize the benefits of nanofactory technology while averting the dangers? Of course it will not. Is it even possible? It had better be. Our future is very uncertain, and it's very near. Much nearer than we might have thought. Let's get started.

POSTSCRIPT

Should Potential Risks Slow the Development of Nanotechnology?

Nanotechnology sounds like the most wild-eyed of science-fiction dreams, and it has become a frequent guest-star in modern science fiction novels. But it seems reasonable to say that nanotechnology will not remain science fiction for very long. Nanotechnologists are not yet close to building the first nanofactories, but nanotechnology is gaining significant attention from government, industry, and investors. Its momentum is growing, as suggested by two recent book titles (among many, many others): Thomas J. Frey, *Nanotechnology: The Future* (CRC, 2009), and Victor E. Borisenko and Stafano Ossicini, *What Is What in the Nanoworld: A Handbook on Nanoscience and Nanotechnology,* 2nd ed. (Wiley-VCH, 2008). The promise of the technology is so great that some are calling for increased government support. See Neal Lane and Thomas Kalil, "The National Nanotechnology Initiative: Present at the Creation," *Issues in Science and Technology* (Summer 2005), and George Allen, "The Economic Promise of Nanotechnology," *Issues in Science and Technology* (Summer 2005). John Balbus et al. update their argument in Scott Walsh et al., "Nanotechnology: Getting It Right the First Time," *Journal of Cleaner Production* (May 2008).

In December 2004, the European Commission published "Towards a European Strategy for Nanotechnology" (http://europa.eu.int/comm/research/industrial_technologies/pdf/nanotechnology_communication_en.pdf), which called for a number of steps designed both to stimulate the development of nanotechnology in Europe and to "integrate societal considerations into the R&D process at an early stage; address any potential public health, safety, environmental and consumer risks upfront by generating the data needed for risk assessment, integrating risk assessment into every step of the life cycle of nanotechnology-based products, and adapting existing methodologies and, as necessary, developing novel ones; [and] complement the above actions with appropriate cooperation and initiatives at international level."

In July 2004, the Royal Society and Royal Academy of Engineering published "Nanoscience and Nanotechnologies: Opportunities and Uncertainties," recommending tighter UK and European regulations and public dialog. In February 2005, the UK government published a lengthy response to the report (http://www.ost.gov.uk/policy/issues/nanotech_final.pdf) that agreed on the need for research and regulation but failed to promise additional money.

Anthony Seaton and Kenneth Donaldson, in "Nanoscience, Nanotoxicology, and the Need to Think Small," *Lancet* (March 12, 2005), comment on the potential health risks of nanomaterials. Rory O'Neill, "Dangers Come in Small

Particles," *Hazards* (July–September 2004), warns that the industry holds the potential for "tomorrow's occupational health calamity." So far, the hazards of nanotechnology are largely speculative; see Gloria Gonzalez, "Nanotechnology Risks Still Largely a Mystery," *Business Insurance* (November 13, 2006). Philip E. Ross, "Tiny Toxins?" *Technology Review* (May/June 2006), notes that the number of commercial products containing nanomaterials is growing rapidly, and some research is already finding worrisome signs of toxicity. There is growing awareness of the need for risk assessment (see Terry J. Allen, "Nanotech: Tiny Particles, Big Risks," *In These Times* [January 24, 2008]) and considerable debate over how to set priorities and fund the necessary research (see Robert F. Service, "Priorities Needed for Nano-Risk Research and Development," *Science* [October 6, 2006]). In February 2007, the United Nations Environment Programme released its *Global Environment Outlook Year Book 2007* (http://www.unep .org/geo/yearbook/yb2007/), which called nanotechnology an "emerging challenge" and noted that it holds great promise but "more research is needed to identify environmental, health and socio-economic hazards."

People such as Bill Joy are sounding strong cautionary notes, but others, such as John Seely Brown and Paul Duguid, "A Response to Bill Joy and the Doom-and-Gloom Technofuturists," *The Industry Standard* (April 13, 2000), are more optimistic. Joy, say Brown and Duguid, far too blithely assumes that very large obstacles in the development of nanotechnology will be overcome in short order. He focuses on hype and oversimplifications (and indeed, the "gray goo" problem is no longer taken seriously at all). He also ignores the role of society, which has shown itself quite capable of controlling the development of technologies in the past. On the other hand, society may not have adequate information in time to make an informed decision on whether to let nanotechnology proceed, perhaps especially considering the speed with which nanotechnology is likely to develop after the first simple assemblers are built. Fariborz Ghadar and Heather Spindler, in "Nanotechnology: Small Revolution," *Industrial Management* (May/June 2005), note that "While scientists and the federal government recognize the potential benefits of nanotechnology and it will not be possible to say that all nanotech applications are safe or are dangerous, it will be important to listen and address public concerns. And although much more data will be available in 10 years that will facilitate the decision, society will be forced to make a decision before then in the absence of complete data. And the adoption of nanotechnologies will be a very diverse and complex problem." The U.S. Environmental Protection Agency has addressed future research needs for risk assessment in a "Nanotechnology White Paper" (February 2007) (http:// www.epa.gov/osa/nanotech.htm). Volker Turk, Claudia Kaiser, and Stephan Schaller, "Invisible but Tangible? Societal Opportunities and Risks of Nanotechnologies," *Journal of Cleaner Production* (May 2008), have addressed some of the issues with "Nanologue, a project that brought together leading research and opinions on the social, ethical and legal implications of nanotechnology applications (NT) in Europe." One result was the NanoMeter, "a web-based tool that allows researchers and product developers (and others interested) to carry out a brief societal assessment of nanotechnological applications prior to market release." See http:// nanometer.nanologue.net/.

ISSUE 11

Are Genetically Modified Foods Safe to Eat?

YES: Henry I. Miller and Gregory Conko, from "Scary Food," *Policy Review* (June/July 2006)

NO: Jeffrey M. Smith, from "Not in My Fridge!" *Ecologist* (November 2007)

ISSUE SUMMARY

YES: Henry I. Miller and Gregory Conko of the Hoover Institution argue that genetically modified (GM) crops are safer for the consumer and better for the environment than non-GM crops.

NO: Jeffrey M. Smith, director of the Institute for Responsible Technology and the Campaign for Healthier Eating in America, argues that GM foods are dangerous to health and should be removed from the marketplace.

In the early 1970s scientists first discovered that it was technically possible to move genes—biological material that determines a living organism's physical makeup—from one organism to another and thus (in principle) to give bacteria, plants, and animals new features and to correct genetic defects of the sort that cause many diseases, such as cystic fibrosis. Most researchers in molecular genetics were excited by the potentialities that suddenly seemed within their grasp. However, a few researchers—as well as many people outside the field—were disturbed by the idea; they thought that genetic mix-and-match games might spawn new diseases, weeds, and pests. Some people even argued that genetic engineering should be banned at the outset, before unforeseeable horrors were unleashed.

Researchers in support of genetic experimentation responded by declaring a moratorium on their own work until suitable safeguards could be devised. Once those safeguards were in place in the form of government regulations, work resumed. James D. Watson and John Tooze document the early years of this research in *The DNA Story: A Documentary History of Gene Cloning* (W. H. Freeman, 1981). For a shorter, more recent review of the story, see Bernard D. Davis, "Genetic Engineering: The Making of Monsters?" *The Public Interest* (Winter 1993).

By 1989 the technology had developed tremendously: researchers could obtain patents for mice with artificially added genes ("transgenic" mice); firefly genes had been added to tobacco plants to make them glow (faintly) in the dark; and growth hormone produced by genetically engineered bacteria was being used to grow low-fat pork and increase milk production by cows. Critics argued that genetic engineering was unnatural and violated the rights of both plants and animals to their "species integrity"; that expensive, high-tech, tinkered animals gave the competitive advantage to big agricultural corporations and drove small farmers out of business; and that putting human genes into animals, plants, or bacteria was downright offensive. See Betsy Hanson and Dorothy Nelkin, "Public Responses to Genetic Engineering," *Society* (November/December 1989).

Thoughts of tinkering with humans themselves have prompted such comments as the following from Richard Hayes, "In the Pipeline: Genetically Modified Humans?" *Multinational Monitor* (January/February 2000): "No one can be sure how the technology will evolve, but a techno-eugenic future appears ever more likely unless an organized citizenry demands such visions be consigned to science fiction dystopias."

Skepticism about the benefits remains, but agricultural genetic engineering has proceeded at a breakneck pace largely because, as Robert Shapiro, CEO of Monsanto Corporation, said in June 1998, it "represents a potentially sustainable solution to the issue of feeding people." Between 1996 and 2005 the area planted with genetically engineered crops jumped from 1.7 million hectares to 90 million hectares.

Many people are not reassured by such data. They see potential problems in nutrition, toxicity, allergies, and ecology. In protest, some people even destroy research labs and test plots of trees, strawberries, and corn. Other people lobby for stringent regulations and even outright bans on the basis of their fears, while others insist that regulation should be based on sound science. See Karen A. Goldman, "Bioengineered Food—Safety and Labeling," *Science* (October 20, 2000), Martin Teitel and Kimberly A. Wilson, *Genetically Engineered Food: Changing the Nature of Nature* (Park Street Press, 2001), and Henry I. Miller and Gregory Conko, "Agricultural Biotechnology: Overregulated and Underappreciated," *Issues in Science and Technology* (Winter 2005).

In the following selections, Henry I. Miller and Gregory Conko of the Hoover Institution argue that genetically modified (GM) crops are safer for the consumer and better for the environment than non-GM crops. People have failed to embrace them because news coverage has been dominated by the outlandish claims and speculations of anti-technology activists. Jeffrey M. Smith, director of the Institute for Responsible Technology and the Campaign for Healthier Eating in America, argues that GM foods are dangerous to health and should be removed from the marketplace.

YES

Henry I. Miller and
Gregory Conko

Scary Food

Like a scene from some Hollywood thriller, a team of U.S. Marshals stormed a warehouse in Irvington, New Jersey, last summer to intercept a shipment of evildoers from Pakistan. The reason you probably haven't heard about the raid is that the objective was not to seize Al Qaeda operatives or white slavers, but $80,000 worth of basmati rice contaminated with weevils, beetles, and insect larvae, making it unfit for human consumption. In regulation-speak, the food was "adulterated," because "it consists in whole or in part of any filthy, putrid, or decomposed substance, or if it is otherwise unfit for food."

Americans take food safety very seriously. Still, many consumers tend to ignore Mother Nature's contaminants while they worry unduly about high technology, such as the advanced technologies that farmers, plant breeders, and food processors use to make our food supply the most affordable, nutritious, varied, and safe in history.

For example, recombinant DNA technology—also known as food biotechnology, gene-splicing, or genetic modification (GM)—is often singled out by critics as posing a risk that new allergens, toxins, or other nasty substances will be introduced into the food supply. And, because of the mainstream media's "if it bleeds, it leads" approach, news coverage of food biotech is dominated by the outlandish claims and speculations of anti-technology activists. This has caused some food companies—including fastfood giant McDonald's and baby-food manufacturers Gerber and Heinz—to forgo superior (and even cost-saving) gene-spliced ingredients in favor of ones the public will find less threatening.

Scientists agree, however, that gene-spliced crops and foods are not only better for the natural environment than conventionally produced food crops, but also safer for consumers. Several varieties now on the market have been modified to resist insect predation and plant diseases, which makes the harvested crop much cleaner and safer. Ironically (and also surprisingly in these litigious times), in their eagerness to avoid biotechnology, some major food companies may knowingly be making their products less safe and wholesome for consumers. This places them in richly deserved legal jeopardy.

From *Policy Review*, 137, June–July 2006, pp. 61–69. Copyright © 2006 by Henry I. Miller and Gregory Conko. Reprinted by permission of the Hoover Institution, Stanford University, and the authors. http://www.policyreview.org.

Don't Trust Mother Nature

Every year, scores of packaged food products are recalled from the American market due to the presence of all-natural contaminants like insect parts, toxic molds, bacteria, and viruses. Because farming takes place out-of-doors and in dirt, such contamination is a fact of life. Fortunately, modern technology has enabled farmers and food processors to minimize the threat from these contaminants.

The historical record of mass food poisoning in Europe offers a cautionary tale. From the ninth to the nineteenth centuries, Europe suffered a succession of epidemics caused by the contamination of rye with ergot, a poisonous fungus. Ergot contains the potent toxin ergotamine, the consumption of which induces hallucinations, bizarre behavior, and violent muscle twitching. These symptoms gave rise at various times to the belief that victims were possessed by evil spirits. Witch-hunting and persecution were commonplace—and the New World was not immune. One leading explanation for the notorious 1691–92 Salem witch trials also relates to ergot contamination. Three young girls suffered violent convulsions, incomprehensible speech, trance-like states, odd skin sensations, and delirious visions in which they supposedly saw the mark of the devil on certain women in the village. The girls lived in a swampy meadow area around Salem; rye was a major staple of their diet; and records indicate that the rye harvest at the time was complicated by rainy and humid conditions, exactly the situation in which ergot would thrive.

Worried villagers feared the girls were under a spell cast by demons, and the girls eventually named three women as witches. The subsequent panic led to the execution of as many as 20 innocent people. Until a University of California graduate student discovered this link, a reasonable explanation had defied historians. But the girls' symptoms are typical of ergot poisoning, and when the supply of infected grain ran out, the delusions and persecution likewise disappeared.

In the twenty-first century, modern technology, aggressive regulations, and a vigorous legal liability system in industrialized countries such as the United States are able to mitigate much of this sort of contamination. Occasionally, though, Americans will succumb to tainted food picked from the woods or a backyard garden. However, elsewhere in the world, particularly in less-developed countries, people are poisoned every day by fungal toxins that contaminate grain. The result is birth defects, cancer, organ failure, and premature death.

About a decade ago, Hispanic women in the Rio Grande Valley of Texas were found to be giving birth to an unusually large number of babies with crippling and lethal neural tube defects (NTDS) such as spina bifida, hydrocephalus, and anencephaly—at a rate approximately six times higher than the national average for non-Hispanic women. The cause remained a mystery until recent research revealed a link between NTDS and consumption of large amounts of unprocessed corn like that found in tortillas and other staples of the Latino diet.

The connection is obscure but fascinating. The culprit is fumonisin, a deadly mycotoxin, or fungal toxin, produced by the mold *Fusarium* and sometimes found in unprocessed corn. When insects attack corn, they open wounds in the plant that provide a perfect breeding ground for *Fusarium*. Once molds get a foothold, poor storage conditions also promote their postharvest growth on grain.

Fumonisin and some other mycotoxins are highly toxic, causing fatal diseases in livestock that eat infected corn and esophageal cancer in humans. Fumonisin also interferes with the cellular uptake of folic acid, a vitamin that is known to reduce the risk of NTDS in developing fetuses. Because fumonisin prevents the folic acid from being absorbed by cells, the toxin can, in effect, induce functional folic acid deficiency—and thereby cause NTDS—even when the diet contains what otherwise would be sufficient amounts of folic acid.

The epidemiological evidence was compelling. At the time that the babies of Hispanic women in the Rio Grande Valley experienced the high rate of neural tube defects, the fumonisin level in corn in that locale was two to three times higher than normal, and the affected women reported much higher dietary consumption of homemade tortillas than in women who were unaffected.

Acutely aware of the danger of mycotoxins, regulatory agencies such as the U.S. Food and Drug Administration and Britain's Food Safety Agency have established recommended maximum fumonisin levels in food and feed products made from corn. Although highly processed cornstarch and corn oil are unlikely to be contaminated with fumonisin, unprocessed corn or lightly processed corn (e.g., cornmeal) can have fumonisin levels that exceed recommended levels.

In 2003, the Food Safety Agency tested six organic cornmeal products and twenty conventional cornmeal products for fumonisin contamination. All six organic cornmeals had elevated levels—from nine to 40 times greater than the recommended levels for human health—and they were voluntarily withdrawn from grocery stores.

A Technical Fix

The conventional way to combat mycotoxins is simply to test unprocessed and processed grains and throw out those found to be contaminated—an approach that is both wasteful and dubious. But modern technology—specifically in the form of gene-splicing—is already attacking the fungal problem at its source. An excellent example is "Bt corn," crafted by splicing into commercial corn varieties a gene from the bacterium *Bacillus thuringiensis*. The "Bt" gene expresses a protein that is toxic to corn-boring insects but is perfectly harmless to birds, fish, and mammals, including humans.

As the Bt corn fends off insect pests, it also reduces the levels of the mold *Fusarium,* thereby reducing the levels of fumonisin. Thus, switching to the gene-spliced, insect-resistant corn for food processing lowers the levels of fumonisin—as well as the concentration of insect parts—likely to be found in the final product. Researchers at Iowa State University and the U.S. Department of Agriculture found that Bt corn reduces the level of fumonisin by as much as 80 percent compared to conventional corn.

Thus, on the basis of both theory and empirical knowledge, there should be potent incentives—legal, commercial, and ethical—to use such gene-spliced grains more widely. One would expect public and private sector advocates of public health to demand that such improved varieties be cultivated and used for food—not unlike requirements for drinking water to be chlorinated and fluoridated. Food producers who wish to offer the safest and best products to their customers—to say nothing of being offered the opportunity to advertise "New and Improved!"—should be competing to get gene-spliced products into the marketplace.

Alas, none of this has come to pass. Activists have mounted intractable opposition to food biotechnology in spite of demonstrated, significant benefits, including reduced use of chemical pesticides, less runoff of chemicals into waterways, greater use of farming practices that prevent soil erosion, higher profits for farmers, and less fungal contamination. Inexplicably, government oversight has also been an obstacle, by subjecting the testing and commercialization of gene-spliced crops to unscientific and draconian regulations that have vastly increased testing and development costs and limited the use and diffusion of food biotechnology.

The result is jeopardy for everyone involved in food production and consumption: Consumers are subjected to avoidable and often undetected health risks, and food producers have placed themselves in legal jeopardy. The first point is obvious, the latter less so, but as described first by Drew Kershen, professor of law at the University of Oklahoma, it makes a fascinating story: Agricultural processors and food companies may face at least two kinds of civil liability for their refusal to purchase and use fungus-resistant, gene-spliced plant varieties, as well as other superior products.

Food for Thought

In 1999 the Gerber foods company succumbed to activist pressure, announcing that its baby food products would no longer contain any gene-spliced ingredients. Indeed, Gerber went farther and promised it would attempt to shift to organic ingredients that are grown without synthetic pesticides or fertilizers. Because corn starch and corn sweeteners are often used in a range of foods, this could mean changing Gerber's entire product line.

But in its attempt to head off a potential public relations problem concerning the use of gene-spliced ingredients, Gerber has actually increased the health risk for its baby consumers—and, thereby, its legal liability. As noted above, not only is gene-spliced corn likely to have lower levels of fumonisin than conventional corn; organic corn is likely to have the highest levels, because it suffers greater insect predation due to less effective pest controls.

If a mother some day discovers that her "Gerber baby" has developed liver or esophageal cancer, she might have a legal case against Gerber. On the child's behalf, a plaintiff's lawyer can allege liability based on mycotoxin contamination in the baby food as the causal agent of the cancer. The contamination would be considered a *manufacturing defect* under product liability law because the baby food did not meet its intended product specifications or level of safety. According to Kershen, Gerber could be found liable "even though all possible care was exercised in the preparation and marketing of the product," simply because the contamination occurred.

The plaintiff's lawyer could also allege a *design defect* in the baby food, because Gerber knew of the existence of a less risky design—namely, the use of gene-spliced varieties that are less prone to *Fusarium* and fumonisin contamination—but deliberately chose not to use it. Instead, Gerber chose to use non-gene-spliced, organic food ingredients, knowing that the foreseeable risks of harm posed by them could have been reduced or avoided by adopting a reasonable alternative design—that is, by using gene-spliced Bt corn, which is known to have a lower risk of mycotoxin contamination.

Gerber might answer this design defect claim by contending that it was only responding to consumer demand, but that alone would not be persuasive. Product liability law subjects defenses in design defect cases to a risk-utility balancing in which consumer expectations are only one of several factors used to determine whether the product design (e.g., the use of only non-gene-spliced ingredients) is reasonably safe. A jury might conclude that whatever consumer demand there may be for non-biotech ingredients does not outweigh Gerber's failure to use a technology that is known to lower the health risks to consumers.

Even if Gerber was able to defend itself from the design defect claim, the company might still be liable because it failed to provide adequate instructions or warnings about the potential risks of non-gene-spliced ingredients. For example, Gerber could label its non-gene-spliced baby food with a statement such as: "This product does not contain gene-spliced ingredients. Consequently, this product has a very slight additional risk of mycotoxin contamination. Mycotoxins can cause serious diseases such as liver and esophageal cancer and birth defects."

Whatever the risk of toxic or carcinogenic fumonisin levels in non-biotech corn may be (probably low in industrialized countries, where food producers generally are cautious about such contamination), a more likely scenario is potential liability for an allergic reaction.

Six percent to 8 percent of children and 1 to 2 percent of adults are allergic to one or another food ingredient, and an estimated 150 Americans die each year from exposure to food allergens. Allergies to peanuts, soybeans, and wheat proteins, for example, are quite common and can be severe. Although only about 1 percent of the population is allergic to peanuts, some individuals are so highly sensitive that exposure causes anaphylactic shock, killing dozens of people every year in North America.

Protecting those with true food allergies is a daunting task. Farmers, food shippers and processors, wholesalers and retailers, and even restaurants must maintain meticulous records and labels and ensure against cross-contamination. Still, in a country where about a billion meals are eaten every day, missteps are inevitable. Dozens of processed food items must be recalled every year due to accidental contamination or inaccurate labeling.

Fortunately, biotechnology researchers are well along in the development of peanuts, soybeans, wheat, and other crops in which the genes coding for allergenic proteins have been silenced or removed. According to University of California, Berkeley, biochemist Bob Buchanan, hypoallergenic varieties of wheat could be ready for commercialization within the decade, and nuts soon thereafter. Once these products are commercially available, agricultural processors and food companies that refuse to use these safer food sources will open themselves to products-liability, design-defect lawsuits.

Property Damage and Personal Injury

Potato farming is a growth industry, primarily due to the vast consumption of french fries at fast-food restaurants. However, growing potatoes is not easy, because they are preyed upon by a wide range of voracious and difficult-to-control pests, such as the Colorado potato beetle, virus-spreading aphids, nematodes, potato blight, and others.

To combat these pests and diseases, potato growers use an assortment of fungicides (to control blight), insecticides (to kill aphids and the Colorado potato beetle), and fumigants (to control soil nematodes). Although some of these chemicals are quite hazardous to farm workers, forgoing them could jeopardize the sustainability and profitability of the entire potato industry. Standard application of synthetic pesticides enhances yields more than 50 percent over organic potato production, which prohibits most synthetic inputs.

Consider a specific example. Many growers use methamidophos, a toxic organophosphate nerve poison, for aphid control. Although methamidophos is an EPA-approved pesticide, the agency is currently reevaluating the use of organophosphates and could ultimately prohibit or greatly restrict the use of this entire class of pesticides. As an alternative to these chemicals, the Monsanto Company developed a potato that contains a gene from the bacterium *Bacillus thuringiensis* (Bt) to control the Colorado potato beetle and another gene to control the potato leaf roll virus spread by the aphids. Monsanto's NewLeaf potato is resistant to these two scourges of potato plants, which allowed growers who adopted it to reduce their use of chemical controls and increase yields.

Farmers who planted NewLeaf became convinced that it was the most environmentally sound and economically efficient way to grow potatoes. But after five years of excellent results it encountered an unexpected snag. Under pressure from anti-biotechnology organizations, McDonald's, Burger King, and other restaurant chains informed their potato suppliers that they would no longer accept gene-spliced potato varieties for their french fries. As a result, potato processors such as J.R. Simplot inserted a nonbiotech-potato clause into their farmer-processor contracts and informed farmers that they would no longer buy gene-spliced potatoes. In spite of its substantial environmental, occupational safety, and economic benefits, NewLeaf became a sort of contractual poison pill and is no longer grown commercially. Talk about market distortions.

Now, let us assume that a farmer who is required by contractual arrangement to plant nonbiotech potatoes sprays his potato crop with methamidophos (the organophosphate nerve poison) and that the pesticide drifts into a nearby stream and onto nearby farm laborers. Thousands of fish die in the stream, and the laborers report to hospital emergency rooms complaining of neurological symptoms.

This hypothetical scenario is, in fact, not at all far-fetched. Fish-kills attributed to pesticide runoff from potato fields are commonplace. In the potato-growing region of Prince Edward Island, Canada, for example, a dozen such incidents occurred in one 13-month period alone, between July 1999 and August 2000. According to the UN's Food and Agriculture Organization, "normal" use of the pesticides parathion and methamidophos is responsible for some 7,500 pesticide poisoning cases in China each year.

In our hypothetical scenario, the state environmental agency might bring an administrative action for civil damages to recover the cost of the fish-kill, and a plaintiff's lawyer could file a class-action suit on behalf of the farm laborers for personal injury damages.

Who's legally responsible? Several possible circumstances could enable the farmer's defense lawyer to shift culpability for the alleged damages to the contracting food processor and to the fast-food restaurants that are the ultimate purchasers of the potatoes. These circumstances include the farmer's having planted Bt potatoes in the recent past; his contractual obligation to the potato processor and its fast-food retail buyers to provide only nonbiotech varieties; and his demonstrated preference for planting gene-spliced, Bt potatoes, were it not for the contractual proscription. If these conditions could be proved, the lawyer defending the farmer could name the contracting processor and the fast-food restaurants as cross-defendants, claiming either contribution in tort law or indemnification in contract law for any damages legally imposed upon the farmer client.

The farmer's defense could be that those companies bear the ultimate responsibility for the damages because they compelled the farmer to engage in higher-risk production practices than he would otherwise have chosen. The companies chose to impose cultivation of a non-gene-spliced variety upon the farmer although knew that in order to avoid severe losses in yield, he would need to use organophosphate pesticides. Thus, the defense could argue that the farmer should have a legal right to pass any damages (arising from contractually imposed production practices) back to the processor and the fast-food chains.

Why Biotech?

Companies that insist upon farmers' using production techniques that involve foreseeable harms to the environment and humans may be—we would argue, *should* be—legally accountable for that decision. If agricultural processors and food companies manage to avoid legal liability for their insistence on nonbiotech crops, they will be "guilty" at least of externalizing their environmental costs onto the farmers, the environment, and society at large.

Food biotechnology provides an effective—and cost-effective—way to prevent many of these injurious scenarios, but instead of being widely encouraged, it is being resisted by self-styled environmental activists and even government officials.

It should not fall to the courts to resolve and reconcile what are essentially scientific and moral issues. However, other components of society—industry, government, and "consumer advocacy" groups—have failed abjectly to fully exploit a superior, life-enhancing, and life-saving technology. Even the biotechnology trade associations have been unhelpful. All are guilty, in varying measures, of sacrificing the public interest to self-interest and of helping to perpetuate a gross public misconception—that food biotechnology is unproven, untested, and unregulated.

If consumers genuinely want a safer, more nutritious, and more varied food supply at a reasonable cost, they need to know where the real threats lie. They must also become better informed, demand public policy that makes sense, and deny fringe anti-technology activists permission to speak for consumers.

Jeffrey M. Smith  **NO**

Not in My Fridge!

It was a bad year for the biotech barons. At a conference in January 1999, the consulting firm Arthur Andersen revealed Monsanto executives' vision of an ideal future—a world in which natural seeds were virtually all extinct and where commercial seeds were genetically modified (GM) and patented. Andersen Consulting then worked backwards from that goal, developing the strategy and tactics to help Monsanto achieve industry dominance in a GM world. At the same meeting another biotech company, apparently with the same aspiration, showed a graph that projected a 95 per cent replacement of all natural seeds by GM varieties in just five years. Within weeks, their ideal future crashed.

By mid-February, Parliament had invited scientist Árpád Pusztai to tell what he knew. Just a few years earlier, in 1996, Pusztai had been given a grant of £1.6 million by the UK government to design a rigorous safety assessment protocol for testing GM foods. In the course of his studies under the auspices of the Rowett Institute in Aberdeen, Pusztai, a pro-GM scientist with a stellar reputation, discovered that the GM potato he was working on caused massive systemic health problems in rats. Virtually every organ in the animals' bodies was affected by eating the GM potato—their brains, livers and testicles were generally smaller, pathological changes in the thymus and spleen were detected and the animals' immune systems were damaged.

Since most GM foods were created using the same process and genetic material, the results raised serious questions about the safety of all GM foods. Pusztai went public in 1998 and paid dearly for his integrity: he lost his job of 35 years, was silenced with threats of lawsuits, his 20-member team was disbanded and the project terminated.

In the same year, the US Food and Drug Administration (FDA) records—44,000 pages of them, kept secret since 1992—revealed that references made by US government scientists to 'unintended negative effects . . . were progressively deleted from drafts of the policy statements (over the protests of Agency scientists)' and that the FDA was under orders from the White House to promote GM crops.

Concern about the safety of GM food was growing. Pusztai's parliamentary invitation forced the Rowett Institute to lift its long-standing gag order. When the scientist finally spoke out about the GM potatoes that had caused such substantial damage to rats, and how the biotech industry had scrambled to protect its reputation by rubbishing his, the press went wild. By week's end they had spewed out 159 'column feet' of text, which, according to one columnist, 'divided society into two warring blocs.' An editorial stated, 'Within a single week the spectre of a food scare has become a full-scale war.'

The resulting overwhelming consumer resistance was too much for the food industry. GM food became a liability and, in April 1999, Unilever publicly committed to removing GM ingredients from its European brands. Within a week, nearly all major food companies followed suit, leaving Monsanto's ideal future in tatters. That rejection by manufacturers has kept nearly all GM foods (other than milk and meat products from GM-fed animals) out of Europe in spite of official approvals of GM varieties by the EU Commission.

But the biotech industry did not roll over. It has steadily pushed its agenda, but more quietly than before. Nearly every natural food crop now has a genetically engineered version produced in a lab somewhere, with at least 172 species grown outdoors in field trials. With pressure from the industry and the US, and in spite of doubts over their impact in terms of health and the environment, the European Commission last year approved new GM crops for cultivation for the first time since the 1999 consumer revolt, and in a vote in June this year, the European Commission allowed accidental GM contamination of organic products at levels up to 0.9 per cent.

Animals Reject GM

Eyewitness reports from farmers and scientists across North America describe how, when given the choice, several varieties of animals—including cows, pigs, deer, elk, raccoons, geese, squirrels, mice and rats—avoid eating GM plants and feed. It's possible the animals instinctively know or sense what we are only just beginning to see.

Lab animals forced to eat GM food showed damage to virtually every system studied. They had stunted growth, bleeding stomachs, abnormal and potentially pre-cancerous cell growth in the intestines, impaired blood cell development, misshapen cell structures in the liver, pancreas and testicles, altered gene expression and cell metabolism, liver and kidney lesions, partially atrophied livers, inflamed kidneys, less developed brains and testicles, enlarged livers, pancreases and intestines, reduced digestive enzymes, higher blood sugar levels, increased death rates, higher offspring mortality and immune system dysfunction.

Reports from the field are similarly alarming. About two dozen US farmers report that GM corn varieties caused thousands of pigs to become sterile. Some also reported sterility among cows and bulls. German farmers link cow deaths to one variety of GM corn, while Filipinos link another variety to deaths among water buffaloes, chickens and horses. When 71 Indian shepherds let their sheep graze on Bt cotton plants after harvest, within five to seven days 25 per cent had died. The 2006 death rate for the region is estimated at 10,000 sheep. This year, more deaths were identified and toxins were also found in Bt cotton fields. Post mortems showed severe irritation and black patches in the intestines and liver of the sheep, as well as enlarged bile ducts. Investigators concluded that preliminary evidence 'strongly suggests the sheep mortality was due to a toxin . . . most probably Bt-toxin.'

Should Humans Be Worried?

The biotech industry argument is that millions have eaten GM foods for years without a problem—but how would it know? There is no surveillance system in place that could identify problems if they did arise. The Canadian government announced in 2002 that it would undertake such monitoring, but abandoned its plans within a year on the grounds that it was too difficult. There are not even human clinical trials. Some GM varieties are approved before any human has ever eaten them.

Soon after GM soya was introduced into the UK, researchers at York Nutritional Laboratory, Yorkshire, reported that allergies to soya had skyrocketed by 50 per cent in a single year. Although no follow-up studies were done, there are many ways in which genetic engineering could be the culprit. Allergic reactions occur when the immune system encounters something it interprets as foreign, different and offensive, and reacts accordingly. All GM foods, by definition, have something foreign and different about them. And several studies show that they provoke reactions.

Although biotech advocates describe genes in terms of Lego, snapping cleanly into place, the process of creating a GM crop can produce massive collateral damage in plant DNA. Native genes can be mutated, deleted or permanently turned on or off, and hundreds may change their levels of protein expression. The result may be an increase in an existing allergen or the production of an entirely new one. Both appear to have happened in GM soya.

Levels of one soya allergen, trypsin inhibitor, were as much as seven times higher in cooked GM soya when compared with a non-GM variety. Another study verified that GM soybeans contain a unique, unexpected protein, not found in controls, that reacts with immunoglobulin E (IgE), the principal antibody involved in allergic reactions. This suggests the potential for dangerous allergic reactions. The same study revealed that one human subject showed a skin-prick immune response to GM soya only, not to natural soya.

In addition, a protein in natural soya cross-reacts with peanut allergies. This means soya may trigger reactions in some people who are allergic to peanuts. This cross-reactivity could theoretically increase in GM varieties. Thus, the doubling of US peanut allergies in the five years immediately after the introduction of GM soya might not be a coincidence.

GM soya also produces an unpredicted side effect in the pancreas of mice—a dramatic reduction in the production of digestive enzymes. If fewer enzymes cause food proteins to break down more slowly, there is more time for allergic reactions to develop. Thus, digestive problems from GM soya might promote allergic reactions to a wide range of proteins, not just to soya.

To make matters worse, the only published human feeding study on GM foods verified that portions of the gene inserted into GM soya transfers into the DNA of human gut bacteria. This means that, years after people stop eating

GM soya, they may still be exposed to its potentially allergenic protein, which is continuously produced inside their intestines.

Monsanto's 'Roundup Ready' GM soya is planted in 89 per cent of US soya acres. A foreign gene from bacteria (with parts of virus and petunia DNA) is inserted, which allows the plant to survive applications of the otherwise deadly Roundup herbicide. Because people aren't usually allergic to a food until they have eaten it several times, we don't know in advance if the protein produced by bacteria, which has never been part of the human food supply, will provoke a reaction.

As a precaution, scientists compare the amino acid sequence of the novel protein with a database of known allergens. If there is a match, according to criteria recommended by the World Health Organization (WHO) and others, the GM crop should either not be commercialised or additional testing should be done. Sections of the protein produced in GM soya are identical to known allergens, but the soybean was introduced before WHO criteria were established, and the recommended additional tests not conducted.

GM corn is also problematic. Rats fed Monsanto's GM corn, for example, were found to have a significant increase in blood ceils related to the immune system. GM potatoes caused the rats' immune system to respond more slowly. And, when produced within GM peas, a harmless protein was transformed into a potentially deadly allergen. The peas and potatoes were not commercialised, but they had passed the superficial tests usually carried out in the approval of most GM crops. Crops that did make it to the market, however, may be triggering immune responses in the unsuspecting population.

Cleaning Up the Food Chain

In 2003, I interviewed GMO campaigners worldwide about their methods and successes, in order to develop a plan for the Institute for Responsible Technology (IRT) that would help remove GMOs from the marketplace. Unlike many other organisations, which are focused on containing GMOs—by limiting the territory of cultivation or preventing new varieties, for instance—IRT's goal is to eliminate the current generation of GM crops, which it believes is unsafe. Intelligent activism from individual consumers and groups could easily accomplish this in as little as 24 months.

The undisputed driver of the GMO doctrine is the United States. The first Bush Administration fast-tracked the GM approval process in 1992, hoping this would increase exports and US dominance of food markets. The opposite ensued, and soon the government was shelling out $3 billion to $5 billion a year in subsidies to prop up prices on the GM crops no-one wanted. Rather than giving up on the unpopular technology, the US tried to force other countries to accept GM, resorting to World Trade Organization (WTO) lawsuits against the European Union, GM food aid for famine-stricken nations, even threats to withdraw funds for AIDS relief if GMOs weren't adopted by African nations.

If GMOs are to implode worldwide, the US must be ground zero.

About 9 out of 10 processed foods in the US contain unlabelled GM ingredients, many produced by the same companies that sell only non-GM products in Europe. Why didn't US consumers react like the Europeans in the wake of the Pusztai scandal? The fact is that the US press did not even mention the story. Project Censored—a group that tracks the news published in independent journals and newsletters and compiles an annual list of stories of social significance that have been overlooked, underreported or self-censored by the major national news media—described it as one of the 10 most underreported events of the year.

Because the US press rarely mentions GM foods at all, if you ask the average American whether he or she has ever eaten a GM food in their life, 60 per cent will so 'no' and 15 per cent will say 'I don't know.' GMOs flourish on the basis of consumer ignorance, but this leaves the biotech industry extremely vulnerable. If some campaign or event were to push this issue above the national radar screen, causing sufficient consumer concern, US manufacturers would respond like their European counterparts and swear off GMOs.

The Power of the Market

The tipping point to trigger a non-GMO food revolution in the US does not require that a majority of shoppers reject GM foods—if even a small percentage started switching brands based on GMO content, major companies would spot the trend, see a loss in market share and respond. This is facilitated by the fact that manufacturers gain no benefits from GM ingredients; requesting their removal is not like asking them to take out sugar or fat. GMOs do not make a product tastier, healthier or more appealing.

Even five per cent of the US population—15 million people or 5.6 million households—making brand choices based on GM content may be more than the critical mass needed to force change. With little exaggeration, Oprah Winfrey could end the genetic engineering of the food supply in 60 minutes. A popular film such as a GMO version of *An Inconvenient Truth* might accomplish it as well.

Even if these things are not forthcoming, however, there are several subgroups within the US that are large enough and receptive enough to drive a transformation. Chief among these are health-conscious shoppers, and they are already being rallied to the cause.

Currently, 28 million Americans buy organic products on a regular basis. Another 54 million are considered 'temperate' organic shoppers. Together they account for approximately 27 per cent of the population. According to a December 2006 poll, 29 per cent of Americans (probably many of the organic buyers) are strongly opposed to GM foods and believe they are unsafe. But most do not conscientiously avoid GM ingredients in their non-organic purchases; they usually don't know how. That's about to change.

In spring 2007, a coalition of food manufacturers, distributors and retailers in the natural products industry, along with the IRT, launched an initiative to remove GM ingredients from the entire natural food sector. This comprehensive initiative—called the Campaign for Healthier Eating in America . . .—will educate consumers about the health risks of GM foods and promote non-GMO brands through in-store non-GMO shopping guides. Within approximately 18–24 months, it is expected that nearly all the food brands sold in natural food markets will have achieved non-GMO status. At that point the campaign will provide in-store, on-shelf labels for retailers to indicate to consumers any of the few remaining holdout products that still 'May contain GM ingredients'.

Shopper education will be provided through GMO-education centres in natural food stores nationwide, as well as regular features on websites and in magazines and newsletters. By providing health-conscious shoppers with information showing that 'Healthy Eating Means No GMOs', and by offering clear choices in the store, brands that do not contain GM ingredients will have the clear advantage.

The mechanics of the sector-wide cleanout is being orchestrated by an organisation called The Non-GMO Project . . . , which is establishing a uniform standard for defining non-GMO and a low-cost, online, third-party verification programme to ensure that farming and production methods meet that standard. The membership of their board of directors illustrates the far-reaching support for this unprecedented initiative in self-regulation. It includes executives from the multi-billion-dollar Whole Foods Market and United Natural Foods, as well as industry leaders such as Eden Foods, Lundberg Family Farms, Organic Valley and Nature's Path.

Organic products are included in this programme: they are not allowed to use GMOs and have been an important oasis for non-GMO shoppers—and yet research shows that some batches of organic seed and crops contain tiny amounts of GM contamination. If unchecked, this can grow over time. By including the organic sector in the campaign, organic producers will use GMO testing methods and procedures that will help clean up seeds and crops and ensure that certified organic foods continue to be a trusted source of non-GMO products. Unlike the recently enacted EU threshold for allowable 'adventitious' contamination of organic products by as much as 0.9 per cent, the standard for non-GMO claims will take into consideration current levels of purity and will in all likelihood require progressively cleaner levels in subsequent years, based on successful efforts to remove GMO contamination.

This initiative, which is akin to an immune response to GMOs by the natural food industry, could easily set the stage for the elimination of GM ingredients throughout the conventional foods industry as well.

Mobilising Support

Health-conscious individuals and groups outside the food industry also have a major role to play in cleaning up the food chain. Parents with young children, for example, are the ones most likely to switch to a healthier diet—for the sake of the children. Such care is warranted, as young, fast-growing bodies are more at risk from potential toxins, allergens and nutritional problems—all three of which are associated with GMOs.

With the epidemics of obesity and diabetes, as well as the increased medication of children for ADHD and depression, the focus on their diets, both at home and at school, is now 'on fire' in the US and elsewhere. Adding compelling information about the impact of GM foods on children's health can leverage the media coverage, community organising, and school-meal reorganisation already taking place. In the US this is the role of the GM-Free Schools campaign . . . , which is active in several states.

On the basis of potential adverse health effects, several healthcare organisations in the US are now providing educational materials to healthcare providers in order to help patients follow the prescription to avoid GM foods. Many religious organisations, too, have denounced GM foods on the basis that such mixing of species is against natural law. They equate the concept of 'GMO' with 'God, Move Over'. Large religious organisations have not yet asked their membership to avoid buying and eating GM foods, however. With the ability to activate millions, religions are the sleeping giants in this debate.

On their own, action by any of these groups is capable of forcing the hand of the US food industry. When company executives learn that a major religion is instructing millions of its followers to avoid their brand, that doctors are prescribing the same, that parents believe the company's foods can hurt children or that millions of trend-setting health-conscious shoppers shun their products, the end is near for GM foods. Over the next two years, through these education-based strategies, the IRT expects the synergy of information and activism to take effect.

A key advantage of addressing the problem of GM food in this way is that it does not rely on governments to step in; it places the mantle of leadership on consumers who are, after all, at the top of our food chain. By making healthier choices for themselves and for their families, they can quite quickly, and quite literally, change the world.

GM-Free Zones?

The advancement of GMOs in Europe and elsewhere has not been without protests. Indeed, the stream of GM crops approved for import have consistently been rejected by the majority of member states. Poland, Greece, northern Austria and, as of June, Ireland are seeking to enforce a ban against planting GM crops, but the European Commission has branded these GM-free zones illegal. Brazil, which grows GM soya, may be introducing corn and cotton starting this year, but approvals are being challenged in the court. Australian states' moratoria on GM crops will expire in 2008 and there is a pitched battle over possible renewals. GM cotton has gained a foothold in India, but thousands of farmer suicides linked to poor crop performance, as well as animal deaths and allergic reactions among cotton workers, are fuelling resistance there. And looming large on the horizon are GM biofuels, the new poster child of the industry, which hopes that biotechnology will be embraced as a solution for global warming.

Decisions being made in Europe and around the world at this time are critical, and will help decide whether the biotech industry can reincarnate its genetically engineered future. The industry paints the picture that agricultural biotechnology is a 'done deal' that must coexist with natural varieties, but this is not the case. GM can be stopped. Given the substantial evidence for adverse health effects and the difficulties of containing GM contamination in the wild, ending the genetic engineering of the food supply appears easier than managing it. . . .

POSTSCRIPT

Are Genetically Modified Foods Safe to Eat?

At first, most of the attention aimed at genetic engineering focused first on its use to modify bacteria and other organisms to generate drugs needed to fight human disease, and second on its potential to modify human genes and attack hereditary diseases at their roots. See Eric B. Kmiec, "Gene Therapy," *American Scientist* (May–June 1999).

Despite some successes, gene therapy has not yet become a multimillion-dollar industry. Pharmaceutical applications of genetic engineering have been much more successful. According to Brian Halweil, in "The Emperor's New Crops," *World Watch* (July/August 1999), so have agricultural applications. Halweil is skeptical, saying that genetically modified foods have potential benefits but that they may also have disastrous effects on natural ecosystems and—because high-tech agriculture is controlled by major corporations such as Monsanto—on less-developed societies. He argues that "ecological" agriculture (e.g., using organic fertilizers and natural enemies instead of pesticides) offers much more hope for the future. Similar arguments are made by those who demonstrate against genetically modified foods and lobby for stringent labeling requirements or for outright bans on planting and importing these crops. See Capulalpum, "Risking Corn, Risking Culture," *World Watch* (November–December 2002). Many protestors argue against GM technology in terms of the precautionary principle; see "GMOs and Precaution in EU Countries," *Outlook on Science Policy* (September 2005).

Many researchers see more hope in genetically modified foods. In July 2000, for example, the Royal Society of London, the U.S. National Academy of Sciences, the Brazilian Academy of Sciences, the Chinese Academy of Sciences, the Indian Academy of Sciences, the Mexican Academy of Sciences, and the Third World Academy of Sciences issued a joint report entitled "Transgenic Plants and World Agriculture" (available at http://www.royalsoc.ac.uk/document.asp?tip=1&id=1448). This report stresses that during the twenty-first century, both population and the need for food are going to increase dramatically, especially in developing nations. According to the report, "Foods can be produced through the use of GM [genetic modification] technology that are more nutritious, stable in storage and in principle, health promoting. . . . New public sector efforts are required for creating transgenic crops that benefit poor farmers in developing nations and improve their access to food. . . . Concerted, organised efforts must be undertaken to investigate the potential environmental effects, both positive and negative, of GM technologies [compared to those] from conventional agricultural technologies. . . . Public health regulatory systems need to be put in place in every country to identify and monitor any potential adverse human health effects."

The worries surrounding genetically modified foods and the scientific evidence to support them are summarized by Kathryn Brown, in "Seeds of Concern," and Karen Hopkin, in "The Risks on the Table," both in *Scientific American* (April 2001). In the same issue, Sasha Nemecek poses the question "Does the World Need GM Foods?" to two prominent figures in the debate: Robert B. Horsch, a Monsanto vice president and recipient of the 1998 National Medal of Technology for his work on modifying plant genes, who says yes, and Margaret Mellon, of the Union of Concerned Scientists, who says no, adding that much more work needs to be done on safety. Jeffrey M. Smith, *Seeds of Deception: Exposing Industry and Government Lies about the Safety of the Genetically Engineered Foods You're Eating* (Chelsea Green, 2003), argues that the dangers of GM foods have been deliberately concealed. Henry I. Miller and Gregory Conko, in *The Frankenfood Myth: How Protest and Politics Threaten the Biotech Revolution* (Praeger, 2004), address at length the fallacy that GM foods are especially risky. Rod Addy and Elaine Watson, "Forget 'Frankenfood', GM Crops Can Feed the World, Says FDF," *Food Manufacture* (December 2007), note that "EU trade commissioner Peter Mandelson said that the inability of European politicians to engage in a rational debate about GM was a source of constant frustration. They were also creating barriers to trade by banning GM crops that had repeatedly been pronounced safe by the European Food Safety Authority." Mac Margolis et al., "Beakers to the Rescue," *Newsweek* (May 19, 2008), is also optimistic about the potential of GM foods to help feed the world. Maywa Montenegro, "Green Revolution 2.0," *Seed* (July/August 2008), argues that the world's food shortages of 2008 indicate that the limits of agriculture to meet needs for food and biofuels are being strained and that genetic engineering holds the seeds of a solution (though not in its current corporate form). Richard Stone, "China Plans $3.5 Billion GM Crops Initiative," *Science* (September 5, 2008), notes that "with questions mounting about China's ability to feed itself . . . not pushing ahead with GM varieties could be more detrimental than any theoretical hazard."

Harihara M. Mehendale, "Genetically Modified Foods: Why the Public Frenzy? Role of Mainstream News Media," *International Journal of Toxicology* (September 2004), blames "the role of the press in spreading misleading facts related to the technology." Robert Falkner, "The Global Biotech Food Fight: Why the United States Got It So Wrong," *Brown Journal of World Affairs* (Fall/Winter 2007), says that food safety fears are a major driver for the antibiotech movement and the government's insistence that a separate regulatory approach is not needed has strengthened "the perception that biotech food is being forced upon reluctant societies."

Is the issue safety? Human welfare? Or economics? When genetically modified corn and other foods were offered as relief supplies to African nations threatened by famine, some accepted the aid. Others, pressured by European activists, turned it down. Robert L. Paarlberg discusses what the U.S. can do to counter resistance to GM foods in "Reinvigorating Genetically Modified Crops," *Issues in Science and Technology* (Spring 2003); he favors addressing the needs of developing countries.

And is the issue only genetically modified food? The July/August 2002 issue of *World Watch* magazine bore the overall title of "Beyond Cloning: The Risks of Rushing into Human Genetic Engineering." The editorial says that human genetic engineering poses "profound medical and social risks." Contributors object to it as unnatural, commercial, a violation of human integrity, potentially racist, and more. Francis Fukuyama, "In Defense of Nature, Human and Non-Human," says, "Anyone who feels strongly about defending non-human nature from technological manipulation should feel equally strongly about defending human nature as well. . . . Nature—both the natural environment around us, and our own—deserves an approach based on respect and stewardship, not domination and mastery."

Internet References . . .

National Aeronautics and Space Administration

At this site, you can find out the latest information on the International Space Shuttle, space exploration, and other space-related news.

http://www.nasa.gov

SETI Institute

The SETI Institute serves as a home for scientific research in the general field of life in the universe, with an emphasis on the search for extraterrestrial intelligence (SETI).

http://www.seti.org

Close Approaches

NASA's Near Earth Object Program lists past and future close approaches to Earth.

http://neo.jpl.nasa.gov/ca/

Near Earth Objects

The Near Earth Object Dynamic Site (NEODyS) provides information on all near earth asteroids (NEAs). Each NEA has its own dynamically generated home page. Note the Risk Page, which presents information on the likelihood of impacts with Earth.

http://newton.dm.unipi.it/neodys/

Space

Many interesting controversies arise in connection with technologies that are so new that they may sound more like science fiction than fact. Some examples are technologies that allow the exploration of space, the detection (and perhaps prevention) of space-based threats, and the search for extraterrestrial intelligence. We have capabilities undreamed of in earlier ages, and they raise genuine, important questions about what it is to be a human being, the limits on human freedom in a technological age, the degree to which humans are helpless victims of fate, and the place of humanity in the broader universe. They also raise questions of how we should respond: Should we accept the new devices and abilities offered by scientists and engineers? Or should we reject them? Should we use them to make human life safer and more secure? Or should we remain, as in past ages, at the mercy of the heavens?

- Is NASA Doing Enough to Protect the Earth from Asteroid and Comet Impacts?
- Will the Search for Extraterrestrial Life Ever Succeed?
- Is "Manned Space Travel" a Delusion?

ISSUE 12

Is NASA Doing Enough to Protect the Earth from Asteroid and Comet Impacts?

YES: J. Anthony Tyson, from "Near-Earth Objects (NEOs)—Status of the Survey Program and Review of NASA's Report to Congress," Testimony before the House Committee on Science and Technology, Subcommittee on Space and Aeronautics (November 8, 2007)

NO: Russell L. Schweickart, from "Near-Earth Objects (NEOs)—Status of the Survey Program and Review of NASA's Report to Congress," Testimony before the House Committee on Science and Technology, Subcommittee on Space and Aeronautics (November 8, 2007)

ISSUE SUMMARY

YES: Physics professor J. Anthony Tyson argues that NASA can fulfill its congressionally mandated mission of surveying near-Earth objects (NEOs) that may pose future hazards to Earth by funding the proposed Large Synoptic Survey Telescope (LSST) project.

NO: Russell L. Schweickart, chairman of the B612 Foundation, argues that NASA should do much more than just survey and catalog NEOs. Not only should it mount a more aggressive survey effort, but it should also accept the job of protecting the Earth from NEO impacts as a public safety responsibility.

Thomas Jefferson once said that he would rather think scientists were crazy than believe that rocks could fall from the sky. Since then, we have recognized that rocks do indeed fall from the sky. Most are quite small and do no more than make pretty streaks across the sky as they burn up in the atmosphere; they are known as meteors. Some—known as meteorites—are large enough to reach the ground and even to do damage. Every once in a while, the news reports one that crashed through a car or house roof, as indeed one did in January 2007 in New Jersey. Very rarely, a meteorite is big enough to make a crater in the Earth's surface, much like the ones that mark the face of the Moon. An example is Meteor Crater in Arizona, almost a mile across, created some 50,000 years ago by a meteorite 150 feet in diameter. (The Meteor

Crater Web site, http://www.meteorcrater.com/, includes an animation of the impact.) A more impressive impact is the one that occurred 65 million years ago; the scar has been found at Chicxulub, Mexico: The results included the extinction of the dinosaurs (as well as a great many other species). Chicxulub-scale events are very rare; a hundred million years may pass between them. Meteor Crater–scale events may occur every thousand years, releasing as much energy as a 100-megaton nuclear bomb and destroying an area the size of a city. And it has been calculated that a human being is more likely to die as the result of such an event than in an airplane crash.

It's not just Hollywood sci-fi, *Deep Impact* and *Armageddon*. Some people think we really should be worried. We should be doing our best to identify meteoroids (as they are called before they become meteors or meteorites) in space, plot their trajectories, tell when they are coming our way, and even develop ways of deflecting them before they cause enormous loss of life. In 1984, Thomas Gehrels, a University of Arizona astronomer, initiated the Spacewatch project, which aimed to identify space rocks that cross Earth's orbit. In the early 1990s, NASA workshops considered the hazards of these rocks. NASA now funds the international Space-guard Survey, which finds about 25 new near-Earth Asteroids every month, and has identified more than 600 over 1 kilometer in diameter (1,000 meters; 1.6 km equals 1 mile); none seem likely to strike Earth in the next century. See Peter Tyson, "Comet Busters," *Technology Review* (February/March 1995), Duncan Steel, *Target Earth: How Rogue Asteroids and Doomsday Comets Threaten Our Planet* (Reader's Digest Association, 2000), David Morrison, "Target Earth," *Astronomy* (February 2002), and David Morrison, "Asteroid and Comet Impacts: The Ultimate Environmental Catastrophe," *Philosophical Transactions: Mathematical, Physical & Engineering Sciences* (August 2006). However, the news periodically issues alarming reports. In 2004, the 130-foot wide asteroid 99942 Apophis looked for a time as if it would strike Earth in 2029 with the equivalent of a 10,000 megaton nuclear bomb. Improved data pushed the date of impact off to 2036. Still more data reduced the probability of an impact in that year to 1 in 45,000. This might seem reassuring, but there are many other large rocks in space, and eventual large impacts on Earth are very likely. David Noland, "The Threat Is Out There," *Popular Mechanics* (December 2006), reviews the story and covers what we might do if this (or another) asteroid takes a closer swing at us. Greg Easterbrook, "The Sky Is Falling," *Atlantic* (June 2008), argues that human society faces so much risk from asteroid and comet impacts that Congress should place a much higher priority on detecting potential impactors and devising ways to stop them.

In the following selections, physics professor J. Anthony Tyson argues that NASA can fulfill its congressionally mandated mission of surveying near-Earth objects (NEOs) that may pose future hazards to Earth by funding the proposed Large Synoptic Survey Telescope (LSST) project (http://www.lsst.org/lsst_home.shtml). Russell L. Schweickart, chairman of the B612 Foundation, whose goal is "to significantly alter the orbit of an asteroid, in a controlled manner, by 2015," argues that NASA should do much more than just survey and catalog NEOs. Not only should it mount a more aggressive survey effort, but it should also accept the job of protecting the Earth from NEO impacts as a public safety responsibility. This must involve ways of deflecting NEOs from Earth-bound paths.

YES

J. Anthony Tyson

Near-Earth Objects (NEOs)—Status of the Survey Program and Review of NASA's Report to Congress

. . . The House Committee on Science has been a leader on a bipartisan basis for over two decades in focusing attention on the need to detect, characterize, and catalog near-Earth asteroids. The passage of the "George E. Brown Jr. Near Earth Object Survey Act" was a landmark piece of legislation that sets a goal of cataloging 90% of NEOs of 140 meters in diameter and larger within 15 years. The Committee is properly looking at the existing and future capabilities for carrying out this goal and expanding the existing Spaceguard program. [The Large Synoptic Survey Telescope] (LSST) adopted the goal of surveying NEOs at the outset as one of its major science capabilities.

Until recently, the discussion of risk associated with an impact of a NEO has been statistical; what is the probability? This is similar to considerations of risk in many other areas such as weather and traffic accidents. What if it were feasible to deploy a system that would alert me of an impending traffic accident well in advance? That would change the very nature of that risk from a probabilistic worry to a deterministic actionable situation. The ability to detect virtually every potentially hazardous near-Earth object and determine its orbit with precision transforms that statistical threat into a deterministic prediction. We face many threats, and virtually all of them are either so complex or unpredictable that they are treated probabilistically even though the social and financial consequences are legion. With a comparatively small investment the NEO risk can be transformed from a probabilistic one to a deterministic one, enabling mitigation.

The First Job: Finding the NEOs

Ground-based optical surveys are the most efficient tool for comprehensive NEO detection, determination of their orbits and subsequent tracking. (Radar also plays an important role once a threatening NEO has been found, in refining its orbit when the NEO is near.) The first job is to find the NEOs which are potentially hazardous (so-called Potentially Hazardous Asteroids) from among the swarm of ten million other asteroids. A survey capable of extending these tasks to NEOs with diameters as small as 140 m, as mandated by Congress, requires a large telescope, a large camera, and a sophisticated data acquisition,

From U.S. House of Representatives, November 8, 2007.

processing and dissemination system. The Congressional mandate drives the requirement for an 8-meter class telescope with a 3000 Megapixel camera and a sophisticated and robust data processing system. These requirements are met by the LSST.

Why is a large telescope required? A typical 140-meter NEO appears very faint (visual magnitude of 25). Multiple NEO detections in a single night are required to estimate its motion, so that its future or past detections can be linked together. This linkage has to be done exceedingly robustly because the near-Earth objects will be outnumbered nearly a thousand to one by main-belt asteroids (between Mars and Jupiter) which present no threat to Earth. By reliably linking detections on multiple nights, the NEO's orbit can be reconstructed and used to compute its impact probability with Earth. Despite their name, NEOs are typically found far from Earth. In principle, very faint objects can be detected using long exposures, but for objects moving as fast as typical NEOs, the so-called trailing losses limit the exposure time to about 30 seconds. In order to detect 140-meter NEOs in 30 seconds, an 8-meter class telescope is required.

Why is a large camera required? The need for a very large field of view comes from the requirement that the whole observable sky should be observed at least every four to five nights. For comparison, we need a field of view thousands of times larger than the Hubble Space Telescope's Advanced Camera for Surveys. With its 10 square degree field of view, LSST will be able to reach the mandated high NEO completeness.

Finding Near-Earth Objects with Ground-based Surveys

Ground-based optical surveys are a very cost-effective tool for comprehensive NEO detection, determination of orbits, and subsequent tracking. A survey capable of extending these tasks to NEOs with diameters as small as 140 m, as mandated by Congress, drives the requirement for a large telescope, a large camera, and a sophisticated data acquisition, processing and dissemination system.

To find a significant fraction of the faint NEOs one must essentially make a movie of the deep sky. Each faint asteroid must be captured in many separate exposures in order for computers to distinguish it from the numerous other asteroids and then piece together its orbit. A large area of the sky (ideally all the sky visible from some location on Earth, at least 20,000 square degrees) must be surveyed rapidly and deeply in order to survey a large volume for these faint asteroids. The ability of a telescope and camera to take rapid deep repeated images of the entire sky is proportional to its "throughput." Throughput (sometimes called etendue) is simply the product of the telescope light collection area (units: square meters) times the camera field of view in a single snapshot (units: square degrees). Thus throughput of a survey facility is measured in units of square meters square degrees. The throughput of LSST is 320 square meters square degrees. High throughput is a necessary condition for such a facility to carry out its mission, but not a sufficient condition: one must also arrange to have high observing efficiency (access to the sky) and highly efficient optics and imaging detectors in the camera, as well as superb image quality.

For an efficient NEO survey, the whole observable sky should be observed at least every four to five nights, with multiple observations per night. In order to do so with exposure time of about 30 seconds per observation, a 10 square degree large field of view is required. Such a large field of view, with pixel size sufficiently small to fully sample the image at a good observing site, implies a multi-billion pixel camera. Indeed, at the time of its completion, the 3.2 billion pixel LSST camera will be the largest astronomical camera in the world.

With a 3.2 billion pixel camera obtaining images every 15 seconds (individual 30 second exposures are split into two 15 second exposures for technical reasons), the data rate will be about 20 thousand gigabytes per night. Not only is this a huge data rate, but the data have to be processed and disseminated in real time, and with exquisite accuracy. It is estimated that the LSST data system will incorporate several million lines of state-of-the-art custom computer code.

State of the LSST Project

The Large Synoptic Survey Telescope (LSST) is currently by far the most ambitious proposed survey of the sky. With initial funding from the US National Science Foundation (NSF), Department of Energy (DOE) laboratories and private sponsors, the design and development efforts are well underway at many institutions, including top universities and leading national laboratories. The main science themes that drive the LSST system design are Dark Energy and Dark Matter, the Solar System Inventory, Transient Optical Sky and the Milky Way Mapping. It is this diverse array of science goals that has generated the widespread excitement of scientists ranging from high-energy physicists to astronomers and planetary scientists, and earned LSST the endorsement of a number of committees commissioned by the National Academy of Sciences.

Fortunately, the same hardware and software requirements are driven by science unrelated to NEOs: LSST reaches the threshold where different science drivers and different agencies (NSF, DOE and NASA) can work together to efficiently achieve seemingly disjoint, but deeply connected, goals. Because of this synergy the Congressional mandate can be reached at only a fraction of the cost of a mission dedicated exclusively to NEO search.

The scientific priority for constructing a large aperture ground based survey telescope was recommended in the astronomy and astrophysics Decadal Survey 2000 report entitled Astronomy and Astrophysics in the New Millennium. Since then, LSST has reached a high state of design maturity. LSST has recently passed the NSF Conceptual Design Review for construction, which puts it on track for transition to Readiness in spring 2008. LSST is a public–private project. To date $44M in private funding has been raised. Twenty-two institutions have joined the effort and have contributed significant in-kind technical labor. LSST R&D continues for another 3 years under NSF support along with in-kind contributions. The project is on track for first light in 2014. It is proposed that the DOE (because of the importance of LSST for addressing the mystery of dark energy) support the $80M cost of constructing the camera. Foreign support now appears likely, and this in-kind would offset the camera cost.

Method of Study: The LSST Operations Simulator

The LSST Operations Simulator was developed to be able to do just the sort of assessment described in this document. It contains detailed models of site conditions, hardware and software performance, and an algorithm for scheduling observations which will, eventually, drive the robotic LSST observatory. . . .

For the currently planned LSST baseline cadence, objects counted as cataloged are observed on 20 different nights on average. A more stringent requirement could decrease the completeness by up to 3%. The completeness is also a function of the assumed size distribution: the flatter the distribution, the higher the completeness. If the latest results for the NEO size distribution by A. Harris are taken into account, the completeness increases by 1–2%. Due to these issues, the completeness estimates have a systematic uncertainty of 2%. Our analysis assumes that no NEOs are known prior to LSST. Current surveys make a negligible contribution to the 90% completeness for NEOs of 140 m and up.

The NEO Survey Completeness Achievable with LSST

The LSST system is the only proposed astronomical facility that can detect 140-meter objects in the main asteroid belt in less than a minute. The LSST system will be sited at Cerro Pachon in northern Chile, with first light scheduled for 2014. In a continuous observing campaign, LSST will cover the entire available sky every four nights, with at least two observations of an NEO per night. Over the baseline survey lifetime of 10 years, each sky location would be observed over 800 times. Two NEO detections in a single night are required to estimate its motion, so that its future or past detections can be linked together. This linkage has to be done exceedingly robustly because the near-Earth objects will be outnumbered a hundred to one by main-belt asteroids which present no threat to Earth. By reliably linking detections on multiple nights, the NEO's orbit can be reconstructed and used to compute its impact probability with Earth.

The currently planned LSST baseline observing cadence on the sky, described in the Major Research Equipment and Facilities Construction proposal submitted to NSF, is simultaneously optimized for all four main science drivers: Characterizing Dark Energy and Dark Matter, the Solar System Inventory, Transient Optical Sky, and the Milky Way Mapping. Computer simulations of LSST observing show that the data stream resulting from this baseline cadence on the sky is capable of providing orbits for 82% of Potentially Hazardous

Asteroids (PHA) larger than 140 meters after 10 years of operations. . . . This baseline cadence spends 5% of the total observing time on NEO-optimized observations in the north region of the ecliptic (plane of the solar system).

Various adjustments to this baseline cadence can boost the completeness for 140 m and larger PHAs to 90%. Based on about 100 different simulations, we find that such adjustments to the baseline cadence or filter choices can have unacceptably large impact on other science programs, if the 90% completeness is to be reached within 10 years from the beginning of the survey. However, with a minor adjustment of the baseline cadence and additional specialized observing for NEOs, this completeness level can be reached with a 12-year long survey, and with a negligible effect on the rest of science goals.

These specialized observations would be of limited use to other science programs, and they require 15% of the observing time. . . .

Conclusions

The ability of LSST to reach the mandated 90% completeness for 140 m and larger PHAs in 10 years by the so-called "dedicated" option described in the 2007 NASA NEO report is supported by our detailed and realistic simulations. An important additional insight from these simulations is that we can deliver the performance of a "dedicated" system by spending 85% of the total observing time on a general survey useful for all LSST science programs, and by specializing only about 15% of the total observing time for NEO surveying. If such an NEO-optimized program is executed for 12 years, the 90% completeness for 140 m and larger PHAs can be reached without a significant negative impact on other science programs.

The current cost estimate for LSST in 2006 dollars is $389M for construction and $37M per year for operations. For a 12-year long survey, 15% of the total cost is $125M. Thus, we could deliver the performance of a full NEO-dedicated LSST to NASA at a small fraction of the total cost to build and operate such a system. This cost is equivalent to 30% of operations, which would commence in 2014. To assure LSST keeps on schedule, about $5M should be spent on optimized NEO orbit software pipeline development in the last phase of R&D and the construction phase, 2009–2014.

Executive Summary

In December 2005 Congress directed NASA to implement a near-Earth object (NEO) survey that would catalog 90% of NEOs larger than 140 meters in 15 years. In order to fulfill the Congressional mandate using a ground-based facility, an 8-meter class telescope equipped with a 3200 Megapixel camera, and a sophisticated and robust data processing system are required. These criteria are met by the Large Synoptic Survey Telescope (LSST). We have carried out over 100 simulations of the LSST operations for a variety of NEO-optimized scenarios. The planned LSST baseline survey cadence on the sky, simultaneously optimized for all main science drivers, is capable of providing orbits for 82% of PHAs larger than 140 meters after 10 years of operation, and is 90%

complete for objects larger than 230 meters. This baseline cadence assumes that 5% of the total observing time is spent on NEO-specialized observing. This is what is currently planned. By increasing this fraction to 15% and by running the survey longer, the Congressional mandate of 90% completeness for NEOs of 140 m and greater size can be fulfilled after 12 years of operation, with 60% completeness level reached after only 3 years.

Note that by operating LSST in this special NEO-enhanced mode we would have the performance equivalent of an LSST fully dedicated to NEO surveying. By supporting only 15% of the total cost, NASA would be essentially getting a NEO-dedicated LSST. This is a key new insight relative to the costing model in the 2007 NASA NEO report to Congress.

Russell L. Schweickart  **NO**

Near-Earth Objects (NEOs)—Status of the Survey Program and Review of NASA's Report to Congress

. . . The impact of near-Earth objects with the Earth is properly described as a cosmic natural hazard of potentially unprecedented dimension, threatening both life and property. Unlike other natural hazards, however, we can in this instance, using current space technology, both predict and prevent the occurrence of such a disaster.

No other natural hazard presents such a wide range of potential destruction, but in no other case are we fortunate enough to have at hand the advanced technology and creative imagination to mitigate such a catastrophic event. The range of explosive impacts we may be called on to prevent extend from the "Tunguska Event" of 1908, approximately a 5 megaton (MT) explosion over Siberia (equivalent to over 300 Hiroshima bombs) up to impacts 100,000 times larger—large enough to destroy civilization and threaten the survival of humanity. We intend to prevent such infrequent but devastating events by slightly and precisely modifying the orbit of a threatening NEO, causing it to pass harmlessly by the Earth. Stated differently, we intend, using available space technology, to slightly alter the workings of the solar system in order to enhance human survival on planet Earth.

To realize such a bold claim we must put in place three critical components of a response system. They are: advanced notice (i.e. an early warning system), a demonstrated deflection capability, and a standing decision process to enable timely action.

The Congress, NASA, and other key global players are to be congratulated for their excellent work in implementing the first phase of the early warning system, the Spaceguard Survey, which has been in operation since 1998. The Congress is to be further commended for its vision in mandating that NASA take the next critical steps as expressed in the George E. Brown, Jr. Near-Earth Object Survey Act of 2005 (the Act). The Act extends the Spaceguard Survey goal, directing NASA to "detect, track, catalogue, and characterize . . . near-Earth objects equal to or greater than 140 meters in diameter . . ." and to "achieve 90 percent completion of [the survey] within 15 years after the date of enactment of this Act."

From U.S. House of Representatives, November 8, 2008.

The Congress also directed that "The Administrator shall transmit to Congress not later than 1 year after the date of enactment of this Act an initial report that provides the following:

(A) An analysis of possible alternatives that NASA may employ to carry out the Survey program, including groundbased and space-based alternatives with technical descriptions.
(B) A recommended option and proposed budget to carry out the Survey program pursuant to the recommended option.
(C) Analysis of possible alternatives that NASA could employ to divert an object on a likely collision course with Earth."

It is NASA's mixed response to these three directives which prompts my testimony here today.

I have been specifically requested to address the following four questions;

1. What are your perspectives on NASA's *Near-Earth Object Survey and Deflection Analysis of Alternatives* Report to Congress? Do you agree or disagree with the report's findings and recommendations?
2. Which, if any, relevant factors, data, or options are not addressed in the report and how should NASA investigate those areas?
3. What does NASA need to do now to understand and mitigate the risks of potential NEO impacts?
4. What governance structures should be established to address potential NEO threats?

1. Perspectives on the NASA Report

My response to the first question is in three parts, corresponding to the three components of the Congressional direction to NASA.

a) Analysis of Survey Program Alternatives

I believe that NASA did a very good job (with the exception of the NASA life cycle cost estimation for the several survey alternatives) in developing and comparing a set of alternative Survey designs to meet the 140-meter goal. While I am not personally qualified to comment on the NASA costing I note that knowledgeable Pan-STARRS and LSST personnel challenge the NASA figures used. These experts claim that the actual costs for both cooperative and dedicated use of such telescopic facilities are considerably lower than those projected by NASA.

One factor not addressed in NASA's analysis of options to meet the revised Survey goal was the capability of various search system options for NEO tracking vice NEO discovery. While all of us in the NEO community strongly support moving aggressively to meet Congress's 140-meter discovery goal the fundamental intent of this enterprise is to protect the Earth from NEO impacts. This ultimate purpose is achieved by both the discovery of NEOs which might pose a threat AND also by tracking them accurately to determine whether or not a deflection campaign is necessary.

It is an unfortunate reality that ground-based telescopic tracking produces, for many challenging NEOs, discontinuous information; data dropouts may last for several years at a time. Should such a critical data dropout occur just as a NEO is found to threaten an impact, the decision on mounting a deflection campaign may well have to be made on the basis of uncomfortably "stale" tracking data. The well-known NEO Apophis, which currently has a 1 in 45,000 probability of collision with the Earth in 2036, is in such a data dropout period at this time. We were last able to see Apophis in August 2006 and we will not see it again until 2011–2012. For Apophis this data interruption is uncomfortable, but not critical since we will see it again before we need to decide on a deflection campaign. This is, however, simply a matter of chance and in many instances in the future we will not be so fortunate.

The orbital phasing responsible for this interrupted tracking can be eliminated by selecting any of several space-based search options in NASA's analysis to augment the ground-based systems. While NASA reports that overall costs for space and ground tracking are comparable (a controversial claim), the tracking quality provided by a telescope in a Venus-like orbit, in particular, is vastly superior. The dual-band IR telescope is especially preferable since it also improves greatly our estimates of NEO mass (and thus impact energy).

In summary, NEO search and discovery is extremely important. NEO tracking, however, is equally important for deciding whether and when to mount a deflection campaign. The dual-band IR telescope in a Venus-like orbit offers both discovery and tracking advantages at a cost comparable to the best ground-based telescopic options.

b) Recommended Program and Supporting Budget

With respect to the second Congressional charge to recommend a program to meet the 140-meter search goal and a budget to support it, NASA failed to respond. NASA opted instead to state the obvious, that ". . . due to current budget constraints, NASA cannot initiate a new program at this time." Of course NASA's tight fiscal situation is precisely why the Congress requested not only a recommended program but also a proposed budget necessary to carry it out.

One can sympathize with NASA's fear of the dreaded "unfunded mandate" from Congress while decrying the Agency's decision to defy the Congressional directive and to delay the initiation of this critical search program. Congress, however, must also recognize and confront the dilemma it imposes on NASA (and other agencies) when it directs action without the specific identification of funds to support the work. Yet given that Congress explicitly directed in its mandate that NASA provide it with a proposed budget to support the program NASA cannot be excused.

I can only urge that **the Congress should again direct NASA in the clearest language possible to comply with the law and recommend a** search program and supporting budget. (Recommendation 1) It is time for the nation to aggressively pursue this urgent NEO program.

c) Analysis of Deflection Alternatives

B612 Foundation believes that NASA's analysis of deflection alternatives, as reported to the Congress, has serious technical flaws. NASA's findings and recommendations misunderstand, mischaracterize, and misrepresent many of the critical issues and options involved in the diversion of a threatening NEO. Furthermore the NASA Report fails to address a number of crucial issues which lie at the very heart of the deflection challenge.

An analysis of the errors of both commission and omission are too numerous and detailed to include in this testimony. I have therefore attached to this written testimony, and urge the Members and their staff to read several documents which address these errors in depth. These documents include:

1. An exchange of correspondence with Congressman Dana Rohrabacher regarding clarification of the intent of the Congress in the nature of the NEOs to be considered for diversion . . . ,
2. An *"Independent Analysis of Alternatives that could be employed to divert a NEO on a likely collision course with Earth."* . . . , and
3. Two detailed critiques of the NASA Report addressing on a point-by-point basis specific errors in the NASA analysis. . . .

To appreciate the depth of the technical errors in the Report, I strongly urge that these appended documents be reviewed in detail. I will summarize here a few of the key points.

Size matters
In examining the technical alternatives for diverting threatening NEOs, NASA selected ". . . a set of five [note: there were actually 7] scenarios representing the likely range of threats." In fact, the set of impact scenarios NASA chose as "typical" were extraordinarily challenging, resulting in a preference for a deflection concept delivering extraordinary capability, i.e. nuclear explosives.

The *least* challenging of the NEOs NASA considered in its analysis is part of a group that comprises just 2% of the potential impact cases. The impact frequency of such an object is once every 35,000 years. The remaining objects considered by NASA range upward to a one-kilometer asteroid (one impact per million years) and a one-kilometer, long-period comet (even more rare).

In fact, objects which hit much more frequently and yet deliver considerable impact energy make up 98% of the likely impact threat. The most likely of these objects to impact is comparable to the Tunguska event of 1908 in Siberian Russia. That event is estimated to have exploded with the force of about 5 megatons of TNT equivalent, or over 300 Hiroshima bombs. Had the Tunguska event been instead the "London event," or "Moscow event," it would have destroyed not just 800 square miles of forest and a few reindeer but an entire city and its population.

As Congressman Dana Rohrabacher stated in his clarification letter to B612 on this subject, "While it is important to understand what technology exists or needs to be developed to divert the larger and more devastating NEOs, the first order of business is to insure that we have a clear understanding of that the options are for the situations we are most likely to encounter."

A random impact occurring directly over a major city is, of course, highly unlikely. Yet when the possibility of such an event and the means of preventing it from occurring are known to exist by the general population it is reasonable to conclude that public pressure on the international community will successfully demand that we initiate a deflection.

Given then a cohort of "most likely NEOs to be deflected" ranging from a Tunguska-like object at the smallest and most frequent end of the scale up to events 100 times less frequent, we find that over 99% of them can be deflected using non-nuclear means.

The need for the availability of nuclear explosions for deflection in extreme cases cannot currently be ruled out, but the likelihood of such a demand materializing over the next several decades is extremely small. Furthermore our search efforts will make the need for such a solution increasingly unlikely over time.

Precision matters

NASA uses the word "effectiveness" in its Report purely as a measure of how much momentum change can be imparted to the asteroid. E.g., in its "Key Findings for Diverting a Potentially Hazardous Object," the first sentence of the first finding states "Nuclear standoff explosions are assessed to be 10–100 times more effective than the non-nuclear alternatives analyzed in this study." The technical term for NASA's undefined word "effectiveness" in this instance is "total impulse," i.e. the amount of momentum imparted to the asteroid in the process of the deflection.

Without doubt the total impulse available is a key measure of any deflection concept. However all of the impulsive (i.e. relatively instantaneous as juxtaposed with slow) deflection techniques evaluated are, while quite powerful, highly uncertain with regard to predicting the precise total impulse delivered. Experts in the field estimate uncertainties ranging from factors of two to five or even higher in the resulting total impulse delivered by either the nuclear or kinetic impact deflection concepts.

Certainly "strength" may well be needed in the deflection of an object on an impact trajectory. The first order of business is, without question, to ensure that the NEO is deflected sufficiently that it miss the planet.

What NASA totally missed however is that whenever an asteroid passes near the Earth (or any planet) it passes through a region in which are scattered hundreds of small impact "keyholes," small areas in Earth's proximity through which if the asteroid passes it will return within a few years and impact the Earth. Any deflected asteroid which misses the Earth must transit this minefield of impact keyholes.

Because the percentage of space taken up by such keyholes is small compared with the space between them, the probability of the NEO passing through one is fairly low. However the consequences of passing through such a keyhole are severe. Thus, whether or not a deflected NEO misses the keyholes cannot be left to chance. A successful deflection must therefore be defined as one which causes the potentially impacting asteroid to not only to miss the Earth but also to miss all impact keyholes. Without this constraint any deflecting agency would be limited to declaring, "we successfully deflected the asteroid away from an impact with Earth . . . and it is unlikely that it will return for an impact any time soon."

A successful deflection requires *both* adequate strength *and* high precision. Immediately following an impulsive deflection the new orbit of the asteroid must be precisely determined and examined for a future keyhole transit. If headed for a keyhole then a small "trim" maneuver can be executed using a weak but precise "slow push" (as NASA refers to it) deflection to avoid that critical passage.

This combination of imprecise strength and precise adjustment is both necessary and sufficient to declare to the world that a fully successful deflection has been achieved. NASA completely missed this essential point in its analysis.

These two key flaws are illustrative of the quality of the analysis on deflection alternatives in the NASA Report. I again refer you to the attachments for greater detail.

2. How Should NASA Now Proceed on These Issues?

I believe that **NASA should produce a supplement to its Report to Congress based on new knowledge which has come to light since it began its analysis. (Recommendation 2)** The state of knowledge of the NEO deflection challenge is increasing very rapidly and NASA has not stayed abreast of recent developments. This is not entirely NASA's fault since it has no assigned responsibility in this critical area. Nevertheless given the Congressional request for an analysis of alternatives, and the urgent need for a legitimate understanding of these options, I urge that NASA revisit this matter. I list below, inter alia, a few suggestions in this regard.

a) NASA should re-examine the NEO deflection challenge utilizing the most likely set of threatening NEOs that we will likely confront. The lower bound of this cohort should lie in the range of the 1908 Tunguska event. (Note: This does not imply a change in the 140-meter search goal. In meeting the 140-meter goal NASA will discover a large fraction of the Tunguska-sized NEO cohort as well.)

b) NASA should examine the need for precision and control in the deflection process taking particular account of the role impact keyholes play during a deflection.

c) NASA should further review and analyze its current (and future) database of NEOs to determine the frequency with which close gravitational encounters occur between the time of NEO discovery and the time of potential impact. In the case where such encounters occur (e.g. Apophis, the most threatening NEO in the current database) analysis shows that a single mission can often be employed to both determine if an impact is indeed threatened and take "slow push" preventive action if necessary. We must understand this class of prospective impacts and capitalize on the potential for a simple and less costly deflection mission.

d) NASA should fully assess the value of a dual-band IR telescope in a Venus-like orbit for search *and* tracking purposes. NASA has already analyzed this instrument's search capability, but it should extend its thinking to evaluate how to use such an instrument to support our impact prevention capability.

e) NASA should correct its faulty analysis of the cost and technological readiness of the Gravity Tractor.

3. What Needs to Be Done to Mitigate the Risks of Potential NEO Impacts?

There are two key actions to be taken that would make significant progress toward protecting the Earth from the potential devastation of NEO impacts. Neither of them is expensive yet both of them are extremely important, even urgent, in light of the anticipated rapid rise in the NEO discovery rate in the near future.

a) **NASA should assign someone in its NEO Program to the specific task of thinking through, analyzing and understanding the NEO deflection challenge. (Recommendation 3)** So long as the NASA effort, and therefore thinking, is restricted to the NEO discovery process only, the government will lack the critical information and understanding needed to protect the Earth from NEO impacts. There is critical linkage between the upstream process of NEO search and orbit analysis and the downstream information needed to deflect NEOs. Absent someone explicitly thinking this through we stand justly accused of focusing on numeric goals for the sake of meeting an abstract quota. I hasten to point out that NASA cannot make such an assignment without being given the explicit responsibility for this critical function.

b) **NASA should validate a basic NEO deflection capability through the execution of a demonstration mission. (Recommendation 4)** While deflection concepts can and indeed must first be worked out conceptually, in an endeavor as critical to public safety as deflecting an asteroid bound for an impact, our ultimate success in such a vital undertaking cannot depend solely on a paper analysis. A demonstration program can be performed on a non-threatening asteroid at a cost no more than that of a typical small scientific mission. This effort need not, and perhaps should not, be undertaken as a US mission per se. The European Space Agency (ESA) has already performed the initial feasibility and design phase of such a mission (though it should be modified to validate the "slow push" component). Were an international partnership agreement negotiated a reasonable cost estimate for a complete NEO deflection demonstration campaign could be performed for about the cost of a single scientific mission.

4. What Governance Structures Should Be Established to Address Potential NEO Threats?

I believe this to be the single most important question of this hearing. Until and unless an explicit assignment of responsibility within government is made to protect the Earth from NEO impacts, no significant advances in our capability will be made, and the US public, and indeed the world public, will remain unnecessarily at risk.

Ironically and somewhat counter intuitively, the full cost of assigning such responsibility and paying for its operations is almost vanishingly small. It is, nevertheless, a sobering responsibility, and an historic one. The very concept of being able to slightly alter the workings of the cosmos to enhance the survival of life on Earth is staggeringly bold. Yet this very capability lies within our technical means today. The missing element, the fatal missing element, is a governmental assignment of responsibility.

I would break this charge into two logical pieces.

a) First it seems to me that there exists today a single logical entity that should be responsible for the analysis, design, manufacturing and testing of a NEO deflection capability. That entity is NASA. NASA is our national space agency and is clearly charged with the development of our national space capability. This is, I believe, a clear and obvious choice.

NEO work in NASA is, however, administratively in an orphaned status. Protecting the Earth from NEO impacts is neither space science nor exploration, although there are elements of both involved. Protecting the Earth from NEO impacts is a public safety activity. Yet today within NASA and its supporting space science and exploration communities the strong perception is that a dollar spent on NEO work is a dollar taken from space science or exploration. This "zero-sum game" presumption cannot be allowed to persist. Yet until explicit responsibility and funding for NEO research, as a public safety responsibility, is assigned to NASA by the Congress, this terrible conflict will persist. I therefore recommend **that the Congress expressly assign to NASA the technical development elements of protecting the Earth from NEO impacts as a public safety responsibility. (Recommendation 5)**

b) The second element is considerably more challenging and controversial. That is, to which agency of government should fall the overall responsibility for protecting the Earth from this infrequent, but devastating natural hazard? This responsibility is greater than and somewhat separate from the technical issues discussed above.

While we have not addressed this matter above I will simply state unequivocally that the NEO mitigation decision process and the policies embedded within it are inherently international. Any NEO deflection will necessarily shift risk, however temporarily, between people and property across the planet.

As we move a NEO away from an Earth impact, we necessarily shift its impact point from one region to another until we complete the deflection.

Given this characteristic, and I ask that you grant this arguendo, the response to a threatening NEO will involve complex and very sensitive international coordination and probably negotiation. This is a planetary challenge, not a national one. The policies, procedures, criteria, thresholds, and agreements which must be addressed are international political challenges and the US involvement will place in the hands of the agency responsible the lives and property of the world's entire population.

It would frankly be presumptuous of me to make a specific recommendation here. Obvious candidates for such a responsibility include the Department of Homeland Security (DHS), the Department of Defense (DoD), and of course NASA. Many other agencies will clearly need to be involved in the decision processes given the potential of evacuation, migration (including cross border), and potentially unprecedented property destruction.

I therefore recommend **that the Congress study the issue of overall governmental responsibility for protection of the Earth from NEO impacts, perhaps with the assistance of specialized policy entities, and ultimately hold public hearings to engage a wide perspective on the issue. (Recommendation 6)**

In closing I would suggest a personal perspective based on having spent the last 6 years of my life studying this issue. NEOs are part of nature. A NEO impact is a natural hazard in much the same way as are hurricanes, tsunamis, floods, etc. NEO impacts are deceptively infrequent, yet devastating at potentially unimaginable levels. NEOs are however not our enemies. We do not need to "defend" against NEOs, we need to protect ourselves from their occasional impact, as we do with other natural hazards.

Unlike other natural hazards, however, NEO impacts can be predicted well ahead of time and actually *prevented* from occurring. If we live up to our responsibility, if we wisely use our amazing technology, and if we are mature enough, as a nation and as a community of nations, there may never again be a substantially damaging asteroid impact on the Earth. We have the ability to make ourselves safe from cosmic extinction. If we cannot manage to meet this challenge, we will, in my opinion, have failed to meet our evolutionary responsibility.

POSTSCRIPT

Is NASA Doing Enough to Protect the Earth from Asteroid and Comet Impacts?

In the debate over the risks of NEO impacts on Earth, there are a few certainties: They have happened before, they will happen again, and they come in various sizes. As Mike Reynolds says in "Earth Under Fire," *Astronomy* (August 2006), the question is not whether impacts will happen in the future. "It's just a matter of when and how big the object will be." Many past craters mark the Earth, even though many more have been erased by plate tectonics and erosion. See Timothy Ferris, "Killer Rocks from Outer Space," *Reader's Digest* (October 2002). Ivan Semeniuk, "Asteroid Impact," *Mercury* (November/ December 2002), says that, "If there is one question that best sums up the current state of thinking about the impact hazard, it is this: At what size do we need to act? In the shooting gallery that is our solar system, everyone agrees we are the target of both cannonballs and BBs. The hard part is deciding where to draw the line that separates them. For practical reasons, that line is now set at 1 kilometer. Not only are objects of this diameter a global threat (no matter where they hit, we're all affected to some degree), they are also the easiest to spot. Under a mid-1990s congressional mandate, NASA currently funds search efforts to the tune of about $3.5 million per year. . . . 'The existing commitment to 1 kilometer and larger is to retire the risk,' says Tom Morgan, who heads NASA's NEO group. 'By the end of this decade we'll be able to tell you if any of these objects presents a threat in the foreseeable future.'" However, as Richard A. Kerr notes, "The Small Ones Can Kill You, Too," *Science* (September 19, 2003). See also Russell L. Schweickart and Clark R. Chapman, "Better Collision Insurance," *American Scientist* (September–October 2005). The risks are very well reviewed in Alan W. Harris, "Chicken Little Was Right! The Risk from an Asteroid or Comet Impact," *Phi Kappa Phi Forum* (Winter/Spring 2006).

What if a "killer rock" does present a threat? In September 2002, NASA held a workshop on *Scientific Requirements for Mitigation of Hazardous Comets and Asteroids,* which concluded "that the prime impediment to further advances in this field is the lack of any assigned responsibility to any national or international governmental organization to prepare for a disruptive collision and the absence of any authority to act in preparation for some future collision mitigation attempt" and urged that "NASA be assigned the responsibility to advance this field" and "a new and adequately funded program be instituted at NASA to create, through space missions and allied research, the specialized knowledge base needed to respond to a future threat of a collision from an asteroid or comet nucleus." The results of the workshop appeared as *Mitigation of Hazardous Impacts Due to Asteroids and Comets* (Cambridge University Press, 2004).

The Organization for Economic Cooperation and Development (OECD) Global Science Forum held a "Workshop on Near Earth Objects: Risks, Policies and Actions" in January 2003. It too concluded that more work is needed. In May 2005, the House Science Committee approved a bill to establish and fund a NASA program to detect and assess near-Earth asteroids and comets down to 100 meters in diameter. See also David H. Levy, "Asteroid Alerts: A Risky Business," *Sky & Telescope* (April 2006). NASA's March 2007 "Near-Earth Object Survey and Deflection Analysis of Alternatives, Report to Congress," argues that though progress is being made, much more would be possible if Congress increased funding.

Given political will and funding, what could be done if a threat were identified? Richard Stone, "Target Earth," *National Geographic* (August 2008), says that "Two facts are clear: Whether in 10 years or 500, a day of reckoning is inevitable. More heartening, for the first time ever we have the means to prevent a natural disaster of epic proportions." There have been numerous proposals, from launching nuclear missiles to pulverize approaching space rocks to sending astronauts (or robots) to install rocket engines and deflect the rocks onto safe paths (perhaps into the sun to forestall future hazards). Several alternatives are discussed in Justin Cunningham, "Collision Course," *Professional Engineering* (December 14, 2005). David L. Chandler, "'Gravity Tractor' Could Deflect Asteroids," *New Scientist* (July 28, 2008), notes that the weak gravitational pull of a nearby spacecraft could be enough to move an asteroid off course. However, Bill Cooke, "Killer Impact," *Astronomy* (December 2004), warns that for the foreseeable future, our only real hope is evacuation of the target zone. All proposed methods require a stronger space program than any nation now has. Lacking such a program, knowing that a major rock is on the way would surely be little comfort. However, given sufficient notice—on the order of decades—a space program might be mobilized to deal with the threat. In *Asteroid Threats: A Call for Global Response* (September 25, 2008), the Association of Space Explorers and its International Panel on Asteroid Threat Mitigation says that lacking appropriate action, "society will likely suffer the effects of some future cosmic disaster [but] [s]cientific knowledge and existing international institutions, if harnessed today, offer society the means to avoid such a catastrophe. We cannot afford to shirk that responsibility."

ISSUE 13

Will the Search for Extraterrestrial Life Ever Succeed?

YES: Seth Shostak, from "When Will We Detect the Extraterrestrials?" *Acta Astronautica* (August 2004)

NO: Peter Schenkel, from "SETI Requires a Skeptical Reappraisal," *Skeptical Inquirer* (May/June 2006)

ISSUE SUMMARY

YES: Radio astronomer and SETI researcher Seth Shostak argues that if the assumptions behind the SETI search are well grounded, signals of extraterrestrial origin will be detected soon, perhaps within the next generation.

NO: Peter Schenkel argues that SETI's lack of success to date, coupled with the apparent uniqueness of Earth, suggest that intelligent life is probably rare in our galaxy and that the enthusiastic optimism of SETI proponents should be reined in.

In the 1960s and early 1970s, the business of listening to the radio whispers of the stars and hoping to pick up signals emanating from some alien civilization was still new. Few scientists held visions equal to Frank Drake, one of the pioneers of the search for extraterrestrial intelligence (SETI) field. Drake and scientists like him utilize radio telescopes—large, dish-like radio receiver–antenna combinations—to scan radio frequencies (channels) for signal patterns that would indicate that the signal was transmitted by an intelligent being. In his early days, Drake worked with relatively small and weak telescopes out of listening posts that he had established in Green Bank, West Virginia, and Arecibo, Puerto Rico. See Carl Sagan and Frank Drake, "The Search for Extraterrestrial Intelligence," *Scientific American* (May 1975) and Frank Drake and Dava Sobel, *Is Anyone Out There? The Scientific Search for Extraterrestrial Intelligence* (Delacorte Press, 1992).

There have been more than 50 searches for extraterrestrial radio signals since 1960. The earliest ones were very limited. Later searches have been more ambitious, culminating in the 10-year program known as the High Resolution Microwave Survey (HRMS). The HRMS, which began on Columbus Day of 1992, uses several radio telescopes and massive computers to scan 15 million radio frequencies per second. New technologies and techniques continue to make the search more efficient. See Seth Shostak, "SETI's Prospects Are Bright," *Mercury* (September/October 2002), and Monte Ross, "The New Search for E.T." *IEEE Spectrum* (November 2006).

At the outset, many people thought—and many still think—that SETI has about as much scientific relevance as searches for Loch Ness Monsters and Abominable Snowmen. However, to Drake and his colleagues, it seems inevitable that with so many stars in the sky, there must be other worlds with life upon them, and some of that life must be intelligent and have a suitable technology and the desire to search for alien life too.

Writing about SETI in the September–October 1991 issue of *The Humanist*, physicist Shawn Carlson compares visiting the National Shrine of the Immaculate Conception in Washington, D.C., to looking up at the stars and "wondering if, in all [the] vastness [of the starry sky], there is anybody out there looking in our direction. . . . [A]re there planets like ours peopled with creatures like us staring into their skies and wondering about the possibilities of life on other worlds, perhaps even trying to contact it?" That is, SETI arouses in its devotees an almost religious sense of mystery and awe, a craving for contact with the *other*. Success would open up a universe of possibilities, add immensely to human knowledge, and perhaps even provide solutions to problems that our interstellar neighbors have already defeated.

SETI also arouses strong objections, partly because it challenges human uniqueness. Many scientists have objected that life-bearing worlds such as Earth must be exceedingly rare because the conditions that make them suitable for life as we know it—composition and temperature—are so narrowly defined. Others have objected that there is no reason whatsoever to expect that evolution would produce intelligence more than once or that, if it did, the species would be similar enough to humans to allow communication. Still others say that even if intelligent life is common, technology may not be so common, or technology may occupy such a brief period in the life of an intelligent species that there is virtually no chance that it would coincide with Earth scientists' current search. Whatever their reasons, SETI detractors agree that listening for extraterrestrial signals is futile. Ben Zuckerman, "Why SETI Will Fail," *Mercury* (September/October 2002), argues that the simple fact that we have not been visited by extraterrestrials indicates that there are probably very few ET civilizations and SETI is therefore futile.

In the selections that follow, Seth Shostak defends SETI and argues that if the assumptions behind the search are reasonable, the search will succeed, perhaps within the next generation. Peter Schenkel, a retired political scientist, argues that SETI's lack of success to date, coupled with the apparent uniqueness of Earth's history and suitability for life, suggests that intelligent life is probably rare in our galaxy. It is time, he says, "to dampen excessive SETI euphoria and to adopt a . . . stand, compatible with facts."

YES

Seth Shostak

When Will We Detect the Extraterrestrials?

Abstract

It has been more than four decades since the first, modern SETI experiment. Many hundreds of star systems have been observed in the radio over wide bandwidth and with impressive sensitivity, and the entire sky has been surveyed in a more restricted mode several times. Optical SETI experiments are underway, and have already scrutinized several thousand nearby stars, looking for nanosecond light pulses.

Still, there is no confirmed signal detection. Given the anticipated improvement in both telescopes and digital electronics applied to SETI, what is the time scale for making such a discovery? In this paper we investigate the rate of stellar surveillance by targeted radio SETI experiments for the foreseeable future, and conclude that it is likely that—if the principal assumptions underlying modern SETI are reasonable—a detection will occur within a single generation.

Introduction

When will SETI succeed is a perennial question which does not, and some would say, cannot, engender reliable answers.* The search has a long history compared with historical exploration efforts, which were typically a decade or so in length—Columbus' four voyages extended over a dozen years, and Cook's reconnaissance of the South Pacific (three voyages) spanned eleven years. In contrast, the first SETI experiment was more than forty years ago (Project Ozma). As has been pointed out, the searches since 1960 have been quite intermittent, and amount to less than two years of continuous observation at sensitivities and spectral coverage comparable to today's experiments. Nonetheless, many SETI researchers are inclined to make the Copernican assumption that our temporal location in the search for signals is mediocre, and that another few decades, or thereabouts, will be necessary for success.

---

*To avoid the ambiguity which some researchers ascribe to the word "success" in SETI, we define it as the unambiguous detection of an artificial, extraterrestrial signal.

Others speak of SETI as a multi-generational project, and encourage a mind-set sympathetic to the "long haul." It is the author's own experience that the most common response by scientists engaged in SETI, when queried as to how long success will take, is to answer with the approximate number of years until their own retirement.

Given the myriad uncertainties of the SETI enterprise, is there any reason to believe that a better prediction could be made, or are such "gut feelings" the best we can hope for? It is the purpose of this brief paper to offer a somewhat more quantitative estimate of when SETI might succeed, based on typical assumptions made by the SETI researchers themselves. Of course, these assumptions could be grossly in error, but the merit of this approach is that the timescales presented here are congruent with SETI's own postulates. To the extent that the arguments made for conducting today's SETI experiments are credible, then the sort of predictions presented here of when a signal might be found are similarly worthy of consideration.

Approach

As for any discovery enterprise, the time required to find a sought-for phenomenon depends on (a) the frequency with which it occurs, and (b) the speed of the reconnaissance. For SETI searches, the first is, crudely, the number of contemporaneous signal generators (transmitters, if you will), and the second is the rapidity with which our telescopes can survey the sky (or, for targeted search strategies, likely locations on the sky) using spectral coverage and sensitivity adequate to find one of these transmitters.

Since the inception of modern SETI, reckoning the number of celestial transmitters has been done using the Drake Equation. The equation computes N, the number of contemporaneous, galactic transmitting sites, as the product of the rate at which intelligent societies arise and the length of time they remain in the transmitting state. As noted, these computations are restricted to our own Galaxy, on the assumption that intelligence in other galaxies would not have the incentive to send signals (or provoke replies) that would be millions of years in transit. In addition, some note that intergalactic messaging, even from nearby nebulae, would require untenable power levels: hundreds to millions of times higher than required for communication over typical intragalactic distances. These arguments have not been considered overly persuasive however, since a number of searches for extragalactic transmitters have been made.

Of possibly greater consequence is the Drake Equation's assumption that searches should be directed to stellar systems capable of hosting Earth-like worlds. Interstellar travel is difficult but not impossible, and it's unclear whether truly advanced intelligences would remain exclusively, or even principally, confined to the solar system of their birth. If migration away from the home star is common to technological intelligence, then targeted SETI searches, which are the most sensitive, could miss the most advanced (and possibly the most easily detected) transmitters.

Number of Stars to Search

With these caveats in mind, we begin by taking a conservative position, and consider the number of (galactic) transmitters predicted by Drake's Equation. It is not the provenance of this paper to evaluate the individual terms of this equation; we are only interested in their product, N. A compilation of published estimates assembled by Dick yields a (logarithmic) average of N ~ 10^5–10^6. (We note that one of Dick's compiled estimates is N = 0.003, which, if correct, would mean that it is overwhelmingly likely that there is nothing and no one to find. Among the SETI research community, this is obviously a minority view.) Drake himself is more conservative, and suggests N ~ 10^4. In the discussion that follows, we adopt a range of values for N of 10^4 to 10^6.

With this range estimate for N, and assuming a disk galaxy with diameter of ~90,000 light-years and half-power disk thickness (locally) of ~1,000 light-years, we can conclude that the nearest transmitter is 200–1,000 light-years away.

How many suitable targets lie within this distance? There are ~10^{11} stars in the Galaxy. Traditionally, 5–10% of these have been considered preferred candidates for harboring intelligence: these comprise, roughly speaking, single F, G or K-type stars at least a few billion years old. The major groups excluded by this historical choice include multiple stars (approximately half of all stars) and M-dwarfs (about 90% of stars). However, recent research has shown that both close double stars and those that are widely separated (tens of AU or more) could host planets in stable orbits. M-dwarfs are presently being reconsidered as SETI targets. It might soon be concluded that only short-lived, massive stars (types A and earlier) can be reliably excluded *ab initio* as SETI targets. Since these comprise only ~1% of all stars, this would mean that virtually the entire stellar complement of the Milky Way would qualify for SETI scrutiny.

However, foreseeable astronomical discoveries may once again narrow the range of interesting stars. The current search for extrasolar planets has shown that ~10% of solar-type stars have detectable worlds, but these are skewed in favor of stars that have higher metallicities. This suggests an obvious target selection criterion. In addition, new space-based interferometers (e.g., NASA's Terrestrial Planet Finder and ESA's Darwin) proposed for deployment in a decade's time will allow not only the direct imaging of Earth-sized worlds, but spectral analyses of their atmospheres. Such techniques could tell us not only which star systems host suitable planets, but could pinpoint worlds that evidence the spectral signatures of life. And, of course, it's still possible that a deeper investigation of the conditions of planets around M-dwarfs could serve to reliably eliminate this very numerous stellar class from consideration.

Consequently, and mindful of this expected progress in our understanding of extrasolar planets, we assume that: (1) for the present decade, all galactic stars remain qualified SETI targets. (2) In the following decade, half of all unobserved stars can be eliminated *a priori* from our SETI target lists, and (3) in the third decade, 90% of unobserved stars can be eliminated. This is, we propose, a conservative projection of progress in choosing which star systems to observe.

Indeed, today's experiments often have more restrictive target lists than we are projecting for 2020 and beyond.

Rate of Target Scrutiny

Having estimated (a) the number of galactic transmitters, and (b) the fraction of star systems that need to be searched, we need only consider the rate at which the search is conducted in order to arrive at our goal: an estimate for when a signal will be found.

We first consider radio searches. Note that large swaths of the celestial sphere have been examined in so-called Sky Survey SETI experiments. The failure (so far) of these experiments to discover a signal, assuming such signals exist, could be due to (a) insufficient sensitivity (note that such sky surveys are typically at least an order-of-magnitude less sensitive than targeted searches, which means that the volume of sky sampled at any given sensitivity level is less by a factor of >60), (b) inadequate spectral coverage, or (c) an inability to monitor specific locations for more than a few seconds, with no facility for making immediate follow-up observations. This precludes detection of all but fully continuous signals.

Targeted searches moderate these shortcomings, but have the disadvantage of being a very slow reconnaissance. This is principally due to the fact that the large telescopes favored for SETI research are only intermittently available. The total number of star systems surveyed to date by the SETI Institute's premier radio search, Project Phoenix (which uses the Arecibo radio telescope), is ~500.

This slow pace of targeted radio searches is about to change. The Allen Telescope Array (ATA), a joint project of the SETI Institute and the University of California at Berkeley, will be a highly sophisticated radio antenna that can be used full-time to make SETI observations. It is anticipated that this instrument will be completed within the current decade. This immediately increases by an order of magnitude the amount of telescope time available for the Institute's targeted searches. In addition, an international consortium is planning the construction of an even larger telescope, the Square Kilometer Array (SKA). If built, this instrument could also be partially dedicated to SETI observations. For the purposes of this paper, we assume that this instrument will double the speed of SETI reconnaissance beginning in the (rather uncertain) year of 2015.

Project Phoenix surveys approximately 50–60 stellar systems annually. The ATA will not only have the benefit of ten times as much observing time as this effort, but will also incorporate multiple beams that allow the simultaneous observation of at least three star systems. In addition, efficiencies in follow-up and wider instantaneous spectral coverage will add at least another factor of 2–3 speed improvement. At a minimum, we can say that, once completed, the ATA will increase the rapidity with which nearby stars are checked for signals by at least two orders of magnitude. In its first year, it will observe considerably more stellar systems than the total investigated by Project Phoenix. We will (conservatively) assume this number to be 1,000 systems, applicable to the year 2006.

The ATA is conceived as an instrument whose capabilities can be expanded as the cost of digital computation continues to decline. According to Moore's Law, a fact-of-life in the field of computing hardware for three decades, the density of transistors on commercially available chips doubles every 18 months. In more practical terms, this means that the cost of computing is halved each 1-1/2 years. The speed (not necessarily the efficacy) of SETI experiments has historically followed this law. . . .

We can expect, therefore, that at least the speed of stellar scrutiny using the ATA will grow at this exponential rate, at least so long as Moore's Law continues to hold. How long might that be? Various pundits, including Moore himself, point to the fact that the further exploitation of silicon technology will likely hit a physical "wall" at which the dimensions of the transistors become nearly molecular in size. An additional (and perhaps more formidable) barrier to the continued reign of this law is the economic cost of new fabrication facilities and even of the chips themselves. On the other hand, foreseeing this technological barrier has stimulated research into optical and quantum computing, and these approaches are expected by many to not only sustain the pace of improvement, but perhaps to accelerate it.

For the purposes of this paper, we adopt widespread industry predictions that Moore's Law in its current form will continue to hold until 2015. Thereafter, we conservatively assume a decrease by half: doubling of computational power per dollar will take 36 months, rather than 18. The speed of SETI reconnaissance is postulated to follow this technological growth.

Having considered at some length the speed and expected improvements in radio SETI searches, we note that several optical SETI experiments are also underway. These look for short ($\leq 10^{-9}$ sec) bursts of photons that could be produced by, for example, a pulsed laser deliberately targeting our solar system. While optical SETI experiments are still relatively new, several thousand star systems have already been observed, and an instrument dedicated to an optical sky survey of the two-thirds of the sky visible from the northern hemisphere is currently under construction.

Despite these encouraging developments, we will not incorporate them into our estimate of when extraterrestrial intelligence will be found. This is because of the very real possibility that optical signals might be either highly intermittent or sent to only small numbers of targets. However, with not-unreasonable assumptions, optical SETI might succeed very soon. Consider a simple example: suppose that an extraterrestrial beacon is set up to serially target all $\sim 10^{11}$ galactic star systems, briefly illuminating their inner solar systems with a burst of nanosecond pulses once every 24 hours. (This brute-force approach would provide each star with a daily kilobit of data, which might be adequate to serve as a "pointer" to other information being served up by this transmitting society.) The observation time per beam for the planned Harvard-Princeton optical sky survey is ≥ 48 seconds, so that the chance of a detection for every sweep of the northern sky (estimated to take 150 days) is $\sim 3 \times 10^{-4}$ N, or >1 for all our estimates for N.

This sunny assessment assumes that all transmitters are detectable by the sky survey. In fact, optical searches for signals from star systems at great distance need to be sensitive in the infrared to defeat the attenuating effect of interstellar dust. Such systems are not yet operational, as they must be space-based. However, there is no technical reason to doubt that they could be deployed within a decade or two. On the other hand, very low transmitter duty cycles may dictate that an effective optical SETI search will require the use of multiple, or possibly all-sky, detectors. Given the newness of optical SETI, and the lack of a body of historical "assumptions" regarding optical signaling, we will not factor such searches into our estimate of when a SETI detection will be made. This is obviously a conservative approach, assuming that optical SETI has any chance at all to succeed.

When a Detection Will Take Place

We now have in hand the requisite parameters to estimate the likely date of a (radio) SETI detection. . . . [We can plot] the number of targeted star systems observed using the ATA with, eventually, the addition of the SKA. . . . [We can then calculate] the volume of space (specified by a maximum distance) in which we've observed all suitable target star systems [and date when we will have observed enough star systems to expect successful SETI. If $N = 10^6$, the date will be about 2015. If $N = 10^4$, the date will be about 2027.] . . .

We remark that this span of dates for a predicted SETI detection extends less than two dozen years forward. Although SETI searches are sometimes referred to as multigenerational projects, our estimate suggests that this isn't the case: success is within the foreseeable future. Among other things, this justifies the efforts being made to plan for a detection, as well as to consider society's likely reaction and what would be a suitable response (if any).

We have tried to make conservative assumptions in this presentation. In particular, a reconnaissance of extrasolar planets, which would chart out their size, orbit, and whether or not they evidence spectral biomarkers, will eventually tightly focus the interest of SETI researchers, reducing (substantially, one assumes) the number of suitable target systems. We have only made a crude correction for this highly likely development. We have also made no assumption that SETI observations, particularly those that reach beyond a few hundred light-years, will concentrate their attentions on the galactic plane, thereby increasing the efficiency of the search.

While we have reckoned on an exponential improvement in technology that governs SETI search speed over the next two-and-a-half decades, this extrapolation is based on four decades in which this has been demonstrably true. To be on the safe side, we have assumed a slowing of this growth beginning in 2015. Finally, we have taken no account of the likelihood that a detection will be made with radio sky surveys, or using optical SETI techniques.

On the other hand, there are many possible reasons why our assessment that a detection will be made within a generation might be wrong. We have not considered the luminosity function or duty cycle of extraterrestrial transmitters, but have instead assumed that the N transmitters estimated by the Drake Equation are all detectable by the ATA and SKA. We have not speculated on the possibility that the frequency coverage of our telescopes is inadequate, nor that the signal types to which they are sensitive are the wrong ones. And, indeed, we do not consider that physical laws of which we are still unaware might dictate a completely different approach to interstellar signaling. And, of course, our range of estimates for N are only considered opinion—and some of that opinion [states] that *no* other contemporary, sentient galactic societies exist.

Nonetheless, we reiterate that the intention of this exercise is to improve upon existing "gut feeling" speculation as to when SETI might expect a detection. While there are a myriad uncertainties attendant upon our estimate that this will occur within two dozen years, we have made this prediction using the assumptions adopted by the SETI research community itself. This community builds equipment and uses strategies that it reckons are adequate to find an extraterrestrial signal. It does this based on more than four decades of thought as to how best to prove the presence of extraterrestrial sentience. If such analyses are well grounded, then such proof will not be long in coming.

Peter Schenkel

 **NO**

SETI Requires a Skeptical Reappraisal

The possible existence of extraterrestrial intelligence (ETI) has always stirred the imagination of man. Greek philosophers speculated about it. Giordano Bruno was burnt on the stake in Rome in 1600, mainly [for] positing the likelihood of other inhabited worlds in the universe. Kant and Laplace were also convinced of the multiplicity of worlds similar to ours. In the latter part of the nineteenth century Flammarion charmed vast circles with his books on the plurality of habitable worlds. But all these ideas were mainly philosophical considerations or pure speculations. It was only in the second half of the twentieth century that the Search for Extraterrestrial Intelligence (SETI) became a scientifically underpinned endeavor. Since the late 1950s distinguished scientists have conducted research, attempting to receive intelligent signals or messages from space via radio-telescopes. Hundreds of amateur astronomers, members of the SETI-League in dozens of countries, are scanning the sky, trying to detect evidence of intelligent life elsewhere in our galaxy. SETI pioneers, such as Frank Drake and Carl Sagan, held the stance that the Milky Way is teeming with a large number of advanced civilizations. However, the many search projects to date have not succeeded, and this daring prediction remains unverified. New scientific insights suggest the need for a more cautious approach and a revision of the overly optimistic considerations.

The standard argument for the existence of a multiplicity of intelligent life runs like this: There are about 200 to 300 billion stars in our galaxy and probably hundreds of millions, maybe even billions of planets in our galaxy. Many of these planets are likely to be located in the so-called "habitable zone" in relation [to] their star, enjoying Earth-favorable conditions for the evolution of life. The physical laws, known to us, apply also to the cosmos, and far-away stellar formations are composed of the same elements as our solar system. Therefore, it is assumed, many should possess water and a stable atmosphere, considered to be basic requisites for the development of life. Such planets must have experienced geological and biological processes similar to those on Earth, leading to the development of primitive life organisms. Then, in the course of time, following a similar course of Darwin's theory of natural selection, these evolved into more complex forms, some eventually developing cognitive capacities and—as in our case—higher intelligence.

From *Skeptical Inquirer*, vol. 30, no. 3, May/June 2006. Copyright © 2006. Used by permission of the Skeptical Inquirer Magazine. http://www.csicop.org.

In other words, it is maintained, our solar system, Earth, and its evolution are not exceptional cases, but something very common in our Milky Way galaxy. Consequently it must be populated by a huge number of extraterrestrial civilizations, many of them older and more advanced than ours.

Considering the enormous number of stars and planets, these seem like fair and legitimate assumptions. It indeed appears unlikely that intelligence should have evolved only on our planet. If many of these civilizations are scientifically and technologically superior to us, contact with them would give mankind a boost in many ways.

These optimistic views are based mainly on the famous Drake formula. . . . It considers the formation of stars in the galaxy, the fraction of stars with planetary systems, the number of planets ecologically suited for life, the fraction of these planets on which life and intelligent life evolves, and those reaching a communicative stage and the length of time of technical civilizations. On the basis of this formula it was estimated that a million advanced civilizations probably exist in the galaxy. The nearest one should be at a distance of about 200 to 300 light-years from Earth. German astronomer Sebastian von Hoerner estimated a number between ten thousand and ten million such civilizations.

But because of many new insights and results of research in a number of scientific fields, ranging from paleontology, geology, biology to astronomy, I believe this formula is incomplete and must be revised. The early optimistic estimates are no longer tenable. A more realistic and sober view is required.

I by no means intend to discredit SETI; the search for extraterrestrial intelligent life is a legitimate scientific endeavor. But it seems prudent to demystify this interesting subject, and to reformulate its claims on a new level, free of the romantic flair that adorns it.

Years ago, I readily admit, I myself was quite taken in by the allegations that intelligence is a very common phenomenon in the galaxy. In books, articles, and on radio and television I advocated the idea that our world, beset by problems, could learn a lot from a civilization more advanced than ours. But, in the meantime, I became convinced that a more skeptical attitude would do reality better justice. There are probably only a few such civilizations in the galaxy, if any at all. The following considerations buttress this rather pessimistic appraisal.

First of all, since project OZMA I in 1959 by Frank Drake, about a hundred radio-magnetic and other searches were conducted in the U.S. and in other countries, and a considerable part of our sky was scanned thoroughly and repeatedly, but it remained disappointingly silent. In forty-six years not a single artificial intelligent signal or message from outer space was received. Some specialists try to downplay this negative result, arguing that so far only a small part of the entire spectrum has been covered, and that more time and more sophisticated equipment is required for arriving at a definite conclusion. Technological and economic criteria may thwart the possibility of extraterrestrial civilizations beaming signals into space over long stretches of time, without knowing where to direct their signals. Or, they may use communication methods unknown to us. Another explanation is that advanced ETI may lack interest in contacting other intelligences, especially those less developed. The argument of the Russian rocket expert Konstantin Tsiolkovski is often quoted: "Absence of evidence is not evidence of absence."

But neither of these arguments, which attempt to explain why we have not received a single intelligent signal from space, is convincing. True, future search projects may strike pay dirt and register the reception of a signal of verified artificial origin. But as long as no such evidence is forthcoming, the possibility of achieving success must be considered remote. If a hundred searches were unsuccessful, it is fair to deduce that estimates of a million or many thousands ETI are unsustainable propositions. As long as no breakthrough occurs, the probability of contact with ETI is near to zero. The argument that advanced extraterrestrials may not be interested in contact with other intelligences is also—as I will show—highly implausible.

Second, as recent research results demonstrate, many more factors and conditions than those considered by the Drake formula need to be taken into account. The geologist Peter D. Ward and the astronomer Donald Brownlee present in their book *Rare Earth* a series of such aspects, which turn the optimistic estimates of ETI upside down.

According to their reasoning, the old assumption that our solar system and Earth are quite common phenomena in the galaxy needs profound revision. On the contrary, the new insights suggest, we are much more special than thought. The evolution of life forms and eventually of intelligent life on Earth was due to a large number of very special conditions and developments, many of a coincidental nature. I'll mention only some that seem particularly important: The age, size, and composition of our sun, the location of Earth and inclination of its axis to it, the existence of water, a stable oxygen-rich atmosphere and temperature over long periods of time—factors considered essential for the evolution of life—and the development of a carbon-based chemistry. Furthermore an active interior and the existence of plate tectonics form the majestic mountain ridges like the Alps, the Himalayas and the Andes, creating different ecological conditions, propitious for the proliferation of a great variety of species. Also the existence of the Moon, Jupiter, and Saturn (as shields for the bombardment of comets and meteorites during the early stages of Earth). Also the repeated climatic changes, long ice ages, and especially the numerous and quite fortuitous catastrophes, causing the extinction of many species, like the one 65 million years ago, which led to the disappearance of dinosaurs but opened the way for more diversified and complex life forms.

Though first primitive life forms on Earth, the prokaryotic bacteria, evolved relatively rapidly, only about 500 million years after the cooling off of Earth's crust and the end of the dense bombardment of meteorites and comets, they were the only life forms during the first two billion years of Earth's 4.6-billion-year history. Mammals—including apes and man—developed much later, only after the extinction of the dinosaurs 65 million years ago. The first human-like being, the Proconsul, emerged in the Miocene Period, just about 18 million years ago. The Australopithecus, our antecessor, dates only 5 to 6 million years. In other words, it took almost 4 billion years, or more than

96 percent of the age of Earth, for intelligence to evolve—an awfully long time, even on the cosmic clock.

In this regard we should note also the caveat of the distinguished biologist Ernst Mayr, who underscored the enormous complexity of human DNA and RNA and their functions for the production of proteins, the basic building blocks of life. He estimated that the likelihood that similar biological developments may have occurred elsewhere in the universe was nil.

The upshot of these considerations is the following: Because of the very special geological, biological, and other conditions which propitiated the evolution of life and intelligence on Earth, similar developments in our galaxy are probably very rare. Primitive life forms, Ward and Brownlee conclude, may exist on planets of other stellar systems, but intelligent life, as ours, is probably very rare, if it exists at all.

Third is the so-called "Fermi Paradox," another powerful reason suggesting a skeptical evaluation of the multiplicity of intelligence in the galaxy. Italian physicist Enrico Fermi posed the annoying question, "If so many highly developed ETIs are out there, as SETI specialists claim, why haven't they contacted us?" I already expressed great doubt about some of the explanations given [for] this paradox. Here I need to focus on two more. The first refers to the supposed lack of interest of advanced aliens to establish contact with other intelligent beings. This argument seems to me particularly untrustworthy. I refer to a Norwegian book, which explains why the Vikings undertook dangerous voyages to far-away coasts in precarious vessels. "One reason," it says, "is fame, another curiosity, and a third, gain!" If the Vikings, driven by the desire to discover the unknown, reached America a thousand years ago with a primitive technology, if we—furthermore—a still scientifically and technically young civilization, search for primitive life on other planets of the solar system and their moons, it is incredible that higher developed extraterrestrial intelligences would not be spurred by likewise interests and yearnings. One of the fundamental traits of intelligence is its unquenchable intellectual curiosity and urge to penetrate the unknown. Elder civilizations, our peers in every respect, must be imbued by the same daring and scrutinizing spirit, because if they are not, they could not have achieved their advanced standards.

A second argument often posited is that distances between stars are too great for interstellar travel. But this explanation also stands on shaky ground. Even our scientifically and technically adolescent civilization is exploring space and sending probes—the Voyager crafts—which someday may reach other stellar systems. We are still far from achieving velocities, near the velocity of light, necessary for interstellar travel. But some scientists predict that in 200 or 300 years, maybe even earlier, we are likely to master low "c" velocities, and once we reach them, our civilization will send manned exploratory expeditions to the nearest stars. Automatic unmanned craft may be the initial attempts. But I am convinced that nothing will impede the desire of man to see other worlds with his own eyes, to touch their soil and to perform research that unmanned probes would not be able to perform. Evidently, civilizations tens of thousands or millions of years in our advance will have reached near c velocities, and they will be able to explore a considerable part of the galaxy. Advanced ETI civilizations would engage in such explorations not only out of scientific curiosity, but in their own interest, for instance for spreading out and finding new habitats for their growing population, or because of the need to abandon their planet due to hazards from their star, and also because with the help of other civilizations it may confront dangers, lurking in the universe, more successfully than alone. The Fermi Paradox should therefore put us on guard, and foster a sound skepticism. Lack of interest in meeting a civilization such as ours is the least plausible reason why we have not heard from ETI.

A little mental experiment illustrates this point. Carl Sagan held once that intelligent aliens would visit Earth at least once every thousand years. But such visits have not taken place. Even extending this period to a million years, we fare no better. Let us assume an extraterrestrial craft landed on Earth any time during the era of the dinosaurs, lasting about 140 million years. It is only logical to assume the aliens would have returned at reasonable intervals to study our world and these fascinating animals, but also to find out if any one of them evolved the capability of reasoning, higher math, and building a civilization. There would have been reason for much surmise. According to paleontologists, Drake stresses, the dinosaur sauronithoides was endowed with such a potential. It was a dinosaur resembling a bird of our size and weight and possessing a mass of brain well above average, and, Drake speculates, if it had survived for an additional ten or twenty million years, it might have evolved into the first intelligent being on Earth. But it didn't happen, because the dinosaurs went extinct due to a cosmic catastrophe. When *Homo australopithecus,* then *Homo faber* and *habilis,* and lastly *Homo sapiens* evolved, shouldn't that have provoked on the part of visiting extraterrestrials a high level of interest? But no such visits are recorded. Only a few mythological, undocumented and highly suspect accounts of alleged visiting aliens exist. It is fair to assume, if advanced aliens had visited Earth during the past 200 million or, at least, during the past 16 million years, they would have left some durable, indestructible and recognizable mark, probably on the moon. But nothing has been detected. The most likely explanation? No such visits took place! There are no advanced extraterrestrial civilizations anywhere in our vicinity. If they existed, they already would have responded to our world's television signals, reaching some 60 light-years into space—another reason invalidating the claim that our galaxy is teeming with intelligence.

Another argument supporting the skeptical point of view sustained here is the fact that none of the detected planets around other stars comes close to having conditions apt for creating and sustaining life. Since Michel Mayor's Swiss group discovered the first planet outside our solar system around the star 51 Pegasi ten years ago, about 130 other planets have been identified within a distance of 200 light-years. Research results show that most are of gaseous composition, some many times the size of Jupiter, some very close to their stars, very hot and with extremely rapid orbital cycles. So far, not one presents conditions favorable for the development of even the most primitive forms of life, not to speak of more complex species. Again it may be argued that only a very tiny fraction of planets were surveyed and future research might strike upon a suitable candidate. This may well be, and I would certainly welcome it. But so far the evidence fails to nourish optimistic expectations. The conditions in our universe are not as favorable for the evolution of life as optimists like to think.

Even if water or fossils of microorganisms should be found underneath the surface of Mars, the importance of such a finding for the theory of a multiplicity of inhabited worlds would be insignificant. Some astronomers think that Titan, the famous moon of Saturn, may have an ocean, possibly of methane. Primitive life forms may exist in it, but this remains to be seen. Even if it does, the evolutionary path from such primitive forms to complex life as human beings is—as we have seen—a long one, studded with a unique sequence of chance and catastrophes.

I am not claiming that we are probably the only intelligent species in our galaxy. Nor do I suggest that SETI activities are a waste of time and money. Though, so far, they have failed to obtain evidence for the existence of ETI, they enrich man's knowledge about the cosmos in many ways. They helped develop sophisticated search techniques, and they contribute decisively to the perception of man's cosmic destiny. Carl Sagan and Frank Drake, the two most distinguished pioneers of SETI, did groundbreaking work. That their efforts and those of other dedicated SETI experts on behalf of this great cause are tinged with a dash of too optimistic expectation is understandable and profoundly human.

However, in the interest of science and sound skepticism, I believe it is time to take the new findings and insights into account, to dampen excessive SETI euphoria and to adopt a more pragmatic and down-to-earth stand, compatible with facts. We should quietly admit that the early estimates—that there may be a million, a hundred thousand, or ten thousand advanced extraterrestrial civilizations in our galaxy—may no longer be tenable. There might not be a hundred, not even ten such civilizations. The optimistic estimates were fraught with too many imponderables and speculative appraisals. What is required is to make contact with a single extraterrestrial intelligence, obtaining irrefutable, thoroughly verified evidence, either via electromagnetic or optical waves or via physical contact, that we are not the only intelligent species in the cosmos. Maybe an alien spacecraft, attracted by our signals, will decide to visit us some day, as I surmised in my novel *Contact: Are We Ready for It?* I would be the first one to react to such a contact event with great delight and satisfaction. The knowledge that we are not alone in the vast realm of the cosmos, and that it will be possible to establish a fruitful dialogue with other, possibly more advanced intelligent beings would mark the biggest event in human history. It would open the door to fantastic perspectives.

But SETI activities so far do not justify this hope. They recommend a more realistic and sober view. Considering the negative search results, the creation of excessive expectations is only grist to the mill of the naysayers—for instance, members of Congress who question the scientific standing of SETI, imputing to it wishful thinking, and denying it financial support. This absolutely negative approach to SETI is certainly wrong, because contrary to the

UFO hoax, SETI (as UCLA space scientist Mark Moldwin stressed in a recent issue of this magazine) is based on solid scientific premises and considerations. But exaggerated estimates fail to conform to realities, as they are seen today, tending to backfire and create disappointment and a turning away from this fascinating scientific endeavor. The dream of mankind to find brethren in space may yet be fulfilled. If it is not, man should not feel sorry for his uniqueness. Rather that circumstance should boost the gratitude for his existence and his sense of responsibility for making the most of it.

POSTSCRIPT

Will the Search for Extraterrestrial Life Ever Succeed?

If the universe is full of intelligent species, why haven't they shown up yet?

Are we in fact alone? Or first? Are the conditions that lead to life and intelligence rare? Are there aliens living in disguise amongst us? Or are we quarantined? Reservationed? Zooed? Or maybe there's nobody there at all—not even us! (Sure, that could be it—if we are just simulations in some cosmic computer.) In *Where Is Everybody? Fifty Solutions to the Fermi Paradox and the Problem of Extraterrestrial Life* (Copernicus Books, 2002), Stephen Webb describes Fermi and his paradox in detail and offers a variety of answers that have been suggested—most seriously, some a bit tongue-in-cheek—for why the search has not succeeded. His own opinion is on the pessimistic side.

The SETI community, however, remains convinced that their effort is worthwhile. *SETI 2020: A Roadmap for the Search for Extraterrestrial Intelligence* (SETI Press, SETI Institute, 2002) is the report of the Search for Extraterrestrial Intelligence (SETI) Science and Technology Working Group, which between 1997 and 1999 developed a plan for the SETI effort through 2020, which will center on multi-antenna arrays, improved multi-channel scanning, and initial efforts to look for infrared and optical signals. The book provides plentiful details, as well as a brief survey of SETI history, the science that backs up the idea that SETI is worth attempting, and the technology that makes SETI even remotely possible. The question of whether life even exists off Earth is surveyed by Brian Vastag, "Will We Soon Find Life in the Heavens?" *U.S. News and World Report* (August 4, 2008).

Naomi Lubick, "An Ear to the Stars," *Scientific American* (November 2002), describes the SETI career of Jill Tarter and discusses new technology being developed for the search. The Terrestrial Planet Finder is discussed by Ray Jayawardhana, "Searching for Alien Earths," *Astronomy* (June 2003). The continuing determination and optimism of the SETI community is described by Richard A. Kerr, "No Din of Alien Chatter in Our Neighborhood," *Science* (February 20, 2004). See also Seth Shostak, "Listening for a Whisper," *Astronomy* (September 2004). In February 2008, SETI researchers met in Arizona to discuss whether the continuing failure to find signs of extraterrestrial intelligence meant they should stop trying. Jill Tarter and Seth Shostak agreed that it is far too early to give up or even to change search methods drastically. See Zeeya Merali, "Is There Anybody Out There? The Hunt for Extraterrestrial Intelligence Has Yielded Barely a Hint of Any Alien Civilisations. Now the Search Is Stepping Up a Gear," *New Scientist* (February 9, 2008).

What if SETI succeeds? Frank Drake noted in *Is Anyone Out There? The Scientific Search for Extraterrestrial Intelligence* (Delacorte Press, 1992) that positive results would have to be reported to everyone, at once, in order to prevent attempts to suppress or monopolize the discovery. Albert A. Harrison, "Confirmation of ETI: Initial Organizational Response," *Acta Astronautica* (August 2003), focuses on the need for a response to success but he is skeptical that an effective response is possible; he says, "Foresight and advance preparation are among the steps that organizations may take to prepare for contact, but conservative values, skepticism towards SETI, and competing organizational priorities make serious preparation unlikely." Should our response include sending an answer back to the source of whatever radio signals we detect? H. Paul Schuch, "The Search for Extraterrestrial Intelligence," *Futurist* (May/June 2003), suggests that there may be dangers in such a move. Those dangers are addressed by Ivan Almar and H. Paul Schuch in "The San Marino Scale: A New Analytical Tool for Assessing Transmission Risk," *Acta Astronautica* (January 2007). A few nonscientists have also begun to consider the implications of successful contact. See, for instance, Thomas Hoffman, "Exomissiology: The Launching of Exotheology," *Dialog: A Journal of Theology* (Winter 2004).

Have the results of SETI to date been totally blank? Researchers have found nothing that justified any claim of success, but there have been a few "tantalizing signals." T. Joseph W. Lazio and Robert Naeye discuss them in "Hello? Are You Still There?" *Mercury* (May/June 2003).

ISSUE 14

Is "Manned Space Travel" a Delusion?

YES: Neil deGrasse Tyson, from "Delusions of Space Enthusiasts," *Natural History* (November 2006)

NO: George W. Bush, from "President Bush Announces New Vision for Space Exploration Program," Office of the Press Secretary (January 14, 2004)

ISSUE SUMMARY

YES: Astronomer Neil deGrasse Tyson argues that large, expensive projects such as space exploration are driven only by war, greed, and the celebration of power. The dream of colonizing space became a delusion as soon as we beat the Russians to the moon, and it remains so.

NO: President George W. Bush argues for his vision of renewed and expanded manned space travel because it improves our lives and lifts the national spirit.

The dream of conquering space has a long history. The pioneers of rocketry—the Russian Konstantin Tsiolkovsky (1857–1935) and the American Robert H. Goddard (1882–1945)—both dreamed of exploring other worlds, although neither lived long enough to see the first artificial satellite, the Soviet *Sputnik,* go up in 1957. That success sparked a race between America and the Soviet Union to be the first to achieve each step in the progression of space exploration. The next steps were to put dogs (the Soviet Laika was the first), monkeys, chimps, and finally human beings into orbit. Communications, weather, and spy satellites were designed and launched. And on July 20, 1969, the U.S. Project Apollo program landed the first men on the moon.

There were a few more *Apollo* landings, but not many. The United States had achieved its main political goal of beating the Soviets to the moon and, in the minds of the government, demonstrating American superiority. Thereafter, the United States was content to send automated spacecraft (computer-operated robots) to observe Venus, Mars, and the rings of Saturn; to land on Mars and study its soil; and even to carry recordings of Earth's sights and sounds past the distant edge of the solar system, perhaps to be retrieved in the distant future by intelligent life from some other world. (Those recordings are attached to the *Voyager* spacecraft, launched in 1977; published as a combination of CD, CD-ROM, and book, *Murmurs of Earth: The Voyager Interstellar Record,* it is now long out of print.) Humans have not left near-Earth orbit for two decades, even though space technology has continued to develop. The results of this development include communications satellites, space shuttles, space stations, and independent robotic explorers such as the *Mariners* and *Vikings,* the rovers *Spirit* and *Opportunity,* and the polar lander *Phoenix*, which finally found water on Mars in July 2008.

Why has human space exploration gone no further to date? One reason is that robots are now extremely capable. Although some robot spacecraft have failed partially or completely, there have been many grand successes that have added enormously to humanity's knowledge of Earth and other planets. Another is money: Lifting robotic explorers into space is expensive, but lifting people into space—along with all the food, water, air, and other supplies necessary to keep them alive for the duration of a mission—is much more expensive. And there are many people in government and elsewhere who cry that there are many better ways to spend the money on Earth.

Still another reason for the reduction in human space travel seems to be the fear that astronauts will die in space. This point was emphasized by the explosion on takeoff of the space shuttle *Challenger* in January 1986, which killed seven astronauts and froze the entire shuttle program for over two and a half years. The point was reinforced by the breakup of *Columbia* on entry February 1, 2003. After the latter event, the public reaction included many calls for an end to such risky, expensive enterprises. See Jerry Grey, *"Columbia*—Aftermath of a Tragedy," *Aerospace America* (March 2003); John Byron, "Is Manned Space Flight Worth It?" *Proceedings* (of the U.S. Naval Institute) (March 2003) (and Richard H. Truly's response in the May issue); and "Manned or Unmanned into Space?" *USA Today* (February 26, 2003), among many others.

In the following selections, astronomer Neil deGrasse Tyson argues that large, expensive projects such as space exploration are driven only by war, greed, and the celebration of power. The dream of colonizing space became a delusion as soon as we beat the Russians to the moon, and it remains so. The Apollo program was the end of an era, not the beginning that many hoped it would prove. In January 2004, President George W. Bush announced a bold plan to send humans to the moon and Mars, beginning as soon as 2015. In this speech, he argues for his vision of renewed and expanded manned space travel because it improves our lives and lifts the national spirit.

YES

Neil deGrasse Tyson

Delusions of Space Enthusiasts

Sometimes innovation gets interrupted.

Human ingenuity seldom fails to improve on the fruits of human invention. Whatever may have dazzled everyone on its debut is almost guaranteed to be superseded and, someday, to look quaint.

In 2000 B.C. a pair of ice skates made of polished animal bone and leather thongs was a transportation breakthrough. In 1610 Galileo's eight-power telescope was an astonishing tool of detection, capable of giving the senators of Venice a sneak peek at hostile ships before they could enter the lagoon. In 1887 the one-horsepower Benz Patent Motorwagen was the first commercially produced car powered by an internal combustion engine. In 1946 the thirty-ton, showroom-size ENIAC, with its 18,000 vacuum tubes and 6,000 manual switches, pioneered electronic computing. Today you can glide across roadways on in-line skates, gaze at images of faraway galaxies brought to you by the Hubble Space Telescope, cruise the autobahn in a 600-horsepower roadster, and carry your three-pound laptop to an outdoor café.

Of course, such advances don't just fall from the sky. Clever people think them up. Problem is, to turn a clever idea into reality, somebody has to write the check. And when market forces shift, those somebodies may lose interest and the checks may stop coming. If computer companies had stopped innovating in 1978, your desk might still sport a hundred-pound IBM 5110. If communications companies had stopped innovating in 1973, you might still be schlepping a two-pound, nine-inch-long cell phone. And if in 1968 the U.S. space industry had stopped developing bigger and better rockets to launch humans beyond the Moon, we'd never have surpassed the Saturn V rocket.

Oops!

Sorry about that. We haven't surpassed the Saturn V. The largest, most powerful rocket ever flown by anybody, ever, the thirty-six-story-tall Saturn V was the first and only rocket to launch people from Earth to someplace else in the universe. It enabled every Apollo mission to the Moon from 1969 through 1972, as well as the 1973 launch of Skylab I, the first U.S. space station.

Inspired in part by the successes of the Saturn V and the momentum of the Apollo program, visionaries of the day foretold a future that never came to be: space habitats, Moon bases, and Mars colonies up and running by the 1990s. But funding for the Saturn V evaporated as the Moon missions wound down. Additional production runs were canceled, the manufacturers' specialized machine tools were destroyed, and skilled personnel had to find work on other projects. Today U.S. engineers can't even build a Saturn V clone. . . .

What cultural forces froze the Saturn V rocket in time and space?

What misconceptions led to the gap between expectation and reality?

Soothsaying tends to come in two flavors: doubt and delirium. It was doubt that led skeptics to declare that the atom would never be split, the sound barrier would never be broken, and people would never want or need computers in their homes. But in the case of the Saturn V rocket, it was delirium that misled futurists into assuming the Saturn V was an auspicious beginning—never considering that it could, instead, be an end.

On December 30, 1900, for its last Sunday paper of the nineteenth century, the *Brooklyn Daily Eagle* published a sixteen-page supplement headlined "THINGS WILL BE SO DIFFERENT A HUNDRED YEARS HENCE." The contributors—business leaders, military men, pastors, politicians, and experts of every persuasion—imagined what housework, poverty, religion, sanitation, and war would be like in the year 2000. They enthused about the potential of electricity and the automobile. There was even a map of the world-to-be, showing an American Federation comprising most of the Western Hemisphere from the lands above the Arctic Circle down to the archipelago of Tierra del Fuego—plus sub-Saharan Africa, the southern half of Australia, and all of New Zealand.

Most of the writers portrayed an expansive future. But not all. George H. Daniels, a man of authority at the New York Central and Hudson River Railroad, peered into his crystal ball and, boneheadedly predicted:

> It is scarcely possible that the twentieth century will witness improvements in transportation that will be as great as were those of the nineteenth century.

Elsewhere in his article, Daniels envisioned affordable global tourism and the diffusion of white bread to China and Japan. Yet he simply couldn't imagine what might replace steam as the power source for ground transportation, let alone a vehicle moving through the air. Even though he stood on the doorstep of the twentieth century, this manager of the world's biggest railroad system could not see beyond the automobile, the locomotive, and the steamship. . . .

Three years later, almost to the day, Wilbur and Orville Wright made the first-ever series of powered, controlled, heavier-than-air flights. By 1957 the U.S.S.R. launched the first satellite into Earth orbit. And in 1969 two Americans became the first human beings to walk on the Moon.

Daniels is hardly the only person to have misread the technological future. Even experts who aren't totally deluded can have tunnel vision. On page 13 of the *Eagle's* Sunday supplement, the principal examiner at the U.S. Patent Office, W.W. Townsend, wrote, "The automobile may be the vehicle of the decade, but the air ship is the conveyance of the century." Sounds visionary, until you read further. What he was talking about were blimps and zeppelins. Both Daniels and Townsend, otherwise well-informed citizens of a changing world, were clueless about what tomorrow's technology would bring. . . .

Even the Wrights were guilty of doubt about the future of aviation. In 1901, discouraged by a summer's worth of unsuccessful tests with a glider, Wilbur told Orville it would take another fifty years for someone to fly. Nope: the birth of aviation was just two years away. On the windy, chilly morning of December 17, 1903, starting from a North Carolina sand dune called Kill Devil Hill, Orville was the first to fly the brothers' 600-pound plane through the air. His epochal journey lasted twelve seconds and covered 120 feet—a distance just shy of the wingspan of a Boeing 757.

Judging by what the mathematician, astronomer, and Royal Society gold medalist Simon Newcomb had published just two months earlier, the flights from Kill Devil Hill should never have taken place when they did:

> Quite likely the twentieth century is destined to see the natural forces which will enable us to fly from continent to continent with a speed far exceeding that of the bird.
>
> But when we inquire whether aerial flight is possible in the present state of our knowledge; whether, with such materials as we possess, a combination of steel, cloth and wire can be made which, moved by the power of electricity or steam, shall form a successful flying machine, the outlook may be altogether different.

. . . Some representatives of informed public opinion went even further. The *New York Times* was steeped in doubt just one week before the Wright brothers went aloft in the original Wright Flyer. Writing on December 10, 1903—not about the Wrights but about their illustrious and publicly funded competitor, Samuel E. Langley, an astronomer, physicist, and chief administrator of the Smithsonian Institution—the *Times* declared:

> We hope that Professor Langley will not put his substantial greatness as a scientist in further peril by continuing to waste his time, and the money involved, in further airship experiments. Life is short, and he is capable of services to humanity incomparably greater than can be expected to result from trying to fly.

. . . You might think attitudes would have changed as soon as people from several countries had made their first flights. But no. Wilbur Wright wrote in 1909 that no flying machine would ever make the journey from New York to Paris. Richard Burdon Haldane, the British secretary of war, told Parliament in 1909 that even though the airplane might one day be capable of great things, "from the war point of view, it is not so at present." Ferdinand Foch, a highly regarded French military strategist and the supreme commander of the Allied forces near the end of the First World War, opined in 1911 that airplanes were interesting toys but had no military value. Late that same year, near Tripoli, an Italian plane became the first to drop a bomb.

Early attitudes about flight beyond Earth's atmosphere followed a similar trajectory. True, plenty of philosophers, scientists, and sci-fi writers had thought long and hard about outer space. The sixteenth-century philosopher-friar Giordano Bruno proposed that intelligent beings inhabited an infinitude of worlds. The seventeenth-century soldier-writer Savinien de Cyrano de Bergerac portrayed the Moon as a world with forests, violets, and people.

But those writings were fantasies, not blueprints for action. By the early twentieth century, electricity, telephones, automobiles, radios, airplanes, and countless other engineering marvels were all becoming basic features of modern life. So couldn't earthlings build machines capable of space travel? Many people who should have known better said it couldn't be done, even after the successful 1942 test launch of the world's first long-range ballistic missile: Germany's deadly V-2 rocket. Capable of punching through Earth's atmosphere, it was a crucial step toward reaching the Moon.

Richard van der Riet Woolley, the eleventh British Astronomer Royal, is the source of a particularly woolly remark. When he landed in London after a thirty-six-hour flight from Australia, some reporters asked him about space travel. "It's utter bilge," he answered. That was in early 1956. In early 1957 Lee De Forest, a prolific American inventor who helped birth the age of electronics, declared, "Man will never reach the moon, regardless of all future scientific advances." Remember what happened in late 1957? Not just one but two Soviet Sputniks entered Earth orbit. The space race had begun.

Whenever someone says an idea is "bilge" (British for "baloney"), you must first ask whether it violates any well-tested laws of physics. If so, the idea is likely to be bilge. If not, the only challenge is to find a clever engineer—and, of course, a committed source of funding.

The day the Soviet Union launched Sputnik 1, a chapter of science fiction became science fact, and the future became the present. All of a sudden, futurists went overboard with their enthusiasm. The delusion that technology would advance at lightning speed replaced the delusion that it would barely advance at all. Experts went from having much too little confidence in the pace of technology to having much too much. And the guiltiest people of all were the space enthusiasts.

Commentators became fond of twenty-year intervals, within which some previously inconceivable goal would supposedly be accomplished. On January 6, 1967, in a front-page story, *The Wall Street Journal* announced: "The most ambitious U.S. space endeavor in the years ahead will be the campaign to land men on neighboring Mars. Most experts estimate the task can be accomplished by 1985." The very next month, in its debut issue, *The Futurist* magazine announced that according to long-range forecasts by the RAND Corporation, a pioneer think-tank, there was a 60 percent probability that a manned lunar base would exist by 1986. In *The Book of Predictions,* published in 1980, the rocket pioneer Robert C. Truax forecast that 50,000 people would be living and working in space by the year 2000. When that benchmark year arrived, people were indeed living and working in space. But the tally was not 50,000. It was three: the first crew of the International Space Station. . . .

All those visionaries (and countless others) never really grasped the forces that drive technological progress. In Wilbur and Orville's day, you could tinker your way into major engineering advances. Their first airplane did not require a grant from the National Science Foundation: they funded it through their bicycle business. The brothers constructed the wings and fuselage themselves, with tools they already owned, and got their resourceful bicycle mechanic, Charles E. Taylor, to design and hand-build the engine. The operation was basically two guys and a garage.

Space exploration unfolds on an entirely different scale. The first moon-walkers were two guys, too—Neil Armstrong and Buzz Aldrin—but behind them loomed the force of a mandate from an assassinated president, 10,000 engineers, $100 billion, and a Saturn V rocket.

Notwithstanding the sanitized memories so many of us have of the Apollo era, Americans were not first on the Moon because we're explorers by nature or because our country is committed to the pursuit of knowledge. We got to the Moon first because the United States was out to beat the Soviet Union, to win the Cold War any way we could. John F. Kennedy made that clear when he complained to top NASA officials in November 1962:

> I'm not that interested in space. I think it's good, I think we ought to know about it, we're ready to spend reasonable amounts of money. But we're talking about these fantastic expenditures which wreck our budget and all these other domestic programs and the only justification for it in my opinion to do it in this time or fashion is because we hope to beat them [the Soviet Union] and demonstrate that starting behind, as we did by a couple of years, by God, we passed them.

Like it or not, war (cold or hot) is the most powerful funding driver in the public arsenal. When a country wages war, money flows like floodwaters. Lofty goals—such as curiosity, discovery, exploration, and science—can get you money for modest-size projects, provided they resonate with the political and cultural views of the moment. But big, expensive activities are inherently long term, and require sustained investment that must survive economic fluctuations and changes in the political winds.

In all eras, across time and culture, only three drivers have fulfilled that funding requirement: war, greed, and the celebration of royal or religious power. The Great Wall of China; the pyramids of Egypt; the Gothic cathedrals of Europe; the U.S. interstate highway system; the voyages of Columbus and Cook—nearly every major undertaking owes its existence to one or more of those three drivers. Today, as the power of kings is supplanted by elected governments, and the power of religion is often expressed in non-architectural undertakings, that third driver has lost much of its sway, leaving war and greed to run the show. Sometimes those two drivers work hand in hand, as in the art of profiteering from the art of war. But war itself remains the ultimate and most compelling rationale.

Having been born the same week NASA was founded, I was eleven years old during the voyage of Apollo 11, and had already identified the universe as my life's passion. Unlike so many other people who watched Neil Armstrong's first steps on the Moon, I wasn't jubilant. I was simply relieved that someone was finally exploring another world. To me, Apollo 11 was clearly the beginning of an era.

But I, too, was delirious. The lunar landings continued for three and a half years. Then they stopped. The Apollo program became the end of an era, not the beginning. And as the Moon voyages receded in time and memory, they seemed ever more unreal in the history of human projects.

Unlike the first ice skates or the first airplane or the first desktop computer—artifacts that make us all chuckle when we see them today—the first rocket to the Moon, the 364-foot-tall Saturn V, elicits awe, even reverence. Three Saturn V relics lie in state at the Johnson Space Center in Texas, the Kennedy Space Center in Florida, and the U.S. Space and Rocket Center in Alabama. Streams of worshippers walk the length of each rocket. They touch the mighty rocket nozzles at the base and wonder how something so large could ever have bested Earth's gravity. To transform their awe into chuckles, our country will have to resume the effort to "boldly go where no man has gone before." Only then will the Saturn V look as quaint as every other invention that human ingenuity has paid the compliment of improving upon.

George W. Bush

President Bush Announces New Vision for Space Exploration Program

Thanks for the warm welcome. I'm honored to be with the men and women of NASA. I thank those of you who have come in person. I welcome those who are listening by video. This agency, and the dedicated professionals who serve it, have always reflected the finest values of our country—daring, discipline, ingenuity, and unity in the pursuit of great goals.

America is proud of our space program. The risk takers and visionaries of this agency have expanded human knowledge, have revolutionized our understanding of the universe, and produced technological advances that have benefited all of humanity.

Inspired by all that has come before, and guided by clear objectives, today we set a new course for America's space program. We will give NASA a new focus and vision for future exploration. We will build new ships to carry man forward into the universe, to gain a new foothold on the moon, and to prepare for new journeys to worlds beyond our own.

I am comfortable in delegating these new goals to NASA, under the leadership of Sean O'Keefe. He's doing an excellent job. I appreciate Commander Mike Foale's introduction—I'm sorry I couldn't shake his hand. Perhaps, Commissioner, you'll bring him by—Administrator, you'll bring him by the Oval Office when he returns, so I can thank him in person.

I also know he is in space with his colleague, Alexander Kaleri, who happens to be a Russian cosmonaut. I appreciate the joint efforts of the Russians with our country to explore. I want to thank the astronauts who are with us, the courageous spacial entrepreneurs who set such a wonderful example for the young of our country.

And we've got some veterans with us today. I appreciate the astronauts of yesterday who are with us, as well, who inspired the astronauts of today to serve our country. I appreciate so very much the members of Congress being here. Tom DeLay is here, leading a House delegation. Senator Nelson is here from the Senate. I am honored that you all have come. I appreciate you're interested in the subject, it is a subject that's important to this administration, it's a subject that's mighty important to the country and to the world.

From The White House Office of the Press Secretary, January 14, 2004.

Two centuries ago, Meriwether Lewis and William Clark left St. Louis to explore the new lands acquired in the Louisiana Purchase. They made that journey in the spirit of discovery, to learn the potential of vast new territory, and to chart a way for others to follow.

America has ventured forth into space for the same reasons. We have undertaken space travel because the desire to explore and understand is part of our character. And that quest has brought tangible benefits that improve our lives in countless ways. The exploration of space has led to advances in weather forecasting, in communications, in computing, search and rescue technology, robotics, and electronics. Our investment in space exploration helped to create our satellite telecommunications network and the Global Positioning System. Medical technologies that help prolong life—such as the imaging processing used in CAT scanners and MRI machines—trace their origins to technology engineered for use in space.

Our current programs and vehicles for exploring space have brought us far and they have served us well. The Space Shuttle has flown more than a hundred missions. It has been used to conduct important research and to increase the sum of human knowledge. Shuttle crews, and the scientists and engineers who support them, have helped to build the International Space Station.

Telescopes—including those in space—have revealed more than 100 planets in the last decade alone. Probes have shown us stunning images of the rings of Saturn and the outer planets of our solar system. Robotic explorers have found evidence of water—a key ingredient for life—on Mars and on the moons of Jupiter. At this very hour, the Mars Exploration Rover Spirit is searching for evidence of life beyond the Earth.

Yet for all these successes, much remains for us to explore and to learn. In the past 30 years, no human being has set foot on another world, or ventured farther upward into space than 386 miles—roughly the distance from Washington, D.C. to Boston, Massachusetts. America has not developed a new vehicle to advance human exploration in space in nearly a quarter century. It is time for America to take the next steps.

Today I announce a new plan to explore space and extend a human presence across our solar system. We will begin the effort quickly, using existing programs and personnel. We'll make steady progress—one mission, one voyage, one landing at a time.

Our first goal is to complete the International Space Station by 2010. We will finish what we have started, we will meet our obligations to our 15 international partners on this project. We will focus our future research aboard the station on the long-term effects of space travel on human biology. The environment of space is hostile to human beings. Radiation and weightlessness pose dangers to human health, and we have much to learn about their long-term effects before human crews can venture through the vast voids of space for months at a time. Research on board the station and here on Earth will help us better understand and overcome the obstacles that limit exploration. Through these efforts we will develop the skills and techniques necessary to sustain further space exploration. To meet this goal, we will return the Space Shuttle to flight as soon as possible, consistent with safety concerns and the recommendations of the Columbia Accident Investigation Board. The Shuttle's chief purpose over the next several years will be to help finish assembly of the International Space Station. In 2010, the Space Shuttle—after nearly 30 years of duty—will be retired from service.

Our second goal is to develop and test a new spacecraft, the Crew Exploration Vehicle, by 2008, and to conduct the first manned mission no later than 2014. The Crew Exploration Vehicle will be capable of ferrying astronauts and scientists to the Space Station after the shuttle is retired. But the main purpose of this spacecraft will be to carry astronauts beyond our orbit to other worlds. This will be the first spacecraft of its kind since the Apollo Command Module.

Our third goal is to return to the moon by 2020, as the launching point for missions beyond. Beginning no later than 2008, we will send a series of robotic missions to the lunar surface to research and prepare for future human exploration. Using the Crew Exploration Vehicle, we will undertake extended human missions to the moon as early as 2015, with the goal of living and working there for increasingly extended periods. Eugene Cernan, who is with us today—the last man to set foot on the lunar surface—said this as he left: "We leave as we came, and God willing as we shall return, with peace and hope for all mankind." America will make those words come true.

Returning to the moon is an important step for our space program. Establishing an extended human presence on the moon could vastly reduce the costs of further space exploration, making possible ever more ambitious missions. Lifting heavy spacecraft and fuel out of the Earth's gravity is expensive. Spacecraft assembled and provisioned on the moon could escape its far lower gravity using far less energy, and thus, far less cost. Also, the moon is home to abundant resources. Its soil contains raw materials that might be harvested and processed into rocket fuel or breathable air. We can use our time on the moon to develop and test new approaches and technologies and systems that will allow us to function in other, more challenging environments. The moon is a logical step toward further progress and achievement.

With the experience and knowledge gained on the moon, we will then be ready to take the next steps of space exploration: human missions to Mars and to worlds beyond. Robotic missions will serve as trailblazers—the advanced guard to the unknown. Probes, landers and other vehicles of this kind continue to prove their worth, sending spectacular images and vast amounts of data back to Earth. Yet the human thirst for knowledge ultimately cannot be satisfied by even the most vivid pictures, or the most detailed measurements. We need to see and examine and touch for ourselves. And only human beings are capable of adapting to the inevitable uncertainties posed by space travel.

As our knowledge improves, we'll develop new power generation propulsion, life support, and other systems that can support more distant travels. We do not know where this journey will end, yet we know this: human beings are headed into the cosmos.

And along this journey we'll make many technological breakthroughs. We don't know yet what those breakthroughs will be, but we can be certain they'll come, and that our efforts will be repaid many times over. We may discover resources on the moon or Mars that will boggle the imagination, that will test our limits to dream. And the fascination generated by further exploration will inspire our young people to study math, and science, and engineering and create a new generation of innovators and pioneers.

This will be a great and unifying mission for NASA, and we know that you'll achieve it. I have directed Administrator O'Keefe to review all of NASA's current space flight and exploration activities and direct them toward the goals I have outlined. I will also form a commission of private and public sector experts to advise on implementing the vision that I've outlined today. This commission will report to me within four months of its first meeting. I'm today naming former Secretary of the Air Force, Pete Aldridge, to be the Chair of the Commission. Thank you for being here today, Pete. He has tremendous experience in the Department of Defense and the aerospace industry. He is going to begin this important work right away.

We'll invite other nations to share the challenges and opportunities of this new era of discovery. The vision I outline today is a journey, not a race, and I call on other nations to join us on this journey, in a spirit of cooperation and friendship.

Achieving these goals requires a long-term commitment. NASA's current five-year budget is $86 billion. Most of the funding we need for the new endeavors will come from reallocating $11 billion within that budget. We need some new resources, however. I will call upon Congress to increase NASA's budget by roughly a billion dollars, spread out over the next five years. This increase, along with refocusing of our space agency, is a solid beginning to meet the challenges and the goals we set today. It's only a beginning. Future funding decisions will be guided by the progress we make in achieving our goals.

We begin this venture knowing that space travel brings great risks. The loss of the Space Shuttle Columbia was less than one year ago. Since the beginning of our space program, America has lost 23 astronauts, and one astronaut from an allied nation—men and women who believed in their mission and accepted the dangers. As one family member said, "The legacy of Columbia must carry on—for the benefit of our children and yours." The Columbia's crew did not turn away from the challenge, and neither will we.

Mankind is drawn to the heavens for the same reason we were once drawn into unknown lands and across the open sea. We choose to explore space because doing so improves our lives, and lifts our national spirit. So let us continue the journey.

POSTSCRIPT

Is "Manned Space Travel" a Delusion?

$\mathbf{A}$fter the *Columbia* tragedy, Stephen L. Petuanch, "No More Shuttles, Please," *Discover* (May 2003), denounced the space shuttle program as too expensive and unsafe. A new generation of shuttles is on the way; see Bill Sweetman, "Space Shuttle: The Next Generation," *Popular Science* (May 2003), and Mark Alpert, "Rethinking the Shuttle," *Scientific American* (April 2003). There are also efforts to develop an affordable spacecraft capable of many safe trips to and from orbit. In October 2004, Bert Rutan's *SpaceShipOne* won the $10 million Ansari X prize by becoming the first private, reusable craft to reach space (though not orbit). See Kathy A. Svitil and Eric Levin, "*SpaceShipOne* Opens Private Rocket Era," *Discover* (January 2005), and Bert Rutan, "Rocket for the Rest of Us," *National Geographic* (April 2005). The next step for private spacecraft is to reach orbit.

When President George W. Bush announced his plan to send humans to the moon and Mars, beginning as soon as 2015, the reaction was immediate. James A. Van Allen asked "Is Human Spaceflight Obsolete?" in *Issues in Science and Technology* (Summer 2004). Andrew Lawler asked "How Much Space for Science?" in *Science* (January 30, 2004). Physicist and Nobel laureate Steven Weinberg, "The Wrong Stuff," *New York Review of Books* (April 8, 2004), argues that nothing needs doing in space that cannot be done without human presence. Until we find something that does need humans on the scene, there is no particular reason to send humans—at great expense—into space. Indeed, the president's Mars initiative may prove to be no more than a ploy to look visionary and force later presidents to face financial realities. John Derbyshire, "Space Is for Science," *National Review* (June 5, 2006), argues that the expense and hazards of putting humans in space do not justify the benefits when much cheaper automated spacecraft (robots) can make all necessary observations. Paul D. Spudis, "Who Should Explore Space? Astronaut Explorers Can Perform Science in Space That Robots Cannot," *Scientific American Special Edition* (January 2008), argues that there is no substitute for human astronauts in installing and maintaining equipment and in conducting field exploration because humans provide skills that are unlikely to be automated in the foreseeable future. Francis Slakey, "Who Should Explore Space? Unmanned Spacecraft Are Exploring the Solar System More Cheaply and Effectively Than Astronauts Are," *Scientific American Special Edition* (January 2008), argues that NASA sends humans into space chiefly for public relations purposes. Unmanned probes are much cheaper and more effective than astronauts, and many scientific organizations have recommended that space science should instead be done through robotic and telescopic missions. See also Louis D. Friedman and G. Scott Hubbard, "Examining the Vision," *American Scientist* (July/August 2008).

The question of whether robots can do the job is particularly relevant because of the success of the Mars rovers, *Spirit* and *Opportunity*, and the *Phoenix* lander. If robots continue to be successful, it seems likely that efforts to promote manned space travel, even from the White House, will meet resistance. Funding for space exploration remains low largely because problems on Earth (environmental and other) seem to need money more urgently than space exploration projects do. The prospects for manned space expeditions to the moon, Mars, or other worlds seem very dim, although Paul D. Spudis, "Harvest the Moon," *Astronomy* (June 2003), asserts that there are four good reasons for putting people at least on the moon: "The first motivation to revisit the Moon is that its rocks hold the early history of our own planet and the solar system. Next, its unique environment and properties make it an ideal vantage point for observing the universe. The Moon is also a natural space station where we can learn how to live off-planet. And finally, it gives us an extraterrestrial filling station, with resources to use both locally and in near-Earth space." See also Paul D. Spudis, "The New Moon," *Scientific American* (December 2003). Nader Elhefnawy, "Beyond *Columbia:* Is There a Future for Humanity in Space?" *The Humanist* (September/October 2003), says that we cannot ignore the wealth of resources in space. Alex Ellery, "Humans versus Robots for Space Exploration and Development," *Space Policy* (May 2003), maintains that although "robotics and artificial intelligence are becoming more sophisticated, they will not be able to deal with 'thinking-on-one's-feet' tasks that require generalisations from past experience. . . . [T]here will be a critical role for humans in space for the foreseeable future." Carl Gethmann, "Manned Space Travel as a Cultural Mission," *Poiesis & Praxis* (December 2006), argues that costs should not be used to reject manned space travel as a pointless option. The dream and the effort are part of our culture, and we should pursue them as far as we can afford to. Arthur Woods, "The Space Option," *Leonardo* (vol. 41, no. 4, 2008), argues that space resources are the most realistic way to ensure future human survival and success. However, an important question is whether the necessary effort and expenditure can be sustained; see David A. Broniatowski and Annalisa L. Weigel, "The Political Sustainability of Space Exploration," *Space Policy* (August 2008). George Whitesides, "The Coming Debate," *Ad Astra* (Summer 2008), argues that the most potent argument for sending humans into space is the role NASA can play in fighting global warming. New President Obama has included increased funding for NASA in the 2010 budget; see "Obama Budget Includes Funding Boost for NASA," *Space.com* (February 26, 2009) (http://www.space.com/news/090226-nasa-obama-2010-budget.html).

Internet References . . .

Center for Democracy & Technology

The Center for Democracy & Technology works to promote democratic values and constitutional liberties in the digital age.

http://www.cdt.org/

Electronic Frontier Foundation

The Electronic Frontier Foundation is concerned with protecting individual freedoms and rights such as privacy as new communications technologies emerge.

http://www.eff.org

MIT Computer Science and Artificial Intelligence Laboratory

In hundreds of diverse projects, the MIT Computer Science and Artificial Intelligence Laboratory works to unlock the secrets of human intelligence, extend the functional capabilities of machines, and explore human/machine interactions.

http://www.csail.mit.edu/

Google Print Library Project

According to Google, the Library Project's aim is to make it easier for people to find relevant books, especially those that are out of print—while carefully respecting authors' and publishers' copyrights. Google's ultimate goal is to create a comprehensive, searchable, virtual card catalog of all books in all languages.

http://books.google.com/googleprint/library.html

The Computer Revolution

*F*ans *of computers have long been sure that the electronic wonders offer untold benefits to society. When the first personal computers appeared in the early 1970s, they immediately brought unheard-of capabilities to their users. Ever since, those capabilities have been increasing. Today children command more sheer computing power than major corporations did in the 1950s and 1960s. Computer users are in direct contact with their fellow users around the world. Information is instantly available and infinitely malleable.*

Some observers wonder about the purported untold benefits of computers. Specifically, will such benefits be outweighed by threats to children (by free access to pornography and by online predators), civil order (by free access to sites that advocate racism and violence), traditional institutions (will books, for example, become an endangered species?), or to human pride (computers have already outplayed human champions at chess, checkers, and go)? Should Google be allowed to make the contents of the world's libraries available to all when they search for information? And if computers can outthink humans at games, how long will it be before they are as intelligent and even conscious as we are?

- Can Machines Be Conscious?
- Is Information Technology a Threat to Privacy?
- Should the World's Libraries Be Digitized?

ISSUE 15

Can Machines Be Conscious?

YES: Christof Koch and Giulio Tononi, from "Can Machines Be Conscious?" *IEEE Spectrum* (June 2008)

NO: John Horgan, from "The Consciousness Conundrum," *IEEE Spectrum* (June 2008)

ISSUE SUMMARY

YES: Christof Koch and Giulio Tononi argue that because consciousness is a natural phenomenon, it will eventually be artificially created. To test for such consciousness, however, will require something other than the classic Turing test.

NO: John Horgan argues that no one has the foggiest idea of what consciousness really is, and it seems highly unlikely that we will ever be able to create an artificial consciousness. "Engineers and scientists should be helping us face the world's problems and find solutions to them, rather than indulging in escapist, pseudoscientific fantasies like the singularity."

The first primitive digital computers were instantly dubbed "thinking machines" because they were able to perform functions—initially only arithmetic—that had always been considered part of the uniquely human ability to think. Some critics of the "thinking machine" label, however, objected that arithmetic is so much simpler than, say, poetry or philosophy (after all, it is only a matter of following a few simple rules) that computers were not thinking at all. Thinking, they said, is for humans only. In fact, if a machine can do it, then it cannot possibly be real thinking. Philosopher John R. Searle, "Is the Brain's Mind a Computer Program?" *Scientific American* (January 1990), argues that mind and consciousness are special. They are what brains—not computers—do. Computers, he says, do no more than manipulate symbols. They do not know what the symbols mean.

In 1950, Alan Turing, an English mathematician and logician, devised a test to determine whether or not a machine was intelligent. The "imitation game" or "Turing test" considered whether or not one could converse with a person and with a computer (through a teletype so that neither could be seen and the human could not be heard) and, after a suitable period, tell which was which. If the computer could pass for an intelligent conversationalist, Turing felt, then it would have to be considered intelligent.

Over the next two decades, computer scientists learned how to program their machines to play games such as chess, solve mathematical theorems, analyze grammar, and perform a number of other tasks that had once been thought doable by thinking humans only. In most cases the machines were not as good at these tasks as humans, but many artificial intelligence (AI) researchers believed it was only a matter of time before the machines matched and even exceeded their creators.

The closest any machine has come to passing the Turing test may have been in the early 1970s, when the late Kenneth Mark Colby, then a Stanford University psychiatrist and computer scientist, programmed a computer to imitate the conversational style of paranoid humans. This was much easier than programming a computer to imitate a nonparanoid human's conversational style because paranoid individuals tend to be very rigid and predictable in their responses. When Colby had psychiatrists interview the programmed computer and a human paranoid (through a teletype, per Turing's criteria), only half could correctly distinguish between computer and human. That is, the computer did indeed come close to passing the Turing test. On the other hand, it was not trying to pass as a normal human being, whose thought processes are far freer, more flexible, and more capable.

Will a computer ever be able to imitate a normal human being? And if it can, will that mean it is really "thinking" or really "intelligent" or really "conscious"? Indeed, many even say that the human mind is nothing more than a program that runs on a biological machine.

Others argue that machines cannot have emotions or appreciate beauty and that computers cannot be self-aware or conscious, no matter how intelligent they may seem to an interrogator. They therefore can never be intelligent or conscious in a human way. However, research in this area has been extraordinarily fruitful. Jean-Pierre Dupuy, *The Mechanization of the Mind* (Princeton University Press, 2000), notes that in the 1940s a small group of mathematicians, engineers, and neurobiologists, working under the rubric of what Norbert Weiner called cybernetics, began to pursue the idea that thinking is a form of computation and thus to be understood as an essentially mechanical or material process. Therefore, everything once taken as uniquely human or spiritual—meaning, purpose, and direction—should be accepted as a matter of physical law, and thus by no means restricted to the human. Besides artificial intelligence, the consequences include conceptual innovations in economics, political science, sociology, and cognitive science. It has also become a major component of the concept of the "singularity," that moment when progress accelerates to the point where we can no longer predict what the next year—or even the next week!—will be like. This may happen when artificially intelligent computers become able to design, improve, and build themselves. Among its prominent features will be conscious computers and transfers of human minds into computers (with subsequent immortality).

Christof Koch and Giulio Tononi argue that because consciousness is a natural phenomenon, it will eventually be artificially created. To test for such consciousness, however, will require something other than the classic Turing test. John Horgan argues that no one has the foggiest idea of what consciousness really is, and it seems highly unlikely that we will ever be able to create an artificial consciousness.

YES    Christof Koch and Giulio Tononi

Can Machines Be Conscious?

Would you sell your soul on eBay? Right now, of course, you can't. But in some quarters it is taken for granted that within a generation, human beings—including you, if you can hang on for another 30 years or so—will have an alternative to death: being a ghost in a machine. You'll be able to upload your mind—your thoughts, memories, and personality—to a computer. And once you've reduced your consciousness to patterns of electrons, others will be able to copy it, edit it, sell it, or pirate it. It might be bundled with other electronic minds. And, of course, it could be deleted.

That's quite a scenario, considering that at the moment, nobody really knows exactly what consciousness is. Pressed for a pithy definition, we might call it the ineffable and enigmatic inner life of the mind. But that hardly captures the whirl of thought and sensation that blossoms when you see a loved one after a long absence, hear an exquisite violin solo, or relish an incredible meal. Some of the most brilliant minds in human history have pondered consciousness, and after a few thousand years we still can't say for sure if it is an intangible phenomenon or maybe even a kind of substance different from matter. We know it arises in the brain, but we don't know how or where in the brain. We don't even know if it requires specialized brain cells (or neurons) or some sort of special circuit arrangement of them.

Nevertheless, some in the singularity crowd are confident that we are within a few decades of building a computer, a simulacrum, that can experience the color red, savor the smell of a rose, feel pain and pleasure, and fall in love. It might be a robot with a "body." Or it might just be software—a huge, ever-changing cloud of bits that inhabit an immensely complicated and elaborately constructed virtual domain.

We are among the few neuroscientists who have devoted a substantial part of their careers to studying consciousness. Our work has given us a unique perspective on what is arguably the most momentous issue in all of technology: whether consciousness will ever be artificially created.

We think it will—eventually. But perhaps not in the way that the most popular scenarios have envisioned it.

Consciousness is part of the natural world. It depends, we believe, only on mathematics and logic and on the imperfectly known laws of physics, chemistry, and biology; it does not arise from some magical or otherworldly quality. That's good news, because it means there's no reason why consciousness can't be reproduced in a machine—in theory, anyway.

From *IEEE Spectrum,* June 2008, part of Special Report: The Singularity. Copyright © 2008 by IEEE Spectrum. Reprinted by permission.

In humans and animals, we know that the specific content of any conscious experience—the deep blue of an alpine sky, say, or the fragrance of jasmine redolent in the night air—is furnished by parts of the cerebral cortex, the outer layer of gray matter associated with thought, action, and other higher brain functions. If a sector of the cortex is destroyed by stroke or some other calamity, the person will no longer be conscious of whatever aspect of the world that part of the brain represents. For instance, a person whose visual cortex is partially damaged may be unable to recognize faces, even though he can still see eyes, mouths, ears, and other discrete facial features. Consciousness can be lost entirely if injuries permanently damage most of the cerebral cortex, as seen in patients like Terri Schiavo, who suffered from persistent vegetative state. Lesions of the cortical white matter, containing the fibers through which parts of the brain communicate, also cause unconsciousness. And small lesions deep within the brain along the midline of the thalamus and the midbrain can inactivate the cerebral cortex and indirectly lead to a coma—and a lack of consciousness.

To be conscious also requires the cortex and thalamus—the corticothalamic system—to be constantly suffused in a bath of substances known as neuromodulators, which aid or inhibit the transmission of nerve impulses. Finally, whatever the mechanisms necessary for consciousness, we know they must exist in both cortical hemispheres independently.

Much of what goes on in the brain has nothing to do with being conscious, however. Widespread damage to the cerebellum, the small structure at the base of the brain, has no effect on consciousness, despite the fact that more neurons reside there than in any other part of the brain. Neural activity obviously plays some essential role in consciousness but in itself is not enough to sustain a conscious state. We know that at the beginning of a deep sleep, consciousness fades, even though the neurons in the corticothalamic system continue to fire at a level of activity similar to that of quiet wakefulness.

Data from clinical studies and from basic research laboratories, made possible by the use of sophisticated instruments that detect and record neuronal activity, have given us a complex if still rudimentary understanding of the myriad processes that give rise to consciousness. We are still a very long way from being able to use this knowledge to build a conscious machine. Yet we can already take the first step in that long journey: we can list some aspects of consciousness that are not strictly necessary for building such an artifact.

Remarkably, consciousness does not seem to require many of the things we associate most deeply with being human: emotions, memory, self-reflection, language, sensing the world, and acting in it. Let's start with sensory input and motor output: *being conscious requires neither*. We humans are generally aware of what goes on around us and occasionally of what goes on within our own bodies. It's only natural to infer that consciousness is linked to our interaction with the world and with ourselves.

Yet when we dream, for instance, we are virtually disconnected from the environment—we acknowledge almost nothing of what happens around us, and our muscles are largely paralyzed. Nevertheless, we are conscious, sometimes vividly and grippingly so. This mental activity is reflected in electrical recordings of the dreaming brain showing that the corticothalamic system, intimately involved with sensory perception, continues to function more or less as it does in wakefulness.

Neurological evidence points to the same conclusion. People who have lost their eyesight can both imagine and dream in images, provided they had sight earlier in their lives. Patients with locked-in syndrome, which renders them almost completely paralyzed, are just as conscious as healthy subjects. Following a debilitating stroke, the French editor Jean-Dominique Bauby dictated his memoir, *The Diving Bell and the Butterfly*, by blinking his left eye. Stephen Hawking is a world-renowned physicist, best-selling author, and occasional guest star on "The Simpsons," despite being immobilized from a degenerative neurological disorder.

So although being conscious depends on brain activity, it does not require any interaction with the environment. Whether the development of consciousness requires such interactions in early childhood, though, is a different matter.

How about emotions? Does a conscious being need to feel and display them? No: *being conscious does not require emotion*. People who've suffered damage to the frontal area of the brain, for instance, may exhibit a flat, emotionless affect; they are as dispassionate about their own predicament as they are about the problems of people around them. But even though their behavior is impaired and their judgment may be unsound, they still experience the sights and sounds of the world much the way normal people do.

Primal emotions like anger, fear, surprise, and joy are useful and perhaps even essential for the survival of a conscious organism. Likewise, a conscious machine might rely on emotions to make choices and deal with the complexities of the world. But it could be just a cold, calculating engine—and yet still be conscious.

Psychologists argue that consciousness requires selective attention—that is, the ability to focus on a given object, thought, or activity. Some have even argued that consciousness is selective attention. After all, when you pay attention to something, you become conscious of that thing and its properties; when your attention shifts, the object fades from consciousness.

Nevertheless, recent evidence favors the idea that a person can consciously perceive an event or object without paying attention to it. When you're focused on a riveting movie, your surroundings aren't reduced to a tunnel. You may not hear the phone ringing or your spouse calling your name, but you remain aware of certain aspects of the world around you. And here's a surprise: the converse is also true. People can attend to events or objects—that is, their brains can preferentially process them—without consciously perceiving them. This fact suggests that being conscious does not require attention.

One experiment that supported this conclusion found that, as strange as it sounds, people could pay attention to an object that they never "saw." Test subjects were shown static images of male and female nudes in one eye and rapidly flashing colored squares in the other eye. The flashing color rendered the nudes invisible—the subjects couldn't even say where the nudes were in the image. Yet the psychologists showed that subjects nevertheless registered the unseen image if it was of the opposite sex.

What of memory? Most of us vividly remember our first kiss, our first car, or the images of the crumbling Twin Towers on 9/11. This kind of episodic memory would seem to be an integral part of consciousness. But the clinic tells us otherwise: *being conscious does not require either explicit or working memory.*

In 1953, an epileptic man known to the public only as H.M. had most of his hippocampus and neighboring regions on both sides of the brain surgically removed as an experimental treatment for his condition. From that day on, he couldn't acquire any new long-term memories—not of the nurses and doctors who treated him, his room at the hospital, or any unfamiliar well-wishers who dropped by. He could recall only events that happened before his surgery. Such impairments, though, didn't turn H.M. into a zombie. He is still alive today, and even if he can't remember events from one day to the next, he is without doubt conscious.

The same holds true for the sort of working memory you need to perform any number of daily activities—to dial a phone number you just looked up or measure out the correct amount of crushed thyme given in the cookbook you just consulted. This memory is called dynamic because it lasts only as long as neuronal circuits remain active. But as with long-term memory, you don't need it to be conscious.

Self-reflection is another human trait that seems deeply linked to consciousness. To assess consciousness, psychologists and other scientists often rely on verbal reports from their subjects. They ask questions like "What did you see?" To answer, a subject conjures up an image by "looking inside" and recalling whatever it was that was just viewed. So it is only natural to suggest that consciousness arises through your ability to reflect on your perception.

As it turns out, though, *being conscious does not require self-reflection.* When we become absorbed in some intense perceptual task—such as playing a fast-paced video game, swerving on a motorcycle through moving traffic, or running along a mountain trail—we are vividly conscious of the external world, without any need for reflection or introspection.

Neuroimaging studies suggest that we can be vividly conscious even when the front of the cerebral cortex, involved in judgment and self-representation, is relatively inactive. Patients with widespread injury to the front of the brain demonstrate serious deficits in their cognitive, executive, emotional, and planning abilities. But they appear to have nearly intact perceptual abilities.

Finally, *being conscious does not require language.* We humans affirm our consciousness through speech, describing and discussing our experiences with one another. So it's natural to think that speech and consciousness are inextricably linked. They're not. There are many patients who lose the ability to understand or use words and yet remain conscious. And infants, monkeys, dogs, and mice cannot speak, but they are conscious and can report their experiences in other ways.

So what about a machine? We're going to assume that a machine does not require anything to be conscious that a naturally evolved organism—you or me, for example—doesn't require. If that's the case, then, to be conscious a machine does not need to engage with its environment, nor does it need long-term memory or working memory; it does not require attention, self-reflection, language, or emotion. Those things may help the machine survive in the real-world. But to simply have subjective experience—being pleased at the sight of wispy white clouds scurrying across a perfectly blue sky—those traits are probably not necessary.

So what is necessary? What are the essential properties of consciousness, those without which there is no experience whatsoever?

We think the answer to that question has to do with the amount of *integrated information* that an organism, or a machine, can generate. Let's say you are facing a blank screen that is alternately on or off, and you have been instructed to say "light" when the screen turns on and "dark" when it turns off. Next to you, a photodiode—one of the very simplest of machines—is set up to beep when the screen emits light and to stay silent when the screen is dark. The first problem that consciousness poses boils down to this: both you and the photodiode can differentiate between the screen being on or off, but while you can see light or dark, the photodiode does not consciously "see" anything. It merely responds to photons.

The key difference between you and the photodiode has to do with how much information is generated when the differentiation between light and dark is made. Information is classically defined as the reduction of uncertainty that occurs when one among many possible outcomes is chosen. So when the screen turns dark, the photodiode enters one of its two possible states; here, a state corresponds to one bit of information. But when you see the screen turn dark, you enter one out of a huge number of states: seeing a dark screen means you aren't seeing a blue, red, or green screen, the Statue of Liberty, a picture of your child's piano recital, or any of the other uncountable things that you have ever seen or could ever see. To you, "dark" means not just the opposite of light but also, and simultaneously, something different from colors, shapes, sounds, smells, or any mixture of the above.

So when you look at the dark screen, you rule out not just "light" but countless other possibilities. You don't think of the stupefying number of possibilities, of course, but their mere existence corresponds to a huge amount of information.

Conscious experience consists of more than just differentiating among many states, however. Consider an idealized 1-megapixel digital camera. Even if each photodiode in the imager were just binary, the number of different patterns that imager could record is $2^{1\,000\,000}$. Indeed, the camera could easily enter a different state for every frame from every movie that was or could ever be produced. It's a staggering amount of information. Yet the camera is obviously not conscious. Why not?

We think that the difference between you and the camera has to do with integrated information. The camera can indeed be in any one of an absurdly large number of different states. However, the 1-megapixel sensor chip isn't a single integrated system but rather a collection of one million individual, completely independent photodiodes, each with a repertoire of two states. And a million photodiodes are collectively no smarter than one photodiode.

By contrast, the repertoire of states available to you cannot be subdivided. You know this from experience: when you consciously see a certain image, you experience that image as an integrated whole. No matter how hard you try, you cannot divvy it up into smaller thumbprint images, and you cannot experience its colors independently of the shapes, or the left half of your field of view independently of the right half. Underlying this unity is a multitude of causal interactions among the relevant parts of your brain. And unlike chopping up the photodiodes in a camera sensor, disconnecting the elements of your brain that feed into consciousness would have profoundly detrimental effects.

To be conscious, then, you need to be a single integrated entity with a large repertoire of states. Let's take this one step further: your level of consciousness has to do with how much integrated information you can generate. That's why you have a higher *level* of consciousness than a tree frog or a supercomputer.

It is possible to work out a theoretical framework for gauging how effective different neural architectures would be at generating integrated information and therefore attaining a conscious state. This framework, the integrated information theory of consciousness, or IIT, is grounded in the mathematics of information and complexity theory and provides a specific measure of the amount of integrated information generated by any system comprising interacting parts. We call that measure Φ and express it in bits. The larger the value of Φ, the larger the entity's conscious repertoire. (For students of information theory, Φ is an intrinsic property of the system, and so it is different from the Shannon information that can be sent through a channel.)

IIT suggests a way of assessing consciousness in a machine—a Turing Test for consciousness, if you will. Other attempts at gauging machine consciousness, or at least intelligence, have fallen short. Carrying on an engaging conversation in natural language or playing strategy games were at various times thought to be uniquely human attributes. Any machine that had those capabilities would also have a human intellect, researchers once thought. But subsequent events proved them wrong—computer programs such as the chatterbot ALICE and the chess-playing supercomputer Deep Blue, which famously bested Garry Kasparov in 1997, demonstrated that machines can display human-level performance in narrow tasks. Yet none of those inventions displayed evidence of consciousness.

Scientists have also proposed that displaying emotion, self-recognition, or purposeful behavior are suitable criteria for machine consciousness. However, as we mentioned earlier, there are people who are clearly conscious but do not exhibit those traits.

What, then, would be a better test for machine consciousness? According to IIT, consciousness implies the availability of a large repertoire of states belonging to a single integrated system. To be useful, those internal states should also be highly informative about the world.

One test would be to ask the machine to describe a scene in a way that efficiently differentiates the scene's key features from the immense range of other possible scenes. Humans are fantastically good at this: presented with a photo, a painting, or a frame from a movie, a normal adult can describe what's going on, no matter how bizarre or novel the image is.

Consider the following response to a particular image: "It's a robbery—there's a man holding a gun and pointing it at another man, maybe a store clerk." Asked to elaborate, the person could go on to say that it's probably in a liquor store, given the bottles on the shelves, and that it may be in the United States, given the English-language newspaper and signs. Note that the exercise here is not to spot as many details as one can but to discriminate the scene, as a whole, from countless others.

So this is how we can test for machine consciousness: show it a picture and ask it for a concise description. . . . The machine should be able to extract the gist of the image (it's a liquor store) and what's happening (it's a robbery). The machine should also be able to describe which objects are in the picture and which are not (where's the getaway car?), as well as the spatial relationships among the objects (the robber is holding a gun) and the causal relationships (the other man is holding up his hands because the bad guy is pointing a gun at him).

The machine would have to do as well as any of us to be considered as conscious as we humans are—so that a human judge could not tell the difference—and not only for the robbery scene but for any and all other scenes presented to it.

No machine or program comes close to pulling off such a feat today. In fact, image understanding remains one of the great unsolved problems of artificial intelligence. Machine-vision algorithms do a reasonable job of recognizing ZIP codes on envelopes or signatures on checks and at picking out pedestrians in street scenes. But deviate slightly from these well-constrained tasks and the algorithms fail utterly.

Very soon, computer scientists will no doubt create a program that can automatically label thousands of common objects in an image—a person, a building, a gun. But that software will still be far from conscious. Unless the program is explicitly written to conclude that the combination of man, gun, building, and terrified customer implies "robbery," the program won't realize that something dangerous is going on. And even if it were so written, it might sound a false alarm if a 5-year-old boy walked into view holding a toy pistol. A sufficiently conscious machine would not make such a mistake.

What is the best way to build a conscious machine? Two complementary strategies come to mind: either copying the mammalian brain or evolving a machine. Research groups worldwide are already pursuing both strategies, though not necessarily with the explicit goal of creating machine consciousness.

Though both of us work with detailed biophysical computer simulations of the cortex, we are not optimistic that modeling the brain will provide the insights needed to construct a conscious machine in the next few decades. Consider this sobering lesson: the roundworm *Caenorhabditis elegans* is a tiny creature whose brain has 302 nerve cells. Back in 1986, scientists used electron microscopy to painstakingly map its roughly 6000 chemical synapses and its complete wiring diagram. Yet more than two decades later, there is still no working model of how this minimal nervous system functions.

Now scale that up to a human brain with its 100 billion or so neurons and a couple hundred trillion synapses. Tracing all those synapses one by one is close to impossible, and it is not even clear whether it would be particularly useful, because the brain is astoundingly plastic, and the connection strengths of synapses are in constant flux. Simulating such a gigantic neural network model in the hope of seeing consciousness emerge, with millions of parameters whose values are only vaguely known, will not happen in the foreseeable future.

A more plausible alternative is to start with a suitably abstracted mammal-like architecture and evolve it into a conscious entity. Sony's robotic dog, Aibo, and its humanoid, Qrio, were rudimentary attempts; they operated under a large number of fixed but flexible rules. Those rules yielded some impressive, lifelike behavior—chasing balls, dancing, climbing stairs—but such robots have no chance of passing our consciousness test.

So let's try another tack. At MIT, computational neuroscientist Tomaso Poggio has shown that vision systems based on hierarchical, multilayered maps of neuronlike elements perform admirably at learning to categorize real-world images. In fact, they rival the performance of state-of-the-art machine-vision systems. Yet such systems are still very brittle. Move the test setup from cloudy New England to the brighter skies of Southern California and the system's performance suffers. To begin to approach human behavior, such systems must become vastly more robust; likewise, the range of what they can recognize must increase considerably to encompass essentially all possible scenes.

Contemplating how to build such a machine will inevitably shed light on scientists' understanding of our own consciousness. And just as we ourselves have evolved to experience and appreciate the infinite richness of the world, so too will we evolve constructs that share with us and other sentient animals the most ineffable, the most subjective of all features of life: consciousness itself.

John Horgan

The Consciousness Conundrum

I'm 54, with all that entails. Gray hair, trick knee, trickier memory. I still play a mean game of hockey, and my love life requires no pharmaceutical enhancement. But entropy looms ever larger. Suffice it to say, I would love to believe that we are rapidly approaching "the singularity." Like paradise, technological singularity comes in many versions, but most involve bionic brain boosting. At first, we'll become cyborgs, as stupendously powerful brain chips soup up our perception, memory, and intelligence and maybe even eliminate the need for annoying TV remotes. Eventually, we will abandon our flesh-and-blood selves entirely and upload our digitized psyches into computers. We will then dwell happily forever in cyberspace where, to paraphrase Woody Allen, we'll never need to look for a parking space. Sounds good to me!

Notably, singularity enthusiasts tend to be computer specialists, such as the author and retired computer scientist Vernor Vinge, the roboticist Hans Moravec, and the entrepreneur Ray Kurzweil. Intoxicated by the explosive progress of information technologies captured by Moore's Law, such singularitarians foresee a "merger of biological and nonbiological intelligence," as Kurzweil puts it, that will culminate in "immortal software-based humans." It will happen not within a millennium, or a century, but no later than 2030, according to Vinge. These guys—and, yes, they're all men—are serious. Kurzweil says he has adopted an antiaging regimen so that he'll "live long enough to live forever."

Specialists in real rather than artificial brains find such bionic convergence scenarios naive, often laughably so. Gerald Edelman, a Nobel laureate and director of the Neurosciences Institute, in San Diego, says singularitarians vastly underestimate the brain's complexity. Not only is each brain unique, but each also constantly changes in response to new experiences. Stimulate a brain with exactly the same input, Edelman notes, and you'll never see the same signal set twice in response.

"This is a wonderful project—that we're going to have a spiritual bar mitzvah in some galaxy," Edelman says of the singularity. "But it's a very unlikely idea."

Neuroscience is indeed thriving. Membership in the Society for Neuroscience has surged from 500, when it was founded in Washington, D.C., in 1970, to almost 40 000 today. New brain journals seem to spring up daily, crammed with data from ever-more-powerful brain probes such as magnetic-resonance imaging and transcranial magnetic stimulation. In addition to such

From *IEEE Spectrum,* June 2008, part of Special Report: The Singularity. Copyright © 2008 by IEEE Spectrum. Reprinted by permission.

noninvasive methods, scientists can stick electrodes in brains to monitor and stimulate individual neurons. Researchers are also devising electrode-based "neural prostheses" to help people with nervous-system disorders such as deafness, blindness, paralysis, and memory loss.

In spite of all those advances, neuroscientists still do not understand at all how a brain (the squishy agglomeration of tissue and neurons) makes a conscious mind (the intangible entity that enables you to fall in love, find irony in a novel, and appreciate the elegance of a circuit design). "No one has the foggiest notion," says the neuroscientist Eric Kandel of Columbia University Medical Center, in New York City. "At the moment all you can get are informed, intelligent opinions." Neuroscientists lack an overarching, unifying theory to make sense of their sprawling and disjointed findings, such as Kandel's Nobel Prize–winning discovery of the chemical and genetic processes that underpin memory formation in sea slugs.

The brain, it seems, is complex enough to conjure fantasies of techno-transcendence and also to foil their fulfillment.

A healthy adult brain contains about 100 billion nerve cells, or neurons. A single neuron can be linked via axons (output wires) and dendrites (input wires) across synapses (gaps between axons and dendrites) to as many as 100 000 other neurons. Crank the numbers and you find that a typical human brain has quadrillions of connections among its neurons. A quadrillion is a one followed by 15 zeroes; a stack of a quadrillion U.S. pennies would go from the sun out past the orbit of Jupiter.

Adding to the complexity, synaptic connections constantly form, strengthen, weaken, and dissolve. Old neurons die and—evidence now indicates, overturning decades of dogma—new ones are born.

Far from being stamped from a common mold, neurons display an astounding variety of forms and functions. Researchers have discovered scores of distinct types just in the optical system. Neurotransmitters, which carry signals across the synapse between two neurons, also come in many different varieties. In addition to neurotransmitters, neural-growth factors, hormones, and other chemicals ebb and flow through the brain, modulating cognition in ways both profound and subtle.

Indeed, the more you learn about brains, the more you may wonder how the damn things work. And in fact, sometimes they don't. They succumb to schizophrenia, bipolar disorder, depression, Alzheimer's disease, and many other disorders that resist explanation and treatment.

Nevertheless, the brain is a computer, singularitarians insist. It just has an extremely messy wiring diagram. According to this perspective, neurons resemble transistors, absorbing, processing, and reemitting the electrochemical pulses known as action potentials. With an amplitude of one-tenth of a volt and a duration of one millisecond, action potentials are remarkably uniform, and they do not dissipate even when zipping down axons a meter long (yes, a full meter). Also called spikes, to reflect their appearance on oscilloscopes, action potentials supposedly serve as the brain's basic units of information.

Within a decade or so, computers will surpass the computational power of brains, many singularitarians say. They base this claim on the assumption that those spikes represent the brain's total computational capacity. If the brain contains one quadrillion synapses processing on average 10 action potentials per second, then the brain performs 10 quadrillion operations per second. At some point in the near future, some singularitarians say, computers will surpass that processing rate and leave us in their cognitive dust unless we embrace them through bionic convergence or uploading.

We've heard such prophesies before. A half century ago, artificial-intelligence pioneers such as Marvin Minsky of MIT and Herbert Simon of Carnegie Mellon University predicted that computers would exceed human intelligence within a generation. Their prophesies inspired sci-fi writers like Arthur C. Clarke—creator of the cybervillain HAL—as well as younger AI visionaries like Kurzweil, Moravec, and Vinge.

But even Minsky admits that computers are still idiot savants. "I wish I could tell you that we have intelligent machines, but we don't," he says. The world's most powerful computers, he acknowledges, lack the common sense of a toddler; they can't even distinguish cats from dogs unless they are explicitly and painstakingly programmed to do so.

Nevertheless, singularitarians are quite right that, if current trends continue, supercomputers will exceed 10 quadrillion operations per second within a decade. IBM's Blue Gene/P supercomputer, introduced nearly a year ago, can be configured to process up to 3 quadrillion operations per second, although no customer has yet ordered one with the full complement of 884 736 processors that would be needed to get that kind of a processing rate. Argonne National Laboratory, in Illinois, is now completing the upgrade of a Blue Gene/P that should be good for around half a quadrillion operations per second.

So would a fully configured Blue Gene/P be cognitive, perhaps like a monkey or a tree frog, if not like us? Of course not. As any singularitarian would agree, intelligence requires software at least as much as hardware. And that software will soon be available, the singularitarians say, because scientists will in the next couple of decades reverse engineer the brain's software, yielding all sorts of benefits. First, the brain's programming tricks will be transferred to computers to make them smarter. Moreover, given the right interface, our brains and computers will communicate as readily as Macs and PCs. And eventually, of course, our personal software will be extracted from our frail flesh and blood and uploaded into advanced robots or computers. (Don't forget to back yourself up on a hard drive!) We'll walk the earth in impervious titanium-boned bodies. Or we'll inhabit impossibly lush virtual paradises specifically created to please and stimulate our disembodied, digital psyches.

Many neuroscientists do assume that, just as computers operate according to a machine code, the brain's performance must depend on a "neural code," a set of rules or algorithms that transforms those spikes into perceptions, memories, meanings, sensations, and intentions. If such a neural code exists, however, neuroscientists still have no idea what that code is. Or, more accurately, like voters in a U.S. presidential primary, researchers have a surfeit of candidates, each seriously flawed.

The first neural code was discovered more than 70 years ago by the British electrophysiologist Edgar Adrian, who found that when he increased the pressure on neurons involved in the sense of touch, they fired at an increased rate. That so-called rate code has now been demonstrated in many different animals, including *Homo sapiens*. But a rate code is a crude, inefficient way to convey information; imagine trying to communicate solely by humming at different pitches.

Neuroscientists have long suspected that the brain employs subtler codes. One of them might be a temporal code, in which information is represented not just in a cell's rate of firing but also in the precise timing between spikes. For example, a rate code would treat the spike sequences 010101 and 100011 as identical because they have the same number of 0 and 1 bits. But a temporal code would assign different meanings to the two strings because the bit sequences are different. That's a vital distinction: the biophysicist William Bialek of Princeton University calculates that temporal coding would boost the brain's information-processing capacity close to the Shannon limit, the theoretical maximum that information theory allows for a given physical system.

Some neuroscientists suspect that temporal codes predominate in the prefrontal cortex and other brain structures associated with "higher" cognitive functions, such as decision making. In these regions, neurons tend to fire on average only one or two times per second, compared with the 100 or more times of sensory and motor neurons.

Other neural-coding theories abound. On a more macro level, researchers are seeking "population codes" involving the correlated firing of many neurons. Edelman, at the Neurosciences Institute, has advocated a scheme called neural Darwinism, in which our recognition of, say, an animal emerges from competition between large populations of neurons representing different memories: Dog? Cat? Weasel? Rat? The brain quickly settles on the population that most closely matches the incoming stimulus. Perhaps because Edelman has cloaked it in impenetrable jargon, neural Darwinism has not caught on.

Wolf Singer of the Max Planck Institute for Brain Research, in Frankfurt, has won more support for a code involving many neurons firing at the same rate and time. Do such synchronous oscillations play a crucial role in cognition and perhaps even underpin consciousness? Singer thinks they might.

Consciousness is not easy to define, let alone create in a machine. The psychologist William James described it succinctly as attention plus short-term memory. It's what you possess right now as you read this article, and what you lack when you are asleep and between dreams, or under anesthesia.

In 1990, the late Nobel laureate Francis Crick and his colleague Christof Koch proposed that the 40-hertz synchronized oscillations found a year earlier by Singer and his collaborator were one of the neuronal signatures of consciousness. But Singer says the brain probably employs many different codes in addition to oscillations. He also emphasizes that researchers are "only at the beginning of understanding" how neural processes "bring forth higher cognitive and executive functions." And bear in mind that it's still a very long way from grasping those functions to understanding how they give rise to consciousness. And yet without that understanding, it's hard to imagine how anyone could build an artificial brain sophisticated enough to sustain and nurture an individual human consciousness indefinitely.

Given our ignorance about the brain, Singer calls the idea of an imminent singularity "science fiction."

Koch shares Singer's skepticism. A neuroscientist at Caltech, Koch was a close friend and collaborator of Crick, who together with James Watson unraveled the structure of DNA in 1953. During the following decade or so, Crick and other researchers established that the double helix mediates an astonishingly simple genetic code governing the heredity of all organisms. Koch says, "It is very unlikely that the neural code will be anything as simple and as universal as the genetic code."

Neural codes seem to vary in different species, Koch notes, and even in different sensory modes within the same species. "The code for hearing is not the same as that for smelling," he explains, "in part because the phonemes that make up words change within a tiny fraction of a second, while smells wax and wane much more slowly."

Evidence from research on neural prostheses suggests that brains even devise entirely new codes in response to new experiences. "There may be no universal principle" governing neural-information processing, Koch says, "above and beyond the insight that brains are amazingly adaptive and can extract every bit of information possible, inventing new codes as necessary."

Theoretical quibbles notwithstanding, singularitarians insist that neural prostheses are already leading us toward bionic convergence. By far the most successful prosthesis is the cochlear implant. During the past few decades, about 100 000 hearing-impaired people around the world have been equipped with the devices, which restore hearing by feeding signals from an external microphone to the auditory nerve via electrodes. But as the deaf memoirist Michael Chorost points out, cochlear implants are far from perfect.

In his 2005 book, *Rebuilt: How Becoming Part Computer Made Me More Human*, Chorost recounts how he learned to live with an implant after losing his hearing in 2001. Although thrilled by the device, which restored his social life, he also recognizes its limitations. Because a cochlear implant provides a crude simulacrum of our innate auditory system, it generally requires a breaking-in period, during which technicians tweak the device's settings to optimize its performance. With that assistance, the brain—perhaps by devising a brand-new coding scheme—learns how to exploit the peculiar, artificial signals. Even then, the sound quality is often poor, especially in noisy settings. Chorost says he still occasionally relies on lip reading and contextual guessing to decipher what someone is saying to him. Cochlear implants do not work at all in some people, for reasons that are not well understood.

By far the most ambitious neural-prosthesis program involves computer chips that can restore or augment memory. Researchers at the University of Southern California, in Los Angeles, have designed chips that mimic the firing patterns of tissue in the hippocampus, a minute seahorse-shaped neural structure thought to underpin memory. Biomedical engineering professor Theodore Berger, a leader of the USC program, has suggested that one day brain chips might allow us to instantly upload expertise. But the memory chips are years away from testing. In rats.

Discussions of memory chips leave Andrew Schwartz cold. A neural-prosthesis researcher at the University of Pittsburgh, Schwartz has shown that monkeys can learn to control robotic arms by means of chips embedded in the brain's motor cortex. But no one has any idea how memories are encoded, Schwartz says. "We know so little about the higher functions of the brain that it seems ridiculous to talk about enhancing things like intelligence and memory," he says. Moreover, he says, downloading complex knowledge directly into the brain would require not just stimulating millions of specific neurons but also altering synaptic connections throughout the brain.

That brings us to the interface problem, the most practical obstacle to bionic convergence and uploading. For now, electrodes implanted into the brain remain the only way to precisely observe and fiddle with neurons. It is a much messier, more difficult, and more dangerous interface than most people realize. The electrodes must be inserted into the brain through holes drilled in the skull, posing the risk of infection and brain damage. They often lose contact with neurons; at any one moment an array of 100 electrodes might make contact with only half that many cells. Scar tissue or blood can encrust the electrode, cells around it might shift their position or die, and electrodes have been known to corrode.

Researchers are testing various strategies for improving contact between neurons and electronics. They are making electrodes out of conducting polymers, which are more compatible with neural tissue than silicon or metal; coating electrodes with naturally occurring glues, called cell-adhesion molecules, which helps cells in the brain and elsewhere stick together; and designing electrode arrays that automatically adjust the position of the electrodes to maximize the reception of neural signals.

At Caltech and elsewhere, engineers have designed hollow electrodes that can inject fluids into the surrounding tissue. The fluids could consist of nerve-growth factors, neurotransmitters, and other substances. The nerve-growth factors encourage cells to grow around electrodes, while the neurotransmitters enhance or supplement electrical-stimulation treatment. Neuroscientists are also testing optical devices that can monitor and stimulate neurons, as well as genetic switches that turn neurons on or off.

To be sure, it's promising work. Terry Sejnowski, a neuroscientist at the Salk Institute for Biological Studies, in San Diego, says the new technologies will make it possible "to selectively activate and inactivate specific types of neurons and synapses as well as record from all the neurons in a volume of tissue." That, in turn, might make it possible to build more effective and reliable neural prostheses.

But again, it's a fantastically long way from there to consciousness uploading. Even singularitarians concede that no existing interface can provide what is required for bionic convergence and uploading: the precise, targeted communication, command, and control of billions of neurons. So they sidestep the issue, predicting that all current interfaces will soon yield to very small robots, or "nanobots." Remember the 1966 motion picture *Fantastic Voyage*? That's the basic idea. But try to imagine, in place of Raquel Welch in a form-fitting wet suit, robotic submarines the size of blood cells. They infiltrate the entire brain, then record all neural activity and manipulate it by zapping neurons, tinkering with synaptic links, and so on. The nanobots will be equipped with some sort of Wi-Fi so that they can communicate with one another as well as with electronic systems inside and outside the body.

Nanobots have inspired some terrific "X-Files" episodes as well as the Michael Crichton novel *Prey*. But they have as much basis in current research as fairy dust.

Steven Rose has nothing against technoenhancement. The neurobiologist at England's Open University wears eyeglasses and is proud of his titanium knee and dental implants. He says a lot can be done to improve the brain's performance through improved drugs, neural prostheses, and perhaps genetic engineering. But he calls the claims about imminent consciousness uploading "pretty much crap."

Rose disputes the singularitarians' contention that computers will soon surpass the brain's computational capacity. He suspects that computation occurs at scales above and below the level of individual neurons and synapses, via genetic, hormonal, and other processes. So the brain's total computational power may be many orders of magnitude greater than what singularitarians profess.

Rose also rejects the basic premise of uploading, that our psyches consist of nothing more than algorithms that can be transferred from our bodies to entirely different substrates, whether silicon or glass fibers or as-yet-unimaginable quantum computers. The information processing that constitutes our selves, Rose asserts, evolved within—and may not work in any medium other than—a social, crafty, emotional, sex-obsessed flesh-and-blood primate.

To dramatize that point, Rose poses a thought experiment involving a "cerebroscope," which can record everything that happens in a brain, at micro and macro levels, in real time. Let's say the cerebroscope (hey, maybe it's based on nanobots!) records all of Rose's neural activity as he watches a red bus coming down a street. Could the cerebroscope reconstruct Rose's perception? No, he says, because his neural response to even that simple stimulus grows out of his brain's entire previous history, including the incident in his childhood when a bus almost ran him over.

To interpret the neural activity corresponding to any moment, Rose elaborates, scientists would need "access to my entire neural and hormonal life history" as well as to all his corresponding experiences. Scientists would also need detailed knowledge of the changing social context within which Rose has lived; his attitude toward buses would be different if terrorists recently had attacked one. The implication of his thought experiment is that our psyches will never be totally reducible, computable, predictable, and explainable. Or, disappointingly enough, downloadable into everlasting new containers.

Perhaps the old joke is right after all: If the brain were simple enough for us to understand, we wouldn't be smart enough to understand it.

Let's face it. The singularity is a religious rather than a scientific vision. The science-fiction writer Ken MacLeod has dubbed it "the rapture for nerds," an allusion to the end-time, when Jesus whisks the faithful to heaven and leaves us sinners behind.

Such yearning for transcendence, whether spiritual or technological, is all too understandable. Both as individuals and as a species, we face deadly serious problems, including terrorism, nuclear proliferation, overpopulation, poverty, famine, environmental degradation, climate change, resource depletion, and AIDS. Engineers and scientists should be helping us face the world's problems and find solutions to them, rather than indulging in escapist, pseudoscientific fantasies like the singularity.

POSTSCRIPT

Can Machines Be Conscious?

Science fiction has played with the idea of "thinking machines" for decades. But is this idea nothing but science fiction? Some scientists do not think so, although they are quick to grant that the technology is not yet nearly ready to produce a convincing example. Still, they are trying, at least in restricted subsets of human intelligence such as game-playing. In February 1996 IBM's "Deep Blue," a chess-playing super-computer, won and drew games against the human world champion Garry Kasparov. It lost the six-game match, but it still demonstrated a skill at something most people are willing to call "thinking" that leaves us breathless. See Monty Newborn, *Kasparov versus Deep Blue: Computer Chess Comes of Age* (Springer-Verlag, 1996).

In May 1997 an improved Deep Blue topped its own performance by trouncing Kasparov 2–1, with 3 draws, and sent the news media into a frenzy. We are, wrote Charles Krauthammer in *The Weekly Standard*, "creating a new and different form of being. And infinitely more monstrous: creatures sharing our planet who not only imitate and surpass us in logic, who have even achieved consciousness and free will, but are utterly devoid of the kind of feelings and emotions that, literally, humanize human beings. Be afraid."

Is chess playing a kind of thinking? When the idea of artificial intelligence was new, workers in the field agreed that it was and set out to achieve it. Even partial success was enough to rouse critics who said that if a machine could do it, it could not be "real" thinking. Deep Blue's complete success, however, seems to have many people *afraid* that chess playing is real thinking and that human primacy in a very fundamental area—in fact, human identity—is now seriously threatened.

Hans Moravec does not feel threatened at all. In *Mind Children* (Harvard University Press, 1988) and its successor, *Robot: Mere Machine to Transcendent Mind* (Oxford University Press, 1998), he forecasts the transfer of human minds into immensely capable machines, and speculates on the replacement of biological intelligence by machine intelligence. Ray Kurzweil, *The Age of Spiritual Machines: When Computers Exceed Human Intelligence* (Viking, 1999), also says that he expects robots to surpass humans.

Not everyone is willing to go so far. Paul M. and Patricia Smith Churchland, "Could a Machine Think?" *Scientific American* (January 1990), "reject the Turing test as a sufficient condition for conscious intelligence [because it is] very important . . . that the right sorts of things be going on inside the artificial machine." In *The Emperor's New Mind: Concerning Computers, Minds, and the Laws of Physics* (Penguin Books, 1991), Roger Penrose, a renowned physicist and mathematician at the University of Oxford in England, concludes, "Is it not 'obvious' that mere computation cannot evoke pleasure or pain; that it cannot perceive poetry or the beauty of an evening sky or the magic of sounds; that it cannot hope or love or despair; that it cannot have a genuine autonomous purpose? . . . Perhaps when computations become extraordinarily complicated they can begin to take on the more poetic or subjective qualities that we associate with the term 'mind.' Yet it is hard to avoid an uncomfortable feeling that there must always be something missing from such a picture."

Most definitions of artificial intelligence do not require that a computer be capable of pleasure, pain, and other feelings, but rather that it be able to do things otherwise reserved to human beings. One prospect for the near future is cars that drive themselves, thanks to advances in sensors and software; see W. Wayt Gibbs, "Innovations from a Robot Rally," *Scientific American Special Edition* (January 2008), and David Kiley, "The Coming of the Car-Bot," *Business Week Online* (July 7, 2008).

On the other hand, people are beginning to talk of a time not too far in the future when human beings will be falling in love with—and perhaps even marrying—robots. See Fred Hapgood, "Deus ex Machina," *Discover* (June 2008), and David Levy, *Love and Sex with Robots: The Evolution of Human-Robot Relationships* (Harper, 2007).

ISSUE 16

Is Information Technology a Threat to Privacy?

YES: Amitai Etzioni, from "Are New Technologies the Enemy of Privacy?" *Knowledge Technology & Policy* (Summer 2007)

NO: Stuart Taylor, Jr., from "How Civil-Libertarian Hysteria May Endanger Us All," *National Journal* (February 22, 2003)

ISSUE SUMMARY

YES: Amitai Etzioni argues that privacy is under attack by new technologies. There is a need for oversight and accountability, but the mechanisms of accountability must not lie in the hands of government.

NO: Stuart Taylor, Jr., contends that those who object to surveillance—particularly government surveillance—have their priorities wrong. Curbing "government powers in the name of civil liberties [exacts] too high a price in terms of endangered lives."

T he Fourth Amendment to the U.S. Constitution established the right of private citizens to be secure against unreasonable searches and seizures. "Unreasonable" has come to mean "without a search warrant" for physical searches of homes and offices, and "without a court order" for interceptions of mail and wiretappings of phone conversations.

Private citizens who—for whatever reason—do not wish to have their communications with others shared with law enforcement and security agencies have long sought ways to preserve their privacy. They therefore welcomed changes in communications technology, from easily tappable copper wires to fiber optics, from analog (which mimics voice vibrations) to digital (which encodes them). But the U.S. Department of Justice sought legislation to require that the makers and providers of communications products and services ensure that their products remain tappable, and in September 1992, the Clinton Administration submitted to Congress the Digital Telephony Act, a piece of legislation designed to prevent advancing technology from limiting the government's ability legally to intercept communications. For a defense of this measure, see Dorothy Denning, "To Tap or Not to Tap," *Communications of the ACM* (March 1993).

Yet people fear the Internet because it makes a huge variety of information available to everyone with very little accountability. Even children can find sites dedicated to pornography, violence, and hate. Marketers can build detailed profiles. Fraud, identity theft, invasion of privacy, and terrorism have taken new forms. Criminals can use encryption (secret codes) to make their e-mail messages and transmitted documents unreadable to anyone (such as law-enforcement personnel with the digital equivalent of wiretap warrants).

In response the Department of Justice developed an Internet wiretapping system called Carnivore. Before it was abandoned in 2004, many people were disturbed by its invisibility and the potential for abuse in its ability to search Internet traffic without a court order and to search for any key words its operators desired. Similar concerns have arisen in connection with new technologies that make it possible to detect chemicals (drugs and explosives) and other signs of wrong-doing, as well as with the growing presence of streetcorner surveillance cameras (see Brendan O'Neill, "Watching You Watching Me," *New Statesman,* October 2, 2006).

But after September 11, 2001, the War on Terrorism began and every tool that promised to help identify terrorists before or catch them after they committed their dreadful acts was seen as desirable. However, when the Department of Defense's Defense Advanced Research Projects Agency (DARPA) proposed a massive computer system capable of sifting through purchases, tax data, court records, and other information from government and commercial databases to seek suspicious patterns of behavior, the objections returned in force. The Total or Terrorism Information Awareness program soon died although many of its components continued under other names; see Shane Harris, "TIA Lives On," *National Journal* (February 25, 2006). Simon Cooper, "Who's Spying on You?" *Popular Mechanics* (January 2005), argues that we are now subject to massively increased routine surveillance and the collection of personal data by both government and business with very few restrictions on how the data are used. Peter Brown, "Privacy in an Age of Terabytes and Terror," *Scientific American* (September 2008), says, "A cold wind is blowing across the landscape of privacy. The twin imperatives of technological advancement and counter-terrorism have led to dramatic and possibly irreversible changes in what people can expect to remain of private life."

In the following selections, Amitai Etzioni argues that privacy is under attack by new technologies. There is a need for oversight and accountability, but the mechanisms of accountability must not lie solely in the hands of government. Stuart Taylor, Jr., contends that those who object to surveillance—particularly government surveillance—have their priorities wrong. Curbing "government powers in the name of civil liberties [exacts] too high a price in terms of endangered lives."

YES

Amitai Etzioni

Are New Technologies the Enemy of Privacy?

Abstract Privacy is one good among other goods and should be weighed as such. The relationship between technology and privacy is best viewed as an arms race between advancements that diminish privacy and those that better protect it, rather than the semi-Luddite view which sees technology as one-sided development enabling those who seek to invade privacy to overrun those who seek to protect it. The merits or defects of particular technologies are not inherent to the technologies, but rather, depend on how they are used and above all, on how closely their use is monitored and accounted for by the parties involved. In order to reassure the public and to ensure accountability and oversight, a civilian review board should be created to monitor the government's use of surveillance and related technologies. Proper accountability requires multiple layers of oversight, and should not be left solely in the hands of the government.

An Arms Race versus a Luddite Imagery

The relationship between privacy and technology should be viewed as akin to the relationship between security and technology or prosperity and technology rather than approached from a Luddite perspective. However, much of the literature on privacy follows this second track. It depicts various technological developments, such as electronic databases, computerized searches, and surveillance instruments, as attacks on privacy. Indeed, the more alarmist accounts speak of a 'surveillance society' and the 'death of privacy.' Although these alarmist critics recognize that there is no way to turn back the clock to a pre-digital age, they bemoan the rise of privacy-invading technologies—criticisms similar in tone and terms to the complaints that the Luddites lodged against the development of industrial equipment, from the loom to the steam engine, in the nineteenth century. And like the Luddites, today's critics have, thus, sought to curb these technological advancements if they cannot be eliminated altogether.

Before showing that such critics misunderstand the relationship between privacy and the new technological developments of the digital age, I should reiterate a point that I have spelled out elsewhere: Privacy is merely one good

From *Knowledge Technology & Policy,* vol. 20, Summer 2007, pp. 115–119 (notes omitted). Copyright © 2007 by MetaPress. Reprinted by permission of Springer Science and Business Media.

among many others. It always has been and needs to be weighed against other goods, without an a priori assumption that privacy should trump all other considerations. If a child is brought to the emergency room with cigarette burns on his body and X-rays reveal that his arm has been broken twice before, ER attendants will suspect that the child has been subject to abuse. And they are required by law (and by all that is decent) to ask various privacy-violating questions of the child and of those who attend to him, including his parents. Here, the wellbeing of the child trumps both his and his parents' right to privacy. Moreover, historical developments, for instance, the rise of the threat of terrorism, change the relative weight one ought to accord to the privacy of those who seek to enter one's country. More generally, it follows that one ought not to consider every privacy reduction as a social or human loss.

As far as the relationship between technology and privacy is concerned, it is best viewed as an arms race between advancements that diminish privacy and those that better protect it—as opposed to a one-sided development in which those who invade privacy overrun those who seek to protect it. Although several new privacy-diminishing technologies exist or are being created, they are countered by other developments designed to better protect privacy. At any given point in time, new devices of both kinds are created, sometimes altering the balance in favor of privacy and sometimes tipping it in favor of the invaders. Moreover, every new mode of attack tends to invite a quest for a new mode of defense—for example, the way in which new computer viruses invite the formation of new security patches.

True, the balance between privacy-invading and privacy-securing technology is changing all of the time. However, if one compares routine communications today to those of say 1975, one finds a significant net *increase* in privacy, largely due to the development of high-powered encryption. In 1975, the routine communications of an ordinary citizen might have included phone calls (easily 'bugged' or listened to on another extension by a jealous spouse) and letters (readily intercepted and steamed open by the authorities or a jealous lover or employee). Other means of routine communications—postcards and cables—were even less secure and private. In contrast, many of today's routine communications are sent electronically, secured by high-powered encryption capabilities programmatically built into many computers—capabilities sure to be found on more PCs in the future. As a result, nowadays, when a person sends a routine email via the Internet, it cannot be easily read, even if intercepted, because not only does it travel in divided packets but it also is likely to be encrypted. In short, it is much more difficult today to violate someone's privacy by accessing and reading a routine communication than it was in the pre-digital era.

Turning to non-routine communications, in the past, some senders were willing to engage in extra measures to ensure privacy, such as using a courier or primitive devices like invisible ink and simple code systems, when dealing with highly sensitive or personal communiqués. Today, all of these measures are still available but so is the high-powered encryption discussed above. Granted, it is true that new developments have occurred, enabling those with the knowledge and means to crack such encryption codes and read messages sent from thousands of miles away, say between bin Laden and his mother in Saudi Arabia. However, such technologies are highly specialized and costly. In short, when scrutinizing the security of today's communications, one must acknowledge that, in general, the current methods of sending routine and non-routine communications prove much more secure than the avenues used in the past, such as the wire or traditional mail.

The same holds true for the storage of information. Medical and financial records are much more secure in encrypted databases than they ever were in locked cabinets, places where such information has historically been stored. This newfound security also applies to other types of information, as long as it is properly encrypted. The absence of such measures reveals more about the extent to which those involved are not seriously privacy-minded, at least for the data at issue, than it does about a threat from new technologies.

All in all, privacy is challenged but far from dead, and various technological developments will continue to enhance it even as others attack it.

Accountability

Advancements in technology are frequently characterized either as boons or anathemas. The same holds true for those technologies that directly impact privacy. However, like most technological developments, those concerning the invasion of privacy cannot be easily lumped into simple categories of good or bad per se, although they are often treated in this manner. Instead, their merits or defects depend on how they are used and, above all, on how closely their use is monitored and accounted for by the parties involved. For example, it makes no sense to seek a ban on cameras in public spaces because someone in London used one to violate the privacy of a couple making out in a car (assuming that they had an expectation of privacy in a car parked in a public space in the first place).

To highlight the point, a simple example will serve: Take the case of electronic toll systems, such as the E-ZPass program used in several parts of the USA. Once an individual enrolls in E-ZPass, he receives an electronic device to place in his car. Each time that he travels through a toll, an antenna picks up on the device, and the appropriate amount is deducted from a prepaid toll account. Proponents of such systems see them as a necessity in the face of ever-increasing traffic and argue that they will revolutionize toll collection by minimizing bottlenecks and the need to build additional booths. But privacy advocates, like Jordana Beebe of Privacy Rights Clearinghouse, assert that such toll collections could encroach on individual liberties and worry over how data will be used. Of E-ZPass, Beebe said, "The primary thing to keep in mind with an E-ZPass is basically you're enabling a tracking system."

Yet one should note first of all that, like many technologies cited by civil liberty groups as sources of privacy violations, such as programs enabling credit card orders over the Internet, E-ZPass participation is voluntary. No one is required to use it. However, millions of Americans find they would rather have the convenience of using these technologies than concern themselves unduly with matters of privacy. Indeed, noted privacy expert Alan Westin divides people into three groups. On one end of the spectrum is a minority of the population (25%) that are 'privacy fundamentalists,' deeply concerned about privacy rights, and on the other end is one-fifth that are 'privacy unconcerned.' The majority (55%) are people that Westin identifies as 'privacy pragmatists,' individuals who tend not to mind personal data collection as long as they feel informed about the solicitor, the possible gains or repercussions of releasing the information, and the safety measures put into place. The comments of the chief executive of the Intelligent Transportation Systems, Neal Schuster, suggest that drivers' reasons for choosing E-ZPass prove consistent with Westin's findings: "We do it because of the convenience and we do it because there are laws that protect us."

In any event, the main issue with E-ZPass is not the technology itself but the ways in which it is used—and that use supervised. As with other technologies, E-ZPass can be employed both in ways that most would find unproblematic and quite beneficial and in a manner that many would find very troubling indeed. Suppose, for example, that a car is recorded going through a designated E-ZPass lane. After it is confirmed that the driver prepaid the toll, that record is immediately erased. Few would mind. However, the response would be vastly different if the record in question were filed away and added to other information about us in some comprehensive government dossier in which information about our travels would be kept for years and would be easily accessed by the police, the media, divorce lawyers, and others.

Clearly, for the issue at hand of privacy invasion and protection, the same technology can be used in very different ways. Still, one more crucial step must be undertaken when analyzing technologies involving privacy (and many others) and that is to move beyond assessing each technology on its own merits. The key question is how much accountability and oversight exists for the use to which the technology is put. To return to the example at hand, assume we are told that E-ZPass is used merely in the minimal way described above—information is immediately erased after verification that the toll has been paid, and the information about who traveled when and where is not otherwise available. Still, we might wonder whether these limitations on the use of the information are observed and, if so, who enforces such curbs and how. One major reason we have laws, policing, and oversight is that we do not automatically trust the authorities to do what is right.

How Can Accountability Be Provided?

To some extent, the needed accountability is already built into the government, and it should not be dismissed. For instance, the Inspector General of the Department of Justice issued two highly critical reports of the FBI in 2003. These reports alerted Congress and the public to the FBI's wrongdoings and pressured it to modify its practices. Furthermore, congressional committees have oversight power. And they correctly demanded more specific information about the usage of various powers provided by certain sections of the Patriot Act in an effort to render the uses of the technologies involved, e.g., wiretapping, more legitimate. However, the record shows that, on their own, these committees cannot provide the needed countervailing force to government agencies hell bent on following their own course in the name of national security.

The press, the next line of defense, has been doing a sound job of regularly reporting about a variety of abuses and about programs with absurd designs, leading the government to send many ideas back to the drawing board and to greatly reform aspects of the no-fly lists, the tracking of foreign students, and airport scanning methods, among others.

Many citizens (me included) find these layers of oversight of value but still insufficient. Such people have an inherently healthy distrust of the government and fear that it would conceal information (the way that the CIA kept some detainees off the books), would doctor it, or would refuse to disclose it—even to Congress. To further strengthen oversight for law enforcement authorities and to reassure the public that they are not running amok, we need a civilian review board. It would be composed of the kind of people who served on the 9/11 Commission: bipartisan, highly respected by the public, able to work together, not in the running for public office, and patriotic. These individuals would need the proper level of security clearance to review detailed records to ensure that nobody is pulling the wool over their eyes. The board would issue regular reports about its generalized findings without revealing specifics about sources and methods. Such oversight would allow one and all to determine whether, in most cases, the search of databases, delayed disclosure, and other new security measures have been employed legitimately and used for good purposes or whether the opposite is the case. Such reports should lead to internal reforms in government agencies, as they will have to expect future rounds of similar audits.

Reliable E-ID

To close, I point to a new technological development that would greatly enhance privacy. New technologies are now being developed and introduced that would allow people to present proof of their identity when communicating via the Internet, much like presenting a passport when crossing national borders. Sometimes referred to as 'digital certificates,' such E-IDs can be provided through a 'certificate authority' or CA, such as GeoTrust or VeriSign. Once established, these digital certificates consist of a variety of information that enables those on the other end of a business transaction to confirm that an individual is who he says he is. The electronic postmark (EPM) extension launched by the US Post Office in partnership with Microsoft and Authenti-Date in October of 2003 is just one example of a technological development that seeks to provide reliable E-IDs. Overall, such E-IDs make it much more difficult for unauthorized persons to gain access to a variety of information, and they will help to minimize identity theft.

The technology behind E-IDs is complex and in flux, and it is not my purpose in this paper to enter into an explanation of its intricacies, especially considering the many different options offered by various vendors. I simply wish to outline the basic concepts of E-IDs as a means by which to provide another example of how some advancements in technology *are helping to safeguard privacy as others infringe upon it.*

Conclusion

In conclusion, privacy is under attack by new technologies, but it is also benefiting from new technologies. Those concerned about privacy should work to improve the regulations controlling the use of these technologies rather than adopt a semi-Luddite position, hoping these technologies will go away or be suppressed. How carefully the use of various technologies is monitored is, as a rule, more important than the capabilities of the technologies themselves. Proper accountability requires multiple layers of oversight. And for that accountability to be fully effective in limiting abuse and building public trust, it cannot be left solely in the hands of the government.

Stuart Taylor, Jr.  **NO**

How Civil-Libertarian Hysteria May Endanger Us All

Someday Americans may die because of Congress's decision earlier this month to cripple a Defense Department program designed to catch future Mohamed Attas before they strike. That's not a prediction. But it is a fear.

The program seeks to develop software to make intelligence-sharing more effective by making it instantaneous, the better to learn more about suspected terrorists and identify people who might be terrorists. It would link computerized government databases to one another and to some non-government databases to which investigators already have legal access. If feasible, it would also fish through billions of transactions for patterns of activities in which terrorists might engage.

But now these goals are all in jeopardy, because of a stunningly irresponsible congressional rush to hobble the Pentagon program in ways that are far from necessary to protect privacy. This is not to deny that, absent stringent safeguards and oversight, the ineptly named "Total Information Awareness" [TIA] program might present serious threats to privacy. It might, for example, subject thousands of innocent citizens and noncitizens alike to unwelcome scrutiny, and might even expose political dissenters to harassment by rogue officials.

But some curbs on potentially dangerous (and potentially life-saving) government powers in the name of civil liberties are not necessary to protect privacy and exact too high a price in terms of endangered lives. Congress's rush to strangle TIA in its infancy is such a case. It makes little more sense than would a flat ban on any and all wire-tapping of phones that might be used by U.S. citizens. Like TIA, wiretapping poses grave risks to privacy if not carefully restricted. So we restrict it. We don't ban it.

The problem with the near-ban on TIA—sponsored by Sens. Ron Wyden, D-Ore., and Charles Grassley, R-Iowa, and known as the Wyden amendment—is that rather than weighing the hoped-for security benefits against the feared privacy costs, and devising ways to minimize those costs, Congress was stampeded by civil-libertarian hysteria into adopting severe and unwarranted restrictions. The Bush administration shares the blame because the person it put in charge of TIA research is Adm. John M. Poindexter, whose record of lying to Congress about the Iran-Contra affair does not inspire trust.

"There are risks to TIA, but in the end I think the risks of not trying TIA are greater, and we should at least try to construct systems for [minimizing] abuse before we discard all potential benefits from technological innovation," says Paul Rosenzweig, a legal analyst at the Heritage Foundation who has co-authored a thoughtful 25-page analysis of the TIA program, including a list of muscular safeguards that Congress could adopt to protect privacy and prevent abuses. Instead of weighing such factors, Rosenzweig says, Congress has "deliberately and without much thought decided to discard the greatest advantage we have over our foes—our technological superiority."

The Wyden amendment seems reasonable enough at first blush. That may be why all 100 senators and the House conferees voted to attach it to the omnibus spending bill that cleared Congress on February 13. The amendment allows pure TIA *research* to continue, if the administration files a detailed report within 90 days or the president invokes national security needs. And the amendment's restrictions on TIA *deployment* have been sold as a temporary move to allow time for congressional oversight.

But such measures, once adopted, are a good bet to become permanent in today's habitually gridlocked Congress, where determined minorities have great power to block any change in the status quo. And the Wyden amendment's impact is likely to be far broader than advertised. It flatly bars *any* deployment of TIA-derived technology, by any agency, with exceptions only for military operations outside the U.S. and "lawful foreign intelligence activities conducted *wholly* [my emphasis] against non-United States persons" (defined to mean nonresident aliens).

The scope of the latter exception is ambiguous. But Rosenzweig fears that it will be read narrowly, and that the Wyden amendment will be read broadly—especially by officials fearful of congressional wrath—as barring virtually *all* uses of TIA technology, even to search the government's own databases for suspected foreign terrorists. This is because virtually all large databases are "mixed": They contain information about U.S. citizens, resident aliens, and nonresident aliens alike.

In any event, the Wyden amendment quite clearly prohibits any use of TIA technology to pursue the unknown but apparently substantial number of U.S. citizens and resident aliens who may be loyal to Al Qaeda, such as suspected dirty-bomb plotter Jose Padilla and the six suspected Yemeni-American "sleepers" arrested in Lackawanna, N.Y., last year. As a technical matter, the FBI, the CIA, and the Department of Homeland Security remain free to develop and deploy similar technology on their own. But they will hesitate to risk charges of evading Congress's will. Not to mention the wastefulness of barring these agencies from building on the TIA technology already developed by the Pentagon.

How did TIA become such a dreaded symbol of Big Brotherism? Part of the reason was well-founded concern that unless strictly controlled, the more exotic uses of TIA, such as surveying billions of transactions involving hundreds of millions of people for patterns deemed indicative of possible terrorist activities, could subject huge numbers of innocent Americans to scrutiny as potential terrorists. But Rosenzweig and others who share these concerns, including officials of the TIA program itself, have already been crafting safeguards. Among them are software designs and legal rules that would block human agents from learning the identities of people whose transactions are being "data-mined" by TIA computers unless the agents can obtain judicial warrants by showing something analogous to the "probable cause" that the law requires to justify a wiretap.

It was largely misinformation and over-heated rhetoric from civil-libertarian zealots—on both the left and the right—that pushed the Wyden amendment through Congress. The misinformation included the false claim that Poindexter would preside over a domestic spying apparatus, and the false suggestion that TIA was poised to rummage through the most private of databases to compile dossiers on millions of Americans' credit card, banking, business, travel, educational, and medical records and e-mails.

To the contrary, Poindexter's job is limited to developing software. And even without the Wyden amendment, TIA would give investigators access only to databases and records—government and nongovernment—that they already have a right to access. Its most basic function would be simply to expedite the kinds of intelligence-sharing that might have thwarted the September 11 attacks, by linking the government's own databases with one another and with any legally accessible private databases. The goal is to enable investigators to amass in minutes clues that now could take weeks or months to collect.

Here's a hypothetical example (adapted from Rosenzweig's analysis) of how as-yet-non-existent TIA technology might help stop terrorists—and how the Wyden amendment might prevent that.

Say the government learns from a reliable informant that the precursor elements of Sarin gas have been smuggled into the United States by unidentified Qaeda operatives via flights from Germany during the month of February. Its first investigative step might be a TIA-based "query" of foreign databases that might help generate a list of possible terrorists. (But the Wyden amendment would bar a TIA-based query for the names of any who might be Americans. And it could be construed as putting entirely off-limits *any* "mixed database" that includes Americans.)

A second step might be a pattern-based query to U.S. government databases to produce a list of all passengers, or perhaps all nonresident aliens, entering the U.S. on flights from Germany during February. (But the Wyden amendment would bar a query for all passengers, and would again pose the mixed-database problem.)

A third query might seek to find which of these passengers' names are also in government databases of known or suspected terrorists. (But the Wyden amendment would pose the same obstacles.)

Fourth, with a list of subjects for further investigation based on these queries, TIA could be used—perhaps after obtaining a judicial warrant—to link to any legally accessible commercial databases to find out whether any of these subjects has bought canisters suitable for deployment of Sarin gas, or rented airplanes suitable for dispersing it, or stayed in the same motels as other subjects of investigation. And so on. (But for the Wyden amendment, that is.)

It is not yet clear whether it is even possible to develop technology powerful enough to do all of this. But it might be possible. Shouldn't we be racing to find out?

POSTSCRIPT

Is Information Technology
a Threat to Privacy?

In July 2008, President Bush signed the revised Foreign Intelligence Surveillance Act, designed to expand the government's warrantless electronic spying activities and ensure retroactive immunity for cooperative telecommunications firms. "According to Bush, the law will be a critical factor in preventing another attack on U.S. soil and vital in securing the safety of the citizens." However, the American Civil Liberties Union (ACLU) promptly filed suit, arguing that the bill lacked essential constitutional safeguards. See "Bush Signs Surveillance Bill as ACLU Seeks Injunction," *CongressDaily AM* (July 11, 2008).

The basic shape of the debate is simple: surveillance and data collection are useful. Government insists that private citizens do not have the right to act in such a way that they cannot be watched, supervised, and punished if government deems it necessary. The issue gained fresh importance in 2005, when the PATRIOT Act came up for renewal (see "'Trust Me' Just Doesn't Fly," *USA Today* [April 13, 2005]) and the federal 2006 budget for surveillance technology and manpower increased greatly (see http://www.epic.org/privacy/budget/fy2006/). Private businesses have very similar attitudes toward employees and even customers; see Stephanie Armour, "Employers Look Closely at What Workers Do on the Job," *USA Today* (November 8, 2006). The Electronic Frontier Foundation (EFF), the Electronic Privacy Information Center (EPIC), and numerous other groups and individuals insist equally strenuously that the right to privacy must come first.

Carnivore and the Total or Terrorism Information Awareness (TIA) program reflect many fears about the Net—that it is a place where evil lurks, where technically skilled criminals use their skills to fleece the unsuspecting public, where terrorists plot unseen, and where technology lends immunity to detection, apprehension, and prosecution. Other technologies—including such old standbys as radar detectors—give advantages to more ordinary people, and law enforcement has long wished for ways to overcome those advantages. Carnivore and Echelon were milestone attempts in the area of communications, although both have been much criticized. See Nat Hentoff, "1984 Is Here," *Free Inquiry* (Spring 2003), John Foley, "Data Debate," *InformationWeek* (May 19, 2003) and Wayne Madsen, "US Insight—The Secrets of DARPA's TIA: The US Government's Electronic Intelligence Snooping Machine," *Computer Fraud & Security* (May 2003). Whitfield Diffie and Susan Landau, "Brave New World of Wiretapping," *Scientific American* (September 2008), discuss the impact of FBI efforts to make voice transmissions over the Internet tappable. Nor is the issue solely American. Yves Poullet, "The Fight against Crime and/or the Protection of Privacy: A Thorny Debate!" *International Review of Law Computers & Technology* (July 2004), discusses the issue from the European standpoint and notes that "there is no worse danger than this cyber-surveillance, which hunts a man down in his most intimate space and raises within him a perpetual and haunting fear of exposure." Concerns over the use of surveillance cameras and RFID chips are expressed by Patrick Tucker, "Fun with Surveillance," *The Futurist* (November–December 2006). James Harkin, "You're Being Watched," *New Statesman* (January 15, 2007), thinks that digital tracking technologies may, overall, be a force for good. Julian Sanchez, "The Pinpoint Search," *Reason* (January 2007), argues that new surveillance technologies pose serious threats to ordinary expectations of privacy. Mark O'Brien, "Law, Privacy and Information Technology: A Sleepwalk Through the Surveillance Society?" *Information & Communications Technology Law* (March 2008), contends that new surveillance technologies can result in an inappropriate imbalance between society's need for surveillance and the individual's need for privacy.

In case anyone should conclude that the only surveillance to worry about comes from government and business, "Move Over, Big Brother," *Economist* (December 4, 2004), outlines how surveillance technology—in the form of camera phones and digital cameras—is now available to everyone. People have attached GPS-enabled phones to cars to track spouses or stalk ex-spouses and used camera phones and digital cameras for industrial espionage and identity theft. They have also used them to record crimes in progress and help law enforcement do its job. The full impact on society, whether for good or bad, is not yet clear.

ISSUE 17

Should the World's Libraries Be Digitized?

YES: Brendan Rapple, from "Google and Access to the World's Intellectual Heritage," *Contemporary Review* (June 2005)

NO: Keith Kupferschmid, from "Are Authors and Publishers Getting Scroogled?" *Information Today* (December 2005)

ISSUE SUMMARY

YES: Brendan Rapple argues that as Google scans, indexes, and makes available for online searching the books of the world's major libraries, it will increase access, facilitate scholarship, and in general benefit human civilization.

NO: Keith Kupferschmid argues that there is no justification in law for Google's massive copying of books. If the Google Print Library Project is allowed to continue, the interests of publishers, authors, and creators of all kinds will be seriously damaged.

When personal computers first came on the market in the 1970s, they were considered useful tools, but their memory was limited to only a few thousand bytes, hard drives were expensive add-ons, and the Internet was two decades away from its present status as a necessity of daily life. But already some people had begun to realize the value of making what had long been available only as print also available in electronic or digital form. Project Gutenberg, founded in 1971 by Michael Hart at the University of Illinois, was busily converting works of classic literature into digital form and making them available on disk. By 1990, a number of small companies were trying to turn electronic publishing into profitable businesses. Almost all are gone, partly because "print on demand" (POD) publishing made it possible to print economically single copies of books stored in electronic form, and partly because the Internet came along and produced an explosion of activity exploiting the new ability to put information of all kinds—including poetry, fiction, comics, and nonfiction of precisely the sort one used to find only on paper—onto "Web pages" that Internet users could access for free. Now, major publishers are making books available in both paper and digital form, and e-books can be downloaded from online booksellers such as Amazon.com.

The Internet Revolution quickly led to the invention of search engines, of which Google is currently the best known and most popular; see Charles H. Ferguson, "What's Next for Google?" *Technology Review* (January 2005). Google's avowed goal is "to organize the world's information and make it universally accessible and useful." Toward this end, it has developed a superlative ability to give those searching for information lists of Web sites, images, scholarly papers, and more. However, though those lists provide access to enormous amounts of valuable information and provide it with speed astonishing to anyone who has ever spent weeks or months researching a topic through a university library, the valuable information is intermingled with a vast amount of garbage. The great flaw of the Internet is that no one checks what goes on Web pages for quality or truth. The traditional publishing industry had its flaws—the vanity presses, for instance, as well as magazines such as the *Weekly World News*—but it had people known as editors who exercised a great deal of quality control. Libraries exerted another level of control through librarians, and the books, magazines, and journals to be found in a university library could generally be trusted. Library collections also extend back for centuries before the Internet existed.

Library collections of course represent a large portion of "the world's information." It was therefore no surprise when Google announced the Google Print Library Project. It would join with a number of large university libraries to scan "millions of books and make every sentence searchable" (see Scott Carlson and Jeffrey R. Young, "Google Will Digitize and Search Millions of Books from 5 Top Research Libraries," *Chronicle of Higher Education,* January 7, 2005). The plan was to begin with older, public domain books, no longer under copyright protection (in the U.S., everything published after 1923 must be presumed to be covered by copyright, meaning that copying requires permission from publishers and/or authors), but to move quickly into copyrighted materials. Older materials would be fully available to Google searchers; copyrighted materials would be available only as short excerpts.

In the following selections, Brendan Rapple argues that the benefits of this effort are enticing. As Google scans, indexes, and makes available for online searching the books of the world's major libraries, it will increase access, facilitate scholarship, and in general benefit human civilization. Keith Kupferschmid argues that there is no justification in law for Google's massive copying of books. If the Google Print Library Project is allowed to continue, the interests of publishers, authors, and creators of all kinds will be seriously damaged.

YES

Brendan Rapple

Google and Access to the World's Intellectual Heritage

I was recently researching the educational views of Vicesimus Knox (1752–1821), headmaster of Tonbridge School, Kent, for thirty-four years. My knowledge of Knox was relatively scant though I knew that his views on liberal education and on the education of females were advanced. Knox was a prolific writer and while his principal educational work was *Liberal Education: Or, A Practical Treatise on the Methods of Acquiring Useful and Polite Learning (1781)*, I realised that his educational views were probably scattered throughout his writings. Less than a year ago my research would have required a laborious and tedious consultation of the multiple microfilm editions of Knox's works owned by my library. Fortunately, however, this library recently purchased *Eighteenth Century Collections Online (ECCO)* a database that aims to include the digital full-text of all significant English-language and foreign-language titles printed in Great Britain during the eighteenth century, together with numerous important works from the Americas. The resource, when complete, will contain the fully searchable text of over 33 million pages from almost 150,000 titles including all the works, as well as variant editions, of Fielding, Burke, Pope, Paine, Franklin, Swift. The titles are based on the authoritative English Short Title Catalogue bibliography, the originals coming from the British Library and other libraries. *ECCO's* searching capabilities are sophisticated. One may search by precise keywords or phrases, specifying that one wishes to search full text, author, title, date, general subject area and more. The books' pages are presented as digital facsimiles or actual images and from the results list and page view one may link directly to different portions of the work, such as the title page, back-of-book index, list of illustrations, an e-Table of Contents.

My search of *ECCO* with Vicesimus Knox as author retrieved 69 texts, including a number of different editions of his 1781 *Liberal Education*. I then performed an advanced search seeking any text with Knox as author that contained the words 'school' or 'learning' or 'education' anywhere in the work. I also limited these results to any text containing the word 'girl' or 'girls' or 'female' or 'females' or 'woman' or 'women' or 'lady' or 'ladies'. This was much more efficient and productive than browsing through reel upon reel of cumbersome microfilm, though I was still required to do that for Knox's post-1800

From *Contemporary Review*, June 2005, pp. 338–343. Copyright © 2005 by Brendan Rapple. Reprinted by permission of the author.

works that I did not have available in print. Before leaving the *ECCO* database I easily located the full-text in digital page image of numerous other eighteenth-century treatises on female education, for example Charles Allen's 1760 *The Polite Lady: Or a Course of Female Education;* the Rev. John Bennett's 1787 *Strictures on Female Education;* Mrs. H. Cartwright's 1777 *Letters on Female Education, Addressed to a Married Lady;* John Moir's 1784 *Female Tuition: Or an Address to Mothers, on the Education of Daughters;* John Rice's 1779 *A Plan of Female Education;* Dublin's Foundling Hospital's 1800 *Rules for Conducting the Education of the Female Children in the Foundling Hospital.*

I found the *ECCO* database so powerful and fascinating that I turned my attention to topics other than female education. It was engrossing to browse through the images of the numerous eighteenth-century editions of Defoe's *Robinson Crusoe,* and I was particularly captivated by the variety and artistic merit of the copious illustrations and the numerous maps delineating Crusoe's voyages. I also came across four editions of *Crusoe* in French. While most of *ECCO*'s 150,000 texts are in English, 443 works are in Welsh, 18 in Dutch, 4322 in French, 76 in German, 429 in Italian, 3712 in Latin, and 45 in Spanish. I was also delighted to access so readily the works of the Edinburgh physician William Cullen and discover his views on nosology, i.e. on the 'systematic arrangement of diseases by classes, orders, genera, and species'. Perhaps I'll sometime investigate in the original text why precisely Cullen made what seems the reasonable claim that 'persons living very entirely on vegetables are seldom of a plump and succulent habit'. I will certainly read the anonymous and scurrilous 1734 text that would undoubtedly not be too congenial to my employers at the Jesuit university where I work: *Love in all its shapes: or, the way of a man with a woman. Illustrated in the various practices of the Jesuits of the Maison Professe at Paris, with divers ladies of Quality and Fashion, at the Court of France.*

Eighteenth Century Collections Online is a wonderful electronic resource that allows one to spend hours in idle enjoyment. For scholars, however, it may become an indispensable tool with the potential to revolutionise radically eighteenth-century scholarship and facilitate innovative multidisciplinary research. It is also an excellent complement to two other powerful electronic databases: *Early English Books Online (EEBO),* which provides full-text access to nearly every English language book published from the invention of printing to 1700, and *Evans Digital Edition,* the full-text digital collection of books, pamphlets, and broadsides printed in America from 1639 to 1800. Those fortunate in having access to all three databases can utilise an admirable digital collection of full-text imprints from the invention of printing to 1800.

⋅⟨❦⟩⋅

The resources and research potential provided by these digital full-text databases come at a high price. They are extremely expensive and only more wealthy academic institutions can afford them. However, in December, 2004 many were surprised by a major new initiative announced by Google that may compete with such costly databases. Google is currently working with the libraries of

Stanford, Harvard, and Oxford Universities, the University of Michigan and the New York Public Library to scan books from their collections digitally, include the content into the Google index and then allow users world-wide to search this content in Google. Different arrangements are being made with the five institutions. All seven million volumes in Michigan's library will be scanned, a task that will take about six years. Stanford has agreed to a pilot phased project, though it seems at this point that all its eight million books will be scanned. Oxford's Bodleian Library will contribute an unspecified, though large, number of its pre-1900 public domain works. NYPL will initially contribute only a subset of its non-copyrighted material. About 40,000 of Harvard's fifteen million volumes will be digitised in its pilot project. The pilot will then be evaluated and a decision made about digitising far larger numbers of Harvard's volumes. Though it is currently unclear how many volumes Google will digitise from the five libraries and make available for searching, the final figure might be as high as thirty million. As Google's press release stated, 'Users searching with Google will see links in their search results page when there are books relevant to their query. Clicking on a title delivers a Google Print page where users can browse the full text of public domain works and brief excerpts and/or bibliographic data of copyrighted material. Library content will be displayed in keeping with copyright law'. The new project is an expansion of the Google Print program, which assists publishers in making their books searchable online. Presently Google locates the books found by a Google Print search at the top of the page indicated by an icon of books to the left.

Many are critical of this new initiative. One influential American author on library matters argues that it will be disastrous for Google users to have access to the full-text of only pre-1923 monographs, that is works in the US public domain, the implication being that users will confine their searches to this material and fail to seek out later works. This seems particularly ironic as for years librarians and others have criticised students' tendency to limit their reading to electronic material much of which is of recent vintage and to ignore older works. Michael Gorman, President-elect of the American Library Association, is also quite critical of the Google initiative. As he argued in an op-ed piece in the *Los Angeles Times* (17 Dec., 2004): 'books in great libraries are much more than the sum of their parts. They are designed to be read sequentially and cumulatively, so that the reader gains knowledge in the reading'. He considers that the results of a Google search of these millions of electronic volumes will be an array of disconnected, frequently meaningless parts of books. Jean-Noël Jeanneney, Président de la Bibliothèque Nationale de France, in a *Le Monde* essay (22 Jan., 2005) criticises what he predicts will be the certain bias in favour of Anglo-Saxon and English language material made digitally available in the Google initiative. M. Jeanneney calls on the European Union to build its own comprehensive digital library programme to balance Google's inevitable Anglo-Saxon view 'with its specific coloring with regard to the diversity of civilisations'.

Still, many are applauding the new venture. Reg Carr, the Director of Oxford University Library Services, observed 'Making the wealth of knowledge accumulated in the Bodleian Library's historic collections accessible to as many people as possible is at the heart of Oxford University's commitment to lifelong learning. Oxford is therefore proud to be part of this effort to make information available to everyone who might benefit from it'. The University of Michigan President, Mary Sue Coleman, observed: 'This project signals an era when the printed record of civilization is accessible to every person in the world with Internet access. It is an initiative with tremendous impact today and endless future possibilities'. As a statement from Harvard University Library declared, looking forward to the future greater involvement by Harvard in the project, 'For users outside of Harvard, the larger project would make accessible the full text of a large number of public-domain books. It would also make the copyrighted portion of the Harvard collection searchable. Including works from the vast Harvard library collection in an information location tool available on the Internet would greatly expand the scope and quality of information available to a worldwide audience of knowledge-seekers'.

❧

Many librarians and teachers have for years been critical of the great range of quality of web content to which Google's search engine points, as well as students' frequent difficulty in authenticating and evaluating material they access on the Internet. Moreover, many contend that far too many students, and others, are unwilling to seek and consult material not available on the web, that is most of the world's information. However, Google's adding to the web these millions of books should result in individuals retrieving more quality hits. It is true that many scholars and students utilise the database *WorldCat,* a catalog of almost sixty million records of diverse materials, a high proportion of which are books, held by libraries throughout the world. However, this is a subscription database and those who do not have access to a major university or public library find it difficult to secure the right to use it. Certainly a number of vast, freely accessible online catalogs exist, for example those of the British Library, the Library of Congress, the Bibliothèque Nationale and others, that point to the existence of millions of monographs. However, it is likely that most individuals do not use these catalogues, and certainly far fewer than those who search Google. Some might say that the goal of Google is grandiose, i.e. 'to organize the world's information and make it universally accessible and useful. Since a lot of the world's information isn't yet online, we're helping to get it there. Google Print puts the content of books where you can find it most easily—right in Google search results'. Nevertheless, to the extent that Google makes some, indeed a great deal, of the world's book information accessible on the web, it is indisputably a great boon. It may not be hyperbolic to predict that Google's initiative will create the world's first great virtual library that will be accessible to all with Internet access.'

Google's initiative is, of course, not the first book digitisation project engaged in by libraries and others. Large digitisation programs providing access to full-text monographic material include the University of Michigan's own *Digital Library Text Collection* that currently provides access to over 32,000 texts; Oxford's *Text Archive* that holds several thousand electronic texts and linguistic corpora in a variety of languages; the *Alex Catalogue of Electronic Texts,* a collection of public domain documents from American and English literature as well as Western philosophy; the Electronic Text Center at the University of Virginia that produces an on-line archive of thousands of SGML-encoded electronic texts. Other well-known projects include *Project Bartleby Archive, Project Gutenberg,* Berkeley's *Literature@SunSITE,* the *Internet Archive Million Book Project* that has the goal of digitising a million books by 2005. Will such projects, small in scale when contrasted with Google's undertaking, survive? It is not yet clear, though it seems unlikely that they will be able to compete with Google unless their digital texts add value that Google's texts do not.

⋅⊙⋅

And what is the future of the large sophisticated digitisation projects discussed earlier, *Early English Books Online, Eighteenth Century Collections Online, Evans Digital Edition/Early American Imprints?* Will libraries continue to expend very considerable funds on full-text collections like these? I think that the answer is yes, at least for the next several years. First of all, they currently exist and scholars want them now. I personally have no wish to indulge my present interest in eighteenth-century female schooling by consulting awkward and inefficient microfilm and microfiche when I have access to databases of digital texts that I can cross-search utilising powerful techniques and that promise to point to new, original, and multidisciplinary research avenues. These databases also have the benefit of being discrete uniform collections. It is unlikely that Google will permit users to select such a distinct body of works that make up, say, *Evans Early American Imprints,* out of all its millions of digitised materials and facilitate advanced searching of this sub-group. Nevertheless, I believe that Google is raising the bar for future digitisation projects. The latter's survival will surely depend on what value, for example scholarly essays, biographical materials, annotations, timelines, bibliographies, images, sound, video etc., they add to mere digitised text to create more attractive packages.

Far from being a destroyer of the written word, the Internet, with Google as a leading vehicle, will prove to be its great support and egalitarian promulgator. In recent months the notion of 'open access' to research has been much in the news and many practical steps have been taken to make research and scholarship freely available to all. Numerous electronic open access scholarly journals have been established. Many institutions have set up freely accessible digital repositories of scholarly resources. The US National Institutes of Health (NIH) has a new policy to facilitate public access to archived publications resulting from NIH-funded, that is tax payer funded, research. In July 2004 the U.K. House of Commons Science and Technology Committee issued a report recommending 'that all UK higher education institutions establish institutional repositories on which their published output can be stored and from which it can be read, free of charge, online'. In October, 2004 the Open Access Team for Scotland issued a declaration stating 'that the interests of Scotland—for the economic, social and cultural benefit of the population as a whole, and for the maintenance of the longstanding high reputation of research within

Scottish universities and research institutions—will be best served by the rapid adoption of open access'. Mention might be made of many other open access initiatives but they all share the goal of supporting free electronic access to scholarly literature.

While most projects focus on providing free access to future scholarship, Google is primarily interested in retrospective coverage, that is making freely available already published material, material that may be hundreds of years old. Still, Google's initiative is very much in the spirit and practice of open access. Indeed, it is a very major open access project, perhaps the most important of all. I have already declared my staunch admiration for the power and scope of such digital full-text databases as *Eighteenth Century Collections Online* and *Early English Books Online*. However, access to these extremely expensive databases is invariably highly restricted. On the other hand, the great potential benefit of Google's plan to digitise millions of the world's books is the democratisation of the dissemination and availability of information and knowledge. Most of the world has no access to major research libraries like those of the United Kingdom and the United States. Indeed most inhabitants of these latter nations themselves do not have ready access to such libraries whether because of reasons of geographic location or certain admission prohibitions. Still, the library situation is much worse in most countries of Africa, Asia, South America and it is unlikely that these countries will ever be able to build libraries on the developed world model. However, it is much more probable that the population of these countries will in the coming years gain greater access to personal or institutional computers that provide Internet access. If Google's promise of digitising and making freely available electronically thirty or more millions of the world's monographs comes to fruition, it will constitute a remarkable vehicle for diffusing in both the developed and developing world much of the world's intellectual heritage. Indeed, it will signal a revolution in the dissemination of information on a par with that of Gutenberg's over five hundred years earlier.

Keith Kupferschmid

 **NO**

Are Authors and Publishers Getting Scroogled?

On Oct. 19, five publishers sued Google claiming that the Google Print Library Project violated their exclusive rights provided by U.S. copyright law. The suit—along with the suit filed by the Authors Guild on Sept. 20—is the culmination of months of debate, pitting publishers and authors against Google. The point of contention is whether Google violates copyright law by digitizing millions of books without the permission of the books' authors and publishers and putting them on its servers to allow them to be searched online.

Over the years, other digitization projects have met with success. For example, the recently announced Open Content Alliance (OCA) is a global collaborative effort of cultural, technology, nonprofit, and governmental organizations that are working to build a permanent archive of multilingual digitized text and multimedia content. Content in the OCA archive will be accessible soon through major Web sites such as Yahoo! and through other search engines.

The OCA will encourage the greatest possible access to and reuse of collections in the archive, while respecting the content owners and contributors. Similarly, Microsoft recently struck a deal with The British Library (BL) to scan 100,000 books from the BL's collection and make them available sometime next year. Unlike Google, however, Microsoft plans to scan copyrighted books only if it first receives permission from the book publishers. Other projects include Project Gutenberg . . . , the U.S. Library of Congress Digital Preservation Program . . . , and Carnegie Mellon's Million Book Project. . . . These efforts all have one thing in common: In each case, the aggregators responsible for digitizing, selecting, organizing, and compiling the content took steps to reach agreement with the copyright owners. Without such agreement, these projects would not have succeeded.

Background on the Google Print Library Project

Google manages two projects intended to make the text of books searchable online. One of the projects is referred to as the Google Print Publisher Program, which is a collaborative effort that enables Google to digitize and make books available for search when Google has received permission from the books'

From *Information Today*, vol. 22, issue 11, December 2005. Copyright © 2005 by Information Today, Inc. Reprinted by permission.

publisher or author. This program—because it operates with the consent of copyright owners whose books are copied by Google—is noncontroversial.

The other project, referred to as the Google Print Library Project, is the focus of lawsuits initiated by The Authors Guild and several publishers. In the Google Print Library Project, which was not disclosed to authors and publishers until earlier this year, Google is working with the libraries of the University of Michigan, Harvard University, Stanford University, and Oxford University as well as the New York City Public Library to digitally scan the books in their collections and make the text of the books searchable online. All of this is done without the copyright owners' permission and is in stark contrast to the approach taken by Google in its Print Publisher Program. Google has not disclosed much information about the internal operations of the Print Library Project. It appears that Google employees will digitally scan the collection of books and then index them using keywords so that they can be searched. When users search for these words, they will be provided with search results that show the title of the book, the number of times the keyword appears in the book, and as many as three "snippets" displaying text from the book that includes those keywords. It is not clear how much text the snippets will display.

But many other questions about the program remain unanswered. For instance, it is not clear how many copies of the books Google will be making and retaining for itself and whether its long-term plans involve uses of the books in addition to those that have been publicly disclosed so far. Google may be making and retaining as many as three or more copies of the book for itself (the scanned copy, the digital copy, and a backup copy). Of course, the libraries will also have a copy. Based on our experiences with other information aggregators, Google is likely to make additional copies while maintaining and operating its database.

And how does Google plan to protect against people abusing its search tool, which could destroy the value of the books? For instance, an individual or a computer program could bombard the Print Library search tool with enough keyword requests to download the heart of a book or substantial portions of it. This so-called gaming of the system occurs frequently with publicly accessible online information. One case was brought against the Internet Archive in which an organization made more than 700 attempts to access Web pages on the Internet Archive Web site. Ninety-two of the attempts were successful at obtaining content.

Similarly, it is not clear what security precautions Google is taking to ensure that its Print Library Project search tool is not hacked in a way that allows the digitized books to be freely downloadable. This past summer, Google shut down its video search tool after it was hacked into and entire movies, such as *The Matrix*, were downloaded.

Once the project became public, numerous groups and publishers cried foul. The first to protest publicly was the Association of American University Presses (AAUP), which issued a public letter to Google containing a list of 16 questions. The questions posed included how long a "snippet" of text will the search engine return in the results, how many digital copies will Google make and store, and how does Google plan to use the copies in the future.

AAUP's letter was followed by a similar letter from the Association of American Publishers (AAP) and a position statement by the Association of Learned and Professional Society Publishers (ALPSP), both demanding that Google terminate the project.

In early August, Google announced that it would be suspending the Google Print Library Project until Nov. 1 due to this criticism. Google requested that publishers provide lists of copyrighted books they do not want included in the Print Library Project. Not surprisingly, the book publishers were pleased about the moratorium, but they weren't happy about Google's attempt to shift the burden of identifying what titles Google would not be allowed to copy onto the shoulders of the authors and publishers.

In September, the Authors Guild initiated a class action suit against Google. In the following month, five publishers filed their own suit against Google, charging Google with large-scale, systematic copyright infringement. Then in November, Google's moratorium on scanning books ended, and Google once again began scanning books. While the controversy over the legality of the Google Print Library Project is not an issue that is going to go away soon, it represents a significant challenge to the future of copyright in the online world.

Why the Google Print Library Project Violates Copyright Law

Under copyright law, the copyright owner of a book is granted the exclusive right to control whether others make copies of the book, distribute it, or display it. These rights extend equally to portions of the book. Basically, if a person other than the copyright owner wants to copy, distribute, or display a book or excerpts from it, permission must be granted from the copyright owner.

There are several exceptions to this general rule. The best known is the fair use exception. This exception permits a person who wants to copy, distribute, or display excerpts from a book to do so without first obtaining the copyright owner's permission if that person can prove two things. First, the person must establish that the use is for purposes of criticism, comment, news reporting, teaching, scholarship or research. Second, the person must show that the use qualifies as a "fair use" after considering the following four factors: (1) the purpose and character of the use, including whether such use is of commercial nature or is for nonprofit educational purposes; (2) the nature of the copyrighted work (in other words, whether the book is fiction or nonfiction); (3) the amount and substantiality of the portion used in relation to the copyrighted work as a whole; and (4) the effect of the use upon the potential market for or value of the copyrighted work.

Defining Fair Use

Google defends its right to manage the Google Print Library Project by asserting that its activities are covered by the fair use exception. Before engaging in any fair use analysis, it should be noted that any such analysis in this case will be extremely difficult because of the sheer volume and variety of books and authors at issue. Fair use claims usually involve a work or a handful of works all owned by one or a few authors. This case, however, involves potentially millions of books owned by millions of different authors and publishers. There does not appear to ever have been any case involving fair use that has been applied on such a broad scale to so many works by so many authors and publishers being copied by one entity. That fact alone may be sufficient cause to deny Google's fair use claim.

Google claims that, although it is copying entire books, such copies are allowed as a fair use because it is making only small excerpts of the books available online and the copies made are only intermediate copies. It cites *Kelly v. Arriba Soft Corp.*, an anomalous case decided in 2003 by the Ninth Circuit, for the proposition that such intermediate copying is permissible under fair use. In the Kelly case, defendant Arriba Soft Corp. operated a visual search engine that retrieved thumbnail images of photos that were already posted on the Internet. By clicking on a thumbnail image, a user was presented with a page containing a full-size image that was imported directly from plaintiff Kelly's Web site. The court concluded that the use of the images constituted a fair use because, among other things, Kelly's use of the images was an artistic one, while Arriba's use was as part of a tool that indexes images on the Web, which was unrelated to any artistic purpose.

Here is a list of factors for fair use.

1. Purpose and Character of the Use.   The first fair use factor requires an analysis of "the purpose and character of the use, including whether such use is of commercial nature or is for nonprofit educational purposes." If the use is educational in nature, it is more likely to be a fair use; if it is more commercial in nature, it is likely not to be.

While Google will argue that its motives are wholly altruistic and educational, that simply is not the case. Google is a commercial for-profit enterprise. It initiated this project because it believes it will increase traffic to its Web site, which will eventually increase Google's advertising revenue. Some 98 percent of Google's revenue is generated through advertising. The nature of Google's use here is commercial, and the first factor should fall in favor of the copyright owners.

In Kelly, the court concluded that the first fair use factor favored Arriba because Arriba's use was neither to "directly promote its [Web site] nor . . . to profit by selling Kelly's images. Instead Kelly's images were among thousands of images in Arriba's search engine database."

Unlike in Kelly, Google's use of the books is directly for the purpose of promoting its own site. If that were not the case, Google would have made the books entirely searchable on the libraries' sites (potentially raising different issues) and would not have to retain copies of the digitized books themselves. Instead, Google is requiring that searches take place on its site, which ultimately results in more advertising revenue for Google. The other noticeable difference from the court's holding in Kelly is that, in this instance, the court will not be considering use of just one copyright owner's works "among thousands" of others, but considering all owners of all books digitized by Google.

While Google will likely claim that the purpose of its Print Library Project search tool is educational in nature (because it helps people locate books on topics of interest), that argument could be made in most copyright infringement cases. Certainly, Napster and Grokster (both lost recent well-publicized copyright infringement cases) could have argued that they were merely making content more available to the masses.

Google may also attempt to convince the courts that its copying is "transformative," another consideration under the first fair use factor. The courts consider a transformative use to be a use that is for a different purpose or of a different character than the use of the copyrighted work, and the use does not supersede the need for the copyrighted work. Courts have uniformly held that merely transferring a work from one medium or format to another is not enough to qualify as a transformative use.

In Kelly, the use was found to be transformative because the thumbnail images made by Arriba Soft were for "improving access to images on the [I]nternet" and not for the artistic purposes of the original. Unlike in Kelly, however, Google is not improving access to material already on the Internet; it is creating access to material that is not on the Internet. By creating access and not simply improving it, Google has merely transferred the books from one medium (print) to another (online) and far exceeded what was considered a transformative use even in Kelly.

2. The Nature of the Work.   The second factor—"the nature of the copyrighted work"—likely favors the authors and publishers. This factor looks at whether the books are factual or more creative in nature. The more creative and expressive the book, the less likely the book can be subject to fair use. Application of this factor is not entirely clear since Google will be copying both fiction and nonfiction books. However, the sheer volume of fictional books designated for copying likely leads to the result that this factor will favor the authors and publishers.

3. The Amount of the Works Used.   The third factor—"the amount and substantiality of the portion used in relation to the copyrighted work as a whole"—favors the copyright owner more than any other factor. Google is copying entire books—lots of them—for the project. The court in Kelly acknowledged that "copying an entire work militates against a finding of fair use" but ultimately found that this factor did not favor either party because "if the secondary user only copies as much as is necessary for his or her intended use, then the factor will not weigh against him or her." Unlike in Kelly, Google is making more copies than necessary. All that is necessary is to make and provide the library with a copy, but Google has kept a copy (and likely numerous copies) for itself.

Google also contends that since users will see only small snippets of the book text and not the complete text of the digitized books, these complete text copies are "intermediate copies," which are allowed under fair use. This argument ignores several facts. First, in cases where the courts have allowed the making of so-called intermediate copies, the copies were deleted immediately after they were used. For example, in Kelly, after Arriba Soft created the thumbnail images from the full-resolution images found online, they immediately deleted any copies of the full-resolution images. Here, Google is retaining permanent copies of the digitized books, so, in fact, they are not intermediate copies at all.

The basic premise of copyright protection is that publishers and authors have the right to control the copying, distribution, and display of their books. The display of the snippet through the Google search engine implicates the reproduction, distribution, and display rights because the snippet is a reproduction of a small portion of the text that is being displayed on users' screens and also is being distributed to them via such displays. Because Google copies the entire book as a precursor to displaying a snippet, Google's copying of the book gives rise to an additional claim of infringement of the reproduction right. This claim applies regardless of whether a snippet is ever displayed. Google would have us focus on the display of the "snippet." The display is important, but, fundamentally, it's the copying of entire books without the explicit permission of authors or publishers that is the first step in the analysis (one which Google is sidestepping).

If, as Google insists, the court may consider only whether a snippet is infringing and not whether the full-text copy of the book is infringing—because the full-text copy from which the snippet is created is what Google terms a "non-infringing intermediate copy"—then the reproduction right will be effectively eviscerated. Under this reasoning, an infringement of the reproduction right could only be possible when there is a corresponding distribution or display. In effect, Google's argument here represents a radical new interpretation of U.S. and international copyright law that undermines the basic premise of copyright law.

4. The Effect on the Market for the Work.   The fourth factor, which is often the most influential on a court's decision, asks whether the use will adversely affect the actual or potential market for the books. This factor looks not only at the user's conduct but, more significantly, at the effect on the market if the use should become widespread. The analysis in Kelly is wholly inapplicable to this case, because in Kelly, there was no actual or potential market for the thumbnail images that competed with Kelly's images. In Google's case, however, there are both actual and potential markets for digitizing these books.

The market for licensing such works to aggregators is on the upswing. As Google has no doubt recognized, the marketplace for information is growing exponentially as users desire access to information faster and easier than ever before. Competition in this marketplace is significant, as aggregators hustle to reach agreement with content providers to put their works online.

Google is trying to become a leader in the information industry by changing the rules, rather than playing by them. While other aggregators generally take great care to first reach agreement with copyright owners to make their content searchable online and then compensate them accordingly, Google is doing neither. If Google succeeds on its fair use claim, it will no longer be necessary for aggregators and others that make nondigital content searchable online to get permission from the owners of that content or to compensate those owners. If upheld, Google's claim will have succeeded in destroying the burgeoning market for information content.

Not only will Google's actions destroy the existing and potential marketplace for information content, they will also succeed in destroying Google's own market. As we know, Google has a counterpart project to its Google Print Library Project, called the Google Print Publisher Program (PPP). Under the PPP, Google reaches agreement with publishers to digitize books and make them searchable and accessible through Google's search engine. If Google's fair use claim is allowed, the PPP will become obsolete. Why would Google take the time, money, and resources to get permission from copyright owners to digitize their content and make it searchable and accessible online if they are allowed to do it legally without making that effort?

From a business standpoint, it would be impossible to justify continuation of the PPP under these conditions, destroying PPP and the value it provides to copyright owners in controlling how their works are made accessible through that program. Even if Google were to continue to operate PPP, it would have little value to book publishers and authors because any negotiating leverage that they would have with Google over how to make their books available would evaporate. If they cannot agree to terms, Google will simply make their books available through the Google Print Library Project.

Holding fair use in favor of Google would turn copyright on its head. It would allow not only Google but countless other less reputable entities to engage in wholesale copying of copyrighted works for the purposes of making those works—or portions of them—accessible online. In essence, the rights of writers and publishers would likely cease to exist in the online world.

Implied License

Google's other claimed legal justification for the PPP is that it has permission—more accurately, implied permission (i.e., an implied license)—to copy any content posted on the Internet for the purposes of allowing people to conduct searches using the Google search engine. Google claims this implied permission emanates from the fact that a Web site operator would not have posted content unless he or she wanted it to be found by users. Google will not copy content located behind a firewall or content located on a Web page that includes an exclusion header telling Google not to copy the Web site. Google is of the opinion that any implied authorization that might exist for Web sites extends to its Google Print Library Project.

If Google's implied license theory holds up in court, the ramifications for publishers and authors, as well as others who create copyrighted works, could be devastating. Google and others could copy any copyrighted content, whether print or digital. Books might be first, but Google (or others) might eventually migrate to copying personal letters and e-mails, print newspapers and magazines, or photographs and video that the authors never intended to be copied or searchable online.

Thankfully, Google's implied license argument seems certain to fail. Even if you assume that Google's implied license theory is correct as applied to Web sites, it does not apply to the books being copied as part of the Google Print Library Project, because (unlike Web site content) the collection of books being copied are not at present generally available at no cost on the Internet. For Google to make these books available, it first has to scan and copy the books and save these digital copies on its servers.

There is no justification for an implied license by the copyright owners of these books that would allow Google to digitize them, save them to its servers, and then make them available for searching.

The Next Step

There appears to be no legal basis justifying Google's massive copying of books to populate its Print Library Project. Nevertheless, digital searching of content—if done correctly—could be of great value to authors, publishers, libraries, users, and Google.

A ruling in favor of Google that allows it to continue to operate the Print Library Project would be a devastating blow to authors and publishers and creators of all kinds and would undermine the purpose and goals of U.S. and international copyright law. As a result, no doubt the interested parties will be watching very closely as the cases filed by the Authors Guild and the publishers proceed toward rulings by the courts. . . .

POSTSCRIPT

Should the World's Libraries Be Digitized?

In 2007, a dozen more university libraries joined the Google project; see Dan Carnevale, "Google Strikes a Deal with 12 Universities to Digitize 10 Million Books," *Chronicle of Higher Education* (June 15, 2007). In 2008, Google announced plans to add foreign libraries to the project, beginning with the municipal library of Lyons, France; see "Google Books Expands Its Non-English Resources," *Nature* (July 24, 2008).

It is interesting to note that Brendan Rapple finds great value in the ability to search through electronic collections of older documents. The particular collections he mentions are comprised of public domain documents bundled and indexed for searching by "aggregators" who do this work for profit. The Google Print Library Project, by making those same documents searchable for free, threatens the business of these companies, many of which belong to the Software and Information Industry Association, which employs Keith Kupferschmid as vice president for intellectual property policy and enforcement.

Clearly, there is money at stake in this issue, and Google is hardly acting out of the goodness of its heart, for it generates revenue by attaching ads to the search pages generated in response to user queries. Publishers and authors of modern works, still protected by copyright, also see money at stake, and John Sutherland, "A New Chapter for Books," *New Statesman* (November 27, 2006), even says new technologies may mean that books face extinction. Steve Seidenberg, "Copyright Clash," *InsideCounsel* (November 2006), describes how in September 2005 the Authors Guild filed a class action suit on behalf of authors and in October 2005 five major publishers filed copyright infringement suits. Google has invoked the "fair-use" exception to copyright protection to support its use of small excerpts from copyrighted works, but critics insist that because Google is keeping illegal copies of the complete work in its computers, it is violating the law. See also Corinna Baksik, "Fair Use or Exploitation? The Google Book Search Controversy," *Libraries & the Academy* (October 2006), and Oren Bracha, "Standing Copyright Law on Its Head? The Googlization of Everything and the Many Faces of Property," *Texas Law Review* (June 2007). Siva Vaidhyanathan, "A Risky Gamble with Google," *Chronicle of Higher Education* (December 2, 2005), says that what Google is doing is valuable but it is work that should be done by libraries rather than private corporations. The libraries themselves seem to see cooperating with the Google project as assisting their existing digitization efforts; see Jill E. Grogg and Beth Ashmore, "Google Book Search Libraries and Their Digital Copies," *Journal of Library Administration* (vol. 47, no. 1/2, 2008). In October 2008, Google settled the lawsuits. According to the Authors Guild press release (http://www.authorsguild .org/advocacy/articles/settlement-resources.attachment/final-press-release_final/ Final%20Press%20Release_final%2010.28.08.pdf), Google will pay $125 million as part of an "agreement [that] promises to benefit readers and researchers, and enhance the ability of authors and publishers to distribute their content in digital form, by significantly expanding online access to works through Google Book Search, an ambitious effort to make millions of books searchable via the Web. The agreement acknowledges the rights and interests of copyright owners, provides an efficient means for them to control how their intellectual property is accessed online and enables them to receive compensation for online access to their works."

Hot on the heels of Google, both Microsoft and Yahoo have announced plans to digitize books and make them available. Jessica Dye, "Scanning the Stacks," *Econtent* (January/February 2006), says that "Critics and detractors of these book digitization projects might disagree on the exact shape [the] future of digital content will take, but all agree that the Internet, with its nearly universal availability, unlimited storage capacity, and powerful search capabilities, needs a comprehensive library. As Google, Yahoo!, and Microsoft begin building the foundations of their online collections, the Internet community will be waiting, watching, and reading between the lines." However, Andrea L. Foster, "Microsoft's Book-Search Project Has a Surprise Ending," *Chronicle of Higher Education* (June 6, 2008), reports that Microsoft has ended its effort. The Yahoo-led Open Content Alliance remains active at http://www.opencontentalliance.org/.

Internet References . . .

Foundation for Biomedical Research

The Foundation for Biomedical Research promotes public understanding and support of the ethical use of animals in scientific and medical research.

http://www.fbresearch.org

Bioethics.net and The American Journal of Bioethics

Bioethics.net, founded in 1993, was the first bioethics Web site. Together with *The American Journal of Bioethics* (AJOB), it has grown to become the most read source of information about bioethics.

http://bioethics.net

National Human Genome Research Institute

The National Human Genome Research Institute directs the Human Genome Project for the National Institutes of Health (NIH).

http://www.genome.gov/

The U.S. Department of Energy Human Genome Project

This site offers a huge amount of information and links on genetics and cloning research.

**http://www.ornl.gov/techresources/
Human_Genome/elsi/Cloning.html**

Ethics

*S*ociety's standards of right and wrong have been hammered out over millennia of trial, error, and (sometimes violent) debate. Accordingly, when science and technology offer society new choices to make and new things to do, debates are renewed over whether or not these choices and actions are ethically acceptable. Today there is vigorous debate over such topics as the use of animals in research and cloning.

- Is "Animal Rights" Just Another Excuse for Terrorism?
- Is It Ethically Permissible to Clone Human Cells?

ISSUE 18

Is "Animal Rights" Just Another Excuse for Terrorism?

YES: John J. Miller, from "In the Name of the Animals: America Faces a New Kind of Terrorism," *National Review* (July 3, 2006)

NO: Steven Best, from "Dispatches from a Police State: Animal Rights in the Crosshairs of State Repression," *International Journal of Inclusive Democracy* (January 2007)

ISSUE SUMMARY

YES: Journalist John J. Miller argues that animal rights extremists have adopted terrorist tactics in their effort to stop the use of animals in scientific research. Because of the benefits of such research, if the terrorists win, everyone loses.

NO: Professor Steven Best argues that the new Animal Enterprise Protection Act is excessively broad and vague, imposes disproportionate penalties, endangers free speech, and detracts from prosecution of real terrorism. The animal liberation movement, on the other hand, is both a necessary effort to emancipate animals from human exploitation, and part of a larger resistance movement opposed to exploitation and hierarchies of any and all kinds.

Modern biologists and physicians know a great deal about how the human body works. Some of that knowledge has been gained by studying human cadavers and tissue samples acquired during surgery and through "experiments of nature". Some knowledge of human biology has also been gained from experiments on humans, such as when patients agree to let their surgeons and doctors try experimental treatments.

The key word here is *agree.* Today it is widely accepted that people have the right to consent or not to consent to whatever is done to them in the name of research or treatment. In fact, society has determined that research done on humans without their free and informed consent is a form of scientific misconduct. However, this standard does not apply to animals, experimentation on which has produced the most knowledge of the human body.

Although animals have been used in research for at least the last 2,000 years, during most of that time, physicians who thought they had a workable treatment for some illness commonly tried it on their patients before they had any idea whether or not it worked or was even safe. Many patients, of course, died during these untested treatments. In the mid-nineteenth century, the French physiologist Claude Bernard argued that it was sensible to try such treatments first on animals to avoid some human suffering and death. No one then questioned whether or not human lives were more valuable than animal lives. In the twentieth century, Elizabeth Baldwin, in "The Case for Animal Research in Psychology," *Journal of Social Issues* (vol. 49, no. 1, 1993), argued that animals are of immense value in medical, veterinary, and psychological research, and they do not have the same moral rights as humans. Our obligation, she maintains, is to treat them humanely.

Today geneticists generally study fruit flies, roundworms, and zebra fish. Physiologists study mammals, mostly mice and rats but also rabbits, cats, dogs, pigs, sheep, goats, monkeys, and chimpanzees. Experimental animals are often kept in confined quarters, cut open, infected with disease organisms, fed unhealthy diets, and injected with assorted chemicals. Sometimes the animals suffer. Sometimes the animals die. And sometimes they are healed, albeit often of diseases or injuries induced by the researchers in the first place.

Not surprisingly, some observers have reacted with extreme sympathy and have called for better treatment of animals used in research. This "animal welfare" movement has, in turn, spawned the more extreme "animal rights" movement, which asserts that animals—especially mammals—have rights as important and as deserving of regard as those of humans. Thus, to kill an animal, whether for research, food, or fur, is the moral equivalent of murder. See Steven M. Wise and Jane Golmoodall, *Rattling the Cage: Toward Legal Rights for Animals* (Perseus, 2000) and Roger Scruton and Andrew Tayler, "Do Animals Have Rights?" *The Ecologist* (March 2001).

This attitude has led to important reforms in the treatment of animals, to the development of several alternatives to using animals in research, and to a considerable reduction in the number of animals used in research. See Alan M. Goldberg and John M. Frazier, "Alternatives to Animals in Toxicity Testing," *Scientific American* (August 1989); Wade Roush, "Hunting for Animal Alternatives," *Science* (October 11, 1996); and Erik Stokstad, "Humane Science Finds Sharper and Kinder Tools," *Science* (November 5, 1999). However, it has also led to hysterical objections to in-class animal dissections, terrorist attacks on laboratories, the destruction of research records, and the theft of research materials (including animals).

In the following selections, journalist John J. Miller argues that animal rights extremists have adopted terrorist tactics in their effort to stop the use of animals in scientific research. Because of the benefits of such research, if the terrorists win, everyone loses. Professor Steven Best argues that new laws against animal rights "terrorism" represent the efforts of animal exploitation industries that seek immunity from criticism. The new Animal Enterprise Protection Act is excessively broad and vague, imposes disproportionate penalties, endangers free speech, and detracts from prosecution of real terrorism. The animal liberation movement, on the other hand, is both a necessary effort to emancipate animals from human exploitation, and part of a larger resistance movement opposed to exploitation and hierarchies of any and all kinds.

YES

John J. Miller

In the Name of the Animals: America Faces a New Kind of Terrorism

Six days after the World Trade Center was destroyed, the New York Stock Exchange rang its opening bell and traders sang "God Bless America" from the floor: They wanted to send a loud-and-clear message to the world that al-Qaeda could not shut down the U.S. economy. Even though the Dow suffered its biggest one-day point-loss in history, the mere fact that buying and selling could resume so quickly marked an inspiring day for capitalism and against terrorism.

On September 7, 2005, however, terrorists struck again, and the NYSE still hasn't recovered. This time, they didn't target a couple of skyscrapers near the exchange, but rather a company called Life Sciences Research (LSR). It had recently qualified for a NYSE listing and its senior management had gathered on Wall Street to celebrate the occasion. Just a few minutes before the first trades were set to occur, NYSE president Catherine Kinney informed her guests that their listing would be postponed. It was immediately obvious to everyone from LSR what had happened: "A handful of animal extremists had succeeded where Osama bin Laden had failed," Mark Bibi, the company's general counsel, would say in congressional testimony the next month.

LSR is better known by the name of its operating subsidiary, Huntingdon Life Sciences (HLS), which is in the business of testing products on animals to assess their safety and comply with government regulations. Most people probably don't like to think about what goes on in these labs—vivisections of monkeys, for instance—but they also appreciate the importance of research whose ultimate goal is the protection and enhancement of human health. About 95 percent of all lab animals are rats and mice, but for animal-rights extremists who believe that "a rat is a pig is a dog is a boy" (as Ingrid Newkirk of People for the Ethical Treatment of Animals once said), the whole endeavor is deeply immoral. And some of them have decided that because the traditional practices of honest persuasion and civil disobedience haven't changed many hearts or minds, they must now adopt a different strategy—something they euphemistically call "direct action." These are efforts to intimidate and harass animal researchers and everyone who comes into contact with them. In recent years, hardcore activists have embraced property destruction and physical assaults. "This is the number-one domestic terrorist threat in America," says Sen. James Inhofe, an Oklahoma Republican. Keeping LSR off the Big Board probably represents their greatest achievement yet.

Red in Tooth and Claw

The animal-rights movement may be wrongheaded, but there's no denying that most of its members are motivated by genuine compassion for animals and a sincere commitment to preventing cruelty. There's also no denying that violence in their name has become a significant problem. Just as the pro-life movement is haunted by the murderers of abortion doctors, the environmental and animal-rights movements are cursed by their own packs of fierce radicals. A year ago, the FBI said that 35 of its offices were conducting more than 150 investigations into "animal rights/ecoterrorist activities." The number of illegal incidents involving these activities has risen sharply, from 220 in the 1980s and 1990s to 363 in just the last five years, according to a recent report by the Foundation for Biomedical Research, an association of businesses and universities that conduct animal research. (By contrast, abortion-clinic violence appears to be subsiding.)

"Other groups don't come close in terms of the financial damage they've done," says John Lewis, an FBI agent who until recently coordinated federal efforts against domestic terrorism. Not even militants in the mold of Timothy McVeigh, the man behind the Oklahoma City bombing in 1995? "We have an acute interest in all of these groups, but when the rubber meets the road, the eco- and animal-rights terrorists lately have been way out in front." Lewis estimates that they've caused around $100 million in damage, mostly property destruction affecting businesses, much of it from arson. This fall, eleven defendants will face trial in Oregon for causing an estimated $20 million in damage in five states.

Although animal-rights terrorism is fundamentally barbaric, its execution has assumed increasingly sophisticated forms. The campaign against Huntingdon Life Sciences began in the United Kingdom seven years ago with the formation of a group called Stop Huntingdon Animal Cruelty, or SHAC. Soon after, SHAC recruited members in the United States to focus on an HLS facility in New Jersey, using methods that were deployed to great effect in the U.K. A federal trial earlier this year—perhaps the most important trial ever held involving animal-rights extremism—put the group's methods on full display.

Many of SHAC's efforts targeted HLS directly. An electronic attack in 2002, for instance, caused the HLS server to overload. But other confrontations involved HLS employees away from work: cars vandalized in driveways, rocks tossed through the windows of homes, and graffiti messages such as "PUPPY KILLER" spray-painted on houses. Descriptions of these incidents were dutifully posted on SHAC's own website, often with an unnerving sense of glee. After a tire-slashing visit to the home of one HLS employee, for example, the SHACtivists seemed pleased that "his wife is reportedly on the brink of a nervous breakdown and divorce." These messages were meant to generate publicity, build a sense of momentum, and serve as models for activists spread across the country. In Britain, one top HLS employee was attacked by a group of hooded men wielding ax handles. "It's only a matter of time before it happens in the United States," warns Frankie Trull, head of the Foundation for Biomedical Research. "Everything they do over there eventually comes over here."

Intimidating employees in their private lives places pressure on HLS itself. But SHAC's harassment didn't stop with HLS employees. They also engaged in "tertiary targeting"—i.e., taking aim at companies with ties to HLS, plus their workers. Dozens of firms decided that doing business with HLS simply wasn't worth it. Deloitte & Touche, which had audited the HLS books, ended its relationship. Lawn gardeners quit. Even a security company that provided services to HLS succumbed to the abuse.

SHAC's methods certainly can be menacing, as transcripts from the trial make clear. One of SHAC's main targets was Marsh, a company that sold insurance to HLS. There was a smoke-bomb attack at an office in Seattle, forcing the evacuation of a high-rise building. In San Antonio, SHAC members glued the locks to a Marsh office and plastered the windows and doors of the building with pictures of a mutilated dog. Once they even stormed inside, screaming threats: "You have the blood of death on your hands! . . . We know where you live! You cannot sleep at night! We will find you!"

And they made good on these threats. Marsh employees were repeatedly harassed at home. There were late-night phone calls: "Are you scared? Do you think the puppies should be scared?" Other calls were more menacing: "We know where you live. You shouldn't sleep at night. You shouldn't rest until the puppies rest." Marion Harlos, who was managing director for Marsh in San Antonio, said that people went through her mail, ordered magazine subscriptions in her name, and rang her doorbell and dashed off in a kind of never-ending Devil's Night. Sometimes protesters would gather in front of her house, banging drums and hollering into megaphones. "They proceeded to parade the neighborhood, shout my name, that of my children," she said. "I was petrified. I was petrified for my children." The kids were kept indoors: "We did not know what was going to take place. Would someone be in the front yard? Would someone be in the back yard? Would someone come up and talk to them? Would someone try and take them?" To make a bad situation even worse, a neighbor threatened to sue Harlos, claiming that the ongoing presence of protesters was hurting property values. Harlos eventually moved.

Sally Dillenback, a Marsh employee in Dallas, had a similarly harrowing experience. A SHAC website published private information, some of it probably obtained by going through her trash: her home address, her car's license-plate number, and even her auto-insurance policy number. Most unsettling, however, was the information about her children: their names, the names of their schools and teachers, and descriptions of their after-school activities. "I felt that my family might be threatened with that kind of information being posted," she testified. The activists certainly didn't leave her alone; they plastered pictures on the side of her house, her mailbox, and her sidewalk. A SHAC website described the strategy: "Let the stickers serve to remind Marsh employees and their neighbors that their homes are paid for in the blood, the blood of innocent animals." On other occasions, animal-rights radicals held protests outside her home with drums and bullhorns. They followed her to church. The scariest moment may have been when Dillenback read an e-mail: "It asked how I would feel if they cut open my son . . . and filled him with poison the way that they, Huntingdon, [were] doing to animals." Her husband bought a semi-automatic shotgun, even though Mrs. Dillenback doesn't like guns: "He was wanting to protect the family."

Pundits in Black Ski Masks

Marsh employees were by no means the only tertiary victims of abuse. Two bombs went off at a California office of Chiron, a biotech company. Nobody was hurt, but the second explosion was delayed—a tactic sometimes used by terrorists to kill first responders. Workers at GlaxoSmithKline, a pharmaceutical company, also had their windows smashed and mail stolen. In one case, SHAC posted information about the spouse of a GSK employee who was undergoing treatment for alcoholism. Another employee was summoned to the Baltimore morgue to identify a dead relative—but when she arrived, she learned the call was a hoax.

Sometimes, the connections between SHAC targets and HLS were so tenuous as to be almost nonexistent. Elaine Perna, a housewife who is married to an executive who retired from the Bank of New York—another company with ties to HLS—confronted SHAC when protesters appeared on her porch. "When I opened the door, they were yelling at me through the bullhorn. One spat at my face through the screen and yelled obscenities at me, about me, about my husband." A defense lawyer's attempt to minimize the incident—"All Ms. Gazzola did was she screamed through the bullhorn, didn't she?"—irritated Perna: "They were yelling at me through a bullhorn, they were calling me effing this and my husband effing that and spitting in my face through a screen. Now, if you think that 'that's all,' you know, you can call it 'that's all.' But to me, it wasn't 'that's all.'" The mayhem didn't stop until the police arrived.

On March 2, a jury convicted six members of SHAC (at press time, sentencing had not yet occurred). This is an important victory, but animal-rights extremism isn't going away—groups such as Hugs for Puppies and Win Animal Rights are now on the scene, continuing their perverse crusade. They certainly don't lack for true believers. In Senate testimony last fall, Jerry Vlasak of the North American Animal Liberation Press Office announced that violence against HLS was "extensional self-defense" in behalf of "non-human animals." Recently, a mysterious full-page advertisement appeared in the *New York Times* and the *Wall Street Journal*. It featured the image of a man in a black ski mask, alongside the words "I Control Wall Street" and a short account of the NYSE fiasco. "Nobody knows who paid for it," says Trull. One theory proposes that a group of institutional investors are responsible; another claims that it's a backhanded attempt by animal-rights activists to raise anxieties even further. HLS still isn't listed.

Several members of Congress have tried to address this species of domestic terrorism by proposing legislation that would toughen the Animal Enterprise Protection Act, a law that was passed before the advent of "tertiary targeting."

At the recent trial, prosecutors secured convictions against SHAC only because they were able to rely on anti-stalking laws. "They had to scour the federal code, looking for violations," says Brent McIntosh, a deputy assistant attorney general at the Department of Justice. "This is an enormous, surreptitious, and interstate conspiracy. We need to strengthen laws against it." Bills to do so have been introduced in both the House and the Senate, but a crowded legislative calendar probably means they won't be debated until a new Congress convenes next year.

The stakes are high. "Five years from now, we don't want to count up another $100 million in losses," says the FBI's Lewis. That's true, although the real costs of animal-rights terrorism aren't really quantifiable: They come in the form of medical discoveries that are delayed or never made, products that aren't approved, and careers that aren't started. Whatever the real price tag, one thing is certain: Each time an animal-rights terrorist wins, people lose.

Steven Best  **NO**

Dispatches from a Police State: Animal Rights in the Crosshairs of State Repression

Welcome to the post-constitutional America, where defense of animal rights and the earth is a terrorist crime.

In the wake of 9/11, and in the midst [of] the neoliberal attack on social democracies, efforts to grab dwindling resources, and crush dissent of any kind, the US has entered a neo-McCarthyist period rooted in witch-hunts and political persecution. The terms and players have changed, but the situation is much the same as the 1950s: the terrorist threat has replaced the communist threat, Attorney General Alfred [*sic*] Gonzalez dons the garb of Sen. Joseph McCarthy, and the Congressional Meetings on Eco-Terrorism stand in for the House Un-American Activities Committee. The Red Scare of communism has morphed into the *Green Scare* of ecoterrorism, where the bad guy today is not a commie but an animal, environmental, or peace activist. In a nightmare replay of the 1950s, activists of all kinds today are surveilled, hassled, threatened, jailed, and stripped of their rights. As before, the state conjures up dangerous enemies in our midst and instills fear in the public, so that people willingly forfeit liberties for an alleged security that demands secrecy, non-accountability, and centralized power. . . .

The bogus "war on terror" has served as a highly-effective propaganda and bullying device to ram through Congress and the courts a pro-corporate, anti-environmental, authoritarian agenda. Using vague, catch-all phrases such as "enemy combatants" and "domestic terrorists," the Bush administration has rounded up and tortured thousands of non-citizens (detaining them indefinitely in military tribunals without right to a fair trial) and surveilled, harassed, and imprisoned citizens who dare to challenge the government or corporate system it protects and represents.

"The Animal Enterprise Protection Act"

While dissent in general has become ever-more criminalized in the dark days of the Bush Reich, animal rights activists especially have been caught in the crosshairs of state repression, targeted by "anti-terrorist" legislation that subverts First Amendment rights to protect the blood money of corporate exploiters. This is because the animal rights/liberation movement is not only one of the most dramatic forms of resistance alive today (such as [is] evident in the dramatic raids, rescues, sabotage, and arson attacks of the Animal Liberation Front, a global movement), but also is an economic threat to postindustrial capital which is heavily rooted in science and research, and therefore dependent upon (it believes) animal experimentation.

In 1992, a decade before the passage of the USA PATRIOT Act, animal exploitation groups such as the National Association for Biomedical Research successfully lobbied Congress to pass a federal law called the Animal Enterprise Protection Act (AEPA). This legislation created the new crime of "animal enterprise terrorism," and laid out hefty sentences and fines for any infringement. The law applies to anyone who "intentionally damages or causes the loss of any property" of an "animal enterprise" (research facilities, pet stores, breeders, zoos, rodeos, circuses, furriers, animal shelters, and the like), or who causes an *economic loss* of any kind. The AEPA defines an "animal rights or ecological terrorist organization" as "two or more persons organized for the purpose of supporting any politically motivated activity intended to obstruct or deter any person from participating in any activity involving animals or an activity involving natural resources." The act criminalizes actions that obstruct "any lawful activity involving the use of natural resources with an economic value."

Like the category of "domestic terrorism" that is a keystone in the USA PATRIOT Act attack on civil liberties, the frightening thing about the AEPA is its strategic vagueness that subsumes any and every form of protest and demonstration against exploitative industries to a criminal act, specifically, to a *terrorist* act. Thus, the actions of two or more people can be labeled terrorist if they leaflet a circus, protest an experimental lab, block a road to protect a forest, do a tree-sit, or block the doors of a fur store. Since, under the purview of the AEPA, any action that interferes with the profits and operations of animal and environmental industries, even boycotts and whistle-blowing could be criminalized and denounced as terrorism. On the sweeping interpretations of such legislation, Martin Luther King, Mahatma Gandhi, and Cesar Chavez would today be vilified and imprisoned as terrorists, since the intent of their principled boycott campaigns was precisely to cause "economic damage" to unethical businesses. And since the AETA, like the legal system in general, classifies animals as "property," their "theft" (read: *liberation*) is unequivocally defined as a terrorist offense.

There already are laws against sabotage and property destruction, so isn't the AEPA just a redundant piece of legislation? No—not once [one] understands its hidden agenda which strikes at the heart of the Bill of Rights. The real purpose of the AEPA is to protect animal and earth exploitation industries from protest and criticism, not property destruction and "terrorism." The AEPA redefines vandalism as ecoterrorism, petty lawbreakers as societal menaces, protestors and demonstrators as domestic terrorists, and threats to their blood money as threats to national security. Powerful economic and lobbying forces, they seek immunity from criticism, to intimidate anyone contemplating protest against them, and to dispatch their opponents to prison.

Free Speech on Trial: The SHAC 7

Hovering over activists' heads like the sword of Damocles for over a decade, the AEPA dropped in March, 2006, with the persecution and conviction of seven members of a direct action group dedicated to closing down the world's largest animal-testing company, Huntingdon Life Sciences (HLS). Exercising their First Amendment rights, activists from the Stop Huntingdon Animal Cruelty (SHAC) campaign ran a completely legal and highly effective campaign against HLS, driving them to the brink of bankruptcy. Since 1999, SHAC activists in the UK and US have waged an aggressive direct action campaign against HLS, notorious for extreme animal abuse (torturing and killing 500 animals a day) and manipulated research data. SHAC roared onto the historical stage by combining a shrewd knowledge of the law, no non-sense direct action tactics, and a singular focus on one corporation that represents the evils of the entire vivisection industry. From email and phone blockades to raucous home demonstrations, SHACtivists have attacked HLS and pressured over 100 companies to abandon financial ties to the vivisection firm. By 2001, the SHAC movement drove down HLS stock values from $15/share to less than $1/share. Smelling profit emanating from animal bloodshed, investment banking firm Stephens Inc. stepped in to save HLS from bankruptcy. But, as happened to so many companies before them, eventually Stephens too could not withstand the intense political heat and so fled the SHAC kitchen. Today, as HLS struggles for solvency, SHAC predicts its imminent demise.

Growing increasingly powerful through high-pressure tactics that take the fight to HLS and their supporters rather than to corrupt legislatures, the SHAC movement poses a clear and present danger to animal exploitation industries and the state that serves them. Staggered and driven into the ropes, it was certain that SHAC's opponents would fight back. Throwing futile jabs here and there, the vivisection industry and the state recently teamed up to mount a major counterattack.

Alarmed indeed by the new form of animal rights militancy, HLS and the biomedical research lobby commanded special sessions with Congress to ban SHAC campaigns. On May 26, 2004, a police dragnet rounded up seven prominent animal rights activists in New Jersey, New York, Washington, and California. Hordes of agents from the FBI, Secret Service, and other law agencies stormed into the activists' homes at the crack of dawn, guns drawn and helicopters hovering above. Handcuffing those struggling for a better world, the state claimed another victory in its phony "war against terror." Using the AEPA, HLS successfully prosecuted the "SHAC 7," who currently are serving prison sentences up to six years.

After the SHAC 7 conviction, David Martosko, the noxious research director of the Center for Consumer Freedom and a fierce opponent of animal rights, joyously declared: "This is just the starting gun." Indeed, corporations and legislators continue to press for even stronger laws against animal rights and environmental activism, as the Bush administration encloses the nation within a vast web of surveillance and a militarized garrison.

In September 2006, the US senate unanimously passed a new version of the AEPA (S3990), significantly renamed the "Animal Enterprise *Terrorism* Act" (AETA). To prevent critical discussion, the Senate fast-tracked the bill without hearings or debate, and just before adjourning for the election recess. In November 2006, the House approved the bill (HR 4239), and President Bush obligingly signed it into law. Beyond the portentous change in name, the new and improved version extends the range of legal prosecution of activists, updates the law to cover Internet campaigns, and enforces stiffer penalties for "terrorist" actions. Created to stop the effectiveness of the SHAC-style tactics that biomedical companies had habitually complained about to Congress, the AETA makes it a criminal offense to interfere not only with so-called "animal enterprises" directly, but also with third-party organizations such as insurance companies, law firms, and investment houses that do business with them.

Thus, the Senate version of the bill expands the law to include "any property of a person or entity having a connection to, relationship with, or transactions with an animal enterprise." The chain of relations, like the application of the law, extends possibly to the point of infinity. As journalist Will Potter notes, "The clause broadens the scope of legislation that is already overly broad." This problem is compounded further with additional vague concepts such as criminalize actions that create "reasonable fear" in the targets of protest, making actions like peaceful home demonstrations likely candidates for "ecoterrorism."

As the Equal Justice Alliance aptly summarizes the main problems with the AETA:

- "It is excessively broad and vague.
- It imposes disproportionately harsh penalties.
- It effectively brands animal advocates as 'terrorists' and denies them equal protection.
- It effectively brands civil disobedience as 'terrorism' and imposes severe penalties.
- It has a chilling effect on all forms of protest by endangering free speech and assembly.
- It interferes with investigation of animal enterprises that violate federal laws.
- It detracts from prosecution of real terrorism against the American people."

ACLU Betrayal

A sole voice of dissent in Congress, Representative Dennis Kucinich (D-Ohio) stated that the bill compromises civil rights and threatens to "chill" free speech. Virtually alone in examining the issue from the perspective of the victims rather than victimizers, Kucinich said: "Just as we need to protect people's right to conduct their work without fear of assault, so too this Congress has yet to address some fundamental ethical principles with respect to animals. How should animals be treated humanely? This is a debate that hasn't come here."

One of the most unfortunate aspects of the passing of this bill was the failure of the American Civil Liberties Union to challenge it. The ACLU did indeed write a letter to Congress about the passing of the AETA, to caution against conflating illegal and legal protest, but the organization failed to challenge the real terrorism perpetuated by animal and earth exploitation industries, and ultimately consented to their worldview and validity.

In an October 30, 2006, letter to Chairman of the House Judiciary Committee F. James Sensenbrenner and Ranking Member John Conyers, the ACLU writes that it "does not oppose this bill, but believes that these minor changes are necessary to make the bill less likely to chill or threaten freedom of speech." Beyond proposed semantic clarifications, the ACLU mainly warns against broadening the law to include legal activities such as boycotts: "Legitimate expressive activity may result in economic damage. . . . Care must therefore be taken in penalizing economic damage to avoid infringing upon legitimate activity."

Thus, unlike dozens of animal protection groups who adamantly reject the AETA *en toto,* the ACLU "does not oppose the bill." In agreement with corporate interests, the ACLU assures the government it "does not condone violence or threats." It thereby dodges the complex question of the legitimacy of sabotage against exploitative industries. The ACLU uncritically accepts (1) the corporate–state definition of "violence" as intentional harm to *property,* (2) the legal definition of animals as "property," and (3) the use of the T-word to demonize animal liberationists rather than animal exploiters. Ultimately, the ACLU sides with the government against activists involved in illegal forms of liberation or sabotage, a problematic alliance in times of global ecocide. The ACLU thereby defends *the property rights* of industries to torture and slaughter billions of animals over the *moral rights* of animals to bodily integrity and a life free from exploitation and gratuitous violence.

The ACLU failed to ask the tough questions journalist Will Potter raised during his May 23, 2006 testimony before the House Committee holding a hearing on the AETA, and to follow Potter in identifying key inconsistencies in bill. Does the ACLU really think that their proposed modifications would be adequate to guarantee that the AETA doesn't trample on legal rights to protest? Are they completely ignorant and indifferent to the fact that the AEPA was just used to send the SHAC 7 to jail for the crime of protesting fraudulent research and heinous killing? And just where was the ACLU during the SHAC 7 trial, one of the most significant First Amendment cases in recent history? Why does the ACLU only recognize violations of the Constitution against human rights advocates? Do they think that animal rights activists are not citizens? Do they not recognize that tyrannical measures used against animal advocates today will be used against all citizens tomorrow? How can the world's premier civil rights institution [be] blatantly speciesist and bigoted toward animals? *Why will they come to the defense of the Ku Klux Klan but not the SHAC 7?* The ACLU's silence in the face of persecution of animal rights activists unfortunately is typical of most civil rights organizations that are too bigoted and myopic to grasp the implications of state repression of animal rights activists for human rights activists and all forms of dissent.

Animal Liberation as a New Social Movement

Corporate exploiters and Congress have taken the US down a perilous slippery slope, where it becomes difficult to distinguish between illegal and legal forms of dissent, between civil disobedience and terrorism, between PETA and Al Qaeda, and between liberating chickens from a factory farm and flying passenger planes into skyscrapers. The state protects the corporate exploiters who pull their purse strings and stuff their pockets with favors and cash.

The right to free speech ends as soon as you begin to exercise it. As the politics of nature—the struggle for liberation of animals and the earth—is the most dynamic fight today, one that poses a serious threat to corporate interests, animal and earth liberationists are under ferocious attack. The growing effectiveness of direct action anti-vivisection struggles will inevitably bring a reactionary and retaliatory response by the corporate–state complex to crack down on democratic political freedoms to protest, as well as new Draconian laws that represent a concerted effort by power brokers to crush the movement for animal liberation.

In the "home of the brave, land of the free," activists are followed by federal agents; their phone conversations and computer activity [are] monitored, their homes are raided, they are forced to testify before grand juries and pressured to "name names," they are targets of federal round ups, they are jailed for exercising constitutionally protected rights and liberties. Saboteurs receive stiffer prison sentences than rapists, bank robbers, and murderers. There has never been freedom of speech or action in the US, but in the post-9/11 climate, where the USA PATRIOT Act is the law of the land, not the Constitution and Bill of Rights, activists are demonized as terrorists—not just the Animal Liberation Front (ALF), Earth Liberation Front (ELF), and SHAC, but also completely legal and peaceful groups like Food Not Bombs and vegan outreach organizations.

The massive police resources of the US state are being used far more to thwart domestic dissent than to improve homeland insecurity. While Big Brother is obsessed with the email, conversations, and meetings of people who know a thing or two about the duties of citizenship, the airlines, railways, subways, city centers, and nuclear power plants remain completely vulnerable to an attack, which, according to the elites, is imminent.

The contemporary animal liberation movement is an *extension of the new social movements,* and as such issues "post-materialist" demands that are not about higher wages but the end to hierarchy and violence, and a new relation with the natural world.

Second, it is a *postindustrial movement,* operating within a global postindustrial society where the primary aspects of the economy no longer center on processing of physical materials as much as information, knowledge, science, and research. Transnational corporations such as Monsanto, pharmaceutical industries such as GlaxoSmithKline, AstraZeneca, Novartis, and Pfizer, and drug testing corporations such as Huntingdon Life Sciences show the importance of science and research for the postindustrial economy, and thus the relevance of the animal liberation movement.

This movement also is an *anti-globalization* movement in that the corporations it attacks often are transnational and global in scope, part of what I call the Global Vivisection Complex (GVC). The GVC is comprised of pharmaceutical industries, biotechnology industries, medical research industries, universities, and testing laboratories, all using animal experimentation to test and market their drugs. As animals are the gas and oil for these corporate science machines, the animal liberation movement has disrupted corporate supply chains, thwarted laboratory procedures, liberated captive slaves, and attacked the legitimacy of biomedical research as an effective scientific paradigm.

Fourth, the animal liberation movement is an *abolitionist movement,* seeking empty cages not bigger cages, demanding rights not "humane treatment" of the slaves, opposing the greatest institution of domination and slavery ever created—the empire of human supremacy over millions of species and billions of animal slaves.

To an important degree, the historical and socio-economic context for the emergence of the animal advocacy movement (in all its diverse tendencies and aspects) is the industrialization of animal exploitation and killing. This is dramatically evident with the growth of slaughterhouses at the turn of the 20th century, the emergence and globalization of factory farming after World War II, and the subsequent growth of research capital and animal experimentation. To this, one would have to add expanding human population numbers, the social construction of carnivorous appetites, and the rise of fast food industries which demand the exploitation and massacre of ever-growing numbers of animals, now in the tens of billions on a global scale. Along with other horrors and modes of animal exploitation, the industrialization, mechanization, and globalization of animal exploitation called into being an increasingly broad, growing, and powerful animal liberation movement.

Animal liberation builds on the great abolitionist struggle of past centuries and is the abolitionist movement of our day. Animal liberationists are waging war against the oldest and last form of slavery to be formally abolished—the exploitation of nonhuman animals. Just as the modern economy of Europe, the British colonies in America, and the United States after the Revolutionary War were once entirely dependent on the trafficking in human slaves, so now the current global economy would crash if all animal slaves were freed from every lab, cage and other mode of exploitation. Animal liberation is in fact the anti-slavery movement of the present age and its moral and economic ramifications are as world-shaking, possible more so, than the abolition of the human slavery movement (which of course itself still exists in some sectors of the world in the form of sweatshops, child sex slavery, forced female prostitution, and the like).

The animal liberation movement is a profound threat to the corporate–state complex and hierarchical society in two ways.

First, it is a serious economic threat, as the planetary capitalist system thrives off animal exploitation with the meat/dairy and biomedical research industries. In the UK, for instance, where the animal rights movement has been particularly effective, drug-makers are the third most important contributor to the economy after power generation and oil industries. The animal rights movement has emerged as a powerful anti-capitalist and anti-(corporate) globalization force in its ability to monkeywrench the planetary vivisection machine and challenge transnational corporations such as HLS, GlaxoSmithKline, and Novartis.

Second, the animal rights movement is a potent ideological and psychological threat. The fight for animal liberation demands radical transformations in the habits, practices, values, and mindset of all human beings as it also entails a fundamental restructuring of social institutions and economic systems predicated on exploitative practices. The philosophy of animal liberation assaults the identities and worldviews that portray humans as conquering Lords and Masters of nature, and it requires entirely new ways of relating to animals and the earth. Animal liberation is a direct attack on the power human beings—whether in premodern or modern, non-Western or Western societies—have claimed over animals, since at least the dawn of agricultural society ten thousand years ago.

Total Liberation

As the dynamics that brought about global warming, rainforest destruction, species extinction, and poisoning of communities are not reducible to any single factor or cause—be it agricultural society, the rise of states, anthropocentrism, speciesism, patriarchy, racism, colonialism, industrialism, technocracy, or capitalism—all radical groups and orientations that can effectively challenge the ideologies and institutions implicated in domination and ecological destruction have a relevant role to play in the global social-environmental struggle. While standpoints such as deep ecology, social ecology, ecofeminism, animal liberation, Black liberation, and the Earth Liberation Front are all important, none can accomplish systemic social transformation by itself. Working together, however, through a diversity of critiques and tactics that mobilize different communities, a flank of militant groups and positions can drive a battering ram into the structures of power and domination and open the door to a new future.

Although there is diversity in unity, there must also be unity in diversity. Solidarity can emerge in recognition of the fact that all forms of oppression are directly or indirectly related to the values, institutions, and *system* of global capitalism and related hierarchical structures. To be unified and effective, however, anti-capitalist and anti-imperialist alliances require mutual sharing, respectful learning, and psychological growth, such that, for instance, black liberationists, ecofeminists, and animal liberationists can help one another overcome racism, sexism, and speciesism.

The larger context for current dynamics in the animal liberation movement involves the emergence of the neoliberal project (as a response to the opening of the markets that was made necessary by the continuous expansion of transnational corporations in the post-war period) which was crucial in the elites' effort to destroy socialism and social democracy of any kind, to privatize all social structures, to gain total control of all resource markets and dwindling resources, and to snuff out all resistance. The animal rights/liberation movement has come under such intense fire because it has emerged as a threat to operations and profits of postindustrial capital (heavily rooted in research and therefore animal experimentation) and as a significant form of resistance. The transnational elite want the fire crushed before its example of resistance becomes a conflagration.

Conversely, the animal liberation movement is most effective not only as a single-issue focus to emancipate animals from human exploitation, but to join a larger resistance movement opposed to exploitation and hierarchies of any and all kinds. Clearly, SHAC and the ALF alone are not going to bring down transnational capitalism, pressuring HLS and raiding fur farms and laboratories will not themselves ignite revolutionary change, and are more rear-guard, defensive actions. The project to emancipate animals, in other words, is integrally related to the struggle to emancipate humans and the battle for a viable natural world. To the extent that the animal liberation movement grasps the big picture that links animal and human oppression struggles as one, and seeks to uncover the roots of hierarchy including that of humans over nature, they can be viewed as a profound new liberation movement that has a crucial place in the planetary struggles against injustice, oppression, exploitation, war, violence, capitalist neo-liberalism, and the destruction of the natural world and biodiversity.

Yet, given the profound relation between the human domination of animals and the crisis—social, ethical, and environmental—in the human world and its relation to the natural world, the animal liberation movement is in a unique position to articulate the importance of new relations between human and human, human and animal, and human and nature.

New social movements and Greens have failed to realize their radical potential. They have abandoned their original demands for radical social change and become integrated into capitalist structures that have eliminated "existing socialist countries" as well as social democracies within the present neoliberal globalization which has become dominant. A new revolutionary force must therefore emerge, one that will build on the achievements of classical democratic, libertarian socialist, and anarchist traditions; incorporate radical green, feminist, and indigenous struggles; synthesize animal, Earth, and human liberation standpoints; and build a global social-ecological revolution capable of abolishing transnational capitalism so that just and ecological societies can be constructed in its place.

Notes

For Feinstein's pathetic capitulation to the Green Scare and her sordid alliance with neo-McCarthyite Senator James "Global Warming is a Myth" Inhofe (R-Okla.), see her press release. . . .

The text of the "Animal Enterprise Protection Act of 1992" is available online.

In states such as Oregon and California, related legislation has already passed which declares it a felony terrorist offense to enter any animal facility with a camera or video recorder "with the intent to defame the facility or facility's owner." See Steven Best, "It's War: The Escalating Battle Between Activists and the Corporate-State Complex," in *Terrorists or Freedom*

Fighters? Reflections on the Liberation of Animals (Lantern Books, 2004), pp. 300–339 (eds. Steven Best and Anthony J. Nocella II).

For a more detailed analysis of the SHAC struggle in the context of political economy, see Steven Best and Richard Kahn, "Trial By Fire: The SHAC 7, Globalization, and the Future of Democracy," *Animal Liberation Philosophy and Policy Journal,* Volume II, Issue 2, 2004 . . .

On the SHAC 7 trial, see Steven Best and Richard Kahn, "Trial By Fire: The SHAC7, Globalization, and the Future of Democracy."

For the text of S3880, the final bill that passed in both houses, see . . .

Will Potter, "Analysis of Animal Enterprise Terrorism Act."

"Why Oppose AETA."

. . . Kucinich also challenged the AETA as being redundant and created a "specific classification" to repress legitimate dissent.

The ACLU letter to Congress is available at . . .

For a list of animal advocacy groups opposed to the AETA, see . . .

For Potter's testimony before the House Committee on the Judiciary Subcommittee on Crime, Terrorism, and Homeland Security see . . .

POSTSCRIPT

Is "Animal Rights" Just Another Excuse for Terrorism?

Much debate about the lethal experiments that were conducted on nonconsenting human subjects by the Nazis during World War II, as well as the ensuing trials of the Nazi physicians in Nuremburg, Germany, has established a consensus that no scientist can treat people the way the Nazis did. Informed consent is essential, and research on humans must aim to benefit those same humans.

As these ideas have gained currency, some people have tried to extend them to say that, just as scientists cannot do whatever they wish to humans, they cannot do whatever they wish to animals. Harriet Ritvo, in "Toward a More Peaceable Kingdom," *Technology Review* (April 1992), says that the animal rights movement "challenges the ideology of science itself . . . forcing experimenters to recognize that they are not necessarily carrying out an independent exercise in the pursuit of truth—that their enterprise, in its intellectual as well as its social and financial dimensions, is circumscribed and defined by the culture of which it is an integral part." The continuing debate is driven by the periodic discovery of researchers who seem quite callous (at least to the layperson's eye) in their treatment of animals (see Kathy Snow Guillermo, *Monkey Business: The Disturbing Case That Launched the Animal Rights Movement* [National Press, 1993]), by the charge that animal rights advocates just do not understand nature or research, and by the countercharge that animal research is irrelevant (see Peter Tatchell, "Why Animal Research Is Bad Science," *New Statesman* (August 9, 2004).

Among books that are pertinent to this issue are F. Barbara Orlans, *In the Name of Science: Issues in Responsible Animal Experimentation* (Oxford University Press, 1993); Rod Strand and Patti Strand, *The Hijacking of the Humane Movement* (Doral, 1993); Deborah Blum, *The Monkey Wars* (Oxford University Press, 1994), and Tom Regan, *Empty Cages: Facing the Challenge of Animal Rights* (Rowman and Littlefield, 2005). Adrian R. Morrison provides a guide to responsible animal use in "Ethical Principles Guiding the Use of Animals in Research," *American Biology Teacher* (February 2003). Barry Yeoman, "Can We Trust Research Done with Lab Mice," *Discover* (July 2003), notes that the conditions in which animals are kept can make a huge difference in their behavior and in their responses to experimental treatments.

Reviewing recent developments in the animal rights movement, Damon Linker, in "Rights for Rodents," *Commentary* (April 2001), concludes, "Can anyone really doubt that, were the misanthropic agenda of the animal-rights movement actually to succeed, the result would be an increase in man's inhumanity, to man and animal alike? In the end, fostering our age-old 'prejudice' in favor of human dignity may be the best thing we can do for animals, not to mention for ourselves." An editorial in *Lancet* (September 4, 2004), "Animal Research Is a Source of Human Compassion, Not Shame," insists that the use of animals in biomedical research is both an essentially humanistic endeavor and necessary. Assistant professor of anesthesiology and radiology at the University of Pittsburgh Stuart Derbyshire writes in "Vivisection: Put Human Welfare First," *Spiked-Online* (June 1, 2004), that the use of animals in research is justified by the search for knowledge, not just the search for medical treatments, and reflects a moral choice to put humans first. Josie Appleton, "Speciesism: A Beastly Concept: Why It Is Morally Right to Use Animals to Our Ends," *Spiked-Online* (February 23, 2006), contends that the development of human civilization has been marked by increasing separation from animals. Humans come first, and it is entirely moral to use animals for our own ends. Torturing animals is wrong, but mostly because it reflects badly upon the torturer. Animal-rights extremists defend the opposing view vigorously, even going so far as to firebomb researchers' homes and cars; see Greg Miller, "Scientists Targeted in California Firebombings," *Science* (August 8, 2008). P. Michael Conn and James V. Parker of the Oregon National Primate Research Center describe in *The Animal Research War* (Palgrave Macmillan, 2008) how animals are used and protected in research and the benefits of their use, while also detailing the movement of terrorist tactics from the United Kingdom to the United States. In their view, "It is extremely important that an informed public know what is really going on and how it impacts on the future of health care and medical advances."

Yet the idea that animals have rights too continues to gain ground. Steven M. Wise finds in *Drawing the Line: Science and the Case for Animal Rights* (Perseus, 2002) that there is a spectrum of mental capacities for different species, which supports the argument for rights. Niall Shanks, in "Animal Rights in the Light of Animal Cognition," *Social Alternatives* (Summer 2003) considers the moral/philosophical justifications for animal rights and stresses the question of consciousness. Jim Motavalli, in "Rights from Wrongs," *E Magazine* (March/April 2003), describes with approval the movement toward giving animals legal rights (though not necessarily human rights). Jeffrey Stinson, "Activists Pursue Basic Legal Rights for Great Apes," *USA Today* (July 15, 2008), describes current efforts to grant such rights to the great apes. Martin Enserink, "Rights for Apes? ¡Si!" *Science* (July 4, 2008), notes that a bill granting these rights has already been approved in Spain. Erin E. Williams and Margo Demello, *Why Animals Matter: The Case for Animal Protection* (Prometheus, 2007), link the mistreatment of animals in labs, slaughterhouses, and other venues with the mistreatment of immigrants and workers. Elisa Aaltola, "Personhood and Animals," *Environmental Ethics* (Summer 2008), discusses whether animals can be considered persons, saying that if they can, this opens new doors for animal ethics.

You can find the benefits of the use of animals discussed on a number of Web sites. Begin with Americans for Medical Progress (http://www.amprogress.org). For lists of specific benefits, visit Michigan State University at http://www.msu.edu/unit/ular/biomed/biomed_index.htm and the Pennsylvania Society for Biomedical Research at http://www.psbr.org/society/ABOUT.htm.

ISSUE 19

Is It Ethically Permissible to Clone Human Cells?

YES: Julian Savulescu, from "Should We Clone Human Beings? Cloning as a Source of Tissue for Transplantation," *Journal of Medical Ethics* (April 1999)

NO: David van Gend, from "Prometheus, Pandora, and the Myths of Cloning," *Human Life Review* (Summer/Fall 2006)

ISSUE SUMMARY

YES: Julian Savulescu, director of the Ethics Program of the Murdoch Institute at the Royal Children's Hospital in Melbourne, Australia, argues that it is not only permissible but morally required to use human cloning to create embryos as a source of tissue for transplantation.

NO: Physician David van Gend argues that not only is the cloning of embryonic stem cells morally indefensible, but recent progress with adult stem cells makes it unnecessary as well.

In February 1997 Ian Wilmut and Keith H. S. Campbell of the Roslin Institute in Edinburgh, Scotland, announced that they had cloned a sheep by transferring the gene-containing nucleus from a single cell of an adult sheep's mammary gland into an egg cell whose own nucleus had been removed and discarded. The resulting combination cell then developed into an embryo and eventually a lamb in the same way a normal egg cell does after being fertilized with a sperm cell. That lamb, named Dolly, was a genetic duplicate of the ewe from which the udder cell's nucleus was taken. Similar feats had been accomplished years before with fish and frogs, and mammal embryos had previously been split to produce artificial twins. It was not long before researchers successfully cloned monkeys and other animals. But the reactions of the media, politicians, ethicists, and lay-people have been largely negative. Dr. Donald Bruce, director of the Church of Scotland's Society, Religion and Technology Project, for example, has argued at some length about how "nature is not ours to do exactly what we like with." Dolly's relatively early death in 2003 has been cited as proof of the risks of cloning.

Many people seem to agree. In 1994 the U.S. National Advisory Board on Ethics in Reproduction called the whole idea of cloning oneself "bizarre . . . narcissistic and ethically impoverished." Arthur Caplan, director of the Center for Bioethics at the University of Pennsylvania, wonders, "What is the ethical purpose of even trying?" Conservative columnist George Will asks whether humans are now uniquely endangered since "the great given—a human being is the product of the union of a man and a woman—is no longer a given" and "humanity is supposed to be an endless chain, not a series of mirrors." Leon R. Kass, "The Wisdom of Repugnance," *The New Republic* (June 2, 1997), argues that human cloning is "so repulsive to contemplate" that it should be prohibited entirely.

Others go further. President Bill Clinton asked the National Bioethics Advisory Commission (see http://bioethics.georgetown.edu/nbac/), chaired by Harold T. Shapiro, president of Princeton University, to investigate the implications of this "stunning" research and to issue a final report by the end of May 1997. He also barred the use of U.S. funds to support work on human cloning. The commission's report called for extending the ban and called any attempt to clone a human "morally unacceptable" for now. Many countries besides the United States agreed, and bans on cloning research were widely imposed.

Yet, says J. Madeleine Nash in "The Case for Cloning," *Time* (February 9, 1998), "hasty legislation could easily be too restrictive." Cloning could serve a great many useful purposes, and further development of the technology could lead to much less alarming procedures, such as growing tissues for transplantation. See Arlene Judith Klotzko, "We Can Rebuild . . . ," *New Scientist* (February 27, 1999). Some of these benefits were considered when George Washington University researchers, using nonviable embryos, demonstrated that single cells could be removed from human embryos and induced to grow into new embryos. If permitted to develop normally, the cells would grow into genetically identical adults. The resulting adults would be duplicates, but only of each other (like identical twins), not of some preexisting adult.

Did Dolly represent something entirely new? For the very first time, it seemed more than science fiction to say it might soon be possible to duplicate an adult human, not just an embryo. But when ethicist John A. Robertson spoke at the National Bioethics Advisory Commission conference held in Washington, D.C., March 13–14, 1997, he said, "At this early stage in the development of mammalian cloning a ban on all human cloning is both imprudent and unjustified. Enough good uses can be imagined that it would be unwise to ban all cloning and cloning research because of vague and highly speculative fears."

In the following selection, Julian Savulescu argues, in part, that because cloned embryos have no moral value beyond that of the cells from which they are cloned, and because human suffering can be relieved, it is not only permissible but morally required to use human cloning to create embryos as a source of tissue for transplantation.

In the second selection, physician David van Gend takes strong exception to the idea that embryos—cloned or not—have no moral value. The cloning of embryonic stem cells, he says, is morally indefensible. In addition, recent progress with adult stem cells makes it unnecessary.

YES

Julian Savulescu

Should We Clone Human Beings?

Introduction

When news broke in 1997 that Ian Wilmut and his colleagues had successfully cloned an adult sheep, there was an ill-informed wave of public, professional and bureaucratic fear and rejection of the new technique. Almost universally, human cloning was condemned. Germany, Denmark and Spain have legislation banning cloning; Norway, Slovakia, Sweden and Switzerland have legislation implicitly banning cloning. Some states in Australia, such as Victoria, ban cloning. There are two bills before congress in the US which would comprehensively ban it. There is no explicit or implicit ban on cloning in England, Greece, Ireland or the Netherlands, though in England the Human Embryology and Fertilisation Authority, which issues licences for the use of embryos, has indicated that it would not issue any licence for research into "reproductive cloning." This is understood to be cloning to produce a fetus or live birth. Research into cloning in the first 14 days of life might be possible in England.

There have been several arguments given against human reproductive cloning:

1. It is liable to abuse.
2. It violates a person's right to individuality, autonomy, selfhood, etc.
3. It violates a person's right to genetic individuality (whatever that is—identical twins cannot have such a right).
4. It allows eugenic selection.
5. It uses people as a means.
6. Clones are worse off in terms of wellbeing, especially psychological wellbeing.
7. There are safety concerns, especially an increased risk of serious genetic malformation, cancer or shortened lifespan.

There are, however, a number of arguments in favour of human reproductive cloning. These include:

1. General liberty justifications.
2. Freedom to make personal reproductive choices.
3. Freedom of scientific enquiry.
4. Achieving a sense of immortality.
5. Eugenic selection (with or without gene therapy/enhancement).

From *Journal of Medical Ethics*, vol. 25, no. 2, April 1999, pp. 87–95 (notes and references omitted). Copyright © 1999 by BMJ Publishing Group. Reprinted by permission.

6. Social utility—cloning socially important people.
7. Treatment of infertility (with or without gene therapy/enhancement).
8. Replacement of a loved dead relative (with or without gene therapy/enhancement).
9. "Insurance"—freeze a split embryo in case something happens to the first: as a source of tissue or as replacement for the first.
10. Source of human cells or tissue.
11. Research into stem cell differentiation to provide an understanding of aging and oncogenesis.
12. Cloning to prevent a genetic disease.

The arguments against cloning have been critically examined elsewhere and I will not repeat them here. Few people have given arguments in favour of it. Exceptions include arguments in favour of 7–12, with some commentators favouring only 10–11 or 11–12. Justifications 10–12 (and possibly 7) all regard cloning as a way of treating or avoiding disease. These have emerged as arguably the strongest justifications for cloning. This paper examines 10 and to some extent 11.

Human Cloning as a Source of Cells or Tissue

Cloning is the production of an identical or near-identical genetic copy. Cloning can occur by fission or fusion. Fission is the division of a cell mass into two equal and identical parts, and the development of each into a separate but genetically identical or near-identical individual. This occurs in nature as identical twins.

Cloning by fusion involves taking the nucleus from one cell and transferring it to an egg which has had its nucleus removed. Placing the nucleus in the egg reprogrammes the DNA in the nucleus to replicate the whole individual from which the nucleus was derived: nuclear transfer. It differs from fission in that the offspring has only one genetic parent, whose genome is nearly identical to that of the offspring. In fission, the offspring, like the offspring of normal sexual reproduction, inherits half of its genetic material from each of two parents. Henceforth, by "cloning," I mean cloning by fusion.

Human cloning could be used in several ways to produce cells, tissues or organs for the treatment of human disease.

Human Cloning as a Source of Multipotent Stem Cells

In this paper I will differentiate between totipotent and multipotent stem cells. Stem cells are cells which are early in developmental lineage and have the ability to differentiate into several different mature cell types. Totipotent stem cells are very immature stem cells with the potential to develop into any of the mature cell types in the adult (liver, lung, skin, blood, etc). Multipotential stem cells are more mature stem cells with the potential to develop into different mature forms of a particular cell lineage, for example, bone marrow stem cells can form either white or red blood cells, but they cannot form liver cells.

Multipotential stem cells can be used as

1. a vector for gene therapy.
2. cells for transplantation, especially in bone marrow.

Attempts have been made to use embryonic stem cells from other animals as vectors for gene therapy and as universal transplantation cells in humans. Problems include limited differentiation and rejection. Somatic cells are differentiated cells of the body, and not sex cells which give rise to sperm and eggs. Cloning of somatic cells from a person who is intended as the recipient of cell therapy would provide a source of multipotential stem cells that are not rejected. These could also be vectors for gene therapy. A gene could be inserted into a somatic cell from the patient, followed by selection, nuclear transfer and the culture of the appropriate clonal population of cells in vitro. These cells could then be returned to the patient as a source of new tissue (for example bone marrow in the case of leukaemia) or as tissue without genetic abnormality (in the case of inherited genetic disease). The major experimental issues which would need to be addressed are developing clonal stability during cell amplification and ensuring differentiation into the cell type needed. It should be noted that this procedure does not necessarily involve the production of a multicellular embryo, nor its implantation in vivo or artificially. (Indeed, cross-species cloning—fusing human cells with cow eggs—produces embryos which will not develop into fetuses, let alone viable offspring.)

A related procedure would produce totipotent stem cells which could differentiate into multipotent cells of a particular line or function, or even into a specific tissue. This is much closer to reproductive cloning. Embryonic stem cells from mice have been directed to differentiate into vascular endothelium, myocardial and skeletal tissue, haemopoietic precursors and neurons. However, it is not known whether the differentiation of human totipotent stem cells can be controlled in vitro. Unlike the previous application, the production of organs could involve reproductive cloning (the production of a totipotent cell which forms a blastomere), but then differentiates into a tissue after some days. Initially, however, all early embryonic cells are identical. Producing totipotent stem cells in this way is equivalent to the creation of an early embryo.

Production of Embryo/Fetus/Child/Adult as a Source of Tissue

An embryo, fetus, child or adult could be produced by cloning, and solid organs or differentiated tissue could be extracted from it.

Cloning as Source of Organs, Tissue and Cells for Transplantation

The Need for More Organs and Tissues

Jeffrey Platts reports: "So great is the demand that as few as 5% of the organs needed in the United States ever become available." According to David K C

Cooper, this is getting worse: "The discrepancy between the number of potential recipients and donor organs is increasing by approximately 10–15% annually." Increasing procurement of cadaveric organs may not be the solution. Anthony Dorling and colleagues write:

> "A study from Seattle, USA, in 1992 identified an annual maximum of only 7,000 brain dead donors in the USA. Assuming 100% consent and suitability, these 14,000 potential kidney grafts would still not match the numbers of new patients commencing dialysis each year. The clear implication is that an alternative source of organs is needed."

Not only is there a shortage of tissue or organs for those with organ failure, but there remain serious problems with the compatibility of tissue or organs used, requiring immunosuppressive therapy with serious side effects. Using cloned tissue would have enormous theoretical advantages, as it could be abundant and there is near perfect immunocompatibility.

There are several ways human cloning could be used to address the shortfall of organs and tissues, and each raises different ethical concerns.

1. Production of Tissue or Cells Only by Controlling Differentiation

I will now give an argument to support the use of cloning to produce cells or tissues through control of cellular differentiation.

The fate of one's own tissue.   Individuals have a strong interest or right in determining the fate of their own body parts, including their own cells and tissues, at least when this affects the length and quality of their own life. A right might be defended in terms of autonomy or property rights in body parts.

This right extends (under some circumstances) both to the proliferation of cells and to their transmutation into other cell types (which I will call the Principle of Tissue Transmutation).

Defending the Principle of Tissue Transmutation
Consider the following hypothetical example:

Lucas I Lucas is a 22-year-old man with leukaemia. The only effective treatment will be a bone marrow transplant. There is no compatible donor. However, there is a drug which selects a healthy bone marrow cell and causes it to multiply. A doctor would be negligent if he or she did not employ such a drug for the treatment of Lucas's leukaemia. Indeed, there is a moral imperative to develop such drugs if we can and use them. Colony-stimulating factors, which cause blood cells to multiply, are already used in the treatment of leukaemia, and with stored marrow from those in remission in leukaemia before use for reconstitution during relapse.

Lucas II In this version of the example, the drug causes Lucas's healthy skin cells to turn into healthy bone marrow stem cells. There is no relevant moral difference between Lucas I and II. We should develop such drugs and doctors would be negligent if they did not use them.

If this is right, there is nothing problematic about cloning to produce cells or tissues for transplantation by controlling differentiation. All we would be doing is taking, say, a skin cell and turning on and off some components of the total genetic complement to cause the cell to divide as a bone marrow cell. We are causing a differentiated cell (skin cell) to turn directly into a multipotent stem cell (bone marrow stem cell).

Are there any objections? The major objection is one of practicality. It is going to be very difficult to cause a skin cell to turn *directly* into a bone marrow cell. There are also safety considerations. Because we are taking a cell which has already undergone many cell divisions during terminal differentiation to give a mature cell such as a skin cell, and accumulated mutations, there is a theoretical concern about an increased likelihood of malignancy in that clonal population. However, the donor cell in these cases is the same age as the recipient (exactly), and a shorter life span would not be expected. There may also be an advantage in some diseases, such as leukaemia, to having a degree of incompatibility between donor and recipient bone marrow so as to enable the donor cells to recognise and destroy malignant recipient cells. This would not apply to non-malignant diseases in which bone marrow transplant is employed, such as the leukodystrophies. Most importantly, all these concerns need to be addressed by further research.

Lucas IIA   In practice, it is most likely that skin cells will not be able to be turned directly into bone marrow cells: there will need to be a stage of totipotency in between. The most likely way of producing cells to treat Lucas II is via the cloning route, where a skin cell nucleus is passed through an oocyte to give a totipotent cell. The production of a totipotent stem cell is the production of an embryo.

Production of an embryo as a source of cells or tissues.   There are two ways in which an embryo could be a source of cells and tissues. Firstly, the early embryonic cells could be made to differentiate into cells of one tissue type, for example, bone marrow. Secondly, differentiated cells or tissues from an older embryo could be extracted and used directly.

Are these permissible?

In England, the Royal Society has given limited support to cloning for the purposes of treating human disease. The Human Genetics Advisory Commission (HGAC) defines this as "therapeutic cloning," differentiating it from "reproductive cloning." Both bodies claim that embryo experimentation in the first 14 days is permitted by English law, and question whether cloning in this period would raise any new ethical issues.

Cloning in this circumstance raises few ethical issues. What is produced, at least in the first few days of division after a totipotent cell has been produced from an adult skin cell, is just a skin cell from that person with an altered gene expression profile (some genes turned on and some turned off). In one way, it is just an existing skin cell behaving differently from normal skin cells, perhaps more like a malignant skin cell. The significant processes are ones of *cellular multiplication* and later, *cellular differentiation*.

If this is true, why stop at research at 14 days? Consider the third version of the Lucas case:

Lucas III   The same as Lucas IIA, but in this case, Lucas also needs a kidney transplant. Therefore, in addition to the skin cell developing blood stem cells (via the embryo), the process is adjusted so that a kidney is produced.

The production of another tissue type or organ does not raise any new relevant ethical consideration. Indeed, if Lucas did not need the kidney, it could be used for someone else who required a kidney (if, of course, in vitro maturation techniques had been developed to the extent that a functioning organ of sufficient size could be produced).

Consider now:

Lucas IV   In addition to the blood cells, all the tissue of a normal human embryo is produced, organised in the anatomical arrangement of an embryo. This (in principle) might or might not involve development in a womb. For simplicity, let us assume that this occurs in vitro (though this is impossible at present).

Is there any morally relevant difference from the previous versions? It is not relevant that many different tissues are produced rather than one. Nor is the size of these tissues or their arrangement morally relevant. If there is a difference, it must be that a special kind of tissue has been produced, or that some special relationship develops between existing tissues, and that a morally significant entity then exists. When does this special point in embryonic development occur?

The most plausible point is some point during the development of the brain. There are two main candidates:

1. when tissue differentiates and the first identifiable brain structures come into existence as the neural plate around day 19.
2. when the brain supports some morally significant function: consciousness or self-consciousness or rational self-consciousness. The earliest of these, consciousness, does not occur until well into fetal development.

On the first view, utilisation of cloning techniques in the first two weeks to study cellular differentiation is justifiable. The most defensible view, I believe, is that our continued existence only becomes morally relevant when we become self-conscious. (Of course, if a fetus can feel pain at some earlier point, but is not self-conscious, its existence is morally relevant in a different way: we ought not to inflict unnecessary pain on it, though it may be permissible to end its life painlessly.) On this view, we should use the drug to cause Lucas IV's skin cells to transmutate and remove bone marrow from these. What is going on in Lucas IV is no different, morally speaking, from cloning. If this is right, it is justifiable to extract differentiated tissues from young fetuses which have been cloned. . . .

I cannot see any intrinsic morally significant difference between a mature skin cell, the totipotent stem cell derived from it, and a fertilised egg. They are all cells which could give rise to a person if certain conditions are obtained. (Thus, to claim that experimentation on cloned embryos is acceptable, but the same experimentation on non-cloned embryos is not acceptable, because the former are not embryos but totipotent stem cells, is sophistry.)

Looking at cloning this way exposes new difficulties for those who appeal to the potential of embryos to become persons and the moral significance of conception as a basis for opposition to abortion. If all our cells could be persons, then we cannot appeal to the fact that an embryo could be a person to justify the special treatment we give it. Cloning forces us to abandon the old arguments supporting special treatment of fertilised eggs.

Production of a Fetus

If one believes that the morally significant event in development is something related to consciousness, then extracting tissue or organs from a cloned fetus up until that point at which the morally relevant event occurs is acceptable. Indeed, in law, a legal persona does not come into existence until birth. At least in Australia and England, abortion is permissible throughout fetal development.

Production of a Child or Adult as a Source of Cells or Tissues

Like the production of a self-conscious fetus, the production of a cloned child or adult is liable to all the usual cloning objections, together with the severe limitations on the ways in which tissue can be taken from donors for transplantation.

Many writers support cloning for the purposes of studying cellular differentiation because they argue that cloning does not raise serious new issues above those raised by embryo experimentation. Such support for cloning is too limited. On one view, there is no relevant difference between early embryo research and later embryo/early fetal research. Indeed, the latter stand more chance of providing viable tissue for transplantation, at least in the near future. While producing a cloned live child as a source of tissue for transplantation would raise new and important issues, producing embryos and early fetuses as a source of tissue for transplantation may be morally obligatory.

Consistency

Is this a significant deviation from existing practice?

1. Fetal Tissue Transplantation

In fact, fetal tissue has been widely used in medicine. Human fetal thymus transplantation is standard therapy for thymic aplasia or Di George's syndrome. It has also been used in conjunction with fetal liver for the treatment of subacute combined immunodeficiency.

Human fetal liver and umbilical cord blood have been used as a source of haematopoietic cells in the treatment of acute leukaemia and aplastic anaemia. Liver has also been used for radiation accidents and storage disorders. The main problem has been immune rejection.

One woman with aplastic anaemia received fetal liver from her own 22-week fetus subsequent to elective abortion over 20 years ago.

Fetal brain tissue from aborted fetuses has been used as source of tissue for the treatment of Parkinson's disease. Neural grafts show long term survival and function in patients with Parkinson's disease, though significant problems remain.

Fetal tissue holds promise as treatment for Huntington's disease, spinal cord injuries, demyelinating disorders, retinal degeneration in retinitis pigmentosa, hippocampal lesions associated with temporal lobe epilepsy, cerebral ischaemia, stroke and head injury, and beta thalassemia in utero using fetal liver. Fetal pancreas has also been used in the treatment of diabetes.

Fetal Tissue Banks

Indeed, in the US and England, fetal tissue banks exist to distribute fetal tissues from abortion clinics for the purposes of medical research and treatment. In the US, the Central Laboratory for Human Embryology in Washington, the National Diseases Research Interchange, and the International Institute for the Advancement of Medicine and the National Abortion Federation, all distribute fetal tissue.

In the UK, the Medical Research Council's fetal tissue bank was established in 1957 and disperses about 5,000 tissues a year.

2. Conception of a Non-Cloned Child as a Source of Bone Marrow: Ayala Case

Not only has fetal tissue been used for the treatment of human disease, but human individuals have been deliberately conceived as a source of tissue for transplantation. In the widely discussed Ayala case, a 17-year-old girl, Anissa, had leukaemia. No donor had been found in two years. Her father had his vasectomy reversed with the intention of having another child to serve as a bone marrow donor. There was a one in four chance the child would be compatible with Anissa. The child, Marissa, was born and was a compatible donor and a successful transplant was performed.

A report four years later noted: "Marissa is now a healthy four-year-old, and, by all accounts, as loved and cherished a child as her parents said she would be. The marrow transplant was a success, and Anissa is now a married, leukaemia-free, bank clerk."

Assisted reproduction (IVF) has been used to produce children to serve as bone marrow donors. It is worth noting that had cloning been available, there would have been a 100% chance of perfect tissue compatibility and a live child need not have been produced.

Objections

While there are some precedents for the proposal to use cloning to produce tissue for transplantation, what is distinctive about this proposal is that human tissue will be: (i) cloned and (ii) deliberately created with abortion in mind. This raises new objections.

Abortion Is Wrong

Burtchaell, a Catholic theologian, in considering the ethics of fetal tissue research, claims that abortion is morally wrong and that fetal tissue cannot be used for research because no one can give informed consent for its use and to use it would be complicity in wrongful killing. He claims that mothers cannot consent: "The flaw in this claim [that mothers can consent] is that the tissue is from within her body but is the body of another, with distinct genotype, blood, gender, etc." Claims such as those of Burtchaell are more problematic in the case of cloning. If the embryo were cloned from the mother, it would be of the same genotype as her, and, arguably, one of her tissues. Now at some point a cloned tissue is no longer just a tissue from its clone: it exists as an individual in its own right and at some point has interests as other individuals do. But the latter point occurs, I believe, when the cloned individual becomes self-conscious. The presence or absence of a distinct genotype is irrelevant. We are not justified in treating an identical twin differently from a non-identical twin because the latter has a distinct genotype.

In a society that permits abortion on demand, sometimes for little or no reason, it is hard to see how women can justifiably be prevented from aborting a fetus for the purpose of saving someone's life. And surely it is more respectful of the fetus, if the fetus is an object of respect, that its body parts be used for good rather than for no good purpose at all.

It Is Worse to Be a Clone

Some have argued that it is worse to be a clone. This may be plausible in the sense that a person suffers in virtue of being a clone—living in the shadow of its "parent," feeling less like an individual, treated as a means and not an end, etc. Thus cloning in the Ayala case would raise some new (but I do not believe overwhelming) issues which need consideration. But cloning followed by abortion does not. I can't make any sense of the claim that it is worse to be a cloned cell or tissue. These are not the things we ascribe these kinds of interests to. Cloning is bad when it is bad for a person. Likewise, arguments regarding "instrumentalisation" apply to persons, and not to tissues and cells.

Creating Life with the Intention of Ending It to Provide Tissue

Using cloning to produce embryos or fetuses as a source of tissue would involve deliberately creating life for the purposes of destroying it. It involves intentionally killing the fetus. This differs from abortion where women do not intend to become pregnant for the purpose of having an abortion.

Is it wrong deliberately to conceive a fetus for the sake of providing tissue? Most of the guidelines on the use of fetal tissue aim to stop women having children just to provide tissues. The reason behind this is some background belief that abortion is itself wrong. These guidelines aim to avoid moral taint objections that we cannot benefit from wrong-doing. More importantly, there is a concern that promoting some good outcome from abortion would encourage abortion. However, in this case, abortion would not be encouraged because this is abortion in a very special context: it is abortion of a *cloned* fetus for medical purposes.

But is it wrong deliberately to use abortion to bring about some good outcome?

In some countries (for example those in the former Eastern bloc), abortion is or was the main available form of birth control. A woman who had intercourse knowing that she might fall pregnant, in which case she would have an abortion, would not necessarily be acting wrongly in such a country, if the alternative was celibacy. When the only way to achieve some worthwhile end—sexual expression—is through abortion, it seems justifiable.

The question is: is the use of cloned fetal tissue the best way of increasing the pool of transplantable tissues and organs?

An Objection to the Principle of Tissue Transmutation

Another objection to the proposal is that we do not have the right to determine the fate of all our cells. For example, we are limited in what we can do with our sex cells. However, we should only be constrained in using our own cells when that use puts others at risk. This is not so in transmutation until another individual with moral interests comes into existence.

Surrogacy Concerns

At least at present, later embryonic and fetal development can only occur inside a woman's uterus, so some of the proposals here would require a surrogate. I have assumed that any surrogate would be freely consenting. Concerns with surrogacy have been addressed elsewhere, though cloning for this purpose would raise some different concerns. There would be no surrogacy concerns if the donor cell were derived from the mother (she would be carrying one of her own cells), from the mother's child (she would be carrying her child again) or if an artificial womb were ever developed.

Should We Give Greater Importance to Somatic Cells?

I have claimed that the totipotent cells of the early embryo, and indeed the embryo, do not have greater moral significance than adult skin cells (or indeed lung or colon or any nucleated cells). I have used this observation to downgrade the importance we attach to embryonic cells. However, it might be argued that we should upgrade the importance which we attach to somatic cells.

This is a *reductio ad absurdum* of the position which gives importance to the embryo, and indeed which gives weight to anatomical structure rather than function. If we should show special respect to all cells, surgeons should be attempting to excise the very minimum tissue (down to the last cell) necessary during operations. We should be doing research into preventing the neuronal loss which occurs normally during childhood. The desquamation of a skin cell should be as monumental, according to those who believe that abortion is killing persons, as the loss of a whole person. These claims are, I think, all absurd.

Yuk Factor

Many people would find it shocking for a fetus to be created and then destroyed as a source of organs. But many people found artificial insemination abhorrent, IVF shocking and the use of animal organs revolting. Watching an abortion is horrible. However, the fact that people find something repulsive does not settle whether it is wrong. The achievement in applied ethics, if there is one, of the last 50 years has been to get people to rise above their gut feelings and examine the reasons for a practice.

Permissive and Obstructive Ethics

Many people believe that ethicists should be merely moral watch-dogs, barking when they see something going wrong. However, ethics may also be permissive. Thus ethics may require that we stop interfering, as was the case in the treatment of homosexuals. Ethics should not only be obstructive but constructive. To delay unnecessarily a good piece of research which will result in a life-saving drug is to be responsible for some people's deaths. It is to act wrongly. This debate about cloning illustrates a possible permissive and constructive role for ethics.

Conclusion

The most justified use of human cloning is arguably to produce stem cells for the treatment of disease. I have argued that it is not only reasonable to produce embryos as a source of multipotent stem cells, but that it is morally required to produce embryos and early fetuses as a source of tissue for transplantation. This argument hinges on:

1. The claim that the moral status of the cloned embryo and early fetus is no different from that of the somatic cell from which they are derived.
2. The claim that there is no morally relevant difference between the fetus and the embryo until some critical point in brain development and function.
3. The fact that the practice is consistent with existing practices of fetal tissue transplantation and conceiving humans as a source of tissue for transplantation (the Ayala case).
4. An argument from beneficence. This practice would achieve much good.
5. An argument from autonomy. This was the principle of tissue transmutation: that we should be able to determine the fate of our own cells, including whether they change into other cell types.

This proposal avoids all the usual objections to cloning. The major concerns are practicality and safety. This requires further study.

The HGAC and The Royal Society have broached the possibility of producing clones for up to 14 days: "therapeutic cloning." Those bodies believe that it is acceptable to produce and destroy an embryo but not a fetus. Women abort fetuses up to 20 weeks and later. We could make it mandatory that women have abortions earlier (with rapid pregnancy testing). However, we do not. Moreover, while the decision for most women to have an abortion is a momentous and considered one, in practice, we allow women to abort fetuses regardless of their reasons, indeed occasionally for no or bad reasons. If a woman could abort a fetus because she wanted a child with a certain horoscope sign, surely a woman should be able to abort a fetus to save a person's life.

I have been discussing cloning for the purposes of saving people's lives or drastically improving their quality. While we beat our breasts about human dignity and the rights of cells of different sorts, people are dying of leukaemia and kidney disease. If a woman wants to carry a clone of her or someone else's child to save a life, it may not be society's place to interfere.

David van Gend

NO

Prometheus, Pandora, and the Myths of Cloning

One of the earliest human trials in regenerative medicine was conducted on a crag high in the Caucasus around the dawn of time. Or not strictly human, since Prometheus was a Titan. But for fraternizing with humans he was pegged out on a high rock where the eagle of Hephaestus ate his liver out each day, and it grew back each night.

With remarkable scientific insight, although without specifying the key role of hepatic stem cells, the Greeks observed that the liver is the one internal organ that has a capacity for vigorous regrowth after trauma.

Prometheus was being punished for his beneficence to humans—for teaching them arts practical and aesthetic, and worst of all for stealing the secret fire of Zeus to give humans comfort in their caves and supremacy over the animals.

To call scientists "Promethean" seems to me a compliment. Their role is to benefit humankind by their labours—and scientists who labor in the field of regenerative medicine using adult stem cells are most authentically Promethean.

The proper term for scientists who violate norms of human relationships and ethics, unleashing destructive forces upon us, is not "Promethean" but "Pandoran." She was the other chapter in Zeus's punishment of Prometheus. Pandora was asexually reproduced, "forged on the anvil of Hephaestus," essentially a laboratory creation like the modern clone. Irresistibly packaged, she wowed the impressionable brother of Prometheus, who accepted her gift of a mysterious box—which, upon being opened, released all sorts of corrupt and harmful things into the world. It is said that one thing only remained in Pandora's box after all the noxious things had emerged: hope, groundless and unreasonable hope.

With cloning, modern Pandorans raise unreasonable hope with their attractively packaged deceit. With obscure motives, they threaten forms of harm to humanity that we are only beginning to understand.

Keeping the lid on Pandora's box is still possible if we can show clearly why cloning is both redundant and wrong.

Why Cloning Is Redundant

A patient of mine with advanced Parkinson's disease hopes to be the first man treated with stem cells from the back of his nose. He is among the dozens of patients with various genetic illnesses whose stem cells have been collected for

From *Human Life Review*, Summer/Fall 2006, pp. 15–16, 21–27 (notes omitted). Copyright © 2006 by David van Gend. Reprinted by permission of the author.

research at the Griffith University Adult Stem Cell Centre, here in Queensland, Australia.

There are cautious, very cautious, grounds for hope for my patient, given that Griffith has successfully used these adult stem cells to treat Parkinson's in rats, and is planning primate trials. If all goes well, human trials will follow.

His case is an example of the true state of stem-cell science, as opposed to its political distortion. In the public mind embryonic stem cells and cloning are the main event, whereas in reality they are a conjurer's sideshow. Adult stem cells are now safely used in 72 human conditions . . . embryonic stem cells remain both unusable and dangerous. The cloning lobby dreams of creating "patient-specific stem cells" for research; adult-stem-cell researchers have already achieved that goal.

Australian cloning advocate Professor Alan Trounson has recently clarified that cloning is not about cell therapies for Parkinson's or spinal injury, but is limited to the modest research goal of creating patient-specific cells for studying disease and developing drugs. That is an important clarification, since the media still pretend that embryonic stem cells, cloned or otherwise, can be used as magic bullets for direct "cell therapy." That has always been false—since, among other things, the risk of tumors inherent in the use of embryonic cells rules out human application. Trounson's revised prospectus for cloning is more honest: "It's not about cells for therapy. This is about cells that give us an opportunity to discover what causes a disease and whether we can interfere with that."

Fine—but even that more realistic goal for cloning has been made redundant, since that is exactly the research capacity Griffith has now achieved with adult stem cells. They possess an expanding range of patient-specific stem cells, easily obtained from patients, readily transformed into the required cell type (brain, muscle, kidney, liver) and useful for genetic study of the disease and development of drugs. These adult stem cells are superior for research because they are cheap, ethically uncomplicated, and free of the genetic damage caused by cloning. And only adult stem cells can be used safely for direct cell therapy without the risk of tumor formation and immune rejection.

Cloning has been left for dead, and Griffith Professor Alan Mackay-Sim has written its obituary telling the Lockhart enquiry into Australia's cloning laws that "it is probable that such stem-cell lines as these will render therapeutic cloning irrelevant and impractical."

If that view is correct, what possible justification is there for pursuing cloning? . . .

Why Cloning Is Wrong

Here is the dual desecration of "research" cloning: not just that a human life is wrongfully killed for the benefit of others, but that a human life is wrongfully created outside of any normal human setting.

To clone is to generate a living human embryo with no mother—think of that! Only an emptied-out female egg is used, with no trace of the mother's genetic identity. And no father, either—for the donor of DNA is not father to the clone, but is instead its identical twin, and could be as anonymous a donor as a piece of human tissue from the laboratory fridge.

Cloning creates a subclass of humans who are nobody's children. Anonymous artifacts, not beloved offspring; scientific objects with no mother or father to defend their interests. The bonds of belonging are broken: A human being is created outside the circle of human kinship and care.

And yet the cloned offspring is a child like any other; if it were allowed to be born, we would care for it as any other orphan. As Australia's religious leaders have pointed out, it would be a lesser evil to let a cloned embryo be born as a child—even considering the sociological distress and genetic disease it will suffer. The greater evil is the one proposed: that it will be created but never allowed to be born, remaining a mere laboratory animal, meat for the consumption of science.

That is not to condone the obvious abuse of "live-birth" cloning. Let Dolly the sheep, Matilda the lamb, or Snuppy the puppy be part of the freak show of cloning, but not a human child. But it is to be clear that the act of asexual reproduction of a human being, regardless of whether the clone lives for days or for years, is an abuse in itself—violating the essential bonds of "blood and belonging" that every human individual needs, willfully creating the world's first absolute orphan. That is a desecration of humanity, and must be condemned as such.

In Australia in 2002, our Parliament was united in condemning cloning—but in 2006, the debate has been reopened. We are at a different stage of the debate than the U.S.; in 2002, we banned cloning but lost the argument over the use of "surplus" IVF embryos, which are now available for research. At that time we argued that there was no good way out for the "surplus" embryos. We advised that it would be a lesser evil to let the current frozen generation of embryos die—acknowledging our shame in allowing them to be stockpiled in the first place, and ensuring it never happened again. We said it was a greater evil to set up a permanent industry exploiting human embryos, since demand would ensure supply: IVF clinics would ensure the ongoing creation of surplus embryos to feed the drug companies.

Our argument failed. In the U.S., there does not appear to be a fixed deadline at which frozen embryos must be thawed out, so they are not so clearly "going to die anyway"; more vividly, the U.S. practice of adopting frozen embryos further negates that fatalistic argument. In Australia, by contrast, the argument that the doomed embryo "may as well be used for research" (in the context of wild claims of miracle cures from the use of embryonic stem cells) carried the majority vote. The prime minister, a fair-minded man, spoke for the misled majority: "I could not find a sufficiently compelling moral difference between allowing embryos to succumb in this way and destroying them through research that might advance life-saving and life-enhancing therapies. That is why, in the end, I came out in favor of allowing research involving excess IVF embryos to go ahead."

But importantly, an ethical line in the sand was drawn between using IVF embryos that were "going to die anyway" and deliberately creating new embryos specifically for destructive research. The PM made this distinction: "It is also my very strong belief that human embryos should not be created for any purpose other than IVF treatment." On this principle a ban on creating embryos "by any means other than by the fertilization of a human egg by human sperm" was passed unanimously by Parliament.

On the same principle, there was a majority vote (non-binding) against all forms of human cloning at the United Nations last year. One delegate expressed the principle as: "No human life should ever be produced to be destroyed for the benefit of another." They saw the inhumanity of creating a cloned human embryo—identical to you or me at that stage of life—with the sole intention of exploiting it for science. Likewise, the creation of a human embryo purely for research is expressly prohibited in Article 18 of the European Convention on Human Rights and Biomedicine.

Australia's Prohibition of Human Cloning Act 2002 provided for periodical review of the legislation, and in late 2005 a six-person committee, handpicked under the auspices of a pro-cloning cabinet minister, predictably recommended overturning the unanimous vote of Parliament and allowing research cloning. This committee acknowledged that cloning creates a human embryo, which could be born as a baby like any of us. But they callously reasoned that the cloned embryo does not really "matter" to anybody, since nobody intends to bring it to birth—therefore let it be cut up for stem cells, used for drug testing, even hybridized with animals, provided it is killed by the age of 14 days.

The question of whether the embryo "matters" goes straight to the heart of this debate. This is the dividing line for public opinion in every legislature around the world. Interestingly, the question is no longer whether the embryo is a human life, but whether that human life "matters." In the words of our Senate report from the 2002 debate: "There is in fact little disagreement that the embryo is a human life and that its life commences at fertilization. The difficulties arise in specifying exactly in what sense it is to be considered 'a life,' and hence what significance should be attached to it."

The committee referred to an earlier Senate report that had reviewed "the biological facts of the matter" and concluded: "Two universally accepted attributes are that the fertilized ovum has 'life' and that it is genetically human (i.e. it is composed of genetic material entirely from the species homo sapiens). It is also generally agreed that it is an entity (a centrally organized unit which has a purposeful independent function as opposed to an organ or tissues). It also has developmental potential."

One can agree on the bare facts—that the embryo is a living individual member of our species—but whether that individual life "matters" depends on the worldview one brings to the debate. And faced with this key question—the meaning of a human life in all its embryonic simplicity—the cultural divide shows up most starkly.

A citizen who believes, as C. S. Lewis put it, that human life is "a transient and senseless contortion on the idiotic face of infinite matter" is unlikely to grant great meaning to a mere embryonic contortion. If ultimately we are all just strangely complex lumps of meat floating in time, then the embryo is just a very small lump of meat, devoid of real meaning.

For those citizens whose worldview gives a deeper context to human life, even the life of the embryo has meaning. To those who share the Christian theory of life, all of us matter, even the "littlest of these His brethren," precisely because we matter to God. Size and age are not a measure of human meaning; what matters is that the individual life is known and loved in God.

On this understanding, a new name is spelled out at conception and written on the palm of God's hand—even if the font is too small for us to read. That name, that genetic identity, will take a lifetime to be fully expressed, but it is the same name we carry for our whole existence: a new character scripted into our vast mystery play, which no other character has the right to erase.

It is vital to engage in the battle for the meaning of the human embryo, for even if there is no hope of persuading card-carrying nihilists, there is always the muddled middle of fellow citizens who can be convinced one way or the other. All future policy on cloning, human-animal hybridization, prenatal eugenics, transgenic manipulation, and other as yet unimagined abuses depends on the dominant view of what the human embryo is, and therefore how we are bound to treat it.

There are four key arguments demeaning the human embryo, which can be rebutted in interesting ways.

First, there are the recurrent dismissive comments that the embryo is "smaller than the full stop at the end of this sentence" (which, being translated into American, refers to a "period"). On this, we should play the scientists on their own ground, reminding them that, according to their own theories, the Universe itself was once "smaller than a period." To cosmologists, the fact that such a tiny entity as the embryonic Universe contained within itself the capacity to unfold into this vast and fruitful cosmos is not a cause for contempt, but intellectual wonder. We need similar eyes of understanding, not of ignorant contempt, when we contemplate the embryonic human. This tiny entity, like the embryonic Universe, is unfolding into the vast and fruitful cosmos of a human being, and deserves a comparable response of intellectual wonder. The only event in the physical world comparable in complexity and wonder to the Big Bang is human conception, which creates the only entity that can know, and therefore in a sense transcend, the Universe itself. The embryonic human is in that sense a greater being than the embryonic universe.

Second, the logic of the culture of death will work backwards from abortion to argue that since the fetus does not matter, the embryo matters even less. . . .

Care is needed here. Policy on how we treat embryos is formed in an entirely different context from policy on abortion. Abortion is portrayed as an act of self-defense against the threatening intruder in the womb. In no way is the laboratory embryo threatening the mother. In the case of the cloned embryo, there is no mother to threaten. Abortion is portrayed as an assertion of moral autonomy over one's private life, often in the context of emotional crisis, while policy on embryonic research is a coldly calculated decision by public committees. The two types of policy must be kept widely separated, and the meaning of the embryo considered on its own merits.

Third, there is the argument that the embryo cannot be considered an individual human being until the stage of possible "twinning" has passed. This is generally taken to be about 14 days of embryonic life. Until that time, we cannot know if the embryo is going to end up as one "entity" or two, which surely casts doubt on its moral status. I admit to finding this a very muddled argument, and it is the phenomenon of cloning itself that finally clears the fog. For with cloning you or I can now undergo "twinning" well past day 14—in fact, tomorrow, if you like. Does that mean that your moral status as a true, unambiguous "individual" today is in question, just because tomorrow you might have split off an identical twin? Is your current "soul" somehow diminished because you have twinned yourself into a clone? The problem is no different for the embryo: If it splits off a twin at day 14 it has merely cloned itself into an identical embryo, a twin that is 14 days younger than the original embryo. So, again, there is a positive way to look at the early embryo: It is a wonder, a marvel, and if it splits off a twin, that is just greater cause for celebration: We now have two marvels, two wonders. At the very least we are looking at one embryonic human; there is the happy chance of a second, younger human being arising a few days later from the phenomenon of natural cloning, or twinning, but that is no cause for downgrading the significance of either life.

Fourth and finally, there is the argument that so many embryos are "wasted" naturally that they surely cannot be considered to have a full human status—even, for some sensible Christian people, full spiritual status in the eyes of God. Estimates vary wildly for embryonic loss, but even if the figure is 30 percent I do not see how the problem is any different from the similar "wastage" of infants in the part of Africa I was born in. Does the fact that some 30 percent died in infancy (including some children of my early missionary ancestors) mean they were not truly human? With all due respect, if God has a problem with taking seriously the moral status of embryos because so many are "wasted," He has the same problem with these wasted African infants, or with the high percentage of Chinese babies wasted through female infanticide. And I remain unconvinced as to why a higher spiritual status should be granted to those of us who, through good luck and good environment, happen to have persisted longer on this earth. None of us matter, in the Christian understanding, unless we matter to God, and it seems wise to give the benefit of the doubt to the most embryonic of these His brethren.

Conclusion

Cloning is wrong.   It violates our humanity and the bonds of love and care to manufacture offspring who have no mother or father. It violates the most basic ethical prohibitions to create an embryo with the intention of destroying it in research. Only the parent-child relationship is the legitimate and humane context in which to create a human embryo.

Cloning is redundant.   Once we have rejected it on ethical grounds, the great consolation is that we do not need cloning anyway; adult stem cells will get us the good things of stem-cell science, leaving cloning "irrelevant and impractical." But we must remember that the scientific argument is strictly secondary: Even if there were additional scientific benefits from cloned-embryo stem cells over the new disease-specific adult stem cells (and there appear not to be) cloning must still be rejected on grounds of basic humanity: fundamental respect for the dignity of a living member of the human species, which rules out creating such a life with its destruction in mind.

In the magnificent new field of regenerative medicine, we can and must be diligent Prometheans, while keeping the lid locked on Pandora's deceitful and dehumanizing gift.

POSTSCRIPT

Is It Ethically Permissible to Clone Human Cells?

Although the cloning debate became vigorous only after the cloning of an adult animal, it is worth stressing that most of the discussion now centers on the cloning of embryos in order to obtain stem cells that can become any cell type or tissue found in the body. The hope is to be able to replace defective cells and cure disease. Ian Wilmut, "The Case for Cloning Humans," *The Scientist* (April 25, 2005), argues that cloning human embryos may offer the best way to understand and treat difficult diseases; Wilmut's team received a license to clone human embryos in February 2005. For a good overview of the stem cell issue, see Rick Weiss, "The Power to Divide," *National Geographic* (July 2005). See also Ronald Bailey, *Liberation Biology: The Scientific and Moral Case for the Biotech Revolution* (Prometheus, 2005).

Leon Kass develops his objections to cloning in "Preventing a Brave New World," *The Human Life Review* (July 2001), and *Life, Liberty and the Defense of Dignity: The Challenge for Bioethics* (Encounter, 2002). He gains support from Mary Midgley, who in "Biotechnology and Monstrosity: Why We Should Pay Attention to the 'Yuk Factor,'" *Hastings Center Report* (September–October 2000), argues that intuitive, emotional responses to things such as cloning have a significance that must not be dismissed out of hand. In *Our Posthuman Future: Consequences of the Biotechnological Revolution* (Farras, Strauss & Giroux, 2002; paperback Picador, 2003), Francis Fukuyama argues for limits on cloning and genetic engineering in order to protect human nature and dignity. David Gurnham, "The Mysteries of Human Dignity and the Brave New World of Human Cloning," *Social & Legal Studies* (June 2005), agrees that cloning threatens human dignity. As a result of such arguments, the United States has banned the use of federal funds for reproductive cloning and severely limited the cloning of embryos to obtain stem cells for either research or treatment purposes. However, some states (e.g., California; see Nigel Williams, "California Ramps Up Stem Cell Plans," *Current Biology* [March 2005]) have chosen to develop their own state-funded research programs. In other countries, progress has been more rapid. See Susan Mayor, "UK and Korean Teams Refine Techniques for Human Cloning," *British Medical Journal* (May 28, 2005).

Speaking to the National Bioethics Advisory Commission (whose report was summarized by chair Harold T. Shapiro in the July 11, 1997, issue of *Science*), Ruth Macklin, of the Albert Einstein College of Medicine, said, "It is absurd to maintain that the proposition 'cloning is morally wrong' is self-evident. . . . If I cannot point to any great benefits likely to result from cloning, neither do I foresee any probable great harms, provided that a structure of regulation and oversight is in place. If objectors to cloning can identify no greater harm than a supposed affront to the dignity of the human species, that is a flimsy basis on which to erect barriers to scientific research and its applications." Nathan Myhrvold argues in "Human Clones: Why Not? Opposition to Cloning Isn't Just Luddism—It's Racism," *Slate* (March 13, 1997), that "Calls for a ban on cloning amount to discrimination against people based on another genetic trait—the fact that somebody already has an identical DNA sequence." There are reasons why cloning—at least of embryonic cells—should be permitted. According to Thomas B. Okarma (interviewed by Erika Jonietz, "Cloning, Stem Cells, and Medicine's Future," *Technology Review*, June 2003), they hold great hope for new and useful medical treatments. And according to Robin Marantz Henig, "Pandora's Baby," *Scientific American* (June 2003), when other reproductive technologies such as *in vitro* fertilization were new, they faced similar objections; now they are routine, and it is likely that someday cloning will be too. Daniel J. Kevles agrees; in "Cloning Can't Be Stopped," *Technology Review* (June 2002), he said that if human cloning can but succeed, it will "become commonplace . . . a new commodity in the growing emporium of human reproduction." Seymour W. Itzkoff, in "Intervening with Mother Nature: The Ethics of Human Cloning," *The Mankind Quarterly* (Fall 2003), calls objections to cloning and related issues "reactionary" and notes that "The cloning of humans and the stem cell production issue are . . . the tip of the iceberg, the slippery slope, or any other metaphor that points to the growing impact of scientific research that could undercut the twentieth-century ideological opposition to viewing human behavior as biologically/genetically determined."

So far, the result of the debate is that research continues but under various regulatory and funding restrictions. See Charles C. Mann, "Braving Medicine's Frontier," *Technology Review* (September 2005). Work with adult stem cells has so far proved disappointing, but see Agneta M. Sutton, "'Yes' to Adult Stem Cells," *Southern Medical Journal* (December 2006). Hopes have also been raised by the 2007 discovery that it is possible to insert certain genes into adult cells and return them to a stem-cell-like state of "pluripotency," meaning that they can differentiate into many kinds of cells. See Constance Holden and Gretchen Vogel, "A Seismic Shift for Stem Cell Research," *Science* (February 1, 2008), and Kazutoshi Takahashi et al., "Induction of Pluripotent Stem Cells from Adult Human Fibroblasts by Defined Factors," *Cell* (November 2007). Ian Wilmut of Dolly fame has shifted his research interests toward making such cells, and cloning critics are now saying there is no further need to clone embryonic cells; see Sally Lehrman, "No More Cloning Around," *Scientific American* (August 2008). On the other hand, Patrick Barry, "Back to the Womb," *Science News* (September 13, 2008), notes that researchers have not yet abandoned work on embryonic stem cells, for only by comparing the two types of stem cells can the nonembryonic stem cells be properly assessed. Michael Fumento, "No, the Stem Cell Debate Is Not Over," *American Spectator* (April 2008), argues that it is premature to say that stem cells of any kind will be medically useful, or that induced pluripotent cells will be any more effective than embryonic or adult stem cells. Insoo Hyun, "Stem Cells from Skin Cells: The Ethical Questions," *Hastings Center Report* (January 2008), argues that there also remain significant ethical issues.

ISSUE 20

Should the Public Have to Pay to See the Results of Federally Funded Research?

YES: Ralph Oman, from Hearing on "The Fair Copyright in Research Works Act," Testimony regarding H.R.6845 before the Subcommittee on Courts, the Internet, and Intellectual Property of the Committee on the Judiciary (September 11, 2008)

NO: Heather D. Joseph, from Hearing on "The Fair Copyright in Research Works Act," Testimony regarding H.R.6845 before the Subcommittee on Courts, the Internet, and Intellectual Property of the Committee on the Judiciary (September 11, 2008)

ISSUE SUMMARY

YES: Ralph Oman, attorney and past register of copyrights, contends, "If the NIH [National Institutes of Health] succeeds in putting all of the NIH-related peer-reviewed articles on its online database for free within one year of publication, the private publishers will be hard-pressed to survive." Allowing private publishers to continue to profit by publishing the results of publicly funded research is the best way to ensure public benefit.

NO: Heather D. Joseph argues that permitting public access to the NIH-funded research results does not threaten the viability of journal publishers. In addition, immediate online access to research results is invaluable to the public.

$\mathbf{A}$ccording to Peter Suber's "Open Access Overview" (http://www.earlham.edu/~peters/fos/overview.htm), "open access" refers to the broad-based movement to put peer-reviewed research articles online, free of charge, and without most copyright and licensing restrictions. According to his "Timeline of the Open Access Movement" (http://www.earlham.edu/~peters/fos/timeline.htm), the movement has roots in the 1960s, well before the Internet came to exist as we know it today. Project Gutenberg (http://www.gutenberg.org/wiki/Main_Page), which makes public-domain novels and other books freely available, was launched in 1971. For many years, the open access movement was no threat to the standard modes of scientific publishing, but by 2004 it was clear that scientific (and other) journals were becoming so expensive that university and college libraries were being forced to cut back on the number of journals they could subscribe to. Pressure was rising to do something about the problem, and open access looked like a possible solution, as exemplified by the Public Library of Science (PLoS). See Theodora Bloom, et al., "PLoS Biology at 5: The Future Is Open Access," *PLoS Biology* (October 28, 2008). In response to a report from the House Appropriations Committee urging the National Institutes of Health (NIH) to require the NIH-funded research reports to be deposited in the NIH's Internet archive, PubMed Central, the NIH Director Elias Zerhouni convened meetings with representatives of academic publishers and others. Publishers expressed concern that making reports freely available would threaten their continued existence. See Jocelyn Kaiser, "House Weighs Proposal to Block Mandatory 'Open Access,'" *Science* (September 19, 2008).

That concern has not diminished. In 2007, legislation mandated that federally funded research reports be given to PubMed Central. The resulting Public Access Policy is described in Robin Peek, "Coming to Grips with the NIH Policy," *Information Today* (September 1, 2008); see also Robin Peek, "The Battle over PubMed Central Continues," *Information Today* (November 1, 2008). Thanks to lobbying by publishers, on September 9, 2008, H.R. 6845, the Fair Copyright in Research Works Act, was introduced to reverse the NIH's policy and forbid other federal agencies from implementing similar policies. The bill was promptly referred to the House Judiciary Committee. It did not come to a vote before that session of Congress ended, but it was reintroduced in 2009. The bill may be moot because in 2009 President Obama signed the Consolidated Appropriations Act, which included a provision making the NIH's Public Access Policy permanent; see Robin Peek, "The Tide Has Changed; Get Over It," *Information Today* (May 1, 2009).

A hearing on the bill was held on September 11, 2008. Publisher representatives such as Martin Frank, executive director of the American Physiological Society, supported the bill arguing, "By protecting copyright for research works, [it] will continue to provide incentives for private-sector investment in the peer review process which helps ensure the quality and integrity of scientific research." In the following selections, Ralph Oman, attorney and past register of copyrights, contends in his testimony, "If the NIH [National Institutes of Health] succeeds in putting all of the NIH-related peer-reviewed articles on its online database for free within one year of publication, the private publishers will be hard-pressed to survive." Allowing private publishers to continue to profit by publishing the results of publically funded research is the best way to ensure public benefit. Heather D. Joseph, executive director of the Scholarly Publishing and Academic Resources Coalition Committee, testifies that permitting public access to the NIH-funded research results does not threaten the viability of journal publishers. In addition, immediate online access to research results is invaluable to the public.

YES

Ralph Oman

The Fair Copyright in Research Works Act

Mr. Chairman and members of the Subcommittee. It is a great honor to appear again before this distinguished panel. It has been a few years since my last appearance.

Thank you for the opportunity to testify on this matter of importance to copyright generally, and to the public, to the research community, to the authors of scientific, technical, and medical articles, and to the publishers of STM journals. I would like to focus on the larger policy issues that undergird the American copyright system and discuss the proposal of the National Institutes of Health that requires recipients of NIH research grants to effectively renounce copyright in their peer-reviewed article manuscripts just 12 months after publication. I will also briefly mention the bill introduced by Chairman Conyers that seeks to moderate the impact of the NIH proposal in a way that will encourage the broadest possible dissemination of high quality, peer-reviewed articles without running roughshod over the rights of authors and copyright owners.

This hearing is important on another level. The language in the appropriations bill that has given rise to this controversy was never vetted by the Judiciary Committee—the committee with intellectual property expertise. With your scrutiny today, the Subcommittee puts this narrow dispute in the larger context of the constitutional mandate—to promote the progress of science for the public interest. Other than celebrating the Judiciary Committee's involvement, I will not comment on the wisdom of legislating on appropriations bills. Into that Serbonian Bog I will not wade.

Instead, I simply applaud your decision, Mr. Chairman, to give a full airing of these issues before your expert Subcommittee. They bear directly on the copyright policies of our government and the incentives to authorship and publication under U.S. copyright law. For reasons I will discuss, the NIH proposal seems short-sighted, counterproductive, damaging to U.S. creativity, which this subcommittee fosters and safeguards, and contrary to the NIH's own interests in encouraging broad public dissemination of peer-reviewed learned articles. The Appropriations Committee, to its credit, sensed that the NIH proposal ventured into sensitive territory and added a very important proviso. That proviso directed the NIH to "implement the public access policy in a manner consistent with copyright law." In my opinion, the NIH has fallen

The U.S. House of Representatives, September 11, 2008.

short of that dictate in several respects, and, with this committee's expert guidance, they should refine their proposal in ways that are true to both the letter and spirit of the copyright law, and the essential policies behind it.

In this debate, three key questions must be answered. First, what policy will result in the broadest dissemination of high quality, peer-reviewed scholarly articles? Second, is it fair for the U.S. government to appropriate the value-added contributions of the private STM publishers? And, third, is the NIH correct in its assumption that the STM publishers will continue to publish their journals even if they lose 50 percent of their paid subscriptions?

Many of my colleagues in academia recognize that the STM publishers perform many vital functions in bringing these articles into the public forum. For one thing, they make substantial investments in the peer-review process. While they do not as a general rule pay the reviewers, the publishers hire in-house teams to support outside specialists. These teams arrange and coordinate effective distribution, stay close to the academic experts in the discipline personally and professionally, follow the literature, and engage in on-going communications with the authors about the reviewers' comments and the incorporation of those comments into the manuscript.

In addition to the peer-review process, the publishers make judgments about which of the manuscripts to publish, depending on their quality and the level of interest in the research itself. They also edit the manuscripts and make them presentable for publication.

My basic concern about the NIH proposal is that it will, sooner rather than later, destroy the commercial market for these scientific, technical, and medical journals. If this dark prophesy comes to pass, who, I wonder, will handle all of these expensive and sensitive administrative details? Some of my academic colleagues are confident that this change in the mechanics of scientific publishing will have little or no impact on the private sector, and that it will remain as robust as ever, even if the NIH freely publishes all of the NIH peer-reviewed article manuscripts shortly after private publication. Some claim that they have "evidence" that STM publishing will continue to flourish. I have not seen that evidence. To me, it suggests an element of wishful thinking. In my experience, Congress is normally reluctant to hang major legislative change in copyright policy on the thin reed of wishful thinking. With the prospect of free copies available in the near term, who in the face of experience and reality can reasonably expect that subscribers to STM journals, faced with their own budgetary constraints and needs, will not look with real favor on alternative free sources? I can't. It is belied by common sense. Certainly, many university and industry librarians will cancel their subscriptions to these learned journals, with some estimates of a cancellation rate approaching 50 percent. With plummeting sales, how could the STM publishers stay in business? This is a critical point, and one that this committee has a special sensitivity to. It really goes to the heart of the matter, in terms of public policy.

It is a basic premise of copyright that the law is designed to benefit the public, not reward authors or publishers. But, as James Madison wrote in the Federalist Papers, "the public good fully coincides" with the rights of authors and copyright owners. With that admonition, we consider the NIH proposal.

It seems clear that Congress would not want the NIH free access policy to cause many or all of the private STM publishers to fade away. Of course, if fair market competition, or a change in the culture of academic publishing, or costly overhead were eventually to drive the private publishers out of business, so be it. It is one thing that they should suffer demise because of changes in the marketplace, and it is another to be brought down by an ill-considered governmental fiat. The NIH does not intend to perform any of the vetting, selection, and editing functions now performed by the learned societies, by the professional organizations, and by the STM publishers, and I doubt if Congress wants to increase their budget so they can take on these additional responsibilities. So the question occurs: who is going to do it? I do not see replacements for the publishers raising their hands to volunteer. For this reason alone, I question the wisdom of the NIH provision. And there are larger issues as well. Experience teaches that as a general rule Congress prefers to keep the hairy snout of the federal government out of the peer-review and manuscript selection process. We live in an open society, and, with a weather eye on the First Amendment, we try to keep the government at arms length from these delicate publication decisions, so as not to skew the process.

That being said, the NIH provision brings back vivid memories of the debate we had in 1980 with the Small Business and University Patent Procedure Act. In that debate, Senator Russell Long, Chairman of the Senate Finance Committee, following the script written by Admiral Rickover, the father of the nuclear submarine, argued in favor of existing government policy—that patents developed with government research money belong to the taxpayers who subsidize the research. Senator Bayh and Senator Dole reasoned that the taxpayers would get a far greater return on their investment if we instead facilitated private sector ownership and commercialization of the inventions, putting these inventions to work for the people. We are about to celebrate the 30th anniversary of Bayh/Dole, and no one is arguing for its repeal.

The same policy arguments apply in the NIH case. If the NIH succeeds in putting all of the NIH-related peer-reviewed articles on its online database for free within one year of publication, the private publishers will be hard-pressed to survive. To me, it seems far more likely that the U.S. taxpayer will achieve the desired objective—the broadest possible dissemination of the peer-reviewed article manuscripts—under the current system. With the private STM publishers running the peer-review process, selecting the articles, and aggressively marketing their journals to libraries and other research institutions, both foreign and domestic, the current system lets the publishers bring their professional judgment and expertise into the process and ensures high quality scholarship. Paid subscriptions keep the current system perking along, without intrusive government involvement, and without an infusion of funds from the government fisc. If the NIH provision is fully implemented, it will almost certainly end this self-policing and self-financing system and get the federal government deeply into the STM publishing business.

Finally, Mr. Chairman, I would like to mention a few related issues. First, I wonder if any of the manuscript articles that the NIH will publish contain preexisting materials that the NIH researcher did not create and therefore does not own. Here, I am thinking of charts, diagrams, photographs, and illustrations. Will the NIH commandeer the rights of those creators as well, or will it require the NIH researcher to clear all of those ancillary rights as part of the "contract." Today, of course, the publishers often help the author clear these rights, including electronic distribution rights. Will the NIH undertake this task if the publishers drop out of the picture?

Second, I wonder if the NIH proposal really serves our international interests. Our trade negotiators are constantly fighting for strong intellectual property protection, which is under siege in many countries around the world. I assume that some of the authors (or at least co-authors) are foreign nationals, and would fall under the protection of the Berne Convention. And I assume some of the impacted publisher/copyright owners are foreign as well. As I will note in a moment, the NIH policy will seriously threaten the protection of American authored and published works in foreign countries. This government edict from the NIH, not promulgated "in a manner consistent with copyright law," has a crippling effect on the value of the copyright in these works. Some of my academic colleagues argue that the Berne Convention has no relevance to the NIH policy. They see it as a simple contract matter, and they note that the researchers get very valuable consideration for their assignment of copyright to the NIH under the contract. Granted, the researchers do receive a generous stipend, averaging $400,000, but that fact also makes the whole arrangement suspect. To a serious researcher, an NIH grant is a matter of life and death professionally. To claim that the assignment of the reproduction right is "voluntary"—the product of a free market negotiation—strikes me as disingenuous.

In fact, the government involvement puts the NIH "contract" in a suspect category in the Berne and TRIPs context. It is not a private contract between commercial interests. Let me draw a hypothetical. The U.S. motion picture industry is now permitted to exhibit theatrically only 10 or so films per year in China. Suppose the government of China were to offer the American film producers a deal: "If you sign a contract waiving your reproduction right, we will allow you to exhibit 100 films a year." The producers would crunch the numbers and calculate the bottom line, even while complaining bitterly that the deal is outrageous and clearly a violation of the spirit of copyright and the Berne Convention. Nonetheless, they might conclude that on balance they would make more money with the proffered deal than they now make with limited access to the huge Chinese market. So, in the end, they might sign on the dotted line. Could the United States take that "contract" to the WTO and press a claim under TRIPs that China is not complying with its treaty obligations? I think so. The ensuing mass piracy of American films in China would be a direct result of this unwaivering government action that diminishes copyright, disguised as a "contract." In any case, the NIH free access policy is an unfortunate international precedent for a country like the United States, whose great strength is intellectual property.

The NIH should reconsider the long term consequences of its proposal. The dedicated researchers who benefit from the NIH grants take great professional pride in being published in prestigious learned journals, all of which constitute a valuable and reliable resource for future research. The NIH itself recognizes that "publication in peer-reviewed journals is a major factor in determining the professional standing of scientists; institutions use publication in peer-reviewed journals in making hiring, promotion, and tenure decisions."

Despite some grumbling about high subscription prices, very few researchers, academics, or librarians are suggesting that the journals have outlived their usefulness. The STM publishers should be given the right to compete fairly in a changing marketplace, in which they will innovate and have the opportunity to flourish on their own merits, as long as their copyrights are protected. Congress should require the NIH to demonstrate convincingly that their free access policy will not jeopardize the existence of the STM publishers and the indispensable role they play in vetting and selecting peer-reviewed articles. Absent that proof, the NIH should rethink their current policy of involuntary assignment. Current law gives the NIH some discretion in implementing their open access policy in a manner consistent with copyright. If the NIH do not amend their policy, Congress should direct them to do so. The Chairman's bill will allow the publishers to continue publishing. It will preserve the STM journals as valuable professional tools for scientific research, thereby promoting the progress of science. By restoring the status quo ante, the Chairman's bill will give the evolving free market a chance to come to grips with the new online technologies without undercutting the incentives that publishers have relied on for two hundred years. I would urge its enactment.

Heather D. Joseph  **NO**

The Fair Copyright in Research Works Act

I am here today because SPARC, ARL, and ATA represent a large number of the users who currently rely on and directly benefit from access to the works that would be affected by this proposed legislation. I am also here having spent fifteen years as a publisher in both not-for-profit and commercial publishing organizations. And finally, I am here as a mother and as a member of the public, with a deep and abiding interest in the results of the research that my tax dollars help to support.

I would like to express my serious reservations about this legislation, and particularly about the negative impact it would have on the advancement of scientific research and on the availability of vital health care information for millions of Americans by overturning the crucially important National Institutes of Health's Public Access Policy.

SPARC, a membership organization of more than 225 college and university libraries in the United States, is dedicated to working collaboratively to expand the dissemination of the results of scholarly research by leveraging the vast new opportunities presented to the academic community in the networked digital environment. ARL represents 123 research libraries in North America. As academic and research libraries, we represent the customer base of the journal publishing industry, providing the majority of the subscription income received by these publishers.

SPARC also serves as the coordinating organization for the Alliance for Taxpayer Access, an alliance of more than 80 libraries, universities, patients advocacy groups, consumer groups, and student organizations who are dedicated to ensuring that a specific subset of scholarly research—specifically the results of research that has been funded using taxpayer dollars—is made freely and rapidly accessible to the public.

U.S. taxpayers underwrite tens of billions of dollars of research each year, and the widespread sharing of the results of this research is an essential component of our government's investment in science. It is only through the use of these findings that funders—and, by extension, taxpayers—obtain value from their investment. Faster and wider sharing of knowledge fuels the advancement of science and accordingly, the return of health, economic, and social benefits back to the public. This is why 33 Nobel Laureates have written in strong support of the NIH Public Access Policy. That letter is included in my written statement.

The U.S. House of Representatives, September 11, 2008.

Yet, despite the fact that the public has paid for this research, colleges, patients, physicians, researchers, and other members of the public frequently cannot access taxpayer-funded research findings because they simply cannot afford to subscribe to all of the journals in which these findings are published.

As the Executive Director of SPARC, I see libraries face this access issue on a daily basis. Even the most well-funded, private university libraries can not afford to subscribe to all of the journals they would like to provide their students. This situation is exacerbated by the continued rapid escalation in price of journal subscriptions, which puts libraries in the position of having to cancel subscriptions. Libraries now routinely find themselves in the position of paying more and more money only to be able to provide their patrons— students, faculty, researchers—with access to less and less.

This is why the organizations that I represent today have enthusiastically supported efforts such as the NIH's which are designed to break this logjam. The NIH Public Access Policy is a simple, effective, and carefully balanced policy. It requires that all investigators funded by the agency submit an electronic version of their final peer-reviewed manuscripts to PubMed Central (PMC), the online archive of the National Library of Medicine, to be made publicly available within twelve months of publication, and in a manner consistent with copyright law.

The policy is designed to create a broadly accessible, permanent archive of the results of NIH-funded research in order to advance the conduct of science and enhance the agency's accountability to the public. In short, this policy ensures that the U.S. taxpayers are able to benefit fully from the research that they have underwritten.

During the extensive public comment periods and discussions that have taken place over the past four years, opponents of the policy have expressed a variety of concerns. Chief among them has been the fear that the policy would create a resource that is competitive with journals, and would ultimately damage publisher revenues. The concern is that their primary customer—academic libraries—will view the availability of an author's manuscript in PubMed Central as an adequate substitute for subscribing to a journal, and will, as result, cancel subscriptions in large numbers. There are several reasons why this fear is unfounded.

First, the current NIH Public Access Policy is a compromise policy that contains safeguards against this happening. Authors who receive NIH funding are required to deposit only their final accepted, peer-reviewed manuscript —the raw, word-processing file—into PubMed Central, rather than the final, copyedited, formatted, enhanced—and copyrighted—version that will ultimately appear in the journal. The final articles with these value-added features remain solely the publishers to distribute and sell as they choose.

Second, the NIH Policy allows an embargo period of up to one year before a manuscript becomes publicly available. In the realm of the extremely fast-moving, crucial biomedical research funded by the NIH, information, after one year, is already old. The value in the articles resulting from this research lies largely in their immediacy.

Finally, there are very few, if any, journals that publish only research articles that have resulted from NIH funding. The vast majority of journals publish articles resulting from other funding sources, along with review articles, editorial material, commentary, and other value-added material.

The findings of recent studies have supported the use of these safeguards. In a 2006 report commissioned by a publishing organization, the Association of Learned and Professional Society Publishers (ALSP) surveyed librarians to determine what factors would prompt them to cancel journal subscriptions.[1] The report concluded that "availability of content via delayed open access was not an important factor in journal cancellations." Specifically, they noted that for availability of material in an archive such as PubMed Central to become a factor in subscription cancellation:

1. The embargo has to be very short. 82% of librarians surveyed noted it had to be 3 months or less, and for 92% it had to be 6 months or less;
2. The raw manuscript, or preprint, is not a substitute for the journal—only 9% saw access to a preprint as an adequate substitute; and
3. Completeness counts—75% of librarians said the archive would have to contain over 90% of a given journal's content before it became a factor in considering cancellation.

The library community does not view this policy as a chance to save money by cutting subscriptions to biomedical journals—but rather as an important opportunity to supplement our journal collections by providing access to additional material that we would not otherwise be able to provide to our patrons. And importantly, libraries strongly support NIH's role in preserving this biomedical literature for future generations of users.

As a publisher, I have seen first hand that the experience of organizations who have voluntarily participated in depositing materials into PubMed Central supports this survey. As a direct example: The American Society for Cell Biology (ASCB), where I served as Publishing Director, has made the research articles from its journal, *Molecular Biology of the Cell*, available on PubMed Central just two months after their publication since 2001. Additionally, the society puts all of the journal's content into the database, not just the fraction supported by NIH funding. Despite this, the revenue generated by *Molecular Biology of the Cell* has increased steadily since 2001. Participation in PubMed Central actually resulted in an increase in the number of articles downloaded from the society's website, increasing the visibility of the journal and the papers published there.

The ASCB is not alone in this experience. There are several hundred other journals also voluntarily depositing content into PubMed Central. . . . None of these would do so if it threatened their core business in any way.

Finally, as a mother and member of the general public, the NIH Public Access Policy addresses the public's rising interest in self-education on health matters and need to see the results of their extensive investments. The information we are talking about today is, after all, generated by a public agency tasked with protecting and improving the public health. The information contained in PubMed Central is not esoteric research of interest only to elite scholars. It is crucial, health-related information that can make a life-or-death difference in the lives of the American public. As of today, the NIH database contains more than 27,500 articles on malaria, 50,000 on AIDS, 41,000 on HIV, 5,000 on health disparities, 2,000 on disadvantaged populations and more than 77,000 on diabetes research. This is a vital resource for individuals looking for health care information at any time of the day, from anywhere, any day of the week.

When my five-year-old son was diagnosed just nine weeks ago, with autoimmune, insulin-dependent Type 1 Diabetes, I did what every member of the patients advocacy groups I represent today predicted I would. I got online and looked for every piece of current information I could get my hands on. I did this from home, at 3 in the morning the night we got home from the hospital, desperate for information that could reassure me that there was something else I could do besides wake my child up twice a night to check his blood sugar for signs of hypoglycemia. I found a 2008 study of continuous glucose monitors, rating parent and patient satisfaction in the prevention of nighttime instances of low blood sugar.[2] Notably, what was available to me was the authors' final manuscript, posted just one month before, available solely because of the NIH Public Access Policy. It was worth the world to me.

Besides serving the interest of the public as just described, the NIH policy also strikes a careful balance between increasing access to the literature and respecting the concerns of publishers, by operating within the current copyright structure. As noted by 45 of law professors who specialize in copyright law, the NIH policy in no way conflicts with U.S. copyright law. The agency receives a non-exclusive license from the researchers they fund, who retain their copyright and are free to enter into traditional publication agreements with journals or to assign these rights to anyone they want, subject to the standard federal purpose license.

Unfortunately, the Fair Copyright in Research Works Act would effectively overturn this important and much needed policy. By prohibiting agencies from making the results of the research they fund public in the manner that they choose, this bill would significantly inhibit our ability to advance scientific discovery. This legislation is not in the best interest of the taxpayers who fund the research nor the scientific community and the public that rely upon it.

References

1. "ALPSP Survey of Librarians on Factors in Journal Cancellation" Mark Ware Consulting Ltd . . .

2. Weinzimer, Stuart MD, c/o DirecNet Coordinating Center, Jaeb Center for Health Research, FreeStyle Navigator™ Continuous Glucose Monitoring System Use in Children with Type 1 Diabetes Using Glargine-based Multiple Daily Dose Regimens: Results of a Pilot Trial," . . .

POSTSCRIPT

Should the Public Have to Pay to See the Results of Federally Funded Research?

According to Walt Crawford, "Open Access: It's Never Simple," *Online* (July/August 2008), one major objection to the traditional mode of scholarly publication—meaning that university and college libraries pay to subscribe to a journal—is that subscriptions have become remarkably expensive. Springer-Verlag's journal prices for 2009 can be seen at http://www.springer.com/librarians/price+lists?SGWID=0-40585-0-0-0; seven of those journals are priced at over $11,000 a year. The prices of Elsevier's titles are listed at http://www.elsevier.com/wps/find/subscriptionpricelist.cws_home/2009subscrippricelistlibr/description; *Life Sciences* cost a library $6,822 for 2009, compared to $4,031 a year in 2000 and $2,325 in 1995. Subscription prices for print journals have grown about 10 percent per year, with electronic access and mixed access being priced even higher. Aggregated (multijournal) electronic-access packages appeared in 2001 to help stabilize prices; see Frances L. Chen, Paul Wrynn, and Judith L. Rieke, "Electronic Journal Access: How Does It Affect the Print Subscription Price?" *Bulletin of the Medical Library Association* (October 2001).

Today aggregated packages (such as EBSCO) are commonplace, with many academic libraries using them to replace paper subscriptions. But even these can be expensive. It is no surprise that libraries are among the strongest backers of the open access movement in the United States and elsewhere (for a Canadian view, see Heather Morrison and Andrew Waller, "Open Access and Evolving Scholarly Communication," *C&RL News* (September 2008)). Some researchers are addressing the concern that open access journals are somehow inferior to subscription journals in terms of quality control by studying their "impact factor" (how often papers are cited); K. A. Clauson, et al., "Open-Access Publishing for Pharmacy-Focused Journals," *American Journal of Health-System Pharmacists* (August 15, 2008), find that impact factors are actually greater for journals with some form of open access. However, Philip M. Davis, "Author-Choice Open-Access Publishing in the Biological and Medical Literature: A Citation Analysis," *Journal of the American Society for Information Science & Technology* (January 2009), finds that the open-access advantage is declining. See also Ji-Hong Park, "Motivations for Web-Based Scholarly Publishing: Do Scientists Recognize Open Availability as an Advantage?" *Journal of Scholarly Publishing* (June 2009).

The pressure for open access does not come only from government agencies such as the NIH. Some see open access as a movement to democratize what has until recently been an elite resource; see Ron Miller, "OPEN ACCESS:

Battles to Democratize Academic Publishing," *EContent* (April 2009). Leslie Chan, Subbiah Arunachalam, and Barbara Kirsop, "Open Access: A Giant Leap towards Bridging Health Inequities," *Bulletin of the World Health Organization* (August 2009), argue that only through open access publishing can the latest research results reach those who need them. Harvard University's arts and sciences faculty "has directly challenged the authority of academic journals to control access to research results" by voting to put faculty work in a free online repository, following similar moves by the Howard Hughes Medical Institute and the Wellcome Trust in London. A comment by Patricia Schroeder of the Association of American Publishers that "publishers may not be as quite as excited to take articles from Harvard" seems more than a little wishful, considering Harvard's reputation. See Andrew Lawler, "Harvard Faculty Votes to Make Open Access Its Default Mode," *Science* (February 22, 2008). In December 2009, Robin Peek, "OAW [Open Access Week] 2009 Exceeds Expectations," *Information Today*, noted that 100 universities have announced plans to require researchers to deposit research information in open access repositories.

Are print journals actually threatened by the open access movement? Many commentators remark that journals offer much more than just research reports. However, they may not prove able to sustain high subscription prices. They will be obliged to adapt, as many are already doing, according to Jennifer Howard, "Scholarly Presses Discuss How They're Adapting to a Brave New E-World," *Chronicle of Higher Education* (July 11, 2008). One such adaptation is publishing books that can be freely downloaded in hope that actual book sales will follow; see John Murphy, "New Entry Tries New Publishing Model," *Research Information* (December 2008). Charles Oppenheim, "Electronic Scholarly Publishing and Open Access," *Journal of Information Science* (vol. 34, no. 4, 2008), expects pressure for open access publishing to continue.

ISSUE 21

Should We Reject the "Transhumanist" Goal of the Genetically, Electronically, and Mechanically Enhanced Human Being?

YES: M. J. McNamee and S. D. Edwards, from "Transhumanism, Medical Technology and Slippery Slopes," *Journal of Medical Ethics* (September 2006)

NO: Maxwell J. Mehlman, from "Biomedical Enhancements: Entering a New Era," *Issues in Science and Technology* (Spring 2009)

ISSUE SUMMARY

YES: M. J. McNamee and S. D. Edwards argue that the difficulty of showing that the human body *should* (rather than *can*) be enhanced in ways espoused by the transhumanists amounts to an objection to transhumanism.

NO: Maxwell J. Mehlman argues that the era of routine biomedical enhancements is coming. Since the technology cannot be banned, it must be regulated and even subsidized to ensure that it does not create an unfair society.

In the early 1970s, scientists first discovered that it was technically possible to move genes—biological material that determines a living organism's physical makeup—from one organism to another and thus (in principle) to give bacteria, plants, and animals new features and to correct genetic defects of the sort that cause many diseases, such as cystic fibrosis. Most researchers in molecular genetics were excited by the potentialities that suddenly seemed within their grasp. However, a few researchers—as well as many people outside the field—were disturbed by the idea. Among other things, they feared that we were on the verge of an era when people would be so modified that they were no longer human. Some critics were also suspicious of the researchers' motives. Andrew Kimbrell, *The Human Body Shop: The Engineering and Marketing of Life*

(HarperSanFrancisco, 1993), thought the development of genetic engineering was so marked by scandal, ambition, and moral blindness that society should be deeply suspicious of its purported benefits.

Since then the idea that human beings will one day be enhanced has grown. The idea now encompasses genetic changes to cure or prevent disease and modify height, muscle strength, and cognitive capabilities, the use of chemicals to improve performance in sports (known and banned as "doping"), and even the incorporation in the human body of electronic and robotic elements to add senses and enhance memory, thinking abilities, strength, and a great deal more. In fact, the idea has become a movement known as transhumanism that "promotes an interdisciplinary approach to understanding and evaluating the opportunities for enhancing the human condition and the human organism opened up by the advancement of technology" (see the Humanity+ site at http://humanityplus.org/). The goal is to eliminate aging, disease, and suffering. The transhumanist vision even extends to "posthumanism," when what human beings become will make present-day humans look like chimpanzees by comparison. It includes the possibility of uploading human minds into computers.

Some people find this vision frightening. Francis Fukuyama, "Transhumanism," *Foreign Policy* (September/October 2004), has called transhumanism "the world's most dangerous idea." Critics find changing human form and capability objectionable because the result is in some sense unnatural. They believe that making some people more capable will exacerbate social distinctions and put those who can afford the changes in the position of old-fashioned aristocracies. Life will be even more unfair than it is today.

Michael Bess, "Icarus 2.0: A Historian's Perspective on Human Biological Enhancement," *Technology and Culture* (January 2008), finds transhumanism in essence dehumanizing: "The technologies of enhancement threaten human dignity precisely because they tempt us to think of a person as an entity that can be 'improved.' To take this step is to break down human personhood into a series of quantifiable traits—resistance to disease, intelligence, and so forth—that are subject to augmentation or alteration. The danger in doing this lies in reducing individuals to the status of products, artifacts to be modified and reshaped according to our own preferences, like any other commodity. In this act, inevitably, we risk losing touch with the quality of intrinsic value that all humans share equally, no matter what their traits may be. In this sense, the well-intentioned effort to enhance a person can result in treating them as a mere *thing*."

In the following selections, M. J. McNamee and S. D. Edwards discuss the idea that even to start on the transhumanist agenda is to set humanity on a "slippery slope" leading to disaster. They argue that of the several types of slippery slope, the one most threatening to transhumanism is the "arbitrary" slippery slope, meaning that the progression from the first change to the last is not based on any sense of the moral good, but only on subjective preference. They argue that this poses a challenge to transhumanism, to show that the changes they embrace *should* be embraced rather than just *can* be embraced. Professor of bioethics Maxwell J. Mehlman argues that the era of routine biomedical enhancements is coming. Since the technology cannot be banned, it must be regulated and even subsidized to ensure that it does not create an unfair society.

YES

M. J. McNamee and
S. D. Edwards

Transhumanism, Medical Technology and Slippery Slopes

No less a figure than Francis Fukuyama recently labelled transhumanism as "the world's most dangerous idea." Such an eye-catching condemnation almost certainly denotes an issue worthy of serious consideration, especially given the centrality of biomedical technology to its aims. In this article, we consider transhumanism as an ideology that seeks to evangelise its human-enhancing aims. Given that transhumanism covers a broad range of ideas, we distinguish moderate conceptions from strong ones and find the strong conceptions more problematic than the moderate ones. We also offer a critique of Boström's position published in this journal. We discuss various forms of slippery slope arguments that may be used for and against transhumanism and highlight one particular criticism, moral arbitrariness, which undermines both forms of transhumanism.

What Is Transhumanism?

At the beginning of the 21st century, we find ourselves in strange times; facts and fantasy find their way together in ethics, medicine and philosophy journals and websites. Key sites of contestation include the very idea of human nature, the place of embodiment within medical ethics and, more specifically, the systematic reflections on the place of medical and other technologies in conceptions of the good life. A reflection of this situation is captured by Dyens who writes,

> What we are witnessing today is the very convergence of environments, systems, bodies, and ontology toward and into the intelligent matter. We can no longer speak of the human condition or even of the posthuman condition. We must now refer to the intelligent condition.

We wish to evaluate the contents of such dialogue and to discuss, if not the death of human nature, then at least its dislocation and derogation in the thinkers who label themselves transhumanists.

One difficulty for critics of transhumanism is that a wide range of views fall under its label. Not merely are there idiosyncrasies of individual academics, but there does not seem to exist an absolutely agreed on definition of

From *Journal of Medical Ethics*, volume 32, 2006, pp. 513–518. Copyright © 2006 by Institute of Medical Ethics. Reprinted by permission of BMJ Publishing Group via Rightslink.

transhumanism. One can find not only substantial differences between key authors and the disparate disciplinary nuances of their exhortations, but also subtle variations of its chief representatives in the offerings of people. It is to be expected that any ideology transforms over time and not least of all in response to internal and external criticism. Yet, the transhumanism critic faces a further problem of identifying a robust target that stays still sufficiently long to locate it properly in these web-driven days without constructing a "straw man" to knock over with the slightest philosophical breeze. For the purposes of targeting a sufficiently substantial target, we identify the writings of one of its clearest and intellectually robust proponents, the Oxford philosopher and cofounder of the World Transhumanist Association, Nick Boström, who has written recently in these pages of transhumanism's desire to make good the "half-baked" project that is human nature.

Before specifically evaluating Boström's position, it is best first to offer a global definition for transhumanism and then to locate it among the range of views that fall under the heading. One of the most celebrated advocates of transhumanism is Max More, whose website reads "no more gods, nor more faith, no more timid holding back. The future belongs to posthumanity." We will have a clearer idea then of the kinds of position transhumanism stands in direct opposition to. Specifically, More asserts,

> "Transhumanism" is a blanket term given to the school of thought that refuses to accept traditional human limitations such as death, disease and other biological frailties. Transhumans are typically interested in a variety of futurist topics, including space migration, mind uploading and cryonic suspension. Transhumans are also extremely interested in more immediate subjects such as bio- and nano-technology, computers and neurology. Transhumans deplore the standard paradigms that attempt to render our world comfortable at the sake of human fulfilment.

Strong transhumanism advocates see themselves engaged in a project, the purpose of which is to overcome the limits of human nature. Whether this is the foundational claim, or merely the central claim, is not clear. These limitations—one may describe them simply as features of human nature, as the idea of labelling them as limitations is itself to take up a negative stance towards them—concern appearance, human sensory capacities, intelligence, lifespan and vulnerability to harm. According to the extreme transhumanism programme, technology can be used to vastly enhance a person's intelligence; to tailor their appearance to what they desire; to lengthen their lifespan, perhaps to immortality; and to reduce vastly their vulnerability to harm. This can be done by exploitation of various kinds of technology, including genetic engineering, cybernetics, computation and nanotechnology. Whether technology will continue to progress sufficiently, and sufficiently predictably, is of course quite another matter.

Advocates of transhumanism argue that recruitment or deployment of these various types of technology can produce people who are intelligent and immortal, but who are not members of the species *Homo sapiens*. Their species type will be ambiguous—for example, if they are cyborgs (part human, part machine)—or, if they are wholly machines, they will lack any common genetic features with human beings. A legion of labels covers this possibility; we find in Dyen's recently translated book a variety of cultural bodies, perhaps the most extreme being cyberpunks:

> . . . a profound misalignment between existence and its manifestation. This misalignment produces bodies so transformed, so dissociated, and so asynchronized, that their only outcome is gross mutation. Cyberpunk bodies are horrible, strange and mysterious (think of *Alien*, *Robocop*, *Terminator*, etc.), for they have no real attachment to any biological structure.

Perhaps a reasonable claim is encapsulated in the idea that such entities will be posthuman. The extent to which posthuman might be synonymous with transhumanism is not clear. Extreme transhumanists strongly support such developments.

At the other end of transhumanism is a much less radical project, which is simply the project to use technology to enhance human characteristics—for example, beauty, lifespan and resistance to disease. In this less extreme project, there is no necessary aspiration to shed human nature or human genetic constitution, just to augment it with technology where possible and where desired by the person.

Who Is for Transhumanism?

At present it seems to be a movement based mostly in North America, although there are some adherents from the UK. Among its most intellectually sophisticated proponents is Nick Boström. Perhaps the most outspoken supporters of transhumanism are people who see it simply as an issue of free choice. It may simply be the case that moderate transhumanists are libertarians at the core. In that case, transhumanism merely supplies an overt technological dimension to libertarianism. If certain technological developments are possible, which they as competent choosers desire, then they should not be prevented from acquiring the technologically driven enhancements they desire. One obvious line of criticism here may be in relation to the inequality that necessarily arises with respect to scarce goods and services distributed by market mechanisms. We will elaborate this point in the Transhumanism and slippery slopes section.

So, one group of people for the transhumanism project sees it simply as a way of improving their own life by their own standards of what counts as an improvement. For example, they may choose to purchase an intervention, which will make them more intelligent or even extend their life by 200 years. (Of course it is not self-evident that everyone would regard this as an improvement.) A less vociferous group sees the transhumanism project as not so much bound to the expansion of autonomy (notwithstanding our criticism that will necessarily be effected only in the sphere of economic consumer choice) as one that has the potential to improve the quality of life for humans in general.

For this group, the relationship between transhumanism and the general good is what makes transhumanism worthy of support. For the other group, the worth of transhumanism is in its connection with their own conception of what is good for them, with the extension of their personal life choices.

What Can Be Said in Its Favour?

Of the many points for transhumanism, we note three. Firstly, transhumanism seems to facilitate two aims that have commanded much support. The use of technology to improve humans is something we pretty much take for granted. Much good has been achieved with low-level technology in the promotion of public health. The construction of sewage systems, clean water supplies, etc, is all work to facilitate this aim and is surely good work, work which aims at, and in this case achieves, a good. Moreover, a large portion of the modern biomedical enterprise is another example of a project that aims at generating this good too.

Secondly, proponents of transhumanism say it presents an opportunity to plan the future development of human beings, the species *Homo sapiens*. Instead of this being left to the evolutionary process and its exploitation of random mutations, transhumanism presents a hitherto unavailable option: tailoring the development of human beings to an ideal blueprint. Precisely whose ideal gets blueprinted is a point that we deal with later.

Thirdly, in the spirit of work in ethics that makes use of a technical idea of personhood, the view that moral status is independent of membership of a particular species (or indeed any biological species), transhumanism presents a way in which moral status can be shown to be bound to intellectual capacity rather than to human embodiment as such or human vulnerability in the capacity of embodiment.

What Can Be Said Against It?

Critics point to consequences of transhumanism, which they find unpalatable. One possible consequence feared by some commentators is that, in effect, transhumanism will lead to the existence of two distinct types of being, the human and the posthuman. The human may be incapable of breeding with the posthuman and will be seen as having a much lower moral standing. Given that, as Buchanan *et al* note, much moral progress, in the West at least, is founded on the category of the human in terms of rights claims, if we no longer have a common humanity, what rights, if any, ought to be enjoyed by transhumans? This can be viewed either as a criticism (we poor humans are no longer at the top of the evolutionary tree) or simply as a critical concern that invites further argumentation. We shall return to this idea in the final section, by way of identifying a deeper problem with the open-endedness of transhumanism that builds on this recognition.

In the same vein, critics may argue that transhumanism will increase inequalities between the rich and the poor. The rich can afford to make use of transhumanism, but the poor will not be able to. Indeed, we may come to think of such people as deficient, failing to achieve a new heightened level of normal functioning. In the opposing direction, critical observers may say that transhumanism is, in reality, an irrelevance, as very few will be able to use the technological developments even if they ever manifest themselves. A further possibility is that transhumanism could lead to the extinction of humans and posthumans, for things are just as likely to turn out for the worse as for the better (e.g., those for precautionary principle).

One of the deeper philosophical objections comes from a very traditional source. Like all such utopian visions, transhumanism rests on some conception of good. So just as humanism is founded on the idea that humans are the measure of all things and that their fulfilment is to be found in the powers of reason extolled and extended in culture and education, so too transhumanism has a vision of the good, albeit one loosely shared. For one group of transhumanists, the good is the expansion of personal choice. Given that autonomy is so widely valued, why not remove the barriers to enhanced autonomy by various technological interventions? Theological critics especially, but not exclusively, object to what they see as the imperialising of autonomy. Elshtain lists the three c's: choice, consent and control. These, she asserts, are the dominant motifs of modern American culture. And there is, of course, an army of communitarians ready to provide support in general moral and political matters to this line of criticism. One extension of this line of transhumanism thinking is to align the valorisation of autonomy with economic rationality, for we may as well be motivated by economic concerns as by moral ones where the market is concerned. As noted earlier, only a small minority may be able to access this technology (despite Boström's naive disclaimer for democratic transhumanism), so the technology necessary for transhumanist transformations is unlikely to be prioritised in the context of artificially scarce public health resources. One other population attracted to transhumanism will be the elite sports world, fuelled by the media commercialisation complex—where mere mortals will get no more than a glimpse of the transhuman in competitive physical contexts. There may be something of a double-binding character to this consumerism. The poor, at once removed from the possibility of such augmentation, pay (per view) for the pleasure of their envy.

If we argue against the idea that the good cannot be equated with what people choose simpliciter, it does not follow that we need to reject the requisite medical technology outright. Against the more moderate transhumanists, who see transhumanism as an opportunity to enhance the general quality of life for humans, it is nevertheless true that their position presupposes some conception of the good. What kind of traits is best engineered into humans: disease resistance or parabolic hearing? And unsurprisingly, transhumanists disagree about precisely what "objective goods" to select for installation into humans or posthumans.

Some radical critics of transhumanism see it as a threat to morality itself. This is because they see morality as necessarily connected to the kind of vulnerability that accompanies human nature. Think of the idea of human rights and the power this has had in voicing concern about the plight of especially vulnerable human beings. As noted earlier a transhumanist may be thought to be beyond humanity and as neither enjoying its rights nor its obligations. Why would a transhuman be moved by appeals to human solidarity? Once the prospect of posthumanism emerges, the whole of morality is thus threatened because the existence of human nature itself is under threat.

One further objection voiced by Habermas is that interfering with the process of human conception, and by implication human constitution, deprives humans of the "naturalness which so far has been a part of the taken-for-granted background of our self-understanding as a species" and "Getting used to having human life biotechnologically at the disposal of our contingent preferences cannot help but change our normative self-understanding."

On this account, our self-understanding would include, for example, our essential vulnerability to disease, ageing and death. Suppose the strong trans-humanism project is realised. We are no longer thus vulnerable: immortality is a real prospect. Nevertheless, conceptual caution must be exercised here— even transhumanists will be susceptible in the manner that Hobbes noted. Even the strongest are vulnerable in their sleep. But the kind of vulnerability transhumanism seeks to overcome is of the internal kind (not Hobbes's external threats). We are reminded of Woody Allen's famous remark that he wanted to become immortal, not by doing great deeds but simply by not dying. This will result in a radical change in our self-understanding, which has inescapably normative elements to it that need to be challenged. Most radically, this change in self-understanding may take the form of a change in what we view as a good life. Hitherto a human life, this would have been assumed to be finite. Transhumanists suggest that even now this may change with appropriate technology and the "right" motivation.

Do the changes in self-understanding presented by transhumanists (and genetic manipulation) necessarily have to represent a change for the worse? As discussed earlier, it may be that the technology that generates the possibility of transhumanism can be used for the good of humans—for example, to promote immunity to disease or to increase quality of life. Is there really an intrinsic connection between acquisition of the capacity to bring about transhumanism and moral decline? Perhaps Habermas's point is that moral decline is simply more likely to occur once radical enhancement technologies are adopted as a practice that is not intrinsically evil or morally objectionable. But how can this be known in advance? This raises the spectre of slippery slope arguments.

But before we discuss such slopes, let us note that the kind of approach (whether characterised as closed-minded or sceptical) Boström seems to dislike is one he calls speculative. He dismisses as speculative the idea that offspring may think themselves lesser beings, commodifications of their parents' egoistic desires (or some such). None the less, having pointed out the lack of epistemological standing of such speculation, he invites us to his own apparently more congenial position:

> We might speculate, instead, that germ-line enhancements will lead to more love and parental dedication. Some mothers and fathers might find it easier to love a child who, thanks to enhancements, is bright, beautiful, healthy, and happy. The practice of germ-line enhancement might

lead to better treatment of people with disabilities, because a general demystification of the genetic contributions to human traits could make it clearer that people with disabilities are not to blame for their disabilities and a decreased incidence of some disabilities could lead to more assistance being available for the remaining affected people to enable them to live full, unrestricted lives through various technological and social supports. Speculating about possible psychological or cultural effects of germ-line engineering can therefore cut both ways. Good consequences no less than bad ones are possible. In the absence of sound arguments for the view that the negative consequences would predominate, such speculations provide no reason against moving forward with the technology. Ruminations over hypothetical side effects may serve to make us aware of things that could go wrong so that we can be on the lookout for untoward developments. By being aware of the perils in advance, we will be in a better position to take preventive countermeasures.

Following Boström's speculation then, what grounds for hope exist? Beyond speculation, what kinds of arguments does Boström offer? Well, most people may think that the burden of proof should fall to the transhumanists. Not so, according to Boström. Assuming the likely enormous benefits, he turns the tables on this intuition—not by argument but by skilful rhetorical speculation. We quote for accuracy of representation (emphasis added):

Only after a fair comparison of the risks with the likely positive consequences can any conclusion based on a cost-benefit analysis be reached. In the case of germ-line enhancements, the potential gains are enormous. Only rarely, however, are the potential gains discussed, perhaps because they are too obvious to be of much theoretical interest. By contrast, uncovering subtle and non-trivial ways in which manipulating our genome could undermine deep values is philosophically a lot more challenging. But if we think about it, we recognize that the promise of genetic enhancements is anything but insignificant. Being free from severe genetic diseases would be good, as would having a mind that can learn more quickly, or having a more robust immune system. Healthier, wittier, happier people may be able to reach new levels culturally. To achieve a significant enhancement of human capacities would be to embark on the transhuman journey of exploration of some of the modes of being that are not accessible to us as we are currently constituted, possibly to discover and to instantiate important new values. On an even more basic level, genetic engineering holds great potential for alleviating unnecessary human suffering. Every day that the introduction of effective human genetic enhancement is delayed is a day of lost individual and cultural potential, and a day of torment for many unfortunate sufferers of diseases that could have been prevented. Seen in this light, *proponents of a ban or a moratorium on human genetic modification must take on a heavy burden of proof* in order to have the balance of reason tilt in their favor.

Now one way in which such a balance of reason may be had is in the idea of a slippery slope argument. We now turn to that.

Transhumanism and Slippery Slopes

A proper assessment of transhumanism requires consideration of the objection that acceptance of the main claims of transhumanism will place us on a slippery slope. Yet, paradoxically, both proponents and detractors of transhumanism may exploit slippery slope arguments in support of their position. It is necessary therefore to set out the various arguments that fall under this title so that we can better characterise arguments for and against transhumanism. We shall therefore examine three such attempts but argue that the arbitrary slippery slope may undermine all versions of transhumanists, although not every enhancement proposed by them.

Schauer offers the following essentialist analysis of slippery slope arguments. A "pure" slippery slope is one where a "particular act, seemingly innocuous when taken in isolation, may yet lead to a future host of similar but increasingly pernicious events." Abortion and euthanasia are classic candidates for slippery slope arguments in public discussion and policy making. Against this, however, there is no reason to suppose that the future events (acts or policies) down the slope need to display similarities—indeed we may propose that they will lead to a whole range of different, although equally unwished for, consequences. The vast array of enhancements proposed by transhumanists would not be captured under this conception of a slippery slope because of their heterogeneity. Moreover, as Sternglantz notes, Schauer undermines his case when arguing that greater linguistic precision undermines the slippery slope and that indirect consequences often bolster slippery slope arguments. It is as if the slippery slopes would cease in a world with greater linguistic precision or when applied only to direct consequences. These views do not find support in the later literature. Schauer does, however, identify three non-slippery slope arguments where the advocate's aim is (a) to show that the bottom of a proposed slope has been arrived at; (b) to show that a principle is excessively broad; (c) to highlight how granting authority to X will make it more likely that an undesirable outcome will be achieved. Clearly (a) cannot properly be called a slippery slope argument in itself, while (b) and (c) often have some role in slippery slope arguments.

The excessive breadth principle can be subsumed under Bernard Williams's distinction between slippery slope arguments with (a) horrible results and (b) arbitrary results. According to Williams, the nature of the bottom of the slope allows us to determine which category a particular argument falls under. Clearly, the most common form is the slippery slope to a horrible result argument. Walton goes further in distinguishing three types: (a) thin end of the wedge or precedent arguments; (b) Sorites arguments; and (c) domino-effect arguments. Importantly, these arguments may be used both by antagonists and also by advocates of transhumanism. We shall consider the advocates of transhumanism first.

In the thin end of the wedge slippery slopes, allowing P will set a precedent that will allow further precedents (Pn) taken to an unspecified problematic terminus. Is it necessary that the end point has to be bad? Of course this is the typical linguistic meaning of the phrase "slippery slopes." Nevertheless, we may turn the tables here and argue that [the] slopes may be viewed positively too. Perhaps a new phrase will be required to capture ineluctable slides (ascents?) to such end points. This would be somewhat analogous to the ideas of vicious and virtuous cycles. So transhumanists could argue that, once the artificial generation of life through technologies of in vitro fertilisation was thought permissible, the slope was foreseeable, and transhumanists are doing no more than extending that life-creating and fashioning impulse.

In Sorites arguments, the inability to draw clear distinctions has the effect that allowing P will not allow us to consistently deny Pn. This slope follows the form of the Sorites paradox, where taking a grain of sand from a heap does not prevent our recognising or describing the heap as such, even though it is not identical with its former state. At the heart of the problem with such arguments is the idea of conceptual vagueness. Yet the logical distinctions used by philosophers are often inapplicable in the real world. Transhumanists may well seize on this vagueness and apply a Sorites argument as follows: as therapeutic interventions are currently morally permissible, and there is no clear distinction between treatment and enhancement, enhancement interventions are morally permissible too. They may ask whether we can really distinguish categorically between the added functionality of certain prosthetic devices and sonar senses.

In domino-effect arguments, the domino conception of the slippery slope, we have what others often refer to as a causal slippery slope. Once P is allowed, a causal chain will be effected allowing Pn and so on to follow, which will precipitate increasingly bad consequences.

In what ways can slippery slope arguments be used against transhumanism? What is wrong with transhumanism? Or, better, is there a point at which we can say transhumanism is objectionable? One particular strategy adopted by proponents of transhumanism falls clearly under the aspect of the thin end of the wedge conception of the slippery slope. Although some aspects of their ideology seem aimed at unqualified goods, there seems to be no limit to the aspirations of transhumanism as they cite the powers of other animals and substances as potential modifications for the transhumanist. Although we can admire the sonic capacities of the bat, the elastic strength of lizards' tongues and the endurability of Kevlar in contrast with traditional construction materials used in the body, their transplantation into humans is, to coin Kass's celebrated label, "repugnant."

Although not all transhumanists would support such extreme enhancements (if that is indeed what they are), less radical advocates use justifications that are based on therapeutic lines up front with the more Promethean aims less explicitly advertised. We can find many examples of this manoeuvre. Take, for example, the Cognitive Enhancement Research Institute in California. Prominently displayed on its website front page . . . we read, "Do you know somebody with Alzheimer's disease? Click to see the latest research breakthrough." The mode is simple: treatment by front entrance, enhancement by the back door. Borgmann, in his discussion of the uses of technology in modern society, observed precisely this argumentative strategy more than 20 years ago:

The main goal of these programs seems to be the domination of nature. But we must be more precise. The desire to dominate does not just spring from a lust of power, from sheer human imperialism. It is from the start connected with the aim of liberating humanity from disease, hunger, and toil and enriching life with learning, art and athletics.

Who would want to deny the powers of viral diseases that can be genetically treated? Would we want to draw the line at the transplantation of non-human capacities (sonar path finding)? Or at in vivo fibre optic communications backbone or anti-degeneration powers? (These would have to be non-human by hypothesis). Or should we consider the scope of technological enhancements that one chief transhumanist, Natasha Vita More, propounds:

> A transhuman is an evolutionary stage from being exclusively biological to becoming post-biological. Post-biological means a continuous shedding of our biology and merging with machines. (. . .) The body, as we transform ourselves over time, will take on different types of appearances and designs and materials. (. . .)
>
> For hiking a mountain, I'd like extended leg strength, stamina, a skin-sheath to protect me from damaging environmental aspects, self-moisturizing, cool-down capability, extended hearing and augmented vision (Network of sonar sensors depicts data through solid mass and map images onto visual field. Overlay window shifts spectrum frequencies. Visual scratch pad relays mental ideas to visual recognition bots. Global Satellite interface at micro-zoom range).
>
> For a party, I'd like an eclectic look—a glistening bronze skin with emerald green highlights, enhanced height to tower above other people, a sophisticated internal sound system so that I could alter the music to suit my own taste, memory enhance device, emotional-select for feel-good people so I wouldn't get dragged into anyone's inappropriate conversations. And parabolic hearing so that I could listen in on conversations across the room if the one I was currently in started winding down.

Notwithstanding the difficulty of bringing together transhumanism under one movement, the sheer variety of proposals merely contained within Vita More's catalogue means that we cannot determinately point to a precise station at which we can say, "Here, this is the end we said things would naturally progress to." But does this pose a problem? Well, it certainly makes it difficult to specify exactly a "horrible result" that is supposed to be at the bottom of the slope. Equally, it is extremely difficult to say that if we allow precedent X, it will allow practices Y or Z to follow as it is not clear how these practices Y or Z are (if at all) connected with the precedent X. So it is not clear that a form of precedent-setting slippery slope can be strictly used in every case against transhumanism, although it may be applicable in some.

Nevertheless, we contend, in contrast with Boström that the burden of proof would fall to the transhumanist. Consider in this light, a Sorites-type slope. The transhumanist would have to show how the relationship between the therapeutic practices and the enhancements are indeed transitive. We know night from day without being able to specify exactly when this occurs. So simply because we cannot determine a precise distinction between, say, genetic treatments G1, G2 and G3, and transhumanism enhancements T1, T2 and so on, it does not follow that there are no important moral distinctions between G1 and T20. According to Williams, this kind of indeterminacy arises because of the conceptual vagueness of certain terms. Yet, the indeterminacy of so open a predicate "heap" is not equally true of "therapy" or "enhancement." The latitude they permit is nowhere near so wide.

Instead of objecting to Pn on the grounds that Pn is morally objectionable (ie, to depict a horrible result), we may instead, after Williams, object that the slide from P to Pn is simply morally arbitrary, when it ought not to be. Here, we may say, without specifying a horrible result, that it would be difficult to know what, in principle, can ever be objected to. And this is, quite literally, what is troublesome. It seems to us that this criticism applies to all categories of transhumanism, although not necessarily to all enhancements proposed by them. Clearly, the somewhat loose identity of the movement—and the variations between strong and moderate versions—makes it difficult to sustain this argument unequivocally. Still the transhumanist may be justified in asking, "What is wrong with arbitrariness?" Let us consider one brief example. In aspects of our lives, as a widely shared intuition, we may think that in the absence of good reasons, we ought not to discriminate among people arbitrarily. Healthcare may be considered to be precisely one such case. Given the ever-increasing demand for public healthcare services and products, it may be argued that access to them typically ought to be governed by publicly disputable criteria such as clinical need or potential benefit, as opposed to individual choices of an arbitrary or subjective nature. And nothing in transhumanism seems to allow for such objective dispute, let alone prioritisation. Of course, transhumanists such as More find no such disquietude. His phrase "No more timidity" is a typical token of transhumanist slogans. We applaud advances in therapeutic medical technologies such as those from new genetically based organ regeneration to more familiar prosthetic devices. Here the ends of the interventions are clearly medically defined and the means regulated closely. This is what prevents transhumanists from adopting a Sorites-type slippery slope. But in the absence of a telos, of clearly and substantively specified ends (beyond the mere banner of enhancement), we suggest that the public, medical professionals and bioethicists alike ought to resist the potentially open-ended transformations of human nature. For if all transformations are in principle enhancements, then surely none are. The very application of the word may become redundant. Thus it seems that one strong argument against transhumanism generally—the arbitrary slippery slope—presents a challenge to transhumanism, to show that all of what are described as transhumanist enhancements are imbued with positive normative force and are not merely technological extensions of libertarianism, whose conception of the good is merely an extension of individual choice and consumption.

Limits of Transhumanist Arguments for Medical Technology and Practice

Already, we have seen the misuse of a host of therapeutically designed drugs used by non-therapeutic populations for enhancements. Consider the non-therapeutic use of human growth hormone in non-clinical populations. Such is the present perception of height as a positional good in society that Cuttler *et al* report that the proportion of doctors who recommended human growth hormone treatment of short non-growth hormone deficient children ranged from 1% to 74%. This is despite its contrary indication in professional literature, such as that of the Pediatric Endocrine Society, and considerable doubt about its efficacy. Moreover, evidence supports the view that recreational body builders will use the technology, given the evidence of their use or misuse of steroids and other biotechnological products. Finally, in the sphere of elite sport, which so valorises embodied capacities that may be found elsewhere in greater degree, precision and sophistication in the animal kingdom or in the computer laboratory, biomedical enhancers may latch onto the genetically determined capacities and adopt or adapt them for their own commercially driven ends.

The arguments and examples presented here do no more than to warn us of the enhancement ideologies, such as transhumanism, which seek to predicate their futuristic agendas on the bedrock of medical technological progress aimed at therapeutic ends and are secondarily extended to loosely defined enhancement ends. In discussion and in bioethical literatures, the future of genetic engineering is often challenged by slippery slope arguments that lead policy and practice to a horrible result. Instead of pointing to the undesirability of the ends to which transhumanism leads, we have pointed out the failure to specify their telos beyond the slogans of "overcoming timidity" or Boström's exhortation that the passive acceptance of ageing is an example of "reckless and dangerous barriers to urgently needed action in the biomedical sphere."

We propose that greater care be taken to distinguish the slippery slope arguments that are used in the emotionally loaded exhortations of transhumanism to come to a more judicious perspective on the technologically driven agenda for biomedical enhancement. Perhaps we would do better to consider those other all-too-human frailties such as violent aggression, wanton self-harming and so on, before we turn too readily to the richer imaginations of biomedical technologists.

Maxwell J. Mehlman

Biomedical Enhancements: Entering a New Era

Recently, the Food and Drug Administration (FDA) approved a drug to lengthen and darken eyelashes. Botox and other wrinkle-reducing injections have joined facelifts, tummy tucks, and vaginal reconstruction to combat the effects of aging. To gain a competitive edge, athletes use everything from steroids and blood transfusions to recombinant-DNA–manufactured hormones, Lasik surgery, and artificial atmospheres. Students supplement caffeine-containing energy drinks with Ritalin and the new alertness drug modafinil. The military spends millions of dollars every year on biological research to increase the warfighting abilities of our soldiers. Parents perform genetic tests on their children to determine whether they have a genetic predisposition to excel at explosive or endurance sports. All of these are examples of biomedical enhancements: interventions that use medical and biological technology to improve performance, appearance, or capability in addition to what is necessary to achieve, sustain, or restore health.

The use of biomedical enhancements, of course, is not new. Amphetamines were doled out to troops during World War II. Athletes at the turn of the 20th century ingested narcotics. The cognitive benefits of caffeine have been known for at least a millennium. Ancient Greek athletes swallowed herbal infusions before competitions. The Egyptians brewed a drink containing a relative of Viagra at least 1,000 years before Christ. But modern drug development and improvements in surgical technique are yielding biomedical enhancements that achieve safer, larger, and more targeted enhancement effects than their predecessors, and more extraordinary technologies are expected to emerge from ongoing discoveries in human genetics. (In addition, there are biomechanical enhancements that involve the use of computer implants and nanotechnology, which are beyond the scope of this article.)

What is also new is that biomedical enhancements have become controversial. Some commentators want to outlaw them altogether. Others are concerned about their use by athletes and children. Still others fret that only the well-off will be able to afford them, thereby exacerbating social inequality.

Banning enhancements, however, is misguided. Still, it is important to try to ensure that they are as safe and effective as possible, that vulnerable populations such as children are not forced into using them, and that they are not available only to the well-off. This will require effective government and private action.

A Misguided View

Despite the long history of enhancement use, there recently has emerged a view that it is wrong. The first manifestation of this hostility resulted from the use of performance enhancements in sports in the 1950s, especially steroids and amphetamines. European nations began adopting anti-doping laws in the mid-1960s, and the Olympic Games began testing athletes in 1968. In 1980, Congress amended the Federal Food, Drug, and Cosmetic Act (FFDCA) to make it a felony to distribute anabolic steroids for nonmedical purposes. Two years later, Congress made steroids a Schedule III controlled substance and substituted human growth hormone in the steroid provision of the FFDCA. Between 2003 and 2005, Congress held hearings lambasting professional sports for not imposing adequate testing regimens. Drug testing has also been instituted in high-school and collegiate sports.

The antipathy toward biomedical enhancements extends well beyond sports, however. Officially, at least, the National Institutes of Health (NIH) will not fund research to develop genetic technologies for human enhancement purposes, although it has funded studies in animals that the researchers tout as a step toward developing human enhancements. It is a federal crime to use steroids to increase strength even if the user is not an athlete. Human growth hormone is in a unique regulatory category in that it is a felony to prescribe it for any purpose other than a specific use approved by the FDA. (For example, the FDA has not approved it for anti-aging purposes.) There is an ongoing controversy about whether musicians, especially string players, should be allowed to use beta blockers to steady their hands. And who hasn't heard of objections to the use of mood-altering drugs to make "normal" people happier? There's even a campaign against caffeine.

If the critics had their way, the government would ban the use of biomedical enhancements. It might seem that this would merely entail extending the War on Drugs to a larger number of drugs. But remember that enhancements include not just drugs, but cosmetic surgery and information technologies, such as genetic testing to identify nondisease traits. So a War on Enhancements would have to extend to a broader range of technologies, and because many are delivered within the patient-physician relationship, the government would have to intrude into that relationship in significant new ways. Moreover, the FDA is likely to have approved many enhancement drugs for legitimate medical purposes, with enhancement use taking place on an "off-label" basis. So there would have to be some way for the enhancement police to identify people for whom the drugs had been legally prescribed to treat illness, but who were misusing them for enhancement purposes.

This leads to a far more profound difficulty. The War on Drugs targets only manufacture, distribution, and possession. There is virtually no effort to punish people merely for using an illegal substance. But a successful ban on biomedical enhancement would have to prevent people from obtaining benefits from enhancements that persisted after they no longer possessed the enhancements themselves, such as the muscles built with the aid of steroids or the cognitive improvement that lasts for several weeks after normal people stop taking a certain medicine that treats memory loss in Alzheimer's patients. In short, a ban on enhancements would have to aim at use as well as possession and sale.

To imagine what this would be like, think about the campaign against doping in elite sports, where athletes must notify anti-doping officials of their whereabouts at all times and are subject to unannounced, intrusive, and often indecent drug tests at any hour of the day or night. Even in the improbable event that regular citizens were willing to endure such an unprecedented loss of privacy, the economic cost of maintaining such a regime, given how widespread the use of highly effective biomedical enhancements might be, would be prohibitive.

A ban on biomedical enhancements would be not only unworkable but unjustifiable. Consider the objections to enhancement in sports. Why are enhancements against the rules? Is it because they are unsafe? Not all of them are: Anti-doping rules in sports go after many substances that pose no significant health risks, such as caffeine and Sudafed. (A Romanian gymnast forfeited her Olympic gold medal after she accidentally took a couple of Sudafed to treat a cold.) Even in the case of vilified products such as steroids, safety concerns stem largely from the fact that athletes are forced to use the drugs covertly, without medical supervision. Do enhancements give athletes an "unfair" advantage? They do so only if the enhancements are hard to obtain, so that only a few competitors obtain the edge. But the opposite seems to be true: Enhancements are everywhere. Besides, athletes are also tested for substances that have no known performance-enhancing effects, such as marijuana. Are the rewards from enhancements "unearned"? Not necessarily. Athletes still need to train hard. Indeed, the benefit from steroids comes chiefly from allowing athletes to train harder without injuring themselves. In any event, success in sports comes from factors that athletes have done nothing to deserve, such as natural talent and the good luck to have been born to encouraging parents or to avoid getting hurt. Would the use of enhancements confound recordkeeping? This doesn't seem to have stopped the adoption of new equipment that improves performance, such as carbon-fiber vaulting poles, metal skis, and oversized tennis racquets. If one athlete used enhancements, would every athlete have to, so that the benefit would be nullified? No, there would still be the benefit of improved performance across the board—bigger lifts, faster times, higher jumps. In any case, the same thing happens whenever an advance takes place that improves performance.

The final objection to athletic enhancement, in the words of the international Olympic movement, is that it is against the "spirit of sport." It is hard to know what this means. It certainly can't mean that enhancements destroy an earlier idyll in which sports were enhancement-free; as we saw before, this never was the case. Nor can it stand for the proposition that a physical competition played with the aid of enhancements necessarily is not a "sport." There are many sporting events in which the organizers do not bother to test participants, from certain types of "strong-man" and powerlifting meets to your neighborhood pickup basketball game. There are several interesting historical explanations for why athletic enhancement has gained such a bad rap, but ultimately, the objection about "the spirit of sport" boils down to the fact that some people simply don't like the idea of athletes using enhancements. Well, not exactly. You see, many biomedical enhancements are perfectly permissible, including dietary supplements, sports psychology, carbohydrate loading, electrolyte-containing beverages, and sleeping at altitude (or in artificial environments that simulate it). Despite the labor of innumerable philosophers of sport, no one has ever come up with a rational explanation for why these things are legal and others aren't. In the end, they are just arbitrary distinctions.

But that's perfectly okay. Lots of rules in sports are arbitrary, like how many players are on a team or how far the boundary lines stretch. If you don't like being all alone in the outfield, don't play baseball. If you are bothered by midnight drug tests, don't become an Olympian.

The problem comes when the opponents of enhancement use in sports try to impose their arbitrary dislikes on the wider world. We already have observed how intrusive and expensive this would be. Beyond that, there are strong constitutional objections to using the power of the law to enforce arbitrary rules. But most important, a ban on the use of enhancements outside of sports would sacrifice an enormous amount of societal benefit. Wouldn't we want automobile drivers to use alertness drugs if doing so could prevent accidents? Shouldn't surgeons be allowed to use beta blockers to steady their hands? Why not let medical researchers take cognitive enhancers if it would lead to faster cures, or let workers take them to be more productive? Why stop soldiers from achieving greater combat effectiveness, rescue workers from lifting heavier objects, and men and women from leading better sex lives? Competent adults who want to use enhancements should be permitted to. In some instances, such as in combat or when performing dangerous jobs, they should even be required to.

Protecting the Vulnerable

Rejecting the idea of banning enhancements doesn't mean that their use should be unregulated. The government has several crucial roles to play in helping to ensure that the benefits from enhancement use outweigh the costs.

In the first place, the government needs to protect people who are incapable of making rational decisions about whether to use enhancements. In the language of biomedical ethics, these are populations that are "vulnerable," and a number of them are well recognized. One such group, of course, is people with severe mental disabilities. The law requires surrogates to make decisions for these individuals based on what is in their best interests.

Another vulnerable population is children. There can be little disagreement that kids should not be allowed to decide on their own to consume powerful, potentially dangerous enhancement substances. Not only do they lack decisionmaking capacity, but they may be much more susceptible than adults to harm. This is clearly the case with steroids, which can interfere with bone growth in children and adolescents.

The more difficult question is whether parents should be free to give enhancements to their children. Parents face powerful social pressures to help their children excel. Some parents may be willing to improve their children's academic or athletic performance even at a substantial risk of injury to the child. There are many stories of parents who allow their adolescent daughters to have cosmetic surgery, including breast augmentation. In general, the law gives parents considerable discretion in determining how to raise their children. The basic legal constraint on parental discretion is the prohibition in state law against abuse or neglect, and this generally is interpreted to defer to parental decisionmaking so long as the child does not suffer serious net harm. There are no reported instances in which parents have been sanctioned for giving their children biomedical enhancements, and the authorities might conclude that the benefits conferred by the use of an enhancement outweighed even a fairly significant risk of injury.

Beyond the actions of parents, there remains the question of whether some biomedical enhancements are so benign that children should be allowed to purchase them themselves. At present, for instance, there is no law in the United States against children purchasing coffee, caffeinated soft drinks, and even high-caffeine–containing energy drinks. (Laws prohibiting children from buying energy drinks have been enacted in some other countries.)

At the same time, it may be a mistake to lump youngsters together with older adolescents into one category of children. Older adolescents, although still under the legal age of majority, have greater cognitive and judgmental capacities than younger children. The law recognizes this by allowing certain adolescents, deemed "mature" or "emancipated" minors, to make legally binding decisions, such as decisions to receive medical treatment. Older adolescents similarly may deserve some degree of latitude in making decisions about using biomedical enhancements.

Children may be vulnerable to pressure to use enhancements not only from their parents, but from their educators. Under programs such as No Child Left Behind, public school teachers and administrators are rewarded and punished based on student performance on standardized tests. Private schools compete with one another in terms of where their graduates are accepted for further education. There is also intense competition in school athletics, especially at the collegiate level. Students in these environments may be bull-dozed into using enhancements to increase their academic and athletic abilities. Numerous anecdotes, for example, tell of parents who are informed by teachers that their children need medication to "help them focus"; the medication class in question typically is the cognition-enhancing amphetamines, and many of these children do not have diagnoses that would warrant the use of these drugs.

Beyond students, athletes in general are vulnerable to pressure from coaches, sponsors, family, and teammates to use hazardous enhancements. For example, at the 2005 congressional hearings on steroid use in baseball, a father testified that his son committed suicide after using steroids, when in fact he killed himself after his family caught him using steroids, which the boy had turned to in an effort to meet his family's athletic aspirations.

Another group that could be vulnerable to coercion is workers. Employers might condition employment or promotion on the use of enhancements that increased productivity. For example, an employer might require its nighttime work force to take the alertness drug modafinil, which is now approved for use by sleep-deprived swing-shift workers. Current labor law does not clearly forbid this so long as the drug is relatively safe. From an era in which employees are tested to make sure they aren't taking drugs, we might see a new approach in which employers test them to make sure they are.

Members of the military may also be forced to use enhancements. The military now conducts the largest known biomedical enhancement research project. Under battlefield conditions, superiors may order the use of enhancements, leaving soldiers no lawful option to refuse. A notorious example is the use of amphetamines by combat pilots. Technically, the pilots are required to give their consent to the use of the pep pills, but if they refuse, they are barred from flying the missions.

The ability of government regulation to protect vulnerable groups varies depending on the group. It is important that educators not be allowed to give students dangerous enhancements without parental permission and that parents not be pressured into making unreasonable decisions by fearful, overzealous, or inadequate educators. The law can mandate the former, but not easily prevent the latter. Coaches and trainers who cause injury to athletes by giving them dangerous enhancements or by unduly encouraging their use should be subject to criminal and civil liability. The same goes for employers. But the realities of military life make it extremely difficult to protect soldiers from the orders of their superiors.

Moreover, individuals may feel pressure to use enhancements not only from outside sources, but from within. Students may be driven to do well in order to satisfy parents, gain admittance to more prestigious schools, or establish better careers. Athletes take all sorts of risks to increase their chances of winning. Workers may be desperate to save their jobs or bring in a bigger paycheck, especially in economically uncertain times. Soldiers better able to complete their missions are likely to live longer.

Surprisingly, while acknowledging the need to protect people from outside pressures, bioethicists generally maintain that we do not need to protect them from harmful decisions motivated by internal pressures. This position stems, it seems, from the recognition that, with the exception of decisions that are purely random, everything we decide to do is dictated at least in part by internal pressures, and in many cases, these pressures can be so strong that the decisions may no longer appear to be voluntary. Take, for example, seriously ill cancer patients contemplating whether or not to undergo harsh chemotherapy regimens. Bioethicists worry that, if we focused on the pressures and lack of options created by the patients' dire condition, we might not let the patients receive the treatment, or, in the guise of protecting the patients from harm, might create procedural hurdles that would rob them of their decisionmaking autonomy. Similarly, these bioethicists might object to restricting the ability of workers, say, to use biomedical enhancements merely because their choices are highly constrained by their fear of losing their jobs. But even if we accept this argument, that doesn't mean that we must be indifferent to the dangers posed by overwhelming internal pressure. As we will see, the government still must take steps to minimize the harm that could result.

Individuals may be vulnerable to harm not only from using enhance-ments, but from participating in experiments to see if an enhancement is safe and effective. Research subjects are protected by a fairly elaborate set of rules, collectively known as the "Common Rule," that are designed to ensure that the risks of the research are outweighed by the potential benefits and that the subjects have given their informed consent to their participation. But there are many weaknesses in this regulatory scheme. For one thing, these rules apply only to experiments conducted by government-funded institutions or that are submitted to the FDA in support of licensing applications, and therefore they do not cover a great deal of research performed by private industry. Moreover, the rules were written with medically oriented research in mind, and it is not clear how they should be interpreted and applied to enhancement research. For example, the rules permit children to be enrolled as experimental subjects in trials that present "more than minimal risk" if, among other things, the research offers the possibility of "direct benefit" to the subject, but the rules do not say whether an enhancement benefit can count as a direct benefit. Specific research protections extend to other vulnerable populations besides children, such as prisoners and pregnant women, but do not explicitly cover students, workers, or athletes. In reports of a project several colleagues and I recently completed for the NIH, we suggest a number of changes to current regulations that would provide better protection for these populations.

Ensuring Safety and Effectiveness

Beginning with the enactment of the Pure Food and Drug Act in 1906, we have turned to the government to protect us from unsafe, ineffective, and fraudulent biomedical products and services. Regardless of how much freedom individuals should have to decide whether or not to use biomedical enhance-ments, they cannot make good decisions without accurate information about how well enhancements work. In regard to enhancements in the form of drugs and medical devices, the FDA has the legal responsibility to make sure that this information exists.

The FDA's ability to discharge this responsibility, however, is limited. In the first place, the FDA has tended to rely on information from highly stylized clinical trials that do not reflect the conditions under which enhancements would be used by the general public. Moreover, the deficiencies of clinical trials are becoming more apparent as we learn about pharmacogenetics—the degree to which individual responses to medical interventions vary depending on the individual's genes. The FDA is beginning to revise its rules to require manufacturers to take pharmacogenetics into consideration in studying safety and efficacy, but it will be many years, if ever, before robust pharmacogenetic information is publicly available. The solution is to rely more on data from actual use. Recently the agency has become more adamant about monitor-ing real-world experience after products reach the market, but this informa-tion comes from self-reports by physicians and manufacturers who have little incentive to cooperate. The agency needs to be able to conduct its own surveil-lance of actual use, with the costs borne by the manufacturers.

Many biomedical enhancements fall outside the scope of FDA authority. They include dietary supplements, many of which are used for enhancement purposes rather than to promote health. You only have to turn on late-night TV to be bombarded with claims for substances to make you stronger or more virile. Occasionally the Federal Trade Commission cracks down on hucksters, but it needs far greater resources to do an effective job. The FDA needs to exert greater authority to regulate dietary supplements, including those used for enhancement.

The FDA also lacks jurisdiction over the "practice of medicine." Consequently, it has no oversight over cosmetic surgery, except when the surgeon employs a new medical device. This limitation also complicates the agency's efforts to exert authority over reproductive and genetic practices. This would include the genetic modification of embryos to improve their traits, which promises to be one of the most effective enhancement techniques. Because organized medicine fiercely protects this limit on the FDA, consumers will have to continue to rely on physicians and other health care professionals to provide them with the information they need to make decisions about these types of enhancements. Medical experts need to stay on top of advances in enhancement technology.

Even with regard to drugs and devices that are clearly within the FDA's jurisdiction, its regulatory oversight only goes so far. Once the agency approves a product for a particular use, physicians are free to use it for any other purpose, subject only to liability for malpractice and, in the case of controlled substances, a requirement that the use must comprise legitimate medical practice. Only a handful of products, such as Botox, have received FDA approval for enhancement use; as noted earlier, enhancements predominantly are unapproved, off-label uses of products approved for health-related purposes. Modafinil, for example, one of the most popular drugs for enhancing cognitive performance, is approved only for the treatment of narcolepsy and sleepiness associated with obstructive sleep apnea/hypopnea syndrome and shift-work sleep disorder. Erythropoietin, which athletes use to improve performance, is approved to treat anemias. The FDA needs to be able to require manufacturers of products such as these to pay for the agency to collect and disseminate data on off-label experience. The agency also has to continue to limit the ability of manufacturers to promote drugs for off-label uses, in order to give them an incentive to obtain FDA approval for enhancement labeling.

An enhancement technology that will increase in use is testing to identify genes that are associated with nondisease characteristics. People can use this information to make lifestyle choices, such as playing sports at which they have the genes to excel, or in reproduction, such as deciding which of a number of embryos fertilized in vitro will be implanted in the uterus. An area of special concern is genetic tests that consumers can use at home without the involvement of physicians or genetic counselors to help them interpret the results. Regulatory authority over genetic testing is widely believed to be inadequate, in part because it is split among the FDA and several other federal agencies, and there are growing calls for revamping this regulatory scheme that need to be heeded.

Any attempt to regulate biomedical enhancement will be undercut by people who obtain enhancements abroad. The best hope for protecting these "enhancement tourists" against unsafe or ineffective products and services lies in international cooperation, but this is costly and subject to varying degrees of compliance.

To make intelligent decisions about enhancement use, consumers need information not only about safety and effectiveness, but about whether they are worth the money. Should they pay for Botox injections, for example, or try to get rid of facial wrinkles with cheaper creams and lotions? When the FDA approved Botox for cosmetic use, it ignored this question of cost-effectiveness because it has no statutory authority to consider it. In the case of medical care, consumers may get some help in making efficient spending decisions from their health insurers, who have an incentive to avoid paying for unnecessarily costly products or services. But insurance does not cover enhancements. The new administration is proposing to create a federal commission to conduct health care cost-effectiveness analyses, among other things, and it is important that such a body pay attention to enhancements as well as other biomedical interventions.

Subsidizing Enhancement

In these times of economic distress, when we already question whether the nation can afford to increase spending on health care, infrastructure, and other basic necessities, it may seem foolish to consider whether the government has an obligation to make biomedical enhancements available to all. Yet if enhancements enable people to enjoy a significantly better life, this may not be so outlandish, and if universal access avoids a degree of inequality so great that it undermines our democratic way of life, it may be inescapable.

There is no need for everyone to have access to all available enhancements. Some may add little to an individual's abilities. Others may be so hazardous that they offer little net benefit to the user. But imagine that a pill is discovered that substantially improves a person's cognitive facility, not just their memory but abilities such as executive function—the highest form of problem-solving capacity—or creativity. Now imagine if this pill were available only to those who already were well-off and could afford to purchase it with personal funds. If such a pill were sufficiently effective, so that those who took it had a lock on the best schools, careers, and mates, wealth-based access could drive an insurmountable wedge between the haves and have-nots, a gap so wide and deep that we could no longer pretend that there is equality of opportunity in our society. At that point, it is doubtful that a liberal democratic state could survive.

So it may be necessary for the government to regard such a success-determining enhancement as a basic necessity, and, after driving the cost down to the lowest amount possible, subsidize access for those unable to purchase it themselves. Even if this merely maintained preexisting differences in cognitive ability, it would be justified in order to prevent further erosion of equality of opportunity.

The need for effective regulation of biomedical enhancement is only going to increase as we enter an era of increasingly sophisticated technologies. Existing schemes, such as the rules governing human subjects research, must be reviewed to determine whether additions or changes are needed to accommodate this class of interventions. Government agencies and private organizations need to be aware of both the promise and the peril of enhancements and devote an appropriate amount of resources in order to regulate, rather than stop, their use.

POSTSCRIPT

Should We Reject the "Transhumanist" Goal of the Genetically, Electronically, and Mechanically Enhanced Human Being?

Josh Fischman, "A Better Life with Bionics," *National Geographic* (January 2010), describes current work in developing prostheses controlled by nerve signals from nerves that have been surgically rerouted to communicate more effectively with the artificial limb's circuitry, a clear example of "improvement" of the human being. He also discusses electronic cochlear implants and artificial retinas. An accompanying editorial comment says, "Bionics is technology at its most ingenious and humane."

Among those who favor transhumanism, few come through more strongly than James Hughes, executive director of the Institute for Ethics and Emerging Technologies (http://ieet.org/). He has argued vigorously that enhancement technologies such as genetic engineering offer "such good that the risks are dwarfed" and finds "faith in the potential unlimited improvability of human nature and expansion of human powers far more satisfying than a resignation to our current limits." See his "Embracing Change with All Four Arms: A Post-Humanist Defense of Genetic Engineering," *Eubios Journal of Asian and International Bioethics* (June 1996). Nicholas Agar, "Whereto Transhumanism? The Literature Reaches Critical Mass," *Hastings Center Report* (May–June 2007), finds that "transhumanism is a movement brimming with fresh ideas. Transhumanists succeed in making the intuitive appeal of posthumanity obvious even if they don't yet have the arguments to compel everybody else to accept their vision." Julian Savalescu and Nick Bostrom (a prominent founder of the transhumanism movement) provide a very positive overview in *Human Enhancement* (Oxford University Press, 2009). Susan Schneider, "Future Minds: Transhumanism, Cognitive Enhancement and the Nature of Persons," in Vardit Ravitsky, Autumn Fiester, and Arthur L. Caplan, eds., *The Penn Center Guide to Bioethics* (Springer 2009), considers the question of whether people who have undergone extreme modifications are still the people they were before. Is personhood affected? Is the soul affected? "There are," she writes, "some serious issues which require working out." James Wilson, "Transhumanism and Moral Equality," *Bioethics* (October 2007), finds that objections to transhumanism on the grounds that enhanced humans will be considered morally superior to unenhanced humans are groundless, for "once we understand the basis for human equality, it is clear that anyone who now has sufficient capacities to count as a person from the moral point of view will continue to count as one even if others are fundamentally enhanced; and it is [a mistake] to think that a creature which had even far greater capacities than an unenhanced human being should count as more than an equal from the moral point of view." David Gelles, "Immortality 2.0," *The Futurist* (January–February 2009), concludes that "skepticism of transhumanism is, arguably, natural. At the deepest level, living forever interferes with everything we understand about the world. . . . But such concerns may not matter any more." The change is already under way, and we may be underestimating how far it will go.

One way in which the change is already upon us appears in the realm of sports. With "Drugs in Sport," J. C. McGrath and D. A. Cowan introduce a special issue of the *British Journal of Pharmacology* (June 2008), containing 11 articles covering how the major groups of drugs used illicitly in sports work and making the case that using drugs to enhance performance "undermines the [fair play] ethos of sport." Steven Kotler, "Juicing 3.0," *Popular Science* (August 2008), notes that athletes are not just abusing steroids. Many enhancement techniques—using reaction time stimulants, hormones that affect muscle, and gene replacement—are going to become commonplace in the next few years. Researchers are already working on ways to detect gene doping and other enhancements; see Ronald Bailey, "Testing Your Strength," *Reason* (April 2007). However, it seems likely that future enhancement techniques may be very difficult to detect. It may be necessary to accept enhancements as a legitimate part of athletics and other realms of endeavor.

Contributors to This Volume

EDITOR

THOMAS A. EASTON is professor of science at Thomas College in Waterville, Maine, where he has been teaching since 1983. He received a B.A. in biology from Colby College in 1966 and a Ph.D. in theoretical biology from the University of Chicago in 1971. He has also taught at Unity College, Husson College, and the University of Maine. He is a prolific writer, and his articles on scientific and futuristic issues have appeared in the scholarly journals *Experimental Neurology* and *American Scientist*, as well as in such popular magazines as *Astronomy, Consumer Reports,* and *Robotics Age*. His publications include *Focus on Human Biology,* 2nd ed., coauthored with Carl E. Rischer (HarperCollins, 1995), *Careers in Science,* 4th ed. (VGM, 2004), and *Taking Sides: Clashing Views on Environmental Issues,* 13th ed. (McGraw-Hill Contemporary Learning Series, 2008). Dr. Easton is also a well-known writer and critic of science fiction.

AUTHORS

ROGER ANGEL is professor of astronomy and optical sciences at the University of Arizona, where he also serves as the director of the Steward Observatory Mirror Laboratory and the Center for Astronomical Adaptive Optics.

JOHN BALBUS is a program director at Environmental Defense in Washington, D.C.

STEVEN BEST is associate professor of philosophy at the University of Texas, El Paso. His most recent book (coauthored with Anthony J. Nocella) is *Igniting a Revolution: Voices in Defense of the Earth* (AK Press, 2006). According to his Web site (http://www.drstevebest.org/), "He has come under fire for his uncompromising advocacy of 'total liberation' (humans, animals, and the earth) and has been banned from the UK for the power of his thoughts."

DAVID L. BODDE is professor and senior fellow at the International Center for Automotive Research, Arthur M. Spiro Center for Entrepreneurial Leadership, at Clemson University.

GEORGE W. BUSH is the former president of the United States.

GEORGE CARLO is a public health scientist, epidemiologist, lawyer, and founder of the Health Risk Management Group. He is chairman of the Carlo Institute and a fellow of the American College of Epidemiology, and he serves on the faculty of the George Washington University School of Medicine. Dr. Carlo has published numerous research articles, commentaries, chapters in books, and health policy papers addressing issues in the health sciences, and he is frequently consulted for television, radio, and newspaper interviews pertaining to public health issues.

GREGORY CONKO is the director of food safety policy at the Competitive Institute. He is the coauthor, with Henry I. Miller, of *The Frankenfood Myth: How Protest and Politics Threaten the Biotech Revolution* (Praeger, 2004).

RICHARD DENISON is a senior scientist at the Environmental Defense Fund in Washington, D.C.

SUSAN E. DUDLEY is the administrator of the Office of Management and Budget's (OMB) Office of Information and Regulatory Affairs.

S. D. EDWARDS is a researcher at the Centre for Philosophy, Humanities and Law in Health Care, School of Health Science, University of Wales, Swansea, UK.

AMITAI ETZIONI is university professor and professor of international affairs, George Washington University, where he is the director of the Institute for Communitarian Policy Studies. His latest book is *How Patriotic Is the Patriot Act? Freedom Versus Security in the Age of Terrorism* (Routledge, 2008).

JAMES R. FLEMING, professor of science, technology, and society at Colby College in Waterville, Maine, is a public policy scholar at the Wilson Center and holds the American Association for the Advancement of Science's Roger Revelle Fellowship in Global Environmental Stewardship.

KAREN FLORINI is a senior attorney at the Environmental Defense Fund in Washington, D.C.

DAVE FOREMAN is the director and senior fellow of the Rewilding Institute. He has been active in wildlife conservation for over 30 years. His books include *Confessions of an Eco-Warrior* (Harmony, 1991) and *Rewilding North America* (Island Press, 2004).

FRANCESCA T. GRIFO is the director of the Union of Concerned Scientists' Scientific Integrity Program.

JOHN HORGAN is an award-winning science journalist and director of the Center for Science Writings at the Stevens Institute of Technology, Hoboken, New Jersey. His latest book is *Rational Mysticism: Dispatches from the Border Between Science and Spirituality* (Houghton Mifflin, 2003).

THE INSTITUTE OF MEDICINE has since its creation in 1970 served as the component of the National Academies that deals with health-related issues.

HEATHER D. JOSEPH is the executive director of the Scholarly Publishing and Academic Resources Coalition Committee.

CHRISTOF KOCH is a professor of cognitive and behavioral biology at California Institute of Technology.

KEITH KUPFERSCHMID is the vice president for intellectual property policy and enforcement for the Software & Information Industry Association (SIIA).

LAWRENCE LESSIG is the C. Wendell and Edith M. Carlsmith Professor of Law at Stanford Law School. His latest book is *Code: Version 2.0* (Basic Books, 2006).

ANNE PLATT McGINN is a senior researcher at the Worldwatch Institute and the author of "Why Poison Ourselves? A Precautionary Approach to Synthetic Chemicals," *Worldwatch Paper 153* (November 2000).

M. J. McNAMEE is a reader in philosophy at the Centre for Philosophy, Humanities and Law in Health Care, School of Health Science, University of Wales, Swansea, UK.

KYLE McSLARROW is the president and chief executive officer of the National Cable & Telecommunications Association.

MAXWELL J. MEHLMAN is the Arthur E. Petersilge professor of law, director of the Law-Medicine Center, and professor of bioethics at Case Western Reserve

University. His latest book is *The Price of Perfection: The Individual and Society in the Era of Biomedical Enhancement* (Johns Hopkins University Press, 2009).

MICHAEL MEYER, the European editor for *Newsweek International,* is a member of the New York Council on Foreign Relations and was an Inaugural Fellow at the American Academy in Berlin. He won the Overseas Press Club's Morton Frank Award for business/economic reporting from abroad in 1986 and 1988 and was a member of the *Newsweek* team that won a 1993 National Magazine Award for its coverage of the Los Angeles riots. He is the author of *The Alexander Complex* (Times Books, 1989), an examination of the psychology of American empire-builders.

HENRY I. MILLER is a research fellow at Stanford University's Hoover Institution. His research focuses on public policy toward science and technology, especially biotechnology. He is the coauthor, with Gregory Conko, of *The Frankenfood Myth: How Protest and Politics Threaten the Biotech Revolution* (Praeger, 2004).

JOHN J. MILLER is *National Review*'s national political reporter. His latest book is *A Gift of Freedom: How the John M. Olin Foundation Changed America* (Encounter Books, 2005).

IAIN MURRAY is a director of projects and analysis and senior fellow in energy, science, and technology at the Competitive Enterprise Institute and the author of *The Really Inconvenient Truths: Seven Environmental Catastrophes Liberals Don't Want You to Know About—Because They Helped Cause Them* (Regnery, 2008).

THE NATIONAL ACADEMY OF SCIENCES (NAS), part of the National Academies (http://www.nationalacademies.org/), is a society of distinguished scholars that analyzes and reports on scientific and technological issues when called upon by government agencies.

RALPH OMAN is Pravel professorial lecturer in intellectual property law and fellow of the Creative and Innovative Economy Center, the George Washington University Law School. He is counsel for the intellectual property practice group of the firm Dechert, LLP, and has served as register of copyrights of the United States and as chief counsel of the Senate Subcommittee on Patents, Copyrights, and Trademarks.

BRENDAN RAPPLE is the Collection Development Librarian in the O'Neill Library of Boston College.

DONALD R. ROBERTS is a professor in the Division of Tropical Public Health, Department of Preventive Medicine and Biometrics, Uniformed Services University of the Health Sciences.

JULIAN SAVULESCU is director of the Ethics Unit of the Murdoch Institute at the Royal Children's Hospital in Melbourne, Australia, and an associate professor in the Centre for the Study of Health and Society at the University of Melbourne. He has also worked as a clinical ethicist at the Oxford Radcliffe Hospitals, and he helped set up the Oxford Institute for Ethics and Communication in Health Care Practice.

PETER SCHENKEL is a retired political scientist interested in the question of what contact with advanced aliens would mean to humanity.

MARTIN SCHRAM is a syndicated columnist, television commentator, and author. His publications include *Mandate for Change*, coedited with Will

Marshall (Berkley Books, 1993) and *Speaking Freely: Former Members of Congress Talk About Money in Politics* (Center for Responsive Politics, 1995).

RUSSELL L. SCHWEICKART is the chairman of the B612 Foundation, whose goal is "to significantly alter the orbit of an asteroid, in a controlled manner, by 2015." As an astronaut, he served as the lunar module pilot for *Apollo 9*, March 3–13, 1969.

SETH SHOSTAK is a senior astronomer at the SETI Institute and the author of *Sharing the Universe: Perspectives on Extraterrestrial Life* (Berkeley Hills Books, 1998).

KRISTIN SHRADER-FRECHETTE is the O'Neill Family Professor, Department of Biological Sciences and Department of Philosophy, at the University of Notre Dame. She is the author of *Taking Action, Saving Lives: Our Duties to Protect Environmental and Public Health* (Oxford University Press, 2007).

JEFFREY M. SMITH is the director of the Institute for Responsible Technology and the Campaign for Healthier Eating in America. He is the author of the International bestseller *Seeds of Deception* (Yes! Books, 2003). His latest book is *Genetic Roulette: The Documented Health Risks of Genetically Engineered Foods* (Yes! Books, 2007).

STUART TAYLOR, JR., is a senior writer and columnist for *National Journal* and a contributing editor at *Newsweek*.

GIULIO TONONI is a professor of psychiatry at the University of Wisconsin, Madison.

MIKE TREDER is executive director of the Center for Responsible Nanotechnology, a nonprofit research and policy group based in New York City.

J. SCOTT TURNER is associate professor of biology at the SUNY College of Environmental Science and Forestry in Syracuse, New York. His latest book is *The Tinkerer's Accomplice: How Design Emerges from Life Itself* (Harvard University Press, 2007).

J. ANTHONY TYSON is astrophysicist and professor of physics at the University of California, Davis, and the director of the Large Synoptic Survey Telescope (LSST) project.

NEIL deGRASSE TYSON is the director of the Hayden Planetarium at the American Museum of Natural History. His latest book is *Death by Black Hole and Other Cosmic Quandaries* (Norton, 2007).

THE UNITED KINGDOM'S NATIONAL RADIATION PROTECTION BOARD JOINED THE HEALTH PROTECTION AGENCY (HPA) as its Radiation Protection Division (http://www.hpa.org.uk/radiation/) on April 1, 2005. The mission of the HPA is to provide better protection in the UK against infectious diseases and other dangers to health, including chemical hazards, poisons, and radiation.

DAVID van GEND is a physician and secretary of the Queensland, Australia, branch of the World Federation of Doctors Who Respect Human Life.

SCOTT WALSH is a project manager at Environmental Defense in Washington, D.C.

ROBERT ZUBRIN is an aerospace engineer and president of Pioneer Astronautics. His latest book is *Energy Victory: Winning the War on Terror by Breaking Free of Oil* (Prometheus, 2007).